Luigi Castiglioni's
VIAGGIO

Libro 16.to

Dello Stato del Connecticut

Cap. I.

Viaggio da Nuova York a New Haven, ad Hartford nel Connecticut, e di là ai Confini col Massachusetts

Avendo lasciato New York la mattina dei 24 d'agosto, e passati i confini fra la Nuova York, e il Connecticut arrivammo a pranzo ad Horse Neck, e nella sera a Norwalk ove si cambiano i cavalli. La strada da Horse Neck a Norwalk è montuosa, e sassosa però le campagne assai fertili principalmente per il frumento. Per diminuire la quantità de sassi che ingombrano il terreno usano gli abitanti di raccoglierli, e formarne un muricciuolo all'intorno delle campagne, che servono invece di siepe per tener lontano il Bestiame siccome in Massachusetts. Norwalk è situato in vicinanza al Braccio di Mare che chiamasi *Devil's*

Luigi Castiglioni's

VIAGGIO

Travels in the
United States of North America
1785–87

Translated and edited by
ANTONIO PACE

with Natural History Commentary and
Luigi Castiglioni's
BOTANICAL OBSERVATIONS
translated by Antonio Pace *and edited by*
JOSEPH & NESTA EWAN

SYRACUSE UNIVERSITY PRESS 1983

First Edition

The preparation of this volume was made possible by a grant from the Translations Program of the National Endowment for the Humanities, an independent federal agency.

This book was published with the assistance of a grant from the National Endowment for the Humanities, an independent federal agency.

Library of Congress Cataloging in Publication Data

Castiglioni, Luigi, 1757–1832.
Luigi Castiglioni's Viaggio-Travels in the United States of North America, 1785–87.

Translation of 2 works originally published together: Viaggio negli Stati Uniti dell'America settentrionale fatto negli anni 1785, 1786 e 1787, and Transunto delle osservazioni sui vegetabili dell'America settentrionale. 1790.
Includes bibliographical references and index.
1. United States–Description and travel–1783–1848. 2. Canada–Description and travel–1763–1867. 3. Botany –United States. 4. Castiglioni, Luigi, 1757–1832. I. Pace, Antonio, 1914– . II. Ewan, Joseph Andorfer, 1909– . III. Ewan, Nesta. IV. Castiglioni, Luigi, 1757–1832. Transunto delle osservazioni sui vegetabili dell'America settentrionale. English. 1983. V. Title. VI. Title: Travels in the United States of North America, 1785–87. VII. Title: Luigi Castiglioni's Botanical observations.
E164.C3513 1983 917.3'043 83-410
ISBN 0-8156-2264-3

Manufactured in the United States of America

Contents

General Introduction, *Antonio Pace* xi

- Preamble xi
- Birth, Family, Early Years, and Education of Luigi Castiglioni xi
- Preparation for the American Voyage: The Road to Paris; England. Departure for America xvi
- Contemporary Reception of the *Viaggio* xix
- Honors and Public Charges Conferred on Castiglioni, Commemoratives xxiii
- The Fortunes of Castiglioni Since the Middle of the Nineteenth Century xxvii
- Castiglioni as an Observer of the American Scene xxix
- The Text, the Translation, and the Present Edition xxxiv

Notes xxxvii

Note on Scientific Author Citations, *Joseph Ewan* xliii

Luigi Castiglioni's *Viaggio*
Translated and edited by Antonio Pace 1

Preface 3

Chapter I Passage from England to America 5

Chapter II The Commonwealth of Massachusetts 13

- A Brief History of the First European Settlements in This Part of America 13
- The City of Boston and Its Environs 16

The Trip to Lancaster and Return to Boston; Thence to Portsmouth in New Hampshire 24
From Portsmouth to Penobscot 28
Past and Present Condition of Massachusetts 42
The Inhabitants of Massachusetts, Their Commerce and Agriculture 49
Chapter III The State of New Hampshire 55
From Portsmouth to the Border of the Territory of Vermont 55
Former and Present Condition of New Hampshire 58
Chapter IV The Territory of Vermont 63
Chapter V Canada 69
Trip from Ticonderoga to Montreal 69
From Montreal to Cataraqui 74
Return from Cataraqui to the Border of New York State 80
Chapter VI The State of New York 85
From Windmill Point to New York City 85
The City of New York 93
History of the Founding of the First Colonies in New York 97
The Former Inhabitants, and the Location of New York 100
The New Form of Government of New York 104
Population, Commerce, and Agriculture of New York 107
Chapter VII From the State of New York to the Border of Georgia 111
From New York City to the Border of North Carolina 111
Continuation of the Trip to the Border of Georgia 117
Chapter VIII The State of Georgia 125
From Purysburg to the City of Augusta 125
Location, Main Rivers and Mountains, and Former Inhabitants of Georgia 130
Division of the State, the Government, Population, Commerce, and Agriculture of Georgia 142
Chapter IX South Carolina 147
Trip from Augusta to the Border of North Carolina 147
Location, and Former Condition of South Carolina 152
Present Condition of South Carolina 158
Chapter X North Carolina 173
From South Carolina to the Virginia Border 173
The Location, and the European Settlements of North Carolina 176

The New System of Government and the Inhabitants of North Carolina 179

Chapter XI Virginia 183

Trip through Virginia from North Carolina to the Maryland Border 183

Location and Climate of Virginia; Its Former Inhabitants, and the European Settlements 190

Present Condition of Virginia 192

Kentucky 199

Chapter XII Maryland 205

Trip through Maryland, from the Virginia Border to the Pennsylvania Border 205

Location and Former Condition of Maryland 206

Present Condition of Maryland 208

Chapter XIII The State of Delaware 211

Chapter XIV Pennsylvania 213

From Philadelphia to Bethlehem 213

Condition of Pennsylvania and a Brief Account of Its Earliest Settlements 217

The New Constitutions of Pennsylvania 219

The City of Philadelphia 223

The Inhabitants of Pennsylvania and Their Trade 229

Chapter XV New Jersey 237

Condition of New Jersey and Its Principal Cities 237

Origin of the Colony of New Jersey and the Present System of Government of This State 239

Present Condition of New Jersey 243

Chapter XVI The State of Connecticut 247

From New York to New Haven and Hartford, and from There to the Massachusetts Border 247

The European Settlements in Connecticut and Its New Form of Government 250

Present Condition of Connecticut 252

Chapter XVII The State of Rhode Island 255

Trip through the State of Rhode Island 255

Former and Present Condition of Rhode Island 259

Chapter XVIII The United States in General 263

The New Federal Government 263

Reflections on the Present Condition of the American Republic 264
Notes 271

Luigi Castiglioni's Botanical Observations

Translated by Antonio Pace
Edited by Joseph and Nesta Ewan 341

Luigi Castiglioni's Place in North American Botany 343
Observations on the Most Useful Plants in the United States 345
References 463
Castiglioni's References 463
Editors' References 467
Index 469

Illustrations

Plate I. Iceberg off the Newfoundland coast. 7
Plate II. Plan of Boston (1) and environs (2-20). 10
Plate III. Plan of the City of Boston. 17
Plate IV. Indian artifacts. 38
Plate V. Plan of New York City. 94
Plate VI. Plan of Charleston. 161
Plate VII. Cultivation and harvesting of rice (figs. 1-3), indigo (figs. 4, 5), and sweet potato (fig. 6). 169
Plate VIII. Cultivation and harvesting of tobacco. 198
Plate IX. Plan of Philadelphia. 224
Plate X. Different rail fences in Virginia (fig. 1) and Pennsylvania (figs. 2, 3). 234
Plate XI. Opossum. 245
Plate XII. Earliest published illustration of Bartram's Franklinia. 382
Plate XIII. Scrub oak, the "Quercus pumila" of Banister (*Quercus ilicifolia* Wang.). 434
Plate XIV. Poison Swamp Sumac (*Rhus vernix* L.). 439

ANTONIO PACE is Professor of Italian Emeritus, University of Washington, and a professional luthier.

JOSEPH EWAN is Ida Richardson Professor of Botany Emeritus, Tulane University, and a Smithsonian Regent Fellow.

General Introduction

Preamble

THE BARRIER of language has too long kept the Milanese patrician traveler and botanist Luigi Castiglioni from proper recognition as an observer of colonial America. The present edition in translation of his *Viaggio negli Stati Uniti dell'America Settentrionale fatto negli anni 1785, 1786, e 1787* (Milano: Marelli, 1790) realizes a promise of more than three decades ago[1] to make accessible to American readers the results of the venture undertaken by the young traveler with the double purpose of seeing with his own eyes the new society in formation beyond the Atlantic after the break with England, and of studying the plant life of the New World with a view to identifying those of its natural productions that might advantageously be introduced in his native country. The main fruit of Castiglioni's two years of residence in America was the *Viaggio,* the bulk of whose two volumes consists of a systematic compendium of information, drawn both from direct observation and secondary sources, on the topography, history, institutions, customs, agriculture, and industry of the individual states from Massachusetts to Georgia, to which is attached a long descriptive appendix of plants deemed worthy of attention and possible adoption in Italy.

Birth, Family, Early Years, and Education of Luigi Castiglioni

An acquaintance with Luigi Castiglioni's person, family background, and the cultural environment in which he was formed helps explain his motivation and the biases that appear in the book that is the main monument to his memory. The general canvas is, understandably, the European Enlightenment, or *Illuminismo,* as the Italians call it—that cheerful moment in the history of western civilization characterized by a dominant faith in the power of man's rational faculty to plumb the physical and moral universe and, through the diffusion of knowledge, to achieve a sort of terrestrial paradise. For many Italians, as for Europeans in general, a conspicuous ingredient of this humanitarian dream was the mirage of America as a providential adumbration of the millenium to come. Milan, the capital of Lombardy and the city in which Castiglioni was born and spent nearly all his life, was one of the centers most actively involved in the social and intellectual ferment of the time. Although the province of Lombardy was an appanage of the House of Austria, liberality and reform were the order of the day, and under the generous rule of Maria Theresa and Joseph II, and the even more progressive and pro-Italian direction of the minister plenipotentiary Count Karl Joseph von Firmian, Milan was abreast of what was going on in the rest of Europe beyond the Alps.

It was in this expansive setting that on the 3rd of October, 1757, a son was born to "the Illustrissimo Signor Don Ottavio Castiglioni and the Illustrissima Signora Donna Teresa Verri," to whom was given three days later in the church of Santa Eufemia the name Luiggi Alessandro Francesco Maria Paolo Gaspare.[2] The child's ancestry was distinguished on both sides. The Castiglionis could trace their lineage back to the Middle Ages, perhaps as far as the eleventh century.[3] Luigi's mother was a member of the large and influential Verri clan and sister of those two sparks of the Milanese Enlightenment, Pietro and Alessandro. As if these connections were not enough, the train of events led to a compounding of family bonds when in 1776 Pietro Verri married his niece Marietta Castiglioni, becoming thereby Luigi's brother-in-law as well as his uncle.[4]

The little that we know about the formative years of Luigi Castiglioni comes from that great epistolary tableau of its time—the correspondence of his two uncles, Pietro and Alessandro Verri.[5] In it, punctuated by a crescendo of exasperated outbursts from Pietro Verri over what appeared to him to be the limitations of his two nephews Luigi and his elder brother Alfonso, one can discern the crystallization of Luigi's adolescent character and his scientific interests. Luigi appears for the first time on April 6, 1776, in the midst of a batch of family news sent by Pietro to his brother in Rome.[6] Recently married to Marietta, Pietro had occasion to speak of his "two fine relatives," Luigi and his brother, pointing to the former as endowed with "more spark and greater sensitivity" but "very timid." In September of the same year[7] Pietro announced that the two lads were thinking of paying Alessandro a visit in

Rome as part of a tour of Italy undertaken "spontaneously" in order to "educate themselves and to learn Italian." "Don't expect them to know the ways of the world, with which they are just becoming acquainted; and you will find them timid and anything but venturesome regarding certain ideas. But they are two good honest beings and fine relatives and friends."

Two months later, in November, 1776,[8] Pietro alludes again to the impending visit, this time yielding a clue as to the reason for the thinly veiled deprecation in his remarks about Luigi and his brother. Even the aftertaste of a pleasant four-day vacation just enjoyed at the Castiglioni country home at Mozzate could not neutralize the acid of Pietro's observations: "Those two brothers, your nephews and my brothers-in-law, are fine lads, discreet, reasonable, affectionate. You will be satisfied with them. They are still such as can come from the hands of Father Sacchi, but they are two essentially unspoiled diamonds." As scions of a well-to-do patrician family the two boys were attending the fashionable Collegio de' Nobili maintained by the Barnabite fathers,[9] and Pietro, a compulsive liberal and reformer, obviously found it increasingly difficult to accept with equanimity the submissiveness inculcated by priestly discipline.

However repressive and enervating in other respects, Luigi's regimen did not stifle his scientific bent. The boy may have sublimated energies otherwise thwarted all the more intensely into uncontroversial scientific pursuits. When Alessandro Verri requested specimens of a beetle (*cornabue* or *cornabò*) not found in the area of Rome, it was Luigi who caught the insects and prepared the box so that they might reach their destination alive.[10] Shortly thereafter, in August, 1777,[11] Pietro asked his brother on behalf of his nephews for seeds from the Botanical Garden of Rome. Pietro's letter discloses that the craze for private pleasure gardens was in full swing among the Milanese; and Littas, Cusanis, and Andreolis were trying their luck with all kinds of botanical oddities. The two Castiglioni brothers also, according to Pietro Verri, were "studying Linnaeus and Tournefort like mad" and had already begun their own plant collection. By December of the same year we find Pietro thanking Alessandro[12] for a box of seeds sent from Rome and describing the joy of "our botanists" at the gift from their uncle. ". . . They have a fine collection of rare and curious simples and possess the language of Linnaeus and Tournefort." With the additional material just received from Rome, containing more than a hundred items unknown in Milan, Pietro predicted that within a year the two boys would have the finest collection in Milan.

The better part of a year would pass before Pietro Verri again mentions the Castiglioni brothers,[13] this time in a paroxysm of frustration and disappointment. His confidence in them, he felt, had been betrayed. It was once his intention to bring up the boys as real friends, and to that end he had associated intimately with them, taught them mathematics, done all in his power to give them proper direction after the death of their father. But now he faced the harsh reality that they had "come out of the Collegio good, honest, apparently reasonable, but with a prodigious passivity, barely daring to have a will." Even harder to swallow was the fact that the despised Father Sacchi was their "hero." To fill Pietro's cup of bitterness to the brim was the further spectacle of the two young nephews in the clutches of yet another priest, a Father Foglia, scathingly characterized by Pietro as a kind of "Tartuffe," who had been administering the Castiglioni estates. In this moment of truth the fact emerges that the tour of Italy contemplated two years earlier was Pietro's idea, an experience he thought "necessary to cure their passivity and to give them an existence." But machinations behind the scenes had thwarted Pietro's plan, causing the trip to be put off. Pietro had done his best to persuade the nephews to be more firm, to travel, and, as an extremely able economist himself, he had urged them to take hold of their languishing patrimony and manage it efficiently. But to no avail. His efforts had brought him only Father Foglia's hate and a certain estrangement and embarrassment in his relationship with his nephews. "Now I realize that it is not possible for us to get along with one another; they are two innocent and passively good doves in the claws of a hawk." Alessandro's suggestion that Pietro not insist but wait for them to come to him, as they inevitably would if they were made of the proper stuff, did not mollify Pietro. The latter's parting blast of September 26, 1778,[14] reaches a peak of causticity: "They are good lads, but of mediocre talent, of no elevation; and, lacking in any kind of energy, they yield to whoever wishes to take the trouble to impose upon them, glad to free themselves of the annoyance of managing their own affairs. They have no whims nor desires, and they find it less troublesome to accept from time to time the little that is given them as pocket money than to put up with the bother of managing their income. . . . They are two doves without a will of their own."

Pietro Verri's strictures must be taken with a grain of salt, especially as regards Luigi Castiglioni. It may be that the two boys lacked the conspicuous open-mindedness and assertiveness that Pietro possessed and would have liked to see in them; and the passivity he deplored may well be attributable, at least in some degree, to their conservative early schooling under clerical mentors. On the other hand, benevolent avuncular exhortations and imprecations may not have been completely lost on the younger nephew, whose greater "spark" and "sensitivity" Pietro had noted in a calmer and perhaps more lucid moment. While Luigi did abandon, possibly at priestly instance, the idea of an educational tour of Italy, not many years would pass before he would undertake at his own initiative the far more challenging and liberating voyage across the Atlantic. Nor, as we shall see, did he remain impervious to currents that ran counter to those of the Old Regime, to judge from his involvement with freemasonry and collaboration in institutions set up in Italy under French rule – compromises unforgivable to his more conservative elder brother Alfonso and which led eventually to an estrangement of many years.[15]

What formal education Luigi Castiglioni received beyond the Collegio de' Nobili can only be conjectured. Particularly unfortunate is the lack of information about his botanical training. We have seen, however, that his passion for botany and command of Linnaean principles appear to have developed from an adolescent interest pursued with his elder brother at a time when private botanical gardens had become fashionable, and wealthy patrician and noble families were vying with one another in adorning their collections with exotic plants. By the time of his great American adventure, Luigi Castiglioni's mastery of his chosen field of knowledge was such as to inspire repeated comment. Sir Joseph Banks, the distinguished naturalist and president of the Royal Society of London, reported to Benjamin Franklin on November 19, 1784, that Castiglioni had impressed him as a "well informed young man."[16] "You will find him a true disciple of Linnaeus," wrote Dr. Aaron Dexter from Boston on June 20, 1785, in presenting the young traveler to the Congregational minister and botanist Manasseh Cutler in Ipswich, Massachusetts[17] – who in turn recorded in his diary that Castiglioni was "an accomplished botanist" from whose knowledge he had "received much advantage."[18] A few days later, in a letter of June 29th to the Rev. Dr. Jeremy Belknap, Cutler had occasion to praise Castiglioni as "a perfect master of Botany."[19] In August of the same year the noted English botanist Jonathan Stokes, whom Castiglioni had met in England, expressed to Cutler his high esteem of the young Italian's ability, but intimating at the same time some sort of student–teacher relationship with Giovanni Scopoli, Professor of Chemistry and Botany at the University of Pavia, whose effects he judged not entirely beneficial:

> . . . He [Castiglioni] is what I would call a botanist of sound principles. He has studied the philosophy of Botany with great attention, and seems to have escaped most of the foibles of his immediate master Scopoli, who is, I think, not less fond of saying something which shall appear new, than of discovering what is really so.
>
> I am apprehensive I spoke too freely to the Count of my opinion of his master. I am fully sensible of the merits of Scopoli, who has deserved much, but I cannot approve of his leading away the attention of the young botanist from the severe distinctive characters of Linnaeus to his own picturesque but often vague diagnosis.[20]

An entry in the diary of Ezra Stiles, president of Yale College, made on August 29, 1786, the day that Castiglioni called on him, must be based upon information obtained from the young traveler and ostensibly corroborates the fact of formal study under Scopoli: "He was educated in the University of Pavia 20 miles from Milan. . . ."[21] A misunderstanding between the two men would appear improbable in the light of Belknap's remark to Manasseh Cutler that Castiglioni "speaks English well."[22] On the other hand, Stiles' statement cannot be reconciled with the absence of Luigi Castiglioni's name from the student and graduation rosters of the University of Pavia during the period that he might have been in attendance.[23] In any case, scraps of correspondence between Scopoli and the Castiglioni brothers show that by the summer of 1784, when Luigi set off on the voyage that would take him to America, the noted professor (brought to the University of Pavia in 1777 by the Empress Maria Theresa in accordance with her plans for developing and strengthening the institution) had become an intimate of the Castiglionis and was on the friendliest of terms with his "dear Cavaliere" Luigi. Scopoli solicitously followed Luigi's peregrinations, corresponding with him and receiving seeds and samples of American flora and fauna.[24] This intimacy could have been the product of a range of relationships from informal association based on common scientific concerns to some kind of patronage of Scopoli by the Castiglionis. The possibility that Luigi in some manner came under the tutelage of Scopoli cannot be ruled out – a speculation perhaps substantiated by a parenthetical comment of Cutler in a letter of February 10, 1786, to Belknap: "Dr. Stokes speaks highly of our Italian Count, and thinks him not inferior in botanical knowledge to the famous Scopoli (the Count's preceptor), whom he visited in a late tour he has made to Italy and Vienna."[25]

Preparation for the American Voyage: The road to Paris; England. Departure for America.

We have no information on Luigi Castiglioni during the half dozen years that follow Pietro Verri's fit of disillusionment and despair with his nephews. He reappears in correspondence attendant upon the travels that would take him eventually to the New World. His itinerary from Italy to England during the second half of the year 1784 and some of the more memorable events of his French sojourn emerge from correspondence with the Lombard mathematician and astronomer Paolo Frisi.[26] Well traveled and affiliated with numerous scientific bodies, among them the Parisian Académie des Sciences and the Royal Society of London, Frisi, then in the last year of his life, was just the person Castiglioni needed to provide him with introductions – a favor Frisi performed presumably with all the more good will and thoroughness for being a longtime friend of Pietro Verri.

The first leg of Castiglioni's journey took him to Paris via Genoa, Nîmes, Montpellier, Toulouse, and Bordeaux. In Genoa, where he arrived on June 4, 1784, Frisi's recommendation admitted him to the company of the most widely known Genoese of the day, the Marquis Agostino Lomellini, Doge of the city in 1762, daring contestant in improvisation with the Arcadian poetess Corilla Olimpica, himself the author of sonnets on astronomy, translator of Watelet's *Art de la peinture,* member of the most illustrious European academies, personal friend of Voltaire and D'Alembert, the latter of whom dedicated to him his *Recherches sur la précession des équinoxes.* However, perhaps not surprisingly, what impressed Castiglioni most was the tour of his host's "vast and delightful garden."[27] In Montpellier, whence he addressed a letter to Frisi on June 29th, he made the acquaintance of the botanist and antiquary De Segnier and of the Abbé Jean-Joseph-Thérèse Roman, historian and translator of Petrarch. After spending some time in Toulouse and Bordeaux, he arrived in Paris around the 20th of July with Frisi's introductions to the Duke de la Rochefoucault-Liancourt, Buffon, Bailly, Condorcet, Franklin, and others.

Castiglioni's stay in Paris was a busy one, notwithstanding the seasonally sluggish tone of the city. He did not succeed in seeing the Duke de la Rochefoucault-Liancourt, Buffon, and Keralio, to whom he had been directed by Frisi, because they were vacationing in the country. But he struck it off very well with the prominent scholar and statesman Jean Sylvain de Bailly, dined with the du Boccages and the Austrian diplomat Count Florimund Mercy d'Argenteau, and attended meetings of the Académie des Sciences, where he transmitted Frisi's greetings to Auguste-Denis Fougereaux de Bondaroy, the mathematician Jacques-Antoine-Joseph Cousin, and Jacques Dominique de Cassini, director of the Paris observatory. Pierre Marie Auguste Broussonet, physician and naturalist, provided him with a letter to Sir Joseph Banks of the Royal Society of London.[28] Castiglioni's reports to Frisi are enlivened by information on sundry contemporary events—the antics of his fellow Milanese, Paolo Andreani; the last rumblings of the Mesmer controversy; the death of Diderot; the visit of Prince Henry of Prussia; the balloon ascensions by the brothers Robert; and the imprisonment of the son of a ballet dancer by the name of Vestri for refusing to favor the Queen with an encore at her request.

The climax of Castiglioni's stay in Paris was the encounter with Benjamin Franklin. Franklin's name turns up for the first time in a letter to Frisi dated August 2, 1784: ". . . Tomorrow I go to M. Bailly's in Challiot and to Mr. Franklin's in Passy. . . . I have not yet seen the latter, but I dined yesterday at Count Mercy's with a very talented and gracious young grandson of his,[29] to whom I revealed my intention of traveling in North America. . . ." Hence we know that on August 3 of that year Castiglioni went to Franklin with the letter penned by Frisi at the end of May, in which the latter, after acknowledging a gift of Franklin's works, presented his young countryman as a "gentleman from one of the most distinguished houses of our city, who plans on making a tour of America in order to see this courageous new nation and to continue his researches on natural history."[30]

The matter-of-fact opening words in the letter Castiglioni addressed to Frisi the day after this first meeting with Franklin reveal little of the excitement that he must have felt in the presence of the best known and most revered personage of the time: "Yesterday morning I went to Mr. Franklin's in Passy, to whom I presented your letter, and who received me with all the cordiality imaginable." Castiglioni went on to communicate to Frisi Franklin's acknowledgment of copies of his works for the American Philosophical Society and special personal greetings, as well as Franklin's promise of an answer to Frisi's last letter with information on the outcome of the official investigation of Mesmer's claims regarding animal magnetism in which he was then much involved. Another tantalizing reference to Franklin occurs in a letter written by Castiglioni from London on the 25th of October to express his gratitude to Frisi for the recommendations that had served so effectively to admit him into the company of so many notable people in Paris: "M. Bailly among others, who unites the most courteous manners with the most sublime erudition, and Mr. Franklin, worth knowing for his affability and character no less than for his fame, showered their attentions upon me, and the latter favored me with letters for London and more distant regions." Franklin, for his part, was very favorably impressed by Castiglioni. In a letter dated Passy, September 26, 1784, which has since somehow found its way into the British Museum, he thanked Frisi for having presented to him "a gentleman so intelligent and so amiable," promising that "If in his American travels I can be of any service to him, he may command me, on his own account as well as in respect to your recommendation."[31]

Frisi's death in November of 1784 abruptly removes his correspondence as a source of information regarding Castiglioni. Fortunately, Luigi's diary, in the possession of a descendant of his elder brother Alfonso,[32] enters most opportunely at this point to fill the void and to give us a good account of what Castiglioni did and what and whom he saw in England, from his arrival in Dover on October 22nd up to the eve of his departure for America in mid-April of the following year.

Castiglioni lost no opportunity to acquire the English language and to acquaint himself with as many aspects as possible of English civilization. His attention ranges in the diary from roads, terrains, houses, agricultural instruments, the arsenal at Portsmouth, the library of Oxford, Blenheim Castle, and the British Museum to details of dress and behavior. He attends a

Quaker meeting, describes an "aerostatic experiment" by Blanchard, sees a presentation of *The Marriage of Figaro* in English and a *commedia dell'arte* at the Covent Garden Theatre, spends an evening as a guest of the Anacreontic Society, is presented at Court, and attends a gala party in honor of the Queen's birthday. Of more pertinent interest to our purpose is the record of his scientific observations and contacts. He lists the trees in the botanical garden at Oxford, and describes the "Holophysikon" of the eccentric naturalist and collector Sir Ashton Lever that was in the process of being sold off by lottery.[33] He takes notes upon the stock of Thomas Martyn, the natural history draughtsman and dealer in shells, insects, and other curiosities, and upon the Linnaean collection of books, manuscripts, and natural productions. He lists the trees and describes in detail the grotto at the country estate of the Duke of New Castle at Twickenham. Castiglioni's reactions to the informal English garden that so intrigued continental Europeans of the day are of interest both to the botanist and the cultural historian. A special attraction for Castiglioni was the royal garden at Richmond with its collection of rare plants, many of them from America.

Castiglioni profited also from the personal relations he was able to establish. At Stoubridge he made the acquaintance of Jonathan Stokes, who, as we have already seen, reported the encounter to Manasseh Cutler. He spent considerable time with the Scottish botanist William Aiton, in charge of Kew Gardens, and with Sir Joseph Banks, on one occasion pointing out to the latter a hitherto unnoticed feature in the pistil of a plant from Kew Gardens. In Bath he dined with the distinguished Roman Catholic prelate and mathematician Charles Walmesley. In Birmingham he met both William Withering, botanist and collaborator with Stokes on the *Flora Anglica,* and Joseph Priestley, recording his personal impressions of the latter.

At the beginning of April, 1785, Castiglioni began to make preparations for the Atlantic crossing. On the 11th he left London to go aboard the *Neptune,* a 240-ton vessel that was to sail for Boston two days later. "Happy me," reads the final sentence of his English diary, "if I can observe things that deserve to pass down to the memory of posterity, and if I shall not have thrown away in vain my labor and my time."

Contemporary Reception of the *Viaggio*

The recognition that came with the publication of the *Viaggio* in 1790 must have made the young Milanese feel that his troubles and expense had not been useless. Comment focused, however, almost exclusively upon the scientific aspects of the work. It is not unlikely that the Austrian censorship, sensitized by the events of the recent French Revolution, discouraged any manifestation of enthusiasm over whatever good things Castiglioni had to say about the new American republic as a government and a society. The notice published in the widely diffused *Opuscoli scelti*[34] and echoed in the *Gazzetta enciclopedica,*[35] both of Milan, set the mood by de-emphasizing all but the botanical importance of the *Viaggio*:

> Many men, like a squirrel that circles about in its cage because it doesn't know what else to do, travel solely to flee from the boredom that afflicts them; and from these the public has no right to expect anything. But from the Signor Cavaliere Castiglioni, who set out from here already learned, and versed especially in the natural sciences; who along the way continued to study, and above all to acquire the languages that he was to speak; who added to the courage to face inconveniences and dangers the penetration and the judgment for recognizing clearly what he was going to see, Italy and his native country expected an account of his travels no less useful than important. And such is the one he has just published. He wastes no time moralizing about human nature, but instructs us pleasantly as he tells us about all that he has observed in those regions where nature is new and has all the vigor of youth. Especially important are his botanical and economic observations on the vegetables, in which he indicates the advantages that are derived from them over there and which we could derive from them. He has done more: a large part of those plants, thanks to his intelligence and concern, seconded by his worthy brother the ingenious and learned Count Alfonso, now flourish where we are. This is really contributing to one's native country by travels, from which others often bring back only vices and fashions.

The ample extract from Castiglioni's botanical appendix accompanying the bibliographical announcement[36] is the first of the citations that will attest the usefulness of the *Viaggio* down to the middle of the nineteenth century. In 1792 the *Antologia romana* edified its readers with Castiglioni's description of the North American sugar maple and the method of making sugar from its sap.[37] Three years later Castiglioni's book, with its rich and suggestive botanical appendix came to the attention of Venetians worried by the depletion of national forests, and the Veronese geologist Giovanni Arduino, in his capacity as Superintendant of Agriculture for Venice, saw fit to transmit to the Superintendant of Public Forests of the Province of Treviso information culled from Castiglioni on the promise of the *Bignonia catalpa* and the *Robinia pseudacacia* as replacements.[38]

The Lombards had themselves turned meantime to Castiglioni for possible suggestions as to what to do about their own dwindling forests. The annual report on agriculture and the crafts submitted in the year 1793 by the Milanese Società Patriotica contained a long chapter on "Heaths and Woods," and in a section titled "Woods: Exotic Plants That Should Be Introduced into Our Region," drew attention to the efforts and success of the Castiglioni brothers in exploiting the possibilities of acclimatizations, and particularly to the repertoir opened by Luigi's voyage to the New World.[39] The following year Carlo Amoretti, secretary of the Società Patriotica, in preparing a second Italian edition of Ludwig Mitterpaker's *Elements of Agriculture,* again voiced the need for saving the forests and praised his countryman Luigi Castiglioni for revealing so many remedial possibilities by his travels, observations, and experiments:

> Among the innumerable gentlemen who travel, very few make as great a contribution to their native country as the distinguished Sig. Cav. Don Luigi Castiglioni has to Lombardy. He, after having covered a large part of Europe, crossed over to America, where, as he examined like a philosopher the customs, commerce, and government of a nascent republic, sought among the products of the vegetation those with which to endow his own country. In his *Travels in North America* . . . he shows clearly how close that was to his heart, and therefore at the end he put an Appendix of "Observations on the Plants of North America"; and not content to conclude from the similarity of climate that they would do well where we are, demonstrated it by deed himself by sending and bringing back with him the seeds of new plants that now populate his family forests.[40]

Mention should be made of the modicum of international attention stirred by Castiglioni's work. A German translation of the *Viaggio* was undertaken, which, however, went no further than the first volume published in 1793.[41] The Spanish botanists Ruiz and Pavón proposed in Castiglioni's honor a genus *Castiglionia* for certain South American plants, but whatever immortality might have accrued from having his name in the botanical nomenclature evaporated when the genus was not sustained by botanists.[42] We are not surprised to find acknowledgment of Castiglioni's contribution to Italian forestry in Jonas Dryander's catalogue of the library of Sir Joseph Banks.[43] The copy of Castiglioni's *Viaggio* in the American Philosophical Society, marked in the hand of John Vaughan, the librarian, must have been sent by the author, but seems to have evoked no comment. Publication of the *Viaggio* might conceivably have set up ripples in America had Castiglioni sent Manasseh Cutler a copy as the latter requested in a letter of December 5, 1792[44] that probably never reached its destination.

With the turn of the century Castiglioni the scientist is quite completely relegated to history. In the year 1819 the author of a description of the city of Milan and its environs deemed it worthwhile to point out to French-speaking visitors the Castiglioni botanical garden in Via di Rugabella and the results of reforestation on the estate at Mozzate.[45] That strange and wonderful peripatetic, polyglot naturalist, and man-of-all-letters Constantine Samuel Rafinesque-Schmalz knew and seems to have drawn upon "Castiglione [*sic*], in Italian 1790," whom he cites in the "Historical Sketch" at the beginning of the second part of his *New Flora of North America,* published in Philadelphia in 1836.[46] Around mid-century concern about a substitute for the common potato after the failure of that crop in Europe would inspire a recollection of Luigi Castiglioni's observations on the *Apios tuberosa* [*Apios americana*].[47] However, the rarity of such references indicates that Castiglioni had lost his contemporary scientific relevance.

As has already been noted, contemporary reactions to the nonscientific content of Castiglioni's *Viaggio* are conspicuous by their absence. A couple of fleeting remarks by Castiglioni's friend Carlo Amoretti are the exception that prove the rule. We have seen that he dismissed Castiglioni's social and political observations with the bare comment: "He wastes no time moralizing about human nature, but instructs us pleasantly as he tells us about all he has observed in those regions where nature is new and has all the vigor of youth." Amoretti is a bit more venturesome in his revision of Mitterpaker's *Elementi di agricoltura,* where he notes that Castiglioni had "examined like a philosopher the customs, laws, commerce, and government of a nascent republic." Other 18th-century references to the *Viaggio* pass over these aspects of the work in complete silence. That such reticence in an age so sensitive to social and political ideas and events was entirely voluntary is hardly credible.

Be that as it may, the century of the Risorgimento seems somewhat more responsive to Castiglioni as an observer of American ways. His fellow Milanese, Carlo Giuseppe Londonio, turning his versatile pen to a history of the English colonies in America, had occasion in 1812 to cite Castiglioni to the effect that the most useful and valuable class of settler in the New World was the frontiersman who lived inland on his own tract of soil; and, as an example of the looseness of manners generated by a frontier society, he could think of no better illustration than Castiglioni's account of "a singular custom practiced in Connecticut," namely, bundling.[48] A few years later an anonymous reviewer of the second edition of Father Giovanni Grassi's *Sundry*

Notes on the Present State of the Republic of the United States of North America saw fit to present the book as the first original work in Italian on that part of the world since "the fine travels in America by our Milanese Cavaliere, Count Luigi Castiglioni."[49] The most generous recognition of Castiglioni as a source of historical and cultural information about America came from Giulio Ferrario in his huge in-quarto compilation on *Ancient and Modern Manners,* lavishly illustrated with aquatints. Ferrario cites Castiglioni repeatedly in his volume dealing with America, and at the end pays tribute to his "illustrious fellow citizen" as one of the authors whose footsteps he had followed closely in his own work.[50]

Honors and Public Charges Conferred on Castiglioni, Commemoratives

The most conspicuous recognition accorded Castiglioni came in the form of membership in various scientific bodies and appointments to public charges. The earliest of these was election to the American Academy of Arts and Sciences in Boston. The minutes of May 30, 1786, record that on that day "Le Comte de Castiglioni, Chevalier de ordere [*sic*] militaire de St. Etienne en Toscane was elected a fellow."[51]

Viewed in retrospect, Castiglioni's association with the Boston Academy appears a comedy of errors. The draft of Manasseh Cutler's letter of December 5, 1792, to Castiglioni opens with the following paragraph:

> Sir:—I did myself the honor, in January, 1786 to nominate you to the American Academy of Arts and Sciences, and at their next meeting you was elected a member. Upon making inquiry, I lately found the Diploma remained in the Secretary's Office, which I have taken, and to prevent further delay, do myself the honor to forward to you. While this infant Society feels itself honored by adding to the list of their Members the respectable name of Le Comte Castiglioni, they hope it will not be displeasing to you. Any communications you may be pleased to make will be gratefully received.[52]

On the title page of his *Viaggio* Castiglioni identifies himself as "Patrician of Milan, Knight in the Order of St. Stephen, P[ope] and M[artyr], Member of the American Philosophical Society of Philadelphia and of the Patriotic Society of Milan," making no reference to the American Academy of Arts and Sciences. He would not have omitted that impressive membership deliberately. Nor does he mention anywhere else his membership in that academy. The only conclusion to be drawn is that Cutler's letter, with the diploma, did not reach Castiglioni, with the result that he never knew of the honor conferred upon him by the hospitable Bostonians whose "pleasant company" he had so much enjoyed in May and June of 1785 and whose "friendly urgings" had persuaded him to linger in their city longer than he intended. It is further commentary on the casual way that such organizations were managed in the early days that the Bostonians soon forgot whom they had elected. When they finally got around to make an official tally of their membership a century later, the "Comte de Castiglioni" elected by their forebears was equated to "Carlo Ottavio Conte di Castiglioni, Tuscany"[53] – Luigi's nephew, who had acquired some distinction as an orientalist and numismatist.

On July 21, 1786, just a few weeks after his election to the American Academy of Arts and Sciences, Castiglioni was made a member of the American Philosophical Society, our oldest American scientific academy. I have discussed elsewhere Castiglioni's relations with the American Philosophical Society.[54] He may have been nominated by Benjamin Rush, whose company he appears to have found especially congenial; or by Franklin, who could have seen in the wealthy young patrician a good opportunity for disseminating information that would redound to the advantage of the newly formed United States. The sponsor may perhaps have been John Vaughan, longtime librarian and corresponding secretary of the Society – from whose hand we have an undated note which, if it is not a recommendation in support of Castiglioni's election, invites comment for its relevance to the latter's self-imposed American mission:

> Count Castiglioni is of a family of very ancient nobility, being a knight of one of the highest orders in Europe. Is of great influence in his country as Nephew to the Gov. of Milan, is devoted to science & related to Father Becharia – has come to this country at his own expence & travelled over a great part of it in examination of its botanical productions.[55]

The inaccuracies and exaggerations in Vaughan's memorandum could be owing to misunderstanding on his part. More likely, they are a byproduct of Castiglioni's strategy for winning concessions. In the first place, Luigi was not a count – at least not until Napoleon so dubbed him in 1810,[56] an honor become dubious and conveniently forgotten after the Congress of Vienna. The title of count was borne properly for the family by Luigi's elder brother Alfonso, upon whom it had been conferred by Maria Theresa in 1774.[57] References to Luigi Castiglioni in his native country previous to the Napoleonic ennoblement limit his honorifics to the modest "don," or at the most, "cavaliere." It was as "le chevalier Castiglioni" that Paolo Frisi introduced his young countryman to Franklin in Paris.[58] Only a little later, during the English sojourn, does the title "count" appear. Sir Joseph Banks, reporting to Franklin on Castiglioni's efforts to improve his English before embarking for America, remarks, "Count Castiglioni I have seen . . .";[59] and Jonathan Stokes, in his letter to Cutler cited above,[60] uses the same title. Allusions to Castiglioni during his residence in America invariably incorporate the nobiliary title. One must conclude that Castiglioni found it expedient to usurp his brother's title as a social lubricant during his travels, for which purpose it clearly served him well.

A similar conclusion may be drawn from Vaughan's qualification of Castiglioni as a "knight in one of the highest orders of Europe" based upon the latter's membership in the order of St. Stephen of Tuscany, of which he was made a "cavaliere" in 1779.[61] The doubtful question whether this order, founded by Cosimo de' Medici in 1562, was one of the highest in Europe[62] is here secondary to the inference that Castiglioni was again apparently seeking to impress a plebeian American.

The same assessment seems inevitable for the representation of Castiglioni as "Nephew to the Gov. of Milan," a historical impossibility because the governor of Milan since 1771 had been Ferdinand, Archduke of Austria. Uncle Pietro's highest civic offices were as counselor and vice president of the "Magistrato Camerale"[63]—a sort of Bureau of Finance—hardly to be equated to the governorship of Milan.

On the other hand, Vaughan's assertion that Castiglioni was "related to Father Beccaria" can be plausibly explained as owing to a mutual misunderstanding. One imagines that Vaughan was the first to bring up the name of Beccaria in some allusion to the Piedmontese professor of physics Giambatista Beccaria, who would have been known to him through the polemic of some years earlier over Franklin's electrical theories. Castiglioni, on his part, hearing the same surname, would presumably have associated it at once with his own countryman, the famous penologist Cesare Beccaria.[64]

At all events, Castiglioni so succeeded in impressing Vaughan with his station in life that a decade and half later, when the latter was casting about for contacts in order to resume the exchange with Italy disrupted by the French Revolution and its aftermath, one of the first names to come to mind was that of the Milanese patrician traveler, botanist, and foreign member of the American Philosophical Society. Accordingly, on July 24, 1802, Vaughan sent him several sets of the third, fourth, and fifth volumes of the *Transactions,* two of them for the Società Patriotica of Milan and the Academy of Sciences of Turin, the others for societies in Florence, Bologna, and Verona, at Castiglioni's discretion.[65]

In 1789, shortly after his return to Italy, Castiglioni was named a member of his native Società Patriotica, an organization founded in 1776 by Maria Theresa of Austria for the purpose of fostering agriculture and the practical arts in Lombardy, and to which Benjamin Franklin and Benjamin Rush already belonged consequent upon suggestions made by Castiglioni when he was in America.[66] In 1792 he presided over the body as its senior administrator ("conservatore anziano"), a duty that could not have continued beyond 1796, when the French invasion brought about the demise of the society.

Other academies subsequently added Castiglioni's name to their membership. After the Academy of Bologna was incorporated under the Napoleonic regime into a centralized Istituto Nazionale di Scienze e d'Arti, Castiglioni was inducted (April 7, 1803) to help fill out the statutory roster of sixty members. However, when the Bolognese academy was reinstated in 1829, Castiglioni's name appears to have been swept out with the other relics of the Napoleonic order.[67] The Italian Academy of Sciences, Letters, and Arts in Leghorn made him an honorary member in 1810.[68] The State Archives of Milan also contain two requests from Castiglioni addressed to the Austrian chancellery in Vienna for permission to accept foreign honors—one of the year 1824 from the Royal Academy of Fine Arts of Copenhagen, the other four years later from the Society for the Advancement of the Liberal and Mechanical Arts of Geneva. Furthermore, the datum cited in the 1831 police report on Castiglioni's masonic sympathies to the effect that he was a "member of the Imperial Royal Academy of Vienna"[69] is in all likelihood a correct indication of yet another honorary affiliation.

Castiglioni held many public charges in the spirit of *noblesse oblige.*[70] In 1803 he was appointed to a commission formed to adapt the traditional coinage to the metric-decimal system; in 1807 he became director of the Royal Printing House; and in 1809 he was made a senator of the Napoleonic Kingdom of Italy. He was president of the Academy of Fine Arts of the city of Milan from 1807 to 1831.[71] He was also named director of the municipal vivarium and served on various other bodies, such as the college of landholders and the heraldic commission. Paradoxically, after Napoleon made him a count in 1810, the Austrian government of the Restoration conferred upon him, in 1819, knighthood in the order of the Iron Cross and appointed him Imperial Chamberlain the following year.[72]

Although Castiglioni, as befitting a member of the landed patriciate, never expected nor received payment for his work, evidence exists that he took his various duties seriously. The State Archives of Milan contain a long report dated September 12, 1815, addressed to the central office of Public Education in which he collaborated with his brother Alfonso to evaluate the prospectus for a work on Italian flora by one Professor Brignoli, who was applying for a subsidy. The same archives preserve several documents having to do with the onerous charge of the presidency of the Academy of Fine Arts, one of them a long detailed description, dated March 11, 1812, of personnel, students, activities, and inventory requested by the Director General of Public Education. The Istituto Lombardo di Scienze e Lettere furnishes from its files clues relative to Castiglioni's activity as a fellow academician. On April 5, 1821, demonstrating extensive knowledge in his hobby of numismatics,[73] he reviewed a work on the money of the ancient Mesopotamian city of Kufa, pointing out the deficiencies of the study and its plagiarisms from his nephew Carlo Ottavio. He also participated as one of six members on a committee appointed at the behest of the Viennese authorities on January 25, 1819, to report on the raw materials and manufactures of the Kingdom of Italy.

The *Gazzetta privilegiata di Milano* records Castiglioni's death on July 19, 1832. His direct descendancy did not go beyond daughter Beatrice who died in 1850, his son Alessandro having died in infancy.[74] Ticozzi, who memorialized Luigi Castiglioni in his continuation of G. B. Corniani's *Secoli della letteratura italiana,*[75] has left us a sympathetic profile of the man, based in all likelihood upon personal acquaintance: "He was always religious and beneficent, frank and polite. He ordered that the money usually spent in final ceremonies be applied to the relief of the humble but self-respecting poor; moreover, he left a considerable grant to the families of all his peasants, whom he had always supported generously in their needs."

The Fortunes of Castiglioni Since the Middle of the Nineteenth Century

Castiglioni's name was not often seen in Europe during the last half of the nineteenth century and the first quarter of the present one. Two historians animated by contemporary Risorgimento fervor, Cesare Cantù and Felice Calvi, mentioned him briefly[76] as a laudable example of the enlightened and revitalized Milanese patriciate of his day. Perhaps more frequent, though hardly less fleeting, is his appearance in such works on botanical history and reference as those of G. A. Pritzel[77] and P. A. Saccardo.[78] P. Amat di San Filippo took particular note of him as a traveler.[79] And Giovanni Casati included Castiglioni in his *Dictionary of Italian Men of Letters*[80] as traveler in America, botanist, and translator of Latin documents on agriculture, antiquities, and numismatics. At some moment in the nineteenth century someone remembered Castiglioni well enough to see that a street was named after him in Milan.[81]

Meantime, American historians began to become aware of the contribution of Castiglioni's *Viaggio* to the social and natural history of their country. The earliest of those to cast an interested glance at Castiglioni's work was the Boston brahmin and littérateur of parts Henry T. Tuckerman. He was also for several decades the only one qualified, by virtue of long residence in Italy and a good working knowledge of the Italian language, to understand fully the contents of the book.[82] Both Sabin and Meisel included Castiglioni within their respective bibliographical purviews.[83] Charles Sprague Sargent refers from time to time to Castiglioni's descriptions.[84] After Tuckerman, C. E. Faxon, in 1891, recommended Castiglioni to his countrymen[85] for "his judicious observations on the social and political conditions of the young republic" and for "his careful notes on its geography and natural history," calling especial attention to Castiglioni's insistence upon "the affinities of our plants with those of Japan and China." W. W. Eggleston's "Trip Across Vermont by Luigi Castiglioni, an Italian Nobleman, in August, 1785"[86] is the first attempt at an integral presentation of a particular portion of the *Viaggio* in answer to rising contemporary interest in local history. And in 1922, A. J. Morrison, as editor of a collection of documents on early travel in Virginia, saw fit to include a translation of part of Castiglioni's account dealing with that state.[87]

Modern scholarly interest in Castiglioni is a crescendo dating from about the third decade of the present century. When Giulio Natali revamped in 1929 his vast survey of eighteenth-century Italian literature published by Vallardi of Milan, he reserved a niche for Castiglioni in his third chapter dealing with "The Philosophic Century."[88] The following year Charles R. D. Miller exhumed and reprinted the eulogy in the *Gazzetta privilegiata di Milano.*[89] In 1934 Giovanni Schiavo drew attention to the important letter from William Bradford, then Attorney General of Pennsylvania, buried in Castiglioni's footnotes attesting the profound impact of Cesare Beccaria's *Crime and Punishment* upon the constitution and penal system of the State of Pennsylvania.[90] In 1941 Nicola Canè recalled Castiglioni to the memory of his fellow Milanese as one who had braved the discomforts and perils of travel to the New World in order to study its society and to bring back for acclimatization such useful plants as the locust, the catalpa, the tulip tree, the thujas, and various species of pine, oak, and nut.[91] Castiglioni figures conspicuously, especially in his American connections, in my survey published in 1945 of the exchange between the American Philosophical Society and Italy[92]; and four years later the late Professor Howard R. Marraro of Columbia University made a detailed study of Castiglioni's journey through Virginia.[93] In the years 1955 and 1957 Hui-Lin Li, of the Morris Arboretum at the University of Pennsylvania, exploited Castiglioni's *Viaggio* for botanical history, appraising the

Italian's pioneering efforts in plant geography and plant introduction and assessing his contributions to botany within a Linnaean framework.[94] In 1957 Thomas D. Clark inserted an extensive biobibliographical note on Castiglioni in his *Travels in the Old South.*[95] As already indicated, my volume on *Benjamin Franklin and Italy,* published in 1958, brought into focus at appropriate points the contacts of the great American with the Italian traveler. The USIS of Milan, assembling in 1963 a display on the theme of "Italian Travelers in the World," highlighted Castiglioni's *Viaggio*, a copy of which was lent for the occasion by the Biblioteca Nazionale Braidense.[96] In 1967 Samuel J. Hough, of the John Carter Brown Library in Providence, R. I., translated and annotated Castiglioni's travels in Rhode Island, New Hampshire, and Vermont.[97] R. Tomaselli, discussing in 1973 the history of the botanical garden at the University of Pavia,[98] cast, as we have seen, some incidental light on Castiglioni's relations with Giovanni Scopoli. Finally, in 1975, I returned to the topic of Castiglioni in behalf of the freshly launched journal *Italian Americana* with a brief *état présent* and a summary collation of a partial manuscript of the *Viaggio* owned, like the English journal, by Count Cesare Brambilla di Civesio, accompanied by a translation of the chapter on Connecticut from this draft.[99]

Castiglioni as an Observer of the American Scene

In undertaking to present to his countrymen the "political birth of a new Republic," Castiglioni did not reckon with the handicaps imposed upon him by temperament, training, and social conditioning. His bent was clearly not for the study of human motivations and behavior, whether individual or social. The evidence from his early years on suggests that Castiglioni was by nature a gentle, compliant, pleasant-mannered individual, too uncertain and diffident to feel much curiosity about the contemporary inner workings, or even the historical behavior, of other human beings. He may consequently have applied all the more vigorously his considerable intelligence to the less intimidating world of nature, especially to that of plants—a choice dictated at least to some extent, as we have seen, by the popularity of the private pleasure garden among the Milanese gentry of the second part of the eighteenth century.

The highly disciplined and rigorously circumscribed education imparted in the Barnabite schools was not the best preparation the young Castiglioni could have had for his venture. It must have contributed to the crystallization of a conservative Roman Catholic outlook that made him incapable of viewing without prejudice the teeming American colonial religious scene. Highly classical and Latinate in content, there would have been little in the curriculum to arouse interest in the history of times nearer to Castiglioni's own. Furthermore, insofar as effective historical writing depends on literary sensitivity and artistry, the Barnabite fathers failed woefully to prepare their ward. An awareness of this deficiency unquestionably underlay Uncle Pietro Verri's scheme to send his two nephews off on the tour of the Italian peninsula which, among other advantages, presumably would have aided them, as he remarked with brutal frankness, "to learn Italian." Since Luigi was then about nineteen years old, it can only be conjectured how much good the junket would have done him. In any case, we must count the *Viaggio*, from a literary point of view, one of the casualties of the age. Italy's centuries-old political fragmentation had obstructed the development of a standard national idiom, and eighteenth-century Milan afforded little opportunity to hear any kind of generally acceptable vernacular. The person destined to point the way to a modern national Italian language, Castiglioni's fellow Milanese Alessandro Manzoni, was but a child of five when the *Viaggio* appeared in 1790. The style of Castiglioni's work smacks strongly of the embalmed classics of the past, particularly the Cinquecento, upon which the Barnabite fathers doubtless based whatever instruction in Italian they gave. Faxon, insensitive to the pedantic archaisms of Castiglioni's language and to its other faults of vocabulary, grammar, and expression, commended the *Viaggio* for its "simple grace" and readability.[100] More valid was the assessment of Cusani, who ascribed the limited success of the work in Italy to its "cold narration and careless style."[101] Certain writers gain in translation. It is hoped that the Englished *Viaggio* below will be, stylistically at least, an improvement on the original.

The narrative that fills all the first volume and half the second volume of Castiglioni's work is simultaneously a journal of his travels, a description of physical America, a history of the separate states of the new republic, and an account of contemporary society in those states. The first of these aspects of the work will interest most the modern reader. The author's prose comes to life when he is telling about objects and scenes before his own eyes or relating episodes and situations experienced. Much of this matter will be useful grist for the historian of early America—for example, Castiglioni's visit to the Penobscot Indian village; the idyllic picture of Mr. Gregory's pioneering family in the depths of the Maine woods; the glimpse of a free negro homesteading family in the St. George wilds; the condition of the roads and inns; the description of various towns and cities; the shocking parallel advertisements for the sale of a horse and a young negro slave; the notes on colonial techniques of agriculture, mining, and manufacture; the eyewitness account of an audience given by Governor William Moultrie of South Carolina to an embassy of Choctaw Indians; the comparative glossary of the Choctaw and Cherokee languages compiled and transmitted to Castiglioni by an unidentified individual; details on the crudity of frontier life; the treatment of slaves; the cultivation of rice and indigo in South Carolina; the raising of tobacco in Virginia; the visits to the Moravian settlements at Bethlehem and Nazareth, Pennsylvania; the proposal to establish a chemistry laboratory in the basement of Philosophical Hall in Philadelphia; the text of the precious letter from William Bradford, then Attorney General of Pennsylvania, acknowledging the indebtedness of the Pennsylvania penal system to the ideas of Cesare Beccaria; the visits to Harvard, Yale, and Princeton Colleges; and the wry appraisal of the New England custom of bundling.

The picture of physical America that emerges from Luigi Castiglioni's journal also retains much of its interest to this day. It is a sober account, often eye-witness, of terrains, mountain ranges, climates, water systems, and forests, punctuated by little excursions into related plant and animal life. Castiglioni does not have the eye of an artist, and he is constitutionally unable to dramatize what he sees; nevertheless much of the material he reports acquires a degree of vividness from being strained through his personal perceptions. After following him along his laborious, and often dangerous, route from his arrival in Boston through the upper New England states into lower Canada, and then successively through the remaining United States of America, one comes off with a strong residual impression of the vastness and variety of the new nation. This aspect of the *Viaggio* makes it a useful complement to the accounts of such travelers as Chastellux, Smyth, Brissot de Warville, Carver, and others, who were for the most part only incidentally concerned with the natural and physical ambiance.

Less valuable is the information Castiglioni provides on the prehistory and history of the early settlements, a deficiency that perhaps should not surprise us, since the highly classical and Latinate content of his formal schooling was not such as to inculcate a knowledge of or interest in the more recent history of the western world, to say nothing of primitive civilizations. Moreover, even if Castiglioni had possessed such an interest, the inadequacies of extant sources of information on the New World would have thwarted the efforts of a historian far more committed and seasoned than he. The most that can be said for this aspect of the historical ingredient of the *Viaggio* is that it stands as one example of the state of European knowledge about America at that time.

Quite disappointing also is Castiglioni's failure to garner more of the history that lay about him. We catch frequent echoes of the Revolutionary War, but Castiglioni adds very little of any significance to what is known about that great event and its immediate aftermath. The more the pity because he apparently had ready access to the presence of many of the protagonists of those heroic days. At the very least, he might have left us a gallery of useful vignettes. We are told, for example, that he met Jefferson in Franklin's home in Passy, but nothing more. Of Franklin, whom Castiglioni saw in Paris and then again in Philadelphia, we have little more than a stylized account. He spent four days with Washington at Mount Vernon, of which the only residue is a stereotype of the American Cincinnatus. From the appendix of American biographies attached to an earlier draft of the *Viaggio*, of which we take note below in the variants, we infer that Castiglioni met in person and associated more or less intimately with such notables as John Adams, Samuel Adams, John Hancock, Robert Morris, Charles Thomson, Nathanael Greene, Henry Knox, and Benjamin Lincoln, but what he says about them is sadly lacking in life and substance.

Castiglioni's political and social observations on the newborn United States also leave much to be desired, vitiated as they are by prejudices inculcated by wealth and position, and, furthermore, made apparently from a wobbly personal political orientation. There was little of the political animal in Castiglioni. Timid and conservative, he was at the same time too sensitive and too intelligent to remain completely indifferent to the beat of contemporary drums, especially in his early years when liberalism and reform were fashionable. In the halcyon days before Italy was caught in the maelstrom of the French Revolution, a measure of freedom of thought and expression was tolerated, so that Castiglioni could with relative impunity act as intermediary between Franklin and the Cremonese printer Lorenzo Manini in the enterprise of printing and diffusing the *Lettere americane* of Gian Rinaldo Carli, even though everyone, including the civil authorities, must have been aware of the thick masonic atmosphere surrounding the operation.[102] The storm had not yet struck when Castiglioni published his *Viaggio*, boldly proclaiming the American Revolution "one of the most memorable events of this century" that might "in time produce important consequences for Europe," incorporating the text of the freshly drafted federal constitution in a chapter that exalted New World humanity and civilization in terms set by Jefferson's *Notes on the State of Virginia,* and closing the account of his travels with an optimistic vision of the future greatness of the United States of America made possible by the recent revolution.

However, that Castiglioni's youthful flirtation with freemasonry and republicanism was not dictated by profound reflection and firm convictions becomes clear from his subsequent political behavior. His political allegiances underwent changes as kaleidoscopic as those that shook Lombardy during the hectic passage from Revolution to Napoleonic era and from Napoleonic era to Restoration. The adolescent meekness and indecision deprecated by

Pietro Verri apparently mellowed into an adult deference and mildness of manner that ingratiated him with whatever government rose to power. We have seen that Castiglioni did not disdain to accept assignments in the Napoleonic regime, for which no doubt the titles of count and senator of the kingdom were rewards. But when the winds began to shift, Castiglioni trimmed his sails accordingly; after the defeat of Leipzig in 1813, he turned his support to the moderate party that sought independence under the rule of Eugene Beauharnais.[103] He managed nonetheless to retain the favor of the Napoleonic government. A report of the year 1814 requested by Napoleon on "upright and enlightened individuals" qualified to serve as consultants on the various branches of administration in a plan to reorganize the Kingdom of Italy included, for the sector Public Education, Universities, and Lyceums, the name of "Luigi Castiglioni, ex-senator, President of the Academy of Fine Arts."[104] It is not surprising, therefore, to see the succeeding Austrian government looking suspiciously into Castiglioni's past. But the same paranoic police who ferreted out Castiglioni's early association with freemasonry closed their report with the paradoxically apologetic characterization: "Excellent in every respect, although as President of the Academy he makes one wish for greater firmness and executive ability. . . . Since the sect [freemasonry] looked for its recruits not only among extremists but also among the educated and the rich, it is possible that Castiglioni, in continuous contact with hotheads, let himself be taken in."[105] In any case, it is significant that Castiglioni's earlier indiscretions did not disqualify him for, nor did he refuse, the high honor of the Austrian Iron Cross and appointment as Imperial Chamberlain.

To the scholarly incapacity ensuing from this intrinsic indifference to matters political must be added the blindness he inherited as the scion of a wealthy patrician family[106] and as the product of an authoritarian and stratified society. Although the notion of a society based upon individual freedom and equality held for him a certain fascination in the abstract, he was unable to fathom its practical implications. He could not understand, and was appalled, for example, by disorders such as the Shays Rebellion in Massachusetts that occurred (1786–87) in the wake of the Revolution. He dutifully assumed the task of summarizing each state Constitution, but his analyses are perfunctory, devoid of profound reflection, and sometimes incorrect in the detail. Even the receipt of the great new federal Constitution directly from the hands of Benjamin Franklin evoked no visible reaction beyond the act of translation with a few bland explanatory notes.

Castiglioni's state-by-state historical, social, and political tableau of the distant nation in formation was foredoomed at best to a very limited success owing to the sheer unavailability of sufficient reliable information. A Tocqueville might have saved the situation by power of insight even in absence of a large fund of established knowledge. But Castiglioni was no Tocqueville. Despite its failings, Castiglioni's *Viaggio,* historical and factual in tone and substance, had the obvious merit of tempering, if not squelching, any impulse a European reader might have felt toward the common fanciful reconstructions of the New World and its inhabitants. Instead of the sophistication and geniality of a Tocqueville, we find a fundamental simplicity and honesty that more often than not mitigate the drabness of the narrative and somehow endow it with a quiet efficacy and charm.

The Text, the Translation, and the Present Edition

The *Viaggio* published in Milan in 1790 is the generally available account of Castiglioni's Atlantic crossing and his two years of travel before his departure from America on a Spanish ship on May 16, 1787. The original journals that he carried through the perils and minor disasters of his wanderings up and down the eastern seaboard of North America appear not to have survived. Extant, however, is a manuscript in Castiglioni's hand that seems to be what remains of a preliminary draft of the *Viaggio*. It draws attention both because of what it reveals about the elaboration of the work and for an appreciable amount of information omitted from the final printed text.[107]

The most conspicuous difference between the published *Viaggio* and the antecedent draft lies in the general plan of the work. The printed *Viaggio* is divided into two "tomes," consisting in all of eighteen chapters, to which is added a botanical appendix entitled "Observations on the Most Useful Plants of the United States," whereas the contents of the manuscript are disposed in three "tomes" comprising all told eighteen "books," plus a final "Capitolo unico" devoted to a series of thumbnail biographies of distinguished Americans, living and dead. Unfortunately, the first tome is missing entirely in the manuscript, and there is a large lacuna at the beginning of the second. The manuscript does not have the long composite botanical appendix. That material we find instead distributed in brief discrete appendices attached to the description of the separate states under the heading of "Natural Productions." Furthermore, the two extant tomes of the draft are interlarded not only with tables of contents but also with other matter, such as glossaries of Indian languages, tables of colonial coinages, weights, and indices of animals and plants, much of which Castiglioni would eventually either omit or weave into the published text. The final "Capitolo unico" of the draft becomes in the printed work an enlarged Chapter XVIII, obviously prompted by the reception of the American Constitution sent hot off the press by Franklin, where Castiglioni presents what must be the first European translation of that famous document; and he replaces the earlier series of disconnected biographies with the concluding essay, "Reflections on the Present State of the American Republic," a more sustained and philosophical appraisal of the New World's accomplishments and promise inspired clearly by Jefferson's *Notes on Virginia.*

Castiglioni may have had in mind an ambitious personal monument in the form of his complete travels.[108] The English diary, obviously intended as printer's copy, is marked "Tom. II" of "Travels to France and England in the Years 1784 and 1785." The last part of the draft *Viaggio* is designated "Tomo Terzo." An index at the end of the fragmentary preceding section is headed "Index of Animals and Plants Described in Tome II." One concludes that at one time Castiglioni projected a first volume for Europe, consisting of a tome each for France and England, and another volume for America, divided presumably into Tome I for the Atlantic crossing, followed by Tomes II and III for the American continent.

A textual comparison of the manuscript and the final *Viaggio* reveals further many differences in detail—usually eliminations from the earlier draft of material that may have seemed to the author, or to others who advised him, excessively personal, controversial, or trivial. Since these deletions are not infrequently of greater interest to the modern reader than what Castiglioni, his counselors, or possibly the censor, judged significant and appropriate for the contemporary Italian public, account will be taken of them in the critical apparatus accompanying the translation.

The version below of Castiglioni's *Viaggio* pretends to nothing more than a simple, readable rendition of the original text. To have attempted more would have been gratuitous, because Castiglioni's prose possesses few qualities worthy of transportation into another language. There would be little virtue in the struggle to find English counterparts for the lamentable idiosyncracies of the original—its ubiquitous Lombardisms, archaisms, polysyndeta, anacolutha, and dangling constructions of every conceivable sort. These are, for the most part, ironed out in the translation. Moreover, long inorganic sentences have been rearranged, and much reparagraphing has been done to make the text more readable. Care has been taken, however, to keep stylistic therapy from distorting the message.

We have tried to keep the documentation of the narrative text at a minimum. Since most of Castiglioni's information on the historical backgrounds, though no doubt new to his Italian public, is now commonplace, it is presented with practically no comment: the modern reader interested in verifying any part of it for whatever reason can generally do so even with such facile tools as the *Encyclopedia Americana,* the *Dictionary of American*

History, the *Dictionary of American Biography,* or the *American Guide Series* of the Federal Writers' Project. Notes, or at least references, are furnished for the more obscure persons, places, objects, and episodes. Persons and places unidentifiable or doubtful after a reasonable search are marked with asterisks in the indices. Proper names are corrected, anglicized, and modernized without further ado, even at the risk of thereby losing clues to contemporary forms and pronunciations. All notes and interpolations not Castiglioni's are set off by square brackets. The bracketed exclamation point in the scientific notes is the botanists' corroborative sign. The variants taken from the Brambilla di Civesio manuscript are headed with the siglum Br, followed by indication of tome and page. In the notes on Chapters XVI and XVII the initials SJH signify matter adopted from the editions of those chapters by Samuel J. Hough. The pagination of the published *Viaggio* of 1790 is given in the translation ([1:1] for example) in order to facilitate reference to the original text.

Antonio Pace

Notes

1. A. Pace, "The American Philosophical Society and Italy," *Proceedings of the American Philosophical Society* 90 (1946): 396, fn. 47.
2. A copy of the birth certificate dated May 6, 1803, exists in the Archivio di Stato of Milan.
3. See P. Litta et al., *Famiglie celebri di Italia,* 15 vols. (Milan &c., 1819–1904), s.v. "Castiglioni."
4. Litta, perhaps confusing the girl's name with that of her mother, gives "Teresa" as the name of Luigi's sister.
5. *Carteggio di Pietro e di Alessandro Verri,* edited by E. Greppi et al., 12 vols. (Milan: Cogliati &c., 1910–42).
6. Ibid. 8 (1934): 71.
7. Ibid., p. 166.
8. Ibid., p. 200.
9. *Gazzetta privilegiata di Milano* (19 July 1832), cited by Charles R. D. Miller, "Luigi Castiglioni," *Philological Quarterly* 9 (1930): 371.
10. *Carteggio Verri* 9 (1937): 60, 67, 70.
11. Ibid., p. 109.
12. Ibid., pp. 131, 133.
13. Ibid., 10 (1939): 76–79.
14. Ibid., p. 87.
15. R. Tomaselli, "Ricorrenze storiche dell'Orto Botanico dell'Università di Pavia negli anni settanta" (rprt. from the *Atti dell'Istituto Botanico e Laboratorio Crittogamico dell'Università di Pavia,* Ser. 6, Vol. 9) (1973): 40, fn. 21.
16. Letter in the Library of the American Philosophical Society.
17. Manasseh Cutler, *Life, Journal, and Correspondence,* edited by W. P. and J. P. Cutler (Cincinnati: Clarke, 1888), 1: 115, fn.
18. Ibid.
19. Ibid. 2: 232.
20. Ibid., pp. 260–61.
21. *The Literary Diary of Ezra Stiles,* edited by F. B. Dexter (New York: Scribners, 1901), 3:236.
22. Ibid. 2: 232.
23. In particular, the "Registro generale de' signori studenti dell'anno 1772, a tutto l'anno 1803"

and the "Elenco generale dei laureati nelle diverse facoltà dall'anno 1772 al 1796," documents in the archives of the University of Pavia.

24. Tomaselli, pp. 18, 55, 56, 65, 71, 77, 80, 85, 113. We may take as a modest monument to this moment in Luigi Castiglioni's career the designation *Stenocorus castillionei* given by Scopoli to an American insect recorded in his *Deliciae florae et faunae insubricae* (Pavia, 1789), 2: Plate 20, with the annotation (p. 40): "In America Septentrionali collegit Ill. Eques Aloysius Castiglioni, et una cum aliis Insectis, Plantisque multis misit Ill. Fratri suo Comiti Alphonso, qui ut omnia sua Insecta, ita et hoc etiam benevole communicavit" (p. 40). While Scopoli doubtless felt himself obliged to name his collaborator and "Maecenas" Count Alfonso, the fact that he goes out of his way to mention the younger brother proves that he also had in mind Sir Luigi.
25. Cutler, *Life, Journal* 2: 237.
26. In the Biblioteca Ambrosiana of Milan, Y.153. sup.
27. The Lomellini garden was of the English pleasure sort, more natural and "philosophic" than the formal continental garden; see Arturo Graf, *L'anglomania e l'influsso inglese in Italia nel secolo XVIII* (Turin: Loescher, 1911), p. 340 ff.
28. *The Banks Letters: A Calendar of the Manuscript Correspondence of Sir Joseph Banks Preserved in the British Museum (Natural History) and Other Collections in Great Britain,* edited by Warren R. Dawson (London: British Museum, 1958), p. 65.
29. William Temple served as Franklin's secretary in Paris.
30. A. Pace, *Benjamin Franklin and Italy* (Philadelphia: American Philosophical Society, 1958), p. 371.
31. Ibid.
32. The ms., entitled "Memorie scritte dal cavaliere Luigi Castiglioni in un viaggio fatto in Francia, e in Inghilterra negli anni 1784. e 1785. Tomo II. Milano 1789," is owned by Count Cesare Brambilla di Civesio of Nervi (Genoa), to whom I am indebted for making it available to me. The hand is obviously that of an amanuensis, but the text bears Castiglioni's own corrections and insertions. Tomo I, which must have contained the French journal, is missing.
33. Cf. W. H. Mullens, "Some Museums of Old London: i, The Leverian Museum," *The Museums Journal* 15 (1915): 123–29, 162–72; also Richard D. Altick, *The Shows of London*, (Cambridge, Mass.: Harvard University Press), pp. 28–33.
34. 13 (1790), "Libri nuovi," p. 17. In all probability the words are from the pen of Carlo Amoretti, Castiglioni's friend and editor of the *Opuscoli scelti.*
35. *Parte letteraria* 11 (1790): 174–75.
36. "Transunto delle osservazioni sui vegetabili dell'America Settentrionale del sig. cav. Luigi Castiglioni," 13 (1790): 269–312.
37. "Sopra l'acero zuccherino dell'America Settentrionale, e il modo di trarre lo zucchero, del sig. cav. Luigi Castiglioni," *Antologia romana* 18 (1792): 14–16.
38. Giovanni Arduino, "Al nobile sig. conte Ascanio Amaltro di Odereo, Soprintendente a Pubblici Boschi della Provincia Trevigiana," *Nuovo giornale d'Italia spettante alla scienza naturale* n.s. 6 (1795): 257–60.
39. *Atti della Società Patriotica di Milano* 3 (1793): xxxiv–cxxix – especially lix–lxviii.
40. *Elementi di agricoltura di Lodovico Mitterpaker di Mettemburg, P. Professore d'Agricoltura nell'Università di Buda, tradotti in italiano, con note relative all'agricoltura milanese; edizione seconda corretta ed accresciuta* (Milano: Galeazzi, 1794), Bk. v, p. 135. Various reviews of this edition of Mitterpaker also paid incidental tribute to Castiglioni: see *Opuscoli scelti* 17 (1794), "Libri nuovi," p. 34, and *Giornale letterario d'Europa* (Venice) 14 (1794): 100–107.

41. *Reise durch die Vereinigten Staaten von Nord-Amerika, in den Jahren 1785, 1786 und 1787, nebst Bemerkungen über die nützlichsten Gewächse dieses Landes.* Aus dem Italienischen von Magnus Peterson. Erster Theil. Mit Kupfern (Memmingen: A Seyler, 1793).
42. The authors' citation accompanying the description of the *Polygamia monoecia Castiglionia* is nevertheless worth repeating here: "*Genus dicatum D. Ludovico Castiglionio, Comiti, qui Arborum exoticarum observandarum et in patria Mediolanensi agro propagandarum studio accensus foederatas Americes Septentrionalis Provincia lustravit, semina collegit, et peregrinationis fructum opere edito cum erudito orbe communicavit.*" See H. Ruiz López and J. Pavón, *Florae peruvianae et chilensis prodromus* (Madrid: De Sancha, 1794); rprt., with bibl. notes, by F. A. Stafleu (Lehre: Cramer, 1965), p. 139. A good account of this botanical expedition to South America is A. R. Steele, *Flowers for the King: The Expedition of Ruiz and Pavón and the Flora of Peru* (Durham, N.C.: Duke University Press, 1964).
43. *Catalogus historico-naturalis Josephi Banks* (Londini: Bulmer, 1796; also New York: Johnson Reprint Corp., 1966, 1: 153).
44. Cutler, *Life, Journal* 2: 296.
45. J. B. de Modène, *Nouvelle description de la ville de Milan, suivie d'une description des environs de la ville et d'un voyage aux trois lacs* (Milan: Pirotta, 1819), pp. 29, 319.
46. Now available in photolithographed rprt. (Cambridge, Mass.: Arnold Arboretum, 1946). The reference to Castiglioni is on p. 6 of the "Historical Sketch."
47. G. Moretti, "Sulla coltivazione dell'*Apios tuberosa* comparativamente a quella del pomo di terra," *Giornale dell'I. R. Istituto di Scienze, Lettere ed Arti* 2 (1850): 81–89.
48. *Storia delle colonie inglesi in America dalla loro fondazione fino allo stabilimento della loro indipendenza* (Milan) 1 (1812), 271–72, 275.
49. *Notizie varie sullo stato presente della Repubblica degli Stati Uniti dell'America Settentrionale* (Milan: Silvestri, 1819), reviewed in *Biblioteca italiana* (Milan) 14 (1819): 130–31.
50. *Il costume antico e moderno: l'America* (Milan: Ferrario, Pt. i 1820), 497.
51. *Memoirs of the American Academy of Arts and Sciences* n.s. 11 (1888): 56.
52. Cutler, *Life, Journal* 2: 295.
53. *Memoirs of the American Academy of Arts and Sciences.*
54. "The American Philosophical Society and Italy," pp. 392–96.
55. Manuscript in the Library of the American Philosophical Society.
56. Tomaselli, "Ricorrenze."
57. Litta, *famigli celebri,* s.v. "Castiglioni." Cf. Tomaselli, "Ricorrenze," p. 38.
58. Pace, *Franklin and Italy,* p. 392.
59. Pace, "The American Philosophical Society and Italy," p. 393.
60. Cutler, *Life, Journal,* pp. 260–61.
61. *Carteggio Verri* 10 (1939): 347.
62. It is interesting that even Luigi's good friend Scopoli was not acquainted with the order. We find him, apparently as he was drawing up the list of patrons for his *Deliciae florae et faunae insubricae,* writing as follows to Alfonso Castiglioni: "Among the titles of Sig. Cavaliere, your brother, I do not understand the two letters 'P.' and 'M.' [Pope and Martyr] and therefore beg you to explain to me what they mean" (Tomaselli, "Ricorrenze," p. 71).
63. Nino Valeri, *Pietro Verri* (Florence: Le Monnier, 1969), pp. 196, 198, 256.
64. While I have not had the opportunity to verify the relations of the Beccaria and Castiglioni families, such a union of nobility and wealth is by no means outside the bounds of either possibility or probability, given the mores and socioeconomic imperatives of the Milanese patriciate; see F. A. Lucini, *La demografia del patriziato milanese* (Fusi: Università di Pavia, 1972). It is noteworthy in this connection that William Bradford, presenting Luigi

Castiglioni with a copy of a recent American translation of Beccaria's masterpiece, called it " a new proof of the veneration that my fellow citizens entertain for the sentiments *of your relative*" (see n39 of Chapter XIV for the text of this letter; italics added).

65. "Journal and Proceedings of the Corr. Sec. Begun 1789," p. 33 (manuscript in the Library of the American Philosophical Society).
66. P. Pecchiai, "La 'Società Patriottica' istituita in Milano dall'imperatrice Maria Teresa: cenni storici," *Archivio storico lombardo* 44, Pt. i (1917): 78, 102.
67. G. B. Ercolani, *Accademia delle Scienze dello Istituto di Bologna dalla sua origine a tutto il MDCCCLXXX* (Bologna: Zanichelli, 1881), pp. 98 and 121 ff.
68. *Atti dell'Accademia Italiana di Scienze, Lettere ed Arti* (Leghorn) 1 (1810): xlv.
69. A. Luzio, "La massoneria sotto il Regno Italico e la Restaurazione austriaca," *Archivio storico lombardo* Ser. V, 4 (1917): 334.
70. The State Archives of Milan preserve his affidavit of July 12, 1803, to the Minister of Internal Affairs of the Cisalpine Republic that he never had enjoyed, nor did at that date enjoy, "any pension or emolument" from his country.
71. A. Caimi, *L'Accademia di Belle Arti in Milano: sua origine, suo incremento e suo stato attuale* (Milan: Lombardi, 1873), p. 22.
72. Tomaselli, "Ricorrenze."
73. Castiglioni was an accomplished numismatist. His extensive collection of Lombard coins, going back to the time of the eastern emperors of the fourth century, willed to the city of Milan under the custody of the Biblioteca Ambrosiana, remains as a material token of his civic philanthropy; see the *Gazzetta privilegiata di Milano,* July 19, 1832.
74. See V. Spreti et al., *Enciclopedia storico-nobiliare italiana: appendice,* Pt. i (Milan: Ed. Soc. An. STIRPE, 1935), p. 552.
75. 2 (1833): 608.
76. See third chapter of Cantù's *L'abate Parini e la Lombardia nel secolo passato* (Milan: Gnocchi, 1854), and Calvi, *Il patriziato milanese,* 2nd ed. (Milan: Mosconi, 1876), p. 221.
77. *Thesaurus literaturae botanicae omnium gentium* (Lipsiae, 1851), Nos. 1744, 1745; 2nd ed., 1872 (rprt. Milan: Goërlich, 1950), Nos. 1595, 1956.
78. *La botanica in Italia: materiali per la storia di questa scienza* (Venice: Ferrari, 1895), p. 47; cf. *Memorie del R. Istituto Veneto di Scienze, Lettere ed Arti* 25 (1895).
79. *Biografia dei viaggiatori italiani: colla bibliografia delle loro opere (Studi biografici e bibliografici sulla storia della geografia in Italia)* (Rome: Tip. Romana), 1 (1882): 525.
80. *Dizionario degli scrittori d'Italia* (Milan: Ghirlanda), 2 (n.d.): 97.
81. Arduino Anselmi, *Milano storica nelle sue vie, nei suoi monumenti* (Milan: Hoepli, 1933), p. 159.
82. See his *America and Her Commentators* (New York: Scribners, 1864), pp. 338–40.
83. Joseph Sabin, *Bibliotheca Americana* (New York: Sabin), 3 (1870): 421: and M. Meisel, *Bibliography of American Natural History: The Pioneer Century, 1769–1865* (New York: Premier Pub. Co.), 3 (1929): 356.
84. *Sylva of North America,* 14 vols. (Boston: Houghton, Mifflin, 1892–1902), passim.
85. "Castiglioni's Travels in the United States," *Garden and Forest: A Journal of Horticulture, Landscape Art and Forestry* 4 (1891): 110–11.
86. Vermont Botanical Club, *Bulletin* 8 (1913): 21–22.
87. "Count Luigi Castiglioni, Chevalier of the Order of St. Stephen, P.M., 1786," in *Travels in Virginia in Revolutionary Times* (Lynchburg, Va.: Bell, 1922), pp. 61–69.
88. *Il Settecento,* pp. 203–204, 244.
89. Article cited in *Carteggio Verri,* p. 200.
90. *The Italians in America Before the Civil War* (New York/Chicago: Vigo Press, 1934), pp. 30–32.

91. "Luigi Castiglioni: uno che conobbe l'America del Nord un secolo e mezzo fa," *L'Ambrosiano* 20 (1941), No. 226 (22 Sept.), p. 3.
92. See Pace, "The American Philosophical Society and Italy."
93. "Count Luigi Castiglioni: An Early Traveller to Virginia," *Virginia Magazine of History and Biography* 58 (1950): 473–91.
94. "Luigi Castiglioni As a Pioneer in Plant Geography and Plant Introduction," *Proceedings of the American Philosophical Society* 99: 51–56; and *Journal of the Washington Academy of Sciences* 47, No. 1 (January 1957).
95. (Norman, Ok.: University of Oklahoma Press) 2 (1956): 92–96.
96. "Due milanesi del '500 e del '700 nell'America del Nord," *Città di Milano* 80 (1963): 238–40.
97. "Castiglioni's Visit to Rhode Island," *Rhode Island History* 26, No. 2: 53–64, and "An Italian Nobleman in New Hampshire and Vermont," *Appalachia* 36: 739–754. The first of these articles was reproduced in the Italian Heritage issue of the *Rhode Islander,* Providence, April 30, 1967.
98. Article cited in Tomaselli, "Ricorrenze."
99. "The Fortunes of Luigi Castiglioni, Traveler in Colonial America, with an Extract from a Recently Discovered Manuscript of His *Viaggio nell'America Settentrionale* (1785–1787)," *Italian Americana* 1 (1975): 246–64.
100. Article cited in "Castiglioni's Travels in the United States."
101. *Storia di Milano* (Milano: Pirotta &c.), 4 (1865): 215.
102. Pace, *Franklin and Italy,* p. 133 ff.
103. Tomaselli, "Ricorrenze."
104. Ettore Verga, "La Deputazione dei collegi elettorali del Regno d'Italia a Parigi nel 1814," *Archivio storico lombardo* Ser. IV, 1 (1904): 320–21.
105. Luzio.
106. Documents relative to the administration of Luigi Castiglioni's numerous properties in and about Milan preserved in the archives of the Biblioteca Trivulziana and at the country home in Mozzate prove, if proof were needed, that he was never in danger of having to earn a livelihood by ordinary employment. The manner in which he entertained William Short, Thomas Jefferson's secretary, during the latter's visit to Milan in October of 1788 furnishes an additional and intimate glimpse into the affluence surrounding the Castiglioni family: see *The Papers of Thomas Jefferson* edited by Julian P. Boyd (Princeton: Princeton University Press), 14 (1958): 41–44.
107. See fn. 99 above. Vol. 22 of the *Dizionario biografico degli italiani,* which is now available, contains an article on Castiglioni by C. Capra supplementing especially what is known of his activity in the events of the revolutionary Cisalpine Republic and the subsequent Napoleonic Kingdom of Italy.
108. An inkling of the importance of his travels in Castiglioni's scheme of things can be gathered from the badly water-damaged group portrait preserved at the family summer villa in Mozzate, where the patriarchal seated central figure of Castiglioni is seen holding in his lap the two volumes of the *Viaggio nell'America Settentrionale.* I owe thanks to the Marquis Camillo Cornaggia Medici, present owner of the villa, for granting me access to various relics of Luigi Castiglioni's life and career.

Note on Scientific Author Citations

Author citations following scientific names, although seldom provided in popular accounts, suggest the story of recognition of a plant or animal: when in the nation's history a species was discovered; often an intimation of its original place of collection; who named it; and its subsequent unchanged or revised classification. Scientific author citations as adopted by botanists and zoologists differ. For example, *Quercus rubra* L. denotes that Linnaeus, upon whose *Species plantarum* (1753) binomial nomenclature of plants officially rests, named this oak, and his scientific name is still valid today. *Tsuga canadensis* (L.) Carr. records that the French botanist Carriere removed the hemlock to a separate genus *Tsuga* although Linnaeus had named the tree *Pinus canadensis* L. Castiglioni used the abbreviation "Lin."

Zoologists in a text do not use the double author citation, merely the author of the original binomial, but not of a subsequent revision. The hummingbird, originally named *Trochilus colubris* Linn., is now referred to as *Archilochus colubris* (Linn.) without reference to the part Reichenbach played in its present classification. Zoologists have adopted "trinomials": subspecies are denoted in three sequential names, for example, *Odocoileus virginianus borealis* Miller (see Chapter V, fn. 20).

Joseph Ewan

Luigi Castiglioni's

VIAGGIO

Travels in the United States of North America

1785–87

Translated and edited by

ANTONIO PACE

Preface

THE REVOLUTION which has taken place in the last few years in North America is one of the most memorable events of this century and may in time produce important consequences for Europe. No wonder, therefore, if after such an epoch reports on things having to do with the United States are more sought after than before and that various travelers have visited this country hitherto little frequented by them. Among these I too was moved by curiosity to see the political birth of a Republic composed of diverse nationalities, scattered over vast provinces far removed from one another, and varied in climate and products.

This was not the only motive, for an object of more immediate utility played a part in my decision. Since experience has shown that the plants of North America from Florida to Canada hold up very well in the climate of Europe, I thought it might be of some advantage to travel through that country, not only to make an abundant collection of seeds, but to investigate the nature of the most useful plants, the manner of cultivating and propagating them, and the uses that are made or can be made of them. Among these I have given greatest attention to trees, a good number of which deserve to be introduced into Lombardy, either because they do well in the most barren terrains, or for their rapid growth, or for the excellent quality of their wood, or, finally, because of other benefits that can be derived from them. I have not, however, omitted those plants which I found celebrated in America as medicinal, although perhaps their efficacy does not always correspond to their reputation; nor those which are of use to industry. I have added a few plants that seemed to me worthy of mention because of the singularity of their form; and, finally, certain shrubs and plants capable of lending new and gracious adornment to our groves and gardens. The observations on plants will be found all together at the end, since it seemed to me best to present them collected in this manner, especially for those who are fond of growing things of this sort. I have tried to exercise even greater care to get the most accurate information on agriculture, since I was convinced that, although our highly intensive cultivation is not to be compared to the first efforts of a country barely populated, so to speak, yet it is always useful to know the farming methods adopted in a climate so similar to ours.

These were the aims of my travels, and they were my principal concern during my stay in America. The readers must not, however, expect to find in this work new discoveries in the plant kingdom, nor a minute botanical description, inasmuch as I thought that the Linnaean name would suffice to indicate clearly the species of the plant under discussion, adding only the synonyms of the authors who were the first to speak about it or who made special mention of it.

The history of animals, and mineralogy, topics of the highest utility, and which are in our day among the most favored sciences, might have been further illuminated by a traveler trained in these subjects; but far from making such a claim for myself, I confess frankly that I have not turned my attention to this aspect of natural history. From all this one can understand that, since this voyage was undertaken by me particularly for my own edification, I have no pretensions beyond giving a sincere account of everything that I myself saw and observed. Should the reader find certain circumstances too minutely described, he must realize that I have preferred to go into excessive detail rather than leave any doubt about the exactness of the facts I report.

With these sentiments I offer this work to the public without any pretension, and I shall be happy indeed if my labor spreads among my countrymen the desire to apply themselves to botany, in view of its true purpose, namely, the practical advantages that can be derived from it for human society.

CHAPTER I

Passage from England to America

[1:1]

On April 13, 1785, I went aboard the 250-ton American vessel *Neptune,* which was to sail from Deal for Boston in Massachusetts. We weighed anchor at half past four, and, borne by a light northeasterly wind, toward evening we passed Dover Castle. During the following days we saw a large number of ships which, because of the easterly winds then prevailing, had not been able to enter the English Channel sooner. On the 18th we made our way out of the Channel, attended almost constantly by a favorable wind, clear sky, and calm sea.

Having passed so-called Land's End and moved out of sight of land, nothing worth observing appeared until the 2nd of May, when, at 49° 8′ latitude and 43° 8′ longitude from London, we fished out a piece of wood that appeared to have been in the water for a long time. This wood [1:2] was American white pine,[1] and in some cracks it contained two wingless insects of the genus *Onisci,* one of which was an inch long and the other half as large. The body was oval, black in color, furnished with 14 feet, and the belly was covered with two oval-shaped coriaceous scales. This insect, described by Rondelet under the name of sea flea,[2] lives commonly near the seashore both in America and in Europe.

The quantity of birds flying around the boat on the 4th led us to suppose ourselves not far from the bank of Newfoundland. In fact, since the color of the sea had changed, we conjectured that we were on the Flemish Cape, a sand bank located at a great depth beneath the water. On French maps it is placed 80 miles to the east of the northernmost point of the great Newfoundland bank. The following morning the sky was covered with clouds and a heavy rain fell until ten; but afterward the fog lifted and the sun appeared. We were then at 48° 7′ latitude and 47° 41′ longitude from London when we perceived at a great distance to the southwest an island, or rather a mountain, of ice. Since our direction was to the northwest, the weather after midday became very cold, toward evening snow fell, and, to our great surprise, at nightfall we found ourselves surrounded by icebergs. Enormous masses 40 [1:3] to 50 feet in length and broad in proportion covered the entire surface of the sea, and, in spite of the greatest precautions, we suffered many and repeated shocks which might perhaps have been fatal to us in a less sturdy boat.[3] Fear of proceeding into a sea thicker with icebergs, or of coming too close to the shore of Newfoundland, toward which we were being taken by the southwest wind, forced us to keep ourselves as far south as the wind permitted. In fact, at four in the morning the icebergs began to thin out, and one saw only small 10- or 12-foot pieces until, at about nine o'clock, the sea seemed completely clear. We were then surprised by a sight less dangerous, but no less unusual. Three islands of ice of huge proportions and height appeared before us, one to the east and the other two to the west, the first of which rose up like a pyramid. Although the cold was not as bitter as the preceding night, it was nevertheless very penetrating, and the thermometer went down to 4° Réaumur below freezing [1:4], the temperature of the water being at the freezing point.

Having left behind the first island of ice, we approached close enough to those situated to the west as to be able to examine them at our leisure. One of these was almost square in form, irregularly capped at the top, and hollow in the middle, so that it resembled the ruins of a dilapidated castle, and the other had the most extraordinary and picturesque shape. It was almost square, and in the center there was an open arch so precisely formed and proportioned to the height of the sheer rise that it could hardly have been made more regular by design (see Plate I). Sea water, entering the hollow of the mass through a hole worn into the opposite side, came forth steadily through this arch in a wide fluctuating stream. The cracks, visible in large number, were tinted a very beautiful azure color, and the peak, terminating in various points, was covered with birds which from time to time flew off to flutter about and come to rest on the sea. These birds, which belong to the genus *Lari,* called gulls by the English,[4] are white with dark spots, with a rather long black beak, and a body the size of a duck. They are often found in the northern seas, and particularly around icebergs, living on the cadavers of large fish.

Right after passing the icebergs we looked [1:5] about us and noticed the horizon covered with thick vapors, and a slope rising in the part of the south toward which we were headed that looked like land not far off. We were however, to our sorrow, soon disabused, since upon proceeding we found ourselves surrounded by icebergs just as the night before (at a presumed latitude

Plate I. Iceberg off the Newfoundland coast.

of 47° 50′, longitude 48° 46′). It was about two o'clock in the afternoon, and the wind was blowing from the northwest in our favor when we were forced to lower almost all our sails in order, insofar as it was possible, to avoid striking those horrid masses. The endless expanse of snow-covered icebergs occupying the entire surface of the ocean as far as the eye could see, the glow of the atmosphere reflecting the whiteness of the snow, and the quantity of sea dogs which, coming out of the water, walked tranquilly about on those reefs of ice, offered to our eyes the horrors of a completely new solitude.

Sea dogs are the smallest of the seals.[5] Their fur is spotted now with black, now with white hair, and sometimes prettily marked with white. They walk slowly on the ice by means of their front flippers, dragging their hind flippers, which join at the end of the body in a sort of tail. Since they have never been disturbed by men in that solitude, they paid little or no attention to the shouts that we intentionally repeated to frighten them; on the contrary [1:6] they approached the boat and calmly turned to look at us.

Everything about me reminded me inevitably of the trip of the renowned Captain Cook, who sailed for a long time in the frozen seas near the poles; and the use he made of the water obtained from ice (which was found to be not only sweet to the taste, but even healthful) persuaded me to try the same experiment. In fact I took some pieces of ice which I melted over the fire, and obtained from it a thoroughly good and sweet water, to the amazement of the sailors, who could not be convinced on the basis of my assertions alone.

More than three hours had passed from the time that the ice had closed in about us when I climbed out on the deck and saw that the horizon appeared light and clear to the south toward which we were headed, and, on the contrary, dark and laden with mists to the north, from which I surmised that we would quickly be out of the ice which was producing the foggy and murky-looking sky. In fact, toward six o'clock in the evening the open sea appeared at some distance ahead, and in a short time we found ourselves out of all danger.

At 9:00 A.M. the thermometer dropped to 3° Réaumur. An iceberg appeared to the northeast, and several others to the east, but at a great distance, and during the rest of the day we saw numerous others scattered about everywhere. An extremely thick fog descended upon us in the evening to renew our fears, and we spent the night not without worry for fear of hitting on our way one of those floating islands, in which case [1:7] we would inevitably have been lost. At daybreak the yards and sails were found to be covered with pieces of ice of considerable size. There were no more icebergs in sight, the sun by dissipating the fog had made the cold milder, and at ten o'clock, having taken a sounding, we found ourselves over the Newfoundland bank at a depth of 35 fathoms.[6] This bank extends from 41° to 50° latitude, and from 49° to 54° of longitude from London. The rich yield of codfish, or *baccalare,* inspired various European nations to send ships there for that purpose, and was the reason for the settlements made on the island of Newfoundland and in the neighboring regions. The sea was quite calm, and the wind having almost completely subsided, we, too, began to fish, and caught more than fifty of those fish. The manner of catching them is very simple, consisting in attaching a big hook to a long cord which is kept suspended some distance from the bottom. A small piece of salted meat, or even the entrails of the same fish, serve as bait, and in a short time one can take a great catch. Among those caught by us was one more than three and a half feet long, in whose stomach were found various starfish with rays mottled with white and reddish color.[7]

[1:8] On the 9th (latitude 44° 13′, longitude 51° 48′) the sky became overcast, and an extremely cold wind blew from the northeast. It increased toward noon, and at two after midnight it shifted to the east and became so strong that we made 9 to 10 miles an hour with only the large sail of the central mast. The sea became more and more stormy, and the water came up over the deck. The wind blew just as violently the following day (latitude 43° 15′, longitude 56° 15′), so that the waves towered like mountains. The wind was unbearable, and we had continual rain and snow, so we spent the whole day in our cabins with windows closed and candles lit, since the constant motion and pitching of the vessel had made most of us sick.

On the morning of the 11th we had the misfortune of losing John Stuart, of English nationality, one of the best sailors on board. Having gone over the side of the boat to fasten a sail, which slipped out of his hand when it was shaken by the wind, he fell into the sea. The captain and his other shipmates ran [1:9] to help him, but on account of the rough sea and the heavy clothes with which he was dressed, and the cold and rain he had suffered, it was impossible for him to swim. The launch could not be put to sea because of the gale; hence ropes were lowered for him to cling to. But after waiting in vain for more than half an hour, we lost all hope, and, spreading sails to the wind, we continued on our way, mourning the death of the poor fellow. This fatal accident spoiled the pleasure that we felt toward evening upon seeing the ocean absolutely calm and the sky perfectly clear. The tranquillity of both sky and sea, favorable wind, and mild weather contributed toward making delightful the day of the 12th, which impressed us as all the more pleasant since the two preceding days had been so grim. In the afternoon (latitude 41° 0′, longitude 60° 36′) we saw a little Irish vessel coming from Londonderry and headed for Boston, that had spent more than 40 days in the passage. Since it had taken the southern route, it had seen only three or four icebergs from a great distance. It would have liked to join us, but since it was not such a fast sailer, we very quickly lost sight of it.

On the 13th the thermometer rose to 11.5° Réaumur, that is, 7.5° above the 7th, and on the 14th it was at 6°. We saw a gannet, another bird of the genus *Lari*,[8] which is found in the neighborhood of [1:10] North American coastal bays. The morning of the 15th was very foggy. Several soundings were taken without finding bottom, and thinking (according to our calculations) that we were not far from Massachusetts Bay, we were much worried for fear of approaching too close to the shores. Toward evening, however, we found bottom at a depth of 85 fathoms. A little later, the fog lifted, and we continued safely on our way favored by a light wind. At daybreak on the 16th of May land was finally sighted, which we recognized as Seguin Island situated 80 miles northeast of Cape Ann. Ships could be seen in the far distance, and the water was covered with marine grasses, of which I collected five different kinds. Some whales from 18 to 20 feet in length were seen coming to the surface and then diving again into the sea, spurting water from their

Plate II. Plan of Boston (1) and environs (2–20).

nostrils. These whales, called grampus and also spermaceti whales[9] by the English (since spermaceti is obtained from their brains), are quite common along the northern coasts of America.

Toward dawn of the 17th we had Cape Ann at a distance of two miles to the northwest, a promontory situated at the northern point of the entrance to Massachusetts Bay, which is closed to the south by another point to which is given the name of Cape Cod. Cape Ann is a fair distance above sea level, and is covered with woods of various sorts of pine and furnished with two beacons which are lit at night [1:11] to facilitate the entrance of ships. The village of the same name [10] is situated further to the south, and is inhabited only by fishermen; but it is located in a delightful bay. From Marblehead, following the coast to the southwest and passing by The Graves and Pullen Point,[11] one enters Boston Bay, one of the most beautiful and charming locations formed by nature.[12] The happy circumstance of a clear, calm sky, tranquil sea, and moderate and favorable wind permitted us to enjoy all the beauties of this place, similar to those described by the poets as the habitat of the Naiads and Nymphs. Many charming islets, almost all of them covered with a varied but vivid green, on which sheep and herds of other animals may be seen, are located in that bay, and the sea between them is deep enough to float the largest ships. Toward the center there is [1:12] Fort William, built by the British and furnished with good defenses, in addition to being situated on a hill surrounded by the ocean. Just beyond the citadel appears the city of Boston in its most charming aspect, its feet festooned with long rows of ships lined up near the shores. At six in the afternoon we anchored, and shortly thereafter we landed, in excellent health after 34 days of passage from Deal.

CHAPTER II

The Commonwealth of Massachusetts

A Brief History of the First European Settlements in This Part of America

[1:13]

BEFORE SPEAKING of Boston and of the republic of which it is the capital, it seems to me necessary to give some idea of the settlements in this part of the world and of the progress of its population. Whoever stops to reflect that the cities and country areas were populated, built, and cultivated within the space of about 150 years by colonies of European poor who had to endure the discomforts of a change of climate, the labors of a nascent agriculture, bloody and almost continuous wars with the ancient Indian inhabitants, and no less frequent internal wars, will surely not fail to be surprised to behold the rapid progress being made by this republic, which is just catching its breath after the long [1:14] and terrible sufferings of the war by which it won its independence from one of the most powerful of European kingdoms.

About the year 1619, as a result of the famous revolution that had taken place in England by which Protestantism was once again embraced, the so-called Presbyterians, who had accepted the doctrine of Calvin and were persecuted in England, fled to Holland.[1] Then it occurred to them to go to America. Having obtained letters patent from King James I, they set sail from Plymouth on the 6th of September, 1620, and after a long and stormy voyage landed on Cape Cod on the 9th of November. Moving further into the bay, they founded New Plymouth, and gave to the region the name of New England. The colonists numbered only 150, and several of them died during the winter from the severe cold. The following spring Massasoit, the *sachem,* or chief, of the Massachuset (the Indians of the regions then occupied by the colonists), having learned from Squanto, an Indian who had been to England, that the English were a powerful and populous nation, visited Governor Carver at New Plymouth and concluded a defensive and offensive alliance with the English; with their help he hoped to conquer the country of the Narraganset, a tribe with which he was then at war. Massasoit also agreed (so say the English) to recognize King James as his sovereign and ceded a part of his country to the new colonists, a procedure adopted by other chiefs who wanted the support of the English in order to conquer [1:15] their enemies, and who likewise declared themselves subjects of the King of England.

At about the same time the Englishman Vernon, accompanied by various emigrants, came to America with the intention of settling in the place called Wessagusset by the Indians, but, unable to get along with the neighboring Presbyterians of New Plymouth since he was of the Anglican religion, he withdrew further to the north where he founded Weymouth, which is now included in Suffolk County. Other Englishmen got together a few years later under the name of the Massachusetts Company and set out from London in 1618 to occupy the region situated between the Charles and Merrimack rivers. Since they had obtained from King Charles I the privilege of making laws provided they were not contrary to those of England, they created their own governor, a certain Craddock, and promulgated some new laws they had drawn up. Among them was one that allowed complete freedom of religion. Nevertheless, because of the diversity of opinions in religious matters, internal dissensions soon arose within the colony, and it split into two parties, one of which established itself in Dorchester (now in Suffolk County), and the other in Charlestown, whence many went over to the peninsula opposite and founded Boston in 1630. Massasoit died during this same year after having, along with his sons Alexander and Metacomet, also called Philip,[2] renewed the alliance with the English.

[1:16] The dissensions over religion did not cease with the separation of the two main parties; on the contrary, new disagreements arose on various points of doctrine. The larger party was that of the Presbyterians, who formed the majority of the colony. Unwilling to put up with the differing views of the other sects, they took advantage of their preponderance to evade the law allowing complete liberty of conscience. Thereafter Presbyterianism was not only the dominant religion, but it was the only one permitted in the colony. Moreover, as if forgetful of the fact that they themselves had just escaped from the persecution aimed at them in England, they became persecutors in America, and the Quakers and Anabaptists from England and the Antilles were imprisoned, banished, and even condemned to death. The spirit of intolerance increased to the point that here, too, witches were created; and as the horrors of the Inquisition were revived in North America, many poor old women were condemned to the fire as witches. Abandoning every other goal not related to this one, they fell back into the most superstitious ignorance and slowed the progress of the colony by driving away Quakers and other dissenters. Then when persecution finally came to an end and new inhabitants had come from various parts, the colonists suffered another blow from the war waged against them by Metacomet, son [1:17] of Massasoit. This lasted for a full two years, in the course of which many inhabitants were massacred by the Indians. But after Metacomet was killed in an attack in 1676 and the Indians were forced to retreat to Canada, peace was reestablished in the region, and from then on the colony began to prosper.

In the year 1691 a royal charter[3] united into a single province the colonies of Massachusetts, New Plymouth, the province of Maine, Sagadahoc, Acadia or Nova Scotia (the half north of Shoal Islands), the islands of Capawach and Nantucket near Cape Cod, and the others directly opposite the abovementioned region to a distance of 10 leagues. The King reserved the right to appoint the governor, lieutenant governor, and secretary, and ordered the creation of 28 councillors, at least seven of whom were to meet as a consultative legal body. On the last Wednesday of May of each year a General Assembly, called the Court, was expected to convene, consisting of the governor, the council, and the representatives of the cities and towns. The latter, who could not be more than two for each city or town, were required to have an income to 40 shillings a year or a personal estate of £50 sterling. The General Assembly had the right to choose the 28 councillors: 18 for the Province of Massachusetts, 6 for Plymouth, 3 for Maine, 1 for Sagadahoc, and 2 others at large. The governor could impose taxes with the consent of the Council, could veto any bill or appointment; [1:18] and he had the power of creating his own Court of Justice. The judges designated for civil and criminal suits were chosen by the General Assembly, which also had the right to draw up new laws, provided they were not contrary to those of England. Suits exceeding £300 sterling were appealed to the crown. To the Crown were reserved trees of more than 24 inches in diameter located on lands not yet sold to private persons, to be used for the navy, with a fine of £100 for anyone who should cut any of them. Finally, any gold or silver that might be discovered in the territory was to belong one-fifth to the inhabitants and four-fifths to the King.

This was more or less the system of government established at that time and which lasted until the outbreak of the recent disturbances, when the inhabitants of Massachusetts, by opposing the stamp tax and others which the English government wished to levy, began and fomented the revolution that ended by establishing the independence of the United States.

The City of Boston and Its Environs

[1:19] Boston, the capital of the State of Massachusetts and one of the largest cities of United America, situated on a peninsula running north and south, is two miles long and a mile and a half wide at its broadest point.[4] Long Wharf, by which one disembarks, is one of the most magnificent in the United States, and is said to be half a mile long. Located there are the shipbuilding yards and various wooden buildings serving as warehouses for all kinds of merchandise.

Beacon Hill, a small elevation on which signals are placed in time of war, is [1:20] in the western part of this peninsula, sloping down to a spacious meadow called the Common where livestock graze.[5] Near it is the public mall adorned with plane trees,[6] lindens and elms, many of which were cut down by the British out of spite when they had to leave the city to their enemies. From the summit of Beacon Hill one dominates the whole peninsula, which is covered on three sides with houses, while only to the northwest is there a space not yet occupied, since that is exposed to the cold winds from the mainland during the winter. Because the city was built on a hill and without a preconceived plan (as was done in other new cities in America), it has winding and irregular streets. They are cobbled with river stones and not well maintained.

The houses, built for the most part of bricks, are not very roomy, but quite clean and in English taste. The roofs are covered with thin slabs of wood of white cedar,[7] which grows in abundance in Massachusetts. These slabs, slender in proportion to their length, are placed one over the other like flat tiles, and the peak of the roof is covered with curved terra-cotta tiles like ours. White cedar wood is best suited for this use since it possesses the property of being light and of holding up better than any other wood under bad weather. The fact of the matter is, however, that some prefer thin sheets of a light black stone discovered a short time ago [1:21] 30 miles from the city, and which can easily be cut, like the slates which we call *lavagne.* This is done not only to make the roofs more durable, but also for the sake of greater safety in case of fire, an event not very rare in a city where there are still many wooden houses. In order to avoid as much as possible such accidents and out of a desire to see the city built more solidly, a law was passed some years ago prohibiting with a fine the building of wooden houses, but the law was never enforced. These houses are built of white pine, whose wood is durable and of a texture halfway between the larch and pinaster.[8] They are covered outside with overlapping boards of the same wood and painted in various colors as is the custom in England. They have two, or at the most

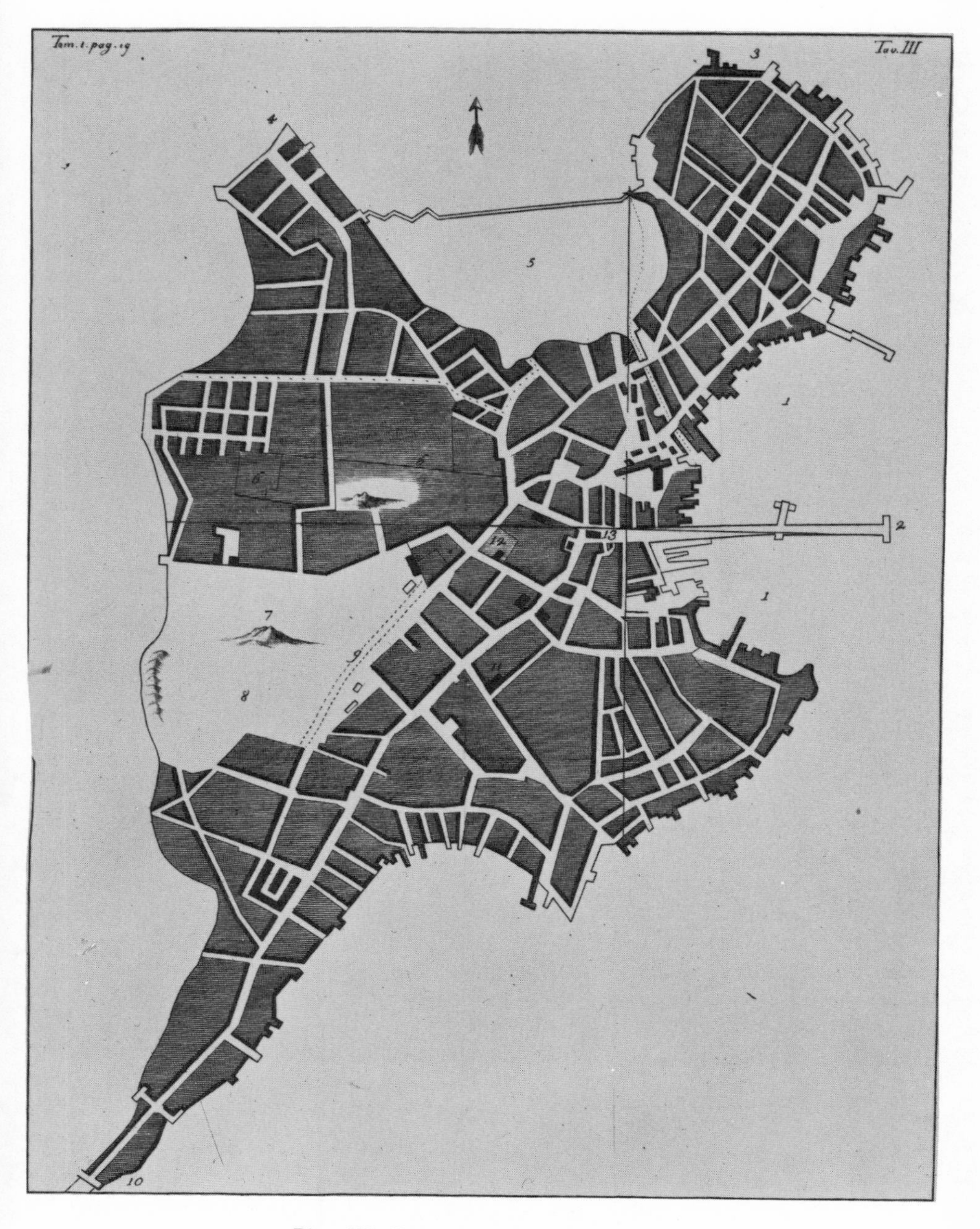

Plate III. Plan of the City of Boston.

three, stories, and on the roof a terrace so that one may enjoy the cool of summer nights. The rooms are small, very simply furnished, and generally adorned with ancestral portraits. The little garden by every house is provided with apple, cherry, and other European fruit trees.

Very frequent in these gardens during the whole summer are those tiny birds called the hummingbird of North America.[9] I was given one in Boston which was only three English inches from the end of its beak to the tip of the tail. The beak [1:22] was slender, a little curved, black in color, an inch in length. Its throat was covered with feathers of a beautiful golden red, followed by others white in color. The rest of the body, as also the wings and feet, were black. The flight of these little birds consists of a continuous and extremely rapid motion of the wings resembling that of certain insects; hence it is difficult to capture them alive without injuring them. They go about the gardens like butterflies sucking honey from the flowers. They like especially the so-called American red jasmine,[10] into whose tube they insert their beaks. They can therefore be captured by suspending a horsehair noose at the opening of the aforementioned flowers in such a way that they are caught when they insert their bills. Once captured, they can be fed on honey or sugar for a few days, but they cannot be kept for a long time. For this reason repeated attempts made up to now to transport them alive to Europe have failed. The nest of these little birds is made of plant fibers, very cleverly woven and covered outside with tiny bits of a kind of lichen. The females differ from the males by being even smaller and without the red feathers which the males have under their throats.

There are various churches in Boston, of which 19 are Presbyterian, 3 Anglican, 3 Quaker, and 2 Anabaptist. Among the Presbyterian churches, or rather of the Congregationalists (a sect not much different from Presbyterianism), the one [1:23] situated in the southern part of the city is very large and beautiful. These congregations, as the name meeting house indicates, have no altar of any sort. Where in our country the main altar is located, there is the pulpit, and beneath it a railing within which stands the minister or cantor who recites the prayers. There also the bread and wine for their communion are prepared. Of the Anglican churches, Trinity is the largest, but made of wood; and the other, formerly called the Royal Chapel, is an old brick building very nicely decorated inside. One cannot say, however, that at the present time this latter church belongs to the Anglicans, since its new minister, Mr. Freeman, not only has changed the liturgy in those places that were not suited to the new system of government, but has even omitted all those prayers in which the Trinity was invoked. As a follower of the famous Priestley, he has revived the opinion of the Unitarians, and instead of ending the prayers with the usual common clause, "Glory be to the Father, the Son,

and the Holy Ghost," he substituted, "Glory be to God alone, incomprehensible, invisible, omnipotent, now and forever. Amen." The churches of the Anabaptists are like those of the Presbyterians, and even simpler in the decorations; and the hall for the assembly of the Quakers is a room provided with seats without any distinction.

The statehouse, built under the government of Queen Anne, as can be seen from an inscription on the door, serves on the ground floor as an exchange for the merchants; and in the upper hall, where the Senate and House of Representatives meet, [1:24] there hangs from the ceiling the wooden figure of a codfish, emblem of the main source of their commerce. The hall, where the public dance is held on Thursdays during the winter, is well adorned. Moreover, the bank and the former gubernatorial residence, which now serves as the treasury, are fair-sized buildings.

The rarely befogged sky and dry and mobile air render the climate healthful, even though it is subject to extreme variations, so that the thermometer, which in summer rises up to 29.5° Réaumur, drops in wintertime to 21° below the freezing point. It is therefore not surprising that, although Boston is situated at latitude 42° 30′, the ocean sometimes freezes out to a distance of two miles from shore, and the ice is such as to support horses. The snow reaches a depth of three feet and sometimes remains for three months. What is more, it is not unusual for the cold to begin at the end of September and last until mid-April, so that there are six months of winter. Spring is very short and ends in May, but in that brief period the vegetation grows rapidly. Summer is sometimes very hot and storms are frequent and violent, so that many houses are provided with lightning rods. Throughout the whole year the transitions from heat to cold are very swift, a very cold day often following a warm one. This instability, against which the inhabitants do not protect themselves adequately, is the source of many diseases, and perhaps the principal cause of the consumptions to which the young women are susceptible here, no less than in England. On the other hand chronic illnesses and apoplexies are more rare than with us.

[1:25] The fare of the Bostonians is frugal, and the tables are covered with few, but substantial, foods, as in England. Meats, butter, and vegetables are excellent, as are fish, among which salmon and mackerel are the most esteemed. Salted cod, or *baccalare,* is not only eaten boiled but also, garnished with fresh butter, and hard-boiled eggs, is eaten on the Sabbath all year around, and many taste no other food on that day, although it is hard to digest and as a consequence causes headaches. When the dinner is over, the bottles are left on the table, and nuts called shellbark,[11] almonds, and raisins are brought on. The most common beverages are cider, spruce[12] beer (made with the tips of a kind of pinaster), and toddy, which is rum mixed with water. But at the tables of the well-to-do they drink Madeira, port, and Bordeaux wines. Before sitting at table punch is served in a large porcelain or silver jug, and the guests drink in turn from the same bowl, beginning always with the master of the house. It must be said, however, that although these liquors are used freely, they are very seldom abused, with the result that drunkenness is less common there than in the other cities of North America.

Since the Bostonians make no distinctions of rank and are completely absorbed in business affairs, they exercise a certain familiarity [1:26] with one another and show a friendship which does not appear simulated. Strangers enjoy a like advantage: they are received with the greatest signs of cordiality and with simple and friendly manners, which makes being with them very pleasant. It is true, however, that during the late war and the subsequent revolution harmony among the citizens was to some degree disturbed because of distinctions between military and political employees.

The main trade is in whale oil, codfish, and lumber, which are shipped to various European ports and to the West Indies. They receive in exchange rum and molasses, which are brandy and the least refined part of sugar. The merchant ships sent to Europe are bound mainly for the ports of England and Ireland, whence on the return they transport to America tools for the crafts or for farming, and other merchandise. Inasmuch as European goods are much more expensive and therefore of lesser weight and volume than those with which the ship was laden, on the return trip a large part of the cargo is taken on credit—a commerce all the more detrimental in that these same goods are not easily sold in America. This ease in obtaining credit is the reason why the inhabitants of the United States, even after independence, prefer English goods to those of France, Germany, and Italy, which, being otherwise less expensive, would suit them better. However, the excessive number of merchants, the scarcity of money in the state, and the difficulty in having it remitted to European correspondents bring it about that commerce [1:27] is not very profitable, and many merchants find it hard to survive. Nevertheless they persist in the same wretched career, instead of moving to the vast nearby countryside and applying themselves to agriculture, the true and perennial source of wealth, and thus effecting their own well-being and that of the state. The mechanical arts have not reached a very high degree of perfection, and the scarcity of population renders manufactured goods so expensive that few prefer them to European ones. Menial tasks are performed by negroes, but the latter are no less happy than the white inhabitants, since they enjoy liberty.[13] The American natives, or Indians, live at a great distance and very rarely come to the city, so that there are many inhabitants who have never seen any of them.

To give an idea of this capital the only topic that remains to be discussed is the state of the sciences, to whose propagation the nearby University, or College, of Cambridge (of which I shall speak below) has contributed greatly. Very seldom does one come upon a citizen of any distinction who does not know at least the names and the uses of the sciences, and who does not show a desire to be informed of new discoveries made in them; and there is perhaps no artisan who does not know how to read, write, and reckon. The Academy of Sciences established there a few years ago has published the first volume of its memoirs which contain various dissertations that would do honor to any literary society. In fact, this completely new city (as compared with European cities)[14] has already [1:28] produced a number of those sublime geniuses that seem scattered by nature over the surface of the earth, but which do not always manifest themselves for lack of means and opportunity. This is the birthplace of the celebrated Benjamin Franklin; of Samuel Adams, who, along with John Hancock, was one of the first to resist the new British impositions; of John Adams, now Minister to England, who played an important part in the treaties of alliance and commerce with France and Holland; of General Knox, who applied himself at the age of 20 to military science and became one of the most informed and active commanders of the American army; and various others, whose military and political talents ought to be better known in Europe.

Charlestown (see Plate II), situated opposite the northern point of the Boston peninsula, is separated from this city by a narrow channel about an eighth of a mile wide which used to be crossed by means of four boats that went continually back and forth from one bank to the other. But since traffic between Boston and Charlestown was very heavy, it was decided in 1785 to build a wooden bridge over this marine channel. This project was carried out the same year, financed by a company of businessmen led by Mr. Thomas Russell, one of the most respected merchants of Boston, indeed of the United States.[15] This undertaking, completed within the short space of a few months, so exceeded general expectations for its solidity, convenience, and beauty, that it astonished the inhabitants and is now the admiration of strangers. The bridge is very [1:29] wide, there being in the middle enough room perhaps for three carriages abreast, and on either side two comfortable walks for pedestrians. At the center a device was constructed for opening the bridge in the middle to allow small boats to pass through from the other side of the channel, which is accomplished in a short time by four men. Since the transportation of products to Charlestown and vicinity has been facilitated thanks to this beautiful and useful structure, the commerce of the capital has increased to some extent.

Charlestown is one of the oldest villages founded by the Europeans in North America, and it was the theater where the hostilities began in the recent war. Little skirmishes had already taken place in Boston and Lexington between English soldiers and the populace, who had no officers nor commanders when the insurgents set out from Boston, went to Bunker Hill (a hillock near Charlestown), and in one night erected a little fort under the command of Dr. Warren. The next morning the English, after crossing the channel between Noddles Island and the continent, landed on the north bank opposite the fort and began the attack. The Americans,[16] almost all of them expert huntsmen, and enjoying the advantage of a dominant height, fired volleys of musket shots at the English, and few of them missing their mark, [1:30] they killed and wounded more than 1000, losing only a very few men themselves. But finally for lack of ammunition they were forced to retreat and to abandon the place to the English. In the retreat more than 100 Americans were wounded and killed, and among those left on the field was their leader, Dr. Warren, a young Boston physician of great promise for his talent and courage. The English, although they were the victors, angered at having had to buy victory at the cost of so much blood from completely untrained men, decided to wreak their vengeance upon Charlestown. With futile barbarism they set fire to it, and since it was composed entirely of old wooden houses, it was very soon utterly destroyed. They thought that with this cruel revenge they could terrify the Americans and thereby stifle the revolution at its birth. But the effect was the contrary of what they expected, since the inhabitants, upon seeing their homes destroyed and all their possessions devoured by the flames, conceived such a hatred for the British that they resolved to defend themselves to the death. Charlestown is now rebuilt with wooden houses, not in rows, although quite pretty to look upon. The hill is covered with a handsome sward formed by lawns divided from each other by picket fences; and from the top of Bunker Hill, where the ruins of the little fort built by the Americans can still be seen, one enjoys the view of the city of Boston and of a part of the mainland.

Near the frequent walls of that region can often be seen that odd species of Indian crab placed by Linnaeus in the genus of *Monoculi* under the name of [1:31] *polyphemus.*[17] These are huge and surpass almost all species of sea crabs, being sometimes about a foot wide. Their shell is flat and almost round, of a not very hard crustaceous substance, the color of ashes, smooth, shiny, and ending in several spikes, some of which can also be seen on their backs. The tail is long and triangular, and the several feet with which they are furnished remain hidden beneath the shell. In America they are called horseshoes, and, perhaps on account of their diagonal form, are believed to be poisonous.

Cambridge (see Plate II), a fairly large town situated near the stream called the Charles River, is, as the crow flies, only a mile and a half from Boston, but since it is divided from that city by an ocean bay, into which the Muddy and Charles rivers empty, one must go by a roundabout way to reach it. There are two roads: the one to the south that goes through Roxbury is seven miles long; and the shorter one, which is three miles long, passes through Charlestown. The latter road, after the construction of the bridge just mentioned, is used most. The terrain near these roads is for the most part sandy and not very productive. Nevertheless, because of the nearness to Boston and the delightfulness of the site, many have built there their country houses, a number of which are elegantly furnished and surrounded by tidy picket fences and charming gardens.

[1:32] Cambridge boasts the oldest university in the United States of America, founded in 1636 under the name of Harvard College. Since that time more than 3000 persons have received their degrees there. The building, made of brick, is very large, and 100 self-supporting students live there. There are six professors: one for theology, one for mathematics and natural philosophy, another for oriental languages, a professor of anatomy and surgery, one of theoretical and practical medicine, and, finally one for chemistry and materia medica. There are, moreover, four teachers called tutors for the English and Latin languages, and geography. The library is furnished with about 10,000 volumes, among which are the ancient classical authors and the most renowned of modern philosophers, in addition to an adequate collection of curious and handsome books. In the physics laboratory there are a number of good pieces of apparatus and a small incipient collection of animals and other natural productions of North America, along with various Indian ornaments and tools. There is also a copy of a presumed Phoenician inscription discovered at Dighton on the Taunton River in the state of which we shall speak below.[18]

On the first day of classes and on graduation day there is a public test of the progress that the students have made in the sciences, and on those days there is a concourse [1:33] of the most distinguished inhabitants of Boston and many from the most distant parts of the state. The ladies (who in America do not disdain attending scientific disputations) likewise assemble there and perhaps by their presence increase in the students the desire to win the approval of the gathering. That same evening, and on the two subsequent ones, there is a public ball, at which the young people seek relief from past occupations in dance and gallantry.

Dorchester (see Plate II), another little village southeast of Boston, is located on a headland called Dorchester Point which extends into the bay. It was famous in the late war because the American army under the command of General Washington was situated in that place, which, dominating from that position the English troops in possession of the city and the fort, compelled them to withdraw. The location could not be more charming, nor the vista more varied, as one enjoys a view of the city and of some pretty little islands. The terrain of the region is stony and uncultivated in many places, only certain knolls being reduced to fields surrounded by wooden fences and by apple orchards, which in that season were all covered with blossoms.

On these trees I noted a quantity of dark-colored worms called caterpillars, which, according to what the inhabitants told me, produce a little moth. Every year they destroy the leaves of the apple trees, so that by midsummer the trees are fully as bare as in winter, and consequently produce very little, and bad, fruit. I was astonished at the carelessness of the [1:34] farmers, who had taken no thought of ridding themselves of this scourge, and I advised Major Swan,[19] the owner of an orchard in that region, to try to destroy those insects by removing their eggs from the trees, which could easily be done in early spring. At that time the trees are rid of their leaves, and the eggs are enveloped in certain nests resembling cocoons scattered here and there over the tree. In fact he tried out this remedy the following year, and it proved so advantageous that he harvested a large quantity of fruit in the fall, although his neighbors came off with nothing owing to the usual devastation wrought by the worms in their apple orchards.

The Trip to Lancaster and Return to Boston; Thence to Portsmouth in New Hampshire

[1:35] On the 6th of June I went from Boston to Lancaster, a town situated 40 miles to the west within the state of Massachusetts, where I had been invited to spend a few days by Mr. Willard,[20] one of the Americans who made the crossing from Europe to America with me. The road from Boston to Lancaster is good enough for the post chaises and gigs that are used in that region. Watertown, Weston, Sudbury, Stow, and Bolton are on the route, and of them only Watertown has the form of a European village. In North America villages are not generally composed of many houses together. On the contrary, the houses are scattered about, each one surrounded by its property, so that their name extends to the whole region, as indicated by the name township. That must have come about because the landowners, having vast stretches of land, located themselves at the center of their farms and were not willing to sacrifice the advantage of having their possessions under their eye to the handsome display of many buildings in one place.[21] [1:36] The clearings that one comes upon from time to time amid the woods are quite well cultivated, and many of them are reduced to fields, or sown to rye and corn, and scattered with apple trees. Grain does not do well here, perhaps on account of the excessive humidity of the atmosphere. Since the spike quickly turns black, the inhabitants had to give up cultivating it. The terrain is uneven, and between the low hills there are very wide valleys where the land is quite productive; and there are fields of thick grass excellent for livestock. In these fields there was a large number of butterflies, most of them common also to Europe, like the Megera, the Jurtina, the Janira, the Antiope, the Argo, and the Comma. I collected only one species, particular to America, namely the Polyxena.[22] This butterfly is black with two rows of yellow spots that edge its wings above and below. It has on its two rear wings a rust-colored spot with a black dot, and a blue band on the upper surface not noted by Fabricius, who was the first to describe it.

On the hills the surface washed by the rains is thin, so that most of the terrains up there are uncultivated. There is also a large number of them along this road. These uncultivated terrains are, however, almost always covered with woods and often inaccessible, off the beaten paths, because of the thickets that [1:37] encumber them. They give some idea of the ancient state of this region, which must have been nothing more than an immense, dark forest. Thus, in fact, it appeared to the eyes of the first colonists, who had to begin their work with the destruction of the trees. This is done by cutting them at the height of about a foot and leaving the trunks on the ground until winter, when everything is burned, and the terrain is enclosed with wooden fences or with a wall about four feet high made of boulders. In the spring one tills as well as possible among the big roots, and rye or corn is sown, both of which produce an abundant crop the same year. In subsequent years the roots are also removed.

The major part of these woods consists of oaks, namely, the red;[23] the white;[24] the dwarf,[25] called scrub oak by the inhabitants; and the type with chestnut leaves;[26] the two pines, that is, the white[27] and the black;[28] and various kinds of pinaster,[29] from which is made spruce beer.

Having crossed a number of small streams by little wooden bridges, among which the Concord at Stow and the Nashua near Lancaster, I arrived at the home of Mr. [1:38] Willard. I intended during my stay to explore the vicinity and collect plants, but the incessantly rainy season kept me from it, and I was barely able to leave the house where I was lodged. Then on the 11th I set out again for Boston, if not satisfied with the few botanical observations, fully content with the hospitality of that good family.

Although I had arranged upon my return to Boston to leave that city at once in order to make a trip to the eastern parts of Massachusetts, the pleasant company of the Bostonians and their friendly urgings kept me in that city for several days, and I finally left for Salem on the 22nd of June. The road, which is very beautiful, and in some places extremely wide, goes by Medford, a pretty little village near Charlestown, and Lynn, another village, which, situated at the foot of a hill covered with red cedars,[30] enjoys the view of the little bay opposite it and the winding course of the Lynn River that empties into the ocean at that point. Salem, capital of Essex County, one of the oldest cities in the State of Massachusetts, and located near the sea, has a port which only small ships can enter. The houses, mostly of wood, are attractive, and there are some brick buildings, among which several Presbyterian churches, an Anglican one, and the Quaker meeting. Its population is said to be 8000 inhabitants, so that this city [1:39] has the right to send four representatives to the General Assembly of the State. Its chief item of commerce is codfish, of which 20,000 to 30,000 barrels are shipped annually.[31] This fish, which as I have already observed elsewhere, is very abundant off the banks of Newfoundland, is dressed where it is caught in the following manner. As soon as it is taken, it is split lengthwise into two halves and quickly arranged in several heaps on the ship, each layer of fish being carefully covered with a layer of salt. They are left this way until the boat arrives in Salem, where the fish is removed from the piles and washed in sea water. Then it is exposed to the sun for eight consecutive days on gratings made especially for that purpose, care being taken to turn it over daily so that it will dry evenly and to bring it in at night. After the eight days it is piled up again inside and left there for about a month, after which it is exposed once more to the sun to dry out thoroughly. When it is completely dry, it is put in barrels, into which it is packed with a press, and loaded onto the ships. The best is caught in the fall or spring. On the other hand, what is caught during the summer is of much inferior quality and is taken to the West Indies, where it serves as food for the negroes.

Upon leaving Salem I passed over the little bay that divides Salem from Beverly, and [1:40] I arrived at Ipswich Hamlet, where I stopped for the night with Mr. Cutler, minister of the Presbyterian church. He, in the hours of leisure left to him by his occupation, has dedicated himself to the study of botany, in which in a short time he has made rapid progress.[32] I experienced an incredible pleasure upon finding in America one who dedicated himself with so much intelligence to the delightful study of natural history, and the following morning we made a brief tour into the country, where I collected a number of curious plants that I had not noted before.

On this occasion we saw various squirrels, animals that are quite common in all parts of Massachusetts, and of which there are three distinct species. The gray squirrel[33] is the largest of them, sometimes the size of a cat. They cause a great deal of damage in the corn fields by opening the ears and eating the tender, sweet kernels. For this reason in some places the farmers were formerly required to kill four of them a year and to bring the heads to a designated person. Elsewhere a bounty of twopence was paid for each squirrel killed.[34] They are killed in the trees with a musket, [1:41] or they are caught alive with snares and traps. They are easily tamed, and are kept in the homes tied to a slender chain to amuse children. These animals are plump and tasty; their flesh is edible, and their hides are sold at a very low price.

Much smaller than the preceding is the striped squirrel,[35] which is no larger than a rat. It is called striped squirrel by the English because of two wide bands of white color that run along its back. They are very abundant in the United States, and are often seen running swiftly among the stones that make up country fences. The skins of these squirrels are highly valued for the pretty contrast made by the two white bands against the dark tobacco color of the rest of the body, and they are used like the rarest furs to make ladies' muffs and tippets.

The flying squirrel,[36] as common in America as in the northern parts of Europe, is even smaller than the striped squirrel, and, by means of a skin extending from the two front legs to the rear ones, has the ability to sustain itself in the air as it descends from one tree to another. In Boston Dr. Clarke gave me a female that was six English inches in length from the tip of the nose to the [1:42] base of the tail, which was four inches long, flat, oval in form, and about an inch wide. The hairs of the back were of a dark gray color, those of the belly, white, and the skin extending along each side of the body, barely visible when the animal was still, was equipped with longer hairs. These squirrels are also easily tamed, and their skins are common and of little value.

Between Ipswich and Newburyport there are 15 miles of beautiful road in the midst of a most delightful country and well cultivated fields. Newburyport is a fairly large town[37] situated in a valley on the shores of the Merrimack River about three miles above the point where it empties into the sea. This river, about a mile wide at that point, is navigable for small ships [1:43] to a distance of 18 miles from its mouth, and to more than 50 for skiffs. Wood comes down to the city by means of rafts from as far as 100 miles.

Newburyport has about 3000 inhabitants, is built partly of wood, partly of brick, and has the advantage of charming environs. Its principal commerce is in salted fish and lumber, which are transported to the West Indies, where they are exchanged for molasses that is distilled to make rum, or aqua vitae. On the 26th I stopped there, held up by an old law that prohibits travel on Sunday. Since the observance of the Sabbath is one of the most deeply inculcated precepts of the Protestant religions (especially of Presbyterianism), on that day not only are play, music, and all kinds of amusement forbidden, but travel likewise, and, at the hour of worship, even strolling. Various persons elected by the people with the title of warden then go about the streets and arrest anyone who dares break these rules. Since they are highly respected in their office, they usually impose fines on transgressors, compelling those who want to travel on Sunday to reveal the reason why they must do so and forcing them to put it off if the motives they give do not seem adequate to them. This law, incompatible with the other principles of liberty and tolerance already established in the United States, no longer exists except in the states of Massachusetts, New Hampshire, Connecticut, and Rhode Island, where Puritanism, the most fanatical of all the sects established in [1:44] America, is strongest. However, in Boston, and also in other cities and villages, these wardens are no longer elected, and strangers enjoy complete liberty.

On the 27th I crossed the Merrimack River opposite the village of Salisbury and went to Hampton on the border between Massachusetts and New Hampshire. From Hampton I went to Greenland and then to Portsmouth. The road is very good and the view of the country, panoramic, but the terrain is sandy and not very fertile. Along the hedges and in the trees that flank the road I saw fluttering about many of those little yellow birds[38] which, on account of their abundance and the resemblance they bear to the Canary sparrow, can be called the North American sparrow. The males are of a beautiful yellow color with the head and wings marked with black, and the female is of a yellowish green resembling in color the *Spinus* or siskin. They are easily caught with traps and tamed, and their song is quite melodious. The so-called bluebird,[39] a kind of wagtail of a most beautiful and vivid blue, and a sort of violet-colored oriole[40] with yellow wings (a bird the size of a thrush called blackbird in Massachusetts), are also quite common.

[1:45] The State of New Hampshire is only 16 miles wide along the seashore and is bordered by Massachusetts on both sides. Hence, in order not to interrupt the story of my travels, I shall reserve for later my account of Portsmouth and its environs, continuing meanwhile to go through that region which, because it is located to the east of New Hampshire, is distinguished by the name of Eastern Massachusetts, and includes the old provinces of Maine and Sagadahoc.

From Portsmouth to Penobscot

[1:46] After a short run to Dover on the Piscataqua River, I left Portsmouth on the 4th of July in the company of Mr. Roland, a marine engineer in Brest sent to America with orders to examine the trees most suitable for ship masts, and above all to visit for that purpose the environs of Penobscot famous for the production of such items. Descending about a mile along the Piscataqua, we crossed it opposite Kittery, the first village belonging to Eastern Massachusetts in the County of York. From Kittery we continued the journey toward Old York, where the river of the same name is crossed by a wooden bridge. In the evening we arrived at Wells and took lodging with Colonel Littlefield,[41] who, after fighting in the recent war, is now completely occupied with farming, and busies himself with increasing the income of his fine estate. He is therefore at the same time a colonel, a farmer, and an innkeeper.

In the neighborhood of Wells one enjoys a wide view of the bay of the same name and of a point of land that juts out to the north. The territories of Old York and Wells are scattered with wretched cabins where the farmers who came to settle a few years ago live with the greatest frugality, since their ordinary food consists of rye bread and [1:47] corn with pork and salted beef, and their beverages of grog and spruce beer. The latter is made by boiling young shoots of white pine[42] until the bark comes off and then mixing this decoction with the proper quantity of molasses. Cider is not so abundant as in the more southern parts of Massachusetts, because orchards are not yet numerous enough, and grog, made with rum mixed with water, is the most common liquor. The distance from Portsmouth to Wells is only 22 miles, and the road is extremely rocky and very bad. But the development of agriculture is quite considerable in view of the short time since the beginning of farming in this region. Wells, like the other townships of Massachusetts, extends over several miles, and the farmers' homes are far apart.

From Wells to Saco the road is mountainous and almost impassable for carriages because of the large stones that encumber it. One sees windmills on elevations and several sawmills situated along the rivers. Fields are few, not yet well cultivated owing to the scarcity of inhabitants, even though the terrain is better than in the other maritime parts of Massachusetts, and grain grows there perfectly well. Where the land is not so productive there are woods of black pine that grows to a height of 25 to 30 feet. The township of Saco, or Biddeford, as the English call it,[43] extends about eight miles. [1:48] The Saco, or Sawco, river, from which it took its name, forms there a fall 25 feet high, and after a short stretch flows into the sea. This town was recently settled by a number of Germans who, after serving in the Hessian troops in behalf of the British, preferred peaceful residence in the forests of America, which they are cultivating, to returning to their native country, from which they were taken to be sold to foreign nations. On the way from Saco to Scarboro one enjoys a wide view over the sea, and, passing by Stroudwater, comes upon Falmouth, capital of Cumberland County. This is one of the oldest cities of Eastern Massachusetts, situated at latitude 43° 50′, 128 miles northeast of Boston, where the Stroudwater and Presumpscot rivers form a very safe bay with two outlets to the ocean. The city is placed on a height extending northward, from which one enjoys the view of the various little islands situated in the bay. But the houses are almost all of wood and the plan is very irregular. The climate of Falmouth is healthful, although very cold in winter. Snow can reach a depth of six feet. Nevertheless, the bay never freezes as happens in the port of Boston, perhaps because the former is more exposed to the open sea and better protected from the northwest winds.

In the year 1775, shortly after the burning of Charlestown, a small village opposite Boston, a British frigate of only 18 cannon entered Casco Bay during the month of October and, catching the inhabitants defenseless, set fire to the city of Falmouth and the ships [I:49] that happened to be in that port. More than 130 homes and many warehouses were consumed by the flames, and about 400 families that were then living there, having lost their personal possessions, moved away. After this catastrophe the Americans decided to defend themselves against a similar surprise and erected a fort on the point of the peninsula whose remains can still be seen. After peace was concluded, many of the former inhabitants returned to Falmouth, and they made the city rise again from the ruins. About 1000 persons are occupied in commerce there at the present time – in codfish, but mainly in lumber and ship masts of white pine, which are cut in the interior regions of the continent and are sometimes up to three feet in diameter.

On the 19th of July we continued the trip on horseback, leaving at Falmouth the carriage that was of no further use to us because of the extremely bad roads, and we reached New Casco situated on the Presumpscot River, which is crossed by a wooden bridge. Then we came upon North Yarmouth, from which one can see the numerous islands of Casco Bay, said to be equal in number to the days of the year. Next we entered a region settled barely 20 years ago. The few farmers who came to settle there live in little cabins made of tree trunks still covered with bark and mortised at the corners, the chinks filled in with clay to stop the wind and rain. These wretched huts are no more than 14 to 16 feet high at the center and 8 to 10 at the walls, and [I:50] covered with a roof made of large pieces of bark of that fir tree called hemlock fir[44] by the English. We had to travel an eight-mile stretch by a muddy path in the midst of the woods, which, encumbered in some spots by large trees that had fallen across it, was almost impassable. The hardships of a disastrous journey in that lonely forest were tempered only by the delightful odor of the sweet fern,[45] a shrub with fernlike leaves, which was very thick in those woods and in bloom. Pines of different kinds, as well as various species of maple – namely, the red,[46] the Pennsylvania,[47] the sugar maple,[48] and the one with variegated bark[49] – are quite common. On the other hand the white nut tree[50] and the sassafras,[51] which are so abundant near Boston, begin to disappear at this point.

Brunswick is a small village on the shores of a little river of the same name, where one sees sawmills of a very simple construction, in which the tree trunks are brought forward little by little [1:51] by the motion of the mill as they are cut and move back as soon as the cut is finished. In this region grasshoppers[52] are so common that they can be heard falling on the ground like drops of water at the beginning of a summer storm. One also finds there the black cricket[53] in the fields, and the white, or house, cricket[54] in the homes.

Five miles from Brunswick we took a boat across New Meadow River, formerly known by the names of Ammareskoghin, or Sagadahoc, and after five more miles we arrived at Bath, once called Georgetown, a little village situated on the shores of the Kennebec River. There they build the ships that are laden with masts and other lumber to be taken to European ports. The Kennebec is navigable for more than 100 miles from its mouth, and its banks are fertile and not infrequently well cultivated. Leaving Bath, one follows the river for about two miles. Then a boat is taken to go to Woolwich. From there one goes around the Sheepscot River, which winds among charming hills, and arrives at Wiscasset Point. This village, since it is situated on a point of land that juts into the river, enjoys a view of the hills about it and receives from the interior by the Sheepscot the lumber that is used there to make ships. Leaving Wiscasset and [1:52] crossing the river, we arrived at Newcastle, where we spent the night.

The following morning, July 13th, we reached Damariscotta, situated on the river of the same name, which we crossed 20 miles above where it empties into the sea. At a distance of nine miles beyond the little Pemaquid, or Broadbay, River, which at that point has salt water because of the tide, we found ourselves at Waldoboro. Out of Waldoboro one enters the thick St. George woods, where the axe of the Europeans has not yet arrived, and therefore there are to be found the so-called hemlock firs and birches of enormous size. This vast expanse of territory covered by thick forests that stop the sun's rays is very damp and swampy. For this reason the narrow, winding path that constitutes the only road is very difficult because of the deep puddles that must be crossed by shaky little bridges of tree trunks not infrequently rotted by the extreme humidity, and because of big rocks and fallen trees that lie across it. There are only a very few cabins in those woods, and in one of them there is a family of negroes who cultivate a little holding and enjoy the priceless advantage of being free and landowners, which their unhappy companions in the more southern parts of America do not achieve. After about seven miles one passes near a tiny lake known as George's Pond, and then comes Warren, a village composed of a few houses and formerly joined to the territory of St. George. Because of the abominable traveling through the woods, we did not arrive there [1:53] until about nine o'clock at night, although we had left Waldoboro at five. We were fortunate indeed to find a guide, otherwise we might have undergone the fate that befell a couple of Englishmen a few days before, who were forced to wander for three days in those woods and would have died of hunger if they had not been found by some woodcutters. There sugar is obtained from a variety of sugar maple[55] called rock maple, that is, *acero de' scogli,* because it grows among stones, and a beverage resembling spruce beer is made from the black birch.[56] Moreover, houses are roofed with the bark of the common birch,[57] and from the yellow birch,[58] the sapwood is removed and used to tan hides.

At the foot of the Penobscot Mountains, which extend from north to south in the bay of the same name, there is situated the village of Camden, 10 miles from Warren. From one of those mountains, which we had climbed, we saw the mountain chain extending to the west and to the north, while to the south we had little Lake Madambeatic, located at the foot of the mountain and east of Penobscot Bay. This mountain is no more than an eighth of a mile high, but it is not easily accessible because of the thickets that occupy the path. At the top there are large stones lying [1:54] about everywhere, and among them grows luxuriantly the *Vaccinium*[59] called blueberry, at that time laden with its berries, which are sweet and tasty. It is a shrub propagated in uncultivated areas as the heather is in Europe.

Wild pigeons,[60] very much like ours, were very common in those woods, where they arrive each year at the beginning of July. These can be seen flying in flocks so thick that often the branches of the densest trees are entirely covered with them. If no other meat happens to be at hand, with a musket one can kill eight or ten of them in a short time, and, roasted with a little butter, they make in no time quite a delicate dish. Their flavor is delicious and they are often very fat, but since they are too common, no one makes much of them, and frequently they are sold at a ridiculously low price. In Carolina and Virginia, through which they pass to retreat during the winter to regions further south, Catesby says that he has seen them for three consecutive days in such great quantity that the branches of the oaks on which they perched broke because of the excessive weight, and the ground was covered with their droppings to the depth of several inches. They feed on acorns, and therefore cause serious damage in places where pigs are raised.

As soon as we had descended the mountain, we returned to Mr. Gregory's home, where we had taken lodging. This was made of tree trunks [1:55] and covered with the bark of hemlock fir. It consisted of only one room, which served as bedroom and kitchen, and a cramped loft fashioned under the peak of the roof to which one climbed by means of a ladder. The floor was made of nothing more than several loosely fastened boards which served as a ceiling for the ground floor room. I spent the night in this not overly magnificent dwelling, and my companion stayed in a nearby house made on the same plan and inhabited by a large family. In the course of the day the ground floor was our apartment where, when the cooking was being done, we had a good fire for preparing supper and baking bread, while in front of the door another fire, of straw, was lighted to drive away the mosquitoes, which exist in infinite number in the uncultivated parts of America during the summer. Hence anyone can imagine what heat we suffered, since it was the month of July, although the cordial and friendly welcome of our hosts made us overlook the discomforts of the habitation.

All the individuals of this good family being busy at some task or other from morning until night, they find in the fruits of their labors a nourishment, if not delicate, certainly abundant and most healthful. Eight cows that graze in their meadows give them enough milk for making cheese and butter and for use in the evening for supper. With corn mixed with rye they make unleavened *crescenze* which they bake at every meal by putting them next to the fire. From time to time they slaughter some of the young beeves, salt part of [1:56] the meat and share part of it with nearby families. They use the hides, after having tanned them with hemlock and birch bark, for making shoes. Their beverages are rum mixed with water, and beer made from spruce or black birch. From Boston they obtain tea, which constitutes their usual breakfast.

Such is the way of life of the inhabitants of these regions, who lack nothing to be the happiest of men. Bound to work which, though continuous, is not laborious, they pass their days in the useful and pleasant activities of agriculture, not only never feeling the torments of poverty, but, what is more, always finding under their own roof the most important things for the main conveniences of life. Lacking churches and ministers and unattached to any particular religion, they read the Bible on Sunday to their children, and adoring the providence of the Supreme Being in his creations, they address to God the prayers inspired by simple and innocent hearts. Untroubled by illusions of grandeur, they live contentedly in their situation, following the tranquil dictates of nature, and Heaven rewards their virtues by making them fathers of many children, who, marrying at the age of 20, form a new settlement near the paternal home. Thus they populate a whole region with the descendants of their own family. Indeed, the increase in population is such that, according to the most careful calculations, it doubles every 18 years, a fact very apparent to a traveler, who finds there [1:57] the homes full of children, of whom there are not infrequently eight or ten in each family.

Leaving the horses at Camden, because they would be useless on the other side of the bay where the roads are not yet passable, we departed on the morning of the 15th in a boat with two sails for Bagaduce, 25 nautical miles away. Since the wind was quite weak and the day foggy, after about an hour's sailing we lost sight of land. Then the wind died down entirely and we turned to the oars. But as the fog became thicker and thicker, cutting off the sight of the islands in the bay, the pilot confessed he did not know in which direction to steer the boat. We remained only a short time in this state of doubt because I remembered having brought with me a little magnetic compass which I used as a guide in the woods. I asked the pilot in what direction Bagaduce was located, which he said was to the northeast, and we aimed the prow toward it. After rowing for five hours, the fog having thinned out, we came upon Long Island,[61] situated in the middle of the bay, which is 18 miles long and settled by 10 or 12 families. Approaching it, we followed the coast from south to north to the point, or cape, from which Bagaduce can be made out. We were delighted with the beautiful view of the beach and the many charming little islands covered with pines that seem to rise from the sea. We then crossed the rest of the bay and [1:58] entered the port toward half past four in the evening.

Bagaduce, an abbreviation for *Major-bag-wa-duce,*[62] a name taken from the Indians, is situated on a strip of land that juts out toward the south. The village is to the northwest in a bay formed by the little Bagaduce River, protected from the winds by some small islands. It can accommodate the largest ships, since it is from 18 to 20 fathoms deep. To the south of the village at the southernmost point one can see on a height Fort George, begun by the British in 1779 and finished at the end of the war. It is square in form and defends equally the port of Bagaduce and the mouth of the Penobscot river, between which it is located. The lower part of the bastions is made of stone and brick, and one can see great walls surmounted by a clay terrace held together by large beams. This fort was occupied by British troops from Halifax, and they remained there until the end of the war, after which they were forced to evacuate it. The Americans tried at first in vain to besiege it, and now, although they know of what advantage it would be to them to have this fort in good condition, because it is the key that opens the passage from the United States to Nova Scotia, still they station there no garrison nor persons assigned to watch over the fortifications. They are allowing it to fall into ruin, to which children contribute not a little by making off with the ironwork and burning the wooden parts.

After looking over the fort and going through the little village in the company of Mr. Lee, one of the principal merchants in those parts, [1:59] we asked him to obtain for us a good boat and men well acquainted with the course of the Penobscot River in order to go up it to the Indian village located

50 miles from its mouth. He found a comfortable sailboat for us with two boatmen. Then the following morning we set out, going around Fort George, and after sailing two miles we reached the mouth of the Penobscot. We arrived late in the evening at the home of Captain Ginn,[63] and the following day at Mr. Treat's, whose home is located near some falls, where navigation of the river ends.

The Penobscot is 2 miles wide at its mouth and navigable upstream for 30 miles, up to some large reefs that traverse it and which remain partly bare at low tide. One also comes upon shallows that prevent the navigation of large boats a few miles from the sea. Above the falls only light birch bark canoes used by the Indians are employed, with which one can go up the river for more than 60 miles. In various spots the river widens so much that it looks very majestic, and it offers many convenient coves where one can easily find shelter from the winds and go ashore. Its waters are salt up to 25 miles from the mouth, and sturgeon, salmon, and other excellent fish are found in it in great abundance. The shores are covered with various species of trees—mainly maples, birches, white pine, fir, and western thuja (there improperly called red cedar), a tree that does not grow in the southern parts [1:60] of Massachusetts. As one goes up the river, few stretches of terrain cleared of trees and rendered productive can be seen, since its banks began to be settled no more than a dozen years ago.

It was our intention to set out for the Indian village the same day, but since it was Sunday and Mr. Treat wanted to hear the sermon that was to be preached by a Presbyterian missionary,[64] he begged us to put off our departure until the following morning and offered to accompany us there. Protestant missionaries are sent every two years out of Boston or other places in Massachusetts to these new settlements that have no churches or ministers. Passing from one region to another, they preach on Sundays, baptize infants, and perform weddings. The first function I happened to see was, in fact, a wedding. The two fiancés, along with the best man and maid of honor, came to the home of Mr. Treat. After a few brief prayers they were married by the missionary, who, at the end of the ceremony, gave the bride a kiss. After him the best man and maid of honor and all the other men present gave the bride their congratulatory kiss, while the groom went about kissing all the women. This custom is common in United America, so that the first visit to brides is called "Go to kiss the bride."[65]

After this ceremony we got into a canoe with Mr. [1:61] Treat and the missionary, and after about two miles we landed on the opposite shore of the river, on whose banks there were many canoes and a large number of people gathered from various parts. The place set for listening to the sermon was a ground floor room where the still dirty straw and the mangers were a sure sign of the use to which it had been put a short time before. To one side there was a broken chair and a table that was to serve as a pulpit for the preacher. Some pine boards held up by stones and pieces of wood constituted the pews for the audience. After all the listeners had congregated, the service began with some prayers, and then the sermon followed. When this was over, we went to a nearby house where, without preliminary ceremonies, in the midst of a crowd of children and in front of a good fire where there was a great kettle, we waited for the dinner hour. No time was lost in preparation. A handsome cod was taken from the kettle and the table was furnished with butter, hard-boiled eggs, and boiled potatoes—which made up the meal, finished off in quick order. We then went back to the barn to hear a second sermon. Afterwards each one got into his canoe and returned to his own home. The evening was spent in edifying moral discussions led by the missionary until, at a late hour, we retired to go to sleep. As soon as I lay down, an infinite number of mosquitoes, which entered with complete freedom through the broken panes of a window, began to land on my face, while other more domestic insects assailed me from every direction, so that I had to [1:62] remain awake all night to defend myself as best I could against so many enemies.

We were ready to set out early on Monday the 18th, but after waiting in vain until half past eight because only two horses could be found in that neighborhood, we began our pilgrimage accompanied by Captain Brewer,[66] Mr. Treat, and the missionary. Up and down we went with our two skinny nags for a distance of five miles, at the end of which we reached the home of Mr. Cobham. We were hardly there before a violent downpour came, accompanied by lightning and thunder. After a little while the rain stopped and, the clouds clearing, we continued our journey on foot along a narrow path much cluttered by shrubs and fallen tree trunks that lay across the way. We finally arrived at the river bank, a little branch of which we crossed in a boat, landing near a sawmill. The island on which the mill is located is several miles long and is called by the Indians *Rum-soconga-manan*, or "Island-between-two-lands." We had no sooner left the mill than a strong wind arose and the storm started up again. We were dressed in summer clothes and, having no place in which to find shelter, we were quickly soaked by the rain which poured down from the sky. Therefore we had to continue on our way in the greatest discomfort, since, in addition to the rain that continued violently and the ruggedness of the path, encumbered as before, we were tormented [1:63] by thousands of gnats[67] and mosquitoes. We finally arrived at the northernmost point of Rum-soconga Island, from which can be seen tiny Penobscot Island, on which Indian Village is situated.

In the woods through which we passed are seen many hemlock firs and thujas, which rise to a height of 30 feet on slender trunks of only two or three inches in diameter. In this wood are found also two carrying places, consisting of a little path on which the Indians walk carrying their canoes on their shoulders in order to avoid going up or down the rapids formed by the rocks in the bed of the river.

As soon as we came in view of Penobscot Island, we called to the Indians, who came to get us in their canoes and took us to their village, where we were introduced by Mr. Treat to one of the chiefs, who took me by the hand and ushered me into his dwelling. He was a man of about 50 years of age, of a small, but sturdy, build. Since he spoke some French, I asked him to have a fire built to dry our clothes, which were all dripping wet. He immediately sent some youths into the nearby wood, who prepared for us a good fire outside his cabin. By that time the rain had stopped completely, and the clouds, borne away by the wind, let fall on the earth the beneficent rays of the sun. So, drawing up to the fire, with the help of the Indians who crowded around us, [I:64] we took off our clothes and let them dry.

Penobscot, or Old Town, as the English call it, on the little island of the same name, is situated, according to the best maps, at latitude 45° 10′ and 50 miles north of the mouth of the river.[68] About 20 Indian families live there in their huts, which they call *wigwams*, arranged in rows and placed close to each other. These huts are made of pine trunks fastened at the corners with strands of bark, and the outside walls, like the roof, are covered with wide pieces of hemlock bark. Inside there are no partitions, and their furnishings consist simply of square pieces of the same bark which serve as seats and some skins or woolen blankets in which they wrap themselves at night to sleep. Woolen blankets, as well as guns and other tools now common among the Indians, are brought to them by European merchants. Before the discovery of America they used—instead of these furnishings—furs, earthen or terracotta receptacles, and sharp pieces of flint that served as arrowheads (Plate IV, Fig. 7), knives, and axes. Every Indian is provided with a gun, a dog, and a canoe—three things that they consider most necessary, and which therefore they conserve with the utmost care. The canoes are made with the greatest skill: the framework is formed of thin strips of wood and then covered with birch[69] bark sewn with roots of the spruce tree. [I:65] They are very light, and a canoe capable of carrying four persons can easily be transported on the shoulders of a single Indian. Instead of oars they use very light wooden paddles, often painted various colors. The two paddlers take their positions, one kneeling at the bow and the other seated in the stern of the canoe. In this manner, swiftly plying the blades in the water, they paddle with great agility, controlling at the same time the course of the little craft; and so great is their skill at this exercise that they descend safely through the rapids. They even dare to make long trips on the sea, following the shore in these fragile craft.

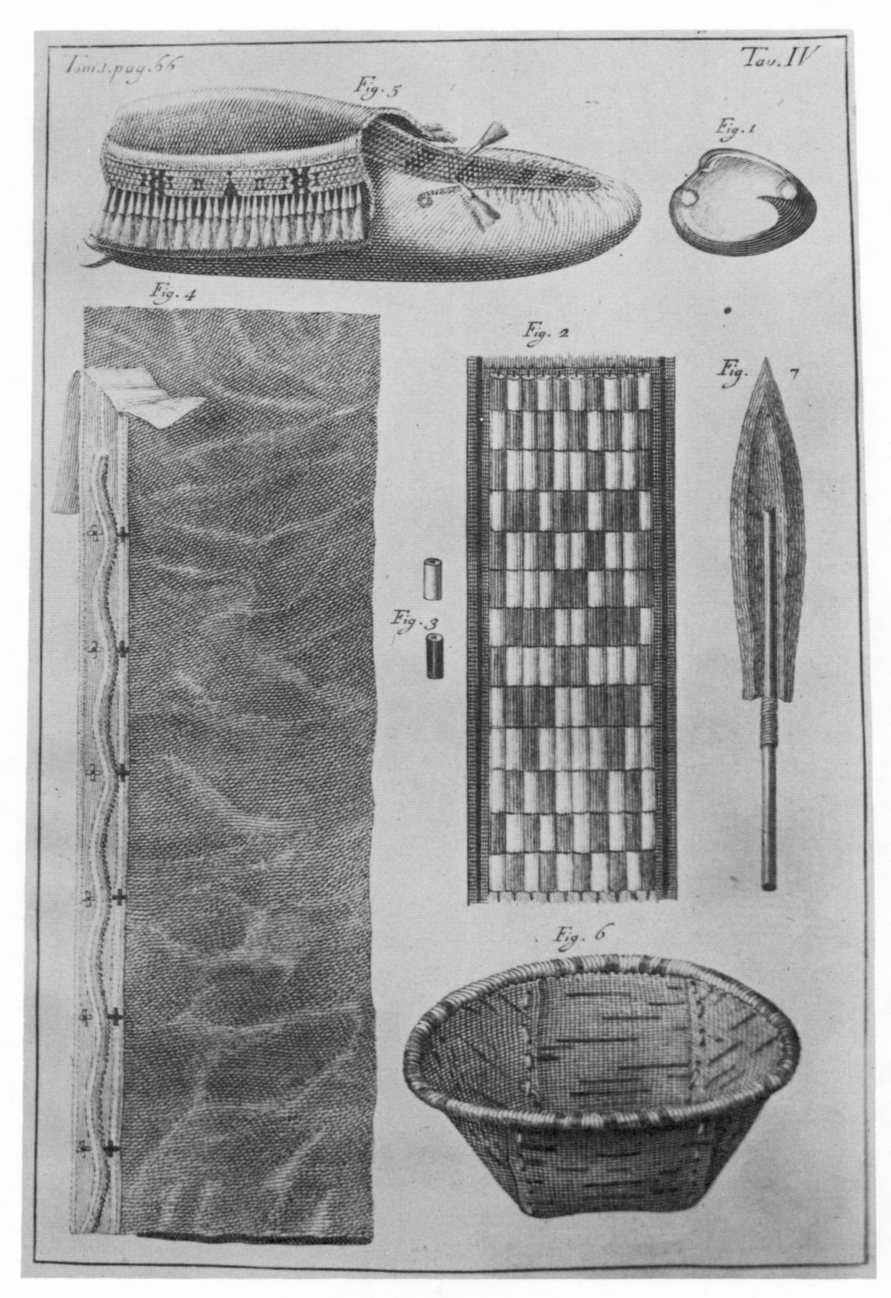

Plate IV. Indian artifacts.

Whenever the wind is favorable, a piece of woolen blanket or canvas, a skin, or, when they have nothing else, a shirt, serves as a sail for them, suspended from a pole that they fasten in the middle of the canoe. They pack very few things in their canoes during trips – namely, some skins to sit on, the woolen blankets they use as beds, and some food. If during the trip they are caught in such a heavy rain that it might fill their little craft and sink it, they go ashore and, lying on the ground, protect themselves against the rain by covering themselves with their canoe bottom side up; and they wait for the end of the storm to continue their journey.

The chiefs, or *sachem*, are chosen from among the oldest of the tribe. They have not only the right of advising and chastising any youth, but also that of distributing the labor of fishing and of the hunt. These Indians are of medium height, regular features, [1:66] and of the color of copper, rendered darker by beaver or deer fat with which they grease their bodies in order to resist better the heat of the sun and also to protect themselves against mosquito bites – which makes them very dirty and ill-smelling. Among the young women there are some who combine a pretty figure with a vivacious face, and the lads are very agile and well proportioned. They descend from the ancient nation of the Abenaki, who once inhabited the regions included under the name of New England, and they are mixed with the descendants of the Mohawk who came from Canada and with offspring of Frenchmen married with Indian women.

Their attire is no longer the ancient one, made of skins, but European dresses and shirts, and uniforms of French and English soldiers. A few wear European-style hats, decorated with feathers. Others always go bareheaded, and their long black, glossy hair is cut short over the upper half of the head, while that of the nape comes down to their shoulders. Some paint their faces red and black in various designs, others have the cartilage of their ears cut and hanging down; and others adorn them with silver rings, which sometimes hang even from their nostrils. They also wear, sometimes across their shoulders, sometimes around their necks, canvas bags covered with *wampum* (Plate IV, Figs. 2 and 3)[70] or tiny bugle beads [1:67] or various colors arranged in patterns. Some have silver bracelets or rings, and others, plaques or medallions of the same metal hanging around their necks. The upper part of their thighs is bare, and they cover their nakedness with a piece of cloth or canvas, ordinarily red in color, which they slip between their thighs and hold up with a band. To this band or belt they attach, by means of a long ribbon, their leggings, that drop from mid-thigh to instep (Plate IV, Fig. 4). These are usually scarlet, and sewn from the outside so that they can be easily put on and taken off, with a strip about two or three finger-breadths wide left beyond the seam which they adorn with *wampum* or bugle beads arranged in patterns. Their shoes (Plate IV, Fig. 5) have neither sole nor heel. They are made of deer or elk skins cured and tanned a hazelnut brown, and very elegantly fashioned. Along the uppers they make an ornamentation with porcupine[71] quills, which they flatten and paint a very pretty red, and on the outside part of the shoe that goes around the instep they put a number of little tassels made of a tin cylinder packed with deer hair colored [1:68] red, which, as they move, produce a pleasing rustle.

The women also wear European dresses, draped over their shoulders and coming down only to their knees, their legs and feet covered with the same stockings and shoes already described above. They, too, wear earrings, bracelets, and similar ornaments, and a few of them have pointed caps decorated with glass beads or *wampum*. When the women are young they have, as I said, pretty, though swarthy, faces, with wide, flat noses; but as they grow old, and perhaps also out of slovenliness, they are utterly disgusting and revolting. Indian women give birth almost without pain. When the children are born, they tie them to a small board with bands, resting their feet on a little piece of wood that joins the board at right angles; and if they are traveling, they carry this behind their shoulders more or less in the same way as the Eskimo do. The occupations of the women consist in raising a little corn, working on the canoes, on stockings, shoes, and other ornaments, and in making birch-bark baskets and pouches, and also dishes and bowls (Plate IV, Fig. 6) that hold water, which they use on their journeys.

The main occupations of the men are fishing and hunting, which provide them with food, and skins, that they then use to buy what they need from European traders. They have a fixed season for the hunt, during which they leave their villages. When they have to [1:69] stay in the woods a long time, they build for themselves temporary huts with tree branches to protect themselves against the inclemencies of the season. Their food consists of maize, or corn, and the flesh of beaver, deer, elk, and other animals, or birds, fish, and shellfish. They preserve meat by drying and smoking it. Their ordinary beverages were formerly water and drinks made from the spruce, sugar maple, or birch; but after the introduction of rum and brandy, they preferred to the other healthy beverages these poisons, which wrought there more devastation than war, smallpox, and plague, and continue still to reduce the population and to pervert the excellent qualities of these tribes. The Abenaki are (like the other Indians) sincere and frank in their behavior, and if they never forget an injury, they are incapable of forgetting a favor. The religion of the inhabitants of this village is Catholicism, and a missionary is sent out of Montreal, who lives among them, baptizes the children, performs weddings, and instructs them in religion. A short time ago, however, a number of the young Indians, persuaded perhaps by some Presbyterian ministers, changed religion. Hence there arose such dissensions between the two parties that the missionary, fearful every night of being killed, withdrew to an island in Penobscot Bay, where he was followed by some of the older Indians.

We remained at Penobscot Village for several hours, and then, since evening was coming on, we got ready to leave. Because traveling on foot was too [1:70] difficult, we decided to descend the river in Indian canoes. Upon asking permission from the chief, he granted it readily, begging us to give some recompense to those who were to escort us. In a short time we saw five canoes launched in the water, in each of which were two Indians. We then got in with them, and passing swiftly through the reefs and rapids, reached Mr. Treat's home. On the following morning, the 19th of July, we left early for Bagaduce, but since the wind was contrary and the tide not always favorable, we were forced to use our oars almost all day long. At dusk a young sea lion[72] came to surface near the boat. One of the boatsmen raised his oar and hit it so squarely in the head that it sank immediately, and then floated dead on the water. But the tide carried us off so that we left it behind and in a short time lost sight of it. These sea lions are quite common in Penobscot River and Bay and are sold at the price of about two Spanish pieces. Their skin is used to cover trunks and from their flesh is obtained a large amount of fuel oil. Finally, at one o'clock after midnight, we entered the port of Bagaduce.

Having satisfied my desire to visit the easternmost parts of the Commonwealth of Massachusetts, and one of the northern extremities of the United States, we took leave of Mr. [1:71] Roland, who had to stop longer at Penobscot, and I embarked in a good sailboat to recross the bay. The sea was rather rough, the wind strong and contrary, and the thick fog kept us from seeing the islands that were supposed to give us our direction, so that we concluded it was dangerous to draw too far away from land, and approached the coast of Long Island. Then, making use of our oars, we followed it for more than 15 miles to its southernmost point, where we went ashore toward eight in the evening. During the day we saw herds of sea lions swimming, mainly in the bays that are found along the coast. On the 20th we did not leave Long Island until ten o'clock on account of the very thick fog, and we arrived at Camden at one in the afternoon, not without danger of losing our way again, inasmuch as, although the fog lifted from time to time, it quickly returned thicker than ever. It is remarkable that, since Penobscot Bay is so subject to fog, no thought is given to providing the boats with a compass and thus avoiding the danger of becoming lost in the bay or going too far out to sea.

At half past four I got my horses back from Mr. Gregory, and for the return to St. George I chose a road nearer to the seashore and less difficult than the one I had taken to come. But although this road was not comparable to the preceding one, it could be described as very bad, since we were often forced to look for tree trunks in the forest to patch up broken bridges so that the horses could pass. At Thomaston we crossed [1:72] the George River in a canoe beside which we led the horses as they swam. The George River at this point is near its mouth, and not far away there are still the ruins of old Fort St. George, from which the region and the river took their name.[73] On calm nights fireflies could be seen flitting about, which are as common in various parts of Massachusetts as in our country. They do not differ essentially in size and color from ours, so that I believe they are a simple variation of the same species.[74]

On the following two days I returned along the same road as before from St. George to Bath on the Kennebec, from where, instead of passing through the Brunswick woods, I took a beautiful and pleasant road along the sea all cleared of trees, bedecked with smiling fields, and rich with houses and inhabitants. On the 26th I went from North Yarmouth to Falmouth, and on the 29th from Falmouth to Kennebunk, where I stayed with Mr. Little, son of the missionary whom I had met at Penobscot.[75]

The next morning I went with him to watch the smelting of the iron that comes from a rich ore of that region.[76] This ore is of the type called muddy, in which the metal is found in the state of ocher. This is dug from a low terrain about seven miles from Kennebunk, and the ore is reddish, friable, and rich. It is [1:73] covered with a large quantity of coal and reduced to a shapeless mass of metal, which, under the mallet, is drawn out into long bars of 50 or 60 pounds in weight obtained from 5 to 6 bushels of ore, each weighing about 50 pounds. Only four bars are produced daily, and an enormous amount of coal is consumed, since the furnace is open and the heat escapes everywhere. The iron is of good quality and is made into utensils and farm tools that formerly were obtained from England.

From Kennebunk I left for Old York and Portsmouth, where I arrived on the evening of the 30th of July, observing along this road many plants of the so-called silk grass,[77] which was in bloom and gave out a very pleasant odor.

Past and Present Condition of Massachusetts

[1:74] When the European settlements in this region began, the Indians who inhabited it were very numerous. The several nations were divided into various tribes. To the east and northeast dwelt the Churchers[78] and Mohagan; to the south the Pequit, or Pequot, and the Narraganset; to the west the Connecticut and the Mohawk; to the north the Aberginians, who divided themselves into Massachuset, Wippanap, and Taratines. The number of these was so large that just the three sagamoreships, or districts of the Massachuset, were separated into seven minor districts counting about 30,000 men. These, however, in a few years were reduced to a little more than 300, not only by a horrible epidemic that raged a little before the colonies were established there, but also by the smallpox introduced by the Europeans, and by the wars they waged with the latter.

During the spring and summer these Indians lived near the seacoast, withdrawing to the interior at the beginning of winter to hunt deer and beaver. They lived on the flesh of bears, deer, cougars, racoons, etc., as well as birds, fish, and oysters, which they dried for provisions. They also preserved crabs [1:75] by smoking them, and moose tongue prepared in this manner was by them deemed the most delicate food. They nourished themselves, too, on birds' eggs, which they boiled in water, and a kind of wild bean[79] with which they used to make a sort of soup by adding corn flour. This grain, which they raised near their villages, they ground and kept in leather bags; and they often ate the still unripe kernels on the cob by roasting them next to the fire. In addition to these foods they also made use of various plant roots, the tiny fruit of the chestnut, blueberries, pumpkins, and melons, which they ate in great abundance. The *tomahawk,* a kind of club ending in a heavy ball, the hatchet furnished with flint instead of iron, bows, and stone-tipped arrows were their arms and principal tools. They were very skillful at shooting the bow, so that they could even kill birds in flight easily.

These Indians were well built, swift of foot, and almost beardless, since they had little beard by nature and plucked that as soon as it appeared. Their clothing consisted of the skins of moose, deer, and beaver, which they wore with the fur inside in winter and outside in summer, painting them various colors and decorating their suits, as well as their stockings and shoes with *wampum* beads, making pretty necklaces even of this sort of money of theirs. Some of them lived to [1:76] a very advanced age, the most common diseases among them being fevers and colds, which they treated by enclosing themselves in a well-insulated cabin and working up a good sweat. Their religion consisted of believing in a benevolent God whom they called Squantam and an evil principle called Abamocho or Cheepie, which, according to them, tormented them with apparitions and diseases. Prayers were addressed to the latter by the *powwows,* their priests, who, like those of the Tartars and the negroes, were at the same time also doctors and necromancers. Today, in Natick, a village near Boston, there are a few descendants of these Indians, who adopted the dress and customs of their neighbors, but since they are very lazy, they live wretchedly on what they can beg. These, and the inhabitants of Penobscot, of whom I have spoken, are the miserable remnants of so many and such numerous nations that used to inhabit this part of America before the arrival of the Europeans.

The Commonwealth of Massachusetts includes the provinces formerly known by the names of Massachusetts, Maine, and Sagadahoc, and the islands called Elizabeth, Martha's Vineyard, and Nantucket, extending from latitude 41° to 46° 30′ and from 67° to 73° longitude from London. Its boundaries are the province of Nova Scotia and Canada to the north, Nova Scotia and the ocean to the east, the states of Connecticut and Rhode Island to the south, and those of New Hampshire and New York to the west. The southern limit of the State of New Hampshire, extending eastward to the seacoast, [1:77] divides this Commonwealth into two portions, one of which, situated to the south, can properly be called Massachusetts, and the other, Eastern Massachusetts, containing the old provinces of Maine and Sagadahoc.[80] Massachusetts proper extends about 120 miles north and south and about 100 east to west. It is divided into 10 districts, or counties, by the names of Hampshire, Berkshire, Essex, Middlesex, Suffolk, Bristol, Plymouth, and Barnstable, Dukes County (which includes the islands of Elizabeth and that of Capawach, or Martha's Vineyard), and, finally, the island of Nantucket, which by itself makes up the tenth county. Eastern Massachusetts extends more than 300 miles from Piscataqua to the St. Croix River,[81] and about 200 from the seacoast to the Canadian border. It is divided into three counties called York, Cumberland, and Lincoln. The seacoast [1:78] is furnished with beautiful and safe bays, as, for example, those of Massachusetts, Saco, Casco, and Penobscot. The region is varied by little hills, but there are few mountains. The principal ones are Agamenticus near Old York, which can be seen from a long distance at sea; the White Mountains situated between New Hampshire and Eastern Massachusetts; and those of Penobscot that extend along the bay of the same name. Numerous rivers, safely navigable for long distances, flow in various parts of the state – for example, the Merrimack, the Kennebec, the Penobscot, and the Connecticut, the last of which comes down from New Hampshire, crosses Massachusetts, and empties into the sea in the state to which it gives its name.

The new Constitutions of Massachusetts were published and went into effect at the beginning of the year 1780, since by that time the temporary form of government adopted at the beginning of the Revolution had come to an end. According to these Constitutions, the legislative power consists of two upper houses, namely, the Senate and the House of Representatives, and these two chambers together form the General Court. The Senate is composed of 31 members chosen from the various counties in the following manner. On the first Monday in April of each year all the male inhabitants over 20 years of age gather in every city and village and vote either by voice or in writing for those senators that are to be elected for [1:79] their county. These votes are sent to the General Court, which meets every year on the last Thursday in May, where the votes are tallied and those individuals who received a majority vote of the people are declared members. The Senate can convene whenever necessary, and it has the right to choose its president and to confirm or reject the new law proposed by the House of Representatives. This body, in imitation of the British House of Commons, is made up of the representatives that each city, town, or village has the right to elect in proportion to the number of its inhabitants. There must be at least 150 taxed heads[82] to have one, 375 to elect two, and so on, 225 additional heads always being required for each new member. These elections are held annually by the people in the same manner as those for senators.

The executive power belongs to a governor, who has a lieutenant, and nine councillors chosen each year from the senators. The governor and lieutenant governor are chosen by the people, whose votes are collected in the various counties and sent to the General Court, where they are nominated according to the majority of votes. However, if the votes are not up to the number required by law for electing one of the candidates without balloting, the House of Representatives chooses two from those nominated by the [1:80] people, and the Senate elects one as governor, leaving to the other the office of lieutenant governor. The governor is also commander of the land and sea troops, and selects the officers at his pleasure. Finally, the judicial power resides in the various tribunals called Courts of Justice. The laws are the same as those in effect in England, and there is no change except in that part in which the latter are opposed to the new form of government. The delegates to the General Congress of the United States are five, elected annually, and they can be recalled at any time, even before the end of their terms, which shows how much power this legislation gives to the people. This form of government, however, in view of the circumstances of this state, seems to me subject to many serious disadvantages, as will be brought out more clearly by my accompanying observations, which, although regarding at various points the conduct of the United States since the war, refer more particularly to the Commonwealth of Massachusetts.

It is no wonder that a nation situated in regions quite removed from Europe, peopled, taught, and held subject by a power which, studiedly inspiring in her a lofty notion of her own Constitution, imbuing her at the same time with a very low opinion of the laws and government of other peoples, should, upon obtaining independence, embrace those principles of government most within the range of her own experience. Such was the case with the American Republic, which, having removed itself from British domination and inadequately acquainted with the advantages of the constitutions of other European nations, embraced [1:81] almost whole those of England, even though they were not the best adapted to the circumstances. The ever flattering, but perhaps often ideal, reputation of a perfect democratic government made them circumspect in granting the title of legislators only to delegates of the people, and two houses were created after those of England.

However, if the delegates of the various cities and districts of an old and powerful nation such as England can be trained politicians, men of wisdom, and wealthy enough to sacrifice part of their private interests to the welfare of the Republic, they are not such in the new and poor American Republic.[83] One hundred and fifty Irish peasants, as lacking in money as they are devoid of knowledge, having no means of self-support in the poor country areas of their wretched native land, go down to the seashore and wait for the first boat to go to America. Arriving in Boston, they betake themselves to the woods of Penobscot or St. George, build their log cabins, and, uniting to form a village, choose one of their number to be a representative in the General Court. The ignorant peasant, leaving his axe behind him, goes to the city, unhappy at interrupting his country labors, which are still on his mind in the midst of his political occupations. He trembles at the very [1:82] mention of "soldier" and "fortification," things which, up to that day, he found only pernicious, and he opposes all kinds of expense. In vain do better educated people try to show him the advantage of the new provisions, since he can never be persuaded that a tax can be advantageous, nor that armed men are necessary to defend him. Upon his return to his cabin he boasts to others of having opposed taxes, and they applaud the person who is the cause of their undoing. Others, who make up perhaps the majority of the members of the Court, are less ignorant men, but may be even more dangerous. Brought up in the country with ideas of an unlimited freedom and informed about the relations between the powers only from the gazettes, which they read avidly, they pass off-hand judgments on even the most complex public affairs, and having become politicians without training or experience, they often cling stubbornly to an opinion from which it is impossible to shake them loose. Men of sense and experience in affairs recognize these defects of present legislation, but since they are for the most part employed as governors or councillors, whose influence extends only to the executive side of the government, they have no way of correcting them. The truth is that in the Senate, one of the two houses composing the General Court, there are also educated people, and this is in fact the only remedy provided for the aforementioned disorder in the new system. Indeed, certain malcontents revealed their desire to destroy this respectable body in order to open the door to unbridled licence.

[1:83] However, to show better the defects of this weak government, it will suffice to tell what happened in Massachusetts in the summer of 1786. Certain inhabitants of the interior, compelled to pay huge taxes to make up for the enormous expenses of the war and the interest on the debts contracted with France and Holland, thought they were being duped by the directors of finance and by the members of the government, imagining that they had used the public money otherwise. Therefore they went, armed, to Springfield and Worcester, the capitals of Hampshire and Berkshire counties, and kept the judges from opening their courts. After these first attempts, which they got out of without punishment, they became bolder and more numerous, and not only opposed the administration of justice in other places but asked the General Assembly to reform various articles of the Constitutions. Their principal demands were that the salary of the governor be reduced, that the Senate be abolished as useless, that the courts of first instance, or, as they are called there, Courts of Common Pleas, be done away with, and, finally, that there be an equal distribution of land among the inhabitants of the Commonwealth, and that all debts contracted up to that time be forgiven: namely, to put it in simpler terms, that the industrious man should lose the fruit of his labors to divide it with the slothful, and that the debtor should defraud his honest creditor of that money which perhaps helped him in his calamaties. This rebellion lasted many months – almost a year, and it might [1:84] have had disastrous results for the state, if the government had not finally decided to put matters right by sending there a regiment under the command of General Lincoln. In a little skirmish that took place with the insurgents, four of them fell on the field of battle; and since their companions had dispersed and their leaders had fled to Canada, the others then once more agreed to obey the government.[84]

When the British were forced to ask for and subscribe to the peace treaty, they ceded to the Americans one of the most beautiful, and most extensive, parts of America. In addition to the established colonies, they yielded, along the seacoast, that portion of the country that extends from Falmouth to the St. Croix River, the places along Lake Champlain, half of lakes Ontario, Erie, Huron, Superior, etc., up to the Lake of the Woods, and from there down along the Mississippi all those regions now inhabited by the Indians to the east of the river so far as Florida. All these places used to be defended by forts made by the British or during the war, which, upon being occupied by American troops, assured the frontiers of the United States. The Forts of Ticonderoga and Crown Point, by defending the navigation of Lake Champlain, secured the boundaries between them and the British in Canada, and would have compelled the latter to submit to the same searches that the Americans undergo at St. John.[85] Fort La Galette on the St. Lawrence [1:85] River could have blocked communication between the lakes and Canada, and those of Oswego and Niagara on the southern shore of Lake Ontario could have inspired the respect of both the British and the Indians.[86] Furthermore, if the Americans had then taken it into their heads to win over the latter by providing them with the merchandise that the British take to them, in time they might perhaps have been in a position to destroy, or certainly at least greatly to reduce the Canada trade.

But what did they do? The war over and the peace signed, the unanimous popular watchword was "liberty." The soldiers who had served in their defense were badly paid, and the people were waiting only the moment of their dismissal in order to relieve themselves of this expense, fearful that their defenders might become their tyrants. This notion assumed such proportions that the great Washington was almost suspected of wanting to set himself up as sovereign, and his resignation was received with applause. The sinew of the Republic and the rising military discipline thus broken, everyone returned [1:86] quietly to his own home, as if the provinces ceded were situated in the midst of the stormiest sea and far from any inhabited part of the globe, and therefore safe for the centuries to come. The British had a very fine port at Bagaduce on Penobscot Bay built during the late war, which, according to the peace treaty, was to have been ceded to the Americans. Consequently, the British asked the Americans repeatedly to send troops to occupy it, but having waited for them in vain for a long time, they finally departed in 1783, destroying the barracks and the magazines as they left. This example made the British more cautious about abandoning such important places that were not occupied by the Americans. Instead of giving up Forts La Galette, Oswego, Niagara, Detroit, etc., they fortified themselves in those places,[87] and built up a substantial new settlement at Cataraqui[88] to facilitate communications between the aforementioned forts. Thus through indolence and ill-advised parsimoniousness the Americans lost this vast area and now are forced to witness their enemies fortifying themselves on their own territories, from whom, on the basis of already established boundaries, they were separated by water.[89]

Having managed their affairs so badly with the British, they did no better with reference to the Indians. These ancient inhabitants of America, although [1:87] devoid of European education, have a natural talent far superior to what we commonly attribute to them. Very unlike the peoples of Sierra Leone, the Gold Coast, and other African regions, who are brought up in the debasement produced by slavery, the courageous and intelligent American Indians abhor the very name of slavery. As the Europeans spread out along the coasts, they forced them to retreat into the interior. Unable to defend themselves on account of superiority in numbers or discipline, they exercised cruel revenge, and, by destroying now one, now another, colonial family, they made them pay in blood for the land occupied. The British were forced to build forts and maintain garrisons on the frontiers to protect themselves from their raids, and at first they had to fight long and bloody wars until the Indians became convinced from experience that they could not destroy the Europeans and turned instead to seek their friendship.

At the outbreak of the war between England and the colonies the Indians did not know how they ought to treat the Americans, namely, whether as friends or as enemies; whether, after the peace, the new republicans would forify the frontier areas; whether they would respect the rights of those nations; and whether, if their friendship were sought, the Americans would enter into a useful and lasting alliance with them. But in that, too, their conduct was contrary to their interests, inasmuch as they allowed the new pioneers, for the most part a bad lot, who had spread out into the interior, to settle at the borders without any control. These people enraged [1:88] the Indians by stealing their canoes, molesting their wives, and intruding into territory not ceded to them, with the result that the natives very often avenged these injuries with the massacre of whole families.[90]

The Inhabitants of Massachusetts, Their Commerce and Agriculture

[1:89] The customs of this people composed of men of various nationalities are not entirely uniform, although in general they differ little from those of the British, from whom the inhabitants for the most part are descended. The hospitality shown equally by the city dwellers of Boston and the farmers of St. George, a certain equality of behavior even between persons of different rank, which, not debasing the poor man, makes him less servilely dependent upon the rich man, an eager desire to become acquainted with the affairs of others less out of idle curiosity than the wish to learn something new, a very strong inclination to become involved in the political administration of the government, and, finally, a keen love of liberty along with a great deal of steadfastness and courage, form the principal character of the inhabitants of Massachusetts. This is upheld by the ideas that the youngsters absorb from their swaddling clothes and from the general application to reading and writing, for which schools are open at public expense in every city, town, and village.

The opinions of the various sects, which once produced in this region not only serious disagreements but even internal wars and cruel persecutions, are now, by virtue of complete freedom of choice, rendered innocuous and peaceful. After the iron rod [1:90] with which they drove away the followers of the other sects was taken from the hands of the Presbyterians, a number of them established themselves there and flourished beyond all bounds after the recent revolution. Among them, that of the Shaking Quakers,[91] recently arisen in America, deserves particular mention. The founder was an Irish woman, who, upon arriving in Boston and declaring herself the Chosen Woman, began to preach a new doctrine and very quickly formed a body of converts, who were persecuted by the people and multiplied rapidly. The main point of their belief is that the end of the world sunken in wicked vices is approaching, and that God sent this woman to be the leader of the chosen people. This is how her followers, who must preach to men penance for the sins committed, call themselves. They summon to penance not only the living, but even the dead, with whom they say they have frequent conversation, as also with the angels and demons. They maintain that they are in a state of resurrection and equal to the angels, since they never commit any sin and dedicate themselves to serving God. They say, on the other hand, that if, seduced by the Devil, they were to neglect their religious exercises, they would die immediately and would never be able to rise again; hence they fight [1:91] continually with the Devil, who is visible to them. These religious exercises consist of laughing, weeping, singing, and jumping in a circle in the fields until they are utterly worn out, and their songs are merely a succession of cries and sounds without articulated words. The violence of these movements is such that sometimes they are seen dripping with sweat even in the most severe winter weather, and often they fall completely exhausted. In this way they believe they are mortifying the flesh and keeping the spirit elevated to celestial matters. Since it is one of the main points of their doctrine to suppose that the end of the world is near, they till the fields to produce only an annual subsistence, and for the same reason do not approve of marriage. The founder of this new sect died two years ago, as the consequence, so they say, of almost continuous drunkenness, from which it can be argued that she was indebted to beer and rum for the ecstasies in which she declared herself absorbed and for the principal points of her singular doctrine. The Shaking Quakers used to be quite numerous not only in this state, but also in those of Vermont and New York. Now, however, since fanaticism has died out with the end of persecution, they are reduced to a small number to be found near Falmouth and Lancaster.[92]

[1:92] The people of Massachusetts are for the most part of fine build, differing from the British only in that they are less rugged and age more quickly. Frank in their personal relationships, they reveal themselves as affable and courteous, and they do not abuse strong liquors as much as the inhabitants of the South. The women, too, are generally of fair and refined features, of ruddy and healthy complexion. But their beauty does not last for many years as in Europe, and for the most part they have bad teeth and thin hair. Before marrying [1:93] they delight in pastimes, but without slighting their housework, at which they keep themselves very busy. They also amuse themselves with music and reading, and they possess a natural vivacity and openness unspoiled by the refinements of gallantry. They marry at between 15 and 18 years of age and then abandon every form of amusement, concerning themselves henceforth only with domestic matters, thus serving as the basis for family happiness by the training they give their children and by their attachment to their husbands, toward whom they maintain the most meticulous loyalty, which not infrequently is not so scrupulously reciprocated. Their winter diversions are sleigh runs in the country, and dancing, which they love so much that they give it up only in old age. During the summer they substitute walking, fishing, horseback riding, and, finally, tea parties after dinner, which resemble our *conversazioni*.

The inhabitants of this state numbered 400,000 at the time of the recent war, but this number must be greatly increased by the emigrants arrived from Europe and by the rapid population growth. The earliest and most substantial settlements are found along the seacoast or on river banks, since in these locations the transportation of goods is easier and commerce is more advantageous. The banks of the Kennebec are inhabited and tilled more than 100 miles from the sea, numerous rich plantations and villages are located on the shores of the Connecticut River; and the Penobscot, although very close to the border, begins to count many inhabitants and to admit [1:94] farming. The first commerce of Massachusetts was in codfish. The construction of vessels necessary for the transportation of this item induced the inhabitants to look for the trees most suitable for such a purpose, and then the tall pines were discovered, and the huge oaks, which in part were used to build ships and in part were sent elsewhere as lumber. This formed a second important line of exportation, which, however, kept diminishing, and even came to an end in the more populated areas where the woods were quickly destroyed. Since this destruction left the land free and open, many turned to cultivating it, and thus there came about a third source of wealth.

The state of agriculture in this part of the world, where the inhabitants are few and the expanse of terrain is vast, is not, nor can it be, equal to that of the populated regions of Europe. Since the first settlers were in general very poor and therefore obliged to obtain subsistence without delay from the land that they undertook to cultivate, they had to think of the easiest means of achieving it. Cattle and other domestic animals that multiply easily and furnish the healthful and solid nourishment of milk and meat were the first concerns of the recently arrived tillers of the soil, who, by cutting down the forests, easily transformed them into the pastures necessary for the maintenance of their livestock. They sowed a tiny amount of corn and a little rye in a part of their holdings to make bread, leaving the rest to grow wild. However, as the population gradually grew and cities of considerable size were founded, such as Boston, Newburyport, Salem, etc., thought began to be taken of means of improving [1:95] cultivation. A huge number of apple trees was planted to provide cider, other kinds of grains were sown, corn and rye fields increased, and the aspect of a sterile forest was changed to that of fruitful and verdant fields. Cherry, plum, and other fruit trees common in Europe multiplied in gardens, where our best leaf vegetables and legumes also were raised. Such was the progress of agriculture in the most populated parts of the state, and not indeed in the reaches more removed from the sea and large rivers, where a very great area is still covered with woods and few grains are obtained from the lands cleared of woods.

The quality of the terrain in the State of Massachusetts is generally not very good, and in particular near the seacoast and on the river banks it can be said that there is nothing worse. In the interior, however, and especially not far from the Connecticut River, the soil is fertile and produces a large quantity of grain. The fields, which are quite abundant along the shore and on the road from Boston to Portsmouth, are often sown with clover[93] and other types of forage grasses, which grow there to a great height but are cut only once a year in the month of July. However, they are often infested with buttercup[94] and with a sort of small white daisy,[95] the first of which is bad for livestock [1:96] when it is not dried, and the second kills all the other better grasses. Wheat is grown only along the Connecticut River and from Wells to Penobscot in Eastern Massachusetts, of two sorts—one which is sown in the fall as we do in our country, and the other (called *marzuolo* in Lombardy and *grano duro* in Tuscany) in the spring. Rye grows abundantly in all terrains and is mixed with corn in making bread. The latter forms the chief staple of country folk, and there are three kinds—red, yellow, and whitish, as well as a variety which grows in Penobscot that has a low stalk and quite a small cob. Potatoes with both white and blue flowers, barley, oats, flax, and hemp are raised in great quantity—especially the latter, widely used for ships' riggings.

Furthermore, on Nantucket Island, situated to the east of Martha's Vineyard, there is a great commerce in whale oil, many ships sailing annually out of that port for whale fishing. Almost all the inhabitants of that otherwise not very productive island subsist on this kind of export. Among them are various Quaker families.

The origin that the Indian inhabitants of these environs ascribed to Nantucket Island is quite curious, and I shall end this section by relating it. At the eastern end of the island of Martha's Vineyard there is a hill made up of earth of various colors known by the name of Gay Head. On its summit can be seen a big hollow [1:97] that looks like the crater of an ancient volcano, and the evident signs of the now extinct subterranean fire are still there. The Indians used to say that before the arrival of the Europeans a certain deity called by them *Manshop* dwelt there, whose wont it was to walk over the reefs and go down to the sea, where he would catch a whale and bring it back with him, roasting it on the coals of the aforesaid volcano and often inviting the Indians to dine with him, or leaving them what was left over from his dinner. The Indians, to show their gratitude to the god, offered him their whole tobacco crop of the island, which was barely enough to fill his pipe. He then began to smoke, and having used up all the tobacco, threw the ashes into the sea, which created Nantucket Island.[96]

CHAPTER III

The State of New Hampshire

From Portsmouth to the Border of the Territory of Vermont

[1:98]

PORTSMOUTH, the capital of the State of New Hampshire, was founded by the colonists of Massachusetts in 1629, and is situated at 71° 11′ longitude from London and at 43° 4′ latitude.[1] At its foot flows the Piscataqua, a majestic river navigable for the largest ships, and which at the distance of three miles from the city empties into the ocean. It contains from 4000 to 5000 inhabitants, and the houses, not at all painted like those of Boston, are generally of wood, as are likewise the public buildings, consisting of five churches,[2] the statehouse, and the public [1:99] dance hall. The streets are winding and unpaved except the one that runs along the river bank. The principal trade is in lumber for the building of ships, which are much esteemed, if not for their durability, at least for their lightness, maneuverability, and inexpensiveness. This trade, which formerly flourished, dropped off a great deal during the war, so that the one hundred forty and more ships which used to be so engaged[3] fell in 1775, when trade with England stopped, to a total loading of a mere 700 tons, including all the ships working out of that port. It is true that thereafter it increased again, and that in 1785 one already counted 32 ships with a total capacity of 3700 tons.

Fifteen miles to the west of Portsmouth is located Dover, an old, but not very important, village. I got there on the 4th of July, 1785, by going up the Piscataqua River, and then the Cocheco, on whose banks it is situated. The banks of the Piscataqua are very high, and in some places they are cultivated; but for the most part they are covered with white pine [1:100] and spruce trees that can be seen standing among the rocks. From time to time one passes by little bays and the mouths of various streams that join the Piscataqua. Here and there the woods on the winding banks of these streams are broken by cultivated lands. After traveling a few miles, one comes upon a very beautiful cone-shaped hill thickly covered with pine trees that you have to go around in order to enter the little Cocheco River. This contains much less water than the Piscataqua and keeps on shrinking up to Dover, where navigation is blocked by large reefs. The water comes down among them and forms a pretty cataract about 30 feet high, near which there is a sawmill that serves to prepare lumber for shipbuilding. The water of the river is salty up to within three miles of Dover, and since there is very little water at low tide, they wait for the reflux to launch their ships, without masts and without ballast, which in this manner go down to the Piscataqua. The environs of Dover are well tilled, and the village is located on a height near a hill from the top of which an immense stretch of territory is revealed to view, and one can see the mountains called the White Hills located about 90 miles to the north.

In this region I came upon some insects, among which especially noteworthy is a certain kind of dark-colored beetle with outer wings marked lengthwise by six bands of gold-colored dots. Fabricius was the first to mention it, calling it *Carabus calidus.*[4]

[1:101] The morning of August 11th I went on to Greenland, Stratham, and Exeter along a very beautiful road in the middle of a well-tilled region. Exeter is situated on a hill at the foot of which runs a stream that empties into the bay of the same name. This was one of the most important strongholds in New Hampshire during the war. Hence the public archives were transferred there lest they should fall into the hands of the British; and the General Court of the state still meets in that place.[5] This town, situated 15 miles southwest of Portsmouth, is the capital of Rockingham County, and formerly it was a center for ship trade and construction. From Exeter I went to Epping, and the following day I continued the trip toward Nottingham, beyond which can be seen on the left some mountains, called Pawtuckaway by the Indians, that run southwest to northeast. From there, passing through Deerfield, Allenstown, and Pembroke, and crossing the Merrimack River, I arrived toward evening at Concord, or Pennacoock,[6] located on the opposite bank of the river.

That day I happened to see, though fleetingly, two snakes of medium length in the woods near the road. One of these was hanging from the branches of a small shrub, and it was of a very pretty green color, so that it could hardly be distinguished from the leaves.[7] These snakes are quite common in the woods, so that if they were poisonous, it would be difficult to avoid them. Fortunately, [1:102] however, they are completely harmless and can be very easily killed. The other species was whitish sprinkled with dark-colored spots, and this is called milk snake in America, because they say it attaches itself to the teats of cows when they are grazing in the fields. This, too, is not poisonous.[8]

Concord (on the Merrimack River at 40 miles from its mouth) is about a mile long, and the houses situated on both sides of the only street are very far from each other. The surrounding terrain is fertile and well tilled, there are many apple orchards, and a great many cattle and horses feed there. The very best land sells at 45 Spanish pieces an acre, and the worst at 2 to 4 pieces. Most of it is cleared, and little grain is sown—but a great deal of rye and corn. Grain yields about 4 bushels an acre,[9] and each bushel ordinarily sells for 1 Spanish piece. A horse is worth about 40 pieces, and a cow from 14 to 15. Concord is far enough from the sea to be safe from invasions, and being situated almost in the center of New Hampshire, many believe that most likely it will in time become the capital.

On the way out of Concord one enjoys the view of the Merrimack, along which the road is laid out, [1:103] and after eight miles one sees a tree-covered islet in the middle of the river, which, splitting into two channels broken by rocks, forms various cascades called by the Indian name *Islehookosit.*[10] Amoskeag Falls eight miles beyond the preceding one is much more beautiful. Its total height is 30 feet, although the water falling as it does step by step from one ledge to the next, it seems less to the eye. The road from Concord to Amoskeag is very beautiful, and very bad compared to the one from Amoskeag to Amherst, a rather large village situated on a hill and furnished with a square surrounded all about by dwellings. In the villages of Wilton and Temple, just as all along the Portsmouth road, one often comes upon talc, which is found in a white calcareous stone sprinkled with spar. This talc occurs for the most part in small pieces, except for that which is found in the two aforementioned villages (which might perhaps compete with that of Russia), where it is used instead of glass in windows. For this purpose it was even shipped elsewhere during the war. Leaving Wilton and going by little Mount Petersboro, I entered a well cultivated valley from which one can make out the Monadnock Mountains to the west. One comes upon many apple orchards on this road, and the region seems wells inhabited, even though it is about 100 miles from the sea. The houses of the farmers are larger than in Eastern Massachusetts, and the more well-to-do among them keep large herds of cattle.

On the morning of the 16th I went up the Monadnock Mountains, leaving the highest peak to the [1:104] north, and after eight miles of laborious traveling, I reached the high point in the road, from which one commands a varied view of the mountains and a beautiful and spacious plain. Dublin is located there, a village composed of a few log cabins and inhabited by poor farmers. Then going down the other side of the mountains, I came upon two little lakes of almost symmetrical form around which there are a few dwellings, and I crossed Goose Brook, a little branch of the Contoocook, a stream that descends amid the rocks forming little cascades. The Monadnock Mountains are covered with beautiful trees, mainly white pine, hemlock, spruce, beeches, birches, alders, and maples. The terrain is entangled with various kinds of brambles, among which can be distinguished the common briar[11] and the raspberry,[12] at that time all laden with fruit. The mountains come to an end a mile beyond Marlboro, and the road is level as far as Keene, quite a large village with wooden houses arranged in a row along the road, and situated among the hills in a pretty valley in whose environs a great deal of grain is harvested.

Eight to ten miles northwest of Keene is Walpole at the foot of the mountains that divide the two rivers, the Connecticut and the Merrimack. This is quite a large village. They keep bees there, and with the honey mixed with water they make a tasty, refreshing drink that [1:105] is used mainly during the warmest summer days.

Continuing my journey, I arrived at the shores of the Connecticut where this river, squeezed between high banks and tumbling along huge rocks, forms a beautiful and majestic waterfall.[13] Over this there was built a few years ago a wooden bridge designed and well executed by a carpenter of that region at the expense of £800 of their currency in order to facilitate communications with the territory of Vermont on the opposite shore. The road runs along the river in the midst of an extremely fertile valley scattered with fields and closed to the east by high pine-covered hills.

Charlestown is a rather large town situated on the banks of the Connecticut, and formerly one of the villages built by the British to defend the frontiers against the Indians. Since it was the fourth along the banks of the river, it was distinguished under the name of Number 4,[14] or otherwise, Fort Stevens, since a fort by that name[15] (now fallen into ruin) was built there. The houses are not systematically arranged, but some of them look nice, and the streets are adorned with beautiful tacamahac or balsam poplar[16] trees, or butternuts.[17] However, since the village is built in a low-lying spot and surrounded by mountains, in August the sky is normally foggy until eight in the morning, shifts from clear weather to rain are frequent and swift, and the storms are very violent.

Former and Present Condition of New Hampshire

[1:106] The first settlements in this territory began in the year 1629 with a certain Wheelwright, who, with other colonists of Massachusetts, bought from the Indians a section of land situated along the Piscataqua River, agreeing to recognize the jurisdiction of Massachusetts; and there he founded Portsmouth and Dover. In the same year Captain Mason obtained from King Charles I the territory between the Piscataqua and Merrimack Rivers, where there was to be established a new colony under the name of New Hampshire. When he arrived in America, he found part of the land granted to him already occupied by Wheelwright. This gave rise to great disputes between him and the inhabitants of Massachusetts which did not come to an end between the latter and Mason's heirs until 1769, when New Hampshire was made into a separate province by the King and the possession of Mason's territory was confirmed for his heirs.[18] After that time we find nothing else in the history of that province worthy of attention beyond the fact that, having later been bought back by the Crown, a special form of government was adopted there which lasted until the recent revolution. The new Constitutions were then published which went into effect in 1784, an interim government having obtained from the beginning [1:107] of the war until that time.

These new laws do not differ much from those of Massachusetts. Here, too, the legislative power resides in the Senate and House of Representatives, which together form the General Court. The Senate consists of 12 persons elected annually by a majority popular vote and confirmed by the General Court on the first Wednesday in June. The House of Representatives is composed of delegates from the cities and villages that have at least 150 tax-paying inhabitants, and 300 more inhabitants beyond the 150, instead of 275 as in Massachusetts, are required in order to have 2 delegates. A president, and five counsellors chosen each year, two from the senators and three from the representatives, at the first session of the General Court, are the heads of the executive power, and the president has the same prerogatives and privileges as appertain to the governor of Massachusetts. The delegates to Congress are chosen in the interval between June and September and can be called on at any time.

New Hampshire extends from latitude 42° 50′ to 46° and by longitude from London from 70° 35′ to 72° 30′. Since it is 100 miles long from north to south and about 140 from east to west, it is divided into five counties or districts bearing the names of Rockingham, Strafford, Hillsborough, Cheshire, and Grafton. Its confines are Canada to the north, part of Massachusetts to the south, Eastern Massachusetts and the ocean to the east, and to the west the territory of Vermont, from which it is separated [1:108] by the Connecticut River. The shoreline extends only 18 miles, from South Hampton to Portsmouth, which is the only port of any significance. The interior of the territory is quite hilly, there being to the northeast the mountains called the White Hills,[19] the Monadnocks and Northfield at a short distance from the Connecticut, besides the Pawtuckaway Mountains and others of lesser height. The principal rivers are the Connecticut, which arises at 45° latitude, divides New Hampshire from Vermont, and passing through the states of Massachusetts and the one to which it gives its name, empties into the ocean; the Merrimack, which originates at the two lakes Winnepesaukee and Kasumpy at 44° latitude and empties into the sea at Newburyport in Massachusetts; and, finally, the Piscataqua, which has a shorter course but widens a great deal near its mouth. It is noteworthy that all these rivers, just as other smaller ones, have a north–south direction, and that navigation is [1:109] everywhere interrupted by frequent and swift falls.

The climate is not different from that of Massachusetts, although the cold in the capital is more severe than that of Boston and the snow falls up to a depth of six feet. Nevertheless, the Piscataqua River never freezes, a fact perhaps attributable to the strength and swiftness of the tide. The heat is not as intense as at Boston since it is tempered by the northeast wind. When this prevails during the months of August and September, it keeps the common and larger species of corn from ripening. The air, however, is healthful throughout the state, and the inhabitants, by their sturdiness, give witness to the benign influence of the climate.

According to the notice published by Congress a few years ago, the inhabitants of this territory come to 150,000. The most important settlements are found along the seacoast where the land is more fertile and trade most active, the regions to the north being mountainous and not very productive. Trade is concentrated almost entirely in Portsmouth and consists in shipbuilding, lumber, masts, clavellated ashes, cod, horses, and cattle; but, as I have observed elsewhere, this trade is now much reduced. Agriculture, which flourishes mainly in the vicinity of the Merrimack and Connecticut Rivers (whose banks are cultivated from Upper Coos[20] down to the Massachusetts border) furnishes in abundance wheat, rye, corn – products, however, that cannot easily be transported elsewhere because [1:110] of the interrupted navigability of the rivers; moreover the method of cultivating the land, like that of Massachusetts, suffers from the same disadvantages because of the scarcity of population. The sciences are not much cultivated owing to the lack of institutes, so that the well-to-do send their children to the college of Cambridge in Massachusetts. There is, of course, a college at Dartmouth, too, near the Connecticut River; but apart from the fact that it was founded for the education of the Indians, its income is too small and its location too inconvenient and remote to keep teachers and to house students there.

Freedom with respect to religion is very great in New Hampshire, and the Constitutions, as in Massachusetts, regard it as the basis of public security. Nevertheless, owing to a residue of hate for Catholics, it is forbidden to elect as senator or president anyone not of Protestant religion, although this law contradicts one of the articles of the Constitutions where the principle is laid down that there must be no distinction of any sort among the various religions established, or to be established, in the state. Among the many sects the most recent is that of the Universalists, so called, who have a church in Portsmouth. The fundamental principle of their belief is that all men are saved, for the reason that, if Christ died to redeem the whole human race, both the good and the wicked must be redeemed from eternal death. Such a soothing doctrine was very quickly embraced by various libertines and vagabonds, [1:111] and the churches of the Universalists were those, if not of the better, certainly of the larger class of the people. Their ministers are for the most part of the lowest origin, and often the blacksmiths and carpenters turned teachers and theologians found themselves much befuddled in sustaining the principles of their shaky religion. Although the people do not seem as well educated as those of Massachusetts because public schools are not so frequent, they have nevertheless the same unlimited ideas of liberty and are easily inclined to rebellion. That is what happened recently at the same time that the disturbances began in Massachusetts, and since I am convinced that the history of this event may be of interest for whomever wishes to know the customs of these peoples, I shall close the present chapter with it.

At the beginning of 1785 the General Court of New Hampshire, moved by the complaints of those who contracted debts at a time that there was not such a scarcity of money, and which they then were unable to repay, passed a law whereby any kind of real and personal property could be used in payment to creditors at a fixed price. But this law had no effect other than to discourage creditors from seeking payment of the sums due them and to render debtors more negligent in paying them. The scarcity continued nevertheless; in fact, the more goods and possessions were substituted for gold and silver as an equivalent in trade, the more money in coin disappeared from circulation, and credit having diminished, the wealthy kept in their money boxes those [1:112] sums that they would otherwise have lent to the needy. Consequently, in August of 1786 about 30 cities and villages presented a petition to the General Court in which they enumerated the disadvantages produced by the scarcity of money and requested an issuance of banknotes. The legislators went along with their petition, fixing the sum of the notes of credit at £20,000 sterling to be lent at 4 percent interest against land as security and payable at a future time at the rate of 6 percent; and this proposal had been referred as early as the 14th of Septmeber to the various cities and localities for their consideration. Then, all of a sudden, on the 20th of September, 450 men, most of them armed, impatient at not yet seeing carried out the desired issuance of bank notes, entered the town of Exeter where the General Court was being held in a church, and presented a petition to this end, dated from the fields of Exeter and signed by Moses French, one of the tenant farmers of Hampstead and leader of the insurgents who assumed the title of moderator. In this document they demanded without delay an answer to the petition. The House of Representatives had selected three commissioners who were to join with three of the Senate in examining it. But the Senate steadfastly refused to concur, adducing as their reason the unfairness of the demands and the small number of thirty villages in comparison with the 200 that compose the state. What is more, they concluded that, even if the whole state were in favor of the petition, the legislative body ought not to deliberate as long as it was [1:113] surrounded by armed men.

The President of the state, General Sullivan, and one of the senators gave the people this answer. But as soon as the insurgents heard the refusal, they surrounded to the beating of drums the church where the legislative body was, crying continually "paper money," "distribution of property," "cancellation of debts," and "suspension of taxes." It continued this way until night, when there was heard a drum in the distance, and a great crowd of people shouting loudly, "For the government, for the government!" At the sound of these voices the insurgents began to flee, even though the president, followed by the whole Court, came out and assured them that he would prevent bloodshed. Nevertheless, the insurgents withdrew to a distant part of the town, and the legislative body, returning calmly to take up the matter again, asked the president to call the state militia to suppress the rebellion. The orders went out at eleven o'clock at night and at daybreak the militia began to march, consisting of 2000 men, of whom 300 on horseback. Led by the president, they advanced against the insurgents, who scattered in fright. Forty of them were made prisoners, the others fled to their cabins, and they would have been according to the laws condemned to an ignominious death had they not, by passing from audacity to fear, asked for grace and pardon, which they in fact obtained.[21]

CHAPTER IV

The Territory of Vermont

[1:114]

CROSSING THE CONNECTICUT RIVER from Charlestown, one enters Rockingham County belonging to Vermont.[1] This region extends from 43° to 45° latitude and from 72° 5′ to 73° 10′ longitude from London. To the north it borders on Canada, to the west and to the south on New York, and to the east on the State of New Hampshire. It was settled not many years ago by various inhabitants of the states of New Hampshire and New York who withdrew to live among these mountains. The populations having then increased, Mr. Colden, at that time Lieutenant Governor of New York, requested that this region be united to his province and divided into two counties under the names of Cumberland and Gloucester. But the Vermonters, who through that union would have been compelled to pay for the land already occupied by them, and who, on the other hand, preferred to be united with the Province of New Hampshire whose capital was not so far away, appealed to the British government, which, however, paid no attention to their complaints. [1:115] Matters were at this point when the Vermonters seized the occasion of the hostilities that had begun in America to declare themselves independent without consulting with the other states.[2] Their new Constitutions were published in 1777 and amended several years later.[3] In accordance with them the legislative power resides in the General Assembly, composed of representatives from cities and villages that have at least 100 tax-paying inhabitants. The election is performed by the free inhabitants over 21 years of age,[4] who vote by written ballot. These votes are collected by the constable, and after they have been examined, the nominations take place on the basis of majority vote. In addition to the General Assembly, there is a deputy governor and a council who duly supervise the execution of the laws. The General Assembly is held annually, now in Bennington, now in Windsor, at one time in Manchester, at another in Rutland.

The first of these, however, which has the largest population, will probably be settled upon as the capital.

On my journey through this territory I left Charlestown on the 30th of August, reaching Wethersfield and then Cavendish, where I spent the night. Along this road recently cut through the woods, dwellings are few and wretched and agriculture is still in its infancy. A little way out of Cavendish one begins to climb the Green Mountains which, traversing the region from north to south, gave it the [1:116] name of Vermont, derived from the French. These mountains are covered with extremely thick woods, where the only road is a narrow path cluttered with stones, with very steep slopes and swampy valleys. Traveling on it, now on horseback, now on foot, we could not make more than two miles an hour. The annoyance of this laborious route was increased by the darkness of that forest and by the unpleasant stench of the marshes. The fungi, moss, and other similar vegetation grow there in great abundance. One often finds great fallen tree trunks so rotten that they collapse under the mere weight of a person. In fact the dampness of these woods that are never penetrated by the rays of the sun is such that sometimes huge trees fall suddenly, roots and all. This phenomenon common to other thick woods in America, which happens even during the calmest summer nights and which I, too, happened to witness, must be attributed to the nature of the soil in which the trees grow. Since this has never been cultivated, it is very hard and almost impenetrable at any depth from the surface. Covered annually by leaves fallen and rotted during the winter, it forms a light layer into which the roots extend by preference. To that fact must be ascribed the consistent observation made by various travelers in America who found that there roots are horizontal in the very same species of plants that have perpendicular roots in Europe.[5] Granted [1:117] this, it is natural that, since the roots are eaten away by the constant humidity of the soil and the tree leans in the direction toward which it is bent by the greater weight of its branches, it will fall without any outside impulse.

The most common trees are elm, spruce, hemlock, sugar maple, Pennsylvania maple, and beech. The soil, fertile in many places, would be suitable for the raising of grains if this region were better inhabited; but since there are not enough people, the best land is sold at 4 Spanish pieces. And 8 pieces an acre are paid to those who undertake to cut the trees and set fire to them. The cabins of the few inhabitants who live there are from five to six miles apart, made of logs, and covered with elm or spruce bark tied to the rafters with strands of the inside bark of elm itself. One of these cabins can be comfortably begun and finished by two men alone within four days.

On the evening of the 21st I arrived at Shrewsbury on the western side of the Green Mountains. From Shrewsbury to Clarendon and from there to Rutland and Castleton was the route that I covered on the 22nd. Clarendon is a rather large village along Otter Creek, which [1:118] comes down from the Green Mountains and flows into Lake Champlain. Rutland is one of the more important towns of the state; and Castleton, situated at the foot of the Green Mountains, stretches out for about two miles. One can see there the ruins of an old fort,[6] and it is only four to five miles away from the South Bay River, which empties its waters into Lake Champlain.

Upon leaving Castleton, one enters upon a new road flooded in various places and therefore almost impassable. I got over it with difficulty, finding myself at various times compelled to go off into the woods. On one of these occasions, the moment I drew away from the trail, I was surprised by an unusual and completely strange buzzing, and turning around to discover the cause, I perceived that it came from a rattlesnake. I was very pleased with this encounter, inasmuch as I had already tried repeatedly to procure for myself one of these curious reptiles. I got off my horse and approached the snake, which I struck too near the tail. I drew back quickly after the blow, and I saw it coil up swiftly, as if to strike. I then left it alone until, no longer afraid of being attacked, it continued slowly on its way. But as soon as it began to go into the wood, I stopped it with a stick, and making my servant hold it down, I struck it until it was dead. Then I put it in a tin box in which I kept fresh the plants I was collecting, and in this manner carried it to Ticonderoga. There I put it in a bottle of rum, and since I was to leave for Canada a few days later, I begged the innkeeper to change the rum from time to time; but since he did not exercise this [1:119] little care, upon my return I found it spoiled and rotted and I had to throw it away, to my great regret.

The rattlesnake, called *caudisono*[7] by the Italians and *serpent à sonnettes* by the French, is common in all uncultivated regions of North America south of latitude 45° and extinct in the more populated areas. They vary in size, and the one killed by me, one of the smaller ones, was two and a half feet long. Its color was dark streaked with black on the back, white on the belly, the scales of which, exposed to the sun, took on a pretty iridescent red-blue tint like mother-of-pearl. Its head was flat and very wide near the neck, the mouth was large and white inside, and the upper jaw was provided with two long, sharp teeth somewhat curved back, that ordinarily lie along the jaw; but since they were mobile at the spot where they are attached, they could be moved away from the jaw to form an obtuse angle with it. The body was thick in the middle and much more slender toward the head; and the tail was furnished with five crotala or flat rings of a dark yellow bony substance inserted into each other.

Although the rattlesnake is extremely poisonous, it is not as dangerous as is thought, inasmuch as it reveals itself to the traveler by means of the rattles which it shakes continuously; and since it is slow and heavy in its gait, it cannot, even when angry, pursue the enemy [1:120] swiftly, and it is capable of shooting forward only half its length. In Vermont the farmers sometimes kill 8 or 10 in a single day, and they are so little afraid of them that a 10- or 12-year-old girl killed 7 on one hill. In Concord Dr. Green assured me that in the 12 years that he has lived there, he never had to attend to anyone bitten by a rattlesnake, although they are very common there. If, however, they are inadvertently touched, if they are disturbed when they are in heat, or if one comes too close after having annoyed them, they strike with remarkable speed. The method that the rattlesnake uses in striking is singular, inasmuch as, when it is threatened, it coils up; then throwing its head back and opening its mouth until its two jaws make a right angle, it hurls itself at its object, which it strikes with its two teeth, by means of which it squirts poison into the wound and then it puts itself again in defensive posture. The strength of this poison varies a great deal in the different seasons. At the height of the summer season it is so virulent that those bitten quickly fall into terrible convulsions and die in a short time. These reptiles must live for a very long time if it is true that the number of their crotala indicates the years of their life, since one is preserved in Philadelphia killed in the summer of 1786 near Fort Allen which had 44 in its tail. These serpents are sometimes found when one digs the ground during the winter, as inert and stiff as a piece of wood, and they become active again when they are brought close to the fire. Many remedies have been tried [1:121] in America with varying success against the bite of this poisonous snake, which will be found mentioned at the end of the work among the plants noted by me, and especially under the entry *Polygala senega.*

To the rattlesnake, as to other big snakes, is regularly attributed the power of enticing birds to come down out of trees to be eaten by them. This fact, already known in Europe, was confirmed to me in America by many trustworthy eyewitnesses, who assured me that a thousand times they had seen little birds and squirrels hopping restlessly from one branch to the next and finally descend to the foot of the tree to yield themselves to the mouth of the snake that was waiting for them there. The celebrated Linnaeus confirms the truth of this fact, adducing the experiment more than once repeated of shutting up rattlesnakes with squirrels. The latter, after having given signs of great agitation, jumped voluntarily into the mouth of the snake.[8] To explain [1:122] the phenomenon with the words charm, sympathy, and antipathy would be substituting an illusion for an enigma. Some said that birds come down fooled by the movement of the tongue of the snakes, which to them seems one of the little worms on which they feed; others, that the fear of the enemy bewilders them, as fear makes men fall into the dangers that they would like to avoid. However, it must be admitted that no satisfactory explanation has yet been given.

Having passed by Fair Haven, the only place that has the form of a village, I saw nothing more beyond four or five wretched huts, in one of which I managed to find a little rye bread and milk. Finally I reached Mount Independence, a high hill on the eastern shore of Lake Champlain, at the top of which can be seen the ruins of the fortifications built there by the Americans. Then crossing Lake Champlain, I arrived toward evening at Ticonderoga, located on the western shore and belonging to the State of New York.

The soil of Vermont is fertile around Lake Champlain, and even in the center of the region, although full of high mountains, there are, here and there, lands excellent for grains. But [1:123] they have not been cleared yet for the lack of inhabitants. As for the inhabitants themselves, since they derive from the colonists of the neighboring provinces, they differ little or not at all from the latter in their customs, except that being without communication with the outside world, they retain a certain uncouthness and lack of culture. The first settlers, people of not too good repute who had fled from the bordering states, created in their neighbors a rather unfavorable opinion of Vermonters, although a great many good and honest farmers subsequently moved in from Massachusetts and Connecticut, attracted by the fertility of the soil, which in their hands becomes more and more productive. However, since the settlements are quite recent, far from the sea, and abounding only in those items that are common also to the neighboring regions, trade in them is not extensive. In fact, toward Lake Champlain (the only outlet for exporting their products) there are the inhabitants of New York, who would be their rivals if the English, who own Canada, should open the way for that traffic. Hence it seems to me that it was better for Vermont to join the states of New York or New Hampshire than to subsist separately with the probability of never succeeding in catching up with the neighboring states on account of its unfavorable situation.

Religious opinions, if such can be called those of a people that attend with complete indifference the churches of the various sects, are the same as are current in the states of Massachusetts and New Hampshire. The sciences are not cultivated at all, and it turns out [1:124] that this region did not produce among its inhabitants any of those distinguished men who contributed toward establishing independence of the United States, unless among them one wishes to include Ethan Allen. This man, having acquired much respect in his own region, assembled at the beginning of the war a company of adventurers and achieved some successes over the British. But subsequently, more courageous than prudent, proceeding into Canada, he tried to lay siege to

Quebec, where he would very quickly have paid the price for his rash undertaking had he not saved himself by flight, while his comrades were made prisoners. Upon his return to his native region, he decided to distinguish himself in literature and published a book entitled *The Oracle of Reason,* in which he threw together passages from various authors favorable to Deism, contributing only a few of his own fresh ideas that are easily recognized for their extravagance.[9]

CHAPTER V

Canada

Trip from Ticonderoga to Montreal

[1:125]

LAKE CHAMPLAIN is about 80 miles long from Lake George to Windmill Point, where it terminates in the Sorel River. This vast expanse of lakeshore lands, for the most part excellent soil, was scarcely inhabited in 1734, but after that time many families settled there, attracted by its fertility and by the low price at which the lands are sold. The trees are similar to those of Massachusetts, New Hampshire, and Vermont. However, at this point certain plants of more southern climates, like sassafras, etc., begin to become rare and even to disappear, and instead one finds thuja and other trees belonging to more northern regions. Bears are very common in the mountains, and the lake abounds in exquisite barbels, perch, and pike, called pickerel by the inhabitants, and other species unknown in Europe.

Although at [1:126] the present time commerce between Canada and the United States is quite negligible, there are boats at Ticonderoga, Crown Point, and other places that serve to transport passengers and livestock. Three kinds of craft are used on this lake, namely, cutters, bateaux,[1] and canoes. The first of these, built like a little ship or skiff and therefore safer in case of a storm, are most comfortable for passengers. The second, with a flat bottom and square sails, serves to transport animals; while canoes, dug out of a single tree trunk, or made of elm or birch bark sewn together, are used only for fishing or to make short trips from one dwelling to another. In winter, however, when navigation is blocked by ice, which happens usually toward the middle of December, they cross the lake in a kind of sled made in the form of a cradle and drawn by one or two horses.

Since no boat was ready, I had to stop over at Ticonderoga the whole of the 24th of August. This fort, built by the French before the cession of Canada and by them called Carillon,[2] is located on a rocky promontory along the shore of the lake. Ethan Allen seized it on the 20th of April, 1775,[3] and in 1777 it was again occupied by British troops that came down from St. John with General Burgoyne. It then fell again under the control of the Americans when Burgoyne was himself made prisoner with his army by General Gates at Saratoga, and thereafter was allowed to fall into ruin. At the present time there are in that place only two families, who established themselves there recently.

[1:127] On the morning of the 25th I amused myself by fishing with hook and line, with considerable success. I caught, among the other fish, two species in my opinion not yet described by naturalists. One of them, called here rock bass because it lives among reefs, belongs to the doree genus, has a white body all covered with black spots.[4] As for the other, called rockfish,[5] it is a small, flat fish of the same genus, adorned on the head with stripes of a very beautiful blue color with a black spot ending in a dark red band at the jaw. Its body is variegated with pretty colors, which, however, as happens with other dorees, disappear at the death of the creature.

Along the shore of the lake and at a short distance from the fort there grows in various places a kind of gooseberry[6] whose fruit, of a deep red, almost black, color, have a sweet and winelike taste, and a tough, thick skin provided with numerous soft and harmless needles.

In the afternoon a boat came [1:128] from Lake George falls with two gentlemen from Albany who stopped off at the house where I was staying. A cutter arrived at almost the same time. Since the wind was favorable, I joined them and we left for St. John in Canada. But we had hardly gone two miles when the wind changed, a very dark night descended upon us, and we anchored off the promontory called Three Mile Point. There, in a wretched dwelling, we found various people engaged in gambling, and we drew up to the fire because the night was damp and cold. When bedtime came, my companions returned to the boat; but I, fearing the moist night air, preferred to remain at the house, where there was a bed and many woolen blankets, which the inhabitants use in trade with the Indians. I was up, however, before dawn on account of the innumerable insects, and as dawn was breaking, I got on the cutter; and we continued our journey with a gentle west wind.

Beyond another promontory called Five Mile Point, one sees mountains rising on the eastern shore. Since they are at some distance, they leave between themselves and the lake a fertile plain belonging to Vermont, whereas to the west the rocky banks rise almost perpendicularly from the water. On one of these that protrudes into the lake is located the fort of Crown Point, built by the British. It, too, was taken by Ethan Allen, recovered by Burgoyne, and then ceded to the Americans; and by them it was abandoned as Ticonderoga had been.[7] Its ruins are at a short distance from those of Fort Frédéric (so called in honor [1:129] of Frédéric Maurepas, Minister of the Navy),[8] built by the French before the cession of Canada and destroyed by the British in 1759. Both of these forts were made of a black calcareous stone that forms the mass of the hill, in which can be seen numerous impressions of sea creatures, especially scallops and ammonites.[9] On the shores of the lake near the fort there is a red sand composed of fragments of granite, and another black-colored one full of iron particles.

Leaving Crown Point, in the evening we reached Gorg Harbor, a little bay protected from the winds, whose banks are still covered with trees and thickets. In only one place could it be seen that the wood had been cut and a cabin built, which was the home of the boatman, who had settled there a few days before with his wife and children. He got off the boat and spent the night with his family. We lay down in the boat under the deck of our little craft, protecting ourselves as best we could against the rain that continued almost all night long. Toward six in the morning of the 27th we left Gorg Harbor with a good south wind and very quickly passed into the great bay where the lake is eight miles wide. We then went by the little islands to the west called The Four Brothers, we saw to the left the island of Valcour, and to the east Grand Isle, 28 miles long and 3 miles wide. There the lake is at its widest, extending 20 miles from one shore to the other. We then came to the point that divides Big Bay from Cumberland Bay, [1:130] where the mountains are lost to view and the country seems level on both sides. In the evening we stopped at a house situated in the same bay. At two after midnight we continued on our way, and, during that day, having seen La Motte Island and got around the headland called Windmill Point[10] with great difficulty on account of the contrary wind, we finally entered the Sorel, or Richelieu, River, which from Lake Champlain descends to St. John and Chambly, emptying into the St. Lawrence at the place called Les Trois Rivières.

The border recently established between the United States and the Province of Canada is two miles above the mouth of the river at 45° latitude. The Isle aux Noix, situated in the middle of the river, is the most advanced outpost of the British, and a captain is stationed there with a company of soldiers. There we had to land and present ourselves to the captain, who deemed it opportune to receive us on the stairs and dismissed us without inviting us to his room. At the end of this ceremony, which we would gladly have done without, we reimbarked. There were still six miles to go before reaching St. John when, all of a sudden, the wind died down, and we were forced to make use of the oars to go up the river.

At dusk a great number of tiny white creatures arose from the river, and attaching themselves to the boat, climbed over our clothing to undergo their transformation. To my great pleasure I saw them, after various movements, stick their heads out from the skin that enveloped them, and then their whole body, helping themselves along with their feet until they freed themselves of their old [1:131] integument and flew off. This is a kind of ephemera, an insect so named on account of the shortness of its life, and which at first sight is by some confused with the mosquito. It is born from the eggs that the mother deposits near water, where it lives in the form of a worm until, in due time, it comes out to some dry spot, and leaving there the skin that covered it, flits about in the form of a little fly.[11] Occupied in these delightful observations, the trip to St. John seemed shorter to me. There we landed.

St. John, located on the Sorel River, was built by the French in 1748 for the defense of the Canadian border and to facilitate the passage of provisions and merchandise from Montreal to Crown Point. In this way they got around the inconvenience of having to load the merchandise on barges and then on ships whenever they left from Fort Chambly situated a few miles further up, where the navigation of the river is interrupted by large rocks. On the other hand, from St. John down to Lake Champlain it is quite clear for ships, of which there are some of 20 cannon that serve to protect the navigation of the lake. At the fort, which is of wood, furnished with palisades and cannon and surrounded by a moat, there resides a major with several companies of soldiers who are responsible to headquarters in Montreal. [1:132] The village is built along the river, composed of log cabins, and the inhabitants are half French and half royalists from New York and Massachusetts who took refuge here after the late revolution.

On the morning of the 29th we hired two *caleches* for Montreal. The *caleche* is a heavy, open chair resting on poles without springs or leather straps, to which one or two horses are attached. Canadian horses are of a French breed, small, badly built, with thick legs, broad, short necks, and ponderous heads; but they are very sturdy and hold up very well under work. Their harness is of quite an ancient form, and they have bells fastened at their necks like our mules. We traveled along the river for about two miles, and then we turned to the left and passed through a wood for an equal stretch, where we were tormented by an innumerable quantity of gnats[12] and mosquitoes, which here they call *marangouins*. Emerging from the wood, one comes upon the village of Savane, located in the middle of an extensive plain reduced to fields in which were grazing a great many horses and rather small, short-horned cows. Moreover, the countryside was full of that kind of wheat that is sown in the spring, which grows there to a height of only two feet and ripens at the beginning of September, forming ears heavily laden with grain.

Leaving Savane, one passes through more [1:133] woods, and then there comes another no less vast and cultivated plain that extends all the way to the St. Lawrence River on the shores of which is situated the village called Laprairie, to which the road leads. This charming plain is closed to the north by two tall mountains, and to the west it is bordered by the St. Lawrence, which, plunging over some falls, then flows majestically by the village of Laprairie and bathes the walls of Montreal on the opposite bank. The villages that one comes upon going from St. John to Laprairie are quite poor, consisting of little wooden houses with straw roofs very high in the center in order to shed the snow. At the dividing lines between one region and the next high crosses are erected, as is the custom in certain places in France and Italy. The village of Laprairie is located on a little eminence and the terrain at its foot is fertile but subject to flooding in late fall when the river freezes at Quebec and the water that comes down from the lakes backs up. These floods sometimes kill livestock that the farmers have not taken the precaution to remove. On the 30th we crossed the St. Lawrence and landed at Montreal. At this spot the river has a swift current and rocks at water level, so that boats run the risk of destruction if they are not guided by experienced helmsmen.

Montreal, the second city of Canada in size and commerce, lies on an island of the St. Lawrence 30 miles long and 12 at its greatest width. The [1:134] city is built on the easternmost point at the foot of a quadrangular mountain and is surrounded by stone walls formerly erected by the French as a defense against Indian raids; but at the present time they are falling into ruin. The streets, cut at right angles, paved with river stones and furnished with sidewalks, but rather narrow ones, and the houses made, indeed, of stone but small, low, and covered with a crude dark-colored lime plaster give the city a melancholy appearance. In order to avoid frequent fires, houses are no longer built of wood, and even the roofs of the churches and of the better dwellings are for that reason covered with tin. One of the most beautiful churches is that of the priests of St. Sulpice, who direct the seminary that furnished parish priests and missionaries. They own all of Montreal Island and collect an annual rent from its houses and lands that amounts to more than one hundred thousand francs a year. The Franciscan monastery is also spacious, although now there is only one brother. In the contiguous garden there are some European vines which, although they mature late in the fall, produce a small quantity of wine. The Jesuits, too, have a boarding school, where they live together wearing their regular costumes. There are three convents in the city, namely, the Soeurs de la Congrégation, the Soeurs Grises, and the Soeurs de l'Hôpital, who attend to the education of girls and assist in the hospitals.

The government of Montreal is dependent on that of Quebec, and there is a commandant with a [1:135] large garrison. The inhabitants are Canadians, that is, French in origin, now mixed with some American royalists from the colonies and a few British. The former are all Catholics and have the same religious liberty they had previously, although various Protestant churches have been introduced for the use of the British and Americans. The climate of Montreal, situated at 45° 27′ latitude, is so cold that the Réaumur thermometer drops to 23° below freezing, and the ice in the river does not begin to melt until the end of March or the beginning of April.

From Montreal to Cataraqui

[1:136] The British government was at that time very sensitive about travelers who wanted to go up the St. Lawrence River, fearing that they might be emissaries sent by the Americans to examine the location and defense of the forts placed on the river and on the lakes, which the British still continued to hang on to in spite of the cession of them agreed upon in the peace treaty. Now since I wished to see those regions, I presented to the commandant, Baron de St. Léger, an open letter from His Excellency Count de Kageneck, then minister of His Imperial Majesty in England, addressed to Baron de Bechlen Bertholf, imperial agent in Philadelphia. Perceiving from this the reason for my travels, he graciously furnished me with letters for the commandants of Cataraqui[13] and Niagara, and issued orders to the corporals of two boatloads of soldiers who had left for Cataraqui a few days before to receive us on board upon my arrival and to show me every consideration. I took with me some salted supplies, some bottles of Burgundy, tea, sugar, biscuits, and several woolen blankets. I left on the morning of the 1st of September in a two-horse carriage, doing the best I could to catch up with the boats, which I hoped to find at the head of Lake St. François. The village of Lachine is the first town that one meets, and then one goes on to [1:137] Pointe Claire, or Pointe de l'Isle, the westernmost tip of the Island of Montreal at about six leagues from the city. From Pointe de l'Isle to Vaudreuil, a village located on the mainland, one drops about three leagues down the St. Lawrence by going around the island called Perrot. Canoes are always ready on both sides for this passage. In the vicinity of Vaudreuil there grows abundantly in the river a kind of rice that the Indians harvest. This is the *Zizania aquatica* of Linnaeus, called wild oats and wild rice by the British inhabitants and *folle avoine*[14] by the French.

Upon landing I immediately notified the captain of militia of that place, sending him the order of the commandant to furnish me with a carriage and horses as soon as possible. In the meantime I amused myself by observing the Indians that had come down the river in great number. These were of the nation of the Ottawa, who live on the banks of a river of the same name that empties into the Lake of Two Mountains, so-called, to the west of the Island of Montreal. They had pitched tents on the shore, where the women were busy repairing old canoes and making new ones. The frame of these light craft is made of two strips of thin white cedar wood[15] that they tie at either end, giving them an oval shape [1:138] by means of three crosspieces fastened at equal distances. Another similar strip forms the keel, which is tied to the part above; and they add other strips along the sides to complete the framework, which they cover with birch bark sewn together with roots of the spruce tree. While the women were busy at this work, part of the men had gone to hunt in the woods, whence they could be heard shouting according to their custom, and others in the river were attending to fishing with hook and line, singing a song that one of them woud strike up and who would be answered by the others in the manner of a chorus. Meantime it was becoming late and time to leave. Not seeing yet the carriage that I had ordered two hours before, I sent my servant to the captain of militia to urge him again. He had not gone very far, however, when I saw him returning to inform me that the carriage was on the way. In fact it arrived a short time afterward, and the driver apologized for the delay, explaining that it was grain harvest time. I then climbed into the carriage, and after a trip of four leagues I arrived at Portage, where I understood the two boats that were to take me to Cataraqui had stopped.

The following morning I put my baggage on one of the boats, and since these had to go up some rapids, I thought it best to continue my journey by carriage as far as Côteau St. François. A wooden fort stands there surrounded by palisades and defended by a few soldiers, and across from it one can see in the river a little island called Prisoners' Island from the fact that during the war more than 300 Americans were held there. The channel that lies between the aforementioned island [1:139] and the fort has a very swift current and is so full of rocks that to go up it boats often lost a whole day, until, at the Crown's expense, a canal was cut through the stone, in which three locks were constructed. About a league beyond Côteau St. François there is the so-called Pointe du Lac at the head of Lake St. François, where I got onto the boat. Lake St. François is only seven leagues long and one wide, and one can say that with it the old Province of Canada ends. The wind was contrary, and since the day was far advanced, I was able to reach by evening only Pointe au Baudet. The following morning we continued from there our voyage into the lake as far as the village of Johnson, at which spot one reenters the river. This village was founded a few years ago by Sir John Johnson, a general in the British army, who formerly owned a fine tract of land on the Mohawk in the State of New York.[16] In the afternoon we met three canoes full of Indians from St. Regis, a village situated on the eastern bank of the river and populated by some Iroquois families, who are Catholic and live by agriculture. Under the name of Iroquois are included in Canada the Indians of the formerly five, now seven, confederated nations that live near Lake Ontario and to the south of the St. Lawrence River. They are distinguished into a) Mohawk, or Canunga; b) Onoyut; c) Onondaga; d) Cayuga, or Cayugae; e) Seneca, or Chenandoane; f) Tuscarora; and g) Saississoga, or Sississogae.

Continuing on our way up the river, we saw a number of tree trunks in the water, on [1:140] some of which there were little heaps of clay in pyramidal form. This was the work of muskrats,[17] animals of the beaver family, like which they built their homes along river banks. They are of the size of a cat, dark-colored, with a pointed nose and a flat, scaly tail, and they give off a strong odor of musk that comes from their liver and genital parts. Toward evening we reached Pointe Maligne, and in the woods I found in bloom rudbeckia with a yellow flower, ceanothus, and various species of sunflower.

The following day we continued our trip slowly because of the swift current in the river. Meanwhile we hooked, in addition to several perch,[18] three different kinds of rather large fish that furnished us our supper. One of these is a new kind of carp called chub by the British and *mulet* by the French Canadians, with a black spine and lateral stripe;[19] the second, resembling our barbel, is called catfish by the British, a name that they give to the European barbel;[20] and, finally, [1:141] the third, called black bass by the British and *achiugan* in Canada, is a kind of doree green above and white in the under parts.[21]

We then passed Long Saut, where the current of the river is very swift. To get by it the eight soldiers that were with us had to jump into the water and pull the boat. On the following day we traversed several other stretches equally difficult and stopped in the evening at Rapide Plat. On the 6th of September we covered, with equal difficulty, only three leagues, as far as the Fallep Islands, so called. On that day we met a little canoe with three Indian women, one of whom, of about 16 years of age and with a pretty face, by her more elegant dress and the quantity of silver rings that she had in her black braids, gave evidence of being a rank superior to the others. They approached the boat, but we had scarcely time to say "*sego*" (the customary greeting among them) before they quickly passed ahead of us, and a little later we lost them from sight, since their extremely light canoe easily overcame the current of the river. Some time later another canoe-full of Indians just returned from the hunt caught up with us, from whom I bought two wild ducks for eight loaves of biscuit, and I might have had them even more cheaply if I had offered them rum.

[1:142] The house in which I had to lodge in the place called Gallop was quite large and new, and its owner very politely obliged me to take his only bed. However, since the room in which it was placed had no door or windowpanes, in the morning I found myself with a heavy head and completely exhausted, sure signs of the tertian fever very common in those parts during the autumn season on account of the great humidity of the climate. After traveling a few miles, we noted Fort La Galette (where the British have a little garrison) situated on land that must have belonged to the Province of New York and located at a short distance from the mouth of the Oswegatchie River, which empties into the St. Lawrence. Beyond the fort the area to the north of the river is still occupied by American royalists. These new settlements extend down as far as the village of Johnson. The inhabitants are furnished with supplies for two years at the expense of the Crown, and they have 100 acres apiece to cultivate. They had also been promised a horse and a cow, but they have not been able to obtain these animals very necessary in that region. And since the flour that the Crown gives them for their daily food is not sufficient, they mix beans with it to make bread. This, with a bit of salted meat that is sold at an exorbitant price, constitutes their entire fare. The houses are of logs, small, low, and often not well protected against bad weather, so that even some of those who recently arrived sleep in tents. The land, generally barren and rocky, especially along the shores of the river, [1:143] responds poorly to their heavy labors, and one sees sadness clearly depicted on the faces of these new colonists who had to leave their cultivated lands in the United States to break new ground.

These settlements come to an end at seven leagues from La Galette, and there are no more habitations to be found for the stretch of 20 leagues to Cataraqui. Over that distance the bed of the river widens considerably and there are, scattered here and there, numerous little islands of varying size and shape called the Thousand Islands by the inhabitants. We spent the night on one of them, using the sail of the boat for a tent and lying around a good fire. We left before daybreak on the morning of the 8th, and after about 15 leagues of favorable sailing we passed from the St. Lawrence River into Lake Ontario and entered Cataraqui.

The fort, formerly called Fort Frontenac by the French, is situated at latitude 44° 50′ on the northern shore of Lake Ontario. The dwellings are located on a tongue of land that forms a little bay to the east in which ships anchor and to the west closes the vaster bay called Kenty, or Kente. The village was populated only in 1783, and one can already count there 40 houses and a proportionate number of inhabitants. A major with various officers and soldiers forms its garrison. They lodge in the old fort while plans are being made to build a new one on a height dominating the lake. The surrounding terrain is extremely barren, livestock is very scarce, and fresh provisions quite meager, so that the officers [1:144] themselves, when they are not furnished with game by the Indians, have to eat salted meat. Milk and butter, two of the most necessary items of British food, are for the same reason very scarce. The latter is transported all the way from Ireland, whence comes also the wheat flour with which more than 2000 persons are maintained from day to day at the expense of the Crown. This fort functions as a very important link between Montreal and the more interior parts of the lakes in Canada, whose commerce is protected by three boats belonging to the Crown that go continually from Cataraqui to Niagara laden with provisions and merchandise. In the environs of Cataraqui there is a kind of serpent called striped snake that is dark on the back with bluish-green horizontal lines, and from two to three feet in length.[22] This snake is quite harmless and hides in the thickets that abound thereabouts.

Six days had already passed since my arrival in Cataraqui, the steadily contrary wind not allowing the ships to leave, when on the evening of the 14th of September they came to notify me that the little sloop *Corwell* was sailing for Niagara. At this news I got out of bed and with no regard for the bad state of my health, the fever never having left me, in a short time I got my things ready, and going down to the shore, went aboard the ship. I was surprised to find there [1:145] four other passengers, namely, two elderly ladies from Quebec, a Catholic priest, and a Frenchman; and since there were only four beds, it is easy to imagine that we were not too comfortably lodged. We set sail toward nine in the evening with a light wind from the east and went out of the port of Cataraqui; but after we had covered only two leagues, the wind changed and blew very strongly all night long. The next morning we found ourselves about a mile away from a little island called Isle aux Canards, and Duck Island by the British. The lake was very rough, and the water came up over the deck. In the course of the day we tried in vain to approach this island from which we had been driven by the wind, and finally we decided to go to Isle aux Chevreuils, where we cast anchor and stopped to wait for a favorable wind. It rained all day long, the wind continued very strong until the following morning, wherefore considering our risky position, we weighed anchor and went to Isle des Renards, called by the British Back Island, or Carleton Island, in whose port we were better protected from the winds. Here, in view of the uncertainty of being able to continue the voyage, and my fever continuing unabated, I thought it best to give up my plan to see Niagara and to return to Cataraqui as quickly as possible. Hence I got off the boat and presented myself to Lieutenant MacLean, the commandant of a little garrison kept there by the British, a courteous young man who welcomed me very hospitably and whom I shall never forget. This island is about six miles in circumference, [1:146] and a few years ago the garrison of soldiers and many of the inhabitants who went to Cataraqui used to be there. There is quite a large wooden fort located on a jutting rock formed of a calcareous stone in horizontal layers very common in the region of Lake Ontario. The village used to be situated below on the lake shore, and you can still see the houses that were abandoned.

On the 17th, with the *Corwell* still at anchor in the port of the island, two Indians arrived paddling a canoe, and since this had to return at once to Cataraqui, I got in with my servant. We covered about three miles in a channel between the various so-called Carleton Islands where the stagnant water is full of rushes, wild rice, and water lilies. Then we landed, one of the Indians took the canoe on his back, the other, the paddles and a part of the baggage, and thus walking about a mile into the woods, we reached another channel where the canoe was again put in the water. At about two in the afternoon we finally entered the port of Cataraqui, where I heard that the frigate *Limnade* was waiting for a favorable wind in order to go to Niagara. My keen desire to see that famous waterfall had almost induced me to seize this new opportunity; but a stronger attack of fever duing the night made it impossible for me to carry out my intention–which would have come to naught anyhow, inasmuch as the frigate, after three hours out of port, had to return because of the contrary wind. At the same time I learned that the sloop *Corwell*, on which [1:147] I had undertaken my first voyage, was still at anchor in the port of Carleton Island.

The navigation of Lake Ontario is very dangerous. Flatboats often founder in it, and even warships are not safe. A few years ago one sank with all the crew. The northwest winds prevail in the winter, so that the passage from Cataraqui to Niagara is extremely difficult, and ships, even after arriving in view of this latter place, are sometimes compelled to go all the way back to Cataraqui, since in that direction there is no bay along the shores of the lake where they can anchor. This lake is about 40 leagues long, and its greatest width from Ganaraski to Irondequac Bay is about 30 leagues, or 90 English miles. Hence from the middle one cannot make out the shores, so that it is like an ocean of fresh water.

On the day of the 22nd of September I finally departed for Montreal in a boat with eight Canadians, gladly leaving a region where everything contributed to making me dejected and ill. Equally averse to satire and adulation,

I would have liked to find that men were virtuous everywhere and to present them as an example for imitation, but inasmuch as I had set for myself the goal of pursuing only the truth, I cannot conceal the disorders of this new population. The officers of the British regiments reorganized at the end of the war, left with nothing to do in America and reduced to half pay, received a portion of land in the Bay of Kenty, and for the first few years they were furnished with the most essential supplies. However, since they were used to [1:148] military life and completely ignorant of agriculture, they left to others the job of attending to their farms. For lack of things to do, they go all the time to Cataraqui and get together with the traders every evening at the inn, the only one there is, where they pass the night among the bottles. Then they sing in loud voices, accompanying their song with yells and shouts and beating the benches and chairs upon the floor without any regard for those unfortunate travelers who seek rest in vain. Nor does the commotion end here, because, as they continue to guzzle wine (if, indeed, such can be called an unhealthy mixture of brandy and other unknown ingredients that has only its color and name), they go mad and beat one another with their fists until, exhausted by their fighting and overcome by sleep and the wine, they sprawl out on the floor to wait for dawn. At daybreak the Indians appear, and intoxicating themselves with brandy, they begin other no less disgusting songs, and sometimes quarrels and squabbles, which are followed in the course of the day by drunken Canadians and other riffraff. Such are the goings on and the amusements of these wretched inhabitants, who pass their days in almost continuous drunkenness just for the pleasure of being crude. Happy Italy and those nations where the abundance of alcoholic beverages does not produce such great abuses, and where drunkenness is regarded among decent people as the most abject of vices!

Return from Cataraqui to the Border of New York State

[1:149] On the 22nd of September we left the port of Cataraqui and went down the St. Lawrence River. That night we slept in the boat, and continuing on our way before dawn, we met a canoe with a family of Indians. There were the father, the mother, two children, and suckling baby, all of them seated on a skin stretched out in the bottom of the canoe. They had spent the whole night fishing. For that purpose they place a torch at the point of the boat to the light of which are drawn the fish that they strike with a kind of harpoon, even throwing it some distance. The Indian had caught several large carp,[23] and some pike,[24] there called *Masko-nan-gi,* which he sold to me for four loaves of biscuit.

At the plantation of Mr. Carey, where we were at dinner, that farmer had harvested a large quantity of ginseng[25] that he was drying in the sun. [1:150] This root, so highly valued in the East Indies and in China, is quite common in the interior of North America, but since these inhabitants do not have the true method of preparing it, American ginseng is considered by the Chinese much inferior to their own.[26] At that same plantation I also saw an eagle, of the size of the Alpine one, of a dark color, with its breast covered with triangular white spots, and yellow feet, which Mr. Carey had caught in that neighborhood. That species of eagle[27] is found in the vicinity of Hudson Bay, and it was described by Edward in his fine work on birds, being a variety of the European tawny eagle.

At night we arrived at Pointe aux Barrils, and on the 24th we went down the Gallop and Rapide Plat passes, where the current is so swift that the general belief in those regions is that one cannot count the trees along the bank during the descent – which, however, is an out-and-out exaggeration. At dusk we discovered a tiny dwelling that looked like a low, narrow corridor, into which we entered to spend the night. But no sooner had we drawn up to the fire than the rain, which had gone on all day long, came in through the loosely connected elm bark that [1:151] formed the roof and began to flood the cabin. By that time I was seized with fever and chills. Nevertheless, since I had to find a better shelter for the night, I had myself taken to the boat, and we dropped down about half a mile to Pointe aux Barbues, where we came upon a place to stay not quite so bad. On the 25th we entered Lake St. François with a favorable wind and continued on our way by sail as far as Pointe au Baudet. The following morning we crossed the rest of the lake, and descending the difficult passes of Côteau du Lac and Le Trou, we reached Soulange, and then Lachine. From there we continued on our way in a carriage to Montreal.

A few days of rest and some medicine quickly restored my health, so that by the 2nd of October I was in condition to continue my travels. As a matter of fact, I crossed the St. Lawrence at Longueuil, went to Laprairie, and the following day went on to St. John, embarking on a cutter that arrived in the evening at Windmill Point, located at the boundary between the Province of Canada and the United States.

The inhabitants of Canada must be distinguished into Britishers, Frenchmen, Americans, and Indians. The first of these are merchants, or soldiers, or people employed in the government; and the second, coming from the French families that settled this country, are the true Canadians. The latter are divided into four classes, comprising the gentlemen, the clergy, the merchants, and the people. Those of the first, who under French domination constituted the nobility, are reduced to a few [1:152] families, which, either for lack of attention to their affairs, or because they were stripped by the government of various privileges that they formerly enjoyed, have now become a restricted class living indolently on the wretched income of the ill-managed possessions. The clergy, both regular and secular, enjoy the same privileges that they had under France, but since the number of Jesuits dropped and the government prevented French ecclesiastics from coming to Canada, the seminaries have deteriorated a great deal, and the clergy and people are generally badly educated. Hence, one can infer why the British tried in vain to establish a philosophical society in Quebec. The third class, on the other hand, namely, the traders who receive protection and encouragement under British rule, find themselves in a better situation and profitably carry on the fur trade that constitutes the main, and practically the only item of exportation. A number of them began as bushrangers,[28] became rich trading with the Indians, and established themselves in Montreal or Quebec, whence they continue the same traffic by means of their agents. It is difficult to imagine what risks these bushrangers run during their annual expeditions among the most remote Indian tribes, since, in order to have first choice of the pelts, they follow them in the hunt and spend days and weeks traveling continuously in the woods, exposed to bad weather, climbing hills and mountains, and crossing swift rivers and stormy lakes. And yet all these difficulties will seem slight compared [1:153] to the constant uncertainty regarding their very existence, inasmuch as the Indians, often drunk with brandy and rum, threaten their lives, so that they live in continual fear of being struck down by their own knives and shot by their own guns. Thus, if the debasement of the Dutch in Japan shows us what power money has over the imagination of men, the intrepidness and deterioration of the Canadian traders are no lesser proof.

The goods that they sell to the Indians are guns, ammunition, woolen blankets, red and blue cloth, shirts, hatchets, knives, scissors, sewing needles, steels, copper vases, tin earrings, bracelets, wampums, glass beads for necklaces, tobacco, colors to paint themselves with, rum, and brandy, in exchange for which they receive furs. The animals whose skins make up the Canada fur trade are many. Certain skins are distinguished into green and pealed, as, for example, those of the moose,[29] deer,[30] reindeer[31] and elk,[32] the latter even being found tanned. [1:154] Beaver[33] pelts are divided in *Castor gras* and *Castor veule,* the former being more highly prized for having been worn by the Indians, so that the hair turns out better in the manufacture of caps. The muskrat[34] and certain other Canadian animals also serve for this purpose. Furs come from the lynx,[35] the cougar[36] (a kind of wildcat), the otter,[37] and two martens called *vison*[38] and *pekan,*[39] [1:155] the *carcajou,*[40] the wolf,[41] and the fox.[42] Of these last, various sorts are counted, namely, red, crossed, black, and silver.

The fourth class, that is, the people accustomed to living with the Indians, greatly imitated their ways. The habit of smoking tobacco is very common among both men and women, who for that purpose carry a short wooden pipe and a raccoon-skin pouch slung across the shoulders in which they keep their supply of tobacco, flints, and agaric that serves as tinder. Among the superstititons that they imitated from the Indians, they are accustomed, when they are traveling on a river in a contrary wind, to throwing a bit of lighted tobacco into the air, saying that this way they give the wind a smoke so that it will be favorable to them. More rational is the method that they picked up from those same Indians of holding up a moistened finger to the wind, distinguishing its direction from the cooler part of the finger. They even imitate the Indians in the tunes of their songs, and are so friendly with them that many married [I:156] Indian women and went to live with them in the woods. Although they are British subjects, they call the King of France by the name of Father even today, and so great is the affection that they have for their former native land that the French troops could easily start a revolution. In fact, they might perhaps have joined the Americans in the late war, if the vigilance of the government and of various members of the ruling class in Canada had not forestalled the danger.

Since the Canadians belong to a sort of republic, as England is, it would seem that they ought to enjoy the advantages of liberty like the other Britishers; but, on the contrary, they are subjects of an absolute government. The King of England, whose power is limited in Europe, is practically a despotic sovereign in Canada, and orders issued in his name have no less weight than in the other monarchies. In short, Canada is treated like a conquered country, and its laws are hardly different from the old ones that used to exist under the French government.

CHAPTER VI

The State of New York

From Windmill Point to New York City

[1:157]

ON THE MORNING of 5 October we came out of the Sorel River into Lake Champlain, and having passed by La Motte Island, skirting along Grand Isle, we arrived toward evening of the next day at Beasson Harbor, a safe and roomy bay located 17 miles north of Crown Point. That night was very cold, and we felt the cold all the more in the house where we were lodged, which, in addition to being full of cracks, was without a roof for about a third of its length, since its owner had removed the boards in order to finish a little sailboat. The contrary wind kept us there the day of the 7th until nine in the evening, when, a favorable wind arising, [1:158] we continued our journey and landed at Ticonderoga at five in the morning. I went at once to examine a quantity of dried plants that I had left there with a part of my baggage when I left for Canada, and I found them all spoiled on account of the humidity caused by the stagnant water that had come in beneath the floor of that miserable dwelling. Thus I had to lose the copious collection of plants that I had very laboriously made in the States of New Hampshire and Vermont, and I also had to throw away the rattlesnake that I had killed, as I have indicated elsewhere.

Since the wind was blowing from the south, I was forced to wait until the following morning, when I decided to go on to the so-called Landing Place[1] on Lake George so as to be ready to leave as soon as the wind became favorable. I sent my servant on with the horses by land, and getting into a canoe with the owner of the house, with both of us paddling, we had a hard time getting around the point of land on which Fort Ticonderoga is located on account of the strong wind and the roughness of the water. Having made it over this stretch, we entered a smooth channel surrounded by high mountains where Lake Champlain has its source from the waters of Wood Creek[2] and those of Lake George, the former coming from the southeast, the latter from the southwest, and joining here. A pretty phenomenon can be observed at the union of these waters. Since that of Wood Creek is [1:159] muddy and whitish and, on the contrary, that of Lake George extremely clear, instead of mixing they remain separated and appear riled on one side and crystal clear on the other.

Going up the channel, we arrived at the cascades of Lake George, and there I continued on my way with my horses as far as the Landing Place. A tiny, ill-protected, and filthy cabin with a hole instead of a window through which the wind blew in beside the fireplace; beside it another similar cabin, and these separated from any other habitation in a lonely valley surrounded by high mountains and exposed to unwholesome vapors emanating from the lake and the neighboring swamps—such was my only shelter. Detained by the contrary wind, I had to remain there the following day also.

During the night thousands of frogs could be heard croaking in the bogs and among them could be easily made out the one particular to America called bullfrog,[3] which, sometimes reaching half a foot in width, surpasses in size all the other species, and with its cry imitates very closely the bellowing of an ox. It is of a whitish color, with palmate feet, the front ones furnished with four toes and the rear with five, by means of which I have seen some of them jump as much as six feet. The French used to prepare a rather delicate dish with them, finding them very juicy and tasty; but the Americans, who have, like the English, a general repugnance for this food, have no use at all for them, so that [1:160] their number has not been reduced a bit, even in the most settled areas. Another species of large frog is the spotted frog,[4] which has a green body covered with dark-colored spots and two circular marks at the ears, from which it got its Linnaean name. Although it is smaller than the preceding, it is nevertheless to be counted among the largest, and its call can be heard at a great distance.

Lake George, formerly called Lake of the Blessed Sacrament by the French, is only 37 miles in length and from 4 to 5 at its greatest width. It is surrounded by high mountains covered with woods and is scattered with little islands. Its water is so clear that the sand can be made out on the bottom at the depth of several feet, and it abounds in excellent fish. It is odd, inasmuch as no river flows into this lake but only little brooks, that it can produce the great quantity of water that descends from its cascades into Lake Champlain. It is probable, therefore, that Lake George is supplied by subterranean rivers.

On the morning of the 11th I was not a little cheered by the news that the wind was favorable and embarking in the afternoon, in the short time of eight hours I reached Fort George located on the other side of the lake. This fort is placed on a height that dominates the lake, and was built by the British for the defense of the borders when the French owned Canada and the territory situated along Lake Champlain. Now it lies [1:161] in ruins, and one can see only a few houses near the shores.[5] I continued my travels to the south on a very good road cut through black pine woods and I saw some sassafras and andromedas, plants that do not grow in the more northerly regions which I had left. In this stretch of country (43° 25′ latitude) I noticed that the sassafras and thuja[6] were shrubs, inasmuch as the former comes very large in the warmer states; and the second I found of the size of a tree in the more northerly regions. Hence these plants do not have all their vigor in this climate for opposite reasons.

As early as 1709 under the government of Queen Anne and during the war with the French, a fort was built on the eastern shore of the Hudson River called Fort Nicholson from the name of a famous English general of those times. In 1711 it was burned by the English themselves when they undertook a naval expedition into Canada. A few years later a new fort (called Fort Edward) was built on the same spot, which, although later destroyed, kept its name in a little village located on the banks of the river. Then one follows the shores of the Hudson, whose waters have a gentle current down to two miles above the village of Saratoga, where the level drops and they flow swiftly among rocks. I crossed the river near the village below this current, and at the distance of one mile from it I saw on a [1:162] hill the remains of the fort of the same name, built by the English to serve as a bulwark for the city of Albany and besieged and taken by the French in 1747. The English, however, before surrendering, set fire to the fort, which burned down in a short time. The route is very beautiful since one can see many well-cultivated fields and a number of houses, whose inhabitants are almost all of Dutch origin; but I found most of the bridges wrecked by an unusual flooding of the river that had occurred a few days before. Here a more temperate climate was suggested to me (43° 5′) by the plane tree, the locust,[7] and white cedar,[8] which do not grow in more northerly places. The extremely sluggish flow of the Hudson in those parts caused it to be given the name of Stillwater, which remained to a village five miles from Saratoga.

In the region about it there is a vast plain where the famous defeat of the British under the command of General Burgoyne took place. He came down from St. John, seized the forts situated along Lake Champlain, and arrived at Fort Edward on the 30th of August, 1777. He left there on the 13th of September, crossed the Hudson River, and occupied the heights of

Saratoga. The American troops commanded by General Gates camped at Stillwater, where they remained until the 7th of October, on which day Burgoyne decided to join battle. The fighting [1:163] was stubborn, the English General Fraser lost his life, and Burgoyne, defeated, retreated on the 10th to Saratoga, where, surrounded by American troops, he surrendered with his whole army on the 16th[9] of the same month. This action, which does all the more honor to the conquerors in that they were not yet allied with the French, was the first blow struck in the direction of American independence.

Upon leaving Half Moon, 14 miles from Saratoga, I abandoned the main road that leads to Albany in order to go to see the famous Cohoes Falls on the Mohawk River. After traveling four miles through the woods, I crossed this river at London's Ferry, and then going down along its banks, I reached the waterfall. This is the most magnificent in North America after those of Niagara and Montmorency in Canada, being 900 feet wide and 75 high. The descent is free on the south side, but broken by large rocks on the north side, so that the water that comes down with majestic smoothness on the one hand is on the other broken up into various streams and cascades, which creates quite a colorful contrast. The impetus of the descent is such that the banks of the river, although twice as high as the waterfall, are constantly sprinkled by a fine rain up to a distance of a hundred feet. The quantity and density of this sprinkling produces the rainbow that is always visible when the sun's rays are [1:164] refracted in it.[10] The banks and the bed of the river are formed of a black stone that becomes friable when exposed to the air, and contains spar and rock crystal. Along the banks of the river one can see handsome establishments; and here begin to appear red cedar,[11] Carolina poplar,[12] and chestnut-leaved oak.[13] As one passes from the shores of the Mohawk to those of the Hudson, a number of little islands come into view, some of which are very well cultivated. At the distance of one mile there finally appears the city of Albany, situated on the banks of the Hudson and on the slope of a verdant hill.

Albany, the second city in the State of New York in size and population, was built in 1614[14] by the Dutch, who called it Fort Orange from the name of a fort situated on the riverbank and whose trees can still be seen. But when the province was conquered by the English under the reign of Charles II, the name was changed to that of Albany, the title of the Duke of York to whom it was ceded by the King, and shortly thereafter it was chartered as a city.[15] The streets, almost [1:165] all of them parallel to the course of the river and cut at right angles by the others that go up the hill, are very wide, adorned with trees, paved in part with cobblestones, and some of them are furnished with a sidewalk. However, since they let livestock go about in them during the summer, and the terrain is by nature clayey, they are very dirty and muddy, especially in the rainy season. Most of the houses are built of brick after the Dutch taste, namely, with a very high peak to the roof, which slopes down sharply on both sides of the house, so that they are neither large nor commodious. The roofs are covered with shingles of white pine or with terra cotta tiles made in the Dutch fashion, and the houses, raised two or three steps above the ground, have wooden seats at the sides of the door where the inhabitants go to cool off on summer nights. In short, the form and distribution of the houses (except for a few built recently in accordance with English taste) give Albany the aspect of one of those ancient cities or villages that we see represented in the paintings of Teniers. The Anglican church, located in the highest part of the city near a fort now destroyed, is made of stone and has a tower with a clock; and the Dutch, the [1:166] oldest of all, is likewise of stone, but of a square, low, and heavy shape, and with a very high roof in the middle of which rises a broad and square belfry. There, too, they preach on Sundays and prayers are recited in Dutch; and there is no other apparent difference from the churches of the Presbyterians except that in the Dutch the women are separated from the men. The townhouse is divided on the upper floor into two halls of medium size, in one of which are held the Courts of Justice, and the other serves for the civic body, consisting of a mayor and aldermen.

The fur trade was formerly the most important business in Albany, especially at the time when the French, who owned Canada, for religious reasons had forbidden their merchants to sell brandy to the Indians because of the disorders that arose daily from the abuse of this liquor. Therefore they preferred to trade with the English in Oswego and Albany, from whom they not only could obtain liquor, but also many other goods more cheaply than in Canada. Among other things the Albanians carried on a great traffic in wampums, a kind of money used by the Indians. Wampums are of two kinds, some white and some blue, made with tiny cylindrical tubes about half an English inch in length, with a very smooth surface. These are obtained (as I have already indicated elsewhere) from a kind of bivalvular shellfish called clam by the English and *porcelaine*[16] [1:167] by the French, which is white inside and has around the edge a patch of deep blue. In addition to the use that the Indians make of these wampums in their negotiations, they serve also as ornaments for both the men and women, who wear them in necklaces or bands on which the white and blue beads are arranged in patterns (Plate IV, Figs. 2 and 3). These bands are also used by them to ratify treaties or to make new ones, and whenever they have important dealings they present some about four English inches wide at the conclusion of each article to preserve the memory of it. The creature that lives in this shell is good to eat. What is more, the Indians considered it such a delicacy that they used to go on purpose to the seashore to gather them, and the first European inhabitants of Long Island made strings of them which, after being dried in the sun, they used to take to Albany to sell to the Indians. The Albany trade with the Indians fell off when the English took possession of Canada, and died out completely after the late war, since the British, by occupying Fort Oswego on Lake Ontario, cut off communications between the Americans and the Indians. Wheat, flour, potash,[17] lumber, ginseng (which is harvested along [1:168] Lake Champlain), and a surreptitious fur trade with Canada, constitute the main items of exportation, for which a great number of yachts are used that go constantly up and down the river between Albany and New York.

The Albanians, almost half of them of Dutch origin, still keep many customs of the nation from which they are descended. Mr. Kalm, talking about them in the second volume of his travels in America,[18] says that they are stingy, concerned only for their own affairs, and that they ask exorbitant prices in dealing with strangers. It must be said, however, either that their customs have changed a great deal, or that Mr. Kalm, informed by the English and the Swedes, judged the life style of the Albanians from that of the gunsmith with whom I was lodged, since, as far as I was concerned, I did not find them any different from the inhabitants of the other cities of this state. The land on which Albany is built belongs to the Van Rensselaer family, whose descendants still keep to this day the title of patroons or *signori*. This manor extends 24 miles along the river, is 12 miles wide,[19] and very profitable to them, since home owners in Albany and farmers of the region are obliged to pay a certain sum. However, since nowadays this is considered exorbitant, it will probably be much reduced.

[1:169] Schenectady, a little city situated on the Mohawk River 16 miles to the northwest of Albany, was formerly one of the best outposts for direct trade with the Indians of the Mohawk Nation, whose villages were located along the same river. The numerous traders who used to live in this city were engaged in a continuous traffic with Albany, which, however, has now completely ceased, and therefore the inhabitants have turned to farming. The city is laid out in various handsome, wide streets, but ever since trade has dropped, it seems quite depopulated.

Having seen the city of Schenectady and spent two days in Albany, I took up my travels again on the 18th of October. Crossing the Hudson River a short distance below the city, I arrived at Kinderhook in the evening, and, the next morning, at Hudson or New City. This city originated from a group of Rhode Islanders and inhabitants of Connecticut who, foreseeing the advantages of this location, obtained permission to found a chartered city there. It is situated on a height, its streets are straight and very wide, and the houses, although of wood, are quite comfortable, and even pleasing to the eye. There were already 200 of them in 1785, which must surprise anyone who stops to consider that the foundations of this new city were laid in 1784, inasmuch as previously there were only two fishermen's cabins.[20] Unfortunately there is no drinking water on the site where it is built, and not having foreseen this eventuality, they had to build a wooden aqueduct that brings in water from a distance of four or five miles. The advantage [1:170] of the location of Hudson consists in its being situated at the end of navigation for large merchant ships, which cannot go up the river as far as Albany, and in the abundance of construction timber that grows on the opposite shore. However, the excessive nearness to the abovementioned city, the trade that has existed for many years between Albany and New York, and the infinite number of little boats that continually go up and down the river, render this advantage quite precarious, so that it is not likely that the city of Hudson will be able to become an important trading post.

On the way from Hudson to Livingston Manor (a stretch of country belonging to the Livingston family of New York) I came upon a freshly killed animal the size of a marten, with a pointed nose, an elongated body, and covered with black hair on its belly and white on its back. Its tail was as long as the animal, wide, flat, and furnished with very long white hair. I would have liked very much to keep it, but so strong was the stench that it gave off that I did not have the courage to take it with me. This animal, which is very common over the whole United States, climbs trees very agilely, and feeds on eggs and newborn birds. When it is pursued, it runs away as fast as it can and tries to climb up a tree. But if it finds itself in danger of being caught, it squirts along with its urine a fluid contained in a separate bladder whose stench is so penetrating and disgusting that men, as well as animals, are forced to give up the pursuit. A single drop of this [1:171] fluid that falls upon clothes defiles them so that they do not lose the odor, unless they are buried in moist earth, in which case they say the stench disappears almost completely within the space of 24 hours. These animals can be easily tamed, and, unless they are very disturbed, they never squirt this fluid. The Indians eat them, taking care, however, to remove the bladder at once, and the pelts, which are not used by the Europeans, serve to make tobacco pouches for the Indians. The *Viverra putorius,* if we can trust the illustration given by Schreber, is an animal very different from the one I saw, which, on the other hand, resembles closely the *Viverra mephitis* represented by Schreber.[21] It might well be that, inasmuch as these animals differ a great deal in their color pattern and perhaps also in the length of hair, they have given rise to numerous ill-known species, as Count Buffon himself states where he speaks of the *chinche.* In New York the species I observed is called skunk.

Poughkeepsie, which one comes upon 10 miles from Rhinebeck and

34 from Livingston Manor, is a fairly large village located on the banks of the Hudson. The governor, the council, and likewise the chamber of the State Assembly resided there during the war, and many families moved there, returning to the city of New York when it was evacuated [1:172] by the British troops.

On the 22nd of October, drawing away somewhat from the river, I reached Fishkill, a village situated in a low valley, and then I began to ascend that chain of mountains which, characterized by the name of the Highlands, crosses the country from east to west. I might here have been able during that day to traverse the most hazardous part of these mountains and to reach the village of Peekskill, if a violent downpour had not compelled me, after going 11 miles, to stop at a bad inn located at one of the highest points in the Highlands. On these mountains one can see many fragments of talc in the stones, which are sandy in nature, and here I found for the first time (latitude 41° 24′) the beautiful tree called tulip tree,[22] which, rising to the height and expanse of a walnut, was at that time laden with mature seeds. This is certainly one of the most valuable of North American trees, combining with the beauty of the leaves and the flowers an aromatic odor and a wood excellent for many uses.[23] Peekskill was the supply depot of the American army during the war, whose stores were seized and destroyed by the British in March, 1777. To the right of the road can still be seen the remains of Fort Independence located on the nearby hill. Three miles away near the river there is Verplanck, a place famous because there on the 30th of March, 1777, the British troops under the command of [1:173] General Vaughan disembarked, who, joining others that landed at Stony Point, took the important Fort Lafayette from the Americans.[24] At this latitude (41° 20′) the large-flowered kalmia[25] grows very abundantly, and about a mile beyond the village of Croton on the banks of a little river of the same name there are huge *Acacia mellifera* trees,[26] which made a pretty sight with their black, hanging, ripe pods.

The mountains of the Highlands come to an end at the village of Tarrytown, and a few miles away there is Philipsborough, another village so called from the name of a rich landholder of that vicinity whose property was confiscated by the State of New York because he had taken the side of the King and retired to England.[27] The house where he lived, one of the most beautiful in those parts, was adorned with a superb garden with greenhouses and rare plants now totally destroyed. Nearby, instead of this garden, I observed in the hedges a few catalpa trees[28] which are probably produced by the seeds of the plants that were formerly in the garden and therefore cannot be considered indigenous at this latitude. This is not the case with the sweet gum tree[29] and the black walnut,[30] found natively in [1:174] various places. Passing between the two hills on which are located the two forts Washington and Lee that were captured by the British between the 15th and 18th November, 1778, I arrived at Kingsbridge. There is a fine wooden bridge over that branch of the Hudson that joins East River and forms Manhattan Island, at the tip of which is the city of New York, where I arrived the evening of the 24th of October.

The City of New York

[1:175] New York, formerly called New Amsterdam,[31] was founded by the Dutch in 1614[32] and conquered by the English in 1664. The following year Governor Nichols granted it a city charter, and afterwards various Englishmen and Germans settled there, so that at the present time it preserves little or nothing of the old Dutch buildings. At the beginning of the late revolution this city was evacuated by the American troops, [1:176] but the English had hardly taken possession of it when fire broke out in a house near the fort and spreading to the adjacent dwellings, very quickly left the fairest part of the city prey to the flames. New York remained in the power of the British until 1783, when they abandoned it to return to Europe. The location is delightful, and excellent for commerce, since it is situated between two navigable rivers, one of which to the east, known by the name of East River, separates it from Long Island, and the other to the west, namely the Hudson, divides it from the State of New Jersey. It dominates equally well the beautiful beaches of the two aforementioned regions, and has before it a wide bay extending all the way to Staten Island, to the east of which there is a strait that opens into the ocean. The fort,[33] now partly destroyed, is located on an eminence, and from it one can see the boats going in and out, which, in order to protect themselves better from the winds, scatter along East River.

The street called Broadway, the widest one, cuts the city from north to south and ends in a circular mall surrounded by iron railings in the middle of which there used to stand, on a pedestal, a bronze statue of George III, which, at the beginning of the war, was knocked down by the people and converted into a cannon.[34] Almost as beautiful is the street called Wall Street, adorned with the marble statue of the celebrated orator and minister the Elder Pitt, later Lord Chatham, which statue lost its head in subsequent disturbances.[35] Broad Street, William Street, Queen Street, and, finally, Hanover Square, [1:177] although they are irregular, surprise the stranger by the number of merchants who have opened shops and stores there, creating more the impression of one of the most flourishing European cities than of the capital

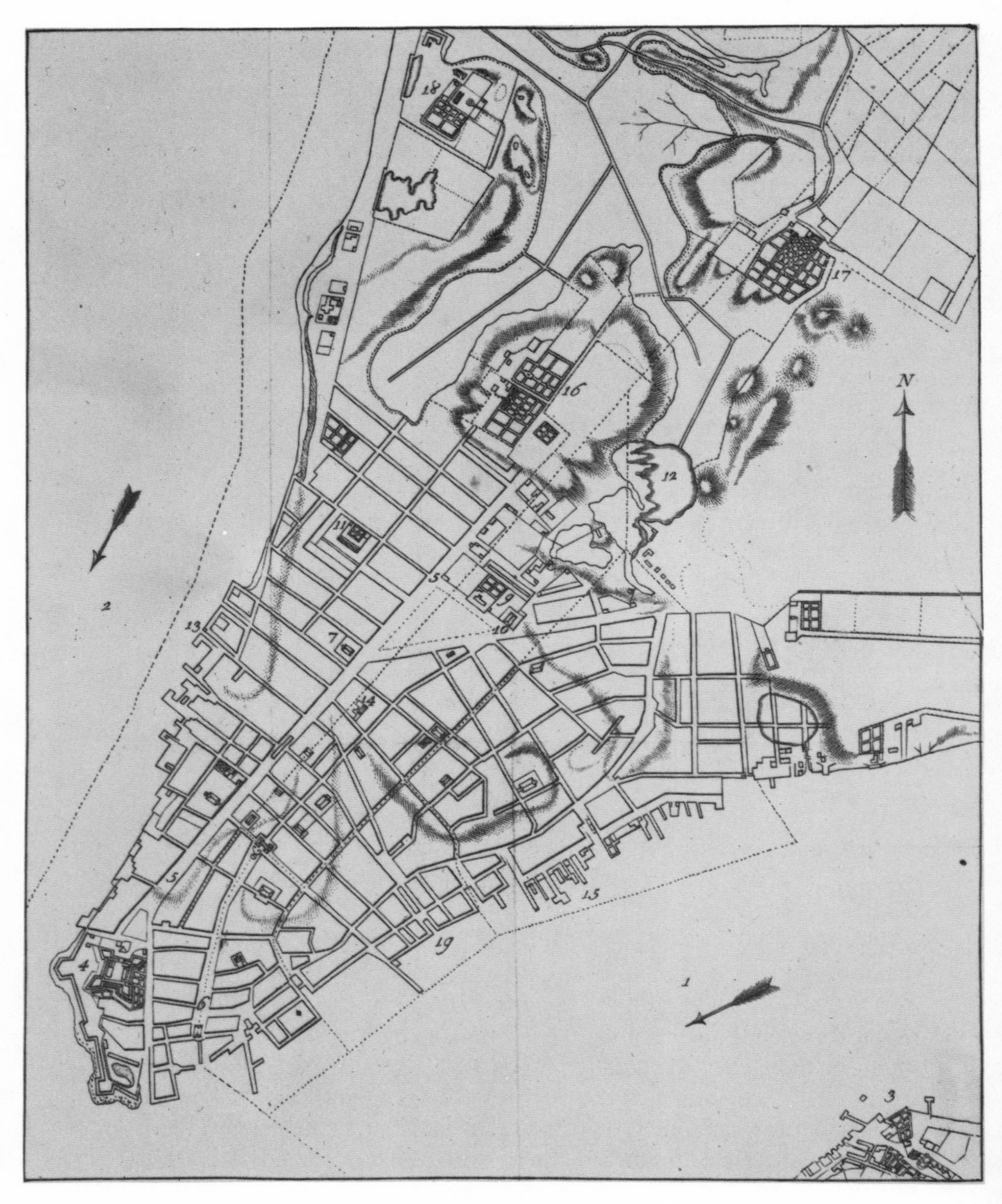

Plate V. Plan of New York City.

of a nascent state. Nevertheless, the number of merchants and excessive importation of goods in proportion to the number of purchasers cause business to languish there as in Boston, and all the more so nowadays because England has imposed new duties on American products and there isn't a steady trade with either France or Spain.

In the various quarters are distributed the churches of the Anglicans, the Presbyterians, the Congregationalists, the Dutch and French Calvinists, the Lutherans, the Assembly of the Quakers and of the Moravians, and a Jewish synagogue. Among all of them, however, the most impressive is the Church of St. Paul of the Anglicans, the façade of which is rich and of good design.[36] The statehouse, where the Congress of the United States and the New York Assembly meet, is a [1:178] very large square building. In the Hall of Congress there are the portraits of Louis XVI, King of France, and of his Queen Consort sent by the King to the United States as a gift. The poorhouse, the penitentiary, and the prison are situated in a large irregular square in the northern part of the city and deserve some consideration, as do also the hospital and the college. Private homes are for the most part built of brick, and many of them in size and taste are not inferior, and perhaps surpass, those of other more populous cities of North America. Each house has a number, and the streets, paved with cobblestones, are distinguished by their names at the corners and illuminated at night. For the convenience of merchants there is a coffeehouse that serves as a bourse where can be found all the gazettes of America, those of London and Paris, and where the vessels that enter or leave the port are carefully registered. Finally, for the amusement of the more well-to-do class of inhabitants, dances are held once a week during the winter in a hall of the city hotel. The theatre is open for two or three months of the year, where English tragedies and comedies are given by a mediocre troop of actors who make a living by going around from one city to another.

The inhabitants are about 22,000, and although no distinction of rank is permitted in the new legislation, they can be considered as divided into four classes. The first is composed of the owners of manors or *signorie,* who having acquired various privileges under English [1:179] government, are considered as the nobility of the city, to whom must be added the richest businessmen. This sort of nobility, who did not want to associate with the other classes of citizens and among whom prejudiced notions of family antiquity were beginning to take root, lost much of their superiority after the late revolution, when persons of no name were elevated to holding the most conspicuous offices of the new republic. The second includes the less wealthy, or less haughty, businessmen and merchants; the third, the artisans; and the fourth, the people.

European culture mixed with American cordiality renders society very pleasant; and the fair sex, attractive to the same degree, although more refined than in Boston, does not have to envy the latter city for beauty of figures and complexions. Some young ladies, however, and mainly those that are considered as of the upper class, excessively given to luxury and to the mad pursuit of fashions, languish in the flower of their years without finding husbands, since young American men want a wife who will manage family affairs carefully, and not one who will wreck them. There is great extravagance at table, and an abundance of carriages, chaises, and horses. Rent and food are very expensive, and drinking water, which is brought every morning from a spring some distance away, is sold in barrels as in Leghorn.[37] There are, it is true, cisterns in the city, the water of which serves for domestic uses, but there are in it often a quantity of insects that produce a revolting tickle in the [1:180] throat and even stomach pains to those that drink it. These insects are *monoculi* of that species described and illustrated by Swammerdam in Plate 31 of his *Biblia Naturae.*[38] I observed some with the microscope on the morning of 5 November in a glass of water freshly taken from the cistern in which these tiny insects could be seen swimming about in great number. Mr. Kalm[39] found many of them in the water of the cisterns of Albany and proved that by mixing in brandy these insects, instead of being adversely affected by it, swam more actively; whence he infers that brandy will have to be used in great quantity to kill the *monoculi* in punch made with that water.

The location of New York – almost at the center of the United States – the fact that it is closer to the European coast than other cities further to the south, and, finally, the year-around open navigation, have caused it to be preferred for the arrival and departure of passenger ships that sail every month for France and England. These ships, well suited to the convenience of passengers, carry regularly letters from one continent to the other and are certainly most useful in maintaining prompt and sure communications between America and Europe. To all the advantages mentioned above is now added that of having become the seat of the Congress of the United States. This political body, composed of the delegates of the various republics, had to move [1:181] from one place to another during the war, and had finally established its seat at Philadelphia.[40] In 1784 some Pennsylvania soldiers, who had for a long time asked Congress in vain for pay owed to them, mutinied and in arms surrounded the house where it was in session. Since Congress was not able to obtain the satisfaction it requested for this insult, it was unwilling to expose its dignity to similar incidents; hence it was deemed opportune to establish itself in New York, as was done shortly thereafter. Along with the Congress, the foreign ministers and other government officials moved to New York, serving considerably to render the seat more brilliant.[41]

The negroes are very numerous and many of them slaves, but in general they are treated gently [1:182] and not crushed by labor. Many would think it much better for the safety of the city not to have so many of them, since there have already been plots, among others one a few years ago, when they planned to burn down the city in order to kill the male inhabitants and marry the widows.[42] Fortunately, the plot was discovered, the leaders were condemned to death, and a law was passed which is still in effect to imprison all negroes found on the streets at night unless they are with their master or sent on an errand by him. This meditated vengeance of the negroes originated solely from the greater harshness with which they were then treated, and from that innate abhorrence that every individual of the human race must feel toward slavery. Surely it is a matter of surprise and pity for a European to read about the sale of slaves here in the newspapers, and all the more so if these notices are compared with those put out for the sale of horses, from which they differ not a bit.[43] Nevertheless it must be said that a society was established here a short time ago, founded [1:183] in order to promote the liberation of the slaves and to protect those who have already obtained freedom. It is presided over by Mr. John Jay,[44] and both he and His Excellency Governor Clinton deserve to be counted among the illustrious men of this city. New York is also the proud depository of the ashes of brave General Montgomery, who, after having taken by assault the fort of St. John and forced Montreal to capitulate, died in defense of American liberty at the siege of Quebec.

History of the Founding of the First Colonies in New York

[1:184] When the Venetian Sebastian Cabot[45] discovered North America in 1497 in the vain attempt at the Northwest Passage, he took possession of it in the name of Henry VII, King of England, by whom he had been engaged on that expedition. Subsequently, Walter Raleigh obtained in 1584 from Queen Elizabeth a patent of ownership of all those lands in North America not occupied by any Christian ruler, and fitting out several ships, he took on board some colonists who landed on Roanoke Island;[46] and in honor of the queen, still unmarried, they gave to the region the name of Virginia.[47] Then when King James I came to the throne of England, disregarding the rights of Raleigh, he granted a new patent for Virginia[48] to two companies. One of them, called the Society of the Adventurers of London,[49] had the right to form colonies from 34° to 41° latitude, and the other, called the Plymouth [1:185] Company, from 41° to 45°. This territory had been distributed in this manner when Henry Hudson, of English nationality, setting out from Holland on the ship *Half Moon* belonging to the Dutch East India Company, discovered Long Island and Manhattan, and went up the nearby river, which from him took the name of Hudson. Upon his return to Amsterdam the Dutch bought from him this new province, and a colony of them left for America in 1614. Settling there along the Hudson River, they gave to the region the name of New Holland and founded the cities of Fort Orange and New Amsterdam.[50] James I, upon being informed of what had happened, protested against the sale made by Hudson and demanded return of the occupied region. But when the Dutch paid no attention to his claim, angered by this snub, he ordered Sir Samuel Argall, then governor of Virginia, to invade and lay waste their new plantations. The Dutch complained at so harsh and unexpected a step; so the King, heeding their pleas, allowed the colonists to remain on their plantations provided they recognized themselves as subjects of England and paid an annual tribute. He even granted Dutch ships coming from Europe permission to stop to take on water and necessary supplies.

The Dutch colonists agreed to these conditions, and they remained for some time, [1:186] until, in the year 1623, encouraged perhaps by protection that they hoped to have from Holland, they refused to pay the customary tribute to the governor of Virginia and erected new forts at their borders. They built a fort on the Delaware River, then called South River, to which they gave the name of Nassau, and another by the name of House of Hope on the Connecticut River, called by them Fresh River. When King Charles I was informed that the Dutch had built forts and considered themselves absolute masters of that territory, he urged the States-General at The Hague in the strongest terms to have everything restored to the previous condition. They answered with assurances that they had in no way authorized what had been done by the colonists, throwing the blame for all that had happened upon the members of the East India Company which was in possession of that territory. Subsequently, Charles I authorized Edmund Loyden, or Ployden,[51] to found a colony to the north in the vicinity of New England, and the Dutch, fearing that it would be difficult to maintain themselves when the power of these neighbors had increased, offered to sell their plantations to the English for the sum of £2500 sterling. However, the disturbances that occurred in England toward the end of the reign of Charles I kept this plan from being carried out, and the Dutch, taking advantage of their disorder, increased the population and strength of the colony.

The Swedes, under the reign of Gustavus Adolphus, had established themselves in America in 1626[52] along the Delaware River, which the Dutch had [1:187] abandoned, and in the territory now taken up by the states of New

Jersey, Pennsylvania, and Delaware. The Dutch looked unfavorably upon the new colonists, and all the more so because the land where they had settled had been previously occupied by them. But since the Swedes had built several forts for their defense, the former did not dare to disturb them until 1654. In this year the ships that were to bring aid to the Swedes were plundered by the Spaniards, and so the Dutch seized this occasion to ask for the repossession of that region. However, by means of several conferences held between General Rising, governor of the Swedes, and Peter Stuyvesant, the Dutch governor, matters seemed to have been restored to tranquility when the following year Stuyvesant himself, going down the Delaware with 6 ships and 600 to 700 men, quickly took possession of the main forts, and then the whole province. The officers and leading inhabitants were taken to New Amsterdam and from there sent back to Sweden; and the people, submitting to the new government, remained in the region.

The conquerors had not enjoyed their usurpations more than nine years when they refused again to pay the customary tribute to Charles II, King of England; and war having been declared in Europe between the two nations, the King sent Sir Robert Carr with 3000 soldiers to America, who in a short time, without opposition, took possession of the whole Dutch province. Entering New Amsterdam, he sent the governor back to Holland along with all those who were unwilling to come under English [1:188] rule, he occupied the forts of the city of Orange and that of Arasapha, and, in a few days, the whole region. The Dutch, annoyed at the loss, avenged themselves by occupying the English colony of Surinam in South America. As a result, at the Peace of Breda in the year of 1667 it was granted to exchange New Holland for that part of Surinam of which the Dutch had taken possession.

Charles II, having become the undisputed owner, gave title to the province situated to the northwest to his brother the Duke of York, who changed the name of New Holland to New York. The eastern one, that is, New Sweden, he gave to Lord Berkeley and Sir John Carteret. The latter, since he owned many lands on the island of Jersey in England, gave to the province the name of New Jersey. Nevertheless, the Dutch did not forget the loss of this territory. On the contrary, in 1673, when they were once more at war with the English, they sent a small squadron to America which without bloodshed again took possession of the province. The inhabitants pledged allegiance to the States-General and the Prince of Orange. But this conquest, made on the 30th of July, was again ceded to the English at the peace treaty signed at Westminster on February 9th of the following year.

The two provinces of New York and New Jersey remained subject to the same government until the year 1681. Then, Lord Berkeley having ceded his portion of New Jersey, the part west of the Delaware River along with a great expanse of [1:189] adjacent territories was given to the celebrated William Penn, from whom it took the name of Pennsylvania. The remainder of New Jersey, which was the larger part, was then separated from New York in 1746 and got its own government. If, however, the province of New York was diminished by these dismemberments, it received a great increase when the English took over Canada, since they added to it the shores of Lake Champlain and of the Sorrel River up to 45° latitude, the vast stretch of land that borders the St. Lawrence River to the northwest, and the southern shore of Lake Ontario. At the outbreak of the recent revolution, it entered the confederation under the name of the State of New York, and since it was situated at the center of the strife, it inevitably suffered a great deal from the English, the Americans, and the Indians. Nor was the war disastrous solely for the many battles that were fought within its territory, but also on account of the loss of a considerable stretch of country to the east of Lakes George and Champlain, which took advantage of the disturbances that arose at the beginning of the revolution and separated, as I have already related, under the name of Vermont.

The Former Inhabitants, and the Location of New York

[1:190] The Indians who used to inhabit the expanse of territory now comprised in this state were the Mohawk, who lived near the river of the same name; the Mohican (perhaps a tribe of the former), who were scattered along the Hudson River; and the Metoac, who held Long Island. The author of the book entitled *Present State of His Majesties Isles and Territories in America,*[53] printed in London in 1687, speaking of these Indians, says that they were well proportioned, copper-colored, with black hair, very skillful in the use of the bow and arrow, that they showed themselves to be very polite with the English and lived in peace with them. From that time on they diminished a great deal in number on account of the continual wars that they waged with other Indian nations, and the epidemic diseases, among which smallpox, to which they were subject. Consequently, the six villages that existed on Manhattan Island at the time of the discovery had dropped to only two by the year 1680.

Their women cultivated a little land for the planting of corn. Moreover, since they nourished themselves mainly on the flesh of deer, polecats, and muskrats, likewise birds, turtles, fish, and clams, they had tents that they [1:191] transported to the spots best for fishing or hunting. Because they were passionate gamblers, they often lost everything they had in the world except the skin with which they covered their loins. Although they were greedy for strong liquors, they did not drink them except when they had enough to get drunk. If the company was too numerous in proportion to the brandy, they chose from among themselves a number proportionate to the quantity of liquor, and the others stood by as peaceful spectators. If then anyone of them gave sign of being drunk before having swallowed his portion, they forced him to gulp the rest, saying that they did not want to deprive him of his due. Murders often resulted, which, according to their custom, were avenged by the relatives and friends of the dead man with the death of the murderer, unless the latter bought himself off at a price, consisting of wampum necklaces.

Their marriages, just as they took place without any preliminary ceremony, inasmuch as it was all over as soon as they agreed on the value of the necklaces that the husband was to pay, so at the slightest disaffection one or the other of the parties would separate and make other arrangements. The women lived apart from their husbands during the time that they were pregnant and giving milk to their babies. If a married woman had relations with another man, that was hardly held against her, provided she had warned her husband beforehand, or one of his closest relatives. But if she failed to take this precaution, she was judged guilty, and sometimes punished even with death. On the other hand, young girls could give themselves [1:192] to anyone even for money, and that was considered by the Indians an entirely free and indifferent matter.

They were very generous and compassionate toward one another, sharing what they had willingly with their friends, and distributing among the others what they won at gambling, or otherwise keeping for themselves the smaller portion. The chiefs, or sachems, when they sat in council, had a guard of armed men, and the people held them in great respect. The priests, like those of the Massachusetts, performed the function of necromancers, and in the opinion of the author worshiped the Devil, who (by virtue either of the industriousness of the priests or the stupid credulity of the bystanders) made his appearance in the form of man, bird, or some other animal.

A tiny remnant of this ancient nation was left on the southern side of Long Island at the time that Mr. Kalm made his trip (namely, 1749), where they lived mainly by fishing, and before the late revolution many of them lived along the Mohawk River in the place where Sir William Johnson had established his residence. But when the war was over, most of them left this region and settled on the shores of Lake Ontario.

The State of New York extends from 40° 30′ to 45° latitude north and from 72° to 76° longitude from London, comprising 290 miles from north to south and about 70 from east to west. It borders on Canada and the St. Lawrence River to the north, on Lake Ontario to the west, on Pennsylvania and in part on New Jersey to the south, on New [1:193] Jersey and the ocean to the south, and on Vermont and the States of Massachusetts and Connecticut to the east. The Hudson River, rising between Lake Champlain and Lake Ontario in the northernmost parts of the state, cuts a long course across it from north to south, and after bathing the shores of the capital, empties into the ocean. It is the most majestic river, and the principal one. Its waters, almost stagnant at Stillwater, are, on the contrary, very swift at Saratoga. The banks, very low in the upper reaches, are extremely high and steep downstream where the river crosses the chain of the Highland Mountains. It appears that in the course of centuries it opened an outlet for itself by cutting almost perpendicularly the rock of which those mountains are composed. Beyond the Highlands the river forms a kind of bay which was called Tappan Zee, and then shrinking near the city of New York, it passes through the strait called The Narrows that divides Long Island from Staten Island and flows into the ocean. The Mohawk River, the second largest, originates a short distance from little Oneida Lake, flows from west to east, and runs into the Hudson near Albany, its navigation interrupted by the pretty falls of Cohoes. A part of the St. Lawrence River and the Lakes George and Champlain, half of which, along with the islands that are found there, was joined to the state, open easy communications with the more interior parts and with Canada. The only seaport on the continent is that of the capital, but others less significant are located on the shores of [1:199] Long Island, which, along with Staten Island, forms a part of New York State.

The country is generally uneven, varied with steep mountains, low and fertile hills, and extensive, marshy terrains. The northernmost section situated north of the Mohawk River between the St. Lawrence and Lake Champlain is even today almost entirely uncultivated on account of the numerous swamps that are found there. But, on the other hand, the fertile banks of the Mohawk, the charming shores of the Hudson, and all the territory toward the south are heavily cultivated and populated. The principal mountains are: to the north, those that lie along the coasts of Lakes George and Champlain; to the west, the mountains of the Mohawks and the Catskills, and, to the east, the Highlands, and that long chain which, running from south to north, separates New York from Connecticut and Massachusetts.

Long Island, divided from Manhattan Island by East River and separated from the State of Connecticut by the arm of the sea called Long Island Sound,[54] is more than 100 miles in length and 12 to 14 at its greatest width. Its terrain is quite fertile except for the ocean side, where, since it is sandy, the region was inhabited only by a few Indians (now totally destroyed), who lived on fish and oysters.[55] [1:195] So great was the quantity of oysters consumed by the Indians that even now huge heaps of shells can be seen near the coasts. In fact, these oysters are excellent and in spite of their abundance furnish a constantly sought-after dish at the tables of the gentry of New York. What is more, since they are considered better than those found on the coasts of the neighboring states, there is a traffic in them, especially with Philadelphia, where every day they are sold in the streets.

Oysters are also put up in New York in a manner called pickled oysters, or marinated oysters, which are shipped to the West Indies. This preparation is performed by opening, washing, and boiling them as soon as they are taken from the sea. Upon being removed from the cauldron, they are spread out on a platter, and when they are somewhat dried out, they are sprinkled with mace, allspice, or black pepper, with the addition of a discreet quantity of vinegar. Then everything is stirred in together in the cauldron with half of the water in which the oysters were boiled, it is placed again over the fire, and when it boils, it is very carefully skimmed. When the liquid has been reduced to a certain density, it is allowed to cool, and then everything is poured into earthen or glass vases which are immediately sealed with the greatest care. The merchants of New York buy them put up in this way in the month of October and send them to the West Indies, where they are sold at a high price. Another method of preserving oysters consists in frying them, putting them in vases, covering them with the butter in which they were fried and closing those vases carefully.[56]

[1:196] Staten Island, a little island to the south of New York, is separated by two channels from Long Island and from the State of New Jersey. There are a number of plantations on it owing to the good quality of the soil.

The climate of New York is as varied as that of the other United States, but differs a great deal in the degrees of cold from the northern end, located at 45° latitude near Canada, to the southern end, which is at only 40° 40′. For that reason the severe cold of the former regions is much more temperate in the capital and on the shores of Long Island.

As I have already said, intermittent fevers are very prevalent in autumn on the shores of Lakes George and Champlain, especially where they are low and inundated, these fevers beginning toward the end of August and lasting until the frosts begin. They are, however, less frequent along the Hudson River (especially in the Highlands), on Long Island, and in New York. But, to tell the truth, it cannot be said that any part of the state is completely free of them, regardless of what the inhabitants say. Since they have an exaggerated notion of the region where they were born, they would often like to deny the existence of them whenever they talk with outsiders about the excellent qualities of their climate.[57]

The New Form of Government of New York

[1:197] The present division of New York is made up of four districts, each of which is subdivided into counties. The eastern district comprises the two counties of Cumberland and Washington, formerly called Charlotte, and both situated near Lake Champlain and Vermont. The western district is composed of the counties of Albany, Columbia, and Montgomery[58] along the Hudson. The middle district contains the counties of Dutchess, Ulster, and Orange, which, situated one to the west and the other two to the east of the Hudson, comprise the mountains of the Highlands and the county north of Westchester and Murderer's Creek. And, finally, the southern district includes the counties of New York, Westchester, Suffolk, Kings, Queens, and Richmond, [1:198] the last of which is on Staten Island and the three preceding on Long Island.

The new form of government adopted after the declaration of independence in 1776 constitutes two legislative bodies, the Senate and the Assembly. The Assembly consists of the representatives of the people, chosen in the following proportion: namely, 9 from the county of New York, 10 from Albany, 7 from Dutchess, 6 from Westchester, 6 from Ulster, 5 from Suffolk, 4 from Queens, 4 from Orange, 2 from Kings, 2 from Richmond, 6 from Montgomery, 4 from Washington, and 3 from Cumberland. The number set by the Constitutions is 70, but the county of Gloucester and part of Cumberland having split off to form the State of Vermont, the representatives were reduced to only 68. They are elected annually by popular ballot, and every male adult inhabitant who has lived at least six months in the state has the right to vote, provided he possesses 20 New York pounds, which amount to about 50 Spanish pieces, or has an annual income of 40 shillings.

The Senate is composed of 24 members chosen from the freemen possessing at least 100 New York State pounds. These are likewise elected by the people, not however by counties as the representatives, but by districts, 3 being chosen from the eastern district, 6 from the western, 6 from the middle, and 9 from the southern. The senators thus elected are divided into classes distinguished under the names of first, second, third, and fourth, each of [1:199] which is made up of 6 senators. Since every year those of the first class complete their terms and a new class is elected, the senators pass successively from one class to the next until they go out of office. This way they remain in office four consecutive years, and a quarter of the membership of the Senate is renewed annually.

All the decisions made by either of the legislative bodies must be approved by the other and then presented for examination and review to a Council composed of the governor, the chancellor, and the judges of the Supreme Court, or at least by two of the latter along with the governor. Then within 10 days the Council refers them back to the legislative body in which they originated, along with its observations in writing. After they have once more been considered, they are rejected or become law when two-thirds of the Senate or the Assembly so deem, notwithstanding the objections presented by the Council. And whenever the Senate and the Assembly are of a different mind about some matter, they confer together and elect committeemen, chosen respectively by ballot in the two chambers, to handle and discuss the differences of opinion that have come about.

The executive power resides in the governor and a Council (different from the one whose duty is the review of the laws) made up of four senators chosen one for each district, and of the lieutenant governor as chairman of the Senate.

The governor is elected by ballot by freeholders in the same way in which the senators [1:200] are elected, and although he is renewed every three years, the same person can be elected again for a second triennium. He is also commander of the land and sea forces, he can call together the Senate and Assembly on extraordinary occasions and prolong the sessions; and he can suspend the execution of the sentence of criminals, provided they are not traitors to country or assassins, in order to seek pardon or softening of the penalty at the first session. The main duties of the governor are: to keep the political bodies informed of the state of affairs, to urge upon them the examination of whatever he believes important to the welfare of the commonwealth, to keep in touch with the Congress of the United States and with the other states, to attend to current dealing with civil and military officials, to see to it that the laws are observed, and to carry out everything that is decided by the legislative authority. The lieutenant governor also remains in office for three years, is president of the Senate, acts for the governor in case of absence, and in case of death continues until the next election. The chancellor and the judges of the Supreme Court remain in office until they reach the age of 60, provided they administer equitably and to the satisfaction of the public. Like the other civil officers they are chosen by a Council composed of four senators selected by the Assembly, led by the governor with the title of president. Finally, the delegates to Congress are chosen every year by the two legislative chambers.

From all this it can be readily seen that the system of government of New York differs principally [1:201] from that of Massachusetts in the election of the members of the Assembly by counties and not by villages. This is much better for the good management of the commonwealth, since it is more likely that 10 persons chosen from all the inhabitants of a county will be knowledgeable enough to be admitted to the legislative bodies than it is that in every poor and recently settled village a man will be found fit for such an important charge. Another very wise provision of the Constitutions of New York is that of leaving the senators at their post for four consecutive years, inasmuch as they can thus be more informed about the matters on which they make decisions. Finally, the review that the Council makes of the laws proposed by the Senate or the Assembly, to whom it refers its observations before they are promulgated, is an excellent remedy to prevent those disorders that might arise from the hasty publication of laws.

Among the many articles to be found in these Constitutions, three seemed to me most remarkable, namely, XXXVII, XXXVIII, and XXXIX, the last two of which reveal how widespread tolerance is with respect to religion, but at the same time how great is the fear that religious opinions may influence directly the government of the Commonwealth.

> XXXVII. The Constitutions order that, whereas it is of great importance to the safety of the State to maintain peace with the Indians, since frauds practised in contracts made [1:202] for their land at an extremely low price have in divers instances been productive of dangerous discontents and animosities, from 1775 on purchases and contracts for the sale of lands made with the said Indians within the limits of this State must be approved by the legislature; otherwise they will be considered null and void.
> XXXVIII. And whereas we are required, by the benevolent principles of rational liberty, not only to expel civil tyranny, but also to guard against that spiritual oppression and intolerance wherewith the bigotry and ambition of weak and wicked priests and princes have scourged mankind, this convention doth further, in the name and by the authority of the good people of this State, ordain, determine, and declare, that the free exercise and enjoyment of religious profession and worship, without discrimination or preference, forever hereafter be allowed, within this State, to all mankind: *Provided,* That the liberty of conscience, hereby granted, shall not be so construed as to excuse actions of licentiousness, or justify practices inconsistent with the peace or safety of this State.
> XXXIX. And whereas the ministers of the Gospel are, by their profession, dedicated to the service of God and the care of souls, and ought not to be diverted from the great duties of their function; therefore, no minister of the Gospel or priests of any denomination whatsoever, shall, at any time hereafter, under any pretence or description whatever, be eligible to, or capable of holding, any civil or military office or place within this State.[59]

[1:203] The Constitutions provide likewise for the control of the militia in time of peace and war, and for the naturalization of foreigners who must in that case renounce all allegiance to foreign rulers or countries.[60]

Population, Commerce, and Agriculture of New York

[1:204] Many and varied reasons concurred to retard for a long time the progress of population in the State of New York, even as it increased in the neighboring provinces, and in 1756 (says Smith[61]) only 100,000 inhabitants were counted there, while those of the little province of Connecticut were more than 133,000. The reasons were, in the first place, the excessive nearness of the French and the Indians, who, making continual raids upon the regions situated in the north, disturbed the new settlements and forced the inhabitants to seek refuge in New Jersey. In the second place, the law passed by the British Parliament to transport criminals there discredited this colony and kept industrious and honest people from settling there.[62]

[1:205] In the third place, the granting of two extensive holdings, or manors, at the time of foundation having caused the price of land to increase exorbitantly and therefore making the former not a landowner but a tenant, only the most wretched element of the people was willing to cultivate it, and these, lacking the means to make it produce well, lived in perpetual mediocrity. The owners of these vast domains, as, for example, the manors or *signorie* of Livingston, Rensselaer, Cortland, Philipse, etc., which occupy a huge expanse of country, went to live in the cities and left agriculture to the poor farmers.[63] Fourth, and lastly, one must list among the reasons [1:206] that held up the growth of population in the State of New York the enmity between the English and the Dutch settled there. At the present time, however, and since before the late war, a number of the causes presented above no longer obtaining, the population has increased to such an extent that the inhabitants were calculated at 250,000 in the report published by the Congress a few years ago.

Among the various nationalities composing this population, the Dutch are those who by their particular customs differ the most from the inhabitants of neighboring states. Although it is already about two centuries since they emigrated from their former homeland, they still preserve their native tongue and continue to make themselves conspicuous by their perhaps too fastidious sense of thrift. Their homes are very neat, they wash often the floors of their rooms and their utensils; but if they are exceedingly diligent in the cleanliness of their homes, they are quite often negligent in that of their person.

The greater inequality in the fortunes of the inhabitants and the less popular form of government has made the first rank citizens there more respected, and maybe has contributed to keeping the ordinary people in a more common ignorance. A poor farmer in Massachusetts does not believe himself inferior to the richest Boston merchant, but imagines himself at the beginning of a career that will take him up to his level in wealth and public influence; and this not ill-founded presumption induces him naturally to educate himself. On the other hand, the New York farmer, deeming himself of a status too different from [1:207] that of the most prominent citizens, limits his aims to a more lowly fortune and neglects to apply himself to study as useless for the tenor of life he has undertaken to follow.

Perhaps these ills are compensated for in part by the advantages that result from them, inasmuch as class distinction, having accustomed the people to a real, or imagined, subjection, has set a limit to excessively free, and even licentious, democracy. As a matter of fact, it is repeated so often in the Constitutions of various states of America that the origin of legislative power resides in the people, that from them alone must depend all the magistrates, etc., that such sentiments have been the reason for disorders that have broken out everywhere, which cannot be prevented and punished by a government that is too weak and limited. If the democratic form is to be judged the best in a republic, it will be so certainly when wise and educated men will be chosen to preside over public affairs, giving them sufficient power, and whose offices terminating after a certain period of time, the new election will be in the hands of the people. But if these legislators are very numerous and by and large ignorant; if the brevity of their offices does not allow them to become experienced; moreover, if the people reserve for themselves excessive authority over them and do not leave to them the management of all business; if, finally, the execution of the laws is neglected and the collection of taxes is obstructed; it will follow that everybody, suiting his own whim, will set himself up as judge and legislator, and consequently the state will find itself in the most dire anarchy. In 1786 a royalist who had returned to his old [1:208] property in New Jersey was seized by the people who, after abusing him verbally, had the cruelty to cut off both his ears. Numerous examples of the same sort could be cited here in which the multitude took upon itself an illicit power in spite of the laws approved by the people themselves.

The trade of the State of New York consists principally of flour, grain, lumber, clavellated ashes, ginseng, horses, and also apples, and linseed, which are shipped to Europe and to the West Indies, from which they receive in return rum, sugar, and molasses. The abovementioned items come down (as

I have already said) from Albany and from other places situated along the Hudson and Mohawk Rivers, or they are produced by the fertile soil of Long Island, on which very handsome properties are to be found. The inhabitants of Lake Champlain subsist for the time being on the fruits of their own lands, but since they are advantageously placed for trade with Canada, they will be able to enrich themselves a great deal if the English–forgetting some day the irreparable loss of the Colonies–consider the independent Americans a friendly nation.

CHAPTER VII

From the State of New York to the Border of Georgia

From New York City to the Border of North Carolina

[1:209]

THE DIVERSIONS of New York City had scarcely caused me to forget the labors of my travels in the North when the already rather advanced season persuaded me to set forth again and to take advantage of the winter, which is the best time to go through the southern states. The wearisome exercise of a long trip on horseback, which, by exposing me to the inclemencies of a rainy climate, could cause me to succumb to the same disease from which I had recently freed [1:210] myself, and the difficulty of carrying with me my books and other necessary things, made me decide to provide myself with a carriage in which I could travel more comfortably. Thus on the morning of November 27, 1785, having crossed the Hudson River with great difficulty on account of the adverse tide, I landed on the opposite shore at Paulus Hook, and I continued the journey to Philadelphia, which I left on the 8th of December and arrived on the 12th at Baltimore in the State of Maryland.[1]

Around Baltimore the terrain is composed of a blood-colored clay very rich in iron which is extracted from it in various smelters in that neighborhood. The terrain is therefore poor and unproductive, and from it was obtained only the wood to be reduced to charcoal for the purpose indicated. Baltimore, the most populous city of Maryland, is located on a hill near the Patapsco, a river that I crossed at the distance of two miles in order to reach Annapolis, the capital of this state. Beyond the river the terrain is sandy, so that the roads are better; but the no less sterile soils are covered with black pine, black oak, and some superb tulip trees. Leaving Annapolis on the 22nd of December, I crossed the Patuxent River at Mount Pleasant and came to the shores of the Potomac, on the opposite bank of [1:211] which is situated the city of Alexandria in the State of Virginia.

Alexandria counts 300 houses and about 3000 inhabitants. Although it is situated at latitude 38° 45′, the Potomac River freezes so solidly that horses can pass over it; but this cold does not last, nor is it the same every year, since there are often winters during which the river never freezes. This burgeoning community has already obtained the name and privilege of city,[2] and as the Potomac River becomes more navigable,[3] it will become one of the most prosperous commercial cities of this state. The public buildings consist of two churches, one Presbyterian, the other Anglican, a Quaker meeting, and the city hall. A number of the buildings are of bricks, which can be obtained at a low price since the neighboring terrain is composed of a soft and tenacious clay. Lime is made from oyster shells, which are found in great abundance in these parts, the whitest of them being chosen for the plaster. The solidity of masonry made with this lime is the same as that of ordinary masonry, but it has the defect of transmitting moisture in rainy weather, attributable to the marine salt that absorbs it from the atmosphere. Regarding the origin of the high piles of oyster shells that one comes upon in various places in North America [1:212] there are two opinions. Some suppose that the Indians regularly brought the shells to a spot decided upon for that purpose, and that they made mounds of them for the burial of the dead, or for the purpose of celebrating there some religious rite, which others believe rather that they were collected by those floods that from time to time disturbed the surface of the globe.

I left Alexandria on the morning of the 25th of December [4] and I reached Mount Vernon, the delightful retreat of the immortal American Cincinnatus. General Washington's house is undistinguished, furnished with two wings that are joined to it by two porticoes, and located in the middle of a spacious yard surrounded by buildings. The view of the Potomac River and of the boats that go up and down it to Alexandria, the spectacle of a broad expanse of cultivated terrain contrasting with the adjacent hills still clad in ancient oaks and lofty pines, contribute to render the site varied and charming.[5] I spent four days there, favored by the General with the greatest hospitality, as he is accustomed to do with strangers, who come in great numbers to admire such a famous personage.[6]

General Washington is about 57 years old, tall, of a sturdy physique and majestic and pleasant mien, and although toughened by military service, he does not give the appearance of being of advanced age. This famous man who opened and brought to a happy conclusion the American war, seemed produced by nature to free America from European subjection and to create an epoch in the history of human revolutions. [1:213] He was born in this country home of his, and coming from one of the best families, he dedicated himself in early youth to the profession of arms. At the age of 17, having been made a major in the regiment of national militia, he exercised his valor against French arms in Canada. Since he distinguished himself there on various occasions, he was promoted to the rank of field adjutant to General Braddock, under whose orders he finished that campaign. He then retired to Mount Vernon with the intention of spending the rest of his days in peace when, the dissensions having begun and he having taken his stand with the defenders of liberty, the reputation acquired in the Canadian war led to a decision in his favor for the difficult assignment of Supreme Commander. In this position, at the beginning of the war he had to suffer discomforts and misery[7] like the most ordinary soldier.[8] When the tides of fortune turned [1:214] for the Americans and their name became more respectable after the capture of Burgoyne, Washington, unchanged in adversity as in the high tide of prosperity, was never seen either disheartened by losses or rendered haughty by victories. The war having been brought to a glorious conclusion, acclaimed as the liberator of his country, even as he beheld himself adored by his soldiers, respected by the people, and protected by a large army, he appeared before Congress, gave up his command, and retired to live privately at home. This action, which crowns the glorious deeds of his busy life, shows that that race of men has not come to an end which knew how to unite the most extensive wisdom with dauntless courage, and to preserve the most rigid virtue at the height of power. After his retirement he did not by any means spend his time in idle repose, but useful to his country in peace as in war, if he laid the foundations of a new republic, he employed his talent in ways to make it flourish. Applying himself to agriculture and presiding over a large number of negroes who under his direction are scarcely aware of being slaves,[9] he put his fields in tiptop condition, sticking to the best products, without multiplying wine and silk, which require an excessively expensive [1:215] cultivation in a country short of farmers. Although he had been brought up in the profession of arms, he did not neglect the study of politics, and even though he has refused the offices that were offered to him in the new government,[10] there is perhaps in America no one who is better informed regarding the present situation of the United States and more honestly desires their prosperity. Heaven grant that, by living for many years, he may long serve as an example of virtue and industry for his fellow citizens, as he served as an example to Europe in the victories that consecrated his name to an eternal fame.

I left Mount Vernon the morning of 29 December and came to Colchester, a little village on the Occoquan, a small stream that empties into the Potomac, and then to Dumfries, where a number of tobacco warehouses can be seen. Aquia, 9 miles from Dumfries, consists of only a few houses, and 14 miles farther on there is Falmouth on the shores of the Rappahannock. Dropping down from there along the river, one perceives Fredericksburg situated on the opposite shore. Like Alexandria, this municipality enjoys the privilege of "city";[11] it is quite extensive, and very active in tobacco trade. The Rappahannock, which empties into Chesapeake Bay, is navigable for small ships, but [1:216] its navigation is sometimes interrupted by ice (latitude 38° 15′), which, however, does not last long.

Upon leaving Fredericksburg one meets along the way numerous plantations, whose owners, called planters, can be distinguished into two classes. The first, namely, that of the richer, is of those who own from 100 to 150 slaves, and live on their lands, where they have in abundance everything necessary for the conveniences of life. They maintain handsome horses, many of which are thoroughbreds, they have gigs and carriages, and they are considered the leading gentry of the district. Their homes are usually quite vast, having in front of them a spacious yard around which are distributed the little homes for negroes, the kitchen, the barns, etc., that are always separated from the house of the owner. The latter does not attend to the direction of the slaves but provides himself with one or two overseers, who preside over the work in the fields in the manner of our *agenti.* The other class of planter consists of those who, having a smaller number of negroes and a smaller amount of land to cultivate, direct the agricultural work themselves. The slaves are either brought over from Africa or were born in the country, and according to their robustness or ability are sold for from 50 to [1:217] 100 Virginia pounds.[12]

If one were to judge the progress of agriculture in this country by the amount of land cleared, one would say that it had arrived at a high degree of perfection. But such is not the case, since a very high proportion of this land is rendered unproductive every year by the cultivation of tobacco, which requires an excellent soil, and in three years so exhausts it that it is necessary to transfer this crop to another terrain. The average planter, who owns from 600 to 700 acres, cultivates only 15 or 20 of them. It is true that the abandoned fields could be made productive by fertilizing them well, but fertilizer is very scarce since the cattle are allowed to wander in the woods, so that a landowner can barely fertilize two or three acres of land. Two acres planted to tobacco produce about 2 hogsheads, or 3000 pounds. A "hog" of tobacco, namely, 1000 pounds, brings from 27 to 39 shillings, so that from 2 acres one earns 117 Virginia shillings.

The following day's trip was 37 miles in the midst of well-tilled country, and where much use is made of peach brandy and persimmon beer. Peach trees are so abundant in Virginia that often, upon cutting away a pine wood, these fruit trees, which previously could not multiply because of the shade, quickly grow in such quantity that in a short time they cover the whole terrain. [1:218] Persimmon beer is obtained from a kind of *Guaiacum* that is quite common in the woods and has a fruit the size of a small apple which would be very good to eat if it did not retain, even when ripe, a disgusting bitterness.[13] The evening of the same day I arrived at Richmond,[14] now the capital of Virginia.[15]

At that time there had been found in this city, at a depth of about 70 feet as a well was being dug, some animal bones, among which some vertebrae larger than those of an ox. I went to the spot to observe the digging, which I found to be situated on the slope of a hill somewhat higher than the other neighboring ones at a short distance from the James River, which there flows very swiftly since it drops more than 70 feet in 5 miles. The earth dug from the well had a strong sulfurous odor and appeared to be composed of the remains of rotted wood, being of an ashen color and turning white in the sun. In this soil I found little pieces that looked like peat, which is very abundant about 13 miles to the southwest along the same river. In it could be seen the impressions of fluvial shells and some black-colored teeth that seemed to belong to some ocean fish.[16] Beyond that, according to [1:219] what they told me, some flint arrowheads and other Indian artifacts were found there. These remains must be of great antiquity, and they show that the Indians had inhabited that region many centuries before.

On the 6th of January I passed through Osborne, an unattractive village located on the Appomattox River, and reached Petersburg. Three villages very close to one another—namely, Petersburg, Blandford on the southern shore of the Appomattox, and Pocahontas on the northern, now united under the single name of Petersburg—form one of the incorporated cities, and one of the busiest, of the State of Virginia. The part that previously formed the village of Pocahontas got its name from Powhatan, an Indian chief. The other two villages, situated south of the river and located on two hills, extend partly into the valley, where there are many other dwellings. A large quantity of tobacco is brought to Petersburg all the way from North Carolina, and since it is of the kind called James River,[17] which is supposed to be the best in the United States, there is a very extensive trade in it with Europe. This advantage is, however, more than counterbalanced by the unhealthfulness of the climate, inasmuch as Petersburg is surrounded by swamps and therefore in one of the most unwholesome locations, and many children die there before reaching adolescence, victims of the damp and contaminated atmosphere.

I was told that in those regions during the summer there is a great abundance of certain birds called soree, a kind of dark-colored [1:220] plover.[18]

These birds live near marshes, and in the months of September and October they feed on wild rice[19] and become so fat that they can hardly fly and are easily killed, even with sticks. Their flesh is quite delicate, and they are in high favor at the tables of the Virginians, where they are as highly regarded as ortolans in our country. Although they are extremely abundant in the fall, at the first frost they suddenly disappear, and since (as I have already said) they can hardly fly by that time, one must say that they hide in the swamps or in tree holes where they spend the winter without food, as it is said that some species of swallows and other birds do.

One mile from Petersbrug there is the home of Colonel Banister, who owns a vast plantation. He is a grandson of the celebrated John Banister who, as Professor of Botany and Librarian at Oxford University, abandoned his occupations in England and came to settle in this part of Virginia, where he collected and described a quantity of rare plants with great care and discrimination. These were described in the *Memoirs of the Curious* published in England in 1707 and in the third volume of the great work by Ray.[20] The courteous hospitality of Colonel Banister having detained me until the [1:221] morning of the 9th, I continued my trip toward the south, and I arrived at Kingston[21] in Dinwiddie County, a rich plantation of Captain Walker.[22]

The next day I called on Dr. Greenway, an Englishman by birth, physician by profession, and an amateur botanist. Having instructed himself in the fundamentals of the Linnaean system, he collected and named more than 600 plants, among which some very rare and not yet described. I examined his fine collection with great satisfaction; and I returned the following day, since Dr. Greenway[23] showed me his descriptions and observations[24] and allowed me to copy several of the more important ones on the medical and economic use that the Indians make of some of these plants.[25]

As one leaves Kingston, he is five miles away from the Nottoway, a little river that joins the Meherrin and goes on to empty into Albemarle Strait. Formerly the Nottoway tribe of Indians lived in this place, whose few descendants now live at Southhampton Courthouse 40 miles away. Crossing Hick's Ford, I stopped in the evening at the home of Major Wall,[26] and the following morning, after 13 miles of travel beyond the stream Meherrin, over which there is a wooden bridge, I reached the border of Virginia and North Carolina, at latitude 36° 30′.

In this region, as likewise in other parts of Virginia and the two [1:222] Carolinas, there are in the woods some very large snakes called mocassin[27] by the inhabitants, whose poison is believed to be no less deadly than that of the rattlesnake. Another very curious kind of snake is the one called in Virginia glass snake,[28] which, if it is struck with a stick, breaks into several pieces, not only at the place where it is hit but also in other parts, since it has vertebrae that break off easily, a property it has in common with the European snake called *Caecilia vulgaria* by Aldrovandi and described by Linnaeus under the name of *Anguis fragilis.*

Continuation of the Trip to the Border of Georgia

[1:223] Halifax, the first city in North Carolina at 16 miles from the border, consists of a few houses.[29] It is situated on the southern shore of the Roanoke River, which at that point flows between high banks covered with trees, thus presenting a wild and melancholy appearance. After a winding course of more than 100 miles, this river empties into Albemarle Sound, and can be navigated by flatboats that carry merchandise from Halifax to Edenton, where it is loaded onto ships. However, the difficulty of going up the river on account of the swift current and the low fertility of the soil render trade rather insignificant, so that all the merchants together ship hardly 100 barrels of tobacco in one year. Rice is raised there only for domestic consumption, and if a few do sow more in moist terrains, since they have not dug canals for irrigating it, it nearly always dies in the warm season unless this happens to be very wet. Pigs are raised very easily in the woods, since they feed on acorns and wild fruit, and their flesh, salted and tightly packed in barrels, is sent to maritime regions and constitutes the most advantageous trade in those parts. As one draws away somewhat from the banks of the river [1:224], the land is sterile, and its few inhabitants subsist by selling resin and pitch that they extract from pine trees, and salt pork. The latter, corn cooked in thin slices, and sweet potatoes[30] are their food, and since grass does not grow in that dry, sandy soil, they feed their horses on corn stalks, and crushed grain takes the place of oats.[31]

After crossing Tar River by a long wooden bridge, one is at Tarboro, a wretched village built in the midst of the woods, which carries on a slender trade in pork. Leaving Tarboro, I crossed the river again, and after 12 miles I arrived at Cobb's Ordinary, or Cobb's Inn, as hotels are called in those parts. The soil is still sandy, and covered with immense woods of black pine, in the midst of which from time to time are found vast swamps that render the climate unwholesome with their putrid exhalations. One sees many trees struck by lightning, and a number of them covered with a green moss[32] that hangs in long strands from the branches. I crossed Tar River for the third time on the 18th, and toward evening I reached Allen's Ordinary. The soil seemed to me less barren—in fact the region is also more populated. In moist and swampy places there is another kind of moss[33] of an ashy color and with slender [1:225] and fleshy fronds hanging in great quantity from the highest oaks. In the course of the day I saw many vultures[34] flying around the swamps looking for dead animals. They are of a mixed gray and black color, with a white beak, and a head adorned with a red fleshy excrescence. They are therefore very similar to turkeys; hence they have sometimes been killed by unskilled hunters who have taken one for the other. Americans call them turkey buzzards[35] and take great care not to kill them on account of the service they render by eating the carcasses of animals and destroying snakes. Since they are never disturbed, they are often seen even in the vicinity of cities, and they rarely flee at the approach of men and dogs.

Before arriving at New Bern, the capital of the state of North Carolina, I crossed the Neuse River by boat. The terrain near this river is swampy, and one sees the Bourbon laurel,[36] the beautiful *Magnolia glauca,* a variety of wax tree[37] that grows up to a height of 12 feet, and, along the banks, the *Yucca filamentosa,* whose leaves, somewhat like those of the marsh reed, are provided on both sides with white, slender, and twisted filaments.

New Bern is situated at the confluence of the two rivers Trent and Neuse, and about it [1:226] a little indigo and rice are raised. The day of the 31st was rainy, and in the afternoon we had a furious storm. The rain continued the whole night and the following day. Such was the heat of the atmosphere that in my bedroom the thermometer went up to 17° Réaumur, although it was the 22nd of January.

I left New Bern on the 24th, always following the Trent River, which is crossed by a bridge at the little village called Trenton.[38] The soil seemed good to me, and I was told that each acre produces from 25 to 30 bushels of corn.[39] In fact, in addition to black pine one sees oaks and other plants that indicate a less barren soil. The marshes and other wet areas are covered with bay, magnolias, andromeda, willow-leaved oaks,[40] smilaxes, and other evergreen trees and shrubs. It goes on this way to 37 miles out of New Bern, where one enters an immense forest[41] whose terrain consists of very white sand. There, too, the few inhabitants engage in the pitch and resin trade.[42] The more industrious among them raise a little cotton and out of it they weave various sorts of fabrics dyed with vegetable juices with which they clothe themselves and from which they make not only men's and women's clothing[43] but even shoes.

In the environs of Sage's Ordinary, 28 miles this side of Wilmington, I saw growing for the first time the handsome shrub called by the inhabitants Japan tree, which is the famous Paraguay tea, otherwise [1:227] known under the name of Jesuit's tea.[44] I was also told that in a nearby field there is found in abundance during the summer that singular plant which has, like the *sen-*

sitiva, the capability of contracting in its leaves and imprisons the flies that land on them, whence it was named flytrap by the British.[45] Likewise in these parts I often came upon those pretty birds called cardinals.[46] They are of the size of a thrush, and to the vivid color of their feathers, which in the male are of a bright cinnabar, they add the sweetness of their song. They can be easily tamed and are kept in cages for many years; some of them have even been taken to Europe. They are not found in northern regions, but they are quite common in Virginia, and especially in the two Carolinas, and are seen flying about in the woods and along the fences enclosing the fields.[47]

Wilmington, another city of North Carolina, is situated on the shores of the Cape Fear River in a valley surrounded by high hills of sand. The houses[48] have a porch in front and are raised several steps above the level of the street, which makes them better ventilated and more healthful. Wilmington has a larger population than New Bern, although it occupies less space because the houses are closer together and the streets are more [1:228] regular.[49] Trade consists of tobacco, pitch, resin, cedar shingles for covering roofs, and other building timbers. The Cape Fear River, so called from the cape or point of land where it enters the sea, is divided into two branches that join beyond Wilmington. The branch called the "northwest" is formed by various brooks and some small rivers that come down from the more northerly parts of this state. It passes near the city of Cross Creek (now called Fayetteville) and is navigable for small boats and rafts up to Wilmington. The other branch, called the "northeast," has a much shorter course and comes down from Dobbs County.

On Sunday the 29th of January a torrential rain fell which continued all day, and the following morning a violent wind sent the roof shingles flying through the air. Luckily it lasted only a short time. Nevertheless, it did cause several accidents. A pilot, a sailor, and three negroes went down with their boats in the river, and a little canoe was transported[50] from the river bank way up to the square. The wind continued with less force the whole day, which was very warm and muggy;[51] but the following day it changed and there was an immediate transition to quite severe cold.

Heading for Charleston[52] out of Wilmington, one crosses the northeast [1:229] branch of the Cape Fear River and then the so-called Causeway. This is a road built at great expense upon the island[53] dividing the two branches of the river, and since it is constructed on a marshy and inundated terrain, it is often impassable when the river is swollen. In order to avoid the trouble and danger, I sent the horses on ahead. Favored by Captain MacAllester with one of his rowboats, we descended with the current and entered a channel called Alligator Creek because of the great quantity of alligators or crocodiles that live in it. Both shores of the channel are covered with evergreen trees,[54] chiefly willow-leaved oaks, andromedas, bay, magnolias, and a kind of dwarf palm[55] with large leaves resembling a fan. There we saw a large white bird, called cormorant[56] in those regions, that lives in ponds near the sea and feeds on fish. After a winding three-mile circuit we came out of the channel, and crossing the northwest branch of the river, we landed at the home of Captain MacAllester.[57] The horses arrived late at night with their harness broken and the carriage much battered, having run the danger of not being able to get out of the deep puddles into which they fell repeatedly.

[1:230] On the 3rd of February I crossed the Lockwood's Folly[58] and the Shallotte, or Charlotte, River,[59] little streams that empty into the sea after a short course, and I reached the border between the two Carolinas. The road from Wilmington to the border is unpopulated and sandy, but various plantations are to be found near the seashore. I left Mr. Vereens' Inn, where I had spent the night, very early the following day in order to get across the so-called Long Bay before high tide. A little further on one crosses a little river (whose waters rise more than six feet at high tide, beyond which the bay begins. This is 15 miles long, and the road is on the beach, which, sloping gently, remains dry during low tide. The fine sand that covers it, almost continuously pounded by the waves, is so hardened that the wheels and the horses leave hardly any imprint upon it, so that they proceed rapidly over it. On the contrary, during high tide when the water covers the road, since one has to get up on the nearby elevation, it is very laborious because of the soft sand. In good weather it is delightful traveling along the shore, since one can enjoy the immense view of the ocean, often varied by the ships and boats that sail along the coast; but when the sea is stormy and the waves advance impetuously upon the beach, then the sight is horrifying, and horses sometimes suffer [1:231] seasickness so badly that they cannot go any further.

Beyond Long Bay[60] I had been told about the house of a certain Mrs. D--- where I could find good lodging. Unfortunately, since there were two or three by the same name, I had to wander about in the woods for more than six miles before finding her home. I finally arrived at a wretched house which I was told was that of Mrs. D---. I got out of the carriage and found the proprietress dining with her overseer. She graciously invited me to share her board;[61] but after having satisfied my appetite, I was very unhappy not to be able to feed my horses, which, not having eaten that day, had the extenuated appearance of Don Quixote's Rosinante. The overseer, whom I begged to give me a little corn for them, answered that he could not do it, and since I did not know whether the lady of the house (who had the reputation of being hospitable) would want to be paid or not, I didn't dare urge any more. Then, when the overseer, at my request to extend my thanks to the proprietress, answered that if I had any bill I could settle it with him, I offered him whatever he wanted provided he gave some corn to my horses. At these words, followed by the payment, the corn was found, which, ground in a mortar, was in a few moments devoured by my famished nags. Then, much more content than before, I climbed back into the carriage and in the evening reached the fine plantation of Mr. Francis Alston.[62]

I covered only four miles on the 6th, dining at the house of Mr. William Alston,[63] [1:232] whose plantation is located on the shore of the Waccamaw River and enjoys the advantage of being regularly irrigated by the same river, which rises every day with the tide. This unusual manner of natural irrigation renders the terrain very productive for rice and indigo, so that this property is considered one of the best of the region.[64] A few years ago the owner had a fine water machine built that activates 12 pistons for shelling rice, one of the first constructed in those parts. The next morning Mr. Alston favored me with his canoe and two negroes, and after covering four miles downstream and crossing the mouths of the Black and Pee Dee rivers, we soon arrived at the city of Georgetown. It is located on a low-lying plain at the confluence of the Waccamaw, Pee Dee, Black, and Sampit rivers, which joining together, form Winyah Bay. Its being situated near four navigable rivers renders it very suitable for an advantageous commerce, and it would have increased in population in a few years if the proximity of Charleston and the damage suffered at the time of the war had not greatly retarded its progress. The city is built on a regular plan, with straight streets and houses quite distant from each other, since many of them were burned down by an English frigate in the late war and have not yet been rebuilt.[65]

Leaving Georgetown on the morning of the 9th[66] of February, I crossed the Sampit River and then arrived at the banks of the Santee, which is divided into two branches by a low and flooded island in the middle of which there is a road made of tree [1:233] trunks that was at that time completely ruined by the water. I was forced, therefore, to[67] enter the channel called Pushingo Creek, which, cutting across the island, communicates with both branches of the river and is so encumbered with trees and winding that one loses a great deal of time in it.[68] I was told that during the summer snakes, which are very abundant, often fall into the boat from the trees hanging over the river. Making my way out of the channel and crossing the southern branch of the river, in two days I reached Bolton's Ferry and then Charleston, capital of South Carolina. The road from Georgetown to Charleston is the most beautiful in the United States, with the exception of the one that goes from Boston to Portsmouth.[69]

On the 20th of March,[70] accompanied by Mr. Henry Middleton, I left Charleston for Savannah. We crossed the Ashley River where the current is very strong, and four miles from the river we found ourselves at the country home of Dr. Drayton, at that time lieutenant governor, in whose garden there are some handsome magnolias and some hedges of Paraguay grass.[71] In these environs can be seen flocks of various species of herons, or *sgarze,* that live on the levees of the rice fields and on the banks of marshes, two of which are most common, namely, the blue heron[72] and the white.[73] The surrounding fields planted to rice are [1:234] irrigated with rain water, which is stored for that purpose in large artificial ponds. The fields are protected by a sturdy embankment from the waters of the river, which, since they are salt, would be harmful to the rice.

By evening we were at the summer residence[74] of Mr. Arthur Middleton, who, having traveled in various parts of Europe, has collected a fair quantity of good paintings. His three-story house has the form of an ancient castle, and laterally there are two wings that according to the plan were to be joined to the structure in the middle to form an extensive habitation. It enjoys the view of the Ashley River and Batavia, vacation place of Commodore Gillon, formerly commander of the American navy, who[75] has built there a house in the Dutch style and established a fine garden[76] with rare plants and some greenhouses. The next day we crossed the Stono River at Randolph's Bridge and stopped to dine at Sandy Hill with Colonel Washington, who distinguished himself in wartime when he was a commander of dragoons. In that area there grow in the woods the Judas tree,[77] the *yucca aloifolia,* the American *lauraceraso,*[78] and the dwarf palm.[79] On the 22nd we crossed the Ponpon, or Edisto, and then the Ashepoo 12 miles from the preceding, and, finally, the Combahee. The water in those rivers is almost level with the shores, and by flooding a great deal of land they form [1:235] wide puddles.[80] Roads[81] have to be built over these out of tree trunks, and since they are very low and badly protected, they are often submerged and ruined by the overflow of rivers and the rain. We found in that condition the Combahee one, which is about a mile long, and which we had to travel on foot in the mud. We were forced to lose a great deal of time to get the carriages and the horses to pass over it, because as we went along we had to place boards under the wheels to keep them from sinking into the soft and swampy terrain.[82] One notes in these woods the azalea,[83] that kind of laurel called sweet bay,[84] and the so-called yellow jasmine, which is the *Bignonia sempervirens* of Linnaeus.

After crossing the Pocataligo, Tully-finny, and Coosawhatchie Rivers, on the morning of the 23rd we dined at Euhawes at the home of Mr. Hayward, and then in the evening at the plantation of Mount Pleasant with Mr. Henry Middleton, with whom I had made the trip from Charleston.[85] During my stay with Mr. Middleton I happened to see an eagle which, after having wheeled about for a long time, plummeted down swiftly upon the water of a nearby fishpond and rose with a fish in its claws, flying off to eat it. This is the *albicilla* eagle,[86] called fishing eagle [1:236] by the Americans, and it lives by the ponds of Virginia and the two Carolinas.

One crosses 16 miles of sandy and barren country to go from Mount Pleasant to Purysburg, a village located on the eastern shore of the Savannah River, which divides South Carolina from Georgia. This village was founded in 1733 by a certain Purry, a native of Neuchâtel, who settled there with 170 Swiss in order to undertake the cultivation of mulberries. However, since this population diminished a great deal in a few years because of the unhealthful climate, the raising of mulberries was completely abandoned, and now Purysburg is reduced to a few houses. At the northwestern edge can be seen a little hill artificially made of oyster and clam shells and located near the river. The big willow-leaved oak trees[87] that grow on top of it, since they are slow-growing plants, show that this little hill is the work of Indians of a remote antiquity.

At Purysburg I was presented with two snakes caught in those environs. One of these, a foot long and of a dark color with a dirty-white belly, is a species not yet described by naturalists.[88] From my examination it does not seem to be poisonous, since I didn't find [1:237] in the upper jaw the two teeth that transmit the poison. I found the other snake equally harmless. It has black rings on its back and the rest is whitish scattered with irregular dark spots. It is almost two feet long.[89] Certain ash-colored lizards are also common here, of the size of our lizard, but with a larger head and with winged toes, that is, furnished at the sides with thin membranes. They have likewise an extremely long fourth toe on their rear feet and two lateral folds. The detailed description that Linnaeus gives of the *Lacerta plica*[90] corresponds very closely with the structure of those I observed.

CHAPTER VIII

The State of Georgia

From Purysburg to the City of Augusta

[1:238]

THE SAVANNAH RIVER comes out of the mountains to the west of Georgia and has an extremely long course during which it absorbs an immense number of little rivers. As a result, when there happens to be steady rains, it floods the adjacent terrains, and precisely this had occurred during the days preceding my arrival.[1] At a distance of seven miles from Purysburg by way of the river there is, on the opposite shore, a village called Abercorn situated on a height where one can land when the Savannah has overflowed its banks. However, since there were only two small canoes, I didn't see how we could ever load onto them the carriage and the horses, when the boatman, full of ideas, looked for some rope [1:239] and with it tied the two boats tightly together. Then he fastened the carriage at the end of one of them, led on the horses, arranged them so that they had their front legs in one canoe and their rear in the other, and thus embarked we went on downstream. Just beyond the height on which Purysburg is situated the terrain is flooded on both sides, and these swamps, which emerge when the water is low, are covered with the most beautiful plants produced by the southern states. They are the retreat of the alligators, which can often be seen swimming in the river and stretched out on the roots of trees near the banks to enjoy the rays of the sun. The alligator, which is a simple variety of crocodile, has a dark brown, almost black, body. It lives on land and in the water, where it feeds on fish, and deposits its eggs on the sand, which open with the heat of the sun. As soon as they are born, the little crocodiles drag themselves down beside the river, in which they live on prey. I found a number of them dead in the woods where they had been carried by the floods and starved to death. They never pursue man when they are on land, and rarely does that happen when they are swimming. On the contrary, they generally run away from whoever is pursuing them, although it is said that they will rush upon those who take to flight. These animals are common in the rivers of Georgia and in those of the two Carolinas, and they are killed only to extract the brain musk. One tries to hit them in the eyes or in the throat, since over the rest of the body their hide is so thick that it resists gun bullets.

When I arrived at Abercorn I got out of the flimsy little boats that [1:240] had taken me there, and I left for Marlborough Grove, the property of General Greene on the bank of the same river. This courageous American commander distinguished himself highly in the southern states for having held out with his little army against British troops very superior in number and training. He is a native of Rhode Island and came to Georgia in the fall of 1785 to settle upon this vast plantation presented to him by the State of Georgia in recompense for his important services.[2]

The next day, the 26th of March, I reached Savannah, the capital of Georgia, in a few hours. This city was founded in the year 1733 by General Oglethorpe, who drew up the plan for it. It did not increase much in wealth or in population until the beginning of the war. At the time of the revolution it was occupied by the American General Howe, who abandoned it in 1778 shortly before the British troops commanded by Lieutenant Colonel Campbell took possession of it. The following year the allied army of Count d'Estaing and General Lincoln laid siege to it, but after the English had defended themselves valiantly against an assault in which the allies lost 894 dead and wounded, the latter raised the siege. Then the English, fearing a new surprise, fortified themselves there, built a wooden fort at the southeastern end near [1:241] the river in order to prevent a disembarkation from that side, and after that held it peacefully until the end of the war.

Savannah is located at 31° 59′ latitude and 80° 41′ longitude from London on a height that dominates the river and from which one enjoys the view of Hutchinson Island opposite it, which is planted to rice and divided into four or five plantations. Along the river there is a sand bank called the Bluff that remains partly dry in winter and serves as a public promenade. Not far from it are the openings of three main streets, each of which crosses the city and has in its center a large square. These streets and squares are not only ornamental but make possible, furthermore, an unobstructed ventilation, and so prove to be quite advantageous in that extremely warm and humid climate. In one of those squares is the statehouse, built of bricks with a portico of four columns, and which suffered much damage during the siege. Opposite this portico there used to be the tomb of Tomochichi, one of the sachems, or Indian chiefs, who was a great friend of the English and went to London at the time of the first settlements, whence he returned laden with gifts. His gratitude and friendship toward the English not only motivated him to keep peace with the colonists, but, when he was about to die, he expressed the desire to be buried among them. His tomb was surrounded by a palisade, which was afterwards destroyed, and now no trace remains of it any longer. The factory formerly erected for silk manufacture and now adapted for use as a theatre, and the churches [1:242] of the Anglicans and Presbyterians, now empty for the lack of ministers, are the buildings most worthy of note, although much damaged by the siege; but the other houses, which are of wood, low, small, and often almost on the point of collapse, give to this city a rather wretched appearance.

The inhabitants are calculated at 1500 whites and 3000 negroes. Some of the principal landowners live quite comfortably, but since most of them were already poor at the time of the settlements, and having lost some of the limited number of slaves they had acquired, they were reduced to a bare sufficiency. They long, however, to keep up with their neighbors the Carolinians, imitating their customs and manners, although in order to do that they have neither enough wealth nor the advantage of a more refined education. The main trade is in rice, indigo, tobacco, and lumber. The raising of rice keeps spreading every year to the distance of 10, 15, and 20 miles from the sea, so that 10,000 barrels were exported in the year 1785. Indigo and tobacco are cultivated in the western regions near Augusta, and lumber is cut in the woods near the sea where live oak[3] grows abundantly, whose wood is one of the most durable for ship building. In exchange for these items, merchandise is received all the way from Europe which formerly was obtained from Charleston at a high price. [1:243] However, the difficulty of going up the river to the city, since there are in these 15 miles sand banks that shift with the floods, and the miserable climate, fatal during the summer to sailors, especially Europeans, along with the small quantity of merchandise, render its commerce quite listless and of small account. On the shores of the Savannah River I frequently found certain beautiful beetles of a golden green color[4] that have a long curved horn on their heads. They form the dung balls, as does in our country the beetle called *pillolario,* in which they deposit their eggs. Along with these I found also certain other beetles similar in color to the preceding except that they were smaller and did not have the horn on their foreheads.[5]

Near Savannah there is a little village consisting of a few inhabitations that from the name of the Indians that lived there in ancient times took that of Yamacraw, and between this and the city there is a wide space called the Common which extends all the way to the banks of the river and could easily be made into a convenient public [1:244] promenade, if it were adorned with trees arranged in avenues. In Yamacraw can be seen a spring of very clear water, over which they are thinking of building baths. Greenage, the country house of Major Washington,[6] where I was on the 28th of March, is situated four miles southeast of the city on the little channel called Augustine Creek, because it goes to St. Augustine, the capital of Eastern Florida. The water is salt, and the channel, clogged with tall swamp grasses, looks very melancholy. In the garden there were several wild orange trees, which easily hold up outside in the warm climates of Georgia and the Carolinas, and nearby I observed for the first time at close range that very beautiful palm, common also in the islands near Charleston, called in Georgia the palmetto tree. Its leaves are very long and comb-like, and as the old leaves fall, they leave various circular scales that surround the trunk. The top of this palm is cut when it is still tender by the inhabitants, who eat it like cabbage, or raw with pepper and salt, or fried with butter; and it tastes like artichoke.[7] Sand flies are common there—tiny insects whose bite produces an [1:245] unbearable itch.

About a mile and a half from Greenage there is a large building where formerly sago powder was made. This substance, easily digestible and very nutritious, and therefore very useful as food, is obtained from the pitch of an East Indian palm called accordingly *sagouifera.* A certain Boswell, who had lived for a long time in the East Indies, had the opportunity to inform himself about the method of making sago, and, having moved to Georgia, spent several years perfecting this product, from which he made a huge profit. At his death he passed the secret on to Dr. Bicrofft, his nephew, from whom I got the following information. The principal ingredient of this substance is the most tender and farinaceous part of sweet potatoes,[8] ground and mixed with a given proportion of the pith of the *sagouifera* palm,[9] for which it occurred to Boswell to substitute that of the palmetto mentioned above. The process is quite long and various instruments are used for the purpose, but since the excellence and perfection of sago depends upon this method of manufacture, and that is a secret, I didn't think I should insist upon a detailed description. Georgia sago, according to what I was assured by various druggists, is not inferior to that of the East Indies, from which it is, however, easily distinguished, since the former is reduced to a fine white-colored powder and the other is in the form of [1:246] little granules.

One of the handsomest properties in the region of Savannah is that of Mr. John Habersham, called Silk Hope, on the little Ogeechee River, and because its banks are low and flooded, the terrain is perhaps more fertile than that of South Carolina. Mr. Habersham's house is ordinary, but his property is vast, in good order, and well cultivated by an adequate number of negroes. There is, moreover, a machine driven by water kept for that purpose at a higher level in an artificial pond, and which activates 12 pistons for shelling rice.

The road from Savannah to Augusta stretches to the northwest at a short distance from the river. It is very sandy, and for 15 miles it is the same one that goes to Charleston. Not far from it is Abercorn, and then Ebenezer, a village situated on a very charming hill on the shores of the river. This latter, founded by a colony of Germans who came with General Oglethorpe, used to be quite populated before the war. But since most of the houses were destroyed by the British, the inhabitants withdrew elsewhere, and only five poor families remain. Nearby there is a fine church built by the German Lutherans who used to be in the village. In the environs, as also in other districts of this region, can be seen many white mulberries,[10] which multiplied upon being transported there from Europe. This culture was promoted by the English [1:247] before the war, who, by paying a high price for Georgia silk, encouraged its propagation; but since the war, whether for lack of this stimulus, or because the tools for spinning silk were destroyed by the enemy army, very few apply themselves to it. To give an idea of the progress that this industry had made before the war, it will suffice to say that Mrs. Postell earned 60 guineas from silk in one year. This industrious lady, who is one of the most diligent cultivators, presented me with some silk she herself had produced, which was of a beautiful silver color, even, and quite fine. The climate, moreover, could not be better suited for mulberries, which grow sturdy and luxuriant without attention or fertilization.

Just beyond Ebenezer one goes down into the valley through which flows the little river called Ebenezer Creek that empties into the Savannah. Since the bed of the Ebenezer is not very deep, the water rises over the banks, and the terrain is flooded for a long stretch when the river swells. Hence for more than two miles the road was covered with water that came up to the horses' bellies. Fifteen miles from Ebenezer is Tukasse-king, a height designated for the building of a village, and 20 miles beyond is the inn of Mr. Pierce, where I arrived the evening of the 7th of April. The region that I covered between Ebenezer and Tukasse-king is scattered with a number of hills, the terrain is sandy and barren, and on the few plantations that are found there only corn and sweet potatoes are raised. The most fertile places are the lowlands, and for that reason subject to [1:248] flooding. Since they can only be planted to rice, they are left uncultivated for the lack of slaves.

In that region I saw in bloom two andromedas, namely, the *paniculata*, and the *nitida* of Bartram, and the handsome halesia shrub,[11] whose flowers resemble white bells, and which grows on the banks of streams. The uplands and the black pine woods were adorned with a great quantity of azaleas,[12] and since among them there were white, red, flesh-colored, and orange flowers, they formed a pleasant variety. In spite of the fact that we were only at the beginning of April, the season was already very temperate, and some butterflies were in evidence, mainly of that American species described by Linnaeus under the name of *plexippus,*[13] which had tobacco-colored wings veined with black, with a black band scattered with white spots at the tips. In that neighborhood I found another pretty butterfly, namely, the *protesilaus*[14] which hardly differs from our European *podalirius*[15] except for its larger size and more vivid colors. On the 8th I reached Beaver Dam, another little river that joins with Briar Creek and flows likewise into the Savannah. After traveling 22 miles in the midst of a barren pine wood where there are only two wretched cabins, I arrived at Mr. Lamberth's Inn. From here the next morning I crossed Briar Creek [1:249] by boat and toward evening arrived at the city of Augusta.

Augusta (latitude 33° 39′ and longitude from London 80° 49′) is the second largest city of Georgia and now the seat of the government of that state. It was founded by General Oglethorpe in 1734, who erected there a fort to defend himself from the Indians, and it was a small village at the time of the war when it was destroyed by English arms. Arisen again from the ruins after the peace, it was decided in 1784 to transfer there the seat of the government as the place nearest to the center of the state, and in the short period of two years it grew so that one already counts there more than 100 houses and about 700 inhabitants. The city is situated in a plain on the southern shore of the Savannah, which is here navigable by big boats. These go down more than 200 miles with indigo, corn, and other products all the way to the city of Savannah, whence they return laden with European goods. However, the difficulty of going back up the river, which takes from seven to eight days, by multiplying the expenses, renders this trade not very profitable. The houses, scattered about half a mile along the river, are all of wood and of ordinary size. Many of them are not of adequate height and have only the ground floor and windows opening at the peak of the roof. Around Augusta the soil in low areas is very productive and cultivated to indigo, which forms the main trade of those regions. There is still a small traffic in skins with the Indians of the Creek nation, who, however, since they are not too friendly with the Georgians, prefer to sell them to the Spaniards of Florida.

Location, Main Rivers and Mountains, and Former Inhabitants of Georgia

[1:250] Georgia extends from 29° to 35° latitude and from 76° to 90° longitude from London; and it is 650 miles wide from east to west and 100 from north to south. It borders on the Savannah River to the north, which divides it from South Carolina, on the east with the ocean, on the south with St. Marys River, and on the west with Louisiana, from which it is separated by the Mississippi. Its southern confines begin with the mouth of St. Marys River to its source; from there directly west to the Apalachicola River, whence, dropping down along this river to 30° latitude, they again proceed in a straight line to the west; and they terminate with the Mississippi. In this immense stretch of country is included Nantchez or Nantchees,[16] a settlement founded long ago by the French and now belonging to the Spanish, who incorporated it in the province of Florida. The principal rivers are: the Savannah, which descends from the more westerly parts, at latitude 34° 54′ flows from northwest to southeast to the city of the same name, and a few miles beyond it empties into the sea; [1:251] the Ogeechee (by others called the Hogohechie), the Altamaha (which, formed by the two rivers Oconee and Ocmulgee, was the old border of Georgia); and, finally, the Satilla and St. Marys Rivers, all of which have the same direction and flow almost parallel to the Savannah, emptying subsequently in the ocean. The other rivers situated to the west of the Appalachian chain of mountains have a different course from north to south, as, for example, the Chattahoochee or Apalachicola, which crosses Florida and empties into the Gulf of Mexico, and the Alabama or Mobile, which runs parallel to the Mississippi. Near the coasts of Georgia there are numerous little islands of various sizes, such as Tybee, Ossabaw, Sapelo, Cumberland, etc., between which and the continent there remains a channel navigable down to the mouth of St. Marys River. The country is level, sandy near the ocean, and clayey in the more internal areas, where it is broken up by charming hills which keep rising toward the north to meet the famous chain that under the various names of Appalachians, Alleghenies, and Blue Mountains cuts across the United States from southwest to northeast.

The climate of Georgia, fully as humid and variable as that of South Carolina, and perhaps hotter, turns out to be very unhealthful in low and flooded places, but excellent for vegetation. However, in the higher locations it is less unwholesome, and the inhabitants there are visibly healthier and sturdier. Spring is ordinarily rainy, especially in March and April; the season is very unstable, and subject to impetuous winds and, not infrequently, to hurricanes during the equinox. The summer [1:252] is hot, the lightning and thunder are terrible and frequent; and it is followed by an extremely rainy fall that is the most dangerous time for maladies. The winter would be the best season, snow and ice being rarely seen, were it also not harmful to the health on account of the great instability of the climate.

The Indian nations that formerly inhabited the now cultivated parts of Georgia, and which still live to the west, are the Creek and the Choctaw.

The Creek, who are divided into Upper, Middle, and Lower Creek with reference to their location in the mountains or on the plain, form even today a numerous, brave, courageous nation, allied with the Spanish and often an enemy of the Americans. The Choctaw, on the other hand, are friendly to the Americans, have a larger population counting about 1200 warriors, but they are not reputed to be as valorous. The latter are no different from northern Indians except that they are perhaps smaller and much darker. They are well built with regular features, except for their forehead which is very sloping, for which reason they were called Flathead Indians by the English. They live west of the Mobile River near the Mississippi.

During my passage from Charleston I was present at the audience that was given by the governor of that city to an embassy of Choctaw.[17] More than 100 Indians of this nation had been present the year before at the peace treaty with the Virginians,[18] and as they were returning to their country, they were surprised [1:253] by the Creek, who killed many of them. Since the Choctaw were then not in a position to avenge themselves, they returned to their homes and arranged to send an embassy to the Carolinians in order to make an alliance with them against the Creek, on whom they wanted to wage war. After a long and disastrous trip, these ambassadors reached Charleston on the 16th of March, 1786, and the next morning they went to the home of General Moultrie, Governor of South Carolina, where they stated the purpose of their mission.[19] The first to speak was Spokohummah[20] (which in their language means red woodpecker), a very old man, who, addressing the Governor, said:

> I came here to see you, to take you by the hand,[21] and to be your brother. Today I see you, and I take you by the hand. I love you and all your people. The Choctaw and the Chickasaw[22] form a single people, and I took you by the hand in the name of the two nations. I am an old man, but I have many youths. We are all your friends. We want to take up the tomahawk[23] for you and be always [1:254] on your side. We have not come to receive gifts,[24] but only to see you, who are the man we love. Whatever it may please you to offer us we shall accept wholeheartedly, but we seek nothing.
>
> We were at the treaty with the Virginians, and we were annoyed by the Creek during our journey. They would like us to join with them against you, whom we love. The Creek have killed some of our nation, which obliged us to travel a long path to see you and to tell you that, if the Creek declare war upon you, we shall take your battles upon ourselves, and we hope to be helped by you [1:255] with arms and ammunition. Tell me what we have to do and we shall do it.

When Spokohummah[25] had finished his speech, Tinctimingo,[26] a young Indian, began to speak thus to the governor:

> Today I see you. My father is the chief of the warriors of our nation. He has sent me to you, the beloved chief of the warriors of your people, and whatever answer you give us, we shall bear it back. The speech that you make shall be repeated to our people, and we shall do your heart's bidding. I came with my people by a long path to see you. We have seen you, and our hearts are joyful and content. I have not come like the serpent with a forked tongue. I have come as a man, and what I say I confirm and defend. Neither my father, nor I, nor any of my people have yet stepped on Spanish soil,[27] nor shall we ever do so. At present I am a youth, but I hope to live and become a man and a warrior.

At the end of Tinctimingo's[28] speech the Indians were dismissed and invited to return the next morning to the governor's house for the answer.[29] He then responded to them in the following terms:

> Friends and brothers. I take you by the hand, because I am glad to see you, and because your nation was always our friend and never [1:256] took up arms against us.[30] I am pleased to hear that the Choctaw and the Chickasaw form a single people. They are powerful warriors,[31] and they have fought in our company against the other redmen.[32]
>
> I regret that the Creek have killed some of your nation, and that you have been forced to make a long detour in order to come to us. If they declare war upon you, our friends from the North will send many people to fight them, they will kill a great number of them, and we shall drive them out of their country. I thank you for the offer to fight for us against the Creek, but I could not bear for us to stand quietly by and watch your people being killed in order to save us. If we need you, you will be notified; we shall give you powder, bullets, and good muskets, and we, too, shall come to fight with you. We shall be brothers, and we shall love one another mutually.

Then turning to Tinctimingo,[33] he continued, saying:

> Brother. I am glad to see you and to hear the speech about the great warrior, your father, that you made to me. I hope that your people and mine will be friends; that the path between us will be open as long as trees grow on the earth and waters flow in the rivers; and

> that you will not listen to the malicious [1:257] rumors circulated against us. I want you and all the red people to live in peace. I am pleased to see you and to receive you as a man, since you say to me that you have come like a man and not like the snake in the grass. I believe that what you say is true, and that you are acting as a man and warrior.

Afterwards he turned toward everyone and said:

> Brothers. I hope that you will watch out for your safety and not pass through the Creek nation. I wish you a good trip, and that you may return safely to your homes.

The embassy thus terminated to the great satisfaction of the Indians, they left the room and promised to return in the afternoon to demonstrate with a dance their pleasure at the confederation formed against the Creek. Various gentlemen of Charleston gathered at the home of the governor, and then the Choctaw arrived toward three in the afternoon accompanied by a great crowd of people. They were seven in number, dressed in a shirt, some with shoes of their making, others barefoot—all, however, with their faces and hair horribly painted red and black.[34] Tinctimingo,[35] the son of the king, or chief, took his stand near the governor and did not enter the dance, believing, perhaps, that his status did not permit him to dance with the others, who, meantime, had arranged themselves in a circle.[36] Spokohummah,[37] the old warrior, led them, and struck up an air that he accompanied with his steps, which the others answered like a chorus, moving constantly in a circle. After eight [1:258] or ten turns a cry, or rather a yell, of joy and then a brief rest served as a pause before beginning another song not much different from the first, but only pronounced more rapidly and accompanied by more rapid steps and more emphatic gesticulations. They moved their bodies, heads, and hands very agilely, dancing almost always hunched over and with their knees bent.[38] After this dance, at the governor's request, they struck up their war song, or rather dance, in which, pretending to fight, they rush upon one another furiously, accompanying the action with horrible yells and fearful contortions of the face.[39] The dance over and evening having arrived, the Indians, weary from their strenuous exercise, were presented with[40] brandy and contentedly left the governor's home.

Apropos of the Choctaw Indians, the reader will welcome here a vocabulary of their language passed on to me by a person who spent a great deal of time with them.[41] Along with this I also got one for the Cherokee, who, although bordering on the former, have an entirely different language.

As for the pronunciation, it is to be observed that the vocabulary was written down by an American and must therefore be pronounced with the English accent. Thus, for example, *ech-nau-té* must be pronounced *ec-no-tí* in Italian, and *aw-busta-hoo-bó, ou-bosta-u-bó;* and inasmuch as in English two *o*'s correspond to the Italian vowel *u*, in order to indicate two separate *o*'s, these are accordingly marked with a line above, as in the word *ōō-kōō-too-she.*

[1:259]	**Choctaw**	**Cherokee**
god	haw-busta-hoo-bó[42]	ech-nau-te
good	chicka-maw	o-see-cyouh
bad	poo-lo	weya-weyouh
body	haw-caw-nip	che-aley
head	nis-co-lo	che-scolah
hair	pa-she	ke-cleh
forehead	ma-sa-na	checa-ante-kana
face	me-shuk	aquoh-kitaje
eyebrows	eno-shu-bah	checa-tes-kana
eyes	ne-shu-skiah[43]	checa-tolah
eyelids	sa-liak-chech	a-checa-tena-chelah[44]
eyelashes	. . . .	too-checa-tles-kelc-keh[45]
nose	be-shuk-kane[46]	chena-solah
nostrils	be-shu-loo[47]	too-chousa-tela-sak[48]
mouth	e-le	cheo-leh
lip	til-be	kana-cut-lah[49]
tongue	sun-lush	kana-kek[50]
tooth	noo-te	chena-tuli-he[51]
chin	nu-tuc-te-hah	che-aneh
neck	coo-lah	cheet-sanee
shoulders	toh-sha	chena-we[52]
chest	ke-shee	chena-tesce
arm	sha-ka-bó[53]	chena-ken[54]
elbow	a-shun-kun-na	chequee-shane
hand	a-buk[55]	aquoh-jane[56]
fist	buk-ta-loo-ko-ché[57]	. . . .
thumb [1:260]	buk-ish-ké	kia-sute-hoo-tanoe
fingers	buk-ko-shé	akota-sute-koo-ane[58]
fingernails	buk-uk-chish	chu-suskeh
navel	haw-lamb-ish	akota-entote[59]
abdomen	. . . .	checa-shane[60]
flanks	ha-tip	chea-tee
groin	ephe-chuc-ubee[61]	chela-sotta
thigh	u-bee	caw-cato
knee	in-galta-haw	chena-gane[62]

leg	hulk-key	chena-shane[63]
anklebone	iea-tito-ko-che	chechu-guala
heel	in-ke-to-bó	cato-kane[64]
foot	eye-lah	coola-sute-noe[65]
toes	u-she	chena-sute-hōō-tanoe[66]
toenail	yock-chish	aquoh-suskeh[67]
suit or dress	lo-hoo-koo[68]	cosa-lanah
underwear	lo-hoo-koo-she	cay-say-eteh
trousers	mallo-foo-kah	asu-loch
skirt	al-koo-naw-fa-liah	asu-noh
woman's short dress	. . . .	squla-cay-octoé[69]
shirt	na-hu-kah	en-whooh
stockings	a-beus-kah	tiloo-fula-skeh[70]
shoes	shoel-ushe	tiloo-shulo-tusta-tleh[71]
fire	lunck	che-le
air [1:261]	make-lech	oo-nol-seh
water	oo-kaw	um-mah
earth	yo-kan-hee	caw-tah
sun	hash-thee[72]	neuto
night	nen-uck	sanoy[73]
moon	hash-nen-uck-jah[74]	sanoy-neuto[75]
stars	fech-ick	no-kusah[76]
sky	shut-ick[77]	kala-lata
day	net-uck	ecah
spring	too-fel-pay	coo-cay[78]
summer	too-fah	coo-yee
autumn	hash-too-lam-um-mah[79]	. . . .
winter	una-foch	coo-lateu
rain	com-bó	caw-es-kek
snow	oo-kōō-too-she	aino-cheh
north	fa-lam-nah	veent-clee
south	oo-kaw-maw-leigh	oo-cana-ich
east	hash-kōō-too-coch[80]	ekah-tay-oie[81]
west	hash-kōō-too-loch[82]	co-saha-ich
man	ha-tuch[83]	skinch
woman	ehoo-you	ak-aieh
girl	che-poo-tah[84]	ak-aieh-chetseh
boy	alla-te-ke[85]	chu-cho-cheh[86]
husband	ehoo-tuch[87]	oo-talleh[88]
wife	ta-ke-che	ak-oo-talleh[89]
child [1:262]	poos-ko-se	ai-oo-talleh[90]
uncle	a-mo-she	a-too-cheh
aunt	ush-kay[91]	a-lo-cheh[92]

mother	ush-kay	ai-cheh
father	un-kay	a-too-teh[93]
brother	te-poo-ba-she[94]	ak-ee-nelea
sister	an-te-ke	an-cato[95]
horse	esu-baw	so-quile
cow	wal-ke	wan-kee[96]
dog	o͞o-phe	kee-tee
deer	a-see	howe
bear	na-tah	yeo-nah
meat	na-pe	howe-yeh
corn	tan-jay	sai-loo
boiled corn	halt-po-nay	cano-lia-hanah[97]
bread	pa-skech	caw-too
eat	im-pah	kul-stinah[98]
drink	ish-ko	te-caw-teta-hé
sleep	no-say	tu-chela-ne
run	maw-le-lay	toto-che so-quile taneh[99]
walk	noo-wah	haw-eneh
work	altoon-hoo	caw-oste-keta-nale
think	wat-tah	chano-lachee
speak	a-num-bul-lay	enetne-halee
love	ehoo-luch	ak-oo-talleech[100]
I	. . . .	Junch[101]
thou	. . . .	ne-hee
he	. . . .	waws-hee[102]
we	. . . .	ne-hato-hee[103]
you [1:263]	. . . .	ne-hee
they	. . . .	ek-hee[104]
America	Virginia	Wooh-tut-lay[105]
Frenchman	fa-lan-chay	kalunt-chech
Spaniard	espa-nay	squa-nah
Englishman	Inglish	Nung-kelesh
Indian	atoka-poo-ho͞o mode[106]	you-weyoh
Cherokee	Che-lo-kee	Chera-quee
Chicksaw	Chi-ca-shaw	Cicka-saw
Creek	Musk-ko-ga *or* Tal-lo po-she	Cowe-tah *or* Coo-soh
when	. . . .	lake-you
thing	natta-hoe	kut-och
how	. . . .	kut-on-stek[107]
where	cut-to-mah[108]	ut-luch
just now	e-moo-nah	coo-hee
breakfast	. . . .	shun-alah-kulsti-nah

dinner	im-pah	ehuh-kulsti-nah
supper	. . . .	suneah-kulsti-nah
Come to lunch.	Aunt-im-pah	. . . .
How are you?	Shiah-tshu?	Tinta-yole-kuh?
Where do you live?	Cut-to-mah-scan-ta?[109]	At-hutto-chaine?
In what country?	To-mah-tiaw-nuin-ta?[110]	Caw-to-etole-chaine-say?[111]
How far? [1:264]	Kōō-a-cut-to-mah?	Law-quoy-enteh?
very well	alt-pe-sah	o-see-you
very bad	eka-choo-cha-mo[112]	aw-leke-kuh[113]
sick	a-ba-kah	. . . .
deer skin	asee-hock-shu-pa[114]	cunna-kay-kowe[115]
bear skin	natah-hock-shu-pa[116]	cunne-kay-yeonah[117]
beaver skin	keeuta-hock-shu-pa	to-yee
otter skin	hoosun-hock-shu-pa[118]	che-yock
yes	yow	ow-ah
no	un-haw-kay-yon	un-tlah
I don't want	I-toe	Unt-tlah-kela
I want	Yo-melodgh-kay	Ow-ah
Go!	I-yah	Hanah
Come!	Nuin-ta	A-hanah
I can't	Yoh-heni-ay-woh	Wye-kee[119]
white[120]	to-hoo-bel[121]	una-kel
black	lo-say	ona-kay
yellow	la-cou-nah[122]	tellon-kay
green	. . . .	it-say[123]
blue	oak-chaw-mau-la	ena-kay
red	hum-mah	keko-kay[124]
mountain	nanna-cho-ho[125]	ot-al-hee[126]
river [1:265]	hat-chaw	aquon-hee[127]
brook	bog-we	neilta-hee
branch of river	bog-issh[128]	slekay-yock
musket	tun-nap-poo[129]	cullo-quah
gunpowder	hit-took	toel-kis-kee
lead	na-pe[130]	cunne
bullets	na-pe[131]	cunne-cune-stiket[132]
pellets	noc-koo-she	tachista ohah-o-see-you[133]
bow	ete-she-ba-taw	echu-luch

arrow	oo-ska-noc-kay[134]	cunne
pipe	chuma-shun-ne-kek[135]	cunna-un-noah[136]
knife	bush-poo	ail-stee[137]
sword	bush-poo-foot-iah	ail-stee-cunne-heetah[138]
ax or mace	i-ske-fuh	cullo-stee
receptacle for boiling water	su-noc	a-cha-ie
tobacco	huck-chuma	cho-lah
flint	ta-su-noc	towes-cola
blanket	an-gee	en-whooh-hōō-tanoe
reed	he-nah	nunno-hee
warrior [1:266]	tuch-kuk	ski-agu-sta
king or chief	min-go	ocho-weyoh-hee
canoe	pe-ne	chew
ship	pe-ne-he-too	chew-aquoh
woolen blanket	shu-ka-bó	chou-stona-nee

It is known that in the Indian languages words are composed of various syllables each of which has most often its own meaning, a fact that can be easily observed even in these two languages. In Choctaw, for example, *hat-tuch* means man; *ehoo-you,* woman; *ehoo-tuch,* husband or man of woman; and *ehoo-luch,* to love. Thus in the same language the sun is called *hash-thee;* night, *nen-uck;* and the moon, *hash-nen-uck-iah,* that is, night sun. Moreover, in the language of the Cherokee, *oo-talleh* means husband; *ak-aieh,* woman; *ak-oo-talleh,* wife; *ak-oo-talleech,* to love; *ai-cheh,* mother; and *ai-oo-talleh,* child. Likewise the sun is called *neuto;* night, *sanoy;* and the compound *sanoy-neuto* (as in the language of the Choctaw) is the word for moon. Also noteworthy are certain odd expressions born out of the poverty of the language. In that of the Cherokee *cunne,* a word that serves to denote both arrow and lead, indicates generically a lethal instrument. In fact, it enters as a constituent not only in *Cunne-cune-stiket,* musket bullets; *ail-stee-cunne-heetah,* sword; and *cunne-un-noah,* pipe or tomahawk; but even in *cunne-kowe* and *cunne-yeonah,* [1:267] that is, deerskin and bearskin, as if to say arrow deer and arrow bear. Various other observations could be made on the roots of the words which are omitted for the sake of brevity.

The vast country situated to the southwest of South Carolina was inhabited by the aforementioned and other Indian nations when it was decided, in the year 1733, to establish there a colony for the relief of the poor of England and Ireland, and also in order to give better protection to the Province of Carolina against the invasions of the Spaniards. Many wealthy and philanthropic gentlemen set up a plan to join in a company and contribute a sum of money to transport the poor to America, and they obtained letters patent from the King on the 9th of June 1732 by which they were authorized to carry out their generous idea. This company was composed of 21 persons who took the name of tutors or trustees of the new colony, and they gave it the name of Georgia in honor of King George II. Not satisfied with having contributed large sums themselves, they tried to obtain other benefactors, stimulating them by depositing the money in the public bank of England and by registering the names of the donors in a book. With this help clothing, arms, and agricultural tools were bought for the colonists and the other things necessary for the new settlement were provided. Toward the middle of August of the same year the trustees met for the first time and elected Lord Percival as their president. Among other things they established that the seal of the society should represent the two rivers, Savannah and Altamaha, which formed the boundaries of Georgia, and that [1:268] in the middle there should be a genius with a cap signifying liberty, a spear in one hand, and in the other a cornucopia with the legend *Colonia Georgia Aug.*; and on the other side several silkworms spinning a cocoon with the motto: *Non sibi sed aliis.* The following November 116 colonists[139] embarked at Gravesend with James Oglethorpe, one of the trustees, and at the beginning of the next year 1733 they arrived at Charleston, where they were received in the most friendly fashion by Mr. Johnson, then governor of Carolina. Oglethorpe, accompanied by William Bull, left for Yamacraw in order to visit the region, and finding a fine height on the shores of the Savannah, he had some small houses built there as best he could, giving to the nascent city the name of the river. Having determined the dwelling place of the new colonists, Oglethorpe turned his attention to dealing with the Indians. Gathering together a number of the so-called Upper Creek and some Yamacraw (tribes that were living there at that time), he passed out many gifts among them and peacefully negotiated the cession of the land. The meeting over, he left for England again, taking with him Tomochichi, the chief or king, with his wife and various other Indians. These, after being presented at the Court and given presents by it, as also by the nobles and citizens, returned to America, passing on to their compatriots a very good idea of the power of the English.

Since the first shipment of beggars collected in England was a mixture of men just as lazy and useless in America as they were before in Europe, the trustees decided to transport there more industrious men who [1:269] would make the new colony flourish. To that end they cast their eyes upon the Germans and Scottish highlanders as sturdy people fit to undertake and bear the labors of breaking new soil. Therefore, after the publication in 1734 at Inverness in Scotland of the terms that were being offered to the new inhabitants of Georgia, 130 Scottish highlanders left for the new province, where they settled on the shores of the Altamaha, building there a village to which they gave the name of New Inverness. At about the same time 170 Germans embarked with the Oglethorpe who had founded the colony, arrived in America, and scattered over various regions. Hence, Georgia got 570 immigrants within three years, 400 of whom English subjects and 170 foreigners. On this trip Oglethorpe brought with him a number of cannon intending to erect forts to protect the frontiers. Upon arriving, he set one up near the Indians, to which he gave the name of Augusta, and another, that he called Frederica, near the Altamaha River.

The obstructed transportation of negroes and other coercive laws imposed by the trustees had long retarded the progress of the colony when it was invaded by Spanish arms in 1742.[140] Oglethorpe (who could be called [1:270] the father of this province), appointed general on that occasion, forced the Spaniards, notwithstanding his inferior forces, to withdraw and reestablished peace there. The peace was broken again ten years later by a certain Bosomworth, an Englishman by birth, who had married an Indian queen and claimed a large stretch of land in Georgia. When this was not granted to him, he incited the Indians to wage a war against the English that lasted until 1762. It was then that the trustees, recognizing the weakness of their administration, ceded the province to the King, who established there a form of government like that of the other colonies.

The situation of Georgia having thus improved, its borders were better protected, when, upon the termination of the war in Canada, the two Floridas were ceded to England at the peace treaty. At that time disagreements arose between the Carolinians and the Georgians as to that portion of country situated between the Altamaha and St. Marys Rivers, which had been granted by the governor to various inhabitants of that province, since according to the concession made by Charles II it belonged to proprietors of South Carolina. However, as a result of the remonstrances made by the Georgians to the Crown of England, the boundary of Georgia was extended south of the Savannah River to the St. Marys, ceding them the region contested by the Carolinians.

[1:271] With these new acquisitions, and with the advantages of a more liberal government, Georgia attained in a few years a better situation. Exportations, which in 1763 had been only 7,500 barrels of rice, 9,633 pounds of indigo, and 1,250 bushels of corn, along with deer and beaver skins, pitch, resin, supplies, and lumber came to no more than £27,021 sterling, in only 10 years amounted to £121,677. Then when the disturbances and the consequent civil war broke out, and since Georgia took part in the confederation, it suffered a great deal from devastations by both parties until, with the attainment of independence, it set itself up as a new state and published its own constitutions.[141]

Division of the State, the Government, Population, Commerce, and Agriculture of Georgia

[1:272] The first division of Georgia was into parishes that took their names from the saint to whom the church was dedicated; but this system was then changed, and the state was divided into 11 counties under the following names: 1) Wilkes County, which includes the country ceded north of the Ogeechee River; 2) Richmond, formerly called St. Paul Parish; 3) Burke, once St. George Parish; 4) Effingham County, in which are found the Parish of St. Matthew and the upper part of that of St. Philip above the Canoochee River; 5) Chatham County, which includes the Parish of Christ Church and the lower part of that of St. Philip: 6) Liberty County, formed from the Parishes of St. John, St. Andrew, and St. James; 7) Glynn, made up from the Parishes of St. David and St. Patrick; 8) Camden County, in which are the Parishes of St. Thomas and St. Mary; and 9) Washington, 10) Greene, and 11) Franklin, recently established in the western regions and so named in honor of the three great [1:273] defenders of American liberty.

The government established after the Revolution is absolutely democratic, and the fundamental laws and the constitutions were drawn up by the people summoned for that purpose. The representatives of the various counties, who are elected each year, make up the only legislative body, namely, the House of Assembly. The election is carried out by ballot in each county, and the right to vote belongs to all the freemen over 20 years of age who own £20 sterling, are liable to pay taxes, and who have lived in the state at least 6 months. Then in order to be elected as a representative, one is required to have lived there 12 months, to be of the Protestant faith, and to own 250 acres of land or to be worth £250 sterling. There are 30 of these representatives, that is, 14 for Liberty County, 4 for the city and port of Savannah, 2 for Sunbury, and 10 more for the rest of the counties taken together.[142] The elections of the representatives takes place each year on the first Tuesday in December, and on the first Tuesday of the following January those elected meet in the city of Augusta in order to proceed with the selection of the governor and the members of the Council—a choice that is made from among the representatives, two of whom are chosen as councillors for each county.

The House of Representatives which, as I have already said, is the sole legislative body, has the power to pass any law not contrary to the Constitutions and to revoke those that turn out to be harmful. The new laws are read three times in the Assembly, but after [1:274] the second reading are sent to the Executive Council for review. This Council must return them with its observations in writing within the space of five days. Its members always vote by counties and not as individuals, and they have the right to select their own president. The governor, who is also the supreme commander of the land and sea troops, has the title of Honorable, remains in office only one year, and cannot be reelected until two years have elapsed. To him is entrusted the executive power, always with the approval of the Council and in accordance with the laws and constitutions of the state. He convenes the Assembly in case of need and can always preside over the Council, except when it is busy with the review of the laws and orders of the Assembly. In the new Constitutions complete freedom of the press is allowed, and any priest or minister is excluded from all public offices. The state seal was changed, too, and instead of that already described, another was formed representing on one side an open volume on which one reads, "The Constitution of the State of Georgia," with the motto *Pro bono publico,* and on the other an elegant house with various habitations in the midst of country and fields with livestock grazing on them, with a winding river, and the exergue *Deus nobis haec otia facit.*

At the end of the war only 10,000 inhabitants could be counted in Georgia, [1:275] a number that increased in a few years to 30,000 because of constant emigration from other states. Settlements exist only between the Savannah and Ogeechee Rivers and in some areas of the Oconee, the other regions further south being still almost completely uninhabited. Since the first colonists who went there from Europe were poor and incapable of undertaking extensive agriculture, they settled along the Savannah River, where they occupied the high, sandy terrain and eked out a wretched subsistence from corn. The trustees also planned to try the cultivation of olives, grapes, and the mulberry. I don't know too well whether the propagation of the first few plants was promoted or whether it proved fruitless, but it is probable that if the cultivation was ever begun, it was very quickly abandoned with no trace of it remaining today. The same is not true of the mulberry, of which various plants exist (as I have already said) even at the present time. After the cession of the province to the Crown it was permitted to transport negroes there, and from then on indigo and rice began to be raised.

The terrain along the seashore and for more than 100 miles toward the west presents a sterile, sandy plain covered with pines in the places distant from the rivers; but on both sides of these there is a low and inundated portion, sometimes quite extensive, and since this is composed of a black, light soil mixed with rotted plants, it is excellent for vegetation. There rice is raised in the places flooded with the help of the high tide, and indigo is sown where the [1:276] land cannot be so easily irrigated. On the barren and sandy highlands they plant corn and sweet potatoes, which serve as food for the negroes. On the other hand in the interior regions the dry and clayey soil is planted to tobacco and corn, which, favored by the fertility of the soil and the warmth of the sun, grow there perfectly. In addition to these valuable products with which Georgia abounds, the lumber business is quite respectable, principally on account of the live oak and black pine, which are reduced to beams and boards by numerous sawmills. Because of these important lines of business activity, the nascent province was already beginning to flourish when, overwhelmed by the troops of both armies, it saw its way to further progress interrupted. For a long time it suffered military devastations which, by destroying homes and possessions and by stripping away or killing the slaves, had by the end of the war almost reduced it to the original state of uncultivated country, until the war finally ended and farming resumed. Nevertheless, since most of the landowners had undergone great losses, the progress of agriculture is very slow and commerce languishes badly.

The inhabitants of Savannah and of other regions not far from the sea, being for the most part native Georgians, are little different (as I have already observed) from their neighbors the Carolinians. But on the other hand those of the interior near Augusta are almost all Virginians, who, drawn by the fertility and the low price of land, left their already cultivated plantations in the [1:277] salubrious climate of the mountains of Virginia. They came to bury themselves in the swamps of Georgia and to subject themselves to the heavy labors of a new agriculture, an effort from which they extract little reward because of the difficulty of transporting goods to the too distant sea ports and the excessive price of European merchandise. The rather unhappy state of their new situation is rendered even worse by the idle life they lead, since, forgetting about agriculture, which was the purpose of their emigration, they occupy themselves with little else but card games and horse races, the usual amusements of Virginians. To the latter the people flock. The artisans make bets on one horse or another which amount to many days' pay, and the horse owners sometimes lose sums exceeding the annual income from their lands. And yet, while this money is being dissipated to the detriment of the wealth and morals of those involved, one can't get them to support public works of the greatest usefulness. Two hundred guineas would be more than enough to dig a canal, which, by diverting the stagnant waters of the lagoons and discharging them into the river, would make the air of the city of Augusta much more healthful and that land fit for cultivation. But it has proved impossible to find capital for such a salutary and profitable enterprise.

If the inhabitants of Augusta are given to idleness and amusements and care little or nothing about their interests, those of the more western regions have even more dissolute ways. Since they are made up of a mixture of people of various [1:278] countries (not infrequently fugitives from the clutches of justice), they can't bear to remain within the limits necessary for a controlled system of society and abandon themselves to the most unrestrained license, in proof of which it will suffice to cite the following case. A famous horse thief, who stole various horses during the war, went to Wilkes County in Georgia in the spring of 1786, where he was recognized by one of the inhabitants and put in prison. When examined by the judges, he was absolved as guilty only of crimes anterior to the peace treaty, in which it is stipulated that all offenses perpetrated by the Whigs and Tories during the war must be pardoned. He was released in accordance with the verdict, and then a number of those people under the leadership of Colonel C______ (well known in America for his turbulent character) seized him again and took him outside of the city of Golphintown to hang him. Upon reaching the place where they intended to carry out this horrid function, they were stopped in their plan by the lack of rope, and they sent a man on horseback to the nearby city to get some. Meantime the wretch tried to escape by flight, but he was very quickly caught by some of the party, who struck him several times in the head with sabers, and he was again put in chains. The news having meanwhile spread about in the city, Mr. Pendelton, attorney general for the state, who happened to be at that time with the judges in that city, moved by such an illegal and barbaric behavior, went to the spot, and arguing for the life of the poor fellow they wanted to sacrifice, with great difficulty succeeded finally in persuading them to reconsign the man to [1:279] prison, where he died the following morning from the wounds received.

It will seem strange that such an assault should remain unpunished in a country which has just published Constitutions most favorable to personal security; but that confirms all the more the defect of the present system which, by limiting too much the executive power, renders it incapable of controlling an already vicious multitude. In spite of these political vices, it is certain that Georgia, aided by the great fertility of a good part of its soil, will in time be able to equal the richest states of United America, especially if it corrects its system of government, and if the inhabitants of Augusta put an end to the disagreements they have with those of Savannah and imitate them instead in being more industrious. But if the multitude continues to nurture itself on strange notions of conquest, if the most sacred treaties with the Indians are broken and land not ceded by them is invaded,[143] if the Spaniards of Florida are provoked by immature pretensions,[144] we shall see Georgia succumb under the weight of these ills which it might have prevented by wise conduct.

CHAPTER IX

South Carolina

Trip from Augusta to the Border of North Carolina

[1:280]

I LEFT AUGUSTA on the 22nd of April, crossed the Savannah again, and then found a good road that took me to the two lakes called "of the Cherokee" from the name of the Indians who used to live there, near the second of which is the inn of a certain Cook. When I entered this dwelling, they asked me whether I was coming from Augusta, and since I answered "Yes," they almost drove me out of the house, inasmuch as the proprietor, as well as his wife and four of his daughters had not yet had smallpox. This disease was very widespread in Augusta, the streets could be seen full of persons afflicted by smallpox, and the people of the surrounding area did not dare to enter the city. However, on the basis of my protestation that I had visited no diseased individual, he received me in his dwelling.

[1:281] Smallpox was introduced into North America from the time that the Europeans began to land there. But after that period, since the inhabitants were scattered, this disease could not become general, so that there were whole populations among whom it had not yet been introduced. Isolated houses were built in maritime cities where those afflicted by smallpox were kept, and the greatest care was taken to keep this scourge of the human race from spreading. During the war the increased movement of people made it much more frequent, so that it was introduced into even the most interior regions, and thereafter inoculation became so general that when smallpox appears, all those who have not had it have themselves inoculated. This is what happened in the city of Augusta, where I myself saw a great many grown men inoculated, who nevertheless continued walking about the streets and attending to their usual occupations. The method that they use is the following: after a preliminary light purge, the inoculating is done by placing the pus in a little incision on the arm, and this operation is often performed by a mother on her children with a light pricking with a needle. It is not dangerous, according to what I was told, and after three days of fever those inoculated take up their ordinary manner of living; exercising no other precaution beyond that of eating wholesome food.

The following day I traveled through a hilly country whose soil is planted to tobacco, grain, and oats, and where one could see blooming in the woods the calycanthus, the large-flowered dogwood, chionanthus, the halesia, and honeysuckle [1:282] with blood-colored flowers.[1] In the course of this day I covered only 15 miles, arriving at the plantation of Mr. Simkins. The large number of cows and horses that could be seen about his home indicated the wealth of the proprietor, although the shabby house did not correspond to the value of the plantation. Mr. Simkins was a member of the Assembly of South Carolina for District Ninety-Six,[2] and according to American custom was called Esquire, a title given in America to those who have held some public office. He received me very cordially, and engaging me in conversation, told me that his plantation had been ruined by the British troops who had burned down the house located on a pretty height near the present habitation, which was serving as a temporary shelter.

From Mr. Simkins' plantation to the village of Ninety-Six, the distance of 27 miles, the country is barren and produces only black oak and pine, so that one encounters no dwelling except in the vicinity of the aforementioned village. There one finds two separate streams under the name of Ninety-Six Creek and Hendless Creek, which could not be crossed by carriage at that time, since they were very full. However, directed by a farmer, we found a narrow path that took us where there was a tree across the [1:283] first stream, and we carried our things over this natural bridge by hand, making the horses swim with the carriage to the other side. In this manner we crossed also the second stream. Ninety-Six, so called from being 96 miles from Fort Prince George and from Keowee, the easternmost villages of the Cherokee nation, is located on a charming hill five miles from the Saluda River and about 170 northwest of Charleston. The old village was situated on the opposite hill and was destroyed in 1780 by the British, who erected fortifications there. The American general Greene laid siege to it in the summer of 1781, and the British garrison, inferior in force, was about to surrender, when an American woman managed to take to the fort a letter informing the commandant that Lord Rawdon was approaching with troop support. With this news the British held the place until the Americans, fearing that they would have to fight too many of the enemy, raised the siege. Shortly thereafter the British themselves evacuated it in order to withdraw to Orangeburg, where they were in a better situation. One can still see the remains of the aforementioned fortifications composed of a ferruginous clay supported by wooden trusses. The new village is composed of some 20 wooden houses and 2 brick buildings, in one of which is held the Court of Justice, and the other serves for a public school of Latin and Greek recently founded there. The country around Ninety-Six is hilly and the soil tough and reddish—excellent for raising tobacco, corn, [1:284] and grain. In a similar terrain, by means of careful culture, grapes produce excellent wines in some parts of Lombardy, and that should succeed better in those regions, where grapevines grow wild in the woods and yield an edible grape. In fact such an attempt was made by some French Protestants, who planted some vineyards in the village of New Bordeaux not far from Ninety-Six, but this cultivation was completely abandoned during the disturbed times of the war.

I left Ninety-Six on the 28th of April, crossed the Saluda River by boat, forded the Rush River, and the next morning entered a steep, narrow way, cut here and there by deep ruts gouged out by water. Hence I had covered barely six miles when my carriage overturned and both shafts broke. I then went back to the nearest dwelling, at a mile from which there was an industrious blacksmith who promised to have the carriage fixed for me by the following day. Meantime I had to stay in that wretched hut, and, what is more, among persons of the worst reputation, as these forest dwellers are. For that reason I kept going to the blacksmith to urge him on, leaving my servant to watch over my things. During these walks through the woods certain insects called ticks, a kind of *zecca*,[3] would fasten themselves to my body. It is of the shape and size of a red-colored bedbug, and as it runs over one's skin it produces a disgusting tickle. [1:285] If one does not take care to remove it, it buries itself in the skin head and all, and as it sucks blood it swells enormously, taking on then a gleaming ashen color. Two of these insects fastened themselves onto one of my arms, and not noticing it until the following day since their sucking doesn't hurt, I had great difficulty in pulling them off, and they left my skin red and sore for several days.

The master of the house where I was staying had spent the whole morning deer hunting. He was one of those hunters called riflemen because they use rifled muskets; and since they are very skillful at target shooting, they are also called marksmen. Deer are quite common in the southern states, where they can often be seen coming out of the woods and looking out on the roads, and they are no different from those of Europe, varying likewise in the size and location of the branchings of their horns.[4] Their flesh is sold at a low price, and since it is the most common food, it is called venison, that is, game. The Indians smoke the meat and eat it dry this way, using the skins tinted in various colors as adornment for shoes, pockets, bags, and other items that they make. The skins of these animals prepared by the Indians are more esteemed than the others because they take care to stretch them immediately after the animal is killed and to remove painstakingly the flesh [1:286] and fat, so that the hair is much more easily preserved. My host spent the afternoon telling about his prowess as a hunter, never inserting anything that had to do with farming, which showed all the signs of being neglected, since just a few acres of land around the house were planted to corn (which prospers in this fertile soil), the only fruit of his agrarian labors, and which served as food for his poor family. That evening I was not able to refuse the bed of my host, and he with his wife and children stretched out on the floor wrapped up in some woolen blankets.

As soon as dawn broke, the carriage having been fixed, I left as quickly as I could. I had traveled barely 10 miles when I found myself on the shore of a wide, swift river, for crossing which there was neither bridge nor boat. This is called the Enoree which, joining Broad River, forms with the Saluda the Congaree at the spot called Friday's Ferry. A short distance away I saw a mill, and directing myself there, the miller told me that in that neighborhood there lived a man who ferried travelers across the river in a little canoe. I sent a message to the home pointed out to me, and a husky young woman appeared who took me across to the other shore in the canoe. Then, with considerable difficulty, she transported the carriage, after having removed the wheels. And with a third trip she carried these across, too, pulling after her the swimming horses. We hadn't gone even four miles when we arrived at the shores of the Tyger River. This one was really not so swift and deep, [1:287] but since there wasn't even a canoe, we had to think about fording it. My servant, an Irishman I had taken on at Augusta, had the bright idea of tying our things to the upper part of the carriage; and getting up on horseback, he entered the river, while I followed with the other horse. Although the water was so deep that it came halfway up my thigh and the carriage was immersed above the seat, we reached the other shore safely. Toward evening we reached Broad River, which we crossed by boat at Fishdam Ford.

Three miles from Broad River there is Sandy Creek, a place known as a nest of thieves and scoundrels. In this country, as in other parts of the United States, one often encounters turkeys[5] in the woods. This bird, one of the most valuable among those domesticated by the efforts of man, is no different in its natural state as far as the flesh is concerned, except that it is darker and has a more exquisite taste. In Charleston they are sold daily in the market. If they are captured alive, they easily become used to being with domestic turkeys, and they propagate in coops. Crossing the two branches of Fishing Creek, I arrived at the home of Colonel Pattens, who, contrary to most of the other inhabitants, received me with every courtesy. He had dinner prepared for me, after which we had the company of two Indians of the Catawba tribe. These Indians, who up until the time of the first settlements [1:288] lived in peace with the Europeans, were reduced to a small number of individuals before the war. They used to live near the Catawba River, where they owned 40,000 acres of land reserved for them by the King of England. During the war they sided with the Americans; hence upon the arrival of the British their village was destroyed and they scattered into the various states. After the peace they returned to the shores of the Catawba and established themselves 10 miles away from their old dwelling place on a stretch of land ceded to them by the State of South Carolina. There are about 200 of them. They raise a little corn and some vegetables. They even go about begging in the neighborhood, getting drunk whenever they can.

Before leaving Colonel Pattens, I got information about crossing the Catawba River. I was told that there were two routes, the shorter of which is that of Old Nation's Ford, where one fords the river, and the other longer one goes where one crosses the river by boat. I was advised, however, to choose the former, since there the water is not very deep and the bed of the river is quite level and smooth; and so I took that direction. After traveling about four miles, we arrived at a plain cleared of trees and near the river, on which formerly stood the village of the Catawba Indians. When we saw that this wide and majestic river had a swift current, we were taken aback for some time. But since we were in a place far from habitations, and trusting the information we had received, we got the carriers ready as at the Tyger and entered [1:289] the river the same way. At first the water came up only to the horses' saddles; but the depth increased when we reached the middle, the carriage began to totter, it toppled into the water, and I saw it carried away immediately by the current. I tried to approach it in order to right it, but I found that impossible. Then, I don't know whether luckily or unluckily, the harness snapped and the carriage broke loose, which my courageous Irishman quickly grabbed by one of the shafts. The depth kept increasing, the water came up almost to my waist, and the swift current was carrying me toward some rocks. Seeing, therefore, that I couldn't give my servant any help, I turned to face the current and tried to gain the shore. All the efforts of my horse were barely sufficient to overcome the rush of the water, but his strength did hold out, until, finding himself where the water was less impetuous, panting, he finally carried me to land. Although I was safe, I found myself, however, alone in the middle of the woods, barelegged, and fearful for the life of my Irishman, so that I ran at once to look for some habitation in order to send him help. I had gone scarcely a mile when I perceived a little house on an elevation. Reaching that place and having asked the owner for help, I ran back to the river without waiting for the people that he promised to send me. A short distance from the disembarkation point I found the other horse with broken harness, and hearing no answer to my calls, I feared that my Irishman was lost. Then, following the shore through the underbrush, I saw him standing in his undershirt in water up to his neck, one hand fastened to a branch of a tree, [1:290] holding back the carriage with the other. I shouted to him that help was coming soon, and in fact shortly afterwards two men arrived who helped him by throwing him ropes, and I recovered the carriage with my things, too—though not without much labor. I lost only a fine collection of dried plants that I had made in the two Carolinas and Georgia, carried away because it was not in the valise. The books and journals, although they were in a leather saddlebag, were so soaked that I was afraid that they were useless, and almost the whole day was spent drying out my baggage. Finally I left, and after eight miles arrived at the Boundary House, on the dividing line between the two Carolinas.

Location, and Former Condition of South Carolina

[1:291] South Carolina extends from 32° to 35° latitude and 78° to 90° longitude from London. It is bounded to the east by the sea, to the west by the Mississippi, to the north its borders with North Carolina are determined in part by the Little River, so-called, and in part by a straight line that extends to the northwest from Little River as far as 35° latitude, and then bending to the west ends at the Mississippi. Finally, it is separated from Georgia to the south by the Savannah River, which, being formed of two branches, one called the Tugaloo and the other the Keowee, gave rise to the dispute still alive between the Georgians and the Carolinians as to which of the two branches should serve as the boundary. If the Keowee were that, as the Georgians would like, nothing would be left to South Carolina in the western parts except a narrow strip of territory, since the source of the Keowee extends beyond latitude 34° 30′, whereas the borders of Carolina reach only to 35°.

Its main rivers are the Savannah, the Santee, and the Pee Dee. The Savannah, which, as I said, is formed by the two rivers, the Tugaloo and the [1:292] Keowee, flows from northwest to southeast and empties into the sea in Georgia a short distance from the city that from it took the name of Savannah. The Santee is formed from the Wateree and Congaree rivers, the first of which comes down from North Carolina, and toward its source is called the Catawba; and the other is formed by the union of the Broad and Saluda rivers. Lastly, the Pee Dee, called Yadkin in North Carolina, is the one that passes near Georgetown. All these rivers, as likewise the other minor ones such as the Coosawhatchie, the Combahee, the Wackcamaw, the Ashley, the Black River, the Stono, etc., flow in their upper reaches amid hills of clayey soil, but descending from there they expand into a sandy plain, and winding about almost at the level of the land, they spread out all around and form, as in Georgia, marshes and deposits that turn out to be very fertile. The mountains that cut across South Carolina from southwest to northeast are a part of the Appalachians, and they separate the regions cultivated by Europeans from those still inhabited by Indians.

The Upper Creek, so called, who are very numerous and good warriors, still live today in the western parts. To the east near the shores of the Mississippi there are the Choctaw, and to the northwest the Cherokee, whose villages are the closest to the present borders of Carolina. Between the Cherokee and the Choctaw there is the nation of the Chickasaw, whose territory extends to a point near the Mississippi. Finally, in the northernmost regions there live, mixed with Europeans, the few individuals descended from the once [1:293] powerful nation of the Catawba. Richard Blome speaks as follows[6] about the nation (probably the Creek), that used to inhabit that part of Carolina occupied by the first colonies:

> The English (so he says) have a perfect Friendship with the natives, and the Proprietors[7] have taken care that no injustice shall be done them; a particular Court of Judicature compos'd of the soberest and disinterested Persons being established by their order, to determine all differences that shall happen between the English and them. They are a People of a ready wit, and though illiterate, are generally found to be of a good understanding. For their keeping an account of Time, they make use of Hieroglyphicks, and instruct their Children in such matters as relate to their Family and Country, which is preserved from one generation to another. Where a Battel hath been fought, or a Colony settled, they raise a small Pyramid of Stone, consisting of the number of the slain, or those setled at the Colony: and for Religious Rites, as Sacrifices, Burials, and the like, they make round Circles with Straws or Reeds, by the differing placing whereof, it is known for what it is made. . . .
>
> They are generally well proportioned, and . . . generally of a good and honest meaning, [1:294] being no ways addicted to Vice or any Extravangancies, and always content themselves with a mean Diet and Apparel for their present subsistance, without taking much care for the time to come. They are much addicted to Mirth and Dancing, and to Acts of Courage and Valour, which they prefer above all other

> Virtues, and are therefore almost continually engaged in War, one Town or Village against another. . . . By which means several Nations have been in a manner quite destroyed since our first Settlement at Ashley River; which keeps them so thin of People, and so divided among themselves, that were they less affected to the English, yet they would have no reason to entertain the least apprehensions of Danger from them, being[8] already too strong for all the Indians that inhabit within five hundred miles of them. . . .
>
> They worship one God as the creator of all things, whom they call Okee, and to whom their High Priest offers Sacrifice, but (as we said of other Indian tribes) believes that he hath something else to do than to mind humane affairs; which they fancy he commits to the Government of less Deities, that is, to good and evil Spirits, to whom their inferior Priests make their Devotions and Sacrifices. They believe the transmigration of Souls; and when any of them dies, their Friends inter with their Corps Provisions and Household-stuff for their Elizium Shades, which they imagine to be beyond the Mountains. . . . They are very superstitious in their Marriages, and from a strange kind of Belief which is entertained amongst them, that from four Women only all Mankind sprang: They divide themselves into like number of Tribes, and have four Burying-places; believing it to be a wicked and ominous thing to mingle [1:295] their Bodies even when dead.

The history of European settlements[9] in this region goes back to the year 1662, although Walter Raleigh tried as early as 1584 to found a colony there without success. Equally fruitless was the attempt made in 1590 by the French Protestants, who, under the protection of Admiral Coligny, had built a fort on the May River in this part of Carolina, at that time called Florida. Some Protestants had already gone there to prepare an asylum for their brethren if they should be forced to flee from Europe. Since this did not come about, the nascent colony was destroyed by some Spaniards from Florida, who were subsequently killed by the Indians. The thought of establishing colonies was carried out, as has been said, in 1662 by Charles II, King of England, who granted this region to eight English gentlemen, limiting its confines from 31° to 36° latitude. This concession was confirmed two years later, and the borders were then extended to 29°, and from the seashore to the Pacific Ocean. Edward Count of Clarendon; George Duke of Albemarle; Lord William Craven; Lord John Berkley; Lord Anthony Ashley; Sir George Carteret; and Sir John Colleton were declared by the King absolute lords and proprietors of this immense regions, the sovereign dominion being reserved for the Crown. Following upon such an ample concession, the proprietors thought to found a colony there, and to form a system of government, to lay out which was selected the celebrated [1:296] John Locke. This contained 120 articles, a number of which are reported here and will serve to give an adequate idea of it.

The province was divided into counties, each of which included eight seigniories, eight baronies, and four tracts, divided each into six colonies. The seigniories, like the baronies and colonies, contained 12,000 acres each. The seigniories belonged to the proprietors, the baronies to the nobility of the region, and the colonies, which contained three fifths of the land, were distributed among the other inhabitants. In this manner he pretended to preserve a certain equality in the government. The nobility in each county was composed of a landgrave and two caciques, who had the right to be members of Parliament, since the former possessed four baronies and the latter two each. All these titles were hereditary, and in the absence of males the eldest female succeeded, and her descendants. At first 12 counties were established, and the first landgraves and caciques were elected by the proprietors and the Palatine Court.[10] It was arranged by the constitutions that as the population increased, 12 more colonies would be formed and a corresponding number of landgraves and caciques would be elected. The eldest of the eight proprietors was called Palatine, and the other seven enjoyed the titles of Admiral, Chamberlain, Chancellor, Constable, Supreme Judge, Grand Administrator, [1:297] and Treasurer, each of which had his own tribunal.

The Palatine presided over the Palatine Court, consisting of the eight proprietors, which had the right of convening the Parliament, pardoning criminals, electing officers, and disposing of the public treasure, with the power of suspending the execution of the orders of the Grand Council and Parliament. The Court of the Chancellery, consisting of the Chancellor and six members with the title of Vice Chancellors, put the seal of the Palatinate on all concession of territory, commissions, and acts of the Palatine Court, and had twelve assistants called Registrars. The Chancellor was head of the Parliament and president of the Grand Council. That of the Supreme Judge, consisting of the latter and 6 judges of the bench, judged all civil and criminal cases, and had 12 assistants called Masters. The tribunal of the Constable was composed of this latter and 6 marshalls, along with 12 assistants with the title of general lieutenants to attend to military affairs. The one of the Admiral, with 6 Consuls and 12 assistants called Proconsuls had the inspection of the ports, docks, and navigable rivers as far as the tide goes, and all the other jurisdictions pertaining to the navy. The Treasury was directed by the Grand Treasurer, and by 6 Vice Treasurers and 12 assistants called Auditors. The Grand Administrator held his tribunal composed of 6 Comptrollers and 12 Engineers or assistants, who regulated commerce, manufactures, public buildings, and matters having to do with water and the measurement of lands. Finally, the last [1:298] council, namely, that of the Grand Chamberlain, with 6 Vice Chamberlains and 12 Executors, supervised ceremonies, heraldry, styles, dress, and games, keeping the records of births, deaths, and marriages.

The Palatine, along with 7 other Proprietors and the 42 councilors of the 7 tribunals, formed the Grand Council in which were settled the controversies that might arise in the separate tribunals, matters of peace or war were decided, and alliances and treaties were made. The Grand Council met the first Tuesday of each month and prepared the agenda that was to be proposed in the Parliament. The Parliament was composed of the Proprietors or their deputies, the landgraves and caciques, and of one inhabitant of each precinct chosen from the landholders. The latter had to have at least 500 acres of land, and no one owning less than 50 acres could vote for his election. This body representing the nation decided all those matters that were not reserved for the Grand Council as above. The new Parliament met on the first Monday of November every other year in the capital city, unless it was otherwise arranged by the Palatine Court. In order to be considered a national, one had to own land in the state, and profess the existence of God and the necessity of a public religion. The ministers of the Anglican Church, the only one recognized by them as true and orthodox, were maintained at public expense and received their keep by order of Parliament. This last article, according to the authors who [1:299] wrote the history of Carolina, was added by one of the Proprietors against the sentiment of Locke.

In spite of the fact that these Constitutions were drawn up in 1663, nothing was done until the year 1667, when the Proprietors fitted out a ship and sent Captain Sayle to examine the coast of Carolina. He was carried by a storm to the Bahama Islands, noted their situation, and particularly that of Providence; and he decided that it, too, had to be ceded to the Proprietors in order to defend the new colony against the attacks of the Spaniards. He then looked over Carolina, where he found many navigable rivers and a level country all covered with forests. Upon returning to England, he made a favorable report on it, and in accordance with his observations about the Bahama Islands, not only these islands but all the islands situated between 22° and 27° of latitude were granted to the Proprietors by the King.

Subsequently, in the year 1699, the said William Sayle sailed from England with two ships on which were many adventurers who were provided with clothing, furniture, manufacturing and agricultural tools, and food by the Proprietors. Although this expedition cost about £12,000 sterling, the number of colonists transported was not considerable, nor was it sufficient for self-defense when necessary against the multitude of Indians who inhabited those immense forests. It is not known exactly where Captain Sayle landed. It is known only that, not satisfied with the first location, he moved further south and chose a point of [1:300] land situated at the confluence of the two rivers, where he laid the foundations of a city called Charlestown in honor of the King. To the two rivers were attached the names of Ashley and Cooper, from that of Lord Ashley Cooper, one of the Proprietors.

In the year 1671 many pilgrims, fleeing from persecution in England, took refuge in Carolina, where they received land to cultivate from the Proprietors. Following their example, a number of Dutchmen from New York who were unhappy with the government of the Duke of York, went to Carolina on the English boats *Blessing* and *Phoenix* and founded on the banks of the Ashley the city of Jamestown, which was destroyed a few years later. New colonies of Protestants arrived from England in 1685 under the reign of James II, and shortly thereafter France, too, contributed toward populating this province by the revocation of the Edict of Nantes.

The intricate form of government established by the philosopher Locke, the continual wars with the Indians, the Spaniards, and the French of Florida, the disturbances arisen because the Anglican religion had been declared dominant, and, finally the unhealthful quality of the climate, would have reduced this colony to nothing in a few years if the Proprietors, moved by the entreaties of the inhabitants and much more by the continual disorders, had not determined to cede the Province to the Crown. This occurred in 1729, at which time an act of the English Parliament was promulgated by which seven of the Proprietors then living ceded to the King not only the government of the Province but also their possessions for the sum of £7500 sterling. [1:301] Only Lord Carteret, the eighth of the Proprietors, in ceding the government of Carolina, wished to reserve for himself, with his heirs and successors, the ownership of the lands with which he was invested by the King.

Carolina was divided at once into two provinces under the name of North and South, and new Constitutions were drawn up much more conformant to those of England and the other American colonies and better suited to promote the flourishing of that region. The new government consisted of a governor, selected by the King, who was the head of the executive power and of the troops, and had that portion of legislative power that belongs to the King of England. The Council was chosen by the King to sustain the prerogatives of the Crown, and the Assembly, composed of the representatives of the people and elected by them, had the rights of the House of Commons. It was up to the governor, as circumstance dictated, to convene, extend, or dissolve the assemblies; he had the power of veto over the bills of both houses, and the bills that were confirmed by him were sent to England for royal approbation.

After this fortunate revolution, emigration from various parts of Europe increased. In 1733 a certain Purry, native of Neuchâtel, who had already been in Carolina, offered his services to the government in transporting there a colony, and he was extended £400 sterling for every 100 emigrants and an adequate expanse of terrain. A little later he returned with 170 Swiss, who went to America and founded Purysburg on the Savannah River, since the government had granted them 40,000 [1:302] acres to cultivate. Then in 1737 there was established another colony, of Irish, who built the city of Williamsburg on the shores of the Santee River. Beyond these almost continual emigrations, the discovery of indigo[11] (a plant much used in dyeing), which in the year 1745 was recognized as among those native to Carolina, served in no small degree to cause this province to flourish. It was very quickly cultivated, and the harvest was so great in just two years that a large quantity of it was sent to Europe. Furthermore, the cultivation of rice, which, although begun in 1730, had never been very extensive, kept increasing and undergoing improvements.

Since the cession of the two Floridas made (as was said above) by France to England after the Canadian war had removed the fear of invasion, it occurred to the government to encourage emigration from Europe. Two territories of 48,000 acres each were designated, one called Mecklenburg, on the Savannah, and the other Londonderry, on the Santee, to be divided up among the new colonists, 100 acres to be given for every man and 50 for every woman or child. Among the many adventurers who went to populate Carolina, there were from 500 to 600 inhabitants of the Palatinate. Enticed by a certain Stumpel, formerly an officer in the Prussian troops, who had promised them the protection of the government, they had come with him to England. But afterwards, abandoned by that fellow, who realized that he was in no position to keep the promises he had made, [1:303] they were about to starve to death when the government learned about their sad plight and shipped them off in 1764 to Carolina; and they settled in the territory of Londonderry. The following year, 1765, Charleston counted about 6000 white inhabitants and 8000 negroes. In the whole province the former were calculated to be upwards of 40,000 and the latter 80,000 to 90,000. Subsequently the population, commerce and wealth of South Carolina grew steadily, and at the beginning of the revolution it was considered the most opulent of the English colonies.

Present Condition of South Carolina

[1:304] The present division of South Carolina is into 20 parishes and 7 districts. The parishes are: 1) St. Philip and St. Michael's in Charleston; 2) Christ

Church to the southeast of the Wando River; 3) St. John's in Berkley to the south of the Santee; 4) St. Andrew southwest of the Ashley River; 5) St. George in the neighborhood of the Edisto; 6) St. James in Goose Creek between the Ashley and Cooper Rivers; 7) St. Thomas and St. Dennis east of the Cooper River; 8) St. Paul, between the Edisto and Stono Rivers; 9) St. Helena, between the Cosaw and Port Royal Rivers and the ocean; 10) St. James, Santee, to the south of the same river; 11) Prince George, Wynyaw, north of the Santee; 12) All Saints; 13) Prince Frederick, to the north of Black River; 14) St. John, in Colleton between the Stono River and the ocean; 15) St. Peter, north of the Savannah; 16) Prince William, between the Coosewhatchie and Combahee Rivers; 17) St. Stephen, west of the Santee; 18) St. Matthew; 19) Orange; 20) and finally, St. David, near the Pee Dee.

The districts are: 1) Wateree to the east of the river of the same name; 2) Ninety-Six, in the internal regions; 3) Saxe-Gotha, south of the Saluda; 4) Broad and Saluda, which is separated into upper, middle, and lower; [1:305] 5) Broad and Catawba, between the rivers of the same name; 6) New Acquisitions, near the North Carolina border; and 7) Savannah and Edisto, located between the rivers of the same name. I have been told latterly, however, that this distribution has been changed, and that the state has been divided into various counties.

The present governmental system that went into effect in 1778 establishes two legislative bodies,[12] namely, the Senate and the House of Representatives, which together form the General Assembly. The Senate is composed of 29 members chosen every two years from the various parishes and districts. The election is carried out by the people on the last Monday of November, and all the freeholders 21 years of age who recognize the existence of God and a future state of reward or punishment have the right to vote, provided they possess 50 acres of land and have lived in the state for a year. The senators must be 30 years of age, of the Protestant religion, must possess the sum of 20,000[13] Carolina pounds, and have lived at least 5 years in the region. The people elect their representatives in the same manner as the senators and in the following proportion: the 2 Charleston parishes, 30; Prince George, 4; All Saints, 20; Saint Matthew, 3; Orange, 3; and the other 16 parishes, 6 each, which makes 96 in all; the district of Saxe-Gotha and the other between Broad and Saluda, 4 each; the districts of [1:306] Wateree, Ninety-Six, Broad and Catawba, and New Acquisitions, 10 each; and, finally, the district between Savannah and Edisto, 6. Hence, in all they are 192. The representatives must be likewise of the Protestant religion and have lived in the Province at least three years.

At the first session of the General Assembly (composed, as I have said, of the Senate and House of Representatives) a governor, lieutenant governor, and eight councilmen, who remain in office for two years, are chosen by ballot from the members of the Assembly, or even from the people. The governor is the commander of the land and sea forces and head of the executive power. At the end of two years he may be reelected after an interval of four years. The Privy Council is composed of the lieutenant governor and eight councillors, four of whom are changed every two years. This tribunal is consulted by the governor whenever he thinks it necessary and in certain cases specified by the Constitutions. The governor has to keep a record of his actions, in which are indicated the affirmative or negative votes of each member, and this record must be presented to the legislative body whenever either of the two chambers requests it. Laws and decrees may originate in either the Senate or the House of Representatives. They may be changed or modified by each of the two bodies in the following manner: if the House proposes a law, it is examined by the Senate, which approves, rejects, or corrects [1:307] it. If the House agrees completely with the opinion of the Senate, the law is promulgated. If they disagree, it is deferred until opinions are conciliated; and the same happens when the Senate is the first to propose. Provisions regarding taxes and other pecuniary contributions may be proposed only by the House of Representatives, and the Senate may reject the tax, but not change it. The delegates to the General Congress of the United States are six, elected by ballot each year. Among the articles of the Constitutions, two regarding religion are noteworthy, and one about the promulgation of laws. In Article XXI priests or ministers of any sect are excluded from public office in imitation of the Constitutions of New York. In Article XXXVIII only the Protestant Christian is declared to be the dominant religion, into which all the Protestant groups of various names may be incorporated provided they agree to subscribe to the following articles: 1) that there is one eternal God and a future state of reward and punishment; 2) that God is publicly to be worshiped; 3) that the Christian religion is the true one; 4) that the holy Scriptures of the Old and New Testament are books of divine inspiration and that they are the rule of faith and practice; 5) that it is lawful and the duty of every man being thereunto called by those that govern, to bear witness to the truth. In Article XLIV it is ordained that no part of the Constitutions may be changed without previous notice of 90 days to the public, and that no changes may be made in it [1:308] without a majority vote of the members of both the Senate and the House of Representatives.

The capital of this state, called Charleston[14] in honor of Charles II, and founded, as has been said, in 1670, counted already in 1677 200 habitations. It then increased in size until 1740, when fire broke out in a house, spread to the neighboring ones, which were of wood; and in spite of all the efforts of the inhabitants and of the sailors who happened to be in port, more than half of them burned down before the fire could be put out. After this

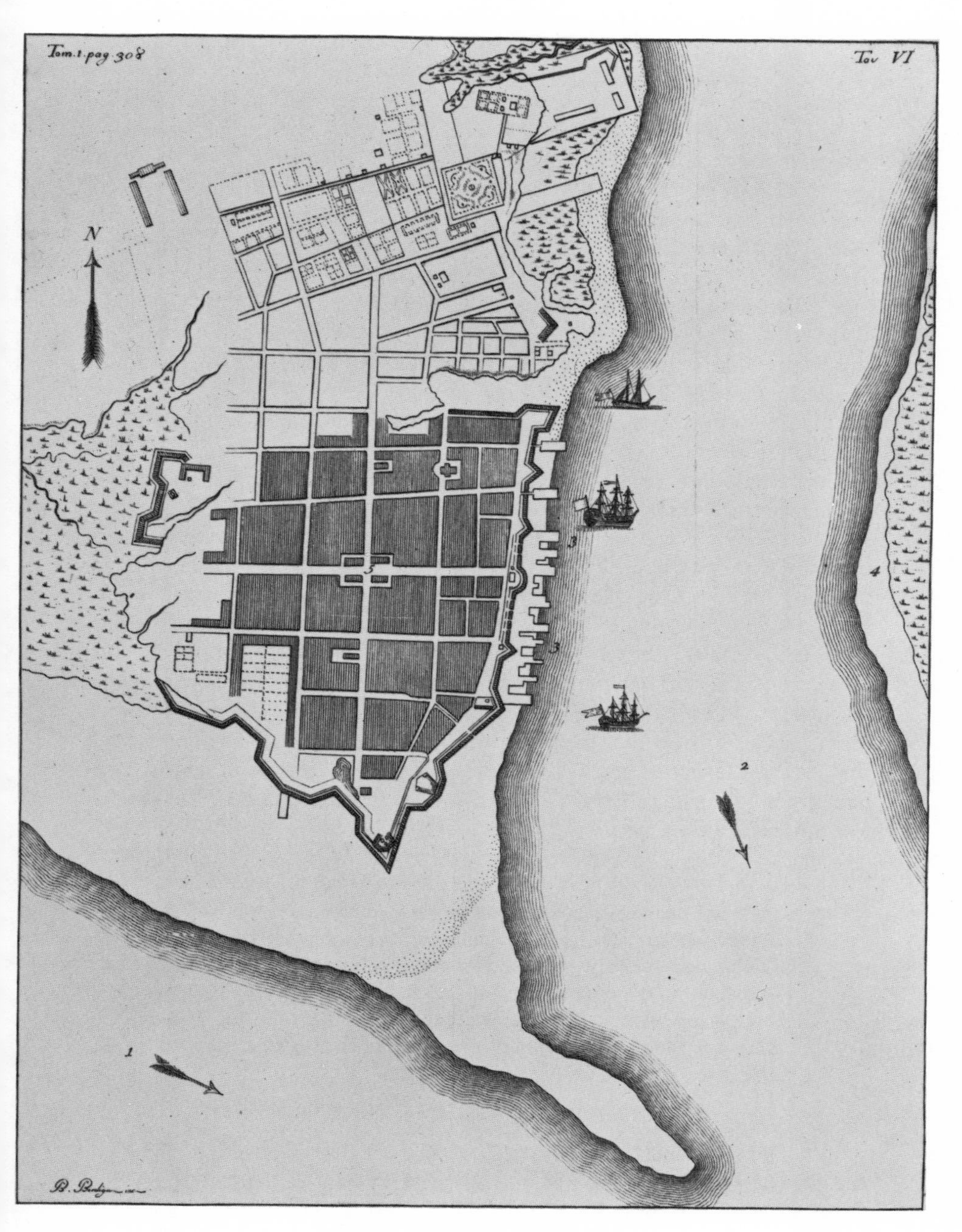

Plate VI. Plan of Charleston.

disaster a terrible hurricane almost entirely destroyed the city again in 1752, water inundated it completely, the houses were left without roofs, big ships that were in the port were dashed against the shore, small boats were tossed way up against the houses, the docks of the port were ruined, and the streets were covered with the wreckage of boats and ships. Many inhabitants lost their lives or were badly injured, and a large quantity of livestock perished in the water. The third and final fatal blow came from the war, [1:309] at which time Charleston had to endure the damages of the siege, when it was taken (on the 11th of May, 1780) by the English generals Clinton and Cornwallis, and further devastation by another fire that burned down many of the finest homes in the most thickly populated section.

Charleston is situated at 32° 40′ latitude on a point formed by two navigable rivers, the Ashley and the Cooper, which join a little above the city and empty into the ocean seven miles below near Sullivan's Island. Along the banks of these rivers there are various wharves where ships can anchor and the necessary warehouses for storing the merchandise. The entrance to the port is defended by Fort Johnson on the little island called James Island and by Fort Moultrie on Sullivan's Island. The streets cut each other at right angles and divide the city into various blocks within which are gardens. Almost at the center of the city at the intersection of two of the widest streets, located at the four corners, are the statehouse, the stock exchange, the market, and a handsome church; and, in the middle, the marble statue representing William Pitt, later Lord Chatham, dressed in a long gown, with the Magna Charta, or English Constitution in his right hand, and in a debating pose. On the pedestal surrounded by iron gates one can read the following inscription [1:310]:

> In grateful memory of his services to his country in general, and to America in particular, the Common's House of Assembly of South Carolina unanimously voted this Statue of the Honorable William Pitt, Esqur., who gloriously exerted himself in defending the Freedom of Americans by promoting the repeal of the Stamp Act in 1766. Time shall sooner destroy this mark of their esteem, than erase from their minds the just sense of his patriotic virtue.

The statehouse, built in 1752, serves both for the Courts of Justice and for the sessions of the Senate and the House of Representatives. The principal churches are those of St. Philip and St. Michael of the Anglicans, adorned by towers with clocks, the church of the Presbyterians, and that of the French Protestants. There are also the congregations of the Anabaptists, the Quakers, the Independents, and a synagogue. The houses number about 1500, many of which are of brick and provided with lightning rods.

The inhabitants of Charleston amount to 5000 whites and 7000 blacks. The leading citizens surpass in luxury and in the imitation of European customs those of the other capitals of the [1:311] United States. Their tables are well provided, and the market abounds in meat and game. Vegetables mature early and copiously, and during the various seasons there are many kinds of excellent fruit, which would be even more abundant if their cultivation were not so careless. In addition, many products are brought there from the Antilles and other southern countries. Oranges come from St. Augustine in Florida, and they are in no way inferior to the renowned Maltese oranges. Coconuts arrive from the Antilles in the winter and spring, at which times they are common in the market. Bananas, the fruit of the *Musa paradisiaca* and *Ananas* arrive in summer, as likewise yams, which are the roots of the *Dioscorea sativa.* These latter are boiled, and they have a flourlike, but almost insipid taste, and differ little from the *Aedos* and the *Tanier,* kinds of roots of other species of *Dioscorea* native to the country. After these plants I cannot omit mentioning two plants transported here and which are now very common in the vicinity of Charleston. The first is the *Melia azedarach,* called there Pride of China, so esteemed for the beauty of its foliage and the fragrance of its flowers. This grows wonderfully in South Carolina and bears every year a large quantity of seeds.[15] The second, quite important, [1:312] is the tallow-tree, transported there from China, and called *Croton sebiferum*[16] by Linnaeus. It resembles very much the black poplar in its leaves and produces clusters of bivalve capsules within which are contained seeds the size of peas. These are covered with a sort of white wax which comes to the surface when melted in boiling water, and, mixed with fat, is used in China for making candles. It is very widespread about Charleston and produces a quantity of seeds, but until now its tallow has not been extracted in America.[17]

The climate of South Carolina is very variable. Spring begins in March and is for the most part dominated by furious winds, especially toward the equinox. April and May are temperate, in June the heat increases, and becomes suffocating in July and August. Then there come from time to time [1:313] violent storms that, by causing a sudden variation, produce many sicknesses. The months of September and October are the most unhealthful, since the air is very hot during the day and cold and humid at night. This is the source of tertian fevers that are regularly suffered by many persons every autumn; pleurisies, and verminous fevers are another scourge of the population that lets up only at the beginning of winter, which, although likewise variable, is the least unhealthful season.[18]

Foremost among the inhabitants of this region are the owners of large plantations in the zones near the sea. These, because of their influence in public bodies, can be regarded as the ones who form the nobility. Some of them, still imbued with the aristocratic distinctions introduced by the complicated system of Locke, insist upon playing up the antiquity of their families, even though their origin is not very remote. They live for the most part in Charleston, visiting their lands two or three times a year; and since most of them [1:314] were raised in England, they resemble the English in their manner of conversing more than they do the other Americans. They are very hospitable, show a great liking for the fine arts, dance, and music, and they imitate European styles—even the most luxurious and extravagant ones. The warm climate brings on a premature adolescence, and one sees there not infrequently lads who behave like full-grown men. However, the degeneration of their bodies is as rapid as their development, for the women do not ordinarily retain their beauty beyond the age of 20, and the men already have white hair and wrinkled skin at 40, or, at the latest, 50. The brevity of life must not, however, be attributed solely to the unhealthful quality of the climate but also to their way of living, since they are not very sensible in their diet, eating a great deal of meat and few vegetables.[19] Likewise, they exercise very little during the day and not infrequently spend their evenings dancing, without worrying about exposing themselves to the damp night air. The abuse of liquors and other excesses also contribute to render more frequent and fatal the diseases that reign alike in the Carolinas, Georgia, and the West Indies. It is a common observation that in the dangerous climes of the American islands the Spaniards enjoy better health than the French, and that the latter are less subject to diseases than the English, which depends only on greater temperance and regularity of living. However, in spite of such gruesome examples, the inhabitants of the cold regions of England, Scotland, and Ireland preserve the same way of life [1:315] in the sweltering atmosphere of the tropics and the equator. The women are dark-complexioned with black and vivacious eyes, so that they seem more like the Spanish than the English from whom they descend; and since they live better regulated lives, they usually live longer.

In addition to the landholders, who live in the capital, there are numerous others who, either for reasons of economy or out of necessity, live all the time in the country on their plantations. The unhealthful location of their plantations has the result that they rarely reach 50 years of age, and they spend their lives in an almost continuous convalescence, in the midst of the sad spectacle of the illnesses of their families. Since they are subject to the bad effects of a bilious humor, they often vent their ill temper on the poor negroes, who, to the shame of mankind, are scarcely reputed to be human beings, and for the slightest failing are exposed to the lash of a slave driver, when the master himself does not take the barbaric pleasure of tormenting them. It is true that some treat their slaves with moderation, but one finds too many of them completely unjust and inhuman. One of them said that he had calculated that, if a negro lived for five years, he repaid amply the money spent to buy him, and consequently he forced his slaves to work at night by the light of pine torches until, exhausted by labor, they were taken by fever and died without any attention. I myself happened to hear an owner, who, to justify his vicious behavior toward negroes, declared without blushing that they were a kind of animal closer to monkeys than [1:316] to man. Those who raise rice and indigo, who are poor, treat their few slaves (if it is possible) with greater cruelty, often letting them go almost completely naked. The idleness in which the masters live often brings it about that they have children by their female slaves who are treated with the cruelest indifference and sold like the others.

Finally, the people of the more internal and mountainous regions (except for a few gentlemen who settled there) are composed of the most vile rabble without the slightest notion of morality, justice, or religion. These wretches live in cabins made of tree trunks, the spaces between which are filled in with clay. The whole family stretches out on one bed that is a nest for innumerable insects. And although the land is fertile, their carelessness is such that in lean years they lack even bread. In fact, these are not the industrious Germans or the sturdy Irish who emigrated in order to live honorably by means of their labor but delinquents who fled from North Carolina, Virginia, and Pennsylvania and hid away in the woods to escape pursuit by the law, and there they continue to lead a vagabond life. These are those riflemen about whom I spoke above, distinguished by their suits of ash-colored cloth decorated with fringes of the same color. A few years ago it was not safe to pass through those parts, where many travelers had been robbed and assassinated; and even today they steal horses and whatever falls into their hands, so that strangers have to exercise a great deal of precaution.

[1:317] The persons who attend to commerce are almost all outsiders and rarely mix in the gatherings of the gentlemen of Charleston. The export trade consists of indigo, rice, tobacco, lumber, pitch and resin, and the imports are wines, rum, sugar, molasses, flour, corn, horses from the north, and various European goods. This trade was once quite profitable, but now on the contrary the state languishes, inasmuch as at the end of the war a great number of British and Scottish merchants moved to the southern states and offered all kinds of goods at credit to the landholders to be repaid with indigo, rice, or tobacco. The latter, enticed by the ease of providing for their needs without having to deal in cash, not only resupplied themselves with the furniture lost in wartime, but even acquired carriages, horses, and other luxury items. When the harvest season came, they were forced to hand over their crops at the price imposed by their creditors; and they found the yield much smaller than the debts previously contracted. This disadvantageous exchange of the richest products of the region for British goods very dear in Europe and much more costly in America brought about such a scarcity of money that even the owners of vast plantations were unable to meet small essential expenses. From that situation originated the unfair law that prevents one from demanding payment from landholders promulgated by the General Assembly of Carolina in the last few years and regularly confirmed under the pretext of poor harvests over several successive years. Hence since the [1:318] landholders are already indebted to British merchants for large sums, and since they do not have the means for supplying themselves elsewhere, they are obliged to depend upon them for the most common European goods, which, on account of the slowness of payment, are sold at an exorbitant price. By means of this cunning strategy the English and Scottish merchants took the direct trade with the southern United States away from the other nations. Hence one can easily see the real reason why English products are preferred by the Americans. However, it can also be added that their better quality contributes to this preference, and all the more so because the merchants of other nations are less wealthy and cannot put off demanding payment of what is due them.

Another reason for the lack of money in Carolina is the excessive importation of negroes. These wretched objects of compassion on the part of any kindhearted person, although they are scorned and treated in the most cruel fashion, are the pride of the landholders, who are more or less respected in proportion to the number of their slaves. Therefore, the moment these unhappy victims arrive from Africa and are set up for sale, a great many people compete in buying them and vie in offering an extravagant price, which, being paid likewise with the produce of the land, brings about the disadvantages mentioned above. In the upper parts of the state, where there are few slaves, money is even more scarce because of the difficulty of transporting the tobacco that they raise and the great expense necessary to send European goods there from the distant seaports.

The first cultivation attempted in South [1:319] Carolina was that of grapes and olives. The region was then not so unhealthful since the exhalations of the swamps were reduced and corrected by the woods that covered them, and only those who lived near ponds suffered from tertian fevers in the fall. But after the cultivation of rice was introduced, with the cutting of the forests and the multiplication of stagnant water, its climate became generally unhealthful. The time of this introduction goes back to the year 1730 when the captain of a ship coming from the East Indies brought with him a small quantity of rice more out of curiosity than with the idea of profit, and he gave it to Mr. Johnson, then governor, who distributed it among several of his friends. In two years alone there was a harvest big enough to send some to Europe, and thereafter its cultivation became much more widespread. However, in view of how harmful it was to the health of the colonists who worked at it, someone had the idea of bringing in negro slaves, whose number increased with the growth of the rice fields.

There are two ways of cultivating rice, namely, in the fields called tide fields and in those called inland fields. The former are situated in marshes near the rivers at some distance from the sea, which are regularly flooded by the river at high tide. These are doubtless the most productive, provided they are not too close to the mouth and therefore subject to salt water, nor too far up, where they are usually damaged by the spring floods. Some of these extremely fertile rice fields, which are sometimes sold for the price (enormous for those regions) of 25 guineas [1:320] an acre, are located on the Waccamaw and on the Pee Dee near Georgetown, and others, not more than two or three miles long on the Santee, Ashley, etc. The other manner of cultivating rice (inland fields) is practiced on lands near the sea, where the river water has a salty taste, and on those that are either far from rivers or subject to flooding, so that they cannot be watered with the help of the tide. This method consists in gathering rain water in large artificially dug ponds and directing it as needed upon the rice fields. Then on lands where the river water is salty, it is held back by rather strong dikes in order to keep it from overflowing. Toward the middle of April, after the earth has been worked over with the hoe, the rice is planted by the negroes in little holes situated at some distance apart in fields divided into wide square areas. They are left dry until the rice reaches a height of about a foot, and then they are flooded. The water is allowed to stand for a few days, after which it is removed. Watering is repeated from time to time as it is needed. However, when the spikes begin to appear, the rice remains under water until it is ripe and ready to be cut, and the weeds that come up in it are pulled out by the negroes.

After the rice has been harvested, it is made into round piles with the spikes carefully placed toward the center, and these piles are left this way during all the fall and even until February and March, at which time the rice is beaten with the flail as is wheat in our country. After the bundles have been beaten, they are taken [1:321] into a wooden chamber situated in the middle of the barnyard and supported by four beams as in some Chinese homes (Plate VII, Fig. 1). In the center of this chamber there is a square opening covered by a wide iron grill (Plate VII, Fig. 2). As a boy rubs the beaten bundles over it, the grains fall through the grill and only the straw remains, which from time to time is cast to one side. Since the floor of this chamber

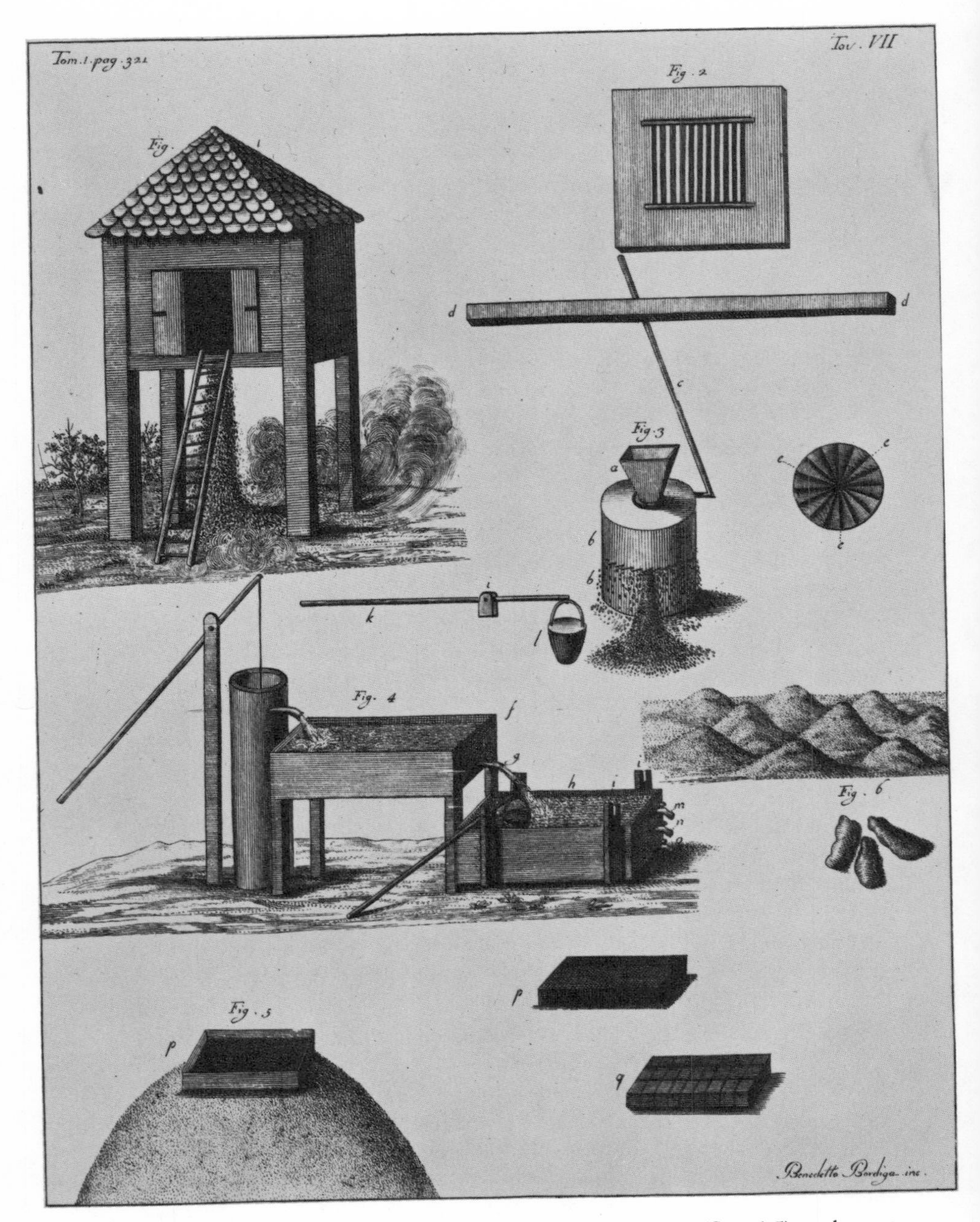

Plate VII. Cultivation and harvesting of rice (figs. 1–3), indigo (figs. 4,5), and sweet potato (fig. 6).

is eighteen or twenty feet from the ground, the rice grains are separated as they fall from the dust and the fragments of straw, which the wind carries off. This has the effect of winnowing. The grain thus separated from the straw and the dust, there remains only to strip off the husk; and to do that, various tools are used. The first consists of a round wooden machine (Plate VII, Fig. 3) with a hopper *a* on top of it that is filled with rice. The rice enters between two wooden cylinders *bb*, which, spun swiftly by the handle *c* that passes through a hole made in the fixed plank *d*, rub the rice between the grooves *eee*, so that the husk is broken and it becomes easier to separate it completely with pestles. This preparatory operation is called "grinding," and it occupies a large number of negroes, each of whom must crack daily about 14 bushels. Afterwards the rice is passed once more through the grills of the winnowing chamber. It is then put under the pestles and completely cleared of husks. Formerly this labor, too, was assigned to slaves, who used to pound it by hand in wooden mortars; but later machines [1:322] were invented activated by one or more horses, and then water mills were adopted on the wealthier plantations. Some of these by activating 12 pestles can husk from 120 to 140 bushels of rice a day. Some people have also tried to activate by water or horses the machine that serves to crack the husk and to spare the negroes this work, but to date it has not been possible to achieve in that manner the perfection of hand labor. The rice is finally removed from the pestles, sifted, and put in large wooden barrrels in which it is taken to the seaports.

On the best lands the harvest is about eight bushels of rice with the husks per acre, and this produces eight barrels[20] of marketable white rice, in addition to the cracked rice called *risino* in Lombardy.[21] Comparing the production of the rice fields of Carolina with ours in Lombardy, one finds the harvest from a given area in America a great deal smaller than ours, which must be attributed to the lack of hands in those regions and also perhaps to the custom of allowing the rice to grow too high, which produces spikes less abundant in grains. The rice of Carolina and Georgia is much larger, whiter, and better husked than that of Lombardy, since the climate is warmer and more diligence is employed in cleaning it. Nevertheless, it is sold at a lower price, [1:323] a barrel of good white rice being worth only 10 Carolina shillings. Ordinarily, edible rice is given no other preparation except to boil it in water and take it this way to the table, where it is mixed with fresh butter. In the country it is used boiled in this manner at lunch and dinner. However, certain thin cakes are also made of it, which are served in the morning with tea or coffee; and it is also prepared in many other ways. The cracked rice serves as food for the negroes, and the powder from the crushed husks makes an excellent fertilizer. Finally, inasmuch as there is a shortage of fodder for horses in this region, they are given rice straw instead of hay and rice itself with the husks still on instead of oats.

Indigo[22] is sown in some places alternately with rice, and in others that previously had been flooded, as well as in dry terrains near marshes. This plant, which had already been cultivated for a long time in the islands of the Antilles, was also found in the year 1745 in the woods of South Carolina. It was quickly cultivated and in a few years became one of the most important sources of income for the region. Different methods have been employed in the various regions in which indigo is raised to extract from it the beautiful blue color useful in dyes. Several of them have already been described; therefore I limit myself to giving a succinct description of the method used in South Carolina in order that it may be compared with the others already published.

After the soil has been well tilled [1:324] with the hoe, furrows are made at the beginning of April two inches deep and a foot and a half from each other, and in them are sown the seeds, which are covered with a bit of earth. If it is a warm season, the little plants begin to appear in 10 or 12 days, and when they have reached some size, the soil around them is worked with the hoe in order to soften it and to eradicate the weeds. When the flowers begin to wilt and fall, the plants are cut off at about one foot above the ground and placed in a wide wooden tank (Plate VII, Fig. 4), which is filled with water from one or more pumps. They are left there for 14 or 15 hours until the surface of the water takes on a deep green appearance and the texture of the plants becomes flaccid and soft. Then the plants are taken from the tank *f*, the spigot *g* is opened, and the colored water is allowed to drop into the square vat, or tank *h*, underneath. At the two sides of this second tank there are two supports *i i* within which moves the rod *k*, to which is attached by means of a movable handle the inverted cone *l* made of heavy wood. Four negroes stir the water continuously with these instruments, pouring in lime water from time to time until a small quantity of indigo matter placed on a dish appears in the form of granules. They then stop their beating, add more lime water and let the mixture settle until the water appears to be entirely limpid and clear, at which time by opening the upper spigot *m* and then successively the other two [1:325] lower spigots *n* and *o*,[23] they empty the water from the tank. The coloring matter then remains deposited on the bottom of the tank itself. It is collected in large pieces of woolen cloth and put into a square, bottomless wooden mold set on a pile of sand (Fig. 5). Upon being compressed there by a weight, the rest of the water comes out through the sand, and the indigo takes on the consistency of fresh cheese. In this condition it is removed from the molds *p p* and cut into square pieces *q* that are thoroughly dried in the sun. These pieces are put in barrels and shipped to Europe. Upon being broken, they acquire the irregular form of commercial indigo.

Indigo is of various qualities, the difference depending not so much on the time of harvest as upon the proportion of lime water and the intelligence of the negroes in its manufacture. The most highly valued, which must be lustrous and of a nice crimson color inside, brings up to one Spanish piece for every Carolina pound of weight. To collect the seeds, which it produces in great abundance, a few feet of it are left without being cut, and they are then kept in a dry place. No more than a bushel of seed is needed for every four acres of land. Indigo is used by the poor inhabitants of the two Carolinas to dye [I:326] suits, stockings, etc., as in Europe, and mixed with milk it forms a beverage that is given to horses afflicted by worms, a disease to which they are subject whenever they are fed on corn.

Tobacco growing has become very widespread (as has already been said) in the western parts of Carolina and Georgia, but since this forms the principal trade of Virginia, I shall reserve talking about it to the description of that State. Grown successfully in many parts of South Carolina is also maize, or corn, and toward the mountains, grain, barley, oats, etc.; and in addition to these even annual cotton, or *bambagia,*[24] is sown for home use. Leafy vegetables, legumes, and other garden vegetables grow very nicely and are so early that lettuce is eaten in the winter, and radishes and asparagus are gathered at the end of March. Pumpkins, cantaloupes, and watermelons which grow wonderfully there are very tasty, but they are believed to be unhealthful in the warm season, and the Indians call them by the same word with which they denote fever.

In the list of edible vegetables of Carolina mention must be made of three other plants grown advantageously there. The first is the *Batata,*[25] called by the inhabitants sweet [I:327] potato, native to Carolina, that is cultivated in the following manner. A raised and sandy terrain near marshes having been chosen, it is tilled in April by negroes, who make many little mounds with the soil (Table VII, Fig. 6). On each of them are planted five or six *batate,* which are covered with a bit of earth. When they have grown, they are weeded; and they require no other care until the harvest of the roots, after which they can be preserved for several months provided they are in a dry place and kept from freezing. These *batate,* which are oblong, of a reddish color outside and greenish inside, are eaten roasted or boiled, puddings are made from them, and cakes that appear as if they were made of sweet almonds and which are served instead of bread in the morning with tea. They are so common that not infrequently they are given as food even to the slaves.[26] The *Hibiscus esculentus* of Linnaeus, an annual herb with mallowlike flower, is the second, which was brought by the negroes from the coasts of Africa and is called okra by them. The fruit, which is a bristly capsule of five sections full of tiny peas, is gathered when it is nearly ripe. Cut into pieces, it is boiled with the flesh of veal, very tasty soups being made of it with the addition of a little tomato, or *pomo d'oro*,[27] [1:328] and Indian pepper.[28] To conclude, the third is the ground nut,[29] a plant brought from the Antilles which produces oblong fruit with a creased and wrinkled skin containing usually two seeds of a pleasant almond flavor when they are roasted over fire. These are served with fruit and eaten with nuts and raisins.

CHAPTER X

North Carolina

From South Carolina to the Virginia Border

[1:329]

HAVING CROSSED THE CATAWBA (as I have already related) and reached Boundary House at the boundary of the two Carolinas, I set out for Charlotte. This village was so named in honor of the reigning Queen of England and is situated at 35° 5′ latitude on a little hill surrounded all about by woods. The soil produces grain, tobacco, and corn in abundance, but the distance from seaports renders them commercially of little advantage. The Court of Justice for Mecklenburg County is held in Charlotte. There is also quite a large wooden [1:330] building that serves as a college.[1] It flourished before the war, and in it were taught the Latin and Greek languages. I came upon two very beautiful butterflies in that area, one of which [2] is very similar to our thistle butterfly, and the other belongs to those called silvery, which are mottled with silver spots under the wings. It is called the vanilla butterfly by Linnaeus[3] because in America its caterpillar feeds on the leaves of this aromatic plant.

Eighteen miles beyond Charlotte I crossed the Rocky River, which flows into the Pee Dee, and after traveling another 23 miles through a fertile and populous region scattered with vast plantations, I arrived at Salisbury. The terrain is everywhere clayey and well cultivated, and the farmers there make use of very long dairy barns divided into three compartments. The two lateral ones serve for the horses and cattle and the middle one as a granary and haymow. Since they are surrounded by a loft, they leave below enough room to admit the wagon and unload it under shelter. These barns are used in some parts of Germany and were introduced into America by the Germans who settled there. Salisbury has about 80 wooden houses and is situated on a charming little hill at [1:331] latitude 35° 40′. In this tiny hamlet is held the Supreme Court of Justice for the district of Salisbury. The countryside is fertile and produces corn and tobacco, which are traded at Fayetteville, a rising city situated on the northwest branch of the Cape Fear River, which is navigable by ship as far as Wilmington. Leaving Salisbury, I crossed the Yadkin River, which afterwards takes the name of Pee Dee, and that same night I reached Salem.

The village of Salem is located on the slope of a fertile hill near one of the branches of the Yadkin River, in whose vicinity the yellow-flowering horse chestnut[4] grows profusely. It was founded by the Moravian Brethren, who still possess it. The Moravians are a Protestant sect whose origin goes way back to the time when the Waldensians were persecuted for having accepted the doctrine of John Huss. Some of his adherents in Moravia followed his doctrine secretly and lived together in Protestant countries, applying themselves particularly to the manual arts and agriculture. From the harmony that reigned among them they took the name of *Fratres Unitatis,* which they later changed to *Unitas Fratrum,* since they did not wish to have a name in common with Catholic monks. The Moravians have a rallying point, since they depend on a synod in Germany, whose principal function is to distribute missionaries who carry the Gospel to the most remote part of the globe, [1:332] and especially to the countries of savages. Their emigration to America took place in 1735 at the time of the first settlements in Georgia as the result of a conversation that arose between Count von Zizendorf, leader of this sect, and General Oglethorpe, who set aside for them a tract of land in the new city of Savannah, to which they went shortly thereafter. However, when the Moravian Brethren refused to take up arms at the time of the wars with the Spaniards of Florida and the Indians, since that was contrary to their religious principles, the Georgians put before them the choice of either arming themselves or of leaving the country. The Moravians chose this latter course, and leaving their possessions, they went to Pennsylvania (the only province in the Colonies where one has always enjoyed perfect freedom of conscience), and there they founded the cities of Nazareth and Bethlehem.[5] The Pennsylvanians furnished them with the money necessary for these settlements; and in order to pay the debts contracted on that occasion, the Moravians decided by law to use their possessions in common and to employ the fruits of their labors to maintain the community, pay their debts, and construct public buildings. Hence it must be noted that common ownership of property is indeed not one of the rules of their institution but simply a particular rule born out of circumstances. In fact this common ownership came to an end in 1762, [1:333] and from that time on each one has enjoyed the advantages derived from his own industry. Since they were extremely dedicated to work, they became wealthy in a short time, and, aided by the Society existing in Germany, they purchased 100,000 acres of land in western North Carolina. That district they called Vacovia. In 1760, 13 Moravian Brethren left Bethlehem to go to the newly acquired land, and as soon as they arrived, they cut down the woods and built a town, to which they gave the name of Bethania. This town, founded without examination, happened to be near some stagnant water, and therefore in an unhealthful location. They chose then some more elevated sites to build the other towns of Salem and Bethabara.

The principal buildings of the village of Salem are the church, two schoolhouses, one for young men of marriageable age and another for young ladies, and the inn—all buildings constructed at public expense. The outlying regions are well cultivated since the Quakers, Anabaptists, and Dunkers were also allowed to settle on the 100,000 acres the Moravians own, who pay a given portion of the harvest to the Society and are allowed to live in peace, provided they are of good character and laudable habits.

The woods near the aforementioned village abound in birds of various kinds, and especially woodpeckers. This species is very copious in North America, and particularly in the southern states, since these birds find easily available food in the worms and insects that [1:334] nest in the rotten trunks of those ancient forests. The largest of all is the white-billed woodpecker, which has a black body and a very handsome crest of red feathers.[6] Catesby gives a drawing of it on Plate 16 of Vol. I and says that the bills of these birds were highly esteemed by the Canadian Indians, who made crowns of them (resembling the *rostrali* of the ancients) for their chiefs and famed warriors. Therefore they bought them at a dear price from the Indians of the southern regions, since these birds were not to be found toward the north. There is another one that has a red head and neck, white belly, and black wings provided below with a white band, and according to Catesby it could be called domestic, inasmuch as it lives in the neighborhood of villages and plantations.[7] All woodpeckers are very harmful to corn, but this latter does perhaps the most damage, so that formerly a bounty was given to those who killed any of them.

I stopped for two days in the village of Salem, and on the morning of the 9th I left for Guilford. This is situated at latitude 36° 10′ and consists of a few wooden habitations built around the house where the Court of Justice is held. Guilford would not be worthy of mention if it were not for the battle of May 24, 1781, engaged in its neighborhood when the American army, [1:335] under the command of General Greene, after a stubborn struggle, was forced to withdraw to Virginia. The loss of the English was 600 men and that of the Americans 400 between the wounded and killed; and the victory remained in doubt, each side boasting of having had the better of it. I then crossed Troublesome and Liver Creeks, and after traveling 43 miles through a cultivated region, I reached the border between North Carolina and Virginia.

The Location, and the European Settlements of North Carolina

[1:336] North Carolina is situated between latitude 35° and 36° 30′ and between 76° and 90° longitude from London. It borders on Virginia to the north, on the ocean to the east, on South Carolina to the south, and the Mississippi River to the west, which separates it from Louisiana. The main rivers are the Cape Fear, Neuse, Pamlico, and Roanoke. Inasmuch as they do not have a long course and since their navigation is frequently interrupted, they do not turn out to be very handy for the transportation of goods. The terrain of the internal and mountainous regions abounds in clay, but near the seashore it is sandy, as in South Carolina, although the marshes near the rivers are not, as in that state, either so extensive or so fertile.

The discovery of this region is due to the ships sent by Queen Elizabeth to cruise before the Spanish islands and coasts of America. As commanders Drake, Hawkins, and Raleigh, employed on this expedition, sailed along the coasts of the Carolinas, at that time not yet distinguished from Florida, they noted their fertility. Upon their return to England they gave such a favorable description of them that it was decided to found a colony there, and Sir Walter Raleigh was chosen to direct [1:337] the undertaking. Raleigh obtained letters patent whereby he was granted the expanse of country between 30° and 40° of latitude, with the option of disposing of it as he pleased and of selling his rights to anyone provided he was an English subject. For the Crown was reserved only the fifth part of the production of the gold or silver mines that might be found there. He formed a company of several friends who contributed to pay the expenses and equipped two ships under the command of captains Philip Amádas and Arthur Barlowe, which set sail in April, 1584, and arrived at the island of Wokoken, or Ocracoke, at north latitude 34° 57′ near Cape Hatteras, which closes the strait of Pamlico. From Ocracoke they crossed over to Roanoke, another island in the strait, now called Albemarle, at latitude 35° 55′. Then, turning back, they landed on the continent, took possession of it in the name of Queen Elizabeth, and (as has been said elsewhere) gave it the name of Virginia. They were received in a friendly manner by the Indians and their king, or chief, Wingina, exchanging knives, axes, and tools for the pelts of beaver and other animals, sassafras and red cedar wood, and a little tobacco.[8] They returned to Ocracoke Island before night and left for England, taking with them two Indians who had [1:338] shown a desire to accompany them.

The profit that was made from the load of those ships inspired Raleigh and his associates to fit out a fleet of seven boats under the command of Sir Richard Grenville, which left Plymouth of the 9th of April, 1585, and arrived on the 16th of the following June at the island of Ocracoke. The flagship foundered upon entering the port, but Grenville saved himself along with all his company and went on to Roanoke Island, when he proceeded to the continent to examine the country. While he was there, one of the Indians stole a silver vessel. Informed of this, Grenville avenged himself by destroying their corn and burning several villages. After this barbarous deed he sailed for Europe, leaving on Roanoke Island a colony of 800 men under the command of Ralph Lane. Desirous of making discoveries, Lane once more went forth upon the continent, where he was welcomed with demonstrations of friendship by the Indian chief Wingina, who, pretending to be a friend of the English, had made a plan to kill them and thus avenge the devastation wrought by Grenville. But when Wingina's intent was discovered by Lane, he retreated with all speed to Roanoke. There, however, the lack of provisions would have forced them to die of hunger if Frances Drake, arriving opportunely, had not taken them aboard his ships and transported them back to England. They had hardly left when Grenville returned with three ships, and not finding the colonists there any longer, he departed from the island, leaving there for some unknown reason only 15 persons.

[1:339] Two years later, namely, in 1587, Raleigh sent three more ships to America with 150 adventurers who were to found the town of Raleigh and form a colony, of which a certain Captain White was to have been governor. When they reached Roanoke, they did not find there any longer the 15 men left by Grenville, and shortly thereafter they were themselves killed by the Indians, against whom they had asked for help from England in vain. All the expeditions of Raleigh having thus ended unhappily, this region remained uncultivated until 1662, when (as has been said) Carolina was ceded to seven proprietors by the King, and the province was populated by two colonies, one of which, after landing at the Ashley River, founded Charleston, and the other settled near the strait of Albemarle.

We have seen how slow the progress of this population was under the government of the Proprietors[9] and how, after Carolina was returned to the power of the King, it was divided into two provinces with the names of North and South. The boundary was set by the Little River directly to the northwest up to 35° and then in a straight line as far as the lands of the Cherokee. Since these confines were not clearly marked, a new line of separation [1:340] was drawn by order of the King whereby York County (at present called New Acquisitions) was incorporated with South Carolina. The State of North Carolina is at the present time divided into 6 districts, each of which includes several counties in the following proportion: the district of Wilmington, 6; New Bern, 6; Edenton, 7; Halifax, 4; Hillsboro, 4; Salisbury, 6—in all, 33 counties.

The capital of North Carolina, called New Bern, is located at latitude 35° 15′ at the confluence of the Trent and Neuse Rivers, which surround it, the former on the south, the other on the north, and after a course of 100 miles empty into the ocean. The city is built on a plain, and the houses, of wood, and not very attractive in appearance, are arranged in a regular pattern but quite distant from one another. In the hot and dry season getting about the city is very uncomfortable because the terrain is sandy and the streets are unpaved. Among the public buildings the only one worthy of note is the erstwhile home of the governor situated in a large square formerly surrounded by a wall.[10] It was built in 1771 under the government of William Tryon (at present a general in the British troops), consisting of a large brick building furnished with two wings with porches and formed after the plan of Buckingham House in London. On the façade is still seen the coat of arms of the King of England in white marble, and in the vestible or main entrance one reads the following curious inscription:

[1:341] *Guli.mo Tryon Arm.ro regnante Provincia. A.D. MDCCLXXI.*
Augusto huic aedificio ea carmina vovit
Guli.mus Draper, balnei Eques, Manila victor.
Rege pio felix diris inimica Tyrannis
Virtuti has aedes libera terra dedit.
Sint domus, & dominus saeclis exempla futuris.
Hinc artes, mores, justitiamque colant.

The inside of this building was much damaged at the time of the war, when the decorations and the paintings were spoiled. Some of the rooms now serve for sessions of the Senate and the House of Commons on the occasion of the General Assembly, others for children's schools, and even for public dances.

Although New Bern is a rather large city and inhabited by followers of various sects, nevertheless there isn't a single church, since the only existing church of the Anglicans was ruined during the war and converted for use as a barn. There is, therefore, in this capital no sign of public worship except two or three times a year whenever it happens that a minister or priest (of any Protestant religion whatever) happens to pass through these parts. In that case prayers are recited in the hall of the Court of Justice, not very roomy, but more than adequate for the few women that attend. To put it briefly, in this city Sunday is different from the rest of the week only in being the most idle day.

The barrenness of the land around the city brings it about that plantations are rare in its vicinity and that few landholders live there. The [1:342] citizens are almost all merchants, for the most part Scotsmen engaged in modest trading, and being of limited fortunes and occupied with their business, they have little to do with strangers. The market is well provided with various kinds of fresh and salted meats; but it lacks vegetables which, since they cannot be raised in the sterile sands of the neighboring region, are shipped from the northern states. They are therefore scarce, very expensive, and very often spoiled and bad. Grog, that is, rum mixed with water, and in some homes Madeira wine, are the commonest drinks. Tea is drunk at breakfast and in the afternoon, although the milk and butter that they take with it are very scarce and not very substantial because of the lack of pasture lands.

The commerce of New Bern consists of pitch, resin, lumber, and salted fish, which, being bulky merchandise and of little value, do not amount to much, all the more because ships of more than 80 tons cannot approach the bay. Although this city was considered the capital of North Carolina before the war, nevertheless the General Assembly is not regularly held there. It transfers itself, according to the desire of the members who compose it, from one city to another of the state. Since the Revolution four cities have enjoyed this prerogative, namely, New Bern, Hillsboro, Halifax, and Cross Creek, now called Fayetteville in honor of the Marquis de Lafayette.

The New System of Government and the Inhabitants of North Carolina

[1:343] The new Constitutions of North Carolina,[11] like those of many other states, establish two legislative bodies, namely, the Senate and the House of Commons, each of which elects its own head or president. The first is composed of the senators chosen every year by the people by ballot in each county from among those inhabitants who have lived there at least one year and possess 300 acres. The members of the second are also elected by ballot, two from each county and one only from each of the cities of Edenton, New Bern, Wilmington, Salisbury, Hillsboro, and Halifax. The Senate and the House of Commons take the name of General Assembly when they are united. Bills are read three times in each of the two houses before they take effect as law, and they must be signed by the president of the Senate or by the speaker, or leader, of the House of Commons. After the annual election, the members of the two houses take up the choice of the governor, who holds office for one year and cannot be confirmed for more than three consecutive years. He must be at least 30 years old, must have lived 5 years in the state, and be the owner of £1000 of currency. [1:344] After the governor has been nominated, they proceed to choose the members of the Council of State, who are seven in number and help the governor carry out the laws of the Assembly. Soldiers in active service or in the pay of the United States, as likewise priests or ministers of the gospel of any denomination, cannot hold other public offices. Also excluded from any public employ are those who deny the existence of God, the truth of the Protestant religion, or the divine authority of the Old and New Testament. The delegates to the General Congress of the United States are chosen each year by ballot in the General Assembly and cannot be confirmed more than three times.

The population of this state is much smaller than that of South Carolina.[12] The inhabitants of the high and mountainous regions, where tobacco is raised, live in great ignorance, and since their knowledge is limited to the environs of their cabins and their few interests, they do not have too high an opinion of the few strangers who pass through those parts. Hence if a traveler in answering their questions reveals that he is not a merchant, or a doctor, or that he does not intend to settle in America, they look upon him suspiciously, thinking it impossible that one might travel solely to educate himself. They are much more confirmed in their opinion if the stranger examines the condition of the villages, if he makes drawings, and if he takes down information. This is what happened to three French officers, among whom there was a colonel who came through Salem after the surrender of Yorktown and Gloucester, when [1:345] Lord Cornwallis was captured. Arriving in the aforementioned village in the evening, they begged one of the Moravian gentlemen to take them to see their manufactures, which he did very reluctantly, fearing (as he himself told me) that they were persons sent by the King of France to explore the country, an idea in which he was confirmed when he saw one of these officers noting on paper the plan of his village. One must be totally ignorant of the present situation in Europe to believe that France, an ally of the Americans, would send three officers to take down the plan of a village of 15 or 20 wooden houses more than 200 miles from the sea without even a moat around it and inhabited by people unable to bear arms as a religious precept.[13]

Indigo and rice are raised in the low places near the sea, especially in the environs of New Bern and Wilmington, but such cultivation is restricted to a small number of landholders who enjoy the possession of a low-lying and fertile terrain near rivers and who have a goodly number of slaves to employ at it. The other inhabitants are generally poor and live in elevated areas, applying themselves to the feeding and raising of herds of swine[14] or extracting resin or pitch from pine trees. The largest herds of swine are found between Halifax and Tarboro, and, as I have already said, they are allowed to wander in the woods, where they feed on the acorns and fruit that fall from the trees. Traveling through these woods, one comes upon them in great numbers as they are being driven to the city in order to salt their flesh and ship it in barrels to the seaports. Since these [1:346] pigs are not artificially fattened, their flesh isn't so viscid and unhealthful, and it doesn't produce those kinds of scurvy and skin diseases to which the too frequent use of salted meats renders one subject. This meat, salted and smoked, is called bacon, and boiled or roasted over coals, it is eaten with butter, eggs, and vegetables, and is very often the only provision found in the inns and in the homes of poor landholders.

Resin and pitch are extracted as the main and almost sole product of a kind of trifoliate pine or black pine[15] that grows everywhere in high, sandy, barren locations. To obtain the resin, the finest trees are chosen and at the height of about half a foot from the ground the bark is cut with an ax until the wood is bared. This wound is about two feet high and its width is in accordance with the girth of the tree, occupying about two thirds of the surface. At the base of the wound a hollow is formed in the wood from which the resin that drips from the wound is collected twice a week. This continues until the tree doesn't yield any more, at which time it shows signs of deterioration, and then dies. Whenever the rain, by wetting the bare wood, impedes the flow, it is scraped again, and this way the draining goes on. Whenever the pitch has been collected in sufficient quantity, it is put in barrels. A mighty small profit is made from this yield, since a very diligent [1:347] negro slave can look after only 3000 pine trees, which at the most can produce 300 barrels of resin; and inasmuch as a barrel sells at about 10 shillings of their money, that is, a Spanish piece and a quarter, the gain turns out to be very small, if one makes allowance for the difficulty and expense of transportation and the cost of the barrels. Pitch is obtained from the same trees after they have been cut and is extracted from the trunks by setting fire to one of the ends, by which means it drips from the opposite end into vessels prepared for that purpose. This item yields even less than the first, both because of the lower price at which it is sold and for the quantity that is lost in the summer, since it comes out through the seams of the barrels when liquified by the heat of the sun.

Some farmers plant cotton and use it for their domestic needs.[16] This plant grows quite well in elevated, sandy, and dry places, and is very useful for the poor inhabitants, because European fabrics and cloth are rare and very expensive. They even plant a little indigo to dye their textiles, and some plant a little rice where the land is naturally inundated by the overflow of rivers, although it dies in years of little rain. In the internal regions[17] bordering on Virginia, grain, rye, barley, oats, corn, flax, hemp, and tobacco are grown. However, grain, which once used to be planted in quantity, is now very scarce, since an insect that destroys it has found its way into the fields. Therefore various landholders of both North Carolina and Virginia had to give up raising it. This is [I:348] an ash-colored curculio (*Curculio* Lin.), and it chews the seeds in the spikes before they ripen.

The difficulties encountered in order to obtain rum and other liquors from the ports led the inhabitants of these parts to make use of beverages made from the fruit of the region. These are two kinds of brandy, one extracted from peaches, which are (as we have said) common in the woods, and the other from a mixture of grain, barley, or rye, which is fermented like beer and then distilled. This latter brandy, known under the name of whiskey, has a medicinal and at first quite disgusting flavor, but the people[18] make great use of it, mixing it with water, and some who are used to it prefer it to the other liquors.

The trade of North Carolina, consisting of pitch, resin, lumber, salted meats, tobacco, and a little indigo and rice, is very sluggish on account of the limited navigability of the rivers. Hence a number of the wealthiest landowners, not finding an outlet for their products in the state, transport them to Charleston in South Carolina or to Petersburg in Virginia; and so the state remains without direct trade with outsiders.[19]

CHAPTER XI

Virginia

Trip through Virginia from North Carolina to the Maryland Border

[1:349]

On the 11th of May, crossing the Dan River three miles from the border of North Carolina, I reached the plantation of Mr. W---. He had been described to me as a zealous Methodist, a sect that differs from the Anglican only in the more strict observance of frequent prayers and whose followers in America are more zealous than educated.[1] His daughter was the wife of the minister, or priest of the Methodists, and both of them lived in the home of the father-in-law.[2] When the time came to go to bed, the family gathered and a hymn was struck up by the minister in a loud voice. Afterwards he read a passage from the Bible in order to give an explanation of it, but arriving at the end of the first verse and perhaps finding himself [1:350] embarrassed, he cut off his sentence saying that, since the hour was late and the night perceptibly shortened, he thought it best for us to go to bed, which we quickly did.

On the 12th I crossed from Paintonborough, called also Halifax Old-Town, and passing over the Banister by a bridge, after traveling 40 miles I reached toward evening the plantation of Colonel Coles, situated a short distance from the Stanton River. I had already seen the Colonel at Richmond and was received by him with the hospitality proper to Virginians. What is more, upon hearing that it was my intention to head toward Philadelphia, he gave me a letter of introduction to his brother Colonel John,[3] whose plantation, located near Charlottesville, is on the way. I looked over with pleasure his thoroughbred horses and various beautiful artificial fields of clover and rye grass, or *falsa segala*.[4]

On the morning of the 14th I took a boat across the Stanton, a river which, joining the Dan and the Banister, then takes the name of Roanoke. When I left the main road, and after winding around for about 20 miles, I barely managed to find shelter for the night in the home of some poor farmers. From there, I stopped at John's Ordinary, and then I reached the house where is held the Court of Justice for Buckingham County, located on top of a high hill at the foot of which flows the Appomatox. I took lodgings for the night with a certain Patterson who owns [1:351] a fine plantation there, and the following day, after traveling for 20 miles, I found myself on the shores of the James River. I was perhaps only a mile away from the river when a very strong wind began to blow, and in a moment the sky was covered with very dark clouds. Thunder and lightning alternated rapidly and kept increasing, and rain and hail came down in torrents. The horses, terrified by the roar of the thunder, the violence of the rain, and the pummeling of the hail, wouldn't budge, and we were able to reach the river only when the storm began to subside. Then from the bank we called for the boatman, who, at the door of his house on the other shore, refused to move[5] until the rain had completely stopped, excusing himself by saying that he had not seen us. Meantime we saw a large snake come out upon the bank from the river. I struck it several times with a club, and believing it dead, I put it on the floor of the carriage, where it recovered from the blows and remained alive for three days, after which I preserved it in brandy. It is very much like the snake called *smiroldo* in Lombardy and is not poisonous. The color of its back is almost black with light, spaced rings, and its belly is white marked with black.[6] On the other side of the James River, which at this place takes the name of Fluvanna, there are some houses, and among them the one in which formerly was held the Court of Justice [1:352] for Albemarle County. There I dried out my clothes, stopped for dinner, and then left for Enniscorthy, the estate of Colonel John Coles four miles away. Another storm, though not as violent as the first one, soaked me a second time, and accompanied by continual lightning, thunder, and rain, I reached the home of the Colonel, who, no less hospitable than his brother, received me very cordially.

Enniscorthy is situated on top of a green and fertile hill from which to the east one enjoys the view of a wide plain through which flows the Fluvanna; to the west are seen the so-called Little Mountains, and to the north those called the Southwest Mountains. Beyond the latter can be perceived the great chain of the Blue Mountains, and at a greater distance, that of the Alleghenies. The exposure of these mountains, protected from the cold northern winds and facing without obstacle due south, is so favorable to vegetation that the trees drop their leaves later in the fall and put forth their leaves and blossoms earlier than in the plain below. Hence certain shrubs (like the calycanthus, for example), which are found only in more southerly regions, grow on these hills and produce ripe seed. From this early vegetation they got the name of Green [1:353] Hills, and both for the fertility of the soil as likewise for their position they can be compared to our hills of Mount Brianza.[7] Therefore mulberries and grapes should do well there. The air is very healthful and the water is good. It has, however, a somewhat chalybeate taste produced by iron mines, which are very common there.

Leaving Enniscorthy on May 18th, I crossed the Rivanna, a river which, joining the Fluvanna, forms the James River, and I began to climb the Southwest Mountains. On that road I killed a snake two feet and seven inches long,[8] of the species that in America is called black snake. They can be found up to five feet long, and if they are disturbed, especially in the season when they are in heat, they move with remarkable speed, and catching up with the enemy, they wind themselves around his legs, bite him, and then flee. Sometimes, however, they don't want to detach themselves at all, and then there is no other way to get rid of them except to cut them to pieces. Their bite produces no bad effect and the pain of the wound is felt for only a short time. To these serpents, as to the rattlesnake, is attributed the faculty of drawing birds and squirrels, which they devour.

Charlottesville is situated in the valley at the foot of the Southwest Mountains only 14 miles [1:354] from Enniscorthy, but since the route over these mountains is very steep and rough, and, moreover, since I had also missed the way, I managed to come down the other side of the mountains only after several hours of wearisome travel, so that I arrived there late toward evening. Charlottesville, a town of a few homes, where now is held the Court of Justice for Albemarle County, is located between the two chains of the Blue and Southwest Mountains. A short distance away from this town is situated the house of Colonel Lewis,[9] with whom on the morning of the 20th of May I climbed to the top of one of the Southwest Mountains, where stands the villa of Monticello belonging to His Excellency Mr. Thomas Jefferson, at present Ambassador of the United States in Paris. The situation of this villa is very pleasant. From it one can enjoy the view of the Blue Mountains, of the hills, and of the plain; and it overlooks numerous plantations beyond the town. The house, designed by the owner, is after the Italian style, with high, spacious rooms—possibly in accordance with too grandiose a concept, with the result that it isn't finished yet. On the slope of the mountains there is a quantity of grapevines, an abundant orchard of the best European fruit trees, and a collection of various plants and most unusual shrubs that he himself collected in the woods of Virginia. However, what renders Monticello most noteworthy is a copious library of the best and rarest English, French, Italian, Greek, and Latin books that Mr. Jefferson gathered, not indeed as a matter of luxury, but for his own edification, since he understands the languages. Mr. Jefferson is known in [1:355] America and in Europe for his talents, and has distinguished himself no less in the sciences than in politics. A few years ago he wrote a number of reflections on Virginia to which he gave the modest title of *Notes,*[10] and which he didn't want to publish. A copy of them was translated and printed in France, so that then he decided to publish them in English, and the work was received with great applause. He also had much to do with affairs relative to the new legislation, and after holding the office of Governor of Virginia and after having been repeatedly a delegate to the General Congress of the United States, he was recently named Minister to the Court of France when the celebrated Franklin returned to America from Paris.

The climb up the Blue Mountains begins 20 miles from Charlottesville.[11] They are of medium height and the crossing is where the little Rockfish River comes down, from which the passage took the name of Rockfish Gap. The route by which one goes up is very narrow in spots and cluttered with large rocks, which make it very difficult for carriages. But neither the steepness nor the length of the route are such that they can be compared at all to the passes of the Appenines, and much less of the Alps. Upon reaching the top, I stopped at Mr. L–'s, who lives at the highest point of the climb, and a short distance from his house I went to the top of one of the peaks, and from there, to my surprise, I saw the valleys and [1:356] high ground covered with numerous plantations. The Southwest Mountains, the ones called Little Mountains, and the Green Mountains could be seen to the east, the Allegheny Mountains to the west, and in between the wide and fertile valley occupied by Augusta County, extending from the Virginia border north to that of Maryland.

A very thick fog came up the next day and a rain began to fall that lasted all day long. Therefore I had to stay on at the home of Mr. L–,[12] and talking with him, he told me, among other things, that many people passed by there on the way to the baths on the other side of the Alleghenies. In lower Virginia the ladies, since they do not in general get much exercise, are subject to all those diseases that come from a soft and sedentary life, as is the case with European ladies, and just like the latter they go to places well known for mineral waters, where, spending their nights at gambling and dancing, they insist upon living methodically as convalescents. While I was spending my time conversing with my host, my Irishman, to dispel the boredom brought on by the rainy weather, was consoling himself with good glasses of hard cider. When evening came and the house was filled with a number of drivers who were crossing the mountains with their wagons, cider was poured in great quantity, and the Irishman became gay and talkative.

Having descended the Blue Mountains and crossed the South River, I reached Staunton on the morning of the 23rd. This village (which is the capital of Augusta [1:357] County) is situated in the middle of the pretty plain that, as I said, lies between the Blue Mountains and the Alleghenies. About it is found limestone, and there are stalactytes near the rivers and brooks. At Staunton I happened to see one of those thrushes called mockingbirds,[13] because they are capable of imitating other birds in their song. They are of the same size as ours, of a darker gray color in their wings, and with a white belly with dark spots. They make their nests among the bushes and are easily raised in cages, since they are much esteemed for their song, principally by the English, who often buy them at an exorbitant price. Mockingbirds are very rare in the northern states of North America, and since they fear the cold, in winter they withdraw toward the south and return only toward the end of spring. In Boston very few of them are to be found even in summer, and therefore they are sometimes sold for up to three and four guineas each. The raising of tobacco, which constitutes the main source of income of the Virginians east of the Blue Mountains, is still in its infancy in these parts, and the land is sown to grain, corn, and hemp. The sturdy and healthy inhabitants do not have the pale hue of those of the southern states, but the freshness and the fine complexion of the northern people. This region was settled first by emigrants from that part of Ireland situated opposite [1:358] northern Scotland, a vigorous race accustomed to living in the middle of the woods; but it was very soon occupied by the Germans from Pennsylvania, who established themselves here.

Among the sights of this region there is a natural bridge about 50 miles from Staunton. This is a wide rock opening in the form of an arch under which flows the water of a little stream. The continuous downpour not only prevented me from going to see this rare phenomenon,[14] but detained me until the 23rd,[15] when, seeing the sky clearing a bit, I proceeded to Middle River. This little stream, which can be forded all year long, was so swollen by the constant rain[16] that other travelers, among whom a transporter of hides from Carolina, had been forced to stop, waiting for the water to recede. Therefore one had to adapt himself to the circumstance, and I went to the home of Captain A--- situated near the river, waiting for the moment I could continue on my way.[17] Meanwhile I kept going down to the river every time the rain permitted it to mark the height of the water with pieces of wood like the Egyptians in order to observe its rise or fall. Finally, during the night of the 28th, it stopped raining, and the following morning the water was considerably lower. My host the captain, or perhaps his wife, tired of having in their home a witness [1:359] to their shiftless lives, advised me to attempt the passage of the river.[18] There were two fords, one quite dangerous near a lock made for a mill,[19] a short distance from a little island covered with bushes; the other further down where the current was swift. Trusting the advice of one who, since he lived on the bank of the river, in my opinion should have known all about it, I asked my Irishmen whether he was willing to try the second passage; and he, who had never known fear, answered yes. So, accompanied by a lot of people, we went to the river bank, and there the Irishman took off his clothes and got into the water with the carriage. He had scarcely pulled away from the bank when the rush of the current dragged him downstream, the carriage overturned, and the horse became entangled in the harness and, being unable to swim, was in danger of going under, so that I, running along the bank with the others, shouted to the Irishman to try to save himself by swimming. He, however, paying no attention to our suggestions, stayed on horseback and continued going downstream, when all of a sudden he jumped into the water and, swimming, drew the horse behind him by the bridle until he found himself with his feet on the ground.[20] From that time on I made a firm resolution not to entrust myself any more to the counsel of those uncouth and brutal people who had already twice put our lives in danger. The master of the house excused himself by saying that he didn't believe the water was so deep, and since I couldn't do anything about it, I pretended to take the excuse as a good one.

The next morning I forded the river near the dam, where the water was not so deep, also because[21] the rain had stopped. When I reached North River, I crossed it in a canoe, making the horses [1:360] swim; and in the evening I stopped at Snap's Inn.

In spite of the almost incessant rains I collected various insects in those thickets, and among them some new ones and others little known by naturalists, for example, a species of beetle[22] with its body all covered with very fine pale yellow hairs and a little roach[23] with segments divided crosswise into two colors, yellow and white, brought to Europe for the first time by Mr. Banks, who found it in New Holland. Quite similar to the latter in colors and size, although of a totally different genus, is a new kind of moth,[24] of those that Linnaeus called twisters, because they form their cocoons by wrapping up leaves of plants. Equally rare seemed to me a species of chrysomela[25] of the size of the rose kind, with segments varying from red to yellowish and marked with three black spots. Finally, among the uncommon ones can be numbered two other insects of the class of those with veined [1:361] wings, that is, the *Catta* ant lion,[26] whose wing veins are spotted with black, and a *Phryganea*[27] with dark-colored wings marked with irregular whitish spots.

Having crossed during the subsequent days the two branches of the dangerous stream called Smith Creek, I entered upon a new road encumbered with the roots of trees and made very bad by the rains. The wheels of my carriage, already repaired so many times, broke in a hundred pieces, so that I barely managed to reach the inn of a certain Macdoval,[28] where I decided to leave the broken carriage and to continue the journey on horseback. I lost some time in this change, and being unable to cross the Shenandoah before night, I set out toward the home of a doctor, from the sight of whom I judged either that he was a doctor of not much reputation or that the inhabitants enjoyed too good health. Upon entering that tiny house which had a floor two or three steps lower than the ground, one found the kitchen – and to the right a little wooden ladder that led to the upstairs apartment, that is, to that triangular space left between the ceiling and the roof. To the left of the kitchen there was a room furnished with two benches, a table, and a little closet containing the library, consisting of a Bible, an old German herbal, and three or four books in the same language, minus the frontispiece [1:362] and index. Beyond this room there was another smaller one with a bolter out of which from time to time there came mice and weevils.[29] An old woman not very clean in the person, the mother of the doctor, by the light of a filthy lantern prepared supper for us, namely, a large dish of sour milk with rye bread and a little butter. After sitting down at table, each one thrust his spoon into the sour soup in the middle, except for me alone. I was satisfied with simple bread.[30] The supper quickly over with, I was taken to the upper floor, where the air entered through the ill-fitted boards; and to the bed[31] prepared for me I preferred to lie on the floor wrapped in my cloak. Beyond the Shenandoah, which we crossed in a canoe, pulling the horses after us as they swam, we found a muddy and stony road, to travel which you cross two streams, Mill Creek and Stony Creek. Leaving behind us Miller's Town, capital of Shenandoah County, and Stower's Town, a town 12 miles from it, after 5 more miles there is Newton to the north of Cedar Creek,[32] and the Winchester. On this road one enjoys a number of beautiful views formed by the Blue Mountains and the Alleghenies.

Winchester, an incorporated town and capital of Frederick County, is one of the most active business centers in Virginia. It has about 200 houses, many of which built of a limestone abundant in those parts, and two churches, one Lutheran, the other Presbyterian. The inhabitants, mostly Germans, trade in grain, flour, and hemp, which they transport to Baltimore and Philadelphia, whence [1:363] they transport European goods that they ship to the more inland regions beyond the Alleghenies. The water of that area, passing through limestone, acquires a purgative quality and produces in persons unaccustomed to it pains in lower abdomen and a precipitate digestion.[33] On the 8th of June I left Winchester, and that evening I stopped at Weathersdon Marsh, called also Charles Town. From there the next day I crossed the Blue Mountains again from west to east. The road is comfortable, following the slope of the valleys, and after eight miles it leads to Harpers Ferry on the Potomac River, which there divides the State of Virginia from that of Maryland.

Location and Climate of Virginia; Its Former Inhabitants, and the European Settlements

[1:364] Virginia, which is the largest of the United States,[34] lies between 36° 30′ and 40° latitude, and extends from 75° to 90° longitude as computed from London. To the north it borders on Pennsylvania and Maryland, on the latter to the east, from which it is separated by Chesapeake Bay, to the south on North Carolina, and on the Mississippi River to the west. The country is level in the areas near the sea, but it very quickly rises to hills, after which come various mountain ranges that have a constant and parallel southwest–northeast direction. The farthest east of these bears the name of Blue Ridge or Blue Mountains, the second is called North Ridge or Alleghenies, and to the west there are other mountain chains that go under the general [1:365] designation of Endless Mountains and form a continuation of the Appalachians. These mountains give rise to many rivers which take different courses, some flowing to the east toward the sea, others emptying into the Mississippi to the west, and, finally, others into the Gulf of Mexico to the south. Among the first is the Potomac, which arises near the Pennsylvania border where Fort Cumberland is and flows into Chesapeake Bay. Its navigation is clear from Alexandria to the sea, but in its upper reaches it is impeded by reefs that often fill up the whole river bed. The Rappahannock, York River, and James River have the same course, terminating likewise in Chesapeake Bay. Those located beyond the mountains that flow from east to west are the Yocchiogenj, the Monongahela, the Greenbrier, the New River, the great Kanawha, the Salt Lick, the Kentucky, and the Bear Grass, all of which flow into the Ohio River, which then empties into the Mississippi. Finally, those that pass between the mountain chains and direct their course from north to south are the North River, the South River, the Cacapon, and the Shenandoah, or Shenadore.

The climate of Virginia is temperate and healthful near the mountains, but warm, humid, and therefore unhealthful in the low regions near the sea,[35] so that fevers and pleurisies are frequent there. Virginia abounds in mineral waters, and the springs of Berkeley and those located beyond the Allegheny Mountains in Augusta [1:366] County, known by the name of Warm Springs and Sweet Springs, are noted for their medicinal qualities.

When the Europeans settled in this region,[36] more than 40 Indian tribes lived there from the sea to the mountains and from the mouth of the Potomac to the southernmost parts of the James River, among whom the most considerable were the Powhatan, the Manahoac, and the Monacan. The tribes that lived on the plain from the shores to the waterfalls were considered Powhatan, and those that were in the mountains were divided into two confederations, the tribes situated at the sources of the Potomac and the Rappahannock being united with the Manahoac, and the others, that occupied the upper reaches of the James River, with the Monacan. These two confederations of mountain Indians were friendly to each other and united in waging war against the Powhatan and the other plains Indians. The territory of the Powhatan and their allies to the south of the Potomac comprised about 8000 square miles, on which were counted 30 tribes and 2400 warriors. Captain Smith says that within 60 miles of Jamestown there were 5000 inhabitants, of whom 1500 were men of arms, so that by computing (says Mr. Jefferson) the number of the Powhatan Indians on this proportion of 3 to 10, 2400 warriors would give a population of 8000 souls scattered over a territory of 8000 [1:367] square miles. In addition to the tribes named above, there were three others, that is, the Nottoway, the Meherrin, and the Tutelo, allied with the Indians of Carolina, thought to be the Chowanoc.

These were the inhabitants of Virginia when, in spite of the unhappy outcome of the attempts made by Sir Walter Raleigh,[37] a society of English noblemen and merchants was formed under the name of the London and Bristol Company, whose object it was to establish a colony in that country. A number of adventurers led by Captain Newport left London at the expense of the Company and reached Chesapeake Bay. There they went up the Powhatoe River, to which they gave the name of James River, and having laid the foundations of Jamestown in honor of James I then reigning, 104 of them remained in the new city, among whom quite a few of good English families. The Powhatan Indians, who lived in those parts, had a certain form of government, and their king ruled over 30 minor kings or chiefs dependent upon him. The English were well received by the Powhatan, who not only furnished them with food and supplies, but helped them to build the city. Nevertheless quarrels arose between the colonists and the Indians, and skirmishes followed, in one of which Captain Smith, who directed the colony, was made prisoner. He was taken before the king who, after offering a [1:368] sacrifice to the god Okee, condemned him to be burned alive. The pyre was already being prepared when Pocahontas, daughter of the king, asked for his life from her father, who granted it in answer to her prayers. He was then not only freed, but united with his liberator, and was respected by the Indians, who regard as one of their nation the prisoners that they allow to live. Smith and Pocahontas later went to England, and when she found there that Smith no longer showed her the affection that he manifested in America, she became disgusted with him and the ingratitude with which she was treated; whereupon, returning to Virginia, she left him and married a certain Mr. Rolfe.[38]

The colonists later occasioned new disturbances among the Indians, and the latter avenged themselves by waging against them such a vigorous war that they were on the point of leaving the country, when Lord Delaware, nominated governor of Virginia, arrived, settled the disputes, and put the colony back in good condition.[39] After returning to England, he undertook a new voyage to America in 1618, but since he died during the crossing, a certain Argall was created his successor by the King. This governor, more intent upon making new discoveries than upon governing the colony well, was recalled and replaced by George Yeardley, who encouraged the raising of tobacco and busied himself with improving the Constitutions, making them more like those of [1:369] England. He created a council in imitation of the Upper House and a General Assembly as counterpart to the House of Commons, and both these bodies sat for the first time in Jamestown in 1620. This can be called the first permanent settlement of the English in North America.

Three years later, when the system introduced by Yeardley was found not to be advantageous, the patent granted to the London and Bristol Company was revoked and the province was placed under the direct control of the Crown. After this change, a large number of adventurers and criminals was transported there, so that the colony began to expand. In 1764 its Council and House of Representatives presented to the King their complaints regarding the Stamp Act; and, along with the other American states, Virginia accepted in 1775 the Declaration of Independence.

Present Condition of Virginia

[1:370] At the present time Virginia is divided into 24 districts, comprising 68 counties.[40] The capital was formerly Williamsburg, but several years ago the government was transferred to Richmond as a city closer to the center of the state, since it is situated at latitude 37° 30′ on the shores of the James River at a distance of about 100 miles from its mouth. Richmond was a tiny village when in 1782 it was designated to be the [1:371] capital. It was then granted a city charter, so that its population grew in a very short time. Now one counts there about 400 houses and 4000 inhabitants. The houses are situated on two hills divided by a stream, over which there is a wide wooden bridge for horses and wagons, and on either side a comfortable walk for pedestrians.[41] Since the streets are unpaved, they are almost impassable in the fall on account of the clayey and sticky terrain. This barely nascent city has no buildings worthy of consideration, and the house in which the delegates to the Assembly convene is very cramped. However, the foundations have been laid for a magnificent statehouse in a handsome site on the hill.[42] The principal trade of Richmond consists of tobacco, which is[43] considered the best in the United States. It is nevertheless unlikely that this capital can have much trade, since it is situated between two cities already well developed commercially, namely, Alexandria and Petersburg. The inhabitants of Richmond are almost all merchants, while the landholders live there only at the time of the General Assembly.

Virginia, like various others of the United States, has a General Assembly made up of two legislative bodies called the Senate and the Chamber of Delegates. The latter is composed of the representatives of the several counties chosen from the freeholders, two for each county and one for each of the cities or townships which are entitled to them. Laws are proposed in this House, and then they are reviewed by the Senate. The senators are [1:372] 24, since this is the number of the districts into which the 68 counties of the state are divided. Every year six senators come to the end of their charge, so that their term of office lasts four years. The governor is elected by ballot by majority vote of the two Houses in joint session and cannot be confirmed for more than three years, after which he may run again only after an interval of four years. The executive power resides in the governor and a council called privy, of eight members, likewise chosen by ballot from the two Houses. Two councilmen are replaced every three years, and each year they elect a president, who, in the event of the death or absence of the governor, takes the title of lieutenant governor of the state. The judges, the attorney general, and the secretary who compose the judiciary tribunals are also chosen by ballot from the two Houses united, that is, the General Assembly. Notable is the law recently promulgated in Virginia whereby an absolute liberty of conscience is established as a matter of principle, whereas in the other states it bears various restrictions. Therefore not only Catholics (who are for the most part excluded from the other Constitutions), but Jews, idolators, Mohammedans–in a word any man of any religion or sect can aspire to the most important offices of the republic.[44]

Since Virginians are mostly planters, that is, landholders and live on their lands, the cities of Virginia are neither very large nor very populous. The plantations, for the most part quite vast, are planted to tobacco by [1:373] black slaves directed by the supervisor, or overseer.[45] The master's house is ordinarily large, well built, and on a good site, either on a hillside or a spacious plain, and all around are the little dwellings of the overseer and the slaves, and likewise the kitchens and the barns, so that the whole complex looks like a small village. A large garden is not lacking, in which vegetables[46] are raised, and also plum trees, cherries, apples, and other fruit trees brought over from Europe.[47] Moreover, many domestic animals are raised, namely, horses, cows, pigs, sheep, chickens, and ducks.[48] The Virginian way of life was succinctly described in the *American Museum*, a periodical published in Philadelphia,[49] and the picture given cannot but be welcome to anyone who desires to know the customs of these people:

> The gentleman of fortune rises about nine o'clock. He perhaps may make an exertion to walk as far as his stables to see his horses, which are seldom more than fifty yards from his house. He returns to breakfast, between nine and ten, which is generally tea or coffee, bread and butter, and very thin slices of venison ham or hung beef. He then lies down on a pallat, on the floor, in the coolest room in the house . . . , with a negro at his head, and another at his feet [1:374], to fan him, and keep off the flies. Between twelve and one, he takes a draught of bombo, or toddy, a liquor composed of water, sugar, rum, and nutmeg, which is made weak, and kept cool. He dines between two and three: and at every table, whatever else there may be, a ham, and greens or cabbage, are always a standing dish. At dinner, he drinks cyder, toddy, punch, port, claret, or Madeira, which is generally excellent here. Having drank some few glasses of wine after dinner, he returns to his pallat, with his two blacks to fan him, and continues to drink toddy or sangaree all the afternoon. . . . Between nine and ten in the evening, he eats a light supper of milk and fruit, or wine, sugar, and fruit, and almost immediately retires to bed, for the night. . . .
>
> The poor negro slaves alone work hard, and fare still harder. It is astonishing and unaccountable to conceive what an amazing degree of fatigue these poor but happy wretches undergo, and can support. The negro is called up about day-break, and is seldom allowed time enough to swallow three mouthfuls of hommininy, or hoe-cake, but is driven out immediately to the field to hard labour, at which he continues, without interruption, until noon. . . . [1:375] About noon is the time he eats his dinner: and he is seldom allowed an hour for that purpose. His meal consists of homminy and salt, and, if his master be a man of humanity, he has a little fat, skimmed milk, rusty bacon, or salt herring, to relish his homminy, or hoe-cake, which kind masters allow their slaves twice a week: but the number of those, it is much to be lamented, is very small; for the poor slave generally fares the worse for his master's riches, which, consisting in land and

> negroes, their numbers increase their hardships, and diminish their value to the proprietor. . . .
>
> They then return to severe labour, which continues in the field until dusk in the evening, when they repair to the tobacco houses, where each has his task in stripping allotted him, which employs him for some hours. If it be found, next morning, that he has neglected, slighted, or not performed his labour, he is tied up, and receives a number of lashes on his bare back, most severely inflicted, at the discretion of those unfeeling sons of barbarity, the overseers, who are permitted to exercise an unlimited dominion over them.
>
> It is late at night before he returns to his second scanty meal, and even the time taken up at it, encroaches upon his hours of sleep. His time for repose and eating never exceed eight hours in the twenty-four.
>
> But instead of retiring to rest, as it might naturally be concluded he would be glad to do, he generally sets out from home, and walks six or seven miles in the night, be the weather ever so sultry, to a negro dance, in which he performs with astonishing agility, and the most vigorous exertions, keeping time and cadence, most exactly, with the music of a banjor [1:376] (a large hollow instrument with three strings), and a quaqua (somewhat resembling a drum), until he exhausts himself, and scarcely has time, or strength, to return home before the hour he is called forth to toil next morning.
>
> When he sleeps, his comforts are equally miserable and limited; for he lies on a bench, or on the ground, with only an old scanty single blanket, and not always even that, to serve both for his bed and his covering. Nor is his clothing less niggardly and wretched, being nothing but a shirt and trowsers, made of coarse, thin, hard, hempen stuff, in the summer, with the addition of a sordid woolen jacket, breeches, and shoes, in the winter.
>
> The female slaves fare, labour, and repose, just in the same manner: even when they breed, which is generally every two or three years, they seldom lose more than a week's work thereby, either in the delivery, or suckling the child.
>
> In submission to injury and insults, they are likewise obliged to be entirely passive, nor dare any of them resist, or even defend himself against the whites, if they should attack him without the smallest provocation; for the law directs a negro's arm to be struck off, who raises it against a white person, should it be only in his own defence. . . .

This picture, though unfortunately true in some respects, is, however (as I have already said), exaggerated, since the indolence and barbarity of the landowners does not generally reach the extreme degree reported here. As a matter of fact, there are many who busy themselves at promoting agriculture and acquiring a scientific education, at which they are capable of succeeding easily, since they are endowed with natural talent and intelligence, as is proved by the Washingtons, the Jeffersons, the Madisons,[50] and many others who became famous [1:377] in military art, sciences and politics; and the hospitality for which the Virginians are so distinguished in America can give only a favorable impression of their character. Their amusements are deer hunting, horse racing, fishing, dancing, and gambling. Hunting is done on horseback, and not without danger, since they pursue the deer through the woods and over places where the terrain is very rough. The horse races, moreover, are finer than elsewhere in America, since the best thoroughbreds are involved. Thus they throw large sums of money into these races, as into card playing, which is very prevalent in the cities and, it may be said, particular to Virginians; and when they are not playing cards, they gamble on tobacco, horses, and all their belongings. Dances are very frequent and numerous in the country, where, inasmuch as the plantations are not far from each other, some 20 or more young ladies can be assembled in a short time, often to dance all night to the music of the violin of a negro; and among the other dances they have the jig, which resembles the dance of our peasants. In the regions of less unhealthful air the Virginians are very sturdy and dark-complexioned, and the women[51] have black, vivacious eyes and white teeth; but their complexion is less beautiful than that of northern women. Young men marry very early, that is, between 14 and 15 years of age, and their marriages for the most part come about by inclination, since there are many occasions, as at dances, where the young people of both sexes can associate freely.

[1:378] The numerous cities of Virginia that are located near the sea or navigable rivers cause the commerce to be distributed over various places, so that no city has many inhabitants or anything much in the way of trade. For this reason it was proposed in the General Assembly to establish two seaports, one to the north, Alexandria, and the other to the south, namely, Norfolk, that should have the privilege of trade with Europe; but since this law would have been damaging to various distant landholders, it was never accepted.

The main, and almost only, item of trade is tobacco,[52] a native plant of that region, used as a medicine by the Indians before the arrival of the Europeans. The cultivation of this plant calls for a great deal of care and employs a large number of slaves during most of the year. One chooses for this purpose a rich, clayey, and somewhat damp terrain, which is covered with wood and cut branches that are set on fire. This serves to fertilize the soil and to destroy the weeds and roots that might interfere with the growth of the tobacco, which is sown there with a light tilling. When the plants have reached a height of about three inches, they are transplanted, after a rainy day, in another plot of the same nature prepared in the manner that I have already said is employed for sweet potatoes,[53] placing a tobacco plant on each little mound of soil. When they begin to grow, one removes those leaves [1:379] that are too close to the ground and might therefore be damaged by the humidity; and when the stalk has reached the height of about a foot, care is taken to remove all the buds that come out of the axils of the leaves and to crush with the fingernails the top of the plant to keep it from getting any taller (Plate VIII, Fig. 1).[54] Only 5, 7, 9, or at the most, 11 leaves are left on each plant, the number depending upon the experience of the cultivators, who leave a larger quantity of leaves on the plants that are more vigorous and which are in a better soil. The plants are weeded from time to time and the spoiled leaves are removed until, at maturity, they are cut off at the foot and placed to dry in the shade, suspended in storehouses made for the purpose (Plate VIII, Fig. 3). Because all the plants do not ripen at the same time, the harvest lasts a long time, generally keeping the negroes busy from the end of August until the middle of September. About 10 weeks after the harvest, when the plants are thoroughly dried, a humid and rainy day is chosen to detach the leaves from the stalk. Gathered into bundles (Plate VIII, Fig. 3), they are tied together by the stems by twisting around them one of the poorer leaves, and bound in this manner they are packed into the barrels as represented in the adjoining figures (Plate VIII, Fig. 4). The James River tobacco, under which name is included all that is raised in the vicinity of this river, is the most highly esteemed in America and is sold at the highest price in Europe.[55]

[1:380] Corn, or maize, is also very common in Virginia, where it grows to a great height and produces very savory white kernels.[56] In the flat country to the east of the mountains bread is ordinarily of this grain, shaped into thin unleavened cakes which, mixed with a little fat or butter,[57] are cooked by bringing them up to the fire; and they turn out light and quite tasty.[58] Peach brandy, a liquor particular to Virginia and the Carolinas, is made there with fruit collected in the woods, where peach trees grow spontaneously and in great quantity. This liquor is very delicate and of good taste provided it is aged a year at least, and it is drunk mixed with sugar or syrup.

Clover[59] fields grow beautifully in this country, and they are very useful for the fine breeds of horses that the wealthier individuals have introduced, buying stallions at a high price in England. The horses that are obtained from one of these and from an English mare are called full-blooded horses, and are the most esteemed. The others, which come from one of these stallions and from a horse born in America are called half-blooded, and although they often turn out as good as the first, they are held in lower esteem. In general, Virginia horses are of [1:381] medium height, bay colored, well shaped, and very

Plate VIII. Cultivation and harvesting of tobacco.

fast runners, but less sturdy and smaller than those of the northern states, and therefore more suited to the saddle than the harness. They serve, as we have already said, for the amusement of racing, which is done according the English custom with the man astraddle and going around a circular space of a mile four times, which not infrequently takes only eight or nine minutes.

Kentucky

[1:382] Kentucky, situated near the Ohio River in the innermost regions of Virginia, has become in America the object of the speculations of schemers and the refuge of those who were unlucky in commerce or lost their credit because of their bad conduct.[60] This fair country extends to the east as far as the foot of the Endless and Allegheny Mountains, where it borders on the other parts of Virginia; to the north it has the Ohio Rivers and the State of Pennsylvania, to the west the Ohio and the Mississippi, and to the south North Carolina, from which it is divided by a line set at 36° 30′ latitude. The thickest settlements are to be found on the Salt Lick, Bear Grass, and Kentucky Rivers, which empty into the Ohio. Among these settlements the oldest goes back to the year 1764, in which a certain Henderson, having heard from hunters about the fertility and beauty of the country they had traveled through near the Ohio, left North Carolina with 100 other inhabitants, and crossing [1:383] the Allegheny Mountains, stopped near the Kentucky River and laid the foundations of Boonesborough.[61] Henderson bought the region from the Indians, formed a social system governed by laws full of good sense, and set himself up as sovereign of that little monarchy. Subsequently others migrated there and founded the village of Harrods; but when the news of this new settlement reached the government of Virginia, it reclaimed the region as part of its own territory, and King Henderson was deposed, receiving 200,000 acres of land as compensation for his sovereignty lost. In order to promote agriculture and to recompense the first colonists, 400 acres[62] were granted to each of those inhabitants who in the preceding years had raised corn, and preference in choosing 1000 acres to those others who had established their homes in more remote parts. Sale was then begun of the land, which from 1779 to 1781 was worth £40 in bank notes, corresponding to the value of a gold guinea, for every 100 acres. After 1781 the price was £160 in bank notes, which, however, in view of the depreciation of the same, was still a gold guinea. In 1784, when the sale ended, between 30 and 40 million acres had been sold, and the state still had about 13 million left.

The first division of this region included only three counties, named Jefferson, Fayette, and Lincoln, the first extending west of the Kentucky River toward the Mississippi, the second east of the Kentucky toward the north [1:384] as far as the Ohio, and the third from the border of the second southward to that of Carolina. Later, since the inhabitants multiplied to the astonishing number of 35,000 persons[63] on account of continuous emigration from the neighboring states, the province as subdivided into seven counties under the names of Jefferson,[64] Nelson, [65] Fayette,[66] Bourbon, Lincoln,[67] Mercer, and Madison.[68]

The Kentucky territory is a vast plain, rising in some places into medium-size hills, and divided by a great many rivers. The most fertile terrain is the most removed from them, where one finds the sugar maple, the Backay (another kind of maple so called), the Virginia cherry, black walnut, and pseudo-acacia.[69] There white-flowering and red-flowering clover grows very high in artificial fields, so that this country is very suitable for the raising of cattle, which during the winter, when hay is lacking, feed on a kind of tender reed[70] that is very abundant in the marshes. The most productive region extends up to 40 miles around the settlements, and its fertility is such that according to many people up to 100 and 120 bushels of [1:385] corn have been harvested per acre,[71] where 50 bushels is considered an average harvest. This was the reason why, along with the low price of the land, the inhabitants of the neighboring states swarmed there; and they still continue to migrate to that place, in spite of the dangers to which they expose themselves.

There are two roads that lead there, one of which goes from Philadelphia to Pittsburgh, where one takes the boat on the Ohio River by which he can descend more than 300 miles to the mouth of the Kentucky. The other crosses the Blue Mountains and the Alleghenies, goes down to the new settlements of North Carolina located on the Clinch River, and then passes through a vast uninhabited region to the shores of the Kentucky. The first road, which is the most convenient for going, is almost impassable for the return trip, since one has to go back up various falls and overcome the rush of the current. For that reason the second one is usually chosen for the return, which is nevertheless very wearisome and quite dangerous because of the continual raids of the Creek and Cherokee Indians, who often surprise and massacre travelers. These Indians have been enemies of the Americans for a long time, so that travelers always go in caravans of 30, 40, or more well-armed persons. At night guards are kept around the tents for warning in case of surprise, and no one dares to wander off by himself. This way they are safe, since the Indians don't pick a fight [1:386] except when the Europeans are fewer than they are. The new settlements are also exposed to their raids and they often take the homes by surprise and kill entire families. Hence, the houses are built not too far from each other, and forts surrounded by stockades are built at a short distance from each village, where all the inhabitants gather for defense in case of surprise.[72]

The poor traveling conditions, the dangers that one meets along the way, and the delay in the carrying out of business—an inevitable consequence of such a great distance from the capital city—have prompted this province to ask the state of Virginia for separation to form the fourteenth republic of the United States. This reasonable request was presented in the session of 1786 to the General Assembly of Virginia, which would have quickly agreed to the separation if certain circumstances had not delayed the concession. It was because various officers of the Virginia troops who received a portion of land in Kentucky country as payment for their services feared, not without reason, that if this were to become a separate republic, they would be compelled by those residents to settle there or to sell their possessions. But after that point was resolved, the following year the separation of Kentucky was effected, which now awaits only the approval of Congress in order to be received into the Union. Later, when this new state is more populated and wealthier, the many inconveniences of travel can be obviated [1:387] by making a new connecting road between the headwaters of the James River, which passes near Richmond, and the Kanhawa, which empties into the Ohio. There is only the distance of 26 miles between these rivers, although it is very rugged, since it crosses a mountain chain. This was the route examined by the same Captain Thompson, who undertook the trip by order of the Virginia Assembly and submitted the plan to them.

Near the mouths of several rivers that discharge into the Ohio one finds bones quite similar to those of Siberia and which, after the most careful observations, were judged to belong neither to the elephant nor to the whale but to an unknown animal to which was given the name of mammoth, in accordance with a tradition of the Indians living around the Ohio.[73] The latter say that in ancient times there were huge animals called by them mammoth (meaning big buffalo in their tongue) which destroyed the bears, elk, deer and other wild animals created for the use of the Indians.[74] The Great Man (i.e., God), upon seeing this, came down to the earth in wrath, and sitting on a mountain in whose stone they say his footprints can still be seen, he hurled his thunderbolts upon these beasts and killed them all except the Great Male, who, turning his forehead against the tempest, shook off the bolts. Then wounded in a flank, he jumped over the Ohio, Wabash, and [1:388] Illinois Rivers, and crossing with one leap the Canadian lakes, withdrew to the northern regions, where they believe he still lives. The extravagance of this account should not surprise anyone who takes into consideration how greatly the truest facts are altered when they are handed down by tradition. Hence it seems probable that the ancient Indians knew these animals, and all the more so because they describe them as carnivores, as the mammoth must have been from the structure of its teeth.

Probably those fortifications discovered a few years ago by Captain Jonathan Heart on the shores of the Muskingum half a mile from the union of this river with the Ohio[75] belong to a less remote epoch, although a very ancient one. A space about a quarter of a mile square, which the aforementioned author calls the "town," can be seen, surrounded by ramparts from 6 to 7 feet high and varying in width from 20 to 40 feet. Each side is divided into four equal parts by three openings, and another is found at each corner of the square. Those in between are the widest, and of these the widest of all is the one that overlooks the Muskingum, which opens upon a passageway that descends gently down to the lower ground, where perhaps in those times the river flowed. The sides of this channel are protected by two ramparts as much as 30 feet high where the ground is lowest, and which are almost level with the ramparts of the town. The bottom of this passageway is [1:389] filled in at the center, perhaps so that it might then serve as a drain for water, and also as a street. At the northwest corner of the town there is a rectangular mound of 148 by 88 feet and 6 feet high, flattened on top, with four symmetrical ramps at the sides corresponding to the opposite openings of the ramparts. Another similar mound of 100 by 80 feet is near the southwest rampart, which differs only in that it is cut way to the center on the rampart side, where the ramp is. Toward the northwest there is a circular rise with four little round excavations around it; and, finally, at the southeast corner a third rectangular mound of 72 by 36 feet, not so high as the preceding ones. A semicircular parapet rises at the southwest corner at the center of which there is a round pile opposite the opening of the rampart. The so-called fortification forms a square near the town with openings in the middle and at the corners, each of which is protected by a circular elevation about 10 feet high, except for the east and west openings, which have two of them, one behind the other. A somewhat oval-shaped little hill, called the pyramid by the author, is 390 feet in circumference and 30 feet high, and surrounded at the foot by a parapet 15 feet wide, 5 feet high, and 759 in outside circumference, where there is an opening that faces toward the fort. In addition to these three principal works, especially in the space between the town and the fortification, there exist other mounds, [1:390] deep moats, and tombs. The latter are little piles of earth in which were found human bones. They came upon a complete skeleton in one of them laid in an east–west direction with many pieces of talc on its chest. In the other tombs the bones were mixed up, some of them scorched, others almost calcified, and in various states of disintegration. In most of the tombs there were other signs of fire, such as vitrified stones and pieces of charcoal; and they found there Indian arrowheads made of flint and fragments of vases that seemed made of oyster shells held together by some sort of cement. The geometrical distribution of the ramparts, their former height, which must have been greater than the present one, are sure proof that they were made by a people not only numerous but socially united, and intelligent in the art of defending themselves, adding the beauty of symmetry to the utility of the arrangement. The modern Indians of that regions gave such vague and inconclusive answers regarding these works that nothing could be got out of them, and they apparently have no tradition on the subject. The large plants growing at the top of the pyramid and on other parts of the ramparts, among which there are white oaks (trees of slow growth) four feet in diameter, and soil quite similar to that of the neighboring woods, namely, composed of the remnants of rotted vegetation, join to give sure proof of the remote antiquity of those fortifications.

It would not be unlikely that such [1:391] works were erected by some colony of Mexicans, peoples who knew very well, according to the literature, the art of fortifying themselves with ramparts and stockades, and all the more so because the promontories here described resemble greatly in their form the temples that they used to have in those regions, that were constructed like truncated pyramids, with the altar placed on top, to which one ascended by means of stairs.[76]

CHAPTER XII

Maryland

Trip through Maryland, from the Virginia Border to the Pennsylvania Border

[1:392]

FROM THE TOWN of Winchester, which I left on the 8th of June, 1786, I went on (as I said) to the Potomac, which divides Virginia from Maryland. Beyond the river the road is put through the less elevated parts of the mountains, and it is neither disastrous nor difficult, then, since it then drops gradually down to Fredericktown from various hills, many of which are quite well cultivated. This is one of the most important towns in the internal regions of the United States, situated at 39° 15′ latitude. The houses are largely of brick, and the main streets, intersecting at right angles, give admittance to other narrower ones. This town was very commercial at the time of the war, when [1:393] communication between the maritime cities was hindered by armies, and now there is still trade in grain, flour, and hemp.[1]

Blackbirds,[2] so called in America because at some distance they appear of that color (although when examined more closely they are really of a dark changing color), are very common in those regions, as unfortunately they are also in the other parts of the United States. These birds fly in thick flocks and one often comes upon them in the fields, where they cause great damage to the corn, on account of which they are called maize thieves by many people. According to Kalm,[3] a bounty was offered in various provinces of America to anyone who killed them, and in the northern colonies they had destroyed them to such a point that hardly any of them were to be seen. But this law (so says the same author) was then abolished in the year 1749, since the grasses in the fields were destroyed by innumerable insects which, according to the observations of inhabitants, served as food for these birds, so that they made up, if not completely, at least in part, for the damage they caused to the fields.

Upon leaving Fredericktown,[4] I crossed the Monocacy River, which empties into the Potomac,[5] and after four miles I reached the city of Baltimore. On this road one passes by bridge over the Patapsco River, whose banks are covered with the handsome shrub of *Kalmia latifolia,* which at that time was laden with crimson flowers. Baltimore is situated at latitude 39° 20′ in the [1:394] valley of the Patapsco River, which discharges into Chesapeake Bay, and although it is not the capital of Maryland, it is certainly the largest and busiest city in that state. Its growth was such that[6] in 20 years, from a small number of houses that once composed it, it grew to the point of having about 7000 inhabitants. The houses extend on the hill toward the north, and between the east and the south they are arranged around a cove formed by the water of the river out to a point of land that encloses it, on which it would have been more practical to build the city, since large ships cannot enter the cove, and the merchandise must therefore be transported in small boats from the river to the city. The main street, called Market Street, is the only one that is paved; and the sidewalks are also of brick, as in Philadelphia. Many of the houses[7] are made of brick and three stories high, among which there is one, placed on the slope of the hill, where the Court of Justice is held. There are two markets, one in the eastern part of the city, built on the model of the one in Philadelphia and situated on low and marshy ground; and the other, at the opposite edge, which, since it is for the most part inhabited by families of French Canadians coming from Acadia and Canada, bears the name of French Town. Baltimore counts various churches of Anglicans, Presbyterians, German Lutherans,[8] etc., and it has also a chapel for Catholics. The inhabitants are for the most part engaged in commerce, since this is the main trading center in Maryland, so that [1:395] out of 1900 houses the stores and shops number 1100.[9]

On the 16th of June[10] I left for Philadelphia, and, in order to avoid the heat of the sun, I chose to make this trip in the public stagecoach which for some years has been leaving Baltimore regularly. By evening we arrived at Joppa, and the following day, passing through Hartford and Charleston, we reached Head of Elk, two miles from where the boundary is set between Maryland and Delaware.

Location and Former Condition of Maryland

[1:396] The borders of Maryland[11] are determined by Pennsylvania to the north, to the east by the State of Delaware and by the sea, to the south by Virginia, and to the west by the Appalachian Mountains. The principal rivers are the Potomac, which separates it from Virginia, and the Susquehanna, which enters Chesapeake Bay. The state is divided by this bay into two parts, distinguished by the names East and West.[12] The region to the east is low and flat, rising to the west in hills that terminate in the chain of the Blue Mountains. There is little or no difference in climate from neighboring Virginia,[13] the level land being unhealthful and the mountainous western part salubrious in the same way.

If the northern states had their origin in the persecution suffered by the Presbyterians in England, Maryland, on the other hand, was populated by persecuted Catholics. Cecil Calvert, Lord Baltimore,[14] Irish by birth, out of a desire to find an asylum for those Catholics who had lost their possessions in the disturbances of the reign of Charles I, asked this king for the proprietorship of that stretch of country in North America lying north of the Potomac River [1:397] discovered as early as 1606, at the time that the first settlements in Virginia were attempted, but which was still inhabited only by Indians. The King made a generous and unlimited cession, granting to Lord Baltimore and his heirs and successors royal jurisdiction, both military and civil, the right to make laws, pardon crimes, coin money, etc. He reserved for the Crown only the fifth part of the gold and silver produced by the mines that might be discovered there, decreeing that as a token of homage he should present at Windsor Castle each year on Tuesday of Ascension week two arrows such as the Indians used. Leonard Calvert, brother of Lord Baltimore, left England in 1633 at the head of 200 Catholics,[15] and upon arriving in Chesapeake Bay set up his colony at the mouth of the Potomac River. From there he went to the village of Yaocomico, where by means of some gifts presented to Weroanco, the chief of those Indians, he was granted permission to live in a part of the aforementioned village, which a short time later was yielded outright to the new colonists. The latter changed the name of Yaocomico to St. Marys, and they gave to the region the name of Maryland in veneration of the Mother of Christ, or, as others maintain, in honor of Henrietta Maria, daughter of Henry IV, King of France and consort of their king, Charles I. The cession of Yaocomico was not the only proof of the favorable welcome of the Indians, since the latter, settling down a short distance from the village, provided them with game. This solicitude of theirs was not entirely altruistic and was aimed at seeking [1:398] the aid of the English against the Susquehanna, a powerful Indian tribe that had declared war upon them. Thus in peace and tranquillity and without bloodshed was born the province of Maryland in America, whose population was increased annually by those Catholics who fled from England in order to escape the penal laws passed against them.[16]

At the outbreak of the civil wars in England the Calverts were deprived of the government of this province, but upon the reseating of Charles

II got it back again. Charles Calvert, son of Lord Baltimore, was governor for 20 years, and during the time of his rule introduced the cultivation of tobacco, a most useful product which formerly was raised only in Virginia. The emigrations from Europe increased from year to year, and thus the Catholics, like the Protestants, enjoyed perfect freedom of conscience, so that in 1687 there were 16,000 inhabitants, an astonishing number if one considers the brief period of time since the founding of the colony.

It would take too much space to mention here the disturbances that the Marylanders suffered subsequently from the wars with the Indians and from the disputes that arose between William Penn and Lord Baltimore over the borders of the respective provinces, and other less important circumstances, which are either found in the history of Pennsylvania or, being too minute, belong rather to the complete history of a country than to a short essay on its origin. There is nothing left for me to add except that Maryland kept its laws under the government of the Calverts until the beginning of the Revolution.

Present Condition of Maryland

[1:399] The General Assembly is here, too, composed of the two legislative bodies, namely, the Senate and the House of Delegates. The latter are chosen annually by the people the first Tuesday in October to the number of 4 for each of the 14 counties into which the state is divided, the requisites being a minimum age of 20 and 500 Maryland pounds' worth of real or personal property. The election of the senators is carried out by a council of representatives chosen by the people on the first of September, two for each county, who meet in the city of Annapolis, and on the third Monday of the same month proceed to elect the senators by ballot. There are 15 of these, 9 from the western part and 6 from the eastern. They must be at least 25 years old and own £1000 of capital; and their office lasts 5 years. The executive power belongs to the governor and a council of five members elected by ballot by the two legislative bodies in the General Assembly. And the governor cannot be confirmed in his charge for more than three years.

The principal cities of this state are Annapolis, Baltimore, and Fredericktown, among which the first bears the title of capital.[17] It is true, however, that the inhabitants of Baltimore, fearing [1:400] that business matters would be neglected in the House of Delegates, wanted the General Assembly transferred to their city as the largest and most active commercially. But in spite of their manipulations the people of Annapolis, anxious to keep for themselves the seat of government, succeeded in thwarting their petitions and in warding off the idea of this change.

Annapolis is located at 38° 55′ latitude on a hill surrounded by the Severn and South Creek Rivers, which join upon entering Chesapeake Bay to form the peninsula upon which is situated the city.[18] The streets are not very regular, but the houses are in general quite impressive and well built. Among them stands out the statehouse placed at the top of the hill, from which one enjoys a very charming view. The ascent to it is by various steps that lead to a large hall with a cupola where the Court of Justice is held, and on either side there are two other halls, the first for the Senate, and the second for the House of Delegates. In this latter can be seen a full-sized portrait of General Washington with his aide de camp Colonel Tilghman (a native of Maryland) and Marquis de Lafayette executed by Mr. Peale,[19] a Philadelphia painter. The upper floor serves for the governor and council, and for the treasury, chancellery, and other state offices. This is the handsomest building of its kind in the southern states. The commerce of this state is insignificant,[20] and the inhabitants, nearly all of them landholders, live so luxuriously and elegantly [1:401] that the society of Annapolis is reputed to be one of the most refined in North America.

Although Catholics were the first inhabitants of Maryland, numerous Protestants came in later, all the sects enjoying complete freedom of conscience. The sciences already begin to flourish, and among other useful institutions two colleges have recently been set up, one under the name of Washington, built in 1783 at Chestertown, and another, which is now being completed, at Baltimore for the teaching of the Greek and Latin languages and mathematics.[21] Marylanders are divided into landholders and merchants. The former either remain on their plantations like the Virginians, from whom they differ little in their customs, or they come to live in Annapolis.[22] The merchants, on the other hand, dwell in large part in Baltimore, and in part they are scattered throughout the various counties.

The number of Maryland inhabitants in 1786 came to 30,000 whites and 83,000 negroes, who are employed at raising tobacco. This item, which there constitutes the main export, is cultivated everywhere, but mainly along the Potomac and other small rivers, since the soil is thin and almost sterile in places too far from water. In addition to tobacco they raise grain, rye, corn, and oats. The grains and tobacco that grow in the more internal parts of the state are transported all the way to Baltimore on certain vehicles called wagons, which are used also in the other nearby [1:402] states. These vehicles have four wheels and very high sides, to which are fastened wooden hoops supporting a cover formed of a thick, heavy canvas, and even black bear skin.[23] Four to six horses are attached, and they often come with their loads of bear, beaver, muskrat, deer, otter, wildcat, and lynx skins from the most distant regions beyond the mountains 300 or 400 miles away. When the drivers have sold their load, they return to the wilds, carrying there salt and the European products which are most needed. On these trips they often employ a month or two, sleeping under the cover of their wagons or upon the bare earth. They very rarely stop at the[24] hotels, and they live on salt pork and a little milk, which they procure from nearby homes. They also nourish themselves on fish, which they roast with lard, whenever they have to stop near some river.[25]

Iron mines are very abundant in Maryland, and the earth is so impregnated with the lime of this metal in the area of Baltimore that in various places it seems to be of a blood-red color. The iron that is extracted is used to make axes, plowshares, and other farming tools, which are manufactured with great perfection. American axes are short and heavy, with the handle set almost in the middle of the iron.[26] With one of these a tree can be cut in less time than with [1:403] European axes, and they have the additional advantage of being more solid and durable. Their shape is not very different from that of the tomahawks, or flint axes of the Indians, so that it seems that they got from them the idea. The plows are simple and without wheels; they are pulled by horses and do not penetrate the soil very deeply.[27]

CHAPTER XIII

The State of Delaware

[2:1]

THIS STATE is the tiniest of the United States, extending only from 38° 35′ to 39° 50′ latitude. I crossed it twice, passing through Christina,[1] a little village founded by the Swedes on the Delaware River, and through the city of Wilmington, which is its capital. This region formerly made up a portion of the Province of New Sweden and was settled in 1628[2] by the Swedes, who ruled there until 1656, when the Dutch took possession of it. After its conquest by the Duke of York, the city of New Castle and the land within the range of 12 miles around was sold by him to William Penn in 1683, to which was added later also the region situated between New Castle and Hoarkill, otherwise called Cape Henlopen. It was then divided into three counties called New Castle, Kent, and Sussex, and formed a part of Pennsylvania until it was ceded in the year 1701[3] by Penn to Edward Shippen, Phineas Pemberton, Samuel Carpenter, Griffith Owen, Caleb [2:2] Pusey, and Thomas Story. Then, although subject to the governor of Pennsylvania, it obtained the right to have a separate Assembly and took the name of Three Delaware Counties, until it broke off completely at the beginning of the disturbances in America.[4] It borders on Pennsylvania to the north, on New Jersey to the east, from which it is separated by the Delaware River, and, to the south, on the State of Maryland. It still preserves the division into three counties, the first, New Castle, near Pennsylvania; the second, Sussex toward Delaware Bay; the third Kent, in the center of the state.

The new constitutions give the legislative power to a House called "of the Assembly" and to a Council, which together form the General Assembly. The House of the Assembly consists of 21 members chosen annually to the number of 7 for each county, and the council is composed of 9 persons who remain in office 9 years, a third of them being replaced every 3 years. The president, or chief magistrate, is chosen by ballot from the General Assembly, and his office lasts three years. The Privy Council, which, along with the president of the state, is at the head of the executive power, is composed of four councillors, two of whom are chosen by the Legislative Council and two by the House of the Assembly; and the delegates to the General Congress of the United States are selected each year by ballot. Priests and ministers of any religion are excluded from holding public offices, as we have said regarding other states; and the introduction and sale of negroes[5] is forbidden [2:3] by law.

The principal cities, indeed the only ones, are those of New Castle and Wilmington. New Castle[6] was built near the Delaware River by the Swedes at the time of the first settlements and was once a very busy city, but now it has declined a great deal and counts barely 150 houses. Wilmington, less depopulated, also owes its origin to the Swedes, who called it Christina. It is situated on a hill that enjoys a fine view of the river; but there are only two or three regular roads there.

The terrain is for the most part fertile and level, broken by low hills, and quite well cultivated. The principal product is grain, and the flour is transported by water, or even by land, to Philadelphia, since there is nowhere in the state a good seaport for trade with Europe. The climate is generally unhealthful, and all the more so in the vicinity of Delaware Bay, where intermittent fevers reign.[7] The inhabitants[8] do not differ from those of Pennsylvania, whose neighbors they are, and the landowners who live out in the country, since they do not have slaves, are not called planters like those of Maryland and Virginia, but farmers, as in neighboring Pennsylvania.[9]

CHAPTER XIV

Pennsylvania

From Philadelphia to Bethlehem

[2:4]

WITHOUT STOPPING to talk about the brief runs that I took into the State of Pennsylvania from Baltimore and Philadelphia, as likewise from Philadelphia to New York, during which trips one passes through some towns of small account, I shall proceed to tell about an excursion of mine to Bethlehem, the dwelling place of the Moravian brothers. On the 20th of July, 1786, I left Philadelphia[1] in the company of Mr. Giuseppe Mussi, a fellow Milanese of ours, a young man of pleasant manners, who has been established there for some years as a merchant. After six miles of good road we arrived at Germantown, a town about two miles long and settled by Germans, who busy themselves with various manufactures. The houses are made of a friable sandstone[2] and shiny because of the quantity of talc mixed in with it. Toward noon we arrived at the house called [2:5] Spring House, where we passed the rest of the day.[3] In the neighborhood I found very frequently *Cephalanthus, Phytolacca, Actaea racemosa,* white and black walnut, Canadian ivy,[4] western briar, American sumac,[5] poison ivy,[6] and the laurels sassafras and benzoin. The next morning we got some birds with the musket, among which the black woodpecker with a red head.[7] It is quite common in this part of Pennsylvania, and large numbers of them can be seen flitting from tree to tree. They make holes in tree trunks with their beaks as our European woodpeckers do, and during the summer they are very harmful out in the cornfields, because, when the kernels begin to ripen, they pierce the leaves that cover the cob, so that the water penetrates and causes it to rot. The female differs from the male in being without the red feathers on its head.[8] We also caught alive, though slightly wounded, another curious bird, called by the inhabitants shag-poke, that is, plague of the shag (a kind of fish similar to pike), and also fish-hook. This is a kind of heron not much different from the *Ardea virescens* of Linnaeus, of which [2:6] it is perhaps a simple variety.[9] It is of a pretty bright blue on the back, with a reddish breast and lores[10] of a yellow color. The pupils of its eyes are black with a yellow iris, and it has a triangular spot of a blueish color on the head. This bird stays around the banks of ponds and streams and thrusts its long neck swiftly toward its prey, which it grabs with its beak and swallows whole. I ascertained this myself, because, upon being turned loose in [2:7] a room, suffering from a wound in an eye, it regurgitated a whole big frog.[11] They make their nests near ponds, where their eggs are often found in the spring; and they can live[12] for a long time without food, as was the case with the one we captured, which remained alive for six days without eating, in spite of the noise and the shaking of the carriage.[13]

Continuing[14] on our way toward eleven in the morning, we reached the inn of Mr. Kichlein that evening. Setting out from there the next day, we arrived at Bethlehem toward dinner time. The region is scattered with very charming hills, some rocky and barren, but on the other hand others fertile and reduced to well-tilled fields sown with wheat, rye, corn, flax, and buckwheat.[15] The houses of the farmers are made of stone and quite comfortable.

Bethlehem was founded by the Moravian brothers and had its origin as follows. A certain Whitefield,[16] a minister of the Anglican Church and later head of the Methodist Society in America, famous for his eloquence and held in high [2:8] esteem by the Americans, bought a piece of land in Pennsylvania and founded there a society under the name of Nazareth for the education of negroes at the same time that the Moravians were forced to flee from their Georgia possessions.[17] Whitefield offered them the management of the school and the enjoyment of the land he had bought; but a little later, differences having arisen between him and John Hager, one of the leaders of the Moravians, over some religious opinions, he took back from them the land granted and forced them to leave. Fortunately, a Pennsylvania gentleman offered to sell them a piece of land located at the confluence of the Lehigh and Delaware Rivers, where in March, 1741, they built a barn and creamery which served also as a church, to which (wishing to allude to the hut in which Jesus Christ was born) they gave the name of Bethlehem. Some time later Whitefield himself, no longer concerned about the plan to educate negroes, sold the land of Nazareth, and it, too, was bought by the Moravians.[18]

The village of Bethlehem is located 53 miles north of Philadelphia on a height that dominates the Lehigh River. It contains about 50 houses unevenly distributed over the hill. The house for the young men of marriageable age[19] is very large, and since it is situated [2:9] on the slope of a hill, it has four stories on one side and only three on the other. In this building there are various dormitories,[20] a hall where they assemble for the private morning and evening prayers, and on top a belvedere from which one enjoys the view of the village, orchards, gardens, and pretty fields that surround it. The house for marriageable girls is likewise very extensive, the private church is very large; the dormitories are airy and very clean, as are also the rooms that serve for the various tasks, especially for spinning cotton and linen and weaving them into ordinary fabrics.[21] The public church, where the Moravians of both sexes assemble on Sundays, is a very large hall, in which the women are separated from the men, and there is a little table with a chair from which the preaching is done. Around this hall there are various pictures representing the passion of Jesus Christ, very poorly executed by one of their brethren.

After seeing these main buildings, I went with Mr. Osley, one of the Moravians, to examine their various manufactures. In the tannery there is a water mill for breaking up into tiny pieces the bark of the white oak,[22] which is there the best of the oaks to take the place of the vallonea, and on the other side of this building there is another mill for pressing the skins, which are dressed as red leathers and black hides. In another place they turn out yellow deerskins,[23] but since these are quite expensive, they don't sell well. The mills mentioned, as likewise those for grinding [2:10] grain, squeezing out linseed oil, and the water pumps that serve[24] for the various manufactures, are driven by the little stream of Manakisy that goes around the village. Beyond those mentioned, there are other manufactures of coarse clothing, woolen socks, cotton, thread, canvases, etc., and likewise the trades of carpenter, turner, blacksmith, hatter, cobbler, tailor, potter, etc. There is only one shop for each craft or trade, and a number of the marriageable youths is turned over to each workman as shopboys.[25]

On Sunday morning, the 23rd, I left for Nazareth, another Moravian village. One goes along by the so-called Kittatinny Mountains on the way to Christian Spring, a rich holding about eight miles from Bethlehem, from which Nazareth is only two miles away.[26] This little village has the shape of a cross, and in the center there is a pump with very good water. The houses are about 30 or 40 in number, built in the style of those of Bethlehem, except that they are less pretentious, apart from the house where the young boys' school is held and the Congregation built by Count Zinzendorf, who expected to end his days there. In that church there are various paintings by the same hand[27] as those of Bethlehem.

In the account of my travels in North Carolina I have already talked about the origin of the Moravians and of their settlements in North America, and now I shall add here only a few notes on their customs. The doctrine of the Moravians is the same as that of Luther, since they [2:11] embraced the so-called Augustan Confession, but their liturgy is quite different and changes according to the pleasure of the German synod. They have missionaries in Greenland and also near Hudson Bay, with whom they correspond, reading in church on Sunday the news they receive from them. It does not appear that the Moravians are much given to study, inasmuch as the only books that are found in their houses are the history of their sect, their missions, catechisms, and prayers. These latter are often formless compilations of absolutely trivial, and sometimes even indecent, verse, as can be inferred from the one given in a footnote by the English translator of the travels of Marquis Chastellux, which he says he copied from their books[28] in Pudsey, England.[29]

[2:12] Male children, as long as they are still boys, live with their relatives, but later (provided they are not necessary for the support of their parents) they enter the training house for marriageable youths where they are instructed in reading and writing and the German and Latin languages, and they are educated in husbandry or in some craft or trade. Girls are shut up in another house where they are trained in female tasks by a number of matrons. They lead a communal life like nuns, the hours of prayer, dinner, supper, etc., regulated by the sound of a bell. The reason that they adduce for raising their children in such a manner is that of preventing the disorders that might arise from the liberty of association between young people of both sexes. However, this life, so monotonous and sedentary, the perhaps excessive application to tasks, and the lack of those amusements and pastimes that are from time to time necessary for young people, render these girls pale and thin so that one could hardly find among them a happy and lively face and a healthy, blooming complexion. It likewise comes about therefrom that, since the young people of both sexes never see one another (being separated even in church and entering by different doors), marriages are not made by inclination but are determined by the parents. This custom which in Europe, and especially in our Italy, produces so many unhappy conjugal ties, does not have the same bad consequences for the Moravians, if we are to believe their reports, and that derives perhaps from the education that they receive, by which they become accustomed to a regulated life, to [2:13] constant occupation, and to a profound respect for their customs. Maybe it is likely that the pale and melancholy faces of the young women, rendered less attractive by their strange headdress consisting of a veil and a little bonnet that covers all the hair, contributes to making the young men still more indifferent in their choice. Usually this is carried out by the father, or the head of the village, who proposes a girl to the young man, and if they are both satisfied, the marriage is set. If, however, the girl refuses twice to marry those who are offered to her, she is condemned to perpetual spinsterhood. The status of the women is distinguished by the color of the ribbon that ties their bonnet under their chin, since the married wear a blue one, widows white, and marriageable girls red.[30]

During the trip back to Philadelphia on the 24th, while we were resting our horses, we killed a robin,[31] a kind of edible thrush with a reddish breast, and a blue wagtail, a very pretty little bird very common in the hedges in America.[32] I also came upon one of the largest moths, very similar to the native one we call *pavonia.* This is a new species, with wings of a dark gray color, and on each of them a half-moon of rusty red with a band of the same color. The ends of the wings are spotted with a pale yellow and black, the tips of the anterior wings being reddish colored with a [2:14] round black spot.[33] I shall add to this one two other butterflies I found in Pennsylvania, namely, the one (called *Phalaena lunus* by Linnaeus) that has yellowish-green wings with a transparent spot surrounded by a reddish line, and a small dark yellow one that has a rather unusual shape representing the outline of a bell.[34]

Condition of Pennsylvania and a Brief Account of Its Earliest Settlements

[2:15] Pennsylvania borders on the north with the State of New York and the Seneca Indians near Lake Erie, on the east likewise with New York and with New Jersey, from which it is separated by the Delaware River, to the south with the States of Delaware, Maryland, and Virginia, and to the west with the Ohio River. It extends from 39° to 44° latitude and from 74° to 81° longitude from London. The main rivers are the Delaware, the Susquehanna, and the Ohio. The Delaware is formed by two branches, called the East and the West. The East originates from little Utsayantha Lake at latitude 42° 26′, 43 miles to the west of the city of Albany. The other (called also the Lehigh) rises from an extensive marsh in Northampton County and joins the other branch in the vicinity of the town of Easton, whence it descends into the bay to which it gives its name. The Susquehanna, a river even larger than the Delaware, takes its origin from Otsego, or Ostega, Lake situated at latitude 42° 47′ west of the city of Albany and 15 miles from the [2:16] Mohawk River. The carrying place between this river and the aforementioned lake is nevertheless calculated to be twenty miles. Lake Otsego is about nine miles long from north to south, and now half a mile and now up to a mile and a half in width. Three miles from the spot where the Susquehanna comes out, another river called Oaks Creek joins it that arises from tiny Canadarago Lake located six miles to the west of the first and equal to about a third of its size. The Susquehanna is navigable up to its source with little flatboats which, handled by just three men, can take on the weight of a ton. They are built of light wood, are readily transported, and can easily be set afloat again whenever they become stranded in shallows. From its source down to the plains of Pennsylvania and Maryland there is no impediment to the passage of boats, but after that the bed of the river widens more than the quantity of its water would warrant, and it does not have adequate depth for convenient navigation. One hundred thiry miles below Lake Otsego there flows into the Susquehanna from the north the Chenango, or Senáchse, River, called also the west branch of the Susquehanna (navigable upstream for 50 or 60 miles by boats of the aforementioned construction), and 50 miles further down the Tioga also joins it, another navigable river whose mouth is located at 42° latitude. The Susquehanna empties into Chesapeake [2:17] Bay after a course of more than 300 miles. Finally, the Ohio (called Allegheny by the Indians and Belle Rivière by the French) comes down the western side of the Allegheny Mountains, joins with the Monongahela at Fort Pitt and empties into the Mississippi after flowing about 1200 miles. It is navigable from Fort Pitt to the new State of Kentucky, which is about 630 miles, and from there to its mouth in the Mississippi.[35]

Pennsylvania, owned first by the Dutch when it was a part of New Holland, was later abandoned by them and occupied by the Swedes. But the latter were again subjected to Dutch rule, and finally it was conquered by the English in 1663.[36] Until that time only the banks of the Delaware were inhabited, and these settlements were a part of New Jersey, whose borders were limited in 1676 to the east bank of the river. That same year the region situated along the west bank was promised by the King of England to Admiral Penn as compensation for services rendered to the Crown. But since the admiral died shortly thereafter, William Penn, the son, requested the execution of the promise made to his father, and after many difficulties finally obtained the concession on March 5, 1681. The limits of the country ceded were: the Delaware River on the east, beginning 12 miles north of New Castle to 43° latitude ("if," so reads the concession, [2:18] "the aforementioned river extends that far north"; from there a straight line westward for five degrees; and from there directly south. The southern limits, finally, were to be determined by a circular line 12 miles from the city of New Castle, which was to be taken as the center.

When William Penn, with various followers of Quakerism, arrived in the new province ceded to him, he gave the region the name of Pennsylvania because of the woods that covered it. He then hoped to live amicably with the Indians, and contrary to the custom of those who had settled in America before him, not believing himself entitled to occupy the country without the consent of the natives, he negotiated with them for the cession of the territory. This act of justice, his simple manners, his honesty and that of his other companions, won him the esteem of the Swedes, the Dutch, and the Indians. The following year Philadelphia was founded, a city systematically planned by Penn himself. At that time the royal concession was also extended. The region situated south of New Castle toward Delaware Bay was added, and the Province was divided into six counties named Philadelphia, Buckingham, Chester, New Castle, Kent, and Sussex, which, taken all together, counted some 4000 inhabitants. In 1685 more than 90 ships arrived in Pennsylvania and the inhabitants reached the number of 70,000, composed of Frenchmen, Dutchmen, Germans, Swedes, Finns, Danes, Scotsmen, Irish, and English, the last alone forming half [2:19] the aforementioned population. Thus the wise laws of William Penn, the consistently preserved freedom of conscience, and the advantageous situation of the Province drew to it new inhabitants from Europe and from the other American colonies. The counties of New Castle, Kent, and Sussex, at first separate, and then joined to Pennsylvania, were ceded by Penn, as we have already said in the history of the State of Delaware, to Edward Shippen and five other partners of his. Pennsylvania and its capital grew in population and wealth, dependent always not on the King but on the heirs of Penn, who kept the title of Proprietors until the beginning of the Revolution. It was they who chose the governor, who was then confirmed by the King. They enjoyed many privileges, owned a great expanse of territory, and received annual tribute from the inhabitants. At the time of the dissensions they kept themselves neutral, but they were nevertheless deprived of their possessions with the pretext that they made them too influential in a republican state. It is indeed true that they were promised a considerable sum of money to recompense them for the serious losses suffered, but no one knows when this promise will be carried out.[37]

The New Constitutions of Pennsylvania

[2:20] It will perhaps not bore anyone to see inserted here the beginning of the Constitutions of Pennsylvania, which, more than the others, breathe the ideas of a pure democracy:[38]

Whereas all government ought to be instituted and supported for the security and protection of the community as such, and to enable the individuals who compose it to enjoy their natural rights, and the other blessings which the Author of existence has bestowed upon man; and whenever these great ends of government are not obtained, the people have a right, by common consent to change it, and take such measures as to them may appear necessary to promote their safety and happiness. And whereas the inhabitants of this commonwealth have in consideration of protection only, heretofore acknowledged allegiance to the king of Great Britain; and the said king has not only withdrawn that protection, but commenced, and still continues to carry on, with unabated vengeance, a most cruel and unjust war against them, employing therein, not only the troops of Great Britain, but foreign mercenaries, savages and slaves, for the avowed purpose of reducing them to a total and abject submission to the despotic domination of the British parliament, with many other acts [2:21] of tyranny, (more fully set forth in the declaration of Congress) whereby all allegiance and fealty to the said king and his successors, are dissolved and at an end, and all power and authority derived from him ceased in these colonies. And whereas it is absolutely necessary for the welfare and safety of the inhabitants of said colonies, that they be henceforth free and independent States, and that just, permanent, and proper forms of government exist in every part of them, derived from and founded on the authority of the people only, agreeable to the directions of the honourable American Congress, We, the representatives of the freemen of Pennsylvania, in general convention met, for the express purpose of framing such a government, confessing the goodness of the great Governor of the universe (who alone knows to what degree of earthly happiness mankind may attain, by perfecting the arts of government) in permitting the people of this State, by common consent, and without violence, deliberately to form for themselves such just rules as they shall think best, for governing their future society; and being fully convinced, that it is our indispensable duty to establish such original principles of government, as will best promote the general happiness of the people of this State, and their posterity, and provide for future improvements, without partiality for, or prejudice against any particular class, sect, or denomination of men whatever, [2:22] do, by virtue of the authority vested in us by our constituents, ordain, declare, and establish, the following *Declaration of Rights* and *Frame of Government,* to be the ***Constitution*** of this commonwealth, and to remain in force therein forever, unaltered, except in such articles as shall hereafter on experience be found to require improvement, and which shall by the same authority of the people, fairly delegated as this frame of government directs, be amended or improved for the design of all government, herein before mentioned.

Beyond that, the following articles found in the same Constitutions are worthy of note:

> XXVIII. The person of a debtor, where there is not a strong presumption of fraud, shall not be continued in prison, after delivering up, *bona fide,* all his estate real and personal, for the use of his creditors, in such a manner as shall be hereafter regulated by law. All prisoners shall be bailable by sufficient sureties, unless for capital offences, when the proof is evident or presumption great.[39]
> XXXII. All elections, whether by the people or in general assembly, shall be by ballot, free and voluntary; And any elector, who shall receive any gift or reward for his vote, in meat, drink, monies, or otherwise, shall forfeit his right to elect for that time, and suffer such other penalties as future laws shall direct. And any person who shall directly or indirectly give, promise, or bestow any such rewards to be elected, shall be thereby rendered incapable to serve for the ensuing year.
> [2:23] XXXV. The printing presses shall be free to every person who undertakes to examine the proceedings of the legislature, or any part of government.
> XXXVIII. The penal laws as heretofore used shall be reformed by the legislature of this state, as soon as may be, and punishments made in some cases less sanguinary, and in general more proportionate to the crimes.
> [2:24] XXXIX. To deter more effectually from the commission of crimes, by continued visible punishments of long duration, and to make sanguinary punishments less necessary; houses ought to be provided for punishing by hard labor, those who shall be convicted of crimes not capital; wherein [2:25] the criminals shall be employed for the benefit of the public, or for reparation of injuries done to private persons. And all persons at proper times shall be admitted to see the prisoners at their labour.
> [2:26] XLIV. A school or schools shall be established in each county by the legislature, for the convenient instruction of youth, with such salaries to the masters paid by the public, as may enable them to instruct youth at low prices: And all useful learning shall be duly encouraged and promoted in one or more universities.

The sole legislative body is the House of the Assembly composed of the representatives of the various counties who are selected annually from the people. The voters are all the white and free inhabitants above 21 years of age who have lived at least one year in Pennsylvania. They gather in each county the second Tuesday in October to elect by ballot their representatives. The latter are numerically proportionate to the population of the county, and the census must be retaken every seven years. In order to be a representative, one must have lived in the state for two years, and one can be reelected only after an interval of four years.

On the fourth Monday in October all the representatives gather in Philadelphia where they are compelled to read and subscribe to the following declaration before taking their places in the Assembly: "I do believe in one God, the creator and governor of the universe, the rewarder of the good and the punisher of the wicked. And I do acknowledge the Scriptures of the Old and New Testament to be given by Divine inspiration."

The representatives are authorized to pass laws that do not conflict with the Constitutions, and for the law to be promulgated, two-thirds of the Assembly must agree. [2:27] However, all the laws that regard directly the welfare of the state are published in the gazettes for a whole year before they go into effect, so that the people can examine them. It is likewise permitted anyone to attend the deliberations of the House of the Assembly except when there is some matter that requires not being revealed and is attended to behind closed doors.

The number of representatives in 1786 was 72, distributed as follows: for the County of Philadelphia, 5; Bucks, 5; Chester, 8; Lancaster, 7; York, 8; Cumberland, 4; Berks, 6; Northampton, 5; Bedford, 2; Northumberland, –; Westmoreland, 3; Washington, 2; Fayette, 1; Franklin, 3; Montgomery, 4; Dauphin, 4; and for the city of Philadelphia, 5.

The executive power is assigned to the Supreme Council of Pennsylvania composed of a president, vice president, and 15 counsellors chosen by the people, one for each county. However, since they have a three-year term of office, they are elected in the following manner: The state is divided into three districts, and one of these elects its counsellors one year, another in the second year, and the last in the third year, so that each year a third of the counsellors are replaced. The president and the vice president are elected annually by the combined votes of the House of Representatives and the Supreme Council from the members of the Council itself.

In addition to these two political bodies, there is one peculiar to Pennsylvania called the Council of Censors. These are elected by the [2:28] people on the second Tuesday of October, two for each county. They remain in office only one year, and they can be reelected only after an interval of seven years. Their duty is to observe whether the Constitutions are enforced, whether the legislative body and the Supreme Council, which holds the executive power, are fulfilling their duties as delegates and custodians of the people, and whether anyone has usurped any right that does not belong to him. They have to investigate whether the taxes have been levied and collected fairly in the various provinces, how the public money has been used, and, finally, whether the laws are enforced impartially. They have therefore the authority to summon for a hearing any person, to examine any document and proceeding, and to stop the course of deliberations, recommending to the legislative body the repeal of such laws as seem to them contrary to the Constitutions. Finally, they can request a convention of persons chosen by the people, to meet two years later in order to amend articles of the Constitutions, specifying the changes that they believe necessary, which must be published in the gazettes six months previously. The delegates to the general Congress of the United States are selected annually.

The City of Philadelphia

[2:29] The origin and the progress of this capital[40] are described by William Penn in a letter addressed to his English friends on the 18th of August 1683.[41] "Philadelphia," he says, "the expectation of those who are interested in this province, is finally begun. It is situated on a peninsula between the two navigable rivers the Delaware and the Schuylkill. The first is a superb and majestic river; but since the other is navigable by ships for a hundred miles above the falls, and because it flows [2:30] northwesterly toward the Susquehanna, probably the main settlements will be made along it. The city, according to the plan, is to be two miles long from one river to the other, and about a mile wide. A very wide street cuts across its middle, at the center of which there is a ten-acre square, at each corner of which will be placed the public buildings, as, for example, the Statehouse, the market, the schools, and some churches. There will be also other squares of eight acres each in the different quarters of the city. Eight streets, with the exception of High Street, will run parallel to the rivers, and twenty, in addition to the central one, will go lengthwise through the city, each fifty feet wide, etc."

The land on which the foundations of this city were laid used to belong to the three Swedish brothers called Svenssöner,[42] that is, sons of Swen, and was exchanged by William Penn for a larger tract about a mile from the city. When Penn wrote the letter above, there were in Philadelphia only 40 houses; but having gone to England on account of the disputes he was having with Lord Baltimore[43] over the boundary with Maryland, he returned to America the following year and found the number of houses increased to 357, many of which, roomy, well built with three floors, had balconies and good cellars. A dock had likewise been built [2:31] which even 500-ton ships could approach, market was held twice a week, two fairs were arranged each year, and there

Plate IX. Plan of Philadelphia.

were seven hotels for the convenience of strangers and those artisans who still had no residence. The hours of work, breakfast, dinner, and supper were marked by the sound of a bell, and after nine in the evening guards went around the city keeping people from walking about the streets or lingering after that time in public places. In the year 1685 Philadelphia counted 600 houses, as is indicated by a letter from Robert Turner written to William Penn,[44] in which he tells him that he had built his own house of brick and that many were imitating him, since those who had wooden ones were not very well satisfied. The population of Philadelphia growing with the years, there were in 1749 2076 houses, which increased to 4474 within 20 years; and although during wartime new homes were not built—on the contrary, a number were destroyed—nevertheless, according to the last calculations, one counts, including the suburbs, about 6000 houses and 40,000 inhabitants.

Philadelphia is situated at 39° 50′ latitude and 75° longitude from London. Its climate cannot be called unhealthful, although it is very variable. In the summer of 1785 the thermometer did not rise beyond 25° Réaumur, but sometimes the heat is much greater, so that the thermometer has been known to go up as high as 32°—which, however, rarely happens, and it lasts only for a few hours. The autumn [2:32] is rainy[45] and the winter very cold, so that the rivers sometime freeze right down to the mouths. In this latter season the cold northwest winds that then begin to blow contribute to the health of the inhabitants and put an end to the tertian fevers, which, however, are not common except in the vicinity of the Schuylkill.[46] One can consider this city, both for beauty and size, the metropolis of the United States. The buildings, notwithstanding the opinion of William Penn, spread much further along the Delaware, where the suburbs of Hartsfield, Kensington, and Southwark are located, and the land toward the Schuylkill still remains unoccupied except for a few country houses.[47] The streets of Philadelphia are very regular, and all intersect at right angles. So-called Front Street, which runs north and south, used to be the nearest to the Delaware River, but now, since a lot of ground has been reclaimed from the river by means of embankments, another street called Water Street has been added, which, however, is not as long as the city. The [2:33] streets parallel to Front Street are called First, Second, Third, Fourth, Fifth, Sixth, Seventh, Eighth, etc. The others are headed east to west, the widest of which, called Broad, and also Market, Street, which cuts through the center of the city, is 100 feet wide; and parallel to this one there are other streets named for the most part after American trees, such as Chestnut, Walnut, and Spruce. They are all cobbled in the middle and have on either side a wide and convenient brick-covered sidewalk, along which are set here and there wooden posts that keep away wagons and horses. Lamps to light the city and pumps with very good water for public use are also placed about. The houses are mostly of three stories, made of bricks, and nice looking, though a little narrow in the façade; and various shops have large glass windows outside, as in England. The public buildings scattered about the various quarters of the city are very numerous, among which the churches of the Catholics, Anglicans, German Protestants, Swedes, Presbyterians, Methodists;[48] likewise the congregations of the Moravian Brothers, the Anabaptists, and Quakers, and a Jewish synagogue.[49] The Town Hall is a fine brick building capped by a [2:34] tower with a clock,[50] and within there are large halls in which are held the Courts of Justice, the Council, and the General Assembly. These open upon the public garden, which is adorned with some beautiful American shrubs.[51] To the right a three-story house is being constructed for the use of the Philosophical Society, and thought has been given to establishing a Chemical Laboratory in the basement.[52] On the other side of the garden near the Town Hall can be seen the prisons, which are quite well ventilated, well lighted, and healthful, and where debtors are kept separate from delinquents.[53] The University, which was formerly the Methodist church,[54] is also a very large building of good construction. The market is a long portico situated in the middle of the street of that name, and is supplied daily with a great quantity and variety of foods; and on Wednesdays and Saturdays, set aside especially for the market, the inhabitants of Pennsylvania, as also those of New Jersey and Delaware, gather there to sell their wares.[55] Outside the city[56] there are two other public buildings – one which is set up to serve as a hospital, and is directed by the Quakers; the other, quite large, is the house for paupers and foundlings, where 250 of these are kept at public expense.

The inhabitants of Philadelphia[57] are divided, as in other American cities, into landholders, merchants, and artisans; and there are also some of those German or Irish immigrants who sell their [2:35] liberty for two or three years. They are obliged to work for the master who payed the expense of their transportation to America; but when this time is over they are free again, and as they are industrious, they find employment in the city, or they go to more interior parts, where they are given land to cultivate. The customs of the people are not different from those of nearby cities, especially New York, except insofar as the Quakers are concerned, who make up most of the population of Philadelphia. This sect, which originated in England shortly before the arrival in America of William Penn, began to spread among the lowest class of the people,[58] who were very soon joined also by some of the more wealthy. A number of them arrived in America with William Penn and began by establishing a complete freedom of conscience. The constant friendship that was seen to reign among the members of that Society, the beneficence that they exercised toward the poor of every faith, their honesty in business transactions, along with their exemplary customs and the patience with which they endured derision and persecutions, made them quickly the object of universal admiration and the model of good and useful citizens.

These virtues were, however, clouded in the eyes of many by some of their opinions and manners contrary to common ideas. Among these (in addition to the difference in their cult of having abandoned the baptism of infants and excluded ministers of the gospel), people considered profane, and even ridiculous, the notion they had that they were inspired by the Holy Spirit, and likewise the convulsions, contortions, and tremulous tone of voice they used in their [2:36] moral discourses, whence they got the name of Quakers, and *Trembleurs* from the French. Their dress was simple, even in the women – of wool, cotton, or linen. They made a point of not following changes in styles, caring only for their convenience and adapting themselves to the seasons. And practicing informality in their personal relationships, they abolished every kind of ceremony. The houses of the Quakers were looked upon as refuges for humanity, and those who were of a different religious persuasion could not help admiring their conduct. They remained so as long as they attracted to themselves the eyes of the multitude; but when the wonder produced by the novelty wore off, their fervor also ceased, and the simplicity of their manners was henceforth constantly altered. Contortions were given up, the pretension of being inspired was abandoned, and only the right common to all to speak up in their churches was maintained. Even the girls, upon seeing that their modest dress was no longer the object of admiration, strove to arouse the attention of the men by adopting dresses of richer fabrics and to show off their beauty by means of a studied simplicity.

These modifications in their principles were not very important until the time of the Revolution, when they became greater and of greater consequence. Since the Quakers consider war the most horrible of evils,[59] they always refused to bear arms, and if a few praised this opinion of theirs, the majority despised it as if coming from their lack of patriotism, fear, or cowardice. The younger [2:37] Quakers were unwilling to put up with this accusation, and quite a few of them abandoned the Society in order to take up arms.[60] This decrease in subjects had not yet altered the principles of their morality, until the multiplicity of disorders and crimes, the natural consequences of a civil war, led astray many of these sectarians and changed the public sentiment, which previously held the very best opinion of them. One must admit, however, that Quakers can still be found who preserve their earlier customs and did not follow the changes produced in the others by the wretchedness of the times.[61]

Among the other reforms of European customs introduced by the Quakers, they have given up the custom of doffing their hats in greeting, substituting for it the handshake; and speaking to one another, they always use the title “Friend,” calling their sect the Society of Friends. The women’s dress is quite plain, but very clean, and they keep their heads covered with a little bonnet, on which, when they leave the house, they wear a kind of silk hat that comes down and covers the neck with an extension in front for protection against the sun’s rays. The amusements of dancing, gambling, and music are forbidden, hence they spend the evening in family conversation; and during the hours of the days when they are not busy both men and women apply themselves to reading, so that their company is very pleasing and instructive. The number of Quakers drops from day to day, since the young ladies marry persons of other sects, with the result that in the course [2:38] of a few generations there will exist in America only the name of a Society to which Pennsylvania owns its flourishing countryside and Philadelphia its preeminence over the other capitals of the United States. The members of the other sects[62] are very fond of strangers, no matter what some travelers say to the contrary, and I was astonished to observe in the winter of the year 1786 the lavishness of their tables, the elegance of their private dancing parties and social gatherings, at which gambling was put to use not to fleecing one another but to varying the entertainment.

The sciences are cultivated in Philadelphia more than in any other part of the United States, and an academy was established under the name of Philosophic Society which began its sessions as early as 1769, although there were literary societies in this city even earlier. Two volumes of its transactions[63] have already been published, containing fine articles. Not many years ago an Agricultural Society was also founded in Philadelphia,[64] to which many farmers of the neighboring countryside belonged. Thus these, like other societies founded for the public welfare, were promoted by the celebrated Benjamin Franklin, to whom America owes so much, and who in his advanced old age continues to be useful to his country both with political discussions and with literary productions always directed to the advantage of humanity. [2:39] His merits in the sciences are too well known in Europe for me to recall them now, but perhaps the principal events of his life are not known to all.

He was born in Boston, which he was forced to leave for having published in the gazettes some articles unfavorable to the inhabitants that displeased the English governor of that province. Withdrawing to Philadelphia, he applied himself to the sciences, not forgetting politics, however, so that he was employed on various occasions. He was one of the keenest defenders of the liberty of the Colonies, and going to England, he gave in Parliament a most eloquent speech to prevent the application of the Stamp Act in America. But all representations having been to no avail, and, in fact, hostilities having already begun, he contributed a great deal to the formulation of the new government. It was he who succeeded in making the Cabinet of Versailles take a role in American affairs, and he acquired great fame with the French both in politics and science, so that he was chosen by the King among the commissaries delegated to examine animal magnetism, since he had made no little contribution toward unveiling the imposture involved. During the last years of his stay in France (at which time I had the good fortune to see him for the first time) he was living in Passy near Paris; but on account of his advanced age and the inconveniences of health, he asked Congress for permission to retire to his native country, which was granted to him, Mr. Jefferson having been elected minister plenipotentiary [2:40] in his stead. Upon his return from Europe, intent as always upon making new researches useful to mankind, he wrote a number of observations having to do with greater safety and comfort during long ocean voyages that were published in the second volume of the *Transactions* of the Philosophical Society of Philadelphia. Upon his arrival in America he was received amid the acclamations of the people; and the new choice of magistrates occurring toward the end of that year 1785, he was elected unanimously president of Pennsylvania, an office corresponding there to that of governor.

The Constitutions of Pennsylvania, which give an almost unlimited freedom to the people, and in which there is a single legislative body, produce an excessively weak and vacillating administration. Seeing its defect, some tried to give the government greater energy and stability by revising and correcting the Constitutions, while others rejected this change as useless. In such a division of opinions, the election of Franklin pleased everyone. The Republicans (such was the name given to those who wanted a reform of the Constitutions), recognizing in him the well-informed statesman, held no doubts about his consent regarding change in the laws that proved inadequate or harmful; and the other party, called the Constitutionalists, believed that he was for upholding those Constitutions that for the most part had come from his own pen. Conscious of the consequences of these differences of opinion, Franklin spoke with all the authority of an ancient legislator, and inclining toward the [2:41] proposed reform, showed that those laws which were excellent during the turmoils of war could be harmful in peace, and that one should do as the good gardener who, in order to have many fruit from a tree, condemns and cuts those very branches at first kept by him with all care in order to make it grow from the roots. If he did not succeed in reconciling the two parties (which was perhaps impossible), he did not fail at least to play the role of a true father of his country and to obtain the prosperity of that Republic that he established and defended with so much ardor. He must be about 80 years old and at that age retains all the vigor of his talent. His face is sincere and venerable, his manner friendly and courteous, and his conversation always instructive. Although he has been employed for many years in public office, he has not thereby increased his wealth, and his neat but simple dress harmonizes perfectly with his character and his writings. In short, he can be said to be one of those rare respectable philosophers who behave according to their pronounced maxims.

The Inhabitants of Pennsylvania and Their Trade

[2:42] Pennsylvania is quite thickly populated, especially in the eastern and southern parts.[65] The principal towns are Bristol, capital of the county of that name, and known for the mineral waters that are found in its neighborhood;[66] Reading; York; and Lancaster, which last, situated 40 miles west of Philadelphia, is the largest and commercially most active town of interior United America. Beyond these, worthy of mention are Carlisle for its college; Fort Pitt, which will very quickly become the center for trade with the settlements on the Ohio; and the towns of Bethlehem and Ephrata, the first, as has been said, inhabited by the Moravians, and the latter by the Dunkers or Dumplers, a sect of Protestants who seek to imitate the ancient anchorites. They have big beards and are dressed in a coarse shirt with wide trousers and a long gown. Their food consists of vegetables, and they busy themselves with tilling the soil, crafts, and manufactures. However, inasmuch as they cannot take wives, their number decreases from day to day, since they cannot find new proselytes among the Americans.

The customs and agriculture of the Pennsylvanians cannot be more precisely described than was done by Dr. Benjamin Rush, a native [2:43] of Philadelphia, who some years ago wrote a letter on this subject to Mr. Benjamin Vaughan, his London friend. This letter was communicated to me by the aforementioned author, and I insert it here below accompanied by some annotations.[67]

> The *first* settler in the woods (says Dr. Rush) is generally a man who has outlived his credit or fortune in the cultivated parts of the state. His time for migrating is in the month of April. His first object is to build a small cabin of rough logs for himself and family. The floor of this cabin is of earth, the roof of split logs; the light is received through the door and, in some instances, through a small window made of greased paper. A coarser building adjoining this cabin affords a shelter to a cow and a pair of poor horses. The labor of erecting these buildings is succeeded by killing the trees on a few acres of ground near his cabin; this is done by cutting a circle round the trees two or three feet from the ground. The ground around these trees is then plowed and Indian corn planted in it. The season for planting this grain is about the 20th of May. It grows generally on new ground with but little cultivation, and yields in the month of October following from forty to fifty bushels by the acre. After the first of September it affords a good deal of nourishment to his family, in its green or unripe state, in the form of what is called roasting ears.[68] [2:44] His family is fed during the summer by a small quantity of grain which he carries with him, and by fish and game. His cows and horses feed upon wild grass or the succulent twigs of the woods. For the first year he endures a great deal of distress from hunger, cold, and a variety of accidental causes, but he seldom complains or sinks under them. As he lives in the neighborhood of Indians, he soon acquires

> a strong tincture of their manners. His exertions, while they continue, are violent, but they are succeeded by long intervals of rest. His pleasures consist chiefly in fishing and hunting. He loves spiritous liquors, and he eats, drinks, and sleeps in dirt and rags in his little cabin. In his intercourse with the world, he manifests all the arts which characterize the Indians of our country. In this situation he passes two or three years. In proportion as population increases around him, he becomes uneasy and dissatisfied. Formerly his cattle ranged at large, but now his neighbors call upon him to confine them within fences to prevent their trespassing upon their fields of grain. Formerly he fed his family with wild animals, but these, which fly from the face of man, now cease to afford him an easy subsistence, and he is compelled to raise domestic animals for the support of his family.[69] Above all, he revolts against the operation of laws. [2:45] He cannot bear to surrender up a single natural right for all the benefits of government, and therefore he abandons his little settlement and seeks a retreat in the woods, where he again submits to all the toils which have been mentioned. There are instances of many men who have broken ground on bare creation not less than four different times in this way, in different and more advanced parts of the state. It has been remarked that the flight of this class of people is always increased by the preaching of the gospel. This will not surprise us when we consider how opposite its precepts are to their licentious manner of living. If our first settler were the owner of the spot of land which he began to cultivate, he sells it at a considerable profit to his successor; but if (as is oftener the case) he was a tenant to some rich landholder, he abandons it in debt;[70] however, the small improvements he leaves behind him generally make it an object of immediate demand to a *second* species of settler.[71]

[2:46] The picture is all too true that Dr. Rush paints of those who, living in the regions furthest removed from the old settlements, have totally uncivilized ways. They amuse themselves with hunting, at which they spend most of the day, and their farming consists entirely in planting that tiny bit of corn that can serve to maintain them. They are so given, as I have already said, to strong drinks that they often end up by getting drunk; and when arguments arise among them, they fight with their fists. To this coarse manner of avenging themselves they add customs even more barbaric and ferocious. If two of them challenge each other to fight, they agree between them whether [2:47] the three following methods of hurting each other are to be permitted: biting, bulking, and gouging. The first of these consists in biting fingers and tearing flesh with the teeth; the second is seizing each other by the most delicate parts and trying in this way to destroy the power to reproduce; and the third, finally, consists in grabbing the adversary by the hair and, putting the thumb at the outside corner of the eye, pressing it with full force until it comes out of its socket.[72]

They are almost always at war with the Indians; and they are the aggressors. They cheat them in contracts, go beyond the boundaries set as limits, steal their canoes, and always bully them whenever they are in greater number. No wonder, therefore, that the Indians, in their efforts to avenge the affronts that they receive continually, often surprise and massacre such ferocious enemies. To give an idea of the character of these backwoods farmers, it will suffice to report the following fact. The Shawnee, or Savannah, Indians, who live near the Sioto or Muskinghum rivers, had a chief, or sachem, whose friendship for the Americans had proved very useful on various occasions. One day when he was playing chess[73] in an American fort with the [2:48] commanding officer, the rumor having spread that a man had been killed by the Savannah Indians, a number of soldiers chosen by the inhabitants ran to the officer's room to avenge themselves upon the sachem. Upon hearing this, he declared to them that, since he had always been a friend of the Americans, if one of his men was the murderer, he would punish him severely or turn him over to their power. The officer himself tried to calm them, but in vain, since they had apparently resolved to kill the sachem. The latter, seeing that he could not persuade them, said very firmly to them, "If you want my life, I have always scorned it, and I scorn it now; but I warn you that my people will avenge my death upon you." He then loosened his clothes and presented his bare breast to their aim, which was immediately pierced by five or six shots. Thereafter the Savannah no longer wanted peace with the Americans, and even now they kill all those who fall into their hands. These things, which often happen in the vast continent of America, if they were known in Europe, would serve to give a better idea of the Indians and to reveal the vices and iniquities of those who pretend to belong to a civilized nation.[74]

> [2:49] This [second] species of settler (continues Dr. Rush) is generally a man of some property. He pays [2:50] one third or one fourth part in cash for his plantation, . . . and the rest in gales or instalments, as it is called here; that is, a certain sum yearly, without interest, till the whole is paid. The first object of this settler is to build an addition to his cabin; this is done with hewed logs; and as sawmills generally follow settlements, his floors are made of boards; his roof is made of what are called clapboards, which are a kind of coarse shingles split out of short oak logs. This house is divided by two floors, on each of which are two rooms; under the whole is a cellar walled with stone. The cabin serves as kitchen to this house. His next object is to clear a little meadow ground and plant an orchard of two or three hundred

apple trees. His stable is likewise enlarged, and, in the course of a year or two, he builds a large log barn, the roof of which is commonly thatched with rye straw. He moreover increases the quantity of his arable land, and instead of cultivating Indian corn alone, he raises a quantity of wheat and rye. . . .[75] This species of settler by no means extracts all from the earth which it is capable of giving. His fields yield but a scanty increase, owing to the ground not being sufficiently plowed. The hopes of the year are often blasted by his cattle breaking through his half-made fences and destroying his grain. His horses perform but [2:51] half the labor that might be expected from them if they were better fed, and his cattle often die in the spring from the want of provision and the delay of grass. . . . This species of settler is seldom a good member of civil or religious society; with a large portion of an hereditary, mechanical kind of religion, he neglects to contribute sufficiently towards building a church or maintaining a regular administration of the ordinances of the gospel. He is equally indisposed to support civil government; with high ideas of liberty, he refuses to bear his proportion of the debt contracted by its establishment in our country. He delights chiefly in company—sometimes drinks spiritous liquors to excess—will spend a day or two in attending political meetings; and thus he contracts debts which . . . compel him to sell his plantation, generally in the course of a few years, to the *third* and last species of settler.

This species of settler is commonly a man of property and good character—sometimes he is the son of a wealthy farmer in one of the interior and ancient counties of the state. His first object is to convert every spot of ground over which he is able to draw water, into meadow. Where this cannot be done, he selects the most fertile spots on the farm and devotes them by manure to that purpose. His next object is to build a barn, which he prefers of stone. This building is in some instances 100 feet in front and 40 in depth. It is made very compact, so as to shut out the cold in winter; for our farmers find that their horses and cattle when kept warm do not require near so much food as when [2:52] they are exposed to the cold. He uses economy, likewise, in the consumption of his wood. Hence he keeps himself warm in winter by means of stoves. . . . His fences are everywhere repaired[76] so as to secure his grain from his own and his neighbor's cattle. But further, he increases the number of the articles of his cultivation, and, instead of raising corn, wheat, and rye alone, he raises oats, buckwheat[77] (the *Fagopyrum* of Linnaeus), and spelts.[78] Near his house he allots an acre or two of ground for a garden, in which he raises a large quantity of cabbage and potatoes. His newly cleared fields afford him every year a large increase of turnips. Over the spring which supplies him with water he builds a milkhouse . . . ; [2:53] he likewise adds to the number and improves the quality of his fruit

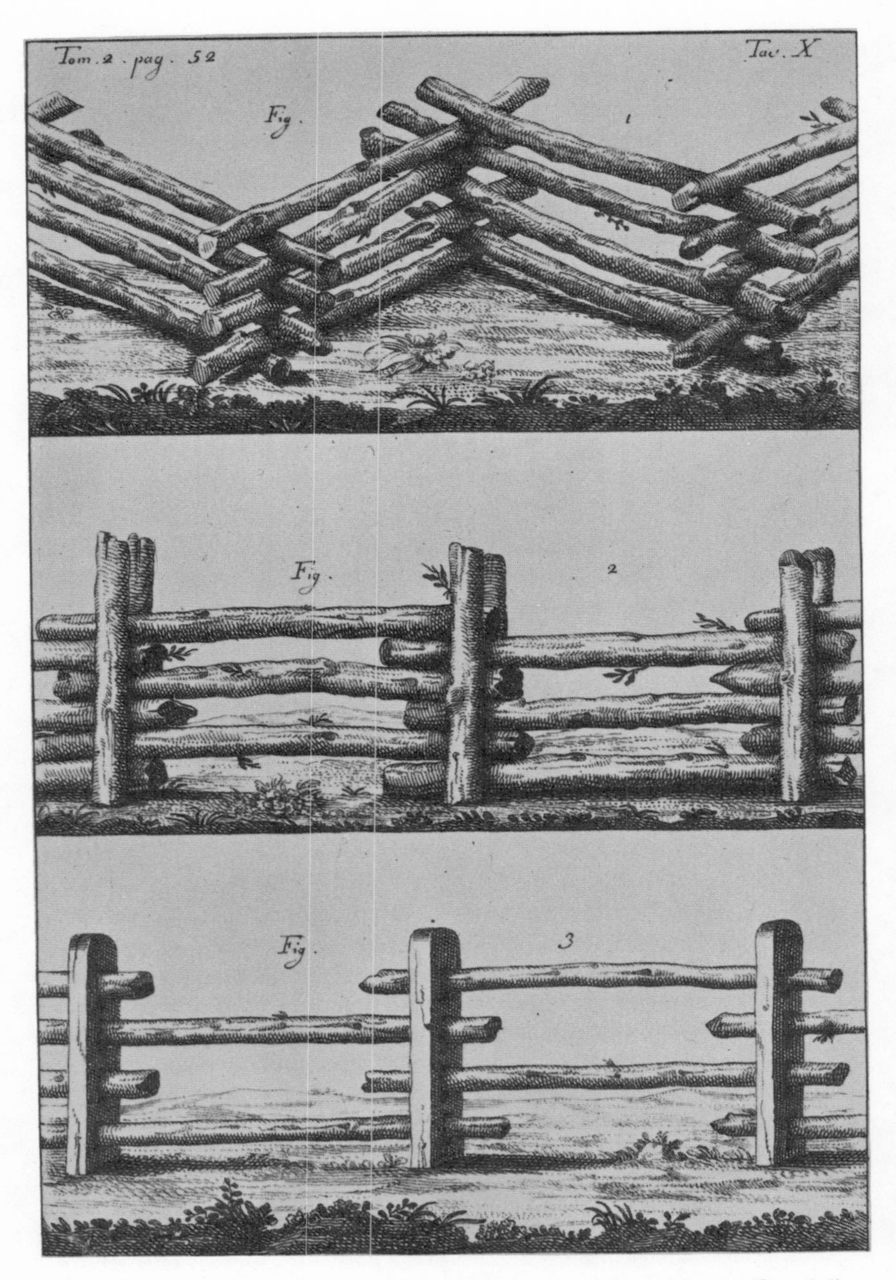

Plate X. Different rail fences in Virginia (fig. 1) and Pennsylvania (figs. 2,3).

trees. His sons work by his side all the year, and his wife and daughters foresake the dairy and spinning wheel to share with him the toils of harvest. The last object of his industry is to build a dwelling house. This business is sometimes effected in the course of his life, but is oftener bequeathed to his son or the inheritor of his plantation; and hence we have a common saying among our best farmers, "that a son should always begin where his father left off"; that is, he should begin his improvements by building a commodious dwelling house, suited to the improvements and value of the plantation. This dwelling house is generally built of stone—it is large, convenient, and filled with useful and substantial furniture. It sometimes adjoins the house of the second settler, but it is frequently placed at a little distance from it. The horses and cattle of this species of settler bear marks in their strength, fat, and fruitfulness of their being plentifully fed and carefully kept. His table abounds with a variety of the best provisions . . .—beer, cider, and home-made wine are the usual drinks of his family. The greatest part of the clothing of his family is manufactured by his wife and daughters. In proportion as he increases in wealth, he values the protection of laws. Hence he punctually pays his taxes towards the support of government. Schools and churches likewise, as the means of promoting order and happiness in society, derive a due support from him; for benevolence and public spirit as to these objects are the natural offspring of affluence and independence. Of this class of settlers are two-thirds of the farmers of Pennsylvania. These are the men to whom [2:54] Pennsylvania owes her ancient fame and consequence. If they possess less refinement than their southern neighbors who cultivate their lands with slaves, they possess more republican virtue. It was from the farms cultivated by these men that the American and French armies were chiefly fed with bread during the late Revolution; and it was from the produce of these farms that those millions of dollars were obtained from the Havanna after the year 1780 which laid the foundation of the Bank of North America and which fed and clothed the American army till the glorious Peace of Paris. . . .

CHAPTER XV

New Jersey

Condition of New Jersey and Its Principal Cities

[2:55]

NEW JERSEY extends from 39° to 42° north latitude and from 74° to 76° longitude from London. It is 195 miles long and 93 wide at its greatest width. It borders upon the State of New York to the north, upon the same state and the ocean to the west, upon Pennsylvania to the west, and the State of Delaware to the south. The main rivers are the Delaware, on the shores of which are found various villages, and which serves as a western border for the state; the Raritan, which comes down from Huntington County, passes by New Brunswick, and empties into the bay to which it gives its name between Sandy Hook and Staten Island; the Passaic, called also the Newark and Second River, [2:56] in which are located some famous falls[1] where the water drops amid rocks from a height of more than 60 feet; and, finally, the Hudson, which sets the boundary of this state to the east. The trip from Philadelphia to New York across New Jersey is ordinarily accomplished in a single day during the summer. There are coaches with six horses that leave each day from both cities, and cover the distance of 92 miles, the horses being changed every 8 to 10 miles. I happened to make this trip several times, both by coach and also with my own horses, having thus more leisure to examine the region.[2] It is level for the most part, broken only by some hills, almost all of them well cultivated, and it is one of the most populous in the United States. One sees beautiful fields and large peach and apple orchards. The fields are enclosed by well-made fences and the farmers' homes are comfortable like those in Pennsylvania. After crossing the Delaware River, the first city that one comes upon is Trenton, located on the shores of the aforementioned river at about 170 miles from its mouth. Although Trenton is not very large nor very populous, it can be considered the capital, since the Council and the Assembly meet there. This city was famous at the time of the war on account of the battle that took place there between the English and American troops.

Princeton, another city situated 12 miles from the preceding one, is known in America [2:57] for the college founded there, considered among the best in the United States. The large building is of stone,[3] and there are many rooms, in each of which are lodged two students, who in winter are provided with wood at the expense of the college. It is run by a president, who is at the same time Professor of Politics and Critical Art;[4] by a vice president, Professor of Moral Philosophy and Theology; and by a third professor, of Physics and Mathematics. In addition to these there are two others with the simple title of Tutors,[5] who teach the Hebraic, Greek, and Latin languages, history, and geography. Then for the rudiments of the Latin, Greek, and English languages there are also two teachers who instruct children. The course of studies is completed in four years. In the first two are taught the languages, history, and geography, and in the next two the principles of the aforementioned sciences[6] are expounded. However, since the limitation of time would not allow the students to get much out of the sciences,[7] they can continue to attend the college and pursue the program they have chosen. Theology lessons are given on Sunday, on which day the students recite the catechism of the religion in which they have been brought up. They are never forced by the directors to change their beliefs, so that this college is preferred by many (principally by the landholders of the southern states) to the others of New Haven and Cambridge.[8] [2:58] Princeton College is under the immediate protection of Congress, having been founded by a society of Presbyterian clergymen, most of them from Pennsylvania and New Jersey.[9] Since its income consists of cash, it fell off greatly with the issuance of bank notes during wartime. The salary of the professors amounts to 400 New Jersey pounds each, that of the trustees is 150, and that of the teachers of the lower schools, 100.[10] Princeton, like the other cities of New Jersey, is not very populous, and there is only one street, from which one enjoys the view of a cultivated surrounding area five miles wide.

In this region, and mainly in the lowlands near the village of the Swedes, one finds an animal called raccoon by the Americans, *espan* by the Germans and Swedes, and *attibro*[11] by the Iroquois Indians. This is a kind of little bear the size of a cat with a pointed nose and rather short legs. Its body is ash-colored, and the rust-colored hairs are black at the ends, so that it seems shaded with black. The head is dark with a white forehead and the eyes are surrounded by a black band. The tail, too, is varied with black and dark rings. It lives in holes in trees and withdraws [2:59] on clear days, coming out only on dark days and wandering about at night to obtain food. It remains sometimes up to six and seven days without taking food. This consists of still unripe corn, but it is also fond of apples, chestnuts, plums, and wild grapes, the last of which it prefers to any other fruit. It has a keen appetite for fowl, and it is caught by putting out as bait a dead hen, or bird, or fish. It is easily tamed, and its flesh is esteemed by some as a very delicious food. A raccoon pelt is sold in Philadelphia for about 20 cents of their money, and hatters use it by mixing its fur with that of beaver. The penis of this animal is curved and of a bony nature, so that it is used in America to make knife handles; and the Indians employ it as a stopper for the pouch in which they carry smoking tobacco.

New Brunswick, 17 miles from Princeton, is located on the south bank of the Raritan, a river navigable by small single-masted boats, and it carries on an active trade with the city of New York. Beyond New Brunswick there is Woodbridge, before reaching which one can see at some distance to the east the little city and port of South Amboy. And then comes Elizabeth Town. This is one of the oldest cities in the state, with two churches—one Anglican, the other Presbyterian—and a city hall, where the General Assembly was sometimes held. The little river that passes through it, whose banks are composed of a reddish limestone, takes its name from the city, is very scant of [2:60] water at low tide, and boats can go up it only at high tide. From Elizabeth Town to the city of New York there are two routes. One of these goes to the point of Newark Bay, called Elizabeth Point, and then crosses the bay to the peninsula on which the city is located. The other, which is most generally chosen, passes through the village of Newark, at a short distance from which one goes down[12] into a low and extensive swamp formed by the waters of the Passaic and Hackensack rivers, which are crossed in boats. Then one gets back to high land up to the distance of a mile from Paulus Hook, where two more very wide swamps are crossed. From Paulus Hook to the city of New York there is only the Hudson River, which has a very wide bed and empties into the sea at a short distance.

Origin of the Colony of New Jersey and the Present System of Government of This State

[2:61] In speaking of the first European settlements in New York, I have already said that the Dutch in 1614 left the shores of the Delaware to take themselves farther northward to the vicinity of the Hudson River. The region they abandoned was occupied 12 years later by the Swedes, whose emigration into America took place in the following manner. Willem Usselinx, a wealthy Swedish merchant, having returned from a trip to North America in 1626, and praising the fertility and beauty of that region, induced King Gustavus Adolphus to publish a proclamation by which he exhorted his subjects to form a commercial company with the title of West India Company. In the General Assembly that was held the following year in Stockholm, a sizable sum was collected for that purpose, among the contributors being the King, the nobility, the army, the bishops, the clergy, and many inhabitants of the provinces. Then the naval officers, the merchants, the agents, etc., were chosen, and it was decided to take on board the ships all those who offered voluntarily.

The fleet departed in 1638 with many Swedish and Finnish [2:62] colonists. They landed at Cape Henlopen,[13] and having purchased from the Indians the territory situated between the aforementioned Cape and the falls of the Delaware River, they gave to the region the name of New Sweden.[14] The Dutch of New Holland looked askance upon the foundation of the Swedish settlements, and all the more so because they had previously occupied the same region, and awaited only a favorable moment to put up opposition, while on the other hand the Swedes, who were aware of the jealousy of their neighbors, thought of fortifying themselves. In the year 1636 David Pietersz de Vries, the Swedish governor, erected a fort two leagues from Cape Henlopen, which he called Hoarkill;[15] another to the west of the Delaware River, named by him Christina;[16] a third on the island of Tinicum, with the name of New Gothenburg; and a fourth, with that of Chester. Although about that time the Swedes and the Dutch united to drive out a colony of Englishmen who had tried to establish themselves on the east bank of the Delaware River, the latter did not give up their claims to the province occupied by the Swedes. In 1654 Johan Printz, governor of the Swedish colony, returned to Europe, leaving the government to his son-in-law John Papegoja, who likewise decided to leave a little later [2:63] and chose Johan Rising to replace him. The latter, seeing how important it was to keep peace with his neighbors, renewed the treaties with the Dutch, the English, and the Indians. But the following year, when the news arrived that the ships meant to bring help to the Swedish colony had been plundered by the Spaniards, the Dutch, disregarding the treaties just renewed, equipped a fleet in order to invade the Swedish territory. This consisted of seven vessels carrying between 6000 and 7000 men under the command of Governor Peter Stuyvesant. Going up the Delaware River, they camped at Helsingburg,[17] a fort that they took from the Swedes, and where they made a few prisoners. They then occupied Trinity Fort, so called, and that of Christina, destroyed the homes, killed the livestock, and sacked New Gothenburg, laying siege to the fort, which was forced to capitulate after 14 days. Having thus come into possession of New Sweden, they sent back to Europe the officials and leading inhabitants as prisoners of war and subjected the people to the Dutch government. The Province of New Sweden was then called New Albion.

From then on the history of this region is intimately connected with that of New York, since they were both conquered by Charles II, King of England, and ceded to the Duke of York, [2:64] his brother, in 1663. The Duke sold New Albion to Lord Berkley and Sir John Carteret, who changed the name of the province to that of New Jersey; and they sent Philip Carteret there as governor after the government had been established in Elizabeth Town.

Then in the year 1680 the colony of New Jersey separated from that of New York, and a particular form of government was established there. In 1681 George Carteret, deathly ill, ordered the sale of East New Jersey [2:65] in order to pay his debts. It was bought by William Penn and eleven other persons called the Twelve Proprietors, who, in the same year, in order to invite foreigners to settle there, had a favorable description of that province published in England. However, during the time that steps were being taken to increase the population of the colony, so many sales and cessions were made by the Proprietors that over a period of years the possessions passed from one family to another without the opportunity to determine their limits. Numerous quarrels arose between the landholders and the Proprietors, so that the latter, to free themselves from continuous annoyances, decided unanimously to cede the province to the Crown, which they did in 1702. New Jersey was then reattached to the government of New York. But after its population increased greatly, it was again separated in 1736, and a particular form of government was established that lasted until the beginning of the Revolution.[18]

Like the other states, the new Constitutions were then formed, in which the power to make laws was granted to a Legislative Council and General Assembly, and the executive power to a governor. The election of the members of the Legislative Council and of the General Assembly is carried out by popular majority vote on the second Tuesday of October of every year in the various counties. Each free inhabitant worth 50 New Jersey pounds who has resided in the county at least one year prior to the election [2:66] has the right to vote; and in each county the elected must be four – one for the Legislative Council and three for the House of the Assembly. In order to be legally elected the members of the Council must have lived one year in the county from which they are chosen and own in real or personal estate at least 100 regional pounds. Furthermore, those who aspire to be members of the Assembly must have an estate of £500 and have lived one year in the county. The Assembly and the Council meet in the city that was agreed upon at the session of the preceding year on the Tuesday immediately following the election of the members, and together they proceed to elect the governor, who is also the head or president of the Council, the chancellor of state, the captain general and commander in chief of all the military forces.

New Jersey is divided into 13 counties, called Sussex, Morris, Bergen, Essex, Hunterdon, Sommerset, Middlesex, Monmouth, Burlington, Glowcester, Salem, Cumberland, and Cape May, so that there are 13 councilmen and 39 members of the Assembly.

Among the most conspicuous of the articles of the Constitutions the following are to be noted:

> XVI. . . . All criminals shall be admitted to the same privileges of witnesses and counsel, as their prosecutors are or shall be entitled to.
> XVII. . . . The estates of such persons as shall destroy their own lives, shall not, for that offence, be forfeited; but shall descend in the same manner, as they would have done, had such persons died in the natural way; [2:67] nor shall any article, which may occasion accidentally the death of any one, be henceforth deemed a deodand, or in any wise forfeited,[19] on account of such misfortune.
> XVIII. . . . No person shall ever, within this Colony, be deprived of the inestimable privilege of worshipping Almighty God in a manner agreeable to the dictates of his own conscience; nor, under any pretence whatever, be compelled to attend any place of worship, contrary to his own faith and judgment; nor shall any person, within this Colony, ever be obliged to pay tithes, taxes, or any other rates, for the purpose of building or repairing any other church or churches, place or places of worship, or for the maintenance of any minister or ministry, contrary to what he believes to be right, or has deliberately or voluntarily engaged himself to perform.
> XIX. . . . There shall be no establishment of any one religious sect in this Province, in preference to another, and . . . no Protestant inhabitant of this Colony shall be denied the enjoyment of any civil right, merely on account of his religious principles; but . . . all persons, professing a belief in the faith of any Protestant sect, who shall demean themselves peaceably under the government, as hereby established, shall be capable of being elected into any office of profit or trust, or being a member of either branch of the Legislature, and shall fully and freely enjoy every privilege and immunity, enjoyed by others their fellow subjects.

[2:68] The general tolerance announced at the beginning of the article renders useless, to say the least, the declaration in favor of Protestants, and it seems rather such favor granted them is a tacit restriction for the others.

In the Constitutions of other states, too, after granting complete freedom of religion, there are restrictions against certain religions, and particularly against Catholics.

Present Condition of New Jersey

[2:69] The eastern coasts of New Jersey, which extend from Sandy Hook to Cape May, are sandy and sterile, producing only red cedar[20] and black pine, but the hilly northern parts are, on the other hand, very fruitful.[21] In the low country near the Delaware River there still survive Swedish settlements in which the unhealthful quality of the climate renders the inhabitants more subject than in the other regions to intermittent fevers, both summer and fall. This disease, common to almost all the American continent in low and flooded spots, doesn't even spare the Indians, although they are less susceptible than the whites, perhaps because of the violence of their exercises and their greater frugality. Europeans who come to America ordinarily suffer these fevers during the first or second year, and their effects are very violent in them. There is no age nor state of robustness that is safe from them, and where they are common, men, women, the old, youths, and even children catch them. They are sometimes daily, sometimes tertian, sometimes quartan, lasting often up to [2:70] five or six months. The ill have a yellowish complexion, pale lips, and dry hands, and even though they eat a great deal, they become thin in short time. If they are tertian or quartan, they can, during cessations of the fever, work and travel without serious inconvenience; but when they are daily, their weakness is such that it makes them incapable of any physical effort.

The best remedy is quinine, and especially the kind recently discovered in the Antilles, which goes under the name of red china,[22] taken in powder form with wine, water, or milk in various doses. However, since these fevers are usually accompanied by a great amount of bile, the doctors advise the taking of tartar emetic, after which they prescribe quinine. Other remedies have also been used with happy results, among which can be listed the following: the bark of the tulip tree, the bark from the roots of the American dogwood,[23] sulphur pulverized and mixed with sugar taken in the evening and the morning; the bark of the peach, and especially that of its roots boiled in water until it is half gone, to be taken in the quantity of a glass each morning before breakfast; decoctions of *Potentilla reptans* and *canadensis* and of the *Caryophyllum*[24] root, as well as the bark of African willow;[25] and, [2:71] finally, mineral spring water impregnated with iron.

Various are the causes reported by Mr. Kalm in his voyage[26] as contributing to produce this malady, all of which, however, seem to me reducible to just two, namely, stagnant water and their manner of living. That the climate of America has no particular tendency to generate this epidemic can be deduced from the fact that this disease is unknown in mountainous regions and those removed from rivers in Massachusetts, New Hampshire, and Connecticut, and that it is common also in Europe in low and marshy places; and inasmuch as it is known also in the cold and temperate climates alike of both continents, from England to Spain and from Florida to Canada, being, however, more frequent, persistent, and dangerous in warm climates. There is no doubt that carelessness in providing oneself with clothes befitting the season, the greater number and size of ponds, and the need to expose oneself to night air, to rapid spells of warmth and cold, and to rain, as well as the excessive use of watermelons, pumpkins, and other watery fruit, render these fevers more frequent in America than in Europe.[27]

In damp and low terrain, in addition to raccoons and muskrats, there is found another animal, common both to Pennsylvania and other [2:72] more southern parts of the United States. This is a kind of *Carigueya,* or *Opossum* (Plate XI) (belonging to the genus *Didelphis* according to Linnaeus), quite common in the provinces south of New York. In the winter of 1786, when I was in Philadelphia, I obtained several of them, both alive and dead, that I was able to examine at my ease. The opossum of these regions[28] has a foxlike head, a pointed snout with a white nose bare at the tip like that of a dog. The ears, round, black, and sometimes rimmed with white, are composed of thin [2:73] cartilege like that of the wings of bats. The whiskers are up to three inches long and turned backwards. The front feet have five toes, of which the lateral ones are shorter and the middle one larger, all with curved claws; and the rear feet have also five toes, but the thumb separate and without a nail. On its body it has two kinds of hair, one short, soft and white in color, spotted with black at the tip, which covers the whole animal, except that it is different in the young, who are all white with black legs. The other hair is twice as long, stiffer, and completely white, and grows on the back, increasing in length toward the tail. This kind of bristle, mixed with black and white hair, gives it an uncertain gray color, whence some authors have said that it seems always dirty and spattered with mud. The tail, hairless and covered with oval scales, makes it possible to hang from the branches of trees like certain monkeys. The soles of the feet are bare and calloused, and these callouses, which form what we call the sole, are six in the front feet and five in the rear. The greatest peculiarity of these animals consists in a sac or pouch they have beneath the belly where the offspring are situated soon after birth and where they withdraw when they are pursued.

Plate XI. Opossum.

The opossum is easily caught since it is not only a slow runner, but when it sees itself pursued and unable to succeed in climbing up a tree, it drops to the ground as if it were dead and allows itself to be carried anywhere, so that many of them are taken to the market in winter. In captivity it is easily [2:74] enraged, and if one brings up some object, it opens its mouth and grinds its teeth, without, however, rushing forward to bite. One of those that I kept alive for a long time, when it was set free in a room, used to hide during the daytime, and jumped and ran around only at night, making a great racket. When I had it seized in order to tie it up, it became so angry that it discharged a great quantity of feces and several drops of black blood came out of its gums; but when the job was done, the blood stopped, and the animal, though sullen, remained quiet. The food that it liked best was meat, which it would take with its hands like monkeys; and it ate also bread, grasses, and legumes. It is very fond of chicken, so that it often raids chicken coops at night; and it laps up water with its tongue like a dog. It gives out a bad odor like that of foxes, which is stronger in females. I had both a male and a female which, although tethered, could approach each other, and after the first greetings, which were quite angry, they seemed to me indifferent. Then since I had to leave for Philadelphia, I left them in the care of a friend, who after a few days wrote me that the female had died. I was very sorry for the loss, all the more because, having examined other dead females with Dr. Foulke, a Philadelphia physician, we needed only this proof to establish certain conjectures of ours on the gestation of these animals still not well understood.[29]

[2:75] The inhabitants of New Jersey are in part Swedes, in part English, Scots, Irishmen, and Germans.[30] They are, as elsewhere, divided into merchants and landholders, the last of whom, the majority, are generally in very mean circumstances. The main trade [2:76] is grain, which is shipped to the two great ports of Philadelphia and New York, since there is in New Jersey no seaport trading directly with Europe.[31] Agriculture has in some places reached a degree of perfection not inferior to that of Pennsylvania, the fields are well cultivated and surrounded by fences, and the houses of the farmers, which are large and comfortable, have a roomy barn that serves as a granary, hayloft, and stable like those of North Carolina. In addition to other cereals, black grain or buckwheat is raised in abundance in New Jersey.[32] It is sown toward the middle of July, since they say that if one sows it earlier, it would continue to bloom the whole summer without producing any seed. This grain is excellent feed for poultry and for fattening swine. From it are made also thin cakes fried with butter that are eaten at breakfast. The stalks are good only for fertilizer, for which purpose they are spread out over the fields.

CHAPTER XVI

The State of Connecticut

From New York to New Haven and Hartford, and from There to the Massachusetts Border

[2:77]

All that remained for me to see in order to complete the tour of the United States were Connecticut and Rhode Island, which, although they are not the most extensive, are, however, among the best from the standpoint of agriculture and population. Therefore I left New York City in public stagecoach on August 28, 1786, and entering the State of Connecticut, I passed between steep heights from Horse Neck to Norwalk.[1] The inhabitants surround the fields with walls of stone, of which there is a great abundance in that region. Norwalk is [2:78] situated near the arm of the sea called Long Island Sound,[2] along which to the north runs the coast of the State of Connecticut and to the south that of Long Island. This village once contained about 200 houses, but it was destroyed in 1781 by the British troops under the command of General Tryon. Although the night was dark, we set out from Norwalk and covered another 13 miles of bad road to reach Fairfield.[3] From there, after three hours of rest, we resumed the trip toward Stratford and arrived in New Haven toward eleven o'clock in the morning. The villages that are found between New York and New Haven are generally small; but even in the most wretched of them are seen always two or three churches, whereby they differ from those of the southern states, where one can hardly find churches in the largest and most populous cities. On this trip I collected two new species of beetle, one of which (resembling the beetle called solstitial) has a shiny and crystalline back with wing casings of a cinnamon color,[4] and the other, smaller and more elongated [2:79], is of a changeable greenish color.[5]

Soon after my arrival in New Haven, I went to visit the president of the University,[6] to whom I had been given letters of recommendation. He showed me the copy of an inscription found on a reef in Massachusetts in a place that is covered by water at high tide on which can be seen various rough sketches of human figures such as children make—circles, curved lines, and triangles that could, with some likelihood, be interpreted as characters. In fact, some of the professors of Cambridge in Massachusetts were of the opinion that the Indians, practicing with bows and arrows in that place, sharpened the flints of their arrows on those reefs, making the abovementioned figures as a pastime. Nevertheless certain men of letters, even European, among whom [2:80] M. Court de Gébelin, to whom the drawing was sent, believed this to be a Phoenician inscription, whereupon they conjectured that that ancient nation had discovered the shores of America as early as that.[7] However, since in other parts of North America similar sketches of men, beaver, and boats can be seen that are certainly the work of Indians, the opinion of the Cambridge professors seems to me very well founded that the supposed inscriptions are nothing more than a complex of capricious figures and signs.

I then went with the President to the chapel adjacent to the University,[8] on the upper story of which is the library, the collection[9] of machines, and the museum. The natural productions in it are few, the most noteworthy being a species of pelican killed in Rhode Island, an American tiger,[10] the horns of a moose killed in Nova Scotia, a piece of petrified wood, and a sample of fine clay discovered in Castleton in the region of Vermont and which was said to be good for making porcelain vases. The few machines were an electrical apparatus with a glass globe, a pneumatic machine, a small sextant, a reflecting telescope, a microscope, and some others that were badly damaged, since they had been buried in the [2:81] College yard in wartime in order to keep them from the hands of the British soldiers. In the same room there is the portrait of King George I and that of Governor Yale, founder of the College. This was built in 1702, and there and in the one of Cambridge in Massachusetts degrees are granted as in the universities of England. The College is governed by a number of individuals called trustees. There is a president, two professors of theology and mathematics, and four readers for the four classes of students, who are divided according to the time they entered the College.[11] The day of the opening of classes and that of the awarding of degrees are celebrated, and on those two days the students give a public demonstration of their progress, with many persons of both sexes participating, as at Cambridge in Massachusetts.[12]

New Haven was founded in 1637 near, as I said, the channel of Long Island, and its port, whose entrance is very narrow, can serve only for small vessels that come and go from the city of New York. In the middle of the port, where the water is deepest, a dock was built, along which are the warehouses. A part of the port remains bare at low tide, and there is a sand bank toward the west almost completely covered by water at high tide. This port is situated to the south of the city, and on the [2:82] opposite side there is a beautiful tilled plain[13] about two miles long terminated by two stony little rises called East and West Rock. In the west hill there is a cave in which some maintain that two of those who took part in the condemnation of Charles I, King of England, hid for a long time, and that finally having come out of this retreat, they took wives, and that their descendants are still living not far from New Haven. The city is divided in a regular way into various streets that end in a large square situated in the center, where the main public buildings are. Toward the west there is the three-story brick College, beside which is the church for the use of the students. In the middle of the square is located the largest Presbyterian church, to one side of it another church of wood and the town hall; and there are also two other churches and a portico for the market. This square is even-sided, surrounded by plane trees, and would be much more beautiful if the terrain were not uneven and if the vast cemetery in front of the main church were removed. In the other parts of the city the houses are all of wood[14] and the streets are unsurfaced and sandy. According to the observations made at the College, New Haven is located at 41° 19′ latitude. Its inhabitants are about 4000, counting the students.

Leaving[15] New Haven, one goes into a charming countryside divided by beautiful cultivated hills, among which there are very fertile valleys reduced [2:83] to fields. Corn, buckwheat, flax, and hemp grow perfectly there, and a quantity of sorghum is also raised. Then come Durham, and Middletown on the shores of the Connecticut River, quite a busy commercial town that has an extensive manufacture of ropes and cables for ships, and, nearby, a rich lead mine[16] that was used during the war, but which is now abandoned. Not far from Middletown is Wethersfield, also situated on the banks of the same river and known in America for the quantity of onions raised in its fields. Their odor can be smelled at some distance from the village, and the ladies, even in elegant little hats adorned with plumes, can be seen in the fields busily gathering the onions and making strings of them, which are sent to the various states and even to Europe. Contiguous to Wethersfield is the city of Hartford, capital of the State of Connecticut. The extensive and industrious farming, the number of villages and houses, and the varied scene of most charming views, reminded me of the delightful hills of the Milanese highlands, to which they yield in no respect, either in beauty or in natural fertility. The insects of Connecticut are not unlike those of Massachusetts, and European butterflies and the various species [2:84] of crickets and locusts are quite frequent. Nevertheless I came upon an insect rather rare in those parts described by Linnaeus as native to the island of Jamaica. This is a kind of beetle with very short horns (or rather jaws) and a small curved horn on its forehead. Its body is black, shiny, with striped wing sheaths, and its abdomen is attached at some distance from the breastplate, for which oddity it was called the interrupted beetle.[17] Not far from this spot I found also two little cerambicids[18] which were sent by me to Europe and described by the distinguished naturalist and my good friend Councilor Scopoli.

Hartford, situated at 41° 50′ latitude and 55° longitude from London, enjoys a very healthful climate,[19] although extremely cold in winter. The Connecticut River is navigable that far for small ships that carry on trade with the Antilles, transporting there horses, lumber, barrels, onions, and salt pork and beef. The city is divided into North and South by the stream called Little River that joins the Connecticut at that point. Its houses are elegant, but almost entirely of wood, and the streets are irregular [2:85] and unpaved.[20] In its environs, which are very fertile,[21] the butternut[22] grows abundantly. After a few days' stay I went on to the pretty village of Windsor, divided by the Connecticut River into East and West, and then leaving the river I soon reached the border between the State of Connecticut and Massachusetts.

The European Settlements in Connecticut and Its New Form of Government

[2:86] John Oldham, Samuel Hill, and several partners were the founders of Connecticut in the year 1633, when, setting out from Massachusetts, they discovered the Connecticut River, which they called Fresh Water River, and settled on its banks. Complaints were lodged because of this new settlement against the colony of New Plymouth by the Dutch of New York, who maintained that that region belonged to their province; but the colony, instead of heeding these complaints, established a trading house there for dealing with the Indians, and two years later informed the Dutch governor that the King of England had granted the river and the neighboring region to his subjects, begging him consequently not to allow houses to be built thereabouts.

The Pequot Indians who lived there[23] had during the two preceding years greatly annoyed the new colonists; hence, to protect themselves against their raids, it was decided to found a city on the banks of the river,[24] to populate which, in the month of June of the following year 1634, [2:87] more than 100 persons left Massachusetts and set out toward the new settlement. Many of these, recently come from England because of religious dissensions, were of good families and not accustomed to the labors and discomforts that they, along with the women and children, had to suffer traveling 100 miles and more in the midst of immense forests guided by the magnetic compass, sleeping in the open, and crossing mountains, rivers, and swamps. The greater part of the new region was situated outside the borders already granted to the jurisdiction of Massachusetts, but they were nevertheless authorized by that colony to set up a new form of government. The emigrants had come from the villages of Roxbury, Dorchester, Cambridge, and Watertown. William Pynchon, at the head of those from Roxbury, founded a village up the river in a place called Aga-wam by the Indians, a name that he changed to that of Springfield.[25] Ludlow, along with those from Dorchester, stopped downstream at Matane-awg, or Cush-an-kamang, which he called Windsor. Hooker and Stone, with those from Cambridge, settled in a place called Suc-kiang, which they named Hartford; [26] and, finally, the emigrants from Watertown founded Wethersfield in the area called Pan-kiang[27] by the Indians, giving to the new colony the name of the river.[28] In 1637 two London merchants named Eaton and Hopkins, a certain Davenport, and various other well-born persons arrived with two large ships from England[29] and bought from the Indians that stretch of territory situated along the seacoast between the [2:88] Hudson and Connecticut rivers. There they founded the city of New Haven in a place called Quinni-piac by the Indians; and they took the regulations of Massachusetts as their model.[30] The region situated between the Connecticut River and Narragansett Bay was after a few years granted to Lords Say and Brook, who, having decided to settle there, sent George Fenwick to America to examine the territory; but having subsequently changed their minds, they ordered Fenwick to sell their rights, which were bought by the people of the Colony of Connecticut.

The inhabitants of Connecticut governed themselves independently of the Crown of England until the year 1661, at which time they petitioned King Charles II to grant them a charter by which they might be declared a British colony under the name of Connecticut, to include the settlements of Connecticut and those of New Haven. They obtained this concession easily from the King, but not so easily the consent of the inhabitants of New Haven, who were opposed to this union. They agreed to it three years later, however, at which time they were incorporated and the new laws went into effect. Since these were very favorable to the people, granting them the power to carry out all the elections of the magistrates, they were not changed in any way after the Revolution and are still valid and in effect.[31] In accordance with them, all the power appertains to two houses, one of which, called the Upper Chamber, is composed of the governor, deputy governor, and 12 assistants or [2:89] councilmen, and the other, called the Lower Chamber, is composed of the representatives of the people. And the two together form the General Assembly. It meets twice a year, namely, in May and October. At the first session the governor, deputy governor, assistants, and secretary are chosen according to the number of votes collected in the various counties since the beginning of April.[32] There are 20 assistants, 10 of whom are in office the first 6 months and the others during the following months. The governor is the captain general of the militia and the deputy governor is his lieutenant.

Present Condition of Connecticut

[2:90] Connecticut is enclosed between 40° 56′ and 42° 6′ latitude and between 54° 29′ and 56° longitude from London. It borders on Massachusetts to the north, on the State of Rhode Island to the east, on New York to the east, and to the south with the ocean channel that divides it from Long Island.[33] The river that gave it its name cuts it almost in two, and on its shores are situated the wealthiest and most populated towns. There are no sizable mountains, but very fertile hills and valleys, except near the southern border, where the terrain is sandy and sterile.

The inhabitants of Connecticut, of Presbyterian faith, since they did not mingle with emigrants of other nations because of their distance from the most frequented ports,[34] still preserve very rigorously their old discipline. The priests, or ministers, are esteemed and feared, and although many new doctrines have spread over other parts of America, they have not penetrated into Connecticut,[35] where there exist only two religions, namely, the Presbyterian and the Anglican. To this might have contributed the general [2:91] education diffused even among the common people of this state, since there are in each town free schools presided over by teachers who often exercise this function without expecting any remuneration from the public. On Sunday the churches are heavily attended and no one stays away except for serious reasons, remaining then shut up in his house and not daring to go out walking during the services. In church hymns are sung in counterpoint by young people of both sexes, often chosen from among the most well-to-do of the region, who answer each other in chorus. Among other customs particular to Connecticut is the one whereby, if it was discovered who was responsible for the pregnancy of an unmarried girl, the delinquent was compelled to make a sort of profession of faith in church in order to be readmitted to the congregation, from which he realized he was banished because of his misdeed.[36] The penalty for adultery was death according to the Constitution, but in the General Assembly of 1784 a new law was promulgated in the following terms:

> Be it enacted by the Governor, Council, and Representatives in General Court assembled, and by the authority of the same, that whosoever shall commit adultery[37] with a married woman, and be therefore convicted before the Superior Court, both of them shall be severely punished by whipping on the naked body, and stigmatized, or burnt on the forehead with the letter A on a hot iron; and each of them shall wear an halter about their necks on the outside of their garments during their abode in this State so as it may be visible, and as often as any of them shall be found without halters worn as aforesaid, they shall upon information, and proof of the same made before a Justice of the Peace, be by him ordered to be whipped not exceeding 30 stripes.

Rape is punished by death, the oath of the raped girl being sufficient proof.

In spite of these extremely severe laws there is in Connecticut a new kind of libertinage that cannot fail to be a surprise to the ears of a European. Many of those who traveled in these regions spoke variously of the ease encountered not only in making friends with girls but even in spending the night with them, a fact contradicted by a number of the inhabitants of the maritime cities of Connecticut and called by them an ancient custom no longer observed. I, too, suspected that the account was exaggerated, until I had the occasion to see incontrovertible proof. I would have foregone speaking of this strange custom[38] were it not that it is connected with the manners of these people and serves to give an idea of their character; hence it seemed necessary to report it.

Love in the United States of America, and especially in the northern states, is not as ardent nor as refined as in most of Europe. [2:93] Abominable vices reduce the strength of amorous emotion in the girls, and the young men daily buy elsewhere the satisfaction of their appetites. From this there results[39] either a total indifference or a brutal avidity in seeking the most delicate manifestations of love. The women, rendered almost insensible, present themselves like statues at the court of Cupid and make modesty and virtue consist[40] in receiving with indifference the warmest testimonials of love. In these parts of Connecticut, if someone enters a house where there is a young lady, and from conversation begins to proceed to embraces, which the modern statue of Pygmalion receives coldly, the parents allow them complete liberty to spend the night together and even to sleep in the same bed; and this custom, which is not, however, common in all families, is called bundling. The young lady accordingly takes off all her clothes except her shift and the lad removes[41] his waistcoat and shoes, and everything is allowed that does not lead to consequences – an agreement requested by the girl[42] and which is said to be strictly observed. Traveling through Connecticut, I found myself in the company of a young man who spent the night with a girl after having courted her not more than six hours, in which time she let herself be kissed in public without showing either pleasure or embarrassment. The morning after, the young man assured me that [43] the girl was very nice and well behaved. All I said was that the same would not have been believed in Europe. A short time afterward I saw the girl just as unruffled as before, although she [2:94] was aware that we knew everything; whereupon I was convinced that this is believed there to be a completely innocent matter that casts no shadow upon the character of the girl. It must be said that these two young people had never seen each other before, and that soon thereafter they separated with the moral certitude of never being together again; so the acquiescence of the girl did not have marriage as the object.

It is difficult to seek out the origin of this custom[44] in a people otherwise so severe unless we were to deduce it from the imitation of the Indians or from the necessity in which the first colonists found themselves to urge young people to marry early in order to increase the population of the colony. In fact, not only in Connecticut, but also in other states, the freedom that is allowed two engaged young people is such that, when promises of marriage are dissolved unexpectedly, often the girls are forced to withdraw to the country to get rid of the premature fruit of their love.

The trade of Connecticut is mainly in horses, wheat, corn, and onions, which are transported to the southern states and to the Antilles,[45] but since it is shared by many and carried on with small ships, it cannot flourish nor make the merchants very rich. Agriculture is more developed than in the other states, since the population there is much larger, with the result that not only are all obliged to exert themselves in order to draw their sustenance from the soil, but quite a few have to leave to look for [2:95] land to farm in the other states. That greatly equalizes the distribution of wealth and causes the state to flourish, so that if the inhabitants of Connecticut cannot equal the luxury of the rich Carolinians, they don't know the discomforts of poverty either. Perhaps the inhabitants of Connecticut[46] owe to their modest fortune and the general education of the people the advantage of not having gotten embroiled in the disastrous uprising of their Massachusetts neighbors and of having kept calm.

CHAPTER XVII

The State of Rhode Island

Trip through the State of Rhode Island

[2:96]

FROM THE CONNECTICUT BORDER[1] I reached Boston by Worcester and Sudbury in two days, and from there, passing through the towns of Roxbury, Dedham, Walpole, and Attleboro, I soon arrived at Rehoboth, a little village worthy of consideration because of some ingenious water engines that are found there. This village is situated in a valley on the shores of the Pawtucket River that forms some falls there and sets the boundary between Massachusetts and the State of Rhode Island.

The city of Providence,[2] not far from Rehoboth, is situated at 41° 49′ latitude and was founded in 1635 by a certain Roger Williams [2:97] in a place formerly called Moshawsik by the Indians. Never thinking that the new settlement might become in time a commercial city, he built some houses at the end of the river on a site ill suited to trade, since big boats could not approach on account of the too shallow water. Nevertheless, with the increase in inhabitants, it became so active commercially as to challenge Newport for the title of state capital. The oldest part of the city is that located east of Providence River, which divides it. In that direction the city extends about a mile from north to south on the slope of a charming hill, and on the height on the west side there are various houses that one approaches by means of a wooden bridge and a wide causeway built over that low terrain formerly flooded by the river. The streets are winding and bumpy, and the best of them that runs along the river is the only one paved. The town hall, the church of the Anabaptists, and the College (quite a vast building situated to the east at the top of the hill) are the most noteworthy edifices.[3]

The inhabitants[4] traffic in lumber, hemp, whale oil, and spermaceti candles, but this useful trade, which once flourished vigorously, was much damaged by the war, and much more at the present time, because with the new emission of notes it very quickly dropped by more than two-thirds, producing great disarray among the merchants.

The ladies[5] enjoy, like those of Newport, the reputation of being among the [2:98] most beautiful in America; but they are subject to losing their teeth early, like those of Boston; and they are likely to die of consumption at an early age. This terrible disease has become even more common in the last few years, and it appears beyond question that it is communicated from one individual to another in the same family. However, in spite of the annual ravages of this malady, the fair sex is so numerous that about seven marriageable girls are counted for each eligible young man. This disproportion arose from the large number of men employed in navigation and of those who go to Virginia and the other southern states in order to make a living.

The climate of Providence does not differ much from that of Boston, except that the cold is less perceptible there in winter and the heat more stifling in summer because this city is situated on high and sandy hills. The soil of the region[6] is almost barren, but the city is nevertheless abundantly provided with meat and poultry that come from Narragansett Bay and from even more distant settlements. Aquatic birds and sea fish are very plentiful, and people generally drink cider as in neighboring Massachusetts.

Seven miles from Providence toward the west there is a rich iron mine belonging to Mr. Brown[7] situated in a low-lying plot of ground surrounded by little hills on which could be seen some young western plane trees. The soil is sandy, covered at the surface with large stones, and to some [2:99] depth mixed with marl, under which is the ore. This is dug from a deep shaft near which there is a fire pump for drawing off the water.[8] This machine was constructed by the brother of the present owner with information that he got out of books about similar machines made in Europe, making some changes very ingeniously adapted to the circumstances of the country. For example, the hot water container and the tube in which the plunger moves are of wood, and the oven is composed of a solid iron box ending in a channel of the same metal that turns in the wooden container at some distance from the walls in order to avoid the danger of setting it on fire. The ingenious maker had hoped to extract the ore from the well with the motion of this machine, but since this operation required a great sacrifice of time and the somewhat rickety building could be endangered by the movement and shock of the wheels, it is not used any longer. The ore extracted from this well was very rich down to a depth of 70 feet, but since at that point it was found to be scarce and of inferior quality, other shafts were sunk at some distance from the preceding one which already furnish better iron.[9] The richness of the ore is such that it yields 50 percent iron at the first smelting. This ore is occasionally mixed with ocher,[10] and sometimes it is of a beautiful shiny [2:100] black,[11] with even small pieces of lead ore[12] mixed in.

The morning of September 18[13] I continued on my way toward Newport, accepting the kind offer of Mr. Brown who insisted upon accompanying me to the village of Bristol. We left Providence at about eleven in the morning and upon crossing the Seekonk River, we were in the State of Massachusetts. Then having visited the two towns of Rehoboth and Barrington and crossing the Warren River near the town of the same name, we reached the peninsula where Bristol is situated. This peninsula, surrounded to the east by Mount Hope Bay and to the west by Providence Bay, is divided in the middle by another small inlet called Bristol Bay, thus forming two tongues of land—one to the west called by the Indian name of Papa-squash, containing several plantations, and the other to the east, where Bristol is situated. This little city was founded by a colony of Englishmen at the time that the first settlements in Narragansett Bay were formed, and it was once quite a busy trading center. However, since the surrounding land is not very fertile and the location less favorable than that of Newport, it lost its old luster and is no longer anything but a poor little village.

[2:101] Mount Hope Bay which, like the other mentioned above, forms part of Narragansett Bay, takes its name from a mountain situated to the east of Bristol where the last sachem of the Narragansett Indians was killed by the colonists; and Papa-squash or Popa-squash point was so named from *popa* (child) and *squash* (woman), since it was the place where in the old days the Indian children and women took refuge in time of war.

From Bristol we went around the bay, and in the evening we went to the Point Pleasant plantation[14] belonging to Mr. Brown. The next day the wind was very strong and against us, and it was a very rainy day. We decided therefore to stop,[15] amusing ourselves the rest of the day by fishing in the intervals during which the rain let up. In addition to several small and very tasty fish,[16] we caught a very curious kind that here goes under the name of toadfish. This fish is of a white color, with spots and dark stripes. It has an elongated shape as long as it is in the water, but as soon as it is put on the ground it begins to puff up so that in a few minutes it becomes almost perfectly round; and continuously breathing air with its mouth, it produces a disgusting grunt.[17] One of these fish caught by us, upon being struck with a stone after it had swelled to a prodigious size, burst with a noise like a swollen bladder;[18] and then it was carelessly [2:102] thrown into the sea. A little later a small fish of the same kind was caught which swelled just like the first. But when it, too, was thrown into the water without examination, upon touching the water it let out the air from its mouth, and resuming its original form, swam swiftly down toward the bottom and disappeared.[19] This phenomenon is common in the species of fish called *orbis* by the ancient Romans because of their round shape and *pesci porci* by the Italians on account of that kind of grunt that they produce from breathing air rapidly through the narrow slit of their gills, as Rondelet says.[20] Although I was not able to examine it carefully because of the heedlessness of my companions, I believe the fish we caught is of the species called *Tetraodon testudineus* by Linnaeus, and which is found in the seas of the East Indies and of America.[21]

On the morning of the 20th[22] we went down Bristol Bay in a little sailboat, and leaving the tiny island called Hog Island to the east, we crossed the channel that divides Papa-squash Bay from Prudence Island.[23] Since the water of the channel was much rougher and the wind was blowing with increasing strength, my companions were afraid that, if we continued our trip as far as Newport, the sea would become too stormy for them to return.[24] Hence we approached Prudence Island, and landing, climbed a hill on [2:103] which is situated another plantation of Mr. Brown,[25] from which one can enjoy the pleasant sight of the island and the continent that form Narragansett Bay. And there we found a large sailboat by which I reached Newport in less than two hours.

This city is situated on a slope at 41° 29′ latitude on a beautiful bay near the southern tip of Rhode Island. The streets are narrow but regular and paved, and the houses almost all of wood and dilapidated.[26] The town hall is not yet finished, and the churches of the various faiths are not very attractive. The inhabitants,[27] although quite impoverished by the great losses suffered in the war, are nevertheless very hospitable, and the ladies are intent upon imitating European luxury.[28] The climate of this city is very temperate and considered one of the most healthful in North America, since the sea air renders the cold less severe and tempers the summer heat. For this reason the gentry of Carolina and the other southern and unhealthful regions come to spend the warm season in Newport. This is the birthplace of Nathanael Greene, about whom I have already spoken during my travels in Georgia, and it might boast another famous soldier in Benedict Arnold, had he not tarnished the fame earned with his courage by betraying his country and trying to turn Washington himself over to the British. Arnold is from one of the oldest families of the State of Rhode Island and was engaged in a lucrative livestock business before the war. After his treachery he went to England, whence, perhaps because of the low esteem in which he [2:104] was held, he left and went to live in Nova Scotia, where they say he has gone back into his old business.

On Monday the 25th of September I returned to Providence[29] and then continued the trip toward Boston, whence I made a run to Plymouth and from there returned to New York. I spent the following winter partly in this latter city and partly in Philadelphia until, spring having arrived, I left New York for Europe on the 16th of May, 1787, on a newly built Spanish brig named the *Galveztown,* which, after 28 days of good sailing, entered the Spanish port of La Coruña.

Former and Present Condition of Rhode Island

[2:105] The ancient inhabitants of this region were the Narragansett Indians, who were divided into various tribes and for the most part lived by fishing. Their number and their unity rendered them formidable for a long time to the first European emigrants until, little by little, as happened in the other settlements, they kept diminishing, so that for some years now there have been no Indians left from this once powerful nation. The first English settlement[30] occurred in the year 1635 in the following manner: Roger Williams, a minister of the church of Plymouth, had spread about many new dogmas; but since these were not well received, he decided to move on to Salem, where for some time he had been wanted as a minister. The magistrates of Salem,[31] who were acquainted with his innovation-loving character, were opposed; but since the people insisted in spite of the opposition of the magistrates, he was chosen for this honorable charge. However, the inhabitants there were satisfied with their choice for only a short time, inasmuch as he wanted the Salem church, the only one he thought orthodox, to separate[32] from the Church of England, and the people were not willing to consent to this innovation. Whereupon he angrily left the Salem church, and even separated from his wife because she attended [2:106] that church. All these disorders notwithstanding, the government would not have been tempted to interfere in this matter if Williams had not persuaded[33] one of the first-rank officers to remove the cross from the King's coat of arms as a mark of anti-Christian superstition. The soldiers, enraged at seeing their flags mutilated in this manner, were no longer willing to assemble for military exercises, and so many conflicts arose from this single[34] cause that the government, after trying in vain to persuade him to retract his fanatical doctrines, found itself obliged to banish him with his followers. It was then that, as we said, he founded the city to which he gave the name of Providence, considering it a refuge providentially given to him.[35] There he had himself rebaptized by a certain Holyman,[36] whom he then rebaptized along with 10 others. Later doubts arose in his mind as to the validity of this second baptism since, according to his odd notion, authority for it from the Apostles could derive only through the intermediary of the ministers of the Anglican Church,[37] which he judged heterodox. Hence he wanted no association with Christians of other sects, convinced that God would send new Apostles, among whom he believed he himself would be included. Having thus become founder, governor, and protector of the new colony, he went to England in 1643, where through Sir Henry Vane, he obtained from the Earl of Warwick a charter of incorporation of the new colony under the title of Providence Plantations. Upon his return, which occurred 48 years after his exile from Massachusetts, being of [2:107] advanced age and having changed his principles and behavior, he preached tolerance toward the other sects and died in the year 1682[38] in the city he had founded, highly esteemed both by the colonists and the Indians.

When the Providence Plantations were founded in the northernmost areas of Narragansett Bay, the islands within it were still inhabited by the Indians. Mr. Coddington, a native Englishman, was the first who in the year 1637 bought from Canonicus, the chief of the Narragansett Indians, Aquidneck Island, whose name he changed to Rhode Island. He was made governor by his followers,[39] which office he held for many years, and although he was originally a zealous Presbyterian, he later adopted a universal tolerance for political ends. This attracted many people of various sects to the island, and principally Quakers, who were then being persecuted elsewhere. The only obstacle to the growth of the colony was the Indians, who disturbed it a great deal for many years, so that the inhabitants asked to be united with those of the other colonies of New England. But since these would not agree, they turned to King Charles II, who joined them to Providence Colony, granting them such ample privileges that the same form of government still exists and was not changed by the Revolution.[40] The General Assembly meets twice a year, at Providence in May and at Newport in October. It is composed of a governor, a deputy governor, and 10 assistants, who form the Upper House; and by the deputies [2:108] of the cities and localities, who compose the House of Commons. All these offices run out in the month of May of each year, at which time new elections are held by the people.

The State of Rhode Island is situated between 41° and 42° latitude and 71° and 72° longitude from London, extending 50 miles from north to south and about 30 from east to west. It touches on Massachusetts to the north and east, Connecticut to the west, and on the sea to the south. The portion of the continent that surrounds Narragansett Bay, formerly known under the name of Providence Plantations, is separated to the southwest from the State of Connecticut by the Pakatuk River and contains the county called Kings County, whose capital is South Kingston. In a direct line northward there is Providence County, with the capital of the same name, to the east, Warwick, containing Bristol peninsula; and to the southeast that little tongue of land situated between the arm of sea called Seaconnet Passage and the Massachusetts border. There are various islands, of which the main ones are three. Rhode Island, properly speaking, the biggest of all, is 16 miles long and 4 to 5 wide at the widest point. Since the terrain is rather hilly, one can enjoy from various places a very beautiful view, especially where it narrows down to only two miles and dominates equally the islands of Cononicut and Prudence, Newport Bay, and a part of the mainland. Cononicut, to the west of Rhode Island, is no [2:109] more than eight miles long and about a mile and a half wide at the widest point.[41] On this island there is only a little village called Jamestown. Finally, Prudence Island, to the north of Cononicut and to the west of Rhode Island and Bristol Bay, is from five to six miles long and not more than a mile wide.[42] Numerous other islands are scattered about the bay, but since they are very small and still uninhabited, deserve no particular mention.

The climate of Rhode Island is very variable. The April season is cold and rainy, but then vegetation develops rapidly in May. The months of June, July, and August are very warm in Providence and in the inland areas, but tempered by the sea breezes in Newport and in the neighboring islands. The months of September and October turn out to be the most delightful, since the sky is usually clear and the air temperate. Nevertheless, dysenteries are prevalent during these months, depending perhaps not so much on the climate as upon the abuse of fruit and the little attention given to protecting oneself against the first cold spells. Winter lasts from November until March, snow falls usually toward the middle of December; but the freezing is not as severe as in Boston.

In the year 1774 the inhabitants of this state reached the number of 59,678, of whom 14,900 were fit for military service.[43] Agriculture [2:110] once thrived vigorously, especially on Rhode Island, which abounded in orchards and was justifiably called the garden of America; but during the time the British troops were in possession of the island, they cut down the fruit trees for firewood, killed the livestock, and ruined the finest farms. Even the sheep, which formerly numbered several thousand, were reduced to a little more than 300 by 1786. On this island they raise corn, flax, hemp, and there are beautiful artificial fields. On Cononicut Island, which is divided into various farms, they make excellent cheeses; and even Prudence Island enjoys a fertile terrain, although farming is more laborious there because of the large quantity of stones that litter the ground. Moreover, Narragansett abounds in fish, and one can count up to 80 different species, among which the tautog, or blackfish, holds the first rank at table.

Horses, corn, lumber,[44] codfish, whale oil, and spermaceti candles constitute the main trade of this state. Newport especially was beginning to flourish again after the war, at which time hopes of its rise were wrecked by the dissensions that broke out in that region in the [2:111] following way. Since Rhode Island was one of the smallest of the United States and had no large and populous cities, the inhabitants of Newport and Providence were by preference employed in the legislative bodies as the persons best versed in politics. The people in the country, viewing this distinction with displeasure, saw to it that in 1786 a plurality of the members of the Assembly was chosen from among themselves and took this occasion to make the new issue of banknotes that they had been contemplating for a long time. Convinced that the opposition against this emission during the preceding years by the legislative body depended only on the fact that most of the members were merchants, they rejoiced at having taken away their influence and did not foresee the disastrous consequences that would result. In fact, these notes, which were not supported by any stable fund, very quickly lost credit, and the law passed to back them up that compelled one to accept them as cash brought all the more ruin to business in Rhode Island.[45] Thus bad [2:112] management by the government brought about the ruin of this state, which, although of limited territory, might have been able to compete with the others in wealth. A thousand errors were made after the first, and among the many, that of not wanting to cooperate in suppressing the rebellion that broke out in Massachusetts—on the contrary, offering free asylum to those rascals, with the result that some scornfully called this region not Rhode Island but Rogues Island[46]—deserved by those who fomented these pernicious innovations.

CHAPTER XVIII

The United States in General

The New Federal Government

[2:113]

IN THE HEAT of the Revolution and amid the confusion of a civil war the Federal Government of the Congress was established, and although the authority granted this political body was quite limited, the general fervor that existed for the common cause brought it about that the orders that emanated from it were executed with the greatest punctuality. But in the tranquillity of peace, zeal dropping off with the cessation of danger, the Congress found itself lacking in strength to carry out its laws, with the result that endless disagreements arose in the administration. It was difficult to obtain from the several states the fulfillment of obligations contracted in the common name by Congress, and amid [2:114] the various disorders commerce, unsupported by public credit, was allowed to languish. These facts demonstrated the need for reforming the Federal Constitution, and for that purpose an Assembly was formed composed of delegates from the various states, whose duty it was to propose a new system. This Assembly held its sessions in Philadelphia, with the celebrated Washington as president, and in September 1787 presented to the Congress the new Constitution. It was examined by the delegates of the people of each state, and having been approved by more than two-thirds of them, will probably go into effect as soon as possible. The United States will, in my opinion, derive great advantages from adopting this Constitution, which (as is expressly stated), while assuring as far as possible the rights of each state, has provided for the interest and security of the union by conferring on the Congress the exclusive power of declaring war, making peace and treaties, of levying general taxes, and of regulating commerce.

Since this is the foundation on which rest the independence and prosperity of the United States, readers will appreciate seeing it inserted here translated as literally as possible, with the addition at each article of those observations that were made by some of the states at the time of ratification. These observations, which regard changes they thought necessary in the aforesaid Constitution, were presented to the Congress, since the states that proposed them had urgently requested their respective delegates to employ every legal [2:115] means to have them inserted into the Constitution, inasmuch as the rule had been set that each state could only reject or accept it without any change.

The ratification of the new Constitution was carried out fully and without any exception by the states of Delaware, New Jersey, Pennsylvania, and Georgia. The ones that added observations were: Massachusetts, New Hampshire, New York, Virginia, and South Carolina. And, finally, those that did not ratify it are: North Carolina and Rhode Island. . . .[1]

Reflections on the Present Condition of the American Republic

[2:152] From the quantity of books that speak of this country and its recent revolution, it seems that they should be perfectly informed about it in Europe; but if one considers that the authors were for the most part moved by partisan spirit excessively to exalt or to disparage the Americans, the reader will be glad to have here in brief a general idea of them based upon my own observations and written with that impartiality that I determined to preserve beforehand. There is much argument in Europe about the quality of the climate and fertility of the land in the United States, about their productions, and, above all, about the system of government, and the industry and customs of those inhabitants, as if, in the vast reaches contained within the limits of this Republic, so many different things could be uniform.

The territory of the United States, extending 1200 miles from north to south and about 1000 at its average width,[2] is divided lengthwise by various contiguous [2:153] mountain chains that begin from the seashore of Massachusetts and end in Florida, running from northeast to southwest. Between these mountains and the sea in the northern provinces there remains a narrow plain scattered with low hills where the soil is quite rich, although rocky. Continuing southward from Pennsylvania to North Carolina, this plain keeps getting wider and lower, and its soil is generally clayey and very fertile. Then in the two Carolinas the plain becomes very broad and lies almost at sea level, but the terrain is largely barren and sandy, [2:154] so that the only places farmed profitably are those rendered fertile by the deposits of the rivers, which there have practically no banks and flood a wide area. It appears, therefore, that this space was taken from the ocean not many certuries ago by means of an immense quantity of matter transported there by the water. Inland to the west of the mountain chains there is an extremely fertile region irrigated by numerous rivers that flow into the Mississippi; and among these one of the main ones is the Ohio, whose banks are now beginning to be settled.

The climate, like the terrain, is quite different in the various provinces, and the snow that reaches a great depth in Massachusetts only occasionally appears, but does not last, in Georgia. Here the constant observation must not be overlooked that under the same degrees of latitude the climate of the United States is colder than that of Europe because of the northwest winds that prevail during the winter. These winds, passing over the immense frozen country of the northern regions, intensify very appreciably the cold on the eastern coast of the new continent. On the other hand, after crossing the ocean, they are much more temperate when they reach the European coasts.[3] The cold in America is such that large rivers freeze over even below 40° latitude, although whenever the northwest winds [2:155] let up, they often thaw even in midwinter. This is the reason for the great inconstancy of the climate in the populated provinces of the United States, where one can shift from the hardest winter to a temperate season in a short time.

The theory of the degeneration of animals in America adopted by Count Buffon and exaggerated by Mr. Pauw[4] and other writers has been recognized as false since the fine work of Mr. Jefferson. This author, in his *Notes on Virginia,* demonstrated plainly how little basis there was for such an opinion; and both Mr. Robertson, in his *History of America,* and Count Carli, in his *Lettere americane,* very clearly proved the same thing. In fact, if cows and horses are quite small in Canada, these same animals in Massachusetts and Pennsylvania match, if they do not surpass, in size those of Europe. Moreover, that America can produce large-bodied animals is proved by the moose, the reindeer, the buffalo, the bear, and above all by those immense bones[5] dug up on the banks of the Ohio quite similar to those from Siberia that belonged to an animal to which was given the name mammoth. The genera of quadrupeds in the United States are almost all common [2:156] to Europe, too, although the species differ somewhat, the most different being the cougar[6] of Buffon,[7] the raccoon, and the opossum,[8] the last of which is perhaps the only one whose genus is not found in Europe. The bird class is much more abundant there, which, as in South America, if they do not commonly have sweet song, are on the other hand dressed in beautifully colored feathers. Amphibians and reptiles are numerous and very varied, and the insects furnish many species still unknown, although there is a goodly number quite like our own.

The vegetable kingdom corresponds to that of the Old World at the same latitudes, and no other fruit trees grow there spontaneously as food for man except peaches and plums. It is noteworthy, however, that plants are quite similar to those of the eastern coasts of northern Asia, and that, for example, the magnolia,[9] illicium,[10] calycanthus,[11] and ginseng,[12] and many others [2:157] too numerous to mention here,[13] grow there as they do in Japan and China. That makes even truer the assertion of Franklin that the two eastern coasts of the Old and New World are very analogous to each other in climate. Certain plant genera abound in species both in America and Europe, especially trees and shrubs such as the oaks, pines, maples, briars, spiraeas, smilaxes, and vacciniums, although the American species are different.[14]

The New World is no less favorable to the propagation of the human species than the Old Continent, and the population of the United States keeps increasing rapidly, especially in the more healthful climates.[15] This increase, however, does not seem so [2:158] rapid in the provinces settled in earlier times, because the emigrations that take place from them to the more inland regions are large and continuous, so that many years must pass before the population of the maritime provinces can equal that of Europe. Nor should that cause any surprise, since in many internal areas one [2:159] finds a fertile soil that costs very little and a much more healthful climate. Emigrations from Europe formerly contributed a great deal to increase the population of those regions, but later, when they were composed of lazy and wicked people, they were more harmful than useful, because emigrants, as Franklin rightfully asserts, should be industrious individuals and skillful in some art or craft in order to succeed, since the notion that to become rich all one needs to do is to go to America is completely false.[16]

Along with the supposed degeneration of animals, it was asserted by some distinguished writers that men are degenerate in America, both in body and mind. But if we reflect upon [2:160] this statement, we shall find it just as erroneous as the first. The ancient inhabitants, that is, the Indians, are perhaps less sturdy than European peasants, but if that is so they are no different than the Chinese, the Negroes, and the East Indians, who are also inhabitants of the Old Continent, yet were not regarded for that reason as degenerate nations. As for the descendants of the Europeans born in America, in healthful climates they reach a very advanced age, and are just as big and strong as their ancestors. The bitter struggles and hardships they have to endure in starting their farms, and the almost incredible ones they put up with during the recent war are a convincing proof.[17] Speaking, moreover, of the talent of the English colonists, who would believe that in the celebrated

History of European Settlements[18] there are these statements?: "Under this foreign sky the mind has become flabby, like the body. Lively and penetrating at an early age, it apprehends readily; but it does not hold up, does not become accustomed to long meditations. It is indeed astonishing that America has not yet produced a good poet, a clever mathematician, a man of genius in a single art or in a single science &c." Without having been in America, knowing [2:161] the names of Washington and Franklin[19] is sufficient to reveal what basis such a strange assertion has. But if to these more famous men one wants to add the others who distinguished themselves in the arts and sciences, as well as in war, the catalogue of the illustrious men of the United States would be a large one. One might cite, for example, the Greenes,[20] the Knoxes,[21] the Clintons,[22] the Lincolns,[23] the Montgomerys,[24] the Putnams,[25] and the Gateses[26] in the military art; the Adamses,[27] the Jays,[28] the [2:162] Madisons,[29] the Jeffersons,[30] and the Paines[31] in the political. Mathematics (contrary to the notion of Abbé Raynal) is one of the sciences most cultivated by Americans as necessary for navigation, and, among others, Williams, Willard, and Rittenhouse distinguished themselves in it. The first, who is a professor at the University of Cambridge in Massachusetts, wrote learned memoirs that were published in the transactions of the American Academy of Boston and determined the latitude of various cities and places of the northern states. The second, president of the aforementioned University, published in the same volume some of his dissertations, and was the correspondent of various European mathematicians, among others the celebrated Euler. And finally the last-named, a mathematician and mechanic, built two ingenious horaries conceived by him that exist at the universities of Philadelphia and Princeton. Benjamin Rush, a Philadelphia doctor, deserves honorable mention for several little treatises that he published on various subjects. And natural history [2:163] owes much to the Bartrams,[32] the Marshalls,[33] the Cutlers,[34] and the Greenways.[35] Among the historians a Belknap, a minister of the Dover church in New Hampshire, wrote the first volume of the history of that country, and a Ramsey in South Carolina that of the late Revolution, received with much praise in America and in Europe. Polite letters, poetry, and the fine arts also have their followers in the United States, and a Hopkinson in Philadelphia is quite well known for his charming and witty productions; and he also has considerable talent in mechanics. The celebrated poem "Macfingal" written in the burlesque and satirical style of "Hudibras," from the pen of Mr. Trumbull of Connecticut, was so applauded even in England that [2:164] several translations were made of it. Of equal merit, although of a completely different style, is the recent poem by Mr. Barlow, also of Connecticut, entitled "The Vision of Columbus." Many highly esteemed poems, and among others the "Happiness of America" (a poem elegantly translated into French by Marquis Chastellux) are productions of the felicitous genius of Colonel Humphrey, who served at the rank of field adjutant under General Washington—not to mention a quantity of other beautiful minor poems that have come out from time to time in the newspapers and gazettes of America. And even painting which, although highly regarded by the English, has never been cultivated by them with great success, seems to have managed to introduce its genius into the United States, since noble talents are seen to flourish there in that art. Mr. Copley, a native of Boston in Massachusetts, who began by painting family portraits in that region, found in England the means for employing his unusual talent in pictures of the death of Lord Chatham, the catastrophe of Brook-Watson, and the death of Major Pierson. As a result, he was commissioned by the City of London to represent in a painting the destruction of the floating batteries under Gibralter. The death of General Wolfe, the return of Regulus, and the portraits of the West family are valued works by Mr. Benjamin West of Philadelphia, now employed by the King of England in the decoration of his Windsor Chapel; and Mr. John Trumbull of Connecticut, now living in Paris, has undertaken to paint the main events of the [2:165] American War, after having produced a happy sample in the Battle of Bunker Hill and the death of General Montgomery. Messrs. Taylor of Philadelphia, Stewart of Rhode Island, and Brown of Boston are also following the career of the first mentioned and have already acquired a reputation in England, the former for his landscapes, the other two for portraits. I do not believe that I have listed here all those that deserve to be known, but I am sure that these are enough to show how well founded the assertion of Abbé Raynal is.

The main objects of exportation of United America are salted fish and lumber in the northern states, tobacco, grain, and flour in the central ones, indigo and rice in the southern states. These items could render commerce very profitable for the United States if the introduction of luxury into the principal cities and the southern regions didn't cause merchandise to be exchanged for more or less unnecessary objects. The general scarcity of real money is owing to that fact, so that they have had to turn to notes, making many people suffer as a consequence. Because of that, many of the most concerned Americans urged that the manufacture of the most indispensable things be introduced into America in order to take care of their main needs. But these aims were largely thwarted because of the scarcity of inhabitants and the ease of acquiring land cheaply, with the result that manual work is very expensive. Nevertheless, America would suffer little from the lack of [2:166] these items if the people that would be employed in producing them applied themselves to agriculture, and if expensive and luxurious European objects were banished from American homes. The progress of Philadelphia, settled by Quakers, as compared with other older cities, proves clearly how much influence simplicity of customs has in promoting the welfare of a newly populated country; and the good farmers of Pennsylvania ought to serve as an example to the other Americans.

A fluctuating system of government, a badly deteriorated commerce, a heavy burden of debts, and the aftermath of a devastating war have given rise to the question whether independence has really been an advantage for the Americans. Certainly among all the European nations England has been the only one to grant to her colonies the broadest privileges, even though the inhabitants of several of them could not at first have expected such a benign government, since they were often fugitives from their motherland for religious or civil dissent, or, indeed, what is more, had been transported to America as punishment. To this gentleness and freedom of government the English owe the greater prosperity of their colonies as compared with those of the other nations. If, however, the Americans had not attempted the Revolution, they would have remained always at the same level of mediocrity; in fact, they could only have deteriorated, since the English government would have continued imposing burdensome taxes on the colonies if it had not found from the outset the strongest [2:167] opposition. However, if the Americans are at present suffering all the disadvantages of a nascent and poor republic and the consequences of a civil war, they have reason to find comfort in the prospect of an improved future situation for themselves. The degree and promptness of future happiness will depend upon how soon a stable and active government is set up, this being the only instrument they still need for achieving it. Their distance from Europe makes them safe from any sudden invasion, and the area and fertility of the land that they own[36] is capable of feeding an immense population, especially in the center of the continent [2:168] where, as I have already indicated, there are vast plains irrigated by many navigable rivers under a temperate and healthful sky. Motivated by these advantages, the United States will flourish very quickly under the auspices of the new government, and they will arrive more easily at that happy era to which they aspire and in which they can distinguish themselves among the most powerful and civilized nations.[37]

Notes

[Castiglioni's notes to the *Viaggio* are those below not enclosed in brackets.]

Chapter I—Passage from England to America

1. *Pinus strobus* Lin. [!]
2. *Oniscus asilus* Lin.
3. The voyage usually made on the passage from England to North America is not exposed to such inconveniences, since ships do not ordinarily go beyond 45° latitude in this season. Furthermore, those that are meant for trips toward the poles are sheathed with copper and protected at the prow with cast iron so massive that they can bump the floating pieces of ice without danger.
4. *Larus canus* Lin. [Perhaps immature *Larus marinus* Linn.]
5. *Phoca vitulina* Lin. [!]
6. The fathom is 6 English feet, so that 35 fathoms are 210 feet, or about 131 Milanese *braccia.*
7. The codfish, or *baccalare* (just as the true stockfish and the *merluccio*), belongs to the genus of the *Gadi* and might be described as follows: *Gadus* (Cod) *tripterygius cirratus albicans, maculis rotundis flavescentibus, linea laterali alba, cauda integra aequali, maxilla superiore longiore.* D. 14, 19, 18. P. 17. V. 6. A. 20, 16. C. 24. *An Gadus callarias*? Lin. [*Gadus morrhua* Linn.]
8. *Larus cataractes* Lin. [Probably the gannet, *Morus bassanus* (Linn.)]
9. *Physeter macrocephalus* Lin. [*Physeter catodon* Linn.]

[10. Modern Gloucester.]

11. The name Bay has been adopted because it is generally known and because it denotes more precisely a small enclosed gulf.
12. Explanation of Plate II, representing Boston Bay:

1) City of Boston	7) Charlestown
2) Dorchester Point	8) Bunker Hill
3) Dorchester	9) Malden
4) The Castle	10) Chelsea
5) Roxbury	11) Lynn
6) Cambridge	12) Pullen Point

13) Deer Island
14) Long Island
15) Spectacle Island
16) Thompsons Island
17) Governors Island
18) Bird Island
19) Noddles Island
20) Hog Island

Chapter II—The Commonwealth of Massachusetts

[1. What Castiglioni adduces at this point as "A Brief History of the First European Settlements in This Part of America" should put the reader on his guard against uncritical acceptance of the historical information presented in the *Viaggio.* In reality, the year of the Pilgrim exodus to Holland is 1608; 1619 is the year of the patent for transfer to the New World. Castiglioni informs his readers that King James I granted the patent, whereas the issuance of such patents was the prerogative of chartered companies, in this instance the London Virginia Company. The Pilgrims needed to apply to the King for permission to worship in their own fashion. This permission was never formally granted; but with the connivance of James I, the Pilgrims managed nevertheless to have their way. Castiglioni's vague allusion to the "famous revolution that had taken place in England by which Protestantism was once again embraced" is presumably to the so-called Elizabethan settlement, whereby the Crown became head of both Church and State. Castiglioni overlooks completely the important fact that the patent granted by the London Virginia Company was for land in the Hudson River region, then in the domain of Virginia. His date for the departure of the *Mayflower,* September 6, 1620, is accurate, but one needs to know that the day so indicated is Old Style, equivalent to September 16, New Style. Moreover, the Pilgrims did not land on November 9/19, as Castiglioni reports; on that day they sighted land—Cape Cod. Then, disregarding the terms of their patent, they decided to settle in Massachusetts Bay. The exploring party landed on December 11/21, the *Mayflower* came up on December 16/26; and the Pilgrims finally landed on 18/28 of the same month. The colonists numbered 102 (Castiglioni says "only 150") of whom 53 died during the first terrible winter, considerably more than the "several" mentioned by Castiglioni. And so on.

Since annotating the parts of the *Viaggio* dealing with the historical background would obviously be tantamount to rewriting them with information now commonplace, they are hereafter reproduced with minimal comment.]

2. These European names are often taken by the Indians, since an exchange of names is with them a sign of friendship.

[3. For the Massachusetts Bay Charter of 1691, as for all similar documents cited by Castiglioni for the different states, see F. N. Thorpe, *The Federal and State Constitutions, Colonial Charters, and Other Organic Laws of the States, Territories, and Colonies Now or Heretofore Forming the United States of America,* 7 vols. (Washington, D.C.: USGPO, 1909).]

4. Explanation of Plate III, representing the city of Boston:

1) The Port
2) Long Wharf
3) Hudsons Point, in the vicinity of which the new bridge has been built
4) Bartons Point
5) Pond of water called Mill Pond
6) Section not yet built up
7) Beacon Hill
8) The Common
9) The Mall
10) Point called Boston Neck where the peninsula joins the mainland
11) Trinity Church
12) Another church called the Royal Chapel
13) Statehouse

[5. The nearly 50 acres of the Boston Common, acquired from an early settler for $150, was long used as communal pasture. Certain residents of Beacon Heights believe to this day that they are legally entitled to pasture a cow on the Common (see *Encyclopedia Americana,* s.v. "Boston," by James Boylan).]
6. *Platanus occidentalis* Lin. [!]
7. *Cupressus thyoides* Lin. [*Chamaecyparis thyoides* (L.) B.S.P.]
8. *Pinus picea* Lin. *Pescia* in Lombardy.
9. *Trochilus colubris* Lin. Hummingbird in English. [*Archilochus colubris* (Linn.)]
10. *Bignonia radicans* Lin. [*Campsis radicans* (L.) Seem.]
11. *Juglans alba* Lin. [*Carya ovata* (Mill.) K. Koch]
12. *Pinus canadensis* Lin. [*Picea glauca* (Moench) Voss]
[13. The northern states abolished slavery soon after the Revolution. According to the 1790 census, there were then about 60,000 free blacks in the United States, including many whose ancestors had never been slaves (*Dictionary of American History,* s.v. "Free Blacks," by John M. McFaul).]
[14. Initiated by John Adams in 1779, chartered by the Massachusetts Legislature in 1780, the American Academy of Arts and Sciences is, after the American Philosophical Society of Philadelphia, the oldest of such bodies founded in America. The first volume of memoirs appeared in 1785.]
[15. The bridge was part of the rebuilding of Charlestown after its destruction by the British in 1778. Thomas Russell was one of the five corporators charged with the construction (see J. F. Hunnewell, *A Century of Town Life: A History of Charlestown, Massachusetts, 1775–1887* (Boston: Little, Brown, 1888), p. 18. History seems not to have corroborated the high opinion of Thomas Russell held in Castiglioni's time, to judge from the absence of his name from the standard biographical collections.]
16. To make the distinction clearer, we shall consistently call the colonists of the United States "Americans," reserving the term "savages" for the natives of that country. [In the present translation the traditional designation "Indian" is used as the equivalent of Castiglioni's *selvaggio.*]
17. *Monoculus polyphemus* Lin. [*Limulus polyphemus* (Linn.)]
18. See Chapter XI, 1, where Yale College in the city of New Haven is discussed.
[19. While the name "Swan" figures frequently in the early history of Dorchester – see Dorchester Antiquarian and Historical Society, *History of the Town of Dorchester, Massachusetts* (Boston: Clapp, 1859), passim – the identity of the Major Swan mentioned by Castiglioni remains uncertain. Two Major Swans, James and Robert, are listed in *Massachusetts Soldiers and Sailors of the Revolutionary War* (Boston: Wright & Potter, 1907) 15: 274 and 278, but no connection with Dorchester appears for either of them.]
[20. Probably Samuel Willard, son of the loyalist Abijah Willard whose property was confiscated. The father never returned after leaving Massachusetts; but the property was apparently repurchased by the family, and his son Samuel, born in 1759, continued to live in Lancaster until his death in 1856; see Abijah P. Marvin, *History of the Town of Lancaster, Massachusetts* (Lancaster, Mass.: Published by the Town, 1879), pp. 299–300, 750).]
21. In Lusatia [an old German marquisate] also, and in certain other parts of Europe villages are composed, as in America, of scattered habitations.
22. *Papilio polyxenes* Fabr., *System. entom.,* p. 444.
23. *Quercus rubra* Lin. [!]
24. *Quercus alba* Lin. [!]
25. *Quercus humilis* Bartr. Catal. [*Quercus laevis* Walt.]
26. *Quercus prinus* Lin. [!]

27. *Pinus strobus* Lin. [!]
28. *Pinus taeda* Lin. [!]
29. *Pinus canadensis* Lin. [*Tsuga canadensis* (L.) Carr.]
30. *Juniperus virginiana* Lin. [!]
31. Last year (1784) 28,000 barrels were shipped. A barrel weighs 112 English pounds.
32. Some of his botanical observations are printed in the transactions of the Boston Academy, which bear the title *Memoirs of the American Academy of Arts and Sciences,* Vol. I, Boston, 1786. [At the time of Castiglioni's visit, Cutler was hard at work on his paper for the *Memoirs* entitled "An Account of Some of the Vegetable Productions Naturally Growing in This Part of America, Botanically Arranged." See W. P. Cutler and J. P. Cutler, *Life, Journals,* and *Correspondence of Rev. Manasseh Cutler*) Cincinnati: Clarke, 1888) 1: 116).]
33. *Sciurus cinereus* Lin. *Petit-gris* (Buffon; Schreber, *Saüghthiere,* Plate 213). [*Sciurus carolinensis* Gmelin]
34. Kalm, *Travels,* London, 1772, Vol. I, p. 75. [1: 52 in the Adolph B. Benson edition of *Peter Kalm's Travels in North America* (New York: Wilson-Erickson, 1937).]
35. *Sciurus striatus* Lin. Schreb., *Saüghthi.,* Plate 219. [The chipmunk, *Tamias striatus* (Linn.)]
36. *Sciurus volans* Lin. [*Sciuropterus volans* (Linn.)]
37. The terms "city," "town," and "village" are entirely arbitrary and used by me in accordance with their respective size and population. The English terms "city" or "borough" are granted only to those cities or towns that are incorporated, that is, having a civic body of magistrates that administers community affairs. In general I have applied the term "city" to all those places where the Supreme Court of Justice is held, and which can be called capitals of the various counties. To the other rather thickly populated places I have given the name of "town," and to small communities that of "village," distinguishing, however, by the English term "cities" those towns that have magistrates, or, as they say, are "incorporated."
38. *Fringilla tristis* Lin. [*Spinus tristis* (Linn.)]
39. *Motacilla sialis* Lin. [*Sialia sialis* (Linn.)]
40. *Oriolus phoeniceus* Lin. [Red-winged blackbird, *Agelaius phoeniceus* (Linn.).]

[41. Doubtless one of the numerous progeny of the Edmund Littlefield who left England about 1630, settling in Wells a few years later: see *Genealogical and Family History of the State of Maine,* edited by G. T. Little (New York: Lewis Historical Pub. Co.), 1 (1909): 101ff. Many of the clan eventually served in the American Revolution. The Colonel Littlefield mentioned by Castiglioni could be Noah Moulton Littlefield, who achieved the rank of lieutenant colonel: see *Massachusetts Soldiers and Sailors of the Revolutionary War* 9 (1902): 881.]

42. *Pinus canadensis* Lin. [*Picea glauca* (Moench) Voss]

[43. The name was changed to Biddeford in 1718 in honor of the English city of Bideford (see A. H. Chadbourne, *Maine Place Names and the Peopling of Its Towns,* Portland, Me.: Bond Wheelwright Co., 1955).]

44. *Pinus abies americana* Marshall, *Arbust. americanum.* [*Tsuga canadensis* (L.) Carr.]
45. *Liquidambar peregrinum* Lin. [*Comptonia peregrina* var. *asplenifolia* (L.) Fern.]
46. *Acer rubrum* Lin. [!]
47. *Acer pensylvanicum* Lin. [!]
48. *Acer saccharinum* Lin. [!]
49. *Acer striatum* Laüth., *Diss. de acere. [Acer spicatum* L.]
50. *Juglans alba* Lin. [*Carya* sp.]
51. *Laurus sassafras* Lin. [*Sassafras albidum* (Nutt.) Nees]
52. *Gryllus locusta caeruleus* Lin.

53. *Gryllus campestris* Lin. [*Gryllus* sp.]
54. *Gryllus domesticus* Lin. [European cricket, sometimes found in U.S.]
55. *Acer saccharinum* Lin. [!]
56. *Betula nigra* Lin. [!]
57. *Betula lenta* Lin. [!]
58. *Betula lenta,* Var. *flava.* [Illegitimate name: *nomen nudum.*]
59. *Vaccinium corymbosum* Lin. [!]
60. *Columba migratoria* Lin. [*Ectopistes migratorius* (Linn.)]
61. Also Winslow's Island.

[62. Major-bigwaduce was the plantation name of Penobscot (see G. J. Varney, *A Gazetteer of the State of Maine* (Boston: Russell, 1881), p. 433).]

[63. To be identified perhaps with the Second Lieutenant James Ginn whose name appears on a list of officers to be commissioned drawn up on July 1, 1776, in Penobscot, and who was commissioned on the 20th of the same month: see *Massachusetts Soldiers and Sailors of the Revolutionary War* 6 (1899): 47.]

[64. This energetic missionary, identified below by Castiglioni as father of Mr. Little at Kennebunk, can be no other than the Reverend Daniel Little. See Edward E. Bourne, *The History of Wells and Kennebunk from the Earliest Settlement to the Year 1820* (Portland: Thurston, 1875), pp. 708–23).]

65. This is still the custom in certain Italian cities.

[66. In all probability Captain John Brewer, one of the region's early settlers after whom the town of Brewer is named: see W. D. Williamson, *A History of the State of Maine* (Hallowell: Glazier, Masters & Smith), 2 (1839): 538–39.

A brief extract, accompanying a map, from a journal of W. S. Carter preserved in the Massachusetts Historical Society creates some uncertainty as to the exact constitution of the party: "Penobscot River at the Head of the Tide about 10 miles North from Owlshead, the Entrance of Penobscot Bay *July 18, 1786.* . . .

"Set off for the Indian Town, so called, in company with the Count de Castiglioni a Noble of Italy, making the Tour of the States and two french gent. with their servants, one Pilot and one Interpreter. . . ."]

67. *Culex pulicaris* Lin. ["*Culex*" is now limited to a mosquito genus.]

[68. Castiglioni's description makes an interesting parallel to the account in Williamson's *History of the State of Maine* 1: 473–74.]

69. *Betula lenta* Lin. [*Betula papyrifera* Marsh. is usually adopted.]
70. *Wampum* (Fig. 3), cylindrical beads pierced through the center, are made with a kind of shell called clams (Plate IV, Fig. 1), which is the *Venus mercenaria* [!] of Linnaeus.
71. *Histrix dorsata* Lin. [*Erethizon dorsatum* (Linn.)]
72. *Phoca vitulina* Lin. [!]
73. This river is very narrow, but quite deep, and navigable for more than fifteen miles from its mouth.
74. *An Lampyris lucida*? Lin. [One or more *Lampyridae*]

[75. Probably David Little, who, less unworldly than his father, made a considerable fortune in Kennebunk through trade, shipbuilding, and farming (Bourne, *History of Wells and Kennebunk,* p. 722).]

[76. Ore brought from Saco, Maryland Ridge, and the western side of Wells road began to be smelted in furnaces set up in 1774 on the island below the lower dam on the Kennebunk River and at the western end of the dam (Varney, *Gazetteer of the State of Maine,* p. 298).]

77. *Asclepias syriaca* Lin. var b [!]

[78. Apparently another name for the "praying," or Christianized Indians.]

79. *An Dolichos polystachyos*? Lin.
80. These provinces, which were populated at the beginning of the settlements made in New England by Sir Ferdinando Gorges, unable to defend themselves against the Indians because the inhabitants were few in number, asked for help from those of Massachusetts, who agreed, on condition, however, that this region be considered as united to their province.
81. The St. Croix River, according to the peace treaty, is supposed to serve as the boundary between the United States and Nova Scotia. But since there are two rivers of the same name, a dispute has arisen between the Americans and the English which has not yet ended.
82. Males from 14 to 60 years of age are subject to paying the head tax.
83. These observations apply only to the form of government of the northern states, and particularly of Massachusetts.
[84. The foregoing analysis of Shays Rebellion of August 1786–February 1787 is typically conservative and simplistic. Castiglioni seems oblivious of the economic depression that wracked American society after the Revolution and the distress of many small property holders who had lost their possessions. He says nothing about the heavy and inequitable taxation that had much to do with the uprising, nor, in the absence of universal franchise, of tempers exacerbated by the impossibility of redress through the ballot. It would have taken a really keen political observer to divine that such an uprising as Shays Rebellion would actually help generate sentiment for a stronger central government and a national constitution.]
85. The effects of Americans are carefully examined at St. John, a British fort on the Sorel River in Canada, and pelts and other contraband articles are confiscated.
86. Since navigation on Lake Ontario is very dangerous, Indian canoes and flatboats, or *bateaux*, are forced to follow the southern shore of the lake, so that all merchandise imported or exported from the upper reaches of the lakes necessarily had to pass near the American forts.
87. The British based themselves on the pretext that the Americans had not carried out certain articles of the peace treaty.
[88. Formerly Fort Frontenac of the French; today Kingston, Ontario.]
[89. Castiglioni was unable to appreciate the complexity of the border fort problem. In actuality it was the British who deliberately delayed the transfer of command because they foresaw a destructive general Indian uprising if the forts were surrendered. The question was not resolved until the Jay Treaty of 1795 (see *DAH*, s.v. "Border Forts, Evacuation of," by M. M. Quaife).]
90. Among the many usurpations of land from the Indians, one of the most unfair was that of the Georgians, who occupied a large part of the country belonging to the Creek nation. The latter, in order to get it back, canvassed the American continent and allied themselves with various nations in order to declare a general war against the Americans. The Georgians, however, gave up part of the territory, and consequently peace was concluded in the summer of 1786. But not before the colonists lost a number of inhabitants, slaughtered by the Indians along the frontier, and the latter suffered the loss of some of their men, killed by the troops of Colonel [Elijah] Clarke, who burned their villages and destroyed their few cornfields.
91. The name Quaker is derived from the English verb "to quake," and to this is added the epithet "shaking," from "to shake," as if they wanted to call themselves "quakers who shake," or, better yet, "Shaking Quakers" [Or Shakers].
92. A gentleman from New York, traveling in the most remote parts of that state, lost his way. After wandering for several hours in the woods, he was overtaken by night and headed for a wretched little cabin that was the only dwelling in that vicinity. Upon entering

it, he was not a little surprised to see gathered there many persons of both sexes who received him politely and made him take a seat near the fire. He had sat there only a few moments when one of those present began to sing, and then one after the other they accompanied him with song, and, getting to their feet, they began to dance in a ring around the room. Then, but too late, he realized he had put up at a church where the Chosen People exercised their rites. The whole night was spent in similar ceremonies, and at dawn, when the singing and dancing stopped, they asked the stranger what he thought of their religion. The stranger, who, after spending a whole day walking in the woods, had not been able to close his eyes once the entire night, with an air of mingled anger and irony, answered, "My dear friends, I couldn't say whether your religion is a good one; but I do assure you that your way of praying to God is certainly the most strenuous of all."

[In June, 1783, the established church of Lancaster adopted a policy of clemency toward their wayward brethren who had been seduced by the persuasions of Mother Ann Lee, resolving: "1. That the said members did not appear to them to be so composed in mind, at the present, as to be capable of receiving any benefit from counsel, reproof or admonition; and therefore, 2. That committing them to the mercy and grace of God, the church would wait until they were become capable of receiving advantage from their Christian endeavors for their recovery" (see Marvin, *History of the Town of Lancaster,* p. 386)].

93. *Trifolium pratense* Lin. [!]
94. *Ranunculus acris* Lin. [! Introduced weed.]
95. *Chrysanthemum leucanthemum* Lin. [! Also an introduced weed.]

[96. Castiglioni might have culled this bit of Indian lore from either the *Columbian Magazine* or the *American Museum* (Philadelphia), both of which carried the identical article, "Origin of the Island of Nantucket: an Indian Tradition," the former in July, 1787, 1:525, the latter the following year, 3:276.]

Chapter III—The State of New Hampshire

[1. The first attempt at a settlement at the Piscataqua River was by Captain John Mason and Sir Ferdinando Gorges in 1623, at Odiorne's Point. In 1629 scattered planters in the Massachusetts Bay Colony bought land in the area and moved in. In 1631 the Council of Plymouth was granted a township with the name of Piscataqua. The present name of Portsmouth was assumed when the General Court of Massachusetts incorporated it as a town in 1653.]

2. Of these, two are Presbyterian, one Anglican, one belongs to the Methodists, and one to the Universalists.
3. List of ships sailing from Portsmouth in the following years:

In 1764	ships 150	In 1769	ships 183
1765	199	1770	142
1766	136	1771	136
1767	180	1772	135
1768	170		

About the same number of ships was engaged from 1772 to September 10, 1775.

4. *Systema entomologiae,* p. 237. [*Calosoma calidum* (Fabr.)?]

[5. The capital was moved from Portsmouth to Exeter in 1775 because of the concentration of Tories in the former city. The State Legislature met there regularly between 1776 and 1784, alternating thereafter between the two cities, a circumstance that gave rise to considerable rivalry and jealousy.]

[6. Concord was founded as the Plantation of Penny Cook by a grant in 1659 from the Massachusetts Bay Colony.]

7. *An Coluber viridissimus?* Lin. [*Opheodrys vernalis* (Harlan). For this and other reptile and fish identifications we are indebted to Harold A. Dundee.]

8. *An Coluber annulatus?* Lin. [*Lampropeltis triangulum* (Lacépède)]

9. Bushel: a measure corresponding to about two Milanese *staia.*

[10. I.e., Hooksett Island.]

11. *Rubus fruticosus* Lin. *Varietas.* [Perhaps *Rubus occidentalis* L.]

12. *Rubus idaeus* Lin. [Probably *Rubus odoratus* L.]

13. Great Falls. [Bellows Falls]

[14. Charlestown was originally granted as "No. 4" by the Massachusetts Bay Colony.]

[15. After the Captain Phineas Stevens who fought off the French and Indians in a decisive battle in 1747 that determined English supremacy in northern New England.]

16. *Populus balsamifera* Lin. [!]

17. *Juglans cinerea* Lin. [!]

[18. For John C. Wheelwright's career as minister of the Gospel and settler, and the tangled tale of the Mason inheritance see Everett S. Stackpole, *History of New Hampshire,* New York: Amer. Hist. Soc. I (1916): 40–45, 303–13.]

19. The mountains called the White Hills were visited in 1784 by several members of the Academy of Boston to determine their height and to examine their productions. Among them were Mr. Cutler for botany, Mr. King for ornithology and the history of other animals, and Mr. Belknap for geography. They had two barometers, quadrants, and other necessary instruments. But after a long and disastrous trip, they stayed only two days in the mountains without being able to make any observations because of the constant rain and the loss of the barometers, which were broken during the trip.

[The identity of "Mr. King" remains a puzzle for the curious. Professor Ewan suspects a lapse on Castiglioni's part. He may have meant the Rev. Daniel Little, who is known to have been a member of the expedition. Mr. Samuel J. Hough ("An Italian Nobleman in New Hampshire and Vermont," *Appalachia* 36 [1967]: 746) equates him to Joshua Fisher, President of the Massachusetts Medical Society—a reasonable conjecture in view of that personage's demonstrable interest in natural history. See Stephen P. Williams, *American Medical Biography* (Greenfield, Mass.: Merriam, 1845), pp. 165–67.

Unfortunately, we do not know the complete make-up of the party engaged in this "first scientific exploration of the White Mountains." A. S. Pease, in his "Notes on the Botanical Exploration of the White Mountains" (*Appalachia* 14 [1917]: 157–78) names, in addition to Manesseh Cutler, Daniel Little, Jeremy Belknap, and Joshua Fisher, also a Colonel (William) Whipple, a Mr. Heard, and two "collegians"—a total of eight. But the résumé of Daniel Little's account of the tour inserted by W. P. and J. P. Cutler into the edition of their grandfather's *Journals and Correspondence* (1: 109) states that, when the party separated, they were "ten in number." This tallies with the inference one draws from the "Description of the White Mountains" by Belknap published in the *American Museum* 3 (1788): 129–32, where we are told that "eight of our company ascended the highest mountain (Washington) on the twenty-fourth of July." If we add to this number the "corpulent" Dr. Fisher and the ailing Rev. Belknap, who Little says did not make the ascent, we are again brought to the number ten, with two members unaccounted for.

Until the unidentified two emerge, the sounder conclusion might be to accept Castiglioni's information, who, after all, must have got his facts directly from Manesseh Cutler.]

[20. Groveton. See Samuel J. Hough, "An Italian Nobleman in New Hampshire and Vermont," *Appalachia* 36 (1967): 746.]

[21. For a more substantial contemporary account of this rebellion see Jeremy Belknap, *The History of New Hampshire* (Boston: Andrews, 1791), 2: 459 ff. Belknap confirms Castiglioni's report that the insurgents were treated with great clemency. His silence as to the identity of the "moderator" or leader, of the rebellion was presumably owing to his reluctance to place a permanent stamp of infamy on a penitent man.]

Chapter IV—The Territory of Vermont

[1. Castiglioni is confused. Windsor and Windham Counties meet across the Connecticut River from Charlestown, and Vermont has no Rockingham County. There is, however, a county by that name in the southeastern corner of New Hampshire, a fact that may underlie Castiglioni's error.]

[2. Frederic F. Van de Water's *The Reluctant Republic* (New York: Day, 1941) is a sprightly account of Vermont's tempestuous emergence.]

[3. Independence was declared at the Windsor convention of 2–8 July, 1777, and a state constitution was then promulgated.]

[4. Vermonters note with pride that theirs was the only early state that imposed no property or income condition for the right to vote.]

5. "The roots of trees in (America) do not penetrate deeply into the soil, but spread out horizontally. I had the opportunity to examine fallen trees in various places, and very rarely did I happen to find any whose roots went down more than a foot." Kalm, Vol. I, p. 13.

[6. Fort Warren. See Samuel J. Hough, "An Italian Nobleman in New Hampshire and Vermont," *Appalachia* 36 (1967): 751.]

7. *Crotalus horridus* Lin. [!]

8. *Vipera caudisona anguis est Americae, cujus caudae crepitaculum ex membranis cartilaginosis, articulatisque connectitur. Sacerdotes nostri a Pensylvania reduces ad unum omnes referunt, hanc Viperam viso in arbore Sciuro ad ejus radices procumbere. Sciurum oculis radiantibus, & rictu hiante, ut solet felis murem contemplari; hunc vero costernatum arborem circumcursare, effugia quaerere, tandem vero velut fascinatum in os anguis insilire. Commenti loco habuere hanc narrationem, eamque genuinae Physicae repugnare crediderunt artium doctores; sed Angli coepere has Viperas vivas caveis eas incluserunt, & laevissimo praetio cuiquam ostenderunt, quod Glirae cavae eidem immissi, undequaque effugia cursu quaesiverint, mox vero Viperae acri obtutu, & ore patulo quasi fascinati demum in gulam ejus se praecipites dederint, adeo ut veritati rei multis testibus comprobatae nullum remaneat dubium (Oratio clar. Lin. de Telluris habitabilis incremento).*

[9. More precisely, *Reason the Only Oracle of Man; Or, A Compenduous System of Natural Religion* (Bennington, 1784).]

Chapter V—Canada

[1. For a description of these indigenous bateaux see W. H. H. Murray, *Lake Champlain and Its Shores,* Boston: DeWolfe, Fiske, 1890, pp. 198–99; cf. *Peter Kalm's Travels in North America,* ed. A. B. Benson (New York: Wilson-Erickson, 1937), 1: 333.]

[2. Fort Carillon was established in 1755 as an outpost for Fort Frédéric.]

[3. Fort Ticonderoga fell before the surprise attack of Ethan Allen and his companions on May 10, 1775.]

4. *Sparus (Bassus) corpore albo nigro-maculato.* D. 11/21 P. 12. V. 1/6 A. 6/16 C. 17. *H. in lacu Champlain. Species nova.*

5. *Sparus (Callo-cephalus) cauda integra radiis dorsalibus XXII.* D. 10/22 P.11. V. 1/6 A. 3/12 C. 17. *Caput lineis caerulescentibus, macula nigra linea purpurea terminata ad apicem maxillae. Corpus pulchre coloratum, at colores cum vita evanescunt. Affinis Sparo virginico.* Lin. *H. in lacu Champlain. Species nova.*

6. *Ribes cynosbati* Lin. [Probably]

[7. For the vicissitudes of this fort, see G. P. Alexander, s.v. "Crown Point," *DAH.*]

[8. Castiglioni is historically correct. The canonization of Fort Frédéric was prompted by the popular compulsion to make its name correspond to the general pattern.]

[9. Kalm has also noted the *Cornua ammonis* of the region (*Travels,* 2: 389, 565).]

[10. Windmill Point, formerly Pointe à la Algonquin, now lies in the western part of the town of Alburgh. See W. H. Crockett, *A History of Lake Champlain,* Burlington (Vt.: McAuliffe Paper Co., 1937).]

11. *Ephemera bioculata* Lin. This species of ephemera seemed to me similar to that which can be seen swarming out of the Arno during the summer, and which children burn with bunches of straw.

12. *Culex pulicaris* Lin. [Genus *Culex* is now applied to mosquitoes.]

[13. This is the name originally given by the French to the region adjacent to the Cataraqui River on Lake Ontario. The military and trading post at the river's mouth, built by Frontenac in 1673, was known both as Fort Frontenac and Fort Cataraqui. The city of Kingston now occupies the site of the fort.]

14. European *folle avoine* is a totally different grass—namely, the *Avena fatua* of Linnaeus.

15. *Cupressus thyoides* Lin. [*Chamaecyparis thyoides* (L.) BSP]

[16. Sir John Johnson (1742–1830), son of the more famous Sir William Johnson (for whom Johnstown, N.Y., was named). As a staunch and active loyalist, Sir John lost his possessions in New York in 1779. He was compensated by a large sum of money and a tract of land in Canada, where he spent the rest of his life. *DAB*]

17. *Castor zibethicus* Lin. Schreb., *Saügth.,* Plate 176. [*Ondatra zibethica* (Linn.)]

18. *Perca fluviatilis* Lin.

19. *Cyprinus* (Chob) *pinna ani radiis decem, dorsali octo.* D. 8. P. 16. V. 8. A. 10. C. 20. *Corpus argenteum linea laterali nigricante, Dorso nigro. H. in Fl. S. Laurentii. Spec. nova.*

20. *Cyprinus barbus?* Lin. D. 7. P. 9. V. 5. A. 23. C. 21. *H. in Fl. S. Laurentii. Pinna dorsalis secunda adiposa.* [*Leucosomus corporalis* Mitchill?]

21. *Sparus (virescens) cauda bifida, corpora virescente subtus albo. Membran. branchiostega radiis* V. D. 9/14 P. 15. V. 5. A. 1/13 C. 17. *H. in Fl. S. Laurentii. Spec. nova.*

22. *Coluber sirtalis* Lin. [*Thamnophis sirtalis* (Linn.)]

23. *Cyprinus carpio* Lin. D. 14. P. 14. V. 9. A. 8. C. 19.

24. *Esox lucius* Lin. D. 20. P. 15. V. 10. A. 17. C. 18. [*Esox* sp.]

25. *Panax quinquefolium* Lin. [!]

26. See article "Ginseng" in Appendix.

27. *Falco fulvus* Lin. *Varietas B. canadensis. Ornitolog. Firentina,* Vol. I, Plate 7. Edward, Vol. I, Table 1. Buffon, *Oiseaux: Aigle* commun. Variété. *Aigle brun.* Note, Vol. I, p. 86, Paris, 1780. [*Aquila chrysaëtos canadensis* (Linn.)]

[28. For this adventurous early American type see article and bibliography by W. E. Stevens in *DAH,* s.v. "*Coureurs de bois.*"]

29. *Cervus alces* Lin. "Elk" in English. *Élan* in French. *Orignal* and *orignac* in Canada. [American moose, *Alces americana* Clinton]
30. *Cervus elaphus* Lin. "Stag" and "deer" in English. *Cerf* in French. [*Odocoileus virginianus borealis* Miller]
31. *Cervus tarandus* Lin. "Rein-" or "moose-deer" in English. *Renne* in French. *Caribou* or *carabou* in Canada. [*Rangifer caribou* Gmelin]
32. *Cervus capreolus* Lin. "Roebuck" in English. *Chevreuil* in French. [Elk, *Cervus canadensis* Erxleben]
33. *Castor fiber* Lin. Eng. "beaver," Fr. *castor.* Beaver were once quite common, not only in Canada, but also in the various parts of the United States, and the number of brooks and streams that still preserve the name of Beaver Creek is very great. However, since these animals cannot defend themselves nor flee, and their pelts are much sought after, they were completely destroyed in the areas frequented by Europeans, both in the United States and in Canada. For this reason I did not have a chance during my various travels in America to see a single one alive, so that it was impossible for me to examine, as was my desire, the singular characteristics of the beaver reported by travelers.
34. *Castor zibethicus* Lin. Eng. "muskrat," Fr. *rat musqué.* Buffon, and in Canada: *ondatra.* [*Ondatra zibethica* (Linn.)]
35. *Felis lynx* Lin. Eng. "wolf-lynx," Fr. *loup-cervier.* [*Lynx canadensis* Kerr]
36. *Felis concolor* Lin. Mantissa and Schreber, *Saügthiere,* p. 394. Eng. "brown cat." Buffon: *Cougar.* They are distinguished into cougars of the North *(pichoux)* and cougars of the South. [*F. concolor* L. was the name given for a South American collection; the northern U.S. species is *Felis concolor couguar* Kerr]
37. *Mustela lutra* Lin. Eng. "otter," Fr. *loutre.* [*Lutra canadensis* (Schreber)]
38. *Mustela vison* Schreber, *Saügthiere,* Plate 127 B. [!] Eng. "mink." Buffon: *vison.*
39. *Mustela canadensis* Schreber, Plate 134. Buffon: *pekan.* [Weasel, *Mustela noveboracensis* (Emmons)]
40. *Ursus luscus* Lin.; and Schreber, p. 530. *Carcajou* or *quincajou* in Canada. [Wolverine, *Gulo luscus* (Linn.)]
41. *Canis lupus* Lin. Eng. "wolf," Fr. *loup.* [*Canis nubilus* Say]
42. Canadian foxes are of various kinds: the red is the common *Canis vulpes* Lin.; the silver is the *Canis cinereo-argenteus* of Brisson and Schreber, *Saügthiere*; and the black and the crossed are the *Canis alopex* Lin., or some variety of the common fox. [*Vulpes fulva* (Desmaret), related forms.]

Chapter VI—The State of New York

[1. The Great Carrying Place, now the town of Fort George, is at the once strategic point where traffic up the Hudson began a 14-mile portage to Lake George.]
2. The Wood Creek stream is also called South Bay.
3. *Rana boans* Lin. [*Rana catesbeiana* Shaw]
4. *Rana ocellata* Lin. [*Rana pipiens* Schreber]
[5. The first substantial fort at this spot, replacing the earlier outpost established by the colonial governor and military organizer Francis Nicholson, was built in 1755 by General Phineas Lyman during the French and Indian Wars and named after him. The name was changed in 1758 to Fort Edward in honor of Edward, Duke of York, grandson of George II. General John Burgoyne's campaign forced abandonment of the stronghold in 1777.]
6. *Thuya occidentalis* Lin. [!]

7. *Robinia pseudoacacia* Lin. [!]
8. *Cupressus thyoides* Lin. [*Chamaecyparis thyoides* (L.) BSP]
[9. Actually, the following day, the 17th of October.]
10. Mr. Kalm saw this waterfall during the summer when the water was low and many rocks were exposed, as can be noted from the illustration added to the second volume of his travels. Kalm, tr. by Mr. Forster, Vol. II, 112. [Pp. 351–52 of Kalm's *Travels in North America,* ed. Benson, 2 (1937).]
11. *Juniperus virginiana* Lin. [!]
12. *Populus heterophylla* Lin. [!]
13. *Quercus prinus* Lin. [!]
[14. As is so often the case, Castiglioni's facts are here a bit shaky. The first foothold of the Dutch, on Castle Island near modern Albany, established in 1613 or 1614, was Fort Nassau. The first colony was not planted at the later Fort Orange until 1624.]
15. The term city, which seems roughly equivalent to *città,* is granted only to those places having a magistrate or a council that represents the community and presides over the maintenance of law and order. This privilege was formerly granted by the King, and now in the United States it is given by the legislative powers of each state.

[Taken by the English in 1664, Albany formed part of the grant made by Charles II to his brother James, Duke of York and Albany, after whom both New York and Albany were renamed. The royal governor of New York, Thomas Dongan, granted Albany a charter in 1686.]
16. *Venus mercenaria* Lin. [!]
17. These are ashes prepared for making lye and soap, and they are sent to England for this purpose since wood ashes are lacking in London. They are distinguished into potash and pearlash, the latter being more refined.
[18. Ed. Benson, 1; 344–45.]
[19. The Van Rensselaer manor was more extensive than Castiglioni indicates. According to the Dongan patent of 1685, the colony of Rensselaerwyck stretched some 23 miles along the Hudson River and ran 24 miles back from each bank – an area of some 700,000 acres.]
[20. The first community, called Claverack Landing, was founded in 1783 by settlers from Massachusetts and Connecticut. The name was changed to Hudson in 1784 in honor of Henry Hudson; and a city charter was granted in 1785.]
21. *Saügthiere,* Plates 121 and 122.
22. *Liriodendron tulipifera* Lin. [!]
23. See article "Tulip Tree" in Appendix.
[24. The British, under Sir Henry Clinton, occupied Stony Point and Verplanck Point on May 31, 1779.]
25. *Kalmia latifolia* Lin. [!]
26. *Gleditsia triacanthos* Lin. [!] Eng. honey locust, Latinized as "Acacia mellifera."
[27. For the history of this manor, destined to be immortalized as the site of Washington Irving's *Legend of Sleepy Hollow,* see the article on Frederick Philipse by Richard E. Day in *DAB.*]
28. *Bignonia catalpa* Lin. [*Catalpa bignonioides* Walt.]
29. *Liquidambar styraciflua* Lin. [!]
30. *Juglans nigra* Lin. [!]
31. Explanation of Plate V, representing the City of New York:

1) River called East River, and also Long Island Sound
2) Hudson River
3) Part of Long Island

4) The fort
5) Broadway
6) Broad Street
7) St. Paul's Church, of the Anglicans
8) Statehouse
9) Poorhouse
10) Prison
11) The College
12) Spring that furnishes drinking water for the city
13) Place from which boats leave that transport passengers to Paulus Hook in New Jersey
14) Theater
15) Dock
16) Ranelagh [Ranelagh Gardens, a resort place.]
17) House of Mr. [Nicholas] Bayard. [Destroyed in the great fire of 1835.]
18) House of Mr. [Leonard] Lispenard. [On Lispenard's Hill, overlooking what became later St. John's Square.]
19) Place from which boats leave that transport passengers to Long Island.

[32. The States-General in The Hague granted the original three-year trading charter to the United New Netherlands Company in 1614. The first colony, New Amsterdam, was found in 1624 by the Dutch West India Company under a charter granted three years earlier.]

[33. Fort Washington, at the north end of Manhattan.]

[34. More exactly, the lead statue of George III that once stood on Bowling Green was melted into bullets for the use of the Revolutionary soldiers. Federal Works Projects, *New York City Guide* (New York: Random House, 1939), p. 59.]

[35. The white marble pedestrian statue by the London sculptor Wilton was erected in 1770 in recognition of Pitt's services to America–especially his role in the repeal of the Stamp Act (Maud W. Goodwin et al., *History of New York*, New York/London: Putnam Sons, 1899, p. 104).]

36. The Catholics had not yet built a church, and they used to gather in a rather inappropriate room, but in the winter of 1785, having bought a lot of adequate size, they laid the foundations of a handsome church where they began to hold services in October of 1786. The Catholic congregation is neither very large nor very rich; nevertheless they all contributed gladly to this laudable undertaking.

[St. Paul's Chapel (1766), of Georgian style, remains the oldest church building in New York City. St. Peter's, under construction at a corner of Barclay and Church Streets at the time of Castiglioni's visit and rebuilt in 1838, stands as the oldest Roman Catholic church in Manhattan.]

[37. Good water was at a premium in old New York. The water from wells was so brackish that even the horses of strangers refused to drink it. The best water came from the great spring called the Tea Water Pump on Chatham St. (now Park Row), and many made a business of distributing it in casks throughout the city (see WPA, *New York City Guide*, p. 213).]

38. *Monoculus pulex* Lin.

[39. *Travels*, ed. Benson, 1: 339–40.]

40. The permanent seat of Congress, according to the latest determinations of that august body, is to be neither Philadelphia nor New York, but a city distant from the seashore which

will be called Confederation City and will be located along the Delaware River in Pennsylvania or in New Jersey toward the center of the United States. The lack of money will delay the execution of this plan, and, as far as can be seen, the Congress will not leave New York very soon.

[A compromise decided the national capital's present location: in 1790 Northern support for a Southern site was won at the price of Southern support for federal assumption of debts incurred by the states during the Revolution.]

41. The diplomatic corps is composed of a minister from Holland, a Spanish chargé d'affaires, two consul generals—one from France and the other from England—and a Swedish consul. His Majesty the Emperor has sent Baron de Bechlen Bertholff to America, but since he has not yet received a public assignment, he is living as a private citizen in Philadelphia.

[42. Castiglioni alludes here presumably to the so-called Negro Plot of 1741 (see Richard B. Morris, s.v., *DAH*).]

43. FOR SALE

Young horse, three years old, well shaped, and trained to the chaise and saddle. Has had the strangles, is docile, sturdy, and is being sold only for need of money. Address inquiry to the printer.

Young negro, twenty years old, well shaped, and trained to work as a cook. Has had smallpox, is serious and active, and is being sold only for lack of employment. Address inquiry to the printer.

[44. The Society for Promoting the Manumission of Slaves and Such of Them As Have Been and May Be Liberated was organized in 1785, with John Jay as president and Alexander Hamilton as secretary.]

[45. The Cabot involved in American explorations was, of course, John, the father of Sebastian.]

46. Roanoke, now included in North Carolina. [Raleigh himself did not participate in the voyage, but sent out a preliminary expedition under Philip Amadas and Arthur Barlow.]

[47. It was the Queen herself who suggested the name Virginia upon the return of the explorers.]

48. Under this name was comprised at that time all the region extending from Nova Scotia to Carolina.

[49. More commonly known as the London Company or the Virginia Company of London. "Adventurer" bore at the time the meaning of "speculative investor." The organization was a joint-stock company.]

50. Now Albany and New York. [In 1614 the States-General of The Netherlands granted Adraien Block and some merchants a three-year charter allowing them to trade in America. Dutch settling in New York did not begin until 1624, when the first families established themselves at Fort Orange near modern Albany. Settlement at New Amsterdam had to await Peter Minuit's famous purchase of Manhattan Island from the Indians in 1626 for 24 dollars' worth of trinkets.]

[51. In all likelihood Sir Edmund Plowden, who in 1632 applied for a grant on Long Island, but was diverted southward and failed in his attempt to found a New Albion in the Delaware valley.]

[52. Twenty-three Swedish soldiers and two officers established Christina on the Delaware in 1638, renamed Wilmington by Thomas Penn.]

[53. An anonymous work by the industrious English publisher and compiler Richard Blome.]

54. Some people called this channel The Devil's Belt.

55. *Ostrea edulis* Lin.

56. Kalm Vol. I, p. 185 [Benson ed., 1: 125–27, 325].
57. These fevers became even more frequent in the capital after the recent war, because when the woods situated to the north of the city were cut down, the way was left clear for the passage of the damp, infectious, exhalations of the swamps near the lakes and the river. For the same reason, that is, the cutting down of the woods, some maintain that winters have become more severe in the city of New York.
58. Columbia, a new county that was split off from that of Albany and of which the city of Hudson is the capital, was so named in honor of the discoverer of America, just as the one formerly called Tryon received its name from General Montgomery.
[59. The present translation of Art. XXXVII reflects Castiglioni's rather free paraphrase of the original text. Arts. XXXVIII and XXXIX are reproduced from F. N. Thorpe's *Federal and State Constitutions,* &c., since their wording closely follows the original.]
60. In the article in which the establishment of the militia is treated, it is stipulated that the Quakers, who as a matter of religion are unwilling to bear arms, can be exempted from this duty by paying instead that sum of money that shall be set by the state legislature.
61. William Smith, *History of [the Province of] New York* [(London: Wilcox, 1757)], p. 207.
62. *The Independent Reflector* ["Of the Transportation of Felons," 1753, No. XVI, pp. 63–66], and Smith. Among the great number of criminals transported from Europe to various British colonies in America, many examples have been seen to prove that the greatest obstacle that a man must face in order to return to virtue after a deed that has publicly shamed him is the certitude that he will never regain the esteem and confidence of his fellow citizens. When this obstacle is removed, experience and remorse not infrequently detach him from vice and make him again a useful member of society. There still lives in the city of New York a man who was branded on a hand in England, and, being unknown in America, so changed his behavior that he acquired for himself, justly, a reputation as an honest and upright man, rising to the position of general in the American army. He confesses that emigration alone was the cause of the change in him, since in America he had won back that right to public opinion that degrading punishment had forever taken from him in England.
63. Nowadays, since these immense possessions are contrary to the principles of a democratic government, holdings of limited size are sold by the state.

Chapter VII—From the State of New York to the Border of Georgia

1. Since I passed hastily over this portion of the states of New Jersey, Pennsylvania, and Delaware, I shall reserve my discussion of them until my return, as I shall do also for the capital cities of Maryland, Virginia, and the two Carolinas.
[2. Alexandria was incorporated in 1779.]
3. The project of making this river navigable was conceived by General Washington, and this great enterprise had already begun at the time of my visit to those regions. [The James River Company was devised in 1785 by Washington to improve navigation on the James River, with the ultimate dream of connecting the headwaters of the James and Kanawha Rivers, providing thereby a connection with the Ohio Valley where Washington owned land. We may surmise that the scheme was a conspicuous topic of conversation at Mount Vernon when Castiglioni passed through.]
[4. In the ms. (Br 1:6) Castiglioni alludes to the wild merrymaking of the evening before, marked by fireworks and the shooting of rifles and pistols, often with dire consequences for young scoundrels who during the day had "sacrificed their reason to Bacchus."]

[5. The ms. account (Br 1:9) embellishes the description by comparing the site to the "enchanted forests of Alcina and the charming country haunts so highly lauded by the story-tellers."]

[6. Apart from the eulogy of Washington which appears at this point, Castiglioni's visit left remarkably little residue. Washington's *Diaries* (ed. J. C. Fitzpatrick, Boston-New York: Houghton Mifflin, 1925, 2: 460) record laconically: "*Sunday, 25th.* Count Castiglioni . . . came here to dinner. . . . *Thursday, 29th.* Count Castiglioni went away after breakfast, on his tour to the Southward." The only positive evidence of personal contact is the brief letter Washington wrote to present the young traveler to Governor William Moultrie of South Carolina (*Writings of George Washington,* edited by J. C. Fitzpatrick, 28: 44, fn., USGPO 1938).]

[7. The ms. (Br 1:9) dramatizes Washington's personal privations: "At least a thousand times he found himself exposed to the harshness of the weather, and his table was often bare of the most ordinary food and most necessary liquids."]

8. The rare courage of the Americans at the beginning of this civil war will serve as an example to future ages of how much can be tolerated by men who are fighting for liberty. Untrained troops are seen leaving their families, undertaking long and laborious expeditions through wild forests and uninhabited mountains in order to face the British troops, at the mention of whom they used to tremble before the Revolution. Lacking clothes and, what is worse, gunpowder, bullets, and cannon, necessity (which is the mother of industry) spurred them to seek these most essential articles, and in a short time some were seen looking over old quarries in order to collect saltpeter, others transformed wood into charcoal, and very soon there were magazines stocked with American powder. The abundant iron mines were put to use; ingots were transformed into muskets and cannon; linen and hemp were grown, which served for clothing for the soldiers and sails for the ships; woolens were woven; and the troops, at first in rags, were suddenly seen in uniform.

[9. The ms. (Br 1:9) reveals Castiglioni's struggle to gloss over the distasteful fact that Washington possessed slaves: "Owner of a large tract of land near his home, he applied himself to agriculture, and presiding over a large number of negroes who work in his fields, he reduced them to the most advantageous state."]

10. In the year 1787, however, he could not refuse the assignment as chairman of an Assembly of the various states gathered in Philadelphia under the name of Convention to propose a new plan of confederation and to remedy the decline in trade.

[11. Fredericksburg was incorporated as a town in 1781; it did not become a city until 1879.]

12. That is, from 75 to 150 *zecchini.*

13. See the article "*Diospyros*" in Appendix.

[14. Br 1:12 "The next day, the last of December, leaving Massey Tavern early, I arrived late at night at Richmond. . . ."

15. We shall talk about Richmond in the chapter in which Virginia is discussed.

16. From their triangular shape they appear to be from a species of dogfish: *Squalus* Lin.

[17. "In trade they distinguish two sorts of tobacco; the first is called Aranokoe, from Maryland and the northern parts of Virginia; this is strong and hot in the mouth, but it sells very well in the markets of Holland, Germany, and the North. The other sort is called sweet scented, the best of which is from James's and York rivers in the southern part of Virginia" (from the anonymous work of the year 1766 composed probably jointly by William and Edmund Burke, *An Account of the European Settlements in America,* London: Dodsley, 2: 199).]

18. *Rallus virginianus* Lin. *Râle de Virginie,* Buffon, *Oiseaux,* Vol. VIII, p. 165, Paris, 1780. The common rail (*Rallus crex* Lin.) is called *re di quaglie* in our country. [*Rallus carolinus*

Linn., now *Porzana carolina* (Linn.), called rail, ortolan, and sora, occurs as a migrant in Virginia. It is seldom seen today in Virginia. Feeding on wild rice, *Zizania aquatica* L., rendered it especially delectable despite its small size. See Alexander Sprunt and E. B. Chamberlain, *South Carolina Bird Life* (Univ. of North Carolina Press, 1949), pp. 196–97.]

19. *Zizania aquatica* Lin. [!]
20. Ray, *Historia plantarum.* [See J. Ewan, s.v. "John Banister," *DSB*]
[21. ". . . A stately two-story house that invites the artistry of some restorer." (Federal Works Project: *Dinwiddie County: The Country of the Apamatica,* Richmond: Dinwiddie County School Board, 1942, p. 235).]
[22. Br 1:14 ". . . to whom I presented a letter of introduction kindly given to me by Col. Banister, his friend and relative."]
[23. Br 1:14 "This gentleman, born in England, and then having come to live in this part of America, endowed with a natural propensity for the study of botany, entered into correspondence with Mr. Gieseke, Professor of Botany in Hamburg, through whom he obtained the works of Linnaeus."]
[24. Br 1:14 ". . . he showed me the careful description of the aforementioned plants, modeled after the Linnaean system. . . ."]
25. These observations will be found inserted at the end of the respective articles.
[26. Br 1:15 ". . . another gentleman, to whom I presented a letter from Captain Walker. . . ."]
27. The mocassin appears to be the *Crotalus durissus* Lin. [A tropical species; ours is *Agkistrodon piscivorus* (Lacépède).]
28. *Anguis ventralis* Lin. [*Ophiosaurus attenuatus* Cope]
[29. Br 1:16 ". . . almost all of wood, and one counts there but one main street."]
30. *Convolvulus batatas* Lin. [*Ipomoea batatas* (L.) Lam.]
[31. Br 1:17 "Twenty-five miles beyond Halifax I stopped at evening at Cottin's Ordinary. This term is used to distinguish the inns of North Carolina, which can with reason be called ordinary—and very ordinary."]
32. This is the *Lichen plicatus* Lin. that also grows in Europe and was called *Muscus arboreus* and *Usnea officinarum* by some old botanists. [In the ms. (Br 1:18) Castiglioni identifies this moss parenthetically as *Lychen barbatus*. Now *Usnea barbata* (L.) Fr.]
33. *Tillandsia usneoides* Lin. [!]
34. *Vultur aura* Lin. [*Cathartes aura septentrionalis* Wied]
[35. Br 1:223–224 "This species of vulture, common in both Virginia and the two Carolinas, took the name 'turkey buzzard' from the resemblance of its feathers to those of the turkey. On the 19th of January, 1786, I saw for the first time four or five of these vultures on the way between Halifax and New Bern. They are of a mingled gray and black color, and they have white beaks and heads covered with a fleshy red-colored excrescence. These birds destroy snakes and feed on cadavers and carrion, which they enjoy so much that they do not flee or draw away even when approached by men and dogs. They have a bad odor, they can be used for nothing, and therefore they are never killed by the inhabitants, who, on the contrary, look very favorably upon them since they purge the country both of cadavers that infest the air and of poisonous animals. Their resemblance to turkeys is so great that a number of foreigners were at first deceived, and knowing that turkeys are common in the woods of the Carolinas, they killed instead some of these vultures and were fooled in their anticipation of a delicate food."]
36. *Laurus borbonia* Lin. [*Persea borbonia* (L.) Spreng.]
37. *Myrica cerifera* Lin. [!]
[38. Br 1:19 ". . . toward evening I reached William's Ordinary, 37 miles from New Bern."]

[39. Br 1:19 "The road is not so sandy, and one sees, mingled in the pines, oaks and other trees that denote a less unproductive terrain."]

40. *Quercus phellos* Lin. [!]

[41. Br 1:20 ". . . of *Pinus taeda*. . . ."]

[42. Br 1:20 ". . . from which they eke out a wretched existence."]

[43. Br 1:20 ". . . which they dye in various colors with the leaves of the colberry, or *Prinos glabrus* [*Ilex glabra* L.], obtaining a reddish-black tint similar to that called *gola di Levante,* which is fixed with copperas; from indigo, which grows in their fields, they extract the color blue, and they make a pretty yellow color with the bark of the hickory (*Juglans alba*) and the laurel *Magnolia glauca*."]

44. *Cassine peragua* Lin. ["Japan tree" may be either *Ilex paraguariensis* St. Hil., "Paraguay tea," in cultivation, which seems possible, or *Viburnum cassinoides* L. (cf. p. 000, below), "Appalachian tea," or a confusion of two or three different plants.]

45. *Dionea muscipula* Lin. [*Dionaea muscipula* Ellis]

46. *Loxia cardinalis* Lin. Eng. red bird. [*Richmondena cardinalis* (Linn.)]

[47. Br 1:21 "Finally, on the 26th, after 28 miles of laborious travel because of the deep sand that covers the road, and passing through uninhabited, sterile, forests as on the day before, I arrived at Wilmington, the most active commercial city in the State of North Carolina."]

[48. Br 1:21 ". . . which are partly wood, partly brick, . . .]

[49. Br 1:21 "However, its location in a low and humid place, and the vapors that emanate from the rice plantations and the uncultivated and inundated lands on the island facing the city make residence there extremely dreary and unhealthful, especially in summer and autumn."]

[50. Br 1:22 ". . . all the way to the Statehouse, striking a poor passerby in the legs."]

[51. Br 1:22–23 ". . . but the following day, the wind shifting to the northwest, the weather became immediately very cold and icy. This rapid succession of rain, heat, and cold in a humid and unhealthful region is the cause for the frequent fatal diseases to which the inhabitants are so subject, whereby sturdy people are seen to waste away with fever in two or three days, look like cadavers, and succumb in a short time in the flower of their age.

"Wednesday afternoon I left on horseback for the Hermitage, a property located eight miles from the city, belonging to Mr. Burguin. This gentleman, at the time of the war, withdrew to England, where he remained until last year, when he returned to America. His house was greatly damaged during the time of dissensions by both the Americans and the British. Since he is considered a loyalist by the former, I don't know whether he will be allowed to remain in this country and to enjoy his income, or whether he will be forced to return to Europe and his property confiscated by the state."]

52. The names of certain cities and villages in England, such as Charleston, Wilmington, Hartford, etc., are often repeated in America and are distinguished only by adding the name of the state in which they are located.

[53. Br 1:23 "This island, quite a vast one and continually flooded by water, is partly sown to rice, but for the most part it is still uncultivated and covered with trees and shrubs. The Causeway, or crossing road, runs from one side to the other of the island for a stretch of about two miles, but, badly built and on a marshy and flooded terrain, it is almost always damaged by the rains or by the overflow from the river, and often impassable. In order to avoid the trouble and danger, I sent my horses and carriage across the Causeway, and through the courtesy of Captain McAllester, who lives on the other side of the river, I, with some other gentlemen, got into a rowboat fitted out for the purpose. Going down the north branch about a mile, we entered a channel called Alligator Creek. . . ."]

[54. Br 1:24 "Among these I noted principally the *Quercus Phellos* or water oak, the sweet bay or *Laurus borbonia,* magnolias, andromedas, and the *Chamaerops americana,* whose large and palmate leaves spread like a fan." (Cf. Br 2:225 "This species of *Chamaerops,* not described by Linnaeus, differs from the European only in having leaves that are blunt at the end and not spiny. It is very common in the ponds and marshes of the two Carolinas, where, owing to the shape of its leaves, it is confused by the inhabitants with the palmetto and *Sabal carolinianum.* I do not know that any use is made of this plant in America."]

55. *Corypha minor* Jacquin, *Amer.* See his article. [*Sabal minor* (Jacq.) Pers.]

56. *An Pelecanus piscator?* Lin. [*Phalacrocorax* sp.]

[57. Br 1:24–25 "My carriage and the horses, however, did not arrive until late at night, and not without danger of remaining buried in the horrid deep pits into which they fell several times, and from which they succeeded laboriously in pulling themselves. Thus my servant, as well as the horses, was all covered with mud, the equipment broken, and the carriage in bad shape. Reflecting upon this condition, I could not help feeling sorry for them, at the same time congratulating myself at having escaped the same fate.

"On the morning of February 2nd I left the home of Captain McAllester, and after going more than eight miles on a completely untraveled road through swamps and puddles, I reached the shores of a wide river where there was no bridge nor boat, and which seemed too deep to ford. I remained for some time in doubt as to what to do, when, leaving my servant in charge of the horses and looking about, I discovered about a quarter of a mile away a small plantation, and walking toward it, I saw a wooden house. When I reached it, I found only some negro slaves who didn't know the road any better than I did. So I waited patiently for the owner to return. When he finally arrived, I accosted him to ask the way. He told me that the road I had taken was completely abandoned after the war, during which the troops had cut the bridge over the river, and that I would have to go back about six miles in order to get on the right road. Thanking him for this advice, I hurried back to where my carriage was, and, doubling back dejectedly over the same wretched route, I stopped toward evening at Mr. Daniel's on the little river, or stream, called Town Creek just three miles from Wilmington."]

[58. Perhaps "Folly" in the sense of "a summer house or pavilion designed for picturesque effect," or possibly some other excessively costly and pretentious structure (cf. *Webster's Third New International Dictionary*). Paul Wilstach, in *Tidewater Virginia*) Indianapolis: Bobbs-Merrill, 1929, pp. 164, 199) lists a Bowman's Folly as "the most pretentious house in Virginia on this side of the bay."]

[59. Presumably Shallotte Inlet.]

[60. Br 1:27 "Crossing Long Bay and seeking a house where I could give my horses something to eat, I asked whether there were an inn in the vicinity and was told that there wasn't any in those parts, but that I might go to a certain Mrs. Dwight's, whose plantation was about two miles away, where I might easily find a little corn for my horses."]

[61. Br 1:28 ". . . and I accepted without much ceremony. . . ."]

[62. Br 1:29 ". . . whose hospitality and kindness amply made up for the labors of the day."]

[63. Br 1:29 ". . . to whom I had a letter of introduction kindly given to me by Captain McAllester in Wilmington."]

[64. Br 1:29 ". . . but the climate is very unhealthful and the inhabitants are subject to many dangerous diseases. I spent the whole day at his plantation, where I saw a fine water machine for shelling rice, and on the morning of the 7th, after having shown me many favors, he insisted upon adding that of offering me his own canoe for going down to Georgetown; and I sent my horses to the nearby plantation of another wealthy gentleman friend of his, Colonel Harriot, where they were to remain until the ferry was ready to leave. Most appreciative of the politeness and civility shown me, I got into the canoe with two negro slaves, and going four miles downstream and then crossing the mouths of the Black and Pee Dee Rivers, reached Georgetown, where I was graciously received at the home of Dr. (Evaring?)."]

[65. Br 1:30–31 ". . . If the commerce of Georgetown receives fresh life and vigor from the handsome and extensive indigo and rice plantations that surround it, the health of the inhabitants is greatly vitiated by them, and the nervous, wormy, putrid, and intermittent fevers destroy the inhabitants in the fairest flower of their age, so that very few reach the age of 50, and at this age they have the appearance of old and decrepit men. However, this decline is attributable not only to the quality of the climate but also to the way of life of the inhabitants. Their breakfast consists not only of tea or coffee, but mainly of salted meats such as ham and salt pork, etc., and both at dinner and supper they use a great deal of meat and few vegetables. Taking very little exercise during the day, they sometimes spend the evening in continuous and exhausting dances, after which they expose themselves heedlessly to the unhealthful and humid night air. The abuse of liquors and other consequent disorders contribute not a little to rendering more fatal and frequent the diseases that reign both in the climates of the Carolinas and in the islands of the Antilles.

"It is a common observation that in the dangerous climate of the American isles the Spaniards enjoy better health than the French, and that the latter are less subject to diseases than the English, which must be attributed solely to the different ways of life. However, in spite of these examples, national prejudices are such and so firmly rooted that the natives or descendants from the temperate lands of England and the gelid climes of Scotland transport and keep their pernicious customs under the warm atmosphere of the tropics and Guinea."]

[66. The 7th, according to Br 1:31.]

[67. Br 1:31–32 ". . . to cross the island by a channel called Pushinghoo Creek, which after a five-mile course opens into the south branch of the Santee."]

[68. Br 1:32 "Coming finally out of the channel and crossing the south branch of the Santee, after traveling about two miles and a half along the river, we arrived at the plantation of Mr. Bowman. Mr. Bowman was educated in Geneva, and in his tour of Europe had made friends with a number of the most famous men of the Old World, whose writings and character he knew. So I spent the evening and the following morning most pleasantly in his home, which I left around dinner time, and after about 27 miles of good road, I stopped at Mr. Scott's inn. From there, on the 11th, I went to Bolton's Ferry, whence I crossed by water to Charleston about three miles away."]

[69. Br 1:32 ". . . and the region about it is very populous."]

[70. Br 1:39–40 "On the 20th of March I finally left Charleston to continue my trip to the south toward Savannah in the company of Mr. Henry Middleton, a very likable young man who received his education in England and is from one of the main families of South Carolina. After 10 miles we crossed the Ashley River, which has there a very strong current, on a 'post,' or ferry, guided by a rope that crosses the river; and after 4 miles we found ourselves at Drayton Hall, the country home of Mr. Drayton (now Lieutenant Governor of South Carolina) on the shores of the Ashley River. The house is very large and made of bricks, and in the garden one sees various magnolias and hedges of *Cassine peragua,* or Indian tea. The surrounding fields are planted to rice and irrigated with rain water, which for that purpose is stored in large ponds or reservoirs, while the river water, which is salt and would be harmful to the growth of rice, is held back by means of a levee or dam. We left Drayton Hall in late afternoon to arrive in the evening at Middleton Place."]

71. *Cassine peragua* Lin. [An ambiguous and confused name. Here probably *Viburnum cassinoides* L. See M. L. Fernald and B. Schubert, *Rhodora* 50 (1948), 169–70.]
72. *Ardea caerulea* Lin. [Possibly the Little blue heron, *Florida caerulea* (Linn.)]
73. *Ardea equinoctialis* Lin. [White heron or Snowy egret *Leucophoyx thula* (Molina)]

[74. Br 1:39 "Middleton Place, at but four miles from Drayton Hall, is the summer home of Mr. Arthur Middleton, a man of fine judgment and discernment who has traveled in various parts of Europe."]

[75. Br 1:39 ". . . having lived a long time in Holland, . . ."]

[76. Br 1:40–41 ". . . on the shores of the river where may be seen various trees and shrubs distributed over the various compartments of the garden, among which the redbud, or *Cercis canadensis,* and wild orange *Prunus (laurocerasus) serratifolia* were laden with flowers. In the vegetable garden I saw some of the best greens and legumes kept in greenhouses, and elsewhere in the garden some models of the Medicean Venus and the satyr of – –.
". . . at dinner time we were at Colonel Washington's at Sand Hill. (. . . but he is not of the same family as, or even related to, the General.) On this road I noted in the woods the *Cercis canadensis,* the *Yucca aloifolia,* the *Prunus serratifolia,* and the *Chamaerops americana.*"]

77. *Cercis canadensis* Lin. [!]
78. *Prunus serratifolia* Lin. [*Prunus caroliniana* (Mill.) Ait.]
79. *Corypha minor.* Jacquin, *Amer.* [*Sabal minor* (Jacq.) Pers.]

[80. Br 1:41 ". . . which, when planted to rice, become very fruitful; but the stagnant water covering the low terrain for several miles about make the air unhealthful and the climate pernicious and deadly."]

[81. Br 1:41 "The roads are for the most part cut through the swamps and made of pieces of wood set crosswise and covered with sand and earth. These are the roads known by the name of 'causeways' and which serve for passage in low and flooded places. . . ."]

[82. Br 1:42 "I saw on this day blooming in the woods the *Laurus aestivalis,* the *Laurus borbonia,* the *Cornus florida,* the *Azalea nudiflora,* and the *Bignonia sempervirens.*"]

83. *Azalea nudiflora* Lin. [*Rhododendron nudiflorum* (L.) Torr.]
84. *Laurus aestivalis* Lin. [*Litsea aestivalis* (L.) Fern.]

[85. Br 1:42 "Here I spent the next day, and on the morning of the 24th I continued my trip toward Purysburg."]

86. *Falco leucocephalus* Lin. Eng. fishing eagle. Buffon, *Oiseaux,* Vol. I, p. 99, Paris, 1780: *pygargue.* [Osprey or Sea eagle, *Pandion haliaetus* (Linn.)]
87. *Quercus phellos* Lin. [!]
88. *Coluber (plumbeus), Scuta abdominalia 127. Squamae subcaudales 50. Corpus supra fuscum, subtus albo-testaceum. Variat vitta testacea pone oculos. H. in Carolina meridionali. Spec. nova.* [Not identifiable: see H. A. Dundee and J. Ewan, *Jour. Herpetology* 13 (1979): 216–17.]
89. *Coluber doliatus* Lin. *Scuta abdominalia 174. Squamae subcaudales 42. Fasciarum paribus XXII. Variat a Linneano annulis lateraliter interruptis. H. in Carolina meridionali.* [? *Lampropeltis triangulum* Lacépède. Alexander Garden sent the specimen described as *C. doliatus* Linn.]
90. Linnaei *Systema naturae,* Edit. XIII, Vol. I, p. 367. [*Anolis carolinensis* Voigt]

Chapter VIII—The State of Georgia

[1. Br 1:45 "Since a great deal of rain had fallen . . . I found the river very high, and was told that on the other side the road was flooded for more than three miles, and that, inasmuch as the terrain was marshy and the causeway in bad condition, it was impossible to pass."]
2. He died in June, 1786, from the malady called sunstroke.
3. *Quercus phellos* Lin. Eng. live oak [Actually *Quercus virginiana* Mill.]
4. *Scarabeus lancifer* Lin. [*Phanaeus vindex?* For an early Virginia account of Dung beetles see Joseph and Nesta Ewan, "De Scarabeis excornibus," in *John Banister and His Natural History of Virginia, 1678–1692* (Urbana, Univ. of Illinois Press, 1970), pp. 301–303.]
5. *Scarabeus festivus?* Lin. It differs from the description of Linnaeus and Fabricius in that it has wing casings of a bronze-green color. The citation of the illustration of Roesel must have been mistaken in both the aforementioned authors. Probably these two species are the two sexes of one, and the *festivus* is the female. [Perhaps the females of the above.]
6. He is an Irishman who settled in America at the time of the war and is related neither to the general nor to the colonel of the same name.
7. *Areca oleracea* Lin. *Chou-palmier* of the French, and cabbage tree of the English. See article on it in Appendix. [*Sabal palmetto* (Walt.) R. & S.]
8. *Convolvulus batatas* Lin. [*Ipomoea batatas* (L.) Lamb.]
9. *Cycas circinalis* Lin. [*Zamia* spp., kunti, or coontie, Florida arrowroots.]
10. *Morus alba* Lin. [!]
11. *Halesia tetraptera* Lin. [*Halesia carolina* L. and/or H. *diptera* Ellis]
12. *Azalea nudiflora* Lin. [*Rhododendron nudiflorum* (L.) Torr.]
13. *Papilio plexippus* Lin. [*Danaus plexippus* (Linn.)]
14. *Papilio protesilaus* Lin. [*Iphiclides podalirius* (Linn.)]
15. *Papilio podalirius* Lin. [*Eurytides protesilaus* (Linn.)]
[16. Doubtless Natchez, the former Fort Rosalie of the French.]
[17. Br 1:32–33 "I cannot help mentioning . . . the special embassy of the Choctaw Indians to Governor Moultrie of Charleston at which I was present and the motives that compelled them to make such a long journey. The Choctaw Indians inhabit the most remote parts to the west near the Mississippi River. They were formerly allies of the English, as they are now of the Americans, and they have about 1200 warriors, or men in condition to take up arms. The Choctaw are united with the Chickasaw, another courageous but not numerous tribe, against the Creek, who, living in the most remote parts of Georgia, are enemies of the Americans and allies of the Spaniards."]
[18. Presumably the Treaty of Hopewell, November 28, 1785, whereby the United States fixed boundaries with and assumed sovereignty over the Cherokee, Choctaw, and Chickasaw.]
[19. Br 1:33 ". . . in the following words, which were translated into English by William Stanley, interpreter of the two languages."]
[20. Br 1:33 ". . . Tinctimingo (or red woodpecker), a very old man and one of the chiefs of the tribe. . . ."]
21. That is, to declare myself your friend.
22. These are Indian allies of the Choctaw who live in the internal regions of South Carolina near the Mississippi.
23. The ax, or hatchet, that the Indians use in war has a handle perforated lengthwise like a reed and often serves also as a smoking pipe. The weapon, by them called *tomahawk*, used to be made of stone or very hard flint, to which they fastened tightly a wooden handle. But now they use iron hatchets brought to them in great abundance by Euro-

peans. When they have killed their enemies with the *tomahawk,* they scalp them – which consists in cutting around the skin of the skull and tearing it off, along with the hair, by means of their teeth. The number of these scalps, which they carry as ornaments, serves to indicate that of the enemy killed. This cruel operation is not infrequently inflicted upon the wounded, but those who do not die as the result of such barbaric treatment are very few. However, the Indian, so inhuman toward prisoners of war, upon whom he often inflicts a slow death by torture, is to the same degree hospitable and affectionate toward his friends, to the point of sharing wholeheartedly with them what he owns.

24. The Indians always expect some gift from the Europeans when they make a treaty. [Br 1:35, fn. ". . . and they would go away very disappointed if nothing were given to them."]

[25. Br 1:35 "Tintimungo."]

[26. Br 1:35 ". . . Spokohomo, a young Indian and son of one of the sachems, or kings, of that nation, stood up and addressed the Governor with these words: . . ."]

27. That is, we are not friends of the Spaniards.

[28. Br 1:36 "Spokohomo's."]

[29. Br 1:36 "Subsequently they gathered again on the 18th of March at the Governor's home, where, in the presence of the Council, he answered their message in the following terms: . . ."]

[30. Br 1:36 "It has been many years since anyone of your nation has been in Charleston, and now you have come again. We are therefore all the more happy to see you, and I hope the path between us will always be open."]

[31. Br 1:36 ". . . they have always been our friends. . . ."]

32. That is what the Indians call one another after the arrival of the Europeans to distinguish themselves from the whites and the blacks.

[33. Br 1:37 "Spokohomo."]

[34. Br 1:38 "Two of them were old and the others husky and well built. They had quite regular features, but somewhat flattened faces. They differed from the northern Indians only in being perhaps smaller and much darker."]

[35. Br 1:38 "Spokohomo."]

[36. Br 1:38 ". . . at the head of which was the old warrior Tomochichi."]

[37. Br 1:38 "Tomochichi then began to move in a circle, striking up an air or musical tone. . . ."]

[38. Br 1:39 ". . . but their movements were almost always uniform and the tune of their airs and songs almost always the same."]

[39. Br 1:39 "This dance, which is always celebrated by the Indians when they declare war upon another nation, serves to arouse martial fury for revenge in their spirits, and when it is celebrated on such occasions, all the warriors assembled for this horrid dance drink the warm blood from the head of a bull killed for the purpose."]

[40. Br 1:39 ". . . rum and brandy."]

[41. This glossary appears in the ms. as an appendix to "Tomo Secondo," pp. 345–53, under the heading: "A Vocabulary of the Most Common Words in the Dialects of the Cherokee and Choctaw Indians, from the Differences in Which It Appears That, Although These Nations Living in the Interior Regions of Georgia and Carolina Are Neighbors, They Have Had a Different Origin."

A footnote by Castiglioni, in addition to warning that the letters must be pronounced according to the rules of English, informs that "the Indians almost detach the last syllable, pronouncing it with a kind of aspiration, as, for example, *Echnaú-tá, Awbustahoó-bó.*"

How to account for the numerous variations between ms. and printed *Viaggio*?

Castiglioni may have had difficulties with the compiler's calligraphy. It is possible, also, that some of the words were taken down originally in more than one form, and that Castiglioni made different choices in his ms. draft and the later printed book.

[42. Br 2:345 "Aubustahoobó."]

[43. Br 2:346 "Neshskiah."]

[44. Br 2:346 "Akekattenakehah."]

[45. Br 2:346 "Toochekotleskelckeh."]

[46. Br 2:346 "Beshockane."]

[47. Br 2:346 "Bechuloo."]

[48. Br 2:346 "Tucheusatelasak."]

[49. Br 2:346 "Canokutlah."]

[50. Br 2:346 "Canuhkek."]

[51. Br 2:346 "Chenutulich."]

[52. Br 2:346 "Chonawe."]

[53. Br 2:346 "Shaekaboh."]

[54. Br 2:346 "Chenoken."]

[55. Br 2:346 "Abuch."]

[56. Br 2:346 "Akayama."]

[57. Br 2:346 "Bachtalookoché."]

[58. Br 2:347 "Akotasotekooane."]

[59. Br 2:347 "Akoteentotte."]

[60. Br 2:347 "Checa-shane."]

[61. Br 2:347 "Ephechucabee."]

[62. Br 2:347 "Chenegane."]

[63. Br 2:347 "Chenescane."]

[64. Br 2:347 "Catekane."]

[65. Br 2:347 "Coolasetaine."]

[66. Br 2:347 "Chenassetahootanoh."]

[67. Br 2:347 "Aquasuskeh."]

[68. Br 2:347 "Laocoh."]

[69. Br 2:347 "Squlakaiouctoé."]

[70. Br 2:347 "Tiloofulaokeh."]

[71. Br 2:348 "Tileshulotustatleh."]

[72. Br 2:348 "Hahthee."]

[73. Br 2:348 "Sanoch."]

[74. Br 2:348 "Hashnenokiah."

[75. Br 2:348 "Saynoineuto."]

[76. Br 2:348 "Noikusah."]

[77. Br 2:348 "Skutick."]

[78. Br 2:348 "Kokay."]

[79. Br 2:348 "Hushtoolahmomah."]

[80. Br 2:349 "Hashkoochuckoch."]

[81. Br 2:349 "Ekuttayoie."]

[82. Br 2:349 "Hashekootooloch."]

[83. Br 2:349 "Hattuch."]

[84. Br 2:349 "Allateke."]

[85. Br 2:349 "Chepootah."]

[86. Br 2:349 "Chuchoch."]

[87. Br 2:349 "Ehuttuch."]

[88. Br 2:349 "Ootalleeh."]
[89. Br 2:349 "Agotalleeh."]
[90. Br 2:349 "Aioteleh."]
[91. Br 2:349 "Hushkay."]
[92. Br 2:349 "Alokeh."]
[93. Br 2:349 "Atoteh."]
[94. Br 2:349 "Tebawbashe."]
[95. Br 2:349 "Anketo."]
[96. Br 2:349 "Wankey."]
[97. Br 2:350 "Canolianah."]
[98. Br 2:350 "Kalistaieneh."
[99. Br 2:350 "Totochesquiletaneh."]
[100. Br 2:350 "Aquatooleach."]
[101. Br 2:350 "Yunch."]
[102. Br 2:350 "Wawseh."]
[103. Br 2:350 "Nehatoe."]
[104. Br 2:350 "Ekeh."]
[105. Br 2:350 "Wohtutlay."]
[106. Br 2:351 "Attockapawhōōmode."]
[107. Br 2:351 "Kuttonstek."]
[108. Br 2:351 "Cuttemah."]
[109. Br 2:351 "Cuttamaschanta."]
[110. Br 2:351 "Tomatiawnuita."]
[111. Br 2:351 "Kawtohetotechainsaye."]
[112. Br 2:351 "Ekachookamo."]
[113. Br 2:351 "Auklekekuh."]
[114. Br 2:352 "Eshockshupe."]
[115. Br 2:352 "Cunnecuh."]
[116. Br 2:352 "Netahockshupa."]
[117. Br 2:352 "Cunnekajyonah."]
[118. Br 2:352 "Hooshunhockshupa."]
[119. Br 2:352 "Wyekih."]
[120. Br 2:352 "United States" appears between "I can't" and "white" as an expression to be translated, but no equivalent is given.]
[121. Br 2:352 "Toohoobeh."]
[122. Br 2:352 "Laconnah."]
[123. Br 2:352 "Itsayee."]
[124. Br 2:352 "Kekokaye."]
[125. Br 2:352 "Nanechoho."]
[126. Br 2:352 "Otalleh."]
[127. Br 2:352 "Aquonee."]
[128. Br 2:352 "Boogishe."]
[129. Br 2:353 "Tunnawpoo."
[130. Br 2:353 "Nappa."]
[131. Br 2:353 "Nappa."]
[132. Br 2:353 "Cunnechunestikeh."]
[133. Br 2:354 "Tachistaohahasesyou."]
[134. Br 2:354 "Ooskenockey."]
[135. Br 2:354 "Chemashunnekek."]

[136. Br 2:354 "Cunnunnoah."]
[137. Br 2:354 "Ailstea."]
[138. Br 2:354 "Yailstecunneheetah."]
[139. See E. Merton Coulter, *A Short History of Georgia* (Chapel Hill: University of North Carolina Press, 1933), p. 21, fn.: ". . . The total number has been variously estimated from 114 to 125."]
140. At about this time General Oglethorpe tried to invade Florida and take St. Augustine, and this attempt would have succeeded if the aforementioned general had not been ill supported by his troops. To avenge themselves for this invasion, the Spaniards then entered Georgia in the year 1742. See *An Impartial History of the War in America*, London, 1780, p. 43.
141. These were accepted at the session of February 5, 1777.
[142. The Georgia Constitution of 1777 does not specify a fixed number of representatives. Here, as elsewhere, the interested reader is referred to a standard text such as Thorpe's *Federal and State Constitutions* for verification of Castiglioni's statements.]
143. See p. 88 [p. 49 of the present translation].
144. Delegates were sent by the Georgians to the Natchez to ask for that place, and upon the refusal of the Spanish, certain individuals expressed the violent idea of occupying it by force.

Chapter IX—South Carolina

1. *Lonicera sempervirens* Lin. [!]
[2. Arthur Simkins. See Edward McCrady, *The History of South Carolina in the Revolution, 1780–1783* (New York: Macmillan, 1902), p. 559.]
3. *Acarus americanus* Lin. [Redbug is an arachnid.]
4. See Buffon, art. "Cerf," and where he speaks of the animals common to both continents. [*Odocoileus virginianus* (Boddaert)?]
5. *Meleagris gallopavo* Lin. [*Meleagris gallopavo americana* Bartram]
6 *The Present State of His Majesties Isles and Territories in America* (London, 1687), p. 156.
7. See below where the government established by Locke is discussed.
8. That is, in 1687. See p. 293 [*of the Viaggio*].
[9. As elsewhere with Castiglioni's thumbnail colonial histories, the reader concerned with the facts is referred here to some standard account such as Edward McCrady's *History of South Carolina*, 4 vols. (New York: Macmillan, 1901–1902).]
10. See below.
11. *Indigofera tinctoria* Lin. [? *Indigofera caroliniana* Mill., one of several native species.]
[12. Castiglioni's description is based upon the Constitution of 1778. He could not have known the revision of 1790 (see F. N. Thorpe, *Federal and State Constitutions* &c., 6: 3258), although he seems to have had wind of modifications.]
[13. An egregious error. The South Carolina Constitution of 1778 specifies "two thousand pounds currency at least, clear of debt" (Thorpe, 6: 3251).]
14. Explanation of Plate VI, representing the city of Charleston:

    1. Ashley River
    2. Cooper River
    3. Docks for ships
    4. Portion of the swampy island called Shutes Folly
    5. Main square, at the corners of which are the four principal buildings, namely, the Statehouse, the Bourse, the Market, and a church; and, in the center, the statue of William Pitt.

15. In Lombardy this tree lives for many years, but it has to be out in the open and protected from the north wind; otherwise it loses almost all its new shoots every winter and never acquires a handsome appearance.
[16. *Sapium sebiferum* (L.) Roxb.]
17. From observing a plant that has survived out-of-doors for more than 20 years at the Villa Crivelli of Mombello, one may be assured that it is easily adaptable in our country. However, this one has never borne either flowers or fruit, perhaps because it is in a dry terrain, so that the attempt should be made to plant it near water as is done in China. The seeds I got from America sprouted easily and in two years had produced vigorous little plants; but the bitter cold of January, 1789, killed those that were not put under cover. This happened because of the tender age of the plants, which had almost herbaceous stems. Notwithstanding all possible precautions taken with the mature plant of Mombello, no one has succeeded in layering it.
18. In the few thermometric observations that I made in Charleston I saw the thermometer, which was at 60° Fahrenheit on the 25th of February, drop to 50° the next day and to 41° the day after that. Hence, whenever the sky is clear, there are quite warm days during the months of January and February; but when the wind blows from the northwest, the air is so cold that water freezes in the pumps.
[19. Br 1:206 "For lunch they eat sausage or ham, or other meat, or salt fish with tea or coffee. For lack of good pastures milk and butter are very scarce, of poor quality, and limited healthfulness.

"Dancing, the only amusement of young people, especially during the winter, is often the cause of many pernicious ailments in this climate, since they generally indulge in this exercise without moderation, consequently exposing themselves heedlessly to the cold night air. Furthermore, the abuse of strong liquors, which they foolishly believe suitable for enduring the summer heat, also weakens their constitutions and renders them subject to terrible disorders that are followed by an early death."]

20. A barrel of rice is 500 English pounds by weight.
21. See *The American Museum* (1788): 317.
22. *Indigofera tinctoria* Lin. [The introduced species.]
23. This is done to remove the water without agitating it, so that it doesn't carry off within itself part of the coloring matter.
24. *Gossypium herbaceum* Lin. Its cultivation has lately become much more extensive.
25. *Convolvulus batatas* Lin. [*Ipomoea batatas* (L.) Lam.] They must not be confused with *patate,* called *pomi di terra,* which are the roots of the *Solanum tuberosum* Lin. [!], nor with the *topinambour,* called also *pero di terra,* which is the *Helianthus annuus* [*Helianthus tuberosus* L.] of the same author.
26. They also serve to make artificial *sago,* as has been said in talking about Georgia.
27. *Solanum lycopersicon* Lin. [!]
28. *Capsicum annuum* Lin. [!] *Peverone* in Lombardy.
29. *Arachis hypogaea* Lin. Eng. ground nut. [The peanut, originally from South America.]

Chapter X—North Carolina

[1. Queen's College, launched under Presbyterian auspices in 1771 at the instigation of Governor William Tryon, never received royal approval. In 1777 the name of the institution was changed to Liberty Hall, which was probably still its designation at the time of Castiglioni's visit. See R. D. W. Connor, *History of North Carolina* (Chicago: Lewis, 1919) 1: 204–205.]

2. *Papilio N. huntera* Fabric., p. 499. *Affinis P. cardui.* Differs from the description of Fabricius by not having the white crisscross on the rear wings, so that the specimen I own resembles more the *Papilio cardui.*
3. *Papilio N. vanillae* Lin.
4. *Aesculus lutes.* [*Aesculus octandra* Marsh.]
5. A more complete account of the settlements and customs of the Moravians will be found in the description of Pennsylvania.
6. *Picus principalis* Lin. Buffon: *Le grand pic noir à bec blanc.* Paris, 1790. [Ivory-billed woodpecker, *Campephilus principalis* (Linn.)]
7. *Picus erythrocephalus* Lin. (Red-headed woodpecker, *Melanerpes erythrocephalus* (Linn.)]
8. This was the first tobacco to go from America to England, where (as happens with novelties) it was immediately believed to be a universal remedy.
9. Moreover, the colonists in North Carolina had to defend themselves against the Tuscarora and Coree Indians, with whom war began in 1712 and ended many years later, when the Indians were dispersed by the troops commanded by Governor Craven.

[10. For the saga of this structure see A. T. Dill, *Governor Tryon and His Palace* (Chapel Hill: University of North Carolina Press, 1955).]

[11. Br 1:209 "The new form of government that was born consequent to the Revolution went into effect on 1777 in accordance with the Constitutions of the state promulgated on December 18, 1776."]

[12. Br 1:211–12 ". . . and Virginia, and can, like the former, be divided into two main classes, namely, the inhabitants of the high and mountainous country and those of the maritime region. The latter, perhaps less depraved, but certainly poorer than those of South Carolina, lack even milk and butter, items of the greatest importance in this sparsely populated region, a fact owing to the necessity of allowing their cows to wander in the woods, since they don't have pastures near their homes.

"The inhabitants of the higher regions are less depraved than those of South Carolina and live in greater abundance (. . . ?) Ignorant, however, and given to idleness and to (. . . ?), they don't care at all about (. . . ?) and often neglect to send their children to school. Limited in their life as they are in their talents, they (leave?) their cabins only for reason of self-interest or money, and if they will travel a hundred miles to make a dollar, they wouldn't go one mile to satisfy their curiosity in observing one of the strangest portents of nature. Accustomed to living by themselves and having seen strangers only in wartime, they judge people on the basis of their own opinion and suspect the most upright men as capable of the basest acts. Nosier than the inhabitants of New England, and goaded, not like them, by a desire to educate themselves, but by some deep-seated, malicious, design, the moment they see a foreigner they ask what country he comes from, where he is going, whether he is sent, whether he has come to settle in America, whether he likes the region, and whether is a doctor or a merchant."]

[13. Castiglioni's sarcasm is more pungent in the ms. version (Br 1:214): "For a ranking officer of the French army to be suspected of the base act of spying is certainly surprising to the ears of a European, but it is not at all so in a region where colonel and peasant (*colonello* and *contadino*) are practically identical titles. It is astonishing, however, in any country of the world that the tiny town of Salem, consisting of 15 to 20 homes, unprovided with arms and fortifications, situated more than 200 miles from the ocean, and inhabited by people who as a matter of religion never take up arms even for their own defense, can believe itself so important to the court of France that spies would be sent expressly to map it out and explore its location. *Oh ignoranza grassa direbbe un cappuccino*!"]

[14. Br 1:215 "Many gentlemen there have several hundred of these animals and make a good profit from them."]

15. *Pinus taeda* Lin. *Varietas echinata.* [More likely *Pinus rigida* Mill.]

[16. Br 1:220 ". . . making it into cloth for sheets, shirts, summer clothes, etc."]

[17. Br 1:220 ". . . more distant from the sea where the land is fertile and clayey, and in the regions near Virginia. . . ."]

[18. Br 1:221 ". . . the most common class of the people. . . ."]

[19. Br 1:222 ". . . Finally, the climate, much like that of South Carolina, is, in the coastal areas, conducive to putrid and bilious diseases; but in the elevated regions, where the air is healthful, the water excellent, and the winter temperate, it is no less salutary than any other of the warmer climates of North America."]

Chapter XI – Virginia

[1. Br 2:231 "This gentleman had been described to me as a very good and hospitable man but a most zealous Methodist, a sect differing from the Anglican only in greater fervor and observation in their prayers, but which in the internal regions of America is composed of men more zealous than educated and much more fanatical than the other sects."]

[2. Br 2:232–33 "Having removed the luggage from the carriage and put the horses in the barn, he began to turn the conversation upon the Algerians, about whose depredations and slave trade they supposed that I, as an Italian, would be informed. But when I explained to him that the slaves, upon giving up the Christian religion and embracing Mohammedanism, are very well treated and often become rich and well-to-do, the good Methodist wondered whether or not it was proper for one to pretend a change of religion in order to obviate the torments of slavery, following in appearance the Mohammedan religion while intending to reassume the Christian religion as soon as he could get out of the Barbary dominions. The poor man didn't remember the Circumcision, and since the daughter of my host was present, I didn't dare mention this little ceremony and waited in silence for the end of the conversation. The good old man asked his son-in-law for his opinion on this temporary change of sect, and the minister, after thinking for a long time and digesting the subject, finally said that he certainly didn't know how to decide such a difficult question. 'But as for me,' he added, 'I would prefer death to giving up the religion I profess.'

"At the end of the conversation on the Algerians there came the hour to go to bed, and, in accordance with the good method of the Methodists, the family gathered around and the minister struck up a hymn which, although sung in a small room where we were no more than nine, counting men, women, servants, and children, they sang loudly enough to be heard two miles away."]

[3. Both of these Coles mentioned by Castiglioni (Isaac and John) must be descendants of the John Coles of Enniscorthy, County Wexford, Ireland, who came to Virginia in 1710 and reputedly built the first house on the site of present-day Richmond (see *NCAB*, 17: 439–440, and *DAB*, s.v. "Edward Coles"); see also *The Encyclopaedia of Virginia Biography*, (New York, 1915).]

[4. Br 2:234–40 "The following day, having awakened early to continue my journey, I was told that one of my horses could not walk and that perhaps the excessive amount of corn he had eaten during the preceding days had swollen his legs and reduced him to that state. But upon closer examination it was discovered that this injury was attributable only to the ignorance of a negro blacksmith who had put two shoes on him the day before. And, in fact, when these were removed, the horse began to walk less painfully. This accident forced me, however, to spend the whole day with the colonel, who, being very fond of horses, showed me his thoroughbreds and various fields sown to English clover, rye grass, etc.

On the 14th the horse was in better condition, and I took leave of Colonel Coles. About a mile from his house we crossed, at Tuquas Ferry, the Staunton River, which, with the Banister and the Dan, form the Roanoke. Beyond the river I left the main road and following the direction kindly given me by the colonel, after about 28 miles of troublesome and tortuous travel on little-frequented roads and sideroads, along which one meets very few habitations, having lost my way and overtaken by nightfall, I sought shelter at the home of some poor farmers, where I spent the night as best I could.

"Leaving early on the morning of the 15th, I went to John's Ordinary and then to Buckingham Court House, where one crosses the Appomattox. The building of the Court of Justice for Buckingham County is located on a high hill at the foot of which there are some farmers' homes in a very charming location. Having covered already 24 miles, I was directed to the plantation of a certain Stewart about 10 miles away where I might stop for the night. His house, so I was told, was right on the road. After going about six miles, I saw a very fine plantation where there were a number of negroes at work, and trusting the directions given me, believing myself at only four miles from Mr. Stewart's home, and since it was already sunset, I thought I could get there before night. The road I entered upon as soon as I passed the plantation was hilly, narrow, and so full of tree stumps cut at about a foot above the ground that only with the greatest difficulty could I steer the carriage between them, at the constant risk of overturning. On either side of the road there was nothing but the thickest woods where there couldn't be heard the voice of a living soul. The night kept getting darker, and having already covered more than four miles, I saw no sign of a habitation. In this uncertainty, continuing slowly on my way, and resigning myself in any case to spending the night in the woods, I met a negro on horseback coming from the direction in which we were headed. As soon as he came up to the carriage, I asked him whether Mr. Stewart's plantation was still far away and whether there were other dwellings on that road. He answered that he didn't know anybody by that name living there, and, moreover, that for more than six miles there were no homes of any sort except an abandoned church about two miles from where we stopped. At this news the only choice left to me was to continue for six miles on the chance of finding a shelter or to turn back more than four miles and seek lodging with the owner of the plantation where we had seen the negroes at work. After some reflection, I deemed it more prudent to double back four miles on my steps than to continue on the way in the uncertainty of finding shelter.

"At this hour the night was very dark and we had to go back over the same bad route over which the carriage, with great difficulty, could be steered during the day. Dreading an upset, as had already happened to me on previous occasions, I entrusted the carriage to my servant, got on horseback, and promised some money to the negro if he would accompany us, fearing that, should some accident should take place, we would have no one to help us. As I was setting out slowly on horseback in the company of the negro, we had not yet gone an eighth of a mile when, startled by the noise, I turned around and saw the carriage and the horse overturned on the ground and the poor Irishman struggling to free himself from the carriage. I quickly dismounted and, aided by the negro, we extricated the servant from the carriage, who, thank heaven, came out of it safe and sound. After this first experiment it would have been rash to continue on our way in the same manner; so I agreed with the suggestion of my servant, namely, to dismiss the negro, hide the carriage in the woods, and continue the trip on horseback after removing the bags. So after dismissing the negro, to whom I gave some money for the help he had lent us in the accident undergone, as soon as he was out of sight my servant went a distance into the woods with the carriage and left it where it could not be seen from the road. Then removing the bags, he mounted on horseback, and, returning to the road, made a mark on a tree so as to be able to find the carriage again the next morning. Then we set out again slowly, leaving to the horses the choice of the route, which we could not make out because of the dense darkness of the night, until, having covered the four miles, we found ourselves near the fence surrounding the plantation toward which we were headed. The dwelling, as far as I could remember from my observation in the afternoon, was situated some distance from the road, and one reached it by a narrow winding lane cut through the woods. Since it was impossible, however, for us to make it out in the dark, we went by it and toward the plantation grounds beyond; so we had to go back, guiding the horses near the wood and steering them in the direction where the lane was. As soon as they reached it, they took it, and in a short time led us to the dwelling. This belonged to a certain Mr. Patterson, who at that hour was already, with his wife, in bed. But getting up quickly, he prepared supper for us very hospitably and set up a bed for me as best he could, and out of the kindness of his heart very quickly made me forget the disasters of the day before.

"My servant was up at dawn and, going into the woods, brought back the carriage, which was found partly damaged by the fall. But it was quickly repaired with rope. I took leave of Mr. Patterson and after traveling 20 miles reached the shores of the James River."]

[5. Br 2:240 ". . . although we could see him idling in the doorway of his house, . . ."]

6. *An Coluber regina?* Lin. [*Lampropeltis getulus* (Linn.) *Scuta abdominalia:* 135. [?] *Squamae subcaudalis:* [?]70.

[7. Br 2:243 ". . . , if the latter were in the simple state of nature."]

8. *Coluber constrictor* Lin. The one I killed had 139 abdominal scutes and 66 tail scales. [Either the racer, or coachwhip, *Masticophis flagellum* (Shaw)]

[9. In all likelihood Colonel Nicholas Lewis, a neighbor of Jefferson in Albemarle County: see H. R. Marraro, "Count Luigi Castiglioni, an Early Traveller in Virginia," *Virginia Magazine of History and Biography* 58 (1950):488 fn.]

10. *Notes on [the State of] Virginia* [Paris, 1785].

[11. Br 2:346 "Leaving Charlottesville on the 21st of May, after about twenty miles of travel I found myself at the foot of the Blue Mountains, which I began to climb."]

[12. Br 2:247–48 ". . . , where I busied myself recompiling my journal and reading an old Bible belonging to my host, and talking with him about various matters. Among other things he told me, he made a great deal of an answer he gave various ladies who continually go by to get to the hot baths and the sweet baths beyond the Alleghenies. In Virginia, where ladies are generally inactive, they suffer all those ills created by idleness and melancholy, and, like our own unoccupied European ladies, under the pretext of recovering their health, go to the baths where, spending their nights at gambling and dancing, they pretend to live as convalescents. Some of these ladies, when they arrive at the foot of the Blue Mountains, fearing that they will be upset if they go up in a carriage, think it best to make the climb on foot. 'When I see these ladies,' Mr. L– said to me, 'I tell them: You might as well return home without taking the trouble of going to the baths, since a lady who can climb this mountain on foot cannot be so afflicted by ills as to need the use of baths.'"]

13. *Turdus polyglottos* Lin. Buffon: *Moqueur.* [*Mimus polyglottos* (Linn.)]

14. The Marquis Chastellux, in his *Travels,* has described it fully, giving four drawings of the same from several points of view. [See *Travels in North America in the Years 1780, 1781 and 1782 by the Marquis de Chastellux,* edited by Howard C. Rice, Jr. (Chapel Hill: University of North Carolina Press, 1963), passim.]

[15. Br 2:250–51 "On the 24th, 25th, and 26th a continuous downpour kept me in Staunton, where the lack of company and any kind of thing to do rendered the hours so long and boring that on the morning of the 27th, the sky having cleared somewhat, although I was assured that I could not cross the Middle River, which flows only five miles from Staunton, I, certain nonetheless that I could make no change for the worse, left, and in a short time reached the shores of the Middle River."]

[16. Br 2:251 ". . . that the water coming out of its bed flooded the land on both sides for a long stretch and it could as a result be forded in no way. . . ."]

[17. Br 2:251 "Captain A---, although an uncouth woodsman, seemed kind and hospitable, but his wife, I don't know why, hated strangers, and although it was profitable for her, she didn't like to put them up in her house. She showed very clearly the annoyance caused by my visit during the next two days that I stayed there. Meantime I kept myself busy reading the Bible, talking about farming with my host, and, from time to time (when the rain permitted) going down to the river and, by means of little sticks of wood, marking the rise or fall of the water like the Egyptians. Often half an inch of difference caused me joy or sorrow, and the stopping of the rain would barely give rise to hope when a new downpour would set me back in the previous situation."]

[18. Br 2:252 ". . . sending my servant on ahead with the carriage."]

[19. Br 2:252–53 ". . . sawmill situated on the opposite shore, was shallower but more dangerous because there was nearby a little island with various shrubs which the carriage could not easily clear if it got entangled in them. The other ford, downstream, was free of such perils; but, on the other hand, it was much deeper and the current swifter."]

[20. Br 2:254 "At this moment the horse had lost his strength, and my Irishman, holding his head out of the water, could hardly keep him alive; and unable easily to free him from the harness, he asked for a knife in order to cut it. One of the men who was with me swam out into the river and, taking him the knife on the other side, they quickly freed the horse, which, to my astonishment, leaped safely onto the bank. The unfortunate accident and my worry for the life of my servant made me (as one might readily guess) postpone my departure to the following day."]

[21. Br 2:255 ". . . because the rain had greatly diminished, and repairing as best we could the carriage, which had suffered during the day before, I continued my journey. After 10 miles of travel I found myself at the North River. . . .

"On the last day of May I took leave of Mr. Snaps, but I had covered barely six miles when, the carriage falling apart, and caught again by the rain, I was forced to stop at the home of Mr. Harnit, where I spent the next two days because of the continuous rain.

"(3 June) The sky having finally cleared, I crossed the two branches of the dangerous torrent called Smith Creek. . . ."]

22. *Cerambyx spinicornis* Lin. *Stenocorus spinicornis* Fabricii, *Syst. entomologiae,* p. 179.

23. *Blatta variegata* Fabricii, p. 273.

24. *Phalaena tortrix (dimidiana) alis luteis apice nigris. Statura ministranae. Cornus nigrum.*

25. *Chrysomela (geographica) thorace violaceo, elytris ruso luteis maculis tribus nigris, media arcuata. Statura tridentatae maculae laterales sub-trigonae. Cryptocephalus* Fabricii.

26. *Myrmeleon catta* Fabricii, p. 312.
27. *Phryganea interrupta* Fabricii, p. 307. *Affinis bilineatae.*

[28. Br 2:256–57 ". . . six miles from the Shenandoah River. Deeming at that point my poor carriage to be in too bad shape to be worth fixing, recalling the various tumbles taken in it, and reflecting on the extremely bad roads that I would have to cover before reaching Winchester, and the difficulty of traveling in those regions with chaises or carriages, I quickly decided to leave my buggy with Mr. Macdoval, and fitting out two of the horses with saddles and loading my baggage on the third, I continued my journey toward the river. The change, however, having taken several hours and it being already late, and also since one couldn't cross the river at night without danger, I thought it best to stop on this side—all the more because, according to what I was told, there dwelt there a certain Dr. N--- who was supposed to be a kind and hospitable man. Having covered about five miles, I found myself near the river, and asking about the dwelling of Dr. N---, a little house was pointed out to me from the appearance of which I concluded at once either that the doctor was an ignoramus or that the region was populated by extraordinarily healthy and sturdy people."]

[29. Br 2:257 ". . . mice and kakuvalachos"(?)]

[30. Br 2:258 ". . . bread with butter, and I gladly yielded to the others my portion of the sour milk."]

[31. Br 2:258 ". . . a filthy mattress with an even filthier blanket were spread out on the floor intended for my bed. . . ."]

[32. Br 2:259 "On the 5th of June I went from Stower's Town to New Town, five miles to the north of the stream called Cedar Creek. . . ."]

[33. Br 2:260 "I myself experienced this annoying affliction during the few days that I stopped there, but I quickly recovered as soon as I passed to the east of the Blue Mountains and stopped drinking the water impregnated with this noxious quality."]

34. Its population is estimated as high as 650,000 in *The American Museum,* Vol. I, p. 294, but this figure seems very much exaggerated, the more common opinion being that it does not exceed 400,000.

[35. Br 2:284–85 ". . . where the inhabitants are frequently subject to pleuritic fevers in winter, to bilious fevers accompanied by *cholera morbus* in summer, which are often fatal and sometimes deprive those stricken of the use of their limbs, and to intermittent or tertian fevers in autumn, which often continue through the following winter. On the other side of the Blue Mountains, however, the climate is good and salutary; but the water is mixed with a large quantity of ferrous calcium which, as I have already noted, produced annoying purges in those who are not used to it. The warm baths and the sweet water of Augusta County about 90 miles west of Staunton beyond the Alleghenies, and likewise the waters of Berkeley, or Berkeley Springs, are highly esteemed by the doctors for the treatment of various maladies."]

36. See Jefferson's *Notes On Virginia.*
37. See "North Carolina," §2.
38. From Rolfe and Pocahontas there descended on the female side Mesdames Bolling, who live a short distance from Petersburg [Br 1:13 ". . . , and they pride themselves on having royal blood in their veins." For the progeny of Pocahontas see Wyndham Robertson, *Pocahontas, alias Matoaka, and Her Descendants,* Richmond, 1887.]

[39. Br 2:263 ". . . Nine ships were sent with Lord Delaware, but only eight arrived at their destination, the ninth, on which were the deputies, having been separated from the fleet and transported to the Bermudas.]

40. The names of the counties are: Amherst, Henrico, Richmond, Prince William, Charlotte, Northumberland, Nansemond, Buckingham, King and Queen, Stafford, Mecklenburg,

Louisa, Monanghela, Dinwiddie, Essex, York, Prince Edward, Fairfax, Goochland, Culpeper, Cumberland, Brunswick, Fauquier, Middlesex, Bedford, Yohagany, Rockingham, Loudoun, Frederick, Northampton, Prince George, Montgomery, Rockbridge, Hampshire, Augusta, Berkley, Greenbriar, Pittsylvania, Surry, Accomack, Westmoreland, Washington, Isle of Wight, Hanover, King George, Gloucester, Fluvanna, Princess Anne, Warwick, Albemarle, Caroline, New Kent, Southampton, Lunenburg, Botetourt, King William, Halifax, Sussex, Spotsylvania, Lancaster, Norfolk, Powhatan, Amelia, Orange, Elisabeth City, Henry, Shenandoah, Chesterfield.

[41. Br 2:269 ". . . The houses are partly on the slope toward the valley and partly on the heights of the hills, and although they are all of wood, some of them appear quite elegant."]

[42. Br 2:269 "The climate of Richmond, situated near the river in quite a warm region, is very unhealthful; and especially in the lower parts of the city the inhabitants are subject to intermittent fevers. Since the weather, however, is not so warm in summer and colder in winter, they are not as fatal as those of New Bern and the other cities of the two Carolinas."]

[43. Br 2:270 ". . . which is grown near the James River and is considered. . . ."]

[44. Br 2:274 ". . . and enjoys all the privileges conferred on the other citizens."]

[45. Br 2:275 ". . . so that the gentry have only the administration and none of the hardship and labor of farming."]

[46. Br 2:275 ". . . the most delicate European vegetables. . . ."]

47. Peach trees are so common the woods of Virginia that no one takes the trouble to cultivate them. [Probably introduced by the Spanish. See Ewan, *Banister,* note 38.]

[48. Br 2:275 ". . . so that they can furnish their tables with milk, butter, and fresh meat all the year around."]

49. Vol. I, No. 3 (March 1787). [Pp. 214–16. The text is somewhat modified here to correspond to Castiglioni's translation.]

[50. Br 2:281 ". . . the Henrys, and many others who became famous in military art, sciences, and legislation are a convincing proof both of their talents and their application. They are, moreover, very hospitable and entertain elegantly, treating strangers in the best manner possible even when not recommended to them, and upon their departure they take it upon themselves to furnish them with letters for their friends."]

[51. Br 2:281–83 ". . . the women are beautiful, witty, and vivacious, and although they do not have the pretty complexion of those of Massachusetts, they have bright black eyes and very beautiful teeth. The men, too, in the less unhealthful regions, seem quite strong and sturdy and dark-complexioned.

"The amusements of the Virginians are deer hunting, horse racing, fishing, dancing, and gambling. Deer hunting, which is done on horseback, is very strenuous, and sometimes dangerous, in this region where they are forced to pursue it through woods and places where the terrain is very bad and rough. The horse races are better than elsewhere in America, since the horses there are much handsomer and more spirited. Dances are frequent and constitute the main amusement of young girls, who often obtain lovers, and thus they [find?] husbands. From this mutual close communication and familiarity passions are aroused so early in both sexes that often girls and youths marry at 14 or 15 years of age. Since the region is in various places very populated, the plantations are so close to each other that in a moment 20 or more girls can be rounded up, who often dance the whole night to the music of a violin played by a negro slave. Among other dances the Virginia jig, so called because it is peculiar to this state, is very much like our peasant *furlana.* Gambling, finally, is much more prevalent in the cities than in the country, and it is a vice that can be said to be peculiar to the Virginians. Gentlemen of good and respectable families often lose time and money at this abominable occupation, and ruin their health and their families. This vice is so inveterate that even children derive pleasure from cards as soon as they begin to distinguish value; and their parents, instead of curbing with their example, excite this passion in them."]

[52. Br 2:285 "Tobacco, *Nicotiana tabacum,* an indigenous North American plant, was known and used by the natives before this continent was discovered by the Europeans as a cure for various maladies. Transported to Europe for this purpose, it was used (as happens with all new remedies) as a universal panacea, and after a while it became a luxury in Europe and an item of commerce for the colonists established in America. The cultivation of this product, which constitutes the wealth of Virginia planters, calls for great knowledge and attention, and employs a large number of slaves throughout most of the year."]

53. See "South Carolina," §5.

[54. Br 2:288 ". . . leaving only a few leaves on each plant, which, receiving very abundant nutriment, grow therefore to a great width."]

55. The tobacco harvested annually in Virginia is valued at the enormous sum of from £6000 to £7000 sterling (*American Museum,* 1788, p. 341) [Br 2:289–290 ". . . but in general this product has deteriorated since its quantity has increased, because many areas of the upper parts of Georgia and the two Carolinas are planted to tobacco."]

[56. Br 2:290 ". . . and much tastier than ours."]

[57. Br 2:290 ". . . instead of mixing it with rye and yeast, which render it sour and disgusting to the palate. . . ."]

[58. Br 2:290–91 ". . . It is also used at breakfast, made into pancakes with butter; or, boiled in water until the kernels open by themselves, and then flavored with a little butter, it is eaten like rice, and called 'hominy.'"

In the low-lying region, although the soil is excellent, wheat cannot be raised, because it is destroyed by a kind of small beetle of the genus of the *Dermestes* or *Bruchus* which eats the heart out of the kernels. These were so numerous that whole fields were destroyed, forcing the owners to give up raising wheat.

The difficulty and expense of obtaining rum and other liquors in regions far from the sea induced the Virginians to make their own brandy from peaches. Peach trees, which grow spontaneously everywhere in Virginia, produce annually a great deal of fruit, which, crushed by a wheel driven by a horse as is done with apples, produce a large quantity of juice, which, passed through a still, comes out as a clear, limpid liquor of excellent flavor and odor. This liquor is very strong, has a pleasing and delicate fragrance, and is drunk mixed with sugar or syrup like maraschino, or simply mixed with water like rum and brandy."]

59. *Trifolium pratense* Lin. [!] [Br 2:291–92 ". . . Fields of clover, rye grass, etc., grow beautifully in Virginia and are much more vigorous and luxuriant than in regions further south. Adding to this advantage the great care and attention exercised in obtaining the finest thoroughbreds and in raising and attending to young horse, the Virginians own the best horses to be found in the United States.

"The wealthy gentlemen, or planters, have obtained, and do obtain, every year from England horses descended from the barbs introduced there many years ago, and whose descendance, like the genealogy of families, is proved by documents. These horses are called by various curious names like 'Achilles,' 'Aeneas,' 'Brilliant,' etc., and they are used not only to breed the mares belonging to the owner himself but are also allowed to breed other mares at a fixed price. The horses obtained from one of these stallions and from an English mare are called 'full-blooded horses.' They are the most esteemed and are sold at a very high price, as in England. The others, called 'half-blooded,' are those obtained from an English stallion and an American mare, and although they often turn out to be just as handsome and as spirited as the former, they are not so esteemed and expensive.

"Virginian horses are in general of medium size, of a bay or Isabel color, very well shaped, spirited, and extremely fast runners. Some of them are still strong and lively at fifteen years of age. They are, however, neither as large nor as sturdy as those of New York and Massachusetts, and they are much more suited to the saddle than to wagons or carriages. The beauty, agility, and spirit of these horses motivated the Virginians to the pastime of races, which take place there not only in the cities but also in the country, and they are very costly to those gentlemen who take an interest in them. The horses run in a circular plain of one mile, and after the fourth circuit the prize is given to those who are the first to pass the box in which the judges are seated, from where the race began. The horses are mounted by a white or negro boy who is weighed before the race begins in order to distribute an equal weight on each horse. The prize consists of 50, and sometimes 100, guineas, disbursed by those who send their horses into the race, and they are paid to the winner. At a given distance from the judges' box there is a stake stuck in the ground that is called 'the distance,' because if any of the horses, after the first time around, hasn't passed this stake while the most active horse has passed the judges' box, he is no longer allowed to continue in race and compete for the prize. The speed with which they run is such that frequently they spin over the four miles in eight minutes, and rarely employ more than nine. The passion for these races is very great; artisans leave their work in order to attend, and some of the competitors wager huge sums on the horses that in their opinion they deem the best.

"The commerce of Virginia, the principal item of which is tobacco, is distributed over the various cities of the state, which, since they are situated on navigable rivers, can send their products to Europe. For this reason there are various commercial cities, and among them no one can reach a really flourishing condition. For that reason the proposal was made in the Assembly to establish two seaports, namely, Alexandria in the north and Norfolk in the south, to which all the products of the state would be funneled. But this law, since it is harmful to various individuals, is not likely to be passed."]

60. The brief description given below of this fertile region not visited by me is based upon the account kindly provided me in Richmond by Captain Thompson, one of the inhabitants of Kentucky.

[Br 2:295 "The brief and incomplete description of this fertile province reported below is based solely upon the account kindly given to me by Captain Thompson, one of the inhabitants of Kentucky, since I myself was unable to visit that new region, both out of fear of being surprised by the Indians and because of the hardships and discomforts of a long journey in a country still completely uncultivated."

George Rogers Clark, in his diary of the return to Williamsburg after the capture of Vincennes, notes at one point that "We slept at Captain Thompson's, whose riches could not keep penury out of doors," from R. L. Kincaid, *The Wilderness Road* (Indianapolis/New York: Bobbs-Merrill, 1947), p. 144. In all probability this is the same person who furnished Castiglioni his information on Kentucky.]

[61. Richard Henderson organized the Transylvania Company for the settlement of Kentucky in 1774. Daniel Boone founded Boonesborough the following year.]

[62. Br 2:296 ". . . merely for the payment of taxes, . . ."]
[63. Br 2:298 ". . . (a surprising total, if one considers the recent date of the first settlements). . . ."]
64. Minister of the United States in Paris.
65. An American general.
66. The Marquis de Lafayette.
67. An American general killed in the Battle of Princeton.
68. Native of Virginia and famous in literature.
[69. Br 2:299 ". . . and, according to the reports of many persons, there are abundant weeping willows, or *Salix babylonica*."]
[70. Br 2:299 ". . . *arundo,* or perhaps *Canna glauca,* . . ."]
[71. Br 2:299 fn. "This assertion seems to me exaggerated, as can easily be determined if one reflects that with a bushel of corn ten acres can be sown, so that this land would produce 1200, etc."]
[72. Br 2:303 "Captain Thompson himself offered me a map he made of a communication road between the headwaters of the James River, which passes near Richmond, and the Kanawha, which flows into the Ohio, by means of which, with only 26 miles of portage, European merchandise and the products of Virginia can be transported into the province of Kentucky. This map, copied from the original kindly lent to me by the author . . . was made by him a few years ago in a trip undertaken into those regions at the order of the Virginia Assembly in order to examine whether it might be possible to render this communication feasible."]
73. See Jefferson's *Notes on Virgina.*
[74. Castiglioni's information about mammoths comes obviously from §6 ("Production mineral, vegetable, and animal") of Jefferson's *Notes on Virginia.* Jefferson does not, however, make the linguistic equation between mammoth and big buffalo; nor does he accept as scientific fact the Indian tradition that these animals were carnivores.]
75. See *Columbian Magazine,* May, 1787 ["Account of Some Remains of Ancient Works on the Muskingum, with a Plan of These Works. By J(onathan) Heart, Capt. in the First American Regiment," pp. 425–27. Some of the measurements given by Castiglioni are at variance with those reported by Heart.

For these curious Indian constructions see H. C. Clyde, *The Mound-Builders,* New York/London: Appleton, 1930, especially pp. 9–13, 261–63, for the Marietta earthworks.]
76. "I have spoken to you about the Pyramids of America on other occasions. Since you know, however, the dimensions and form of those of Egypt, I shall tell you what we have from Gemelli Carreri on those of Mexico located toward the north. So the one that was supposed to have been raised to the moon had a base 650 palms long on two sides and 500 on the other two. It was 200 palms high and all of stone, with stairs dug into the stone itself like those of Egypt. Bishop Somarica had both the statue of the moon and that of the sun taken down. The pyramid of the latter was larger than that of the moon. The base on two sides was 650 palms long, 1000 on the other two, and it was about 250 palms high, etc. The general name with which the inhabitants distinguish such pyramids is *Cou.* They ascribed their construction to the Ulmeci, who were said to have been the first inhabitants of that country, having come by sea from the Orient. [Gian Rinaldo] Carli, *Lettere americane* [nuova edizione corretta ed ampliata colla aggiunta della Parte III or per la prima volta impressa. Cremona: Manini, 2 (1782): 39, Pt. II, Letter iii (not vii as indicated in Castiglioni's *Viaggio*)]. See also Clavigero, *Storia del Messico,* "Notice" inserted at the end of Tome II.

Chapter XII – Maryland

[1. Br 2:236 ". . . which are transported here for sale from the internal regions of the state."]

2. *Gracula quiscula* Lin. [Purple grackle, crow blackbird, *Quiscalus quiscula* (Linn.)]

[3. *Travels in North America,* ed. A. B. Benson, New York: Wilson-Erickson, 1937, 1: 248–50.]

[4. Br 2:326 ". . . on the 10th. . . ."]

[5. Br 2:326 ". . . and the following day, after traveling about twenty-four miles and crossing the Patapsco River over a bridge, I reached Baltimore toward dinner time."]

[6. Br 2:326 ". . . that now one counts there more than 1900 houses and about 7000 inhabitants."]

[7. Br 2:327 ". . . and very elegant. In various parts of the city, however, they are not distributed regularly but scattered about here and there at some distance from each other, except in Market Street and some others, which are regular. The aforementioned Market Street is the only one paved, with a cobblestone surface and brick sidewalks as in Philadelphia. The other streets, since they are not paved and the terrain is clayey, are very dirty, muddy, and almost impassable in wet and rainy weather.

"The main buildings are the courthouse, made of bricks on the slope of the hill, the two markets. . . ."

[8. Br 2:328 ". . . which is now being finished, in addition to a chapel for Catholics and other religious congregations and societies."]

[9. Br 2:328 "Since this is the principal trading center in the state, the products of the more distant western parts, consisting mainly of tobacco, wheat, flour, skins of various kinds, etc., are brought there."]

[10. Br 2:328 ". . . after dinner, I left for Philadelphia in the public stagecoach in order to avoid the heat of the sun. I left orders for my servant to come there with my horses."]

[11. Br 2:333 "The State of Maryland extends from 37° to 40° latitude and from 75° to 79° longitude from London, comprising more than 150 miles in length and 140 at the widest part."]

[12. Br 2:333 ". . . each . . . subdivided into seven counties."]

[13. Br 2:341 ". . . and in low and marshy regions intermittent or tertian fevers are common in autumn and putrid and bilious fevers during the summer. In the more northern parts, however, the climate is better, especially where the Potomac River flows among the Blue Mountains and near the Pennsylvania border."]

[14. Castiglioni confuses the various Calverts. Leonard Calvert was the father of George Calvert, first Lord Baltimore, who launched the Avalon colony and obtained the Maryland Charter. Cecil, his son and heir, became sole proprietor of the newly created American Palatinate upon his father's death in 1632.]

[15. Actually, the number and religious affiliations of those taken on board remain problematical. See M. P. Andrews, *History of Maryland: Province and State* (Garden City, N.Y.: Doubleday-Doran, 1929), pp. 22–24.]

[16. Br 2:331 ". . . It very quickly became one of the most flourishing colonies. . . ."]

[17. Br 2:340 "There is little appreciable commerce at present, and Baltimore can be said to be the only city in which trade is in a flourishing condition."]

[18. Br 2:334 "This city contains only about 300 houses and 2000 inhabitants. . . ."]

[19. Br 2:334 ". . . a mediocre American painter, . . ."]

[20. Br 2:335 ". . . since Annapolis is too close to the city of Baltimore, which can be called the commercial city of the state. The inhabitants are for the most part owners of vast estates and numbers of negro slaves, and live so luxuriously and elegantly that the society of Annapolis is reputed to be one of the most civilized and refined in North America. The ladies follow more the European fashions than those of Virginia, and they are very elegant, witty, and vivacious. Dances, *conversazioni*, and other pastimes fill the recreational hours during the various seasons of the year, and gatherings turn out to be all the more pleasant in that the inhabitants are friends and know one another."]

[21. Washington College, founded in 1706, still exists as a coeducational institution. The Baltimore academy mentioned by Castiglioni proved ephemeral: "The youth of Baltimore intended for the learned professions hitherto were sent abroad, and mostly to schools in Pennsylvania; but now an academy was established under the patronage of the Rev. Doctors Carroll, West, and Allison on Charles Street, where Edward Langworthy taught the classics, and Andrew Ellicott of Joseph, Surveyor of the United States, the mathematics, natural philosophy, &c., which unfortunately was not long continued." J. T. Scharf, *The Chronicles of Baltimore* (Baltimore: Turnbull Bros., 1874), p. 243.]

[22. Br 2:340–41 ". . . where they spend in pastimes and amusements the hours they do not employ in their private businesses or state government. Horse races, dances, and gatherings constitute, as in Virginia, the diversions of the wealthier gentry.

The merchants live mostly in Baltimore, or scattered over the various parts of the state in order to furnish the inhabitants with European goods, in payment of which they receive tobacco that they send to the seaports. The difference in condition of the inhabitants of the two main cities has given rise to complaints and disorders, the inhabitants of Baltimore believing that the landholders who populate Annapolis, the capital, are too concerned with their own interests and neglect those of the merchants in the laws passed by the legislative body. For this reason, and out of the desire to promote the city in which they live, the merchants wanted the state Chamber to reside in Baltimore, adducing, in order to persuade people to make the change, various reasons, among which the greater size of this city and the ease of providing oneself with European goods in a trading place; but in spite of their maneuvers, the inhabitants of Annapolis, eager to keep the seat of government in their city, succeeded in thwarting their urgings and in killing the idea of this pernicious change."]

[23. Br 2:338 "Wagons are wide, they can hold a great quantity of merchandise, and three or four men who sleep in them. There they are protected from the sun and rain. Four to six horses are hitched to them according to the weight of the load and the length of the journey."]

[24. Br 2:339 fn. ". . . public inns or hotels, where food is too expensive. . . ."]

[25. Br 2:339 fn. "Everyone in Europe knows how harmful to the health eating salt meat is and what the fatal consequences are. In America, however, whether it be the different quality of climate, the mixing of salt meat with milk and butter, or the spirituous liquors they use, it is certain that many families who feed themselves all year around on salt meat are strong, sound, and sturdy, and don't have the slightest sign of scurvy or similar ailment."]

[26. Br 2:339 ". . . which adds more force to the blows of the axe."]

[27. The following note in the appendix to the second volume of the ms. (Br 2:365–66) accompanies a comparative chart of the currencies of Maryland, Virginia, the two Carolinas, and Georgia:

"**NOTE:** Gold coins are cut and reduced in weight in order to keep them from being exported, and since in Virginia there are no copper coins and they have no value, Spanish *pesos*, French *écus*, and other small silver coins are cut into halves, quarters, eighths, sixteenths, etc., without any rule for determining their weight. In the states of Maryland and the Carolinas this cut silver has no value, but in North and South Carolina there is paper money, which, however, has lost a great deal of its intrinsic value.

"English coins are copper, and they are current in the various states, held to a varying value in accordance with that of the other coins. In Maryland an English copper, that is, an English halfpenny, is worth 1 penny, and 12 of them make a shilling. In South Carolina and Georgia, on the other hand, 2 coppers are a penny and, 24 of them, that is, 12 pennies, make a shilling.

"During the time that the English owned North America, coppers were minted in Virginia dating from 1773. On one side was GEORGIUS III. REX with the crowned head of the King, and on the other the royal escutcheon surrounded by the words VIRGINIA 1773. Latterly, in Annapolis, a certain Chalmers, goldsmith, made some silver shillings and put on them his name–CHALMERS ANNAPOLIS."]

Chapter XIII – The State of Delaware

[1. Br 3:3 "On the 17th of June, having crossed the border near Head of Elk, I reached Christiana, an old village founded by the Swedes on the Delaware River and beyond the city of Wilmington. This is the most populous city in the state and now the capital. . . . It is situated on a hill that enjoys a charming view of the river and is composed of many houses. There are only two or three regular streets, which go down the hill and end right at the river, on both sides of which there are other homes scattered over the heights."]

[2. The first Swedish group, under Peter Minuit, arrived in 1638.]

[3. The three Lower Counties, so called, chose to be a separate colony of the Crown and set up their own Assembly in 1704, though without a separate designation and still formally under Penn's governors.]

[4. Br 3:7 ". . . and it took from the nearby river the name of the State of Delaware."]

[5. Br 3:5 ". . . negroes, Indians, or mulattoes, brought in from any part of the world. . . ."]

[6. Br 3:4 ". . . which vies with Wilmington for the title of capital, . . ."]

[7. Br 3:3–4 "The climate of Wilmington, situated near the Delaware Bay, whose stagnant water renders the air unhealthful, produces there a great quantity of putrid and intermittent fevers."]

8. According to the latest published notices, they add up to about 35,000.

[9. In the ms. (Br 3:5) the last paragraph reads as follows: "Since there isn't any city that has a good seaport, the commerce of the state is very secondary. Products are loaded onto sloops, or small single-masted ships, that go up the bay and the river as far as Philadelphia, where the products are offered at the market, and they return laden with merchandise. Many are also transported in wagons, since the trip is very short and the roads quite good.

"There is nothing left for me to say about the manners and customs of the inhabitants because, connected and almost united with the Pennsylvanians, they don't differ from them in any essential respect. The natural products are likewise the same. I didn't have time to observe any particular animal or plant during my brief run through this state."]

Chapter XIV – Pennsylvania

[1. Br 3:9 ". . . I left Philadelphia in a rented two-horse carriage accompanied by Mr. Giuseppe Mussi. . . ."]

[2. Br 3:9–10 ". . . mixed with a large quantity of mica, and some of them are very comfortable and elegant. The market is almost in the center of the village, and the houses are distributed about a number of charming hills that offer very beautiful points of view. Leaving Germantown, we reached Spring House toward dinner time, where, on account of the meanness and balkiness of one of our horses, we were unable to continue our trip, and compelled to stay all night and to send our unharnessed horses back to the city for better ones in the morning."]

[3. Br 3:10–11 "In an excursion I made in the afternoon I noted in the hedges the *Cephalanthus occidentalis,* the *Phytolacca decandra,* and the *Actaea racemosa* in bloom, and, among the more curious trees, the *Juglans alba* and *nigra,* the *Hedera quinquefolia,* the *Rubus occidentalis,* the *Rhus toxicodendron* and *glabrum,* and the *Laurus sassafras* and *benzoin.*

"The next morning, since the horses had not yet arrived, we decided to amuse ourselves by killing some birds that could be seen flitting about in large numbers near the road. The first one killed was the red-headed woodpecker, described by Linnaeus under the name of *Picus pileatus niger, crista rubra, temporibus alisque albis maculis. Differt* (he says) *a Pico martio quod tempora alba, maculae aliquot parvae in alis albae, caput magis late coccineum. Mas tenia secundum mandibulam inferiorem. Mas foeminaque crista rubra.*"]

4. *Hedera quinquefolia* Lin. [*Parthenocissus quinquefolia* (L.) Planch.]
5. *Rhus glabrum* Lin. [!]
6. *Rhus toxicodendron* Lin. [!]
7. *Picus pileatus* Lin. [*Dryocopus pileatus* (Linn.)]
8. Linnaeus is mistaken when he says *Mas foeminaque crista rubra.*
9. *Ardea an virescens?* Lin. *A. occipite nudo, dorso viridi-nitente, pectore rutescente, loris luteis. Rostrum nigrum, oculi nigri, iride flava, caput supra maculatum, macula triangulari cinereo-caerulescente. Alae concolores, secundariae ferrugineo marginatae. Pedes fusci. Ungue medio introrsum serrato. H. ad stagna, & rivulos.*

Length of beak	2½ English inches
Length of outstretched neck, including the beak	10½ inches
From end of beak to tip of tail with neck in normal position	12 inches
From tip to tip of outstretched wings	24 inches
Length of legs	6½ inches

The comb-like dentated claw is common to various *Ardeae,* just as one finds in some of them that sort of yellowish necklace of short feathers around the breast that I noted in this species. [Probably immature Green heron, *Butorides virescens* (Linn.)]

10. The so-called lores (*Lora* of Linnaeus) are the skin that surrounds the opening of the beak at its base.

[11. Br 3:13 "Upon closer examination I noticed that the claw of the middle toe was provided on the inside face with comb-like teeth bestowed by nature upon this bird for the purpose of cleaning its beak and smoothing down the feathers of the neck and wings, or perhaps to provide relief from the stings of insects that sometimes torment it. (Note: This comb is common particularly to those species called *Ardeae* by Linnaeus, which he distinguished by their possession of a middle toe equipped with *serrata: ungue intermedio introrsum serrato.* Another peculiarity consists in a collar of short yellowish-colored feathers around its breast, covered, however, by other feathers."]

[12. Br 3:13 ". . . and where the young can live. . . ."]

[13. Br 3:13 ". . . carriage, to which the cage was fastened."]
[14. Br 3:14 "Our horses having finally arrived, we continued. . . ."]
15. *Polygonum fagopyrum* Lin. [*Fagopyrum sagittatum* Gilib.]
16. Whitefield went to America with General Oglethorpe, founder of the Colony of Georgia. He was at that time a very zealous Methodist, and founded near Savannah, with contributions collected in America and Europe, a hospital, which, since it was located in an unhealthful site, was later abandoned. The Methodists esteem his sermons very highly, and they consider him practically a saint. [Br 3:15–16, fn. "This Whitefield is held in the highest esteem by the Americans, and his sermons are praised as the productions of one possessing a natural eloquence. The Methodists, the most methodical and bigoted of the Anglicans, consider him almost a saint. Of his works I have seen only the description of a voyage of his to America written after the style and functions of the missionaries in the Indies, who in their journals say: 'Today, through my prayers to God, I have saved the soul of a poor dying man who otherwise would have died unshriven,' etc., with other detailed descriptions of his virtuous deeds that to many seem dictated more by the ambition to appear saintly than by a sincere spirit of religion. . . ."]
17. See "North Carolina." [Br 3:15 "At about this time the Georgians found themselves forced to take up arms against the Spaniards in Florida; and since the Moravians, who then lived in Georgia were unwilling to arm themselves in defense of the state, they were driven from their possessions and took refuge in Pennsylvania."]
18. See Crantz, *Historia Fratum Unitatis.*
19. See Chapter X on North Carolina, p. 000.
[20. Br 3:17 ". . .in which 20 to 30 beds are disposed in two rows, . . ."]
[21. Br 3:17–18 "The chapel, or private church for the girls is quite large, and many musical instruments, such as harpsichords, violins, violoncellos, etc., can be seen there, which they use to accompany the voice in hymns and prayers on festive days. The dormitories are very spacious and kept extremely clean; and on the ground floor there are the refectory and the various cooking facilities, so that this building, admittance to which is forbidden to the young men, has all the appearance of one of our cloisters for nuns."]
22. *Quercus alba* Lin. [Which takes the place of the European *Q. cerris* L.]
[23. Br 3:18 ". . .for trousers, saddles, gloves, etc., . . ."]
[24. Br 3:19 " . . .serve for use of the laundry, for drinking water, and for various manufactures and trades. . . ."]
[25. Br 3:19 "The houses in Bethlehem are in large part of stone, small, but very comfortable; and they contain only one family."]
[26. Br 3:20 "Christian Spring, a rich holding that they own in a broad and beautiful plain about eight miles from Bethlehem, is cultivated by more than 30 marriageable young men of this Society, who live there all the time."]
[27. Br 3:20 " . . .hand and of the same merit as those of Bethlehem, and the village contains also craftsmen of the various trades. After listening to a German sermon and prayers in the morning, we left again for Bethlehem, whence we proceeded in the afternoon 10 more miles toward Philadelphia."

The painter for whose work Castiglioni shows so little enthusiasm is the Danzig artisan John Valentine Haidt, 1700–80: see G. A. Howland, "John Valentine Haidt, A Little Known Eighteenth Century Painter," *Pennsylvania History*, 8 (1941), 304–13.]

[28. Br 3:24 " . . .in 1773. . . ."]
29. Here is the original. . . . The reference is to the Blessed Virgin. . . :

And she so blessed is,
She gives him many a kiss:
Fix'd are her eyes on him;
Thence moves her every limb;
And since she him so loves,
She only with him moves:
His matters and his blood
Appear her only good.

[See Howard C. Rice, Jr., ed., *Travels in North America in the Years 1780, 1781 and 1782 by the Marquis de Chastellux* (Chapel Hill, N.C.: University of North Carolina Press, 1963) 2: 644–45.]

[30. Br 3:25 "Their religion (as we have already said) is Lutheran, but some people believe, inasmuch as they venerate images and crucifixes, that they are secretly Roman Catholics—which, however, is completely unfounded. Whatever may be their beliefs, it is certain that they live together with great exemplariness, and that they are for others modes of industry and work."]

31. *Turdus migratorius* Lin. [!]

32. *Motacilla sialis* Lin. [Bluebird, *Sialia sialis* (Linn.)]

33. *Phalaena attacus (Diana) Alis patentibus griseo-fuscis; macula lunata ferruginea. Statura, & magnitudo Ph. pavonia majoris. Corpus fuscum, abdomine subtus albo nigro maculato. Alae macula lunata, fasciaque disci ferrugineis; anticae fascia terminali, undulata, pallida, apice rubra, oculo nigro; posticae fascia terminali pallido-testacea, linea, punctisque fuscis. H. in Pensilvania. Spec. nov.* [*Hyalophora cecropia* (Linn.) Our thanks to J. M. Kingsolver.]

34. *Phalaena emargana. Pyralis emargana* Fabric., *System. entom.*, p. 651. [Br 3:25 "Toward evening we reached Germantown, and the following morning, Philadelphia."]

[35. Castiglioni says in a footnote (Br 3:32–34) that he rewrote the material on the Delaware and Susquehanna Rivers after receiving "various notices . . . from Mr. (Simeon) De-Witt, a New York State engineer and geographer, who found himself *in loco* last year to set the boundaries with the State of Pennsylvania."]

36. See Vol. I, p. 184 ff.

37. The Penn family is divided into two branches. Of the elder son there is left only a single descendant, namely, the younger Mr. John Penn, who has traveled a great deal in Europe, and even in Italy, and who, having dedicated himself to study, lives in quite complete retirement in Philadelphia. Of the other branch there are two brothers, Richard and John, both of whom were governors of Pennsylvania.

[38. In the ms. (Br 3:60) Castiglioni introduces the topic of the government of Pennsylvania with the following words: "The Pennsylvania Constitutions being the freest and most independent, and those thought to preserve intact popular liberty, I deem it appropriate to report here in their entirety various articles from them."]

39. My fellow citizens cannot but be pleased at knowing how much influence the book *On Crimes and Punishments* has had in establishing the penal laws of the various American constitutions; and I am convinced that they will read with pleasure a letter written to me by the attorney general of the State of Pennsylvania upon sending me a copy of this book printed in Philadelphia a few years ago.

Philadelphia, August 10, 1786

I have the honor to present you with an American copy of the famous book on *Crimes and Punishments* that will be delivered to you by the bearer of this letter. It is a new proof of the veneration my countrymen harbor for the opinions of your famous relative. I should like it to be known by the author of this book, so well received in the Old World, that his efforts to extend the domain of humanity have been crowned in the New World with the happiest success. Long before the recent Revolution this book was common among lettered persons of Pennsylvania, who admired its principles without daring to hope that they could be adopted in legislation, since we copied the laws of England, to whose laws we were subject. However, as soon as we were free of political bonds, this humanitarian system, long admired in secret, was publicly adopted and incorporated by the Constitution of the State, which, spurred by the influence of this benign spirit, ordered the legislative bodies to render penalties less bloody and, in general, more proportionate to the crimes. The necessity of establishing our political existence and the concerns that multiply about a nascent republic kept the legislative bodies from undertaking this beneficial reform, but under the pressure of public opinion that it be no longer deferred, those august tribunals have turned their hand to this important task. A plan has already been drafted and approved, and it has been published in order to see the reaction of the citizens; and all that remains is for the coming session of the General Assembly to give it legal force. Then, when this change in our penal laws has taken place, the lash, branding, mutilation, and death will be replaced by strenuous and continuous labor for variable periods of time, and instead of one hundred sixty capital crimes in the country from which we have recently separated, there will be only four in Pennsylvania. Then a happy new era will begin, and I dare hope that, instructed by experience, Pennsylvania will persevere in these ideas until that point of perfection is approached at which *every punishment will be public, immediate, and mandatory, the smallest possible in the given instance, proportionate to the crime, and determined by the laws.*

One must attribute mainly to this excellent book the honor of this revolution in our penal code. The name of Beccaria has become familiar in Pennsylvania, his authority has become great, and his principles have spread among all classes of persons and impressed themselves deeply in the hearts of our citizens. You yourself must have noticed the influence of these precepts in the other American states. The tyranny of prejudice and injustice has fallen, the voice of a philosopher has stilled the outcries of the masses, and although a bloody system may still survive in the laws of many of our states, nevertheless the beneficent spirit sown by Beccaria works secretly in behalf of the accused, moderating the rigor of the laws and tempering justice with compassion.

I am,

Respectfully yours,
WILLIAM BRADFORD, Jr.

[For a very readable account in English of Beccaria's life, work, and influence, see Marcello Maestro, *Cesare Beccaria and the Origins of Penal Reform* (Philadelphia: Temple University Press, 1973), esp. p. 137 ff., for his impact upon early American thought.]

40. Explanation of Table IX, representing the city of Philadelphia:

1) Plan of the aforementioned city according to the design of William Penn
2) Delaware River

3) Schuylkill River
4) Large ten-acre square
5) Four more of eight acres
6) Hartsfield
7) Kensington
8) Southwark
9) Portion of the State of New Jersey
10) A little island, exposed when the water is low.

N.B. The suburbs of Hartsfield, Kensington, and Southwark did not exist in the old plan of Penn, but the city extended toward the west to the Schuylkill. The dotted lines indicate Penn's design, and the others denote the city as constructed at present.

[41. Castiglioni paraphrases *A Letter from William Penn Proprietor and Governour of Pennsylvania in America, to the Committee of the Free Society of Traders of that Province, Residing in London, Containing a General Description of Said Province. . .* , London: Sowle, 1683.]

[42. About 1654 the Dutch government granted 800 acres fronting on the Delaware River for a settlement known as Wicaco to Swen Gondersen, Swen Swensen, Oele Swensen, and Andries Swensen. See J. F. Watson and W. P. Hazard, *Annals of Philadelphia and Pennsylvania in the Olden Times* (Philadelphia: Stoddart 1879) 3: 24.]

43. See Chapter XII, §2.

[44. Robert Turner was a wealthy draper and fellow Quaker who settled in Philadelphia. The letter is of June 3, 1685. See Watson and Hazard, *Annals,* (1881) 1: 49.]

[45. Br 3:58 " . . .and the months of August, September, and October are considered the most unhealthful. The intermittent, or tertian, fevers, so common in the southern regions, are there not so frequent, and they reign for the most part only near the Schuylkill. The winter is very cold, and snow begins to fall usually toward the middle of December. . . ."]

46. On the 3rd of November, 1786, I crossed the Delaware on the ice, and on the 11th of the same month, the thermometer having dropped to 19° below freezing, horses could cross safely. There was a cold spell on the 5th of February, 1788 (*American Museum,* Vol. III, p. 199), when the thermometer sank to the same point. What is more surprising is the fact that the day before it stood at 3° above freezing, so that within the space of seven hours it dropped 22° Réaumur, an almost unheard-of thing in other countries.

[47. Br 3:40 "What is built up in Philadelphia, and marked all in black and without punctuation in Drawing and Table I (unfortunately missing in the ms.), does not cover half the area intended by William Penn. On the contrary, buildings have extended along the Delaware and formed the suburbs of Kensington, Ball's Town, and Southwark."]

[48. Br 3:43 " . . .Methodists, or New Light. . . ."]

[49. Br 3:43–44 ". . . and a synagogue for the Jews, all different from one another, are very remarkable for the size and beauty of their buildings."]

[50. Br 3:44 " . . .not yet finished, however, in accordance with the design." (The facing page of the ms. bears a frontal sketch of Independence Hall.)]

[51. Br 3:47 " . . .trees and shrubs from more southern parts of the United States and divided by various little alleys where on warm summer days the ladies go to get some fresh air."]

[52. Br 3:47 " . . .and, on the other two floors, the meeting hall, the library, the cabinet for the equipment, the museum, etc."]

[53. Br 3:47 "The prisoners are not shut up, as in various parts of Europe, in unhealthful subterranean cells, but in healthful and airy rooms, and provided daily with adequate food."]

[54. Br 3:47 "The University, another noteworthy building, was formerly one of the Methodist churches, and now instruction is given there to a number of young men in belles-lettres and sciences, in which they give a public demonstration each year at the beginning of July." The "New Building" at Arch and Fourth Streets, erected for the famous evangelist preacher George Whitefield, had passed into the possession of "Hell-fire" Gilbert Tennent and his Presbyterian flock before becoming the site of the Academy and Charitable School of Philadelphia and eventually the College of Philadelphia, today the University of Pennsylvania. See E. P. Oberholtzer, *Philadelphia: History of the City and Its People* (Philadelphia: Clarke, 1, 1912), pp. 178–79.]

[55. Br 3:44 "However, although this Market is superior to all the other American markets for its attractiveness and abundance, unfortunately its location in the middle of one of the broadest streets of the city constricts it and cuts off the beautiful view of the river."]

[56. Br 3:47–48 "Outside the city there are two other public places, namely, the Hospital and the Almshouse. The former is a building in the form of a cross, not yet completed according to the design. . . , surrounded by another stretch of wall near which there is a number of beautiful oriental plane trees. The director of this Hospital is a Quaker, and the patients are looked after with great care and cleanliness. The latter is formed by two magnificent three-story wings ending at the corners in two towers and joined at the center by a stretch of wall leading to the inside courtyard formed by the two buildings. This building, called the Almshouse, contains the paupers of the city, foundlings, and various sick people, who in all do not exceed the number of 250, kept there at public expense." (Castiglioni's sketches of the Hospital and the Almshouse appear on p. 49 of the ms.)]

[57. Br 3: 48, 51 "The inhabitants of Philadelphia amount. . . , according to the best estimates, to about 40,000, a number that is increased every year by German and Irish emigrations from Europe. They arrive 100 or 150 at a time by ship and indenture themselves for two or three years to a master who pays the captain money for their passage. At the end of the three years they are free, and if they are industrious and honest, they can easily find some job in the city, or they move to the more internal parts of the state where they are given land by the owners for beginning a new settlement. The Germans, good and honest workers who left their native land not because of crimes but for lack of employment, are the most successful in creating an adequate status for themselves in a few years. But this is not so with the Irish, who, being for the most part the dregs from prisons, become thieves and criminals, and multiply in America thefts and other crimes formerly almost unknown, so that their entry should be stopped by the government as harmful to the public peace of the state."]

[58. Br 3:52 " . . .but the simplicity of their manner and customs, their good morality, and perhaps also the persecution they suffered, very quickly increased the number of their proselytes, among whom began to be counted many persons respectable for their talents and family. . . . Arriving there in America, they won the friendship of the Indians, established a complete freedom of conscience, and although persecuted, they did not become persecutors. An unalterable friendship among the various members of this Society, the humaneness with which they helped the poor of every kind, patience in putting up with ridicule and persecution, their even conduct, honesty, and probity in business, very soon made them the admiration of good people and the model of useful and industrious citizens. These virtues of theirs were obscured, however, in the eyes of many by certain opinions and customs contrary to the ordinary way of thinking. . . .

"The dress of the Quakers was plain; they wore large round hats, and they made a point of not following changes in fashion, but dressing in the most comfortable manner and the one best adapted to the season. The women wore simple, plain, dresses of wool, cotton, or linen, and covered their heads with a little bonnet on which, when they went out, they placed a hat that came down over the nape and extended around to protect the face from the rays of the sun. When they spoke with one another they always used the term 'Friends' and the second person singular. In this reform of European manners, they did not fail to abolish the inconvenient custom of doffing their hats in greeting one another; and they replaced this ceremonious habit with the friendly gripping of the hand. They likewise left optional the acts of sitting down, standing up, entering or leaving a house, asking for food and drink when one is hungry or thirsty, and looking for lodgings, without the need for so many ceremonious lies. The hospitality, kindness, and simplicity of their customs caused the homes of the Quakers to be respected as refuges for humanity, and even those who differed from them in many opinions could not help admiring their outstanding virtues."]

[59. Br 3:55 "Since the Quakers, out of humanitarian principle, consider war as contrary to that friendship and brotherhood that ought to unite all the peoples of the world. . . ."]

[60. Br 3:55 ". . . and they preferred the love of glory and the security of their country to the passive and censured conduct of the individuals of their sect."]

[61. Br 3:56 "The doctrine of the Quakers as explained in *The Apology* published by Mr. Barclay (one of the individuals of this sect) consists mainly in believing that all men, of whatever religion or country, are called to penance by God through the Holy Spirit, that these calls are frequent, and that the goodness of God never tires, regardless of whether men either do or do not hear his words, or, repentant, fall again into their misdeeds, until, if they remain unremittingly deaf to his voice, engulfing themselves evermore in sins, he overwhelms them with their errors and eternal perdition. They believe, moreover, that the sacraments were nothing but symbols, and that therefore they are not to be repeated in the Church of Christ."]

[62. Br 3:57 "The principal gentlemen of the other sects do not differ in urbanity, politeness, and consideration for foreigners from those of the other larger American cities, and although it is said generally that the Philadelphians, in imitation of the Quakers, live to themselves and do not like the company of strangers, I must say for the sake of truth that, within the circle of my acquaintances, I experienced no example of such unsociable conduct. On the contrary, I beheld with amazement, in my stay in Philadelphia during the winter of 1786, the lavishness of their tables, the elegance and magnificence of their private dances, social gatherings, and dinners given in turn by various well-to-do gentlemen. If at these parties there was gambling, it served only to render the *conversazione* more varied, since very small sums were placed at stake, more to interest the person in the game than out of a base, pernicious, and vicious desire for gain."]

63. *Transactions of the American Philosophical Society Held at Philadelphia for Promoting Useful Knowledge* (Philadelphia, Vol. I, 1771, Vol. II, 1786).

[64. Castiglioni doubtless saw the article in *The American Museum,* 3 (1788): 172–75, that made public the "Laws of the Philadelphia Society for Promoting Agriculture; As Revised and Enacted by the Said Society on the Tenth Day of January, 1786," along with a notice of "Premiums Proposed by the Philadelphia Society for Promoting Agriculture (pp. 176–79). He must have been struck by the similarities of this organization with his own Milanese Società patriotica.]

[65. Br 3:69 "The main products are wheat, flour, corn, rye, buckwheat, flax, hemp, etc. Wheat, the richest and most lucrative product, is converted into flour and shipped to the eastern parts of Massachusetts, the two Carolinas, Georgia, the East Indies, and Spain. Since this item is the principal export of the state, great care is taken that none of bad quality is shipped in order not to harm the credit already acquired; and there are inspectors whose duty it is to examine flours and to forbid the exportation of those of inferior quality."]

[66. Br 3:70 ". . . Germantown, populated by Germans, famous for various manufactures and for elegant carriages made there, Carlisle, which has a university, or college, called Dickenson College. . . ."]

[67. The translation given here is an amalgam of Rush's original text and Castiglioni's version. For the critical background of the Rush letter, see the collection of his *Letters* as edited by L. H. Butterfield, Philadelphia: American Philos. Soc., 1 (1951): 400–407.]

68. The unripe ears, stripped of their husks, are roasted in the fire, and the kernels are eaten after being covered with butter. [Castiglioni expatiates upon this American delicacy in his ms. (Br. 3:72–73): "When the corn is not completely ripe, but the grains are already formed on the ear, the latter are picked, brought close to the fire and roasted all around. Thus roasted, these ears are taken, still warm, from the fire, covered with fresh butter, and eaten, extracting the kernels with the teeth until they are all gone. The sweet milky juice found in the various seeds of cereal plants when they are not completely ripe not only renders the aforementioned kernels soft and flexible, but adds to a pleasant and very welcome flavor. This item of food is found alike on the tables of poor farmers and the wealthiest gentlemen and is generally highly appreciated."]

69. Pigs are the animals they choose by preference, salting and smoking the meat, which, fried and mixed with wild herbs, or boiled without seasoning, is their most common food. [In the ms. (Br 3:75) Castiglioni adds: ". . . and often the only food with which these people nourish themselves throughout the whole year."]

70. [Castiglioni paraphrases part of a note by Rush:] "If the first settler is unable to purchase, he takes a tract of land for several years on a lease, and contracts, instead of paying annual rent for it, to clear fifty acres of land, and to build a house and a barn, and to plant an apple orchard on it."

71. [Castiglioni again quotes in paraphrase:] "The unoccupied lands are sold by the state for about six guineas per hundred acres. But as the first settlers buy them from persons who had purchased them from the state, they are sold for a much higher price. The quality of the soil – its vicinity to mills, courthouses, churches, and navigable water – the distance to the seaports of Philadelphia or Baltimore – and the nature of the roads all play a part in rendering the price more or less considerable. Likewise the quantity of land cleared and made tillable and the nature of the improvements influence the price to the second and third settlers. Hence, what cost the first one only a quarter of a guinea, or at the most 2 guineas per acre, is sold at 1 to 10 guineas to these later ones."

72. Traveling through the interior regions of the United States, one often sees persons with fingers and eyes lost in these barbaric duels. [For a contemporary description of one of these brutal encounters see *The American Museum,* 1 (1787): 471–72.]

73. Some Indians are much given to this game, which they learned from the Europeans.

74. Here are other more recent facts. In a letter from an inhabitant of the city of Savannah in Georgia to a friend of his in Philadelphia dated December 8, 1787, there is the following paragraph: "Since your departure from this country, we have been engaged, and are now in a war with the Creek Indians. Small parties have penetrated as low down as the Canoochee, killed our citizens, and done other damage. It is my firm belief, that it might have been stopped in the first stage, had the executive of this country brought to trial a Col. Alexander, who murdered eight or nine Indians on their hunting grounds"; *American Museum* (1788): 101–102.

Another letter, of May 16, 1788, dated Pittsburgh in Pennsylvania: ". . . The news of this country is confined to Indian affairs, and three fourths of the accounts have very little truth in them. It is expected there will be a general attendance of the Indians at the treaty—at present there are no appearances of hostile intentions among the savages. Some boats were attacked in March last about 600 miles down the Ohio, and some people killed and others taken . . . ; from circumstances attending this matter, it is conjectured some white men were principal agents in the affair"; *American Museum* (1788): 593.

N.B. In these boats there were, among others, a botanist and a mineralogist sent to America by the King of France to examine the natural products here. The first was killed and the other captured.

75. Rye does not serve in Pennsylvania, as it does in Massachusetts, for making bread, but instead it is allowed to ferment and from it is distilled a liquor called whiskey.
76. The quantity of wood found on a piece of freshly cleared land and the difficulty in consuming it lead people in America to prefer fences to hedges for enclosing fields. They are made in different ways in the various parts of the United States. In the Carolinas and in Virginia, for example, they are made in a zigzag form (Plate X, Fig. 1), and although they are unsightly and occupy part of the public thoroughfares, they are preferred to the others because they require very little work. In Pennsylvania, on the other hand, and in the other middle states, they are better constructed (Plate X, Figs. 2 and 3). Finally, in the northernmost states, as in Massachusetts, in places where stones abound and wood is not so plentiful, little walls of uncemented stones are made around the fields, as is also the custom in our country in mountainous areas.
77. *Polygonum fagopyrum* Lin. Lombard *frajna.* [*Fagopyrum sagittatum* Gilib.]

[78. Castiglioni translates spelts as *sorgo* (i.e., sorghum), with the footnote, "*Holcus sorgum* Lin. Lombard *melica.*"]

Chapter XV—New Jersey

1. Passaic Falls.

[2. Br 3:112 ". . . and the cities. Dispensing with the itinerary that I have provided on other occasions, I shall satisfy myself with noting in order everything of interest both in the cities and the country.

"It is my belief that my friends will welcome here the description of the region between Philadelphia and New York as found in the repeatedly cited Professor Kalm. . . ." (The substance of the quotation that Castiglioni inserts at this point can be found in *Peter Kalm's Travels in North America,* ed. A. B. Benson, New York: Wilson-Erickson, 1937, 1: 118.)]

[3. Br 3:113–14 "The building of the College is of stone, of three stories, vast, magnificent. . . ."]

[4. Br 3:114 ". . . Criticism, . . ."]

[5. Castiglioni equates the *Tutori* of his text to Trustees in a footnote.]

[6. Br 3:114 ". . . a general idea of the various sciences."]

[7. Br 3:114–15 "Limitation of time not permitting them to go very deeply into philosophical discoveries, at the end of the course many of the students remain at their own expense, and having decided to pursue a particular philosophical and theological science, they continue their study, thus becoming teachers of it."]

[8. Br 3:115 "This freedom of thought in allowing each one to follow his own opinions and a strict moral discipline bring it about that many gentlemen, principally inhabitants of the South, prefer Princeton College to those of New Haven and Cambridge in New England."]

[9. Br 3:115 ". . . and it maintained itself by means of donations made by the inhabitants of the various United States."]

[10. Br 3:115–16 "Founded, as I have already said, with contributions from the various states, it is not at all dependent upon the government of New Jersey, and it established itself at Princeton only because this city is situated almost exactly at the center of the United States in a very good and healthful climate."]

11. *Ursus lotor* Lin. Schreber, Saügthiere, Part iii, p. 521, Table 146. Buffon: *raton,* Vol. VIII, Table 43, and *Suppl.,* Vol. III, Ed. in 4°, Paris. [*Procyon lotor* (Linn.)]

[12. Br 3:117–18 ". . . onto a causeway built across a wide swamp, which leads to the Passaic, or Second, River. From this river, across a similar swamp, one reaches another called Hackensack Swamp, beyond which the terrain rises again up to about a mile from Paulus Hook, where two other very wide marshes must be crossed.

"It being late at night when we left Newark, the marshes near the aforementioned river were covered with a very thick fog and emitted a disgusting stench. Mosquitoes, or *Culex pipiens,* were innumerable, and we were concerned about the drowsiness that the weariness from traveling had brought upon us. (The Passaic and Hackensack Rivers, flowing through the same valley, join in Newark Bay, which connects with the ocean.)

"From Paulus Hook one crosses the Hudson, or North River, from which can be perceived the city of New York, situated along both banks."]

[13. Castiglioni's fn., Br 3:120: "Cape Henlopen, called also Cape James, is situated at the mouth of the Delaware at latitude 38° 46′."]

[14. Reference to any of numerous readily available modern histories of New Jersey—e.g., the two volumes by John E. Pomfret, *The Province of West New Jersey* and *The Province of East New Jersey* (Princeton, N.J.: Princeton Univ. Press, 1956 and 1962), or R. P. McCormick, *New Jersey from Colony to State, 1609–1789* (Princeton, N.J.: Van Nostrand, 1964)—will quickly set straight the inaccuracies of Castiglioni's summary of the tangled early history of this colony.]

15. This fort was destroyed, and in the same spot was built a village called Lewes Town, now capital of Sussex County in the State of Delaware.

16. Now Wilmington, one of the main trading places in the State of Delaware.

17. Now Salem, capital of a county by that name in New Jersey.

[18. The two Jerseys were merged in 1702 as a united Royal Colony administered by the governor of New York. But the governor's commission recognized the political independence of the Colony, and the two Jerseys maintained separate capitals, the legislature meeting alternately in Perth Amboy and Burlington until after the Revolution.]

19. In England there is a law by which the weapon used by the suicide to take his life is confiscated.

20. *Juniperus virginiana* Lin. [!]

[21. Br 3:128–37 "The climate of this state is not at all different from those of New York and Pennsylvania, except that in New Jersey that disease that goes under the name of 'fever and aigue' is more common. Since this disease, which can almost be called general in the United States of America, has been accurately described by Mr. Kalm in his *Travels in America,* I deem it well to report here the entire section of the aforementioned author on the subject. Speaking of Raccoon, a tiny village in the State of New Jersey populated by Swedes, he expresses himself as follows. . . ." (Castiglioni goes on to cite Kalm at length on the topic of what today we know to be malaria: see Kalm's *Travels in America,* ed. Benson, 1:191–95.)]

22. *Cinchona caribaea* [Jacq. = *Exostema caribaea* (Jacq.) Roem. & Schult.]

23. *Cornus florida* Lin. [!]

24. *Geum rivale* Lin. [!]

25. *Salix babylonica* Lin. [!] [Br 3:141–42 "In addition to all these remedies reported by Mr. Kalm, and various other less effective ones, there was discovered recently in America another bark as excellent, according to what they say, as quinine, namely, that of the weeping or African willow. This discovery was made in the following manner: Mr. (Thomas) Hutchins, a United States geographer, happened last year to be in the internal regions of Virginia near the shores of the Ohio in order to mark off the border divisions with the Indians. The season being warm and rainy, a number of his people caught these fevers and were incapacitated for work. The distance they were from any city or town where quinine could be obtained made them turn industriously to experimenting with various plants of that region to find a remedy for these fevers. They then made a strong decoction from the bark of the African willow (*Salix babylonica*), which grows abundantly on the shores of the Ohio. Taken daily, in a few days it restored their health. This experiment, according to what I have heard from trustworthy persons, was repeated in various places by the same Mr. Hutchins with equal success.
    "The pleurisies called 'stitches' and 'burning' are likewise quite common in America and often destroy many inhabitants." "Weeping willow" is native to China.]
26. Kalm, *Travels,* I, 292.
[27. Br 3:139–40 "These fevers are of the putrid and nervous kind. They come on usually with a chill, followed by a hot fever that lasts for several hours. The afflicted have a yellowish color, pale lips, dry hands, and suffer a general physical weakness. They are depressed, and even though they may eat a great deal, they become thin in a short time. When these fevers are tertian or quartan, they can work and travel in the interludes without great inconvenience, but when they are quotidian, on the other hand, debilitation is such as to render them unfit for any exertion. The onset of the fever is indicated by a painful sensation of cold about the knees and fingers, accompanied by a general weakness. This is followed by a similar and more painful sensation of cold in the small of the back, which, spreading to the shoulders and then dropping to the stomach, produces that convulsive tremor called the chill of the fever. As soon as this is over, the temperature begins. The patient then feels relieved and sweats easily until the fever leaves him completely. (These symptoms were constantly with me when I had the fever in Canada.)"]
28. *Didelphis marsupialis* Lin. Schreber, *Saügthiere*, Plate 145* with the asterisk. [*Didelphis virginiana* Kerr]
    N.B. This is the true opossum of the United States, to which belong many of the synonyms given by Mr. Schreber to his *Didelphis opossum*; but the figure of Plate 145 (without asterisk) does not resemble this animal. The specimens I observed had the following proportions:

		[in.]
From the tip of the snout to tip of the tail English feet	1	2
From shoulders to base of tail	1	
Tail		10
Front feet		
Arm		2½
Forearm		2
Paw		1½
Rear feet		
Thigh		2¾
Leg		3½
Foot		2¼

29. The females we examined had not yet borne young and the reproductive organs were very small. The anus of the opossum is very large, the vagina extremely tiny, and the rectal intestine very wide and composed of a very thin membrane. Above it there is a long, narrow, canal divided in its upper part into three branches (see Plate XI, Fig. 3), the middle one ending in the urethra of the bladder, the lateral ones connected with the two urethras. The Fallopian tubes extend to the fimbria, beneath which are situated the two ovaries. Their gestation period must be quite brief, since the uteruses and the vagina are made of a very thin substance and do not seem capable of much stretching; and perhaps for that reason it happens that the young come out still almost shapeless from the womb of the mother to attach themselves to the nipples. These are arranged in a circle inside the pouch and do not have (as some used to suppose) any connection with the organs of reproduction. A pouch (Fig. 2) is snug against the belly of animals still young, and at the bottom of it there are some small glands from which oozes a viscous fluid with a musklike odor. The two bones joined in the form of a bow (Plate XI, Fig. 4) that support the pouch are called *ossa marsupialia* by Tyson in the anatomy of these animals. The outside of the cranium is concave on both sides so as to form a ridge along the head; and the brain is very small in proportion to the head, with the lateral hollows filled with fat. [Edward Tyson, 1650–1708, M.D., F.R.S., who published his treatise in *Philosophical Transactions* in April 1698]

[30. Br 3:147 "The inhabitants of New Jersey, being composed of Swedes, Englishmen, Scots, Dutch, and Germans, do not have particular manners and customs, and especially in the cities, since they are in continuous communication with the cities of New York and Philadelphia; they differ from the inhabitants of these cities only in being less wealthy and enjoying less luxury."]

[31. Br 3:147–48 ". . . and because of this second-rate trade, the expenses of the government, and the limited fortune of the inhabitants, some of them would like to see themselves united to one of the adjoining states—Pennsylvania or New York.

"The eastern shores of New Jersey, extending from Sandy Hook to Cape May, are nothing more than a barren desert of sand producing only *Juniperus virginiana* cedars and pines; and the northern parts are quite mountainous and rocky. The best and richest settlements are therefore along the shores of the Delaware and in the internal country, where wheat, rye, oats, corn, flax, etc., are grown very abundantly and perfectly. In some places agriculture is taken to a degree of perfection not inferior to that of Pennsylvania. The fields are well cultivated, surrounded by fences, the farmers' homes are very comfortable, and on each plantation there is a dairy barn which serves for the storage of grain and hay, and in which is arranged also the stable for livestock. Professor Kalm, in Vol. I, p. 174, speaking of these dairy barns, describes them thus: . . . ." (Castiglioni quotes at this point Kalm's paragraph on these barns: cf. Kalm's *Travels in America,* ed. Benson, 1: 118–19.)]

32. *Polygonum fagopyrum* Lin. [*Fagopyrum sagittatum* Gilib. The account here of the uses made of buckwheat in New Jersey is based on Kalm's *Travels,* which Castiglioni cites at greater length on this topic in his ms., Br 3:150–51. Cf. Kalm's *Travels in America,* ed. Benson, 1: 183–84.]

Chapter XVI—The State of Connecticut

[1. Br 3:167 ". . . where the horses are changed. The road from Horse Neck to Norwalk is mountainous and rocky; the fields, however, are very fertile, especially for wheat. To reduce the quantity of stones that litter the ground, the inhabitants are accustomed to gather them up to make little walls about the fields which serve to keep livestock away as in Massachusetts."]

[2. Br 3:167–68 ". . . called Devil's Belt, or Long Island Sound."]

[3. Br 3:168–69 ". . . where I intended to rest. (Fairfield suffered the same fate as Norwalk and was destroyed by General Tryon.) Barely three hours after we turned in we were awakened to continue our journey, but, instead of attaching four horses to the carriage, they attached only two, and, moreover, these were so skinny and weak that we lost three hours covering just the 10 miles to Stratford. Crossing there the river that takes its name from the aforementioned village, we found a good carriage with four horses to take us to New Haven. The road being better and the horses very good, these 13 miles were run in a short time, and descending from a hill into a very charming and well-cultivated plain, we arrived in New Haven toward eleven in the morning. There I left my companions, who continued on their way to Boston, and I remained behind to observe the sights of the region."]

4. *Scarabeus (vitreus) scutellatus inermis, thorace viridi nitidissimo, elytris levibus, pedibusque testaceis.*

Clypeus inermis fuscus. Antennae clava nigra. Thorax vitreus quasi vernice nitens, marginibus elytrorum colore. Scutellum elytris concolor. Elytra lucida, subrufa, abdomine breviora, abdomine apice fusco-nigrum, extremitate elytris concolore. Corpus subtus lucidum, annulis albido testaceis notatum, alibi nigricans. Pedes lucidi, elytris concolores, tibiis edentulis.

Accedit Cetoniae micanti Fabricii. Habitus Scarabei solstitialis. Spec. nova.

5. *Scarabeus (albiventris) exscutellatus inermis oblongus, capite thoraceque nigris, elytris viridinitentibus, abdomine subtus apiceque albo.*

Clypeus rotundatus. Antennae rufae. Thorax punctulatus niger. Elytro tenuissimo griseo villo, lente conspicuo, quasi polline adspersa, fundo viridi translucente, striis tribus, inter strias subtilissime, denseque punctulata. Abdominis apex albus linea nigra distinctus, subtus pilis tenuissimis albis. Pedes testacei, tibiae posticae angulo prominente.

Statura, & habitus Carabi minoris. Spec. nova.

[6. Br 3:169–73 "On the same day of my arrival I went to present myself to Dr. Stiles, president of the University, to whom I had a letter of introduction. He is a man of about 60 years of age, lean, thin, and of short stature. Having read the letter that I presented to him, he began by asking whether or not I was a merchant, whether I had come to America for business or pleasure, whether I was interested in literary things. 'Because,' he added, 'before speaking I like to know the inclinations of my new acquaintance.' (Fn. of Castiglioni: The inquisitiveness of the inhabitants of Connecticut is familiar to all who have had occasion to travel in that province. Dr. Franklin, having arrived at an inn after traveling many miles and wanting something to eat, made in vain his request of the innkeeper, who kept pestering him with various questions. He finally told him to gather his wife, his children, and the whole family in that room. When they were all assembled, the Doctor said to them: 'I am Benjamin Franklin. I come from Boston, and I am going to New York.' And then he explained the reasons for undertaking this trip and answered all the questions that were put to him. Having finished his discussion, he turned to the innkeeper and said: 'Now I have satisfied your curiosity, and I hope you will give me something to eat.') To these queries I answered that I was not a merchant, that I had come to America solely out of curiosity, and that I had made some study of natural history, particularly botany. 'That being the case,' he answered, 'please excuse me a moment.' And leaving the room, he returned very quickly with a little machine, a book, and a paper package. The machine was a kind of three-wheeled wagon that by means of three wings arranged in a circle around an axis was made to go in the direction from which the wind was blowing—a device that, fitted to a boat, would make it move against the wind and against the current.

After that he showed me an inscription that he himself had discovered near the sea in the State of Rhode Island. This inscription, or rather hieroglyphic characters or figures, is carved on a reef that remains almost entirely covered with water at high tide. Near it, however, there are various other shorter ones whose signs are less definite. As for the first, of which he showed me the design, it consists of various human figures [figures], curved lines [curve], triangles △, and others that might resemble characters, but which could have been made by accident or as a joke. Certain professors of Cambridge University in Massachusetts, after examining this inscription, were content to call the characters *lusus Indianorum,* supposing that that was probably one of the beaches where the Indians used to go to practice shooting with their bows, sharpening their arrows on these reefs and forming in this manner those abstract representative figures. Nevertheless, some European scholars, among whom was M. Court de Gébelin, author of *Le Monde primitif* and victim of magnetism, to whom this inscription was sent, thought the characters were Punic, or that at least they bore a great resemblance to those used by this nation. I leave to others to determine whether it is more likely that some Carthaginians or Phoenicians discovered the shores of America, as seems to be proved by the abovementioned inscriptions, or whether the Indians, amusing themselves at making bad drawings, accidentally formed curved lines, circles, and crosses that show some similarity to Phoenician and Carthaginian characters.

Finally, the President let me see the drawing he had recently received of a vast fortification discovered on the shores of the Ohio. There is in this place quite a vast main fort of a square shape surrounded by ramparts with other minor fortifications. Near these were found tombs full of bones and skeletons distributed around a center like the points of a star. This curious method of arranging the bodies and the vast fortifications, which one cannot believe is the work of Indians, have given rise to various conjectures, some supposing that these are works of the Spaniards or the French, who had inhabited Louisiana and Florida for a long time, and others going back to more remote times and giving the credit for these works to peoples living on this continent before the Indians (see the descriptions and drawing of these fortifications in the *Columbian Magazine* of May, 1787)."

Edmund B. Delabarre's *Dighton Rock* (New York: Neale, 1928), is a fascinating analysis of the historical and psychological problems posed by this curious monument.]

7. Court de Gébelin, *Monde primitif,* Vol. VIII, p. 561, Plate 1.

[8. Br 3:173 ". . . where, on the ground floor there is the meeting place for evening and morning prayers. . . ."]

[9. Br 3:173 ". . . the laboratory for machines and natural history. In the library there are some scientific books, not, however, too modern, various scholastic books and ancient authors, and a large number of Protestant theologians and holy fathers."]

10. *Felis concolor.* Linnaei *Mantissa,* & Schreber, *Saügthiere*.[!]

[11. Br 3:177 "At this college, as at the one in Cambridge, Massachusetts, the degrees of *Academiae magister* and doctor are conferred as in English universities."]

[12. Br 3:177 "The two main celebrations are Commencement, or beginning of classes, and Election, on which days the students give public proof of their progress by delivering orations in Greek, Latin, and English, and by answering questions on physics, mathematics, and theology before being admitted to the various degrees. At that time a great many gentlemen and ladies gather from the towns near New Haven, and for three days there is a public evening ball."]

[13. Br 3:175 ". . . divided into pleasant fields surrounded by wooden fences, . . ."]

[14. Br 3:176 ". . . many of them very beautiful and elegant, . . ."]

[15. Br 3:178 "I left New Haven at ten in the morning of August 31st in a very comfortable carriage and arrived at dinner time at Durham 27 miles away. For about 12 miles out of New Haven the road is very sandy, but thereafter the terrain is fertile and clayey. The countryside is most charming, broken up by beautiful cultivated hills between which lie extremely fertile valleys reduced to fields."]

16. This is of the sort called *Galaena plumbi granulosa* by the naturalists.

17. *Lucanus interruptus* Lin.

18. *Cerambix tornator* Scop., *Delic. insub.*, Pt. ii, Plate 20, Fig. 1. *Stenocorus castillionei* Scop., *Delic. insub.*, Pt. ii, Plate 20, Fig. 2.

[19. Br 3:181 ". . . the inhabitants are healthy and sturdy, and the fair sex is noted both for shapeliness and rosy complexion."]

[20. Br 3:180 "The most beautiful one runs parallel with the river, where the best houses are."]

[21. Br 3:181 ". . . especially toward the northwest on the road to Albany."]

22. *Juglans cinerea* Lin. [!]

[23. Br 3:183 ". . . had killed a number of the new colonists. . . ."]

[24. Br 3:183 ". . . and Mr. Hooker, jealous of the superiority that a certain Mr. Cotton, a Presbyterian minister, had acquired in Massachusetts, sought to move there with his friends, which was granted him, though not without difficulty."]

[25. Br 3:184 ". . . because he was a native of a village by that name in England; . . ."]

[26. Br 3:184 ". . . the name of Mr. Stone's native place in England."]

[27. *Py-quag,* according to *Encyclopedia Americana,* s.v. "Wethersfield."]

[28. Br 3:185 "However, in spite of the fact that (as I have already said) they had obtained permission to settle there by the Massachusetts Colony, they very quickly agreed to form a separate political body, established their own laws and constitutions, and gave to the new colony the name of the river."]

[29. Br 3:185 ". . . and, although invited by the colonists to settle in Massachusetts, they refused their offers, . . ."]

[30. Br 3:185–86 ". . . and they set themselves up as a colony, which took the name of the capital city. The Colony of Connecticut, and that of New Haven, were continuing to govern themselves with their own laws when Fenwick, a pious man from a respectable English family, arrived in America to take possession in the name of Lords Say and Brook of the country belonging to them situated between the Connecticut and Narragansett Bay where they had decided to settle; but then changing their minds and no longer thinking of moving to America, they ordered George Fenwick to sell their rights, which were bought in 1644 by the people of Connecticut."]

[31. Br 3:187 "Connecticut is divided into six counties, and each county contains various cities and villages, each of which has the right to have two representatives at the General Court, or Assembly. This Assembly is distinguished into two bodies, namely, the Upper Chamber and the Lower Chamber."]

[32. Br 3:147–48 "At the beginning of April the votes are collected in the various cities and villages submitted by the inhabitants on pieces of paper with the names of the persons that they want elected to one or the other of the aforementioned offices. These are sent to the General Assembly on the second Thursday in May, and from them are selected the governor, deputy governor, treasurer, and secretary by majority vote. As for the assistants, 20 are chosen, of whom 10 assume office after the first 6 months. The representatives, who are also elected by the people in the manner indicated above, remain in office only 6 months and are changed at the two sessions of May and October."]

[33. Br 3:189 "The climate is very cold in the winter and more temperate in the summer; and although New Haven and the other maritime cities are subject to tertian fevers in autumn, the more internal parts of the state are very healthful, and Hartford is considered one of the most salubrious cities in America."]

[34. Br 3:189 ". . . and because the population of the state is so abundant that it does not admit many new settlements, . . ."]

[35. Br 3:190 ". . . where the uniformity of principles and prejudices, and a general education, have blocked innovations. The reading of the Bible, which they do regularly on Sundays, and the sermons, or preachings, which they listen to on mornings and evenings of festive days, make them masters in the principles of the Christian religion; and the art of reading and writing, taught in a public school built in every village that all the children attend, make it possible for every inhabitant to participate equally in the education imparted.

"On Sundays hymns in counterpoint are sung in church, and boys and girls of the most respectable families do not consider it beneath them to join in the singing."

36. I happened to see this ceremony one Sunday in a church in the city of Hartford.

[37. Castiglioni's note in ms., Br 3:199: "By 'adultery' is understood in this country only the breach of faith of the wife toward the husband, and 'adulterer' is the name given to one who has an affair with the wife of another man; but breach of faith of the husband toward his wife is not considered at all, otherwise you would see nearly all the husbands in America with ropes around their necks."]

[38. Br 3:191 ". . . which might be offensive to the ears of sensitive readers, . . ."]

[39. Br 3:192 ". . . in persons of both sexes. . . ."]

[40. Br 3:192 ". . . not indeed in preventing, but in receiving and not returning. . . ."]

[41. Br 3:194 ". . . removes only his suit and stockings. Here I must say, along with Tassoni in his *Secchia rapita:*

Gli abbracciamenti, i baci, e i colpi lieti
Tace, la Musa casta, e vergognosa."

(A suggestive reticence from the description of Venus' revenge on her jealous husband Vulcan in the seventeenth-century mock epic of Alessandro Tassoni, *The Rape of the Bucket,* Canto II, Stanza 57.)]

[42. Br 3:194 ". . . before granting this community of bed, . . ."]

[43. Br 3:194 ". . . that he had not slept all night long, but he assured me that the girl was still intact, and that he had found her very well behaved and modest."]

[44. Br 3:196 "This custom of bundling derives perhaps from the need the first colonists found themselves in to receive one another in their little cabins and to spend the night there when settlements were few and far between, or also from their need to persuade young people to marry early. . . ."]

[45. Br 3:199 "From there are obtained in exchange molasses for making rum, sugar, coffee, etc."]

[46. Br 3:199–200 "More uniform in their opinions than the inhabitants of the other states, they have given more thought than all others to promoting public education, and perhaps to this and to the general low level of wealth they owe the fact that they did not become embroiled in the unfortunate revolution of their neighbors, the inhabitants of Massachusetts, and did not, like them, disturb the peace of the state."]

Chapter XVII—The State of Rhode Island

[1. Br 3:201 "From the Connecticut border, after two days of travel, through Worcester, Sudbury, etc., I reached Boston where, entertained by the hospitality of my old friends and acquaintances, I stayed until the 11th of September, after which, renting a two-seated carriage, I left for Providence. On this route one comes upon the villages of Roxbury, Dedham, Walpole, and Attleboro, where I spent the night; and the following morning I arrived in Providence."]

[2. Br 3:211–12 "Providence, a city situated at latitude 41° 49′, was founded in 1635 by Roger Williams, who went there with his followers after having embraced and preached Anabaptist dogma and having been persecuted in Salem, Massachusetts, where he had settled originally with his followers. The motive for their flight being solely to enjoy free exercise of their religion, and never suspecting that the new settlement might become of some consequence in the future, they built a few houses at the end of the river in a situation least adapted for commerce, since there was at that spot a shoal that prevented large ships from approaching; and they laid the foundations of the city which, considered by them as an asylum furnished by God for their refuge, they called Providence. However, the inhabitants increasing little by little, and various other sects settling there, this city became much more flourishing and commercial. Now it disputes the title of capital with Newport and is one of the most populous in the state. It is situated on the so-called Providence River, which divides the city into East and West."]

[3. Br 3:203 ". . . to which may be added various handsome brick homes and other very elegant ones of wood."]

[4. Br 3:203–204 "The inhabitants of this city are mostly merchants, and the main trade consists of lumber, hemp, etc., which are sent to the Antilles, for which they receive in exchange molasses that is distilled into rum or brandy. This useful trade, which flourished in Providence after the ruin of the Newport trade owing to the fatal consequences of the recent war, was much hindered and greatly damaged at the present time by a new issue of paper money, which, unsupported by any public funds, very quickly dropped by two thirds of its value and did so much harm to the progress of this city that a number of merchants were forced to close their doors."]

[5. Br 3:204–205 "The ladies of Providence are lovable, courteous, and very beautiful, and have, along with those of Newport, the reputation of being the belles of America. A perfectly fine and white complexion, rosy cheeks, pretty eyes, and a charming and vivacious figure conjoined with keen wit and intelligence, are endowments not infrequently found united in the fair sex of this part of America. It is, however, regrettable that many of them in the fairest flower of their years lose their teeth, and many of them die of consumption. The former defect, which they share with the women of Boston, results perhaps from the use of hot and dense tea, from the frequent eating of sweet and sugary things, from feeding on roasted corn and then exposing oneself to excessive cold in the winter, as a consequence of which the tooth enamel, already worn by too warm and corrosive substances, rots away completely. This opinion seems corroborated by observation, since usually the upper teeth, being more exposed to the cold, are all corroded, while the lower ones, which remain covered by the lip, are all intact. Consumption, a terrible disease that has already carried off so many fair victims in their most florid youthful age, and which perhaps results from the little care that they take to protect themselves against the rigors of winter, has become even more common in the last three years or so and is transmitted from one member to another within the same family."]

[6. Br 3:206 "The soil about the city is very barren and sandy, but the inhabitants are nevertheless furnished with good provisions. Beef, veal, lamb, and pork are excellent, there is an abundance of fowl and aquatic birds, and a great variety of salt-water fish. The most common liquors are rum, brandy, and cider, as in the other states of New England."]

[7. Br 3:206 "On the morning of the 14th I went with Messrs. Brown and Francis, (two of) the wealthiest merchants of this city, to a rich iron mine seven miles from Providence belonging to the said Mr. Brown and visited a few years ago by the Swedish mineralogist Baron d'Hormelin. . . ."]

[8. Br 3:207 "This machine was constructed under the direction of the late N. Brown, brother of the present, who was endowed with a natural talent for mechanics. It is very remarkable both for having been conceived by one who had never before seen a machine of that sort and for the new way in which it was built."

Samuel J. Hough's annotations to this chapter in his article "Castiglioni's Visit to Rhode Island," *Rhode Island History,* 26 (1967): 53–64 illumine various points of interest to the Rhode Island historian. For example, the Mr. Brown mentioned by Castiglioni is John Brown, 1736–1803, main owner of the Cranston iron bogs, opened in 1765. The brother who devised the steam engine was Joseph Brown, 1733–85. The second Brown estate, to which Castiglioni refers below, was acquired from the state after being confiscated from Joseph Wanton, the last royalist governor of Rhode Island.]

[9. Br 3:208 "This iron is found in metallic form, the ore is very rich and abundant, and a barrel of iron is obtained from two of ore at the first smelting. Mixed with the iron are found now and then fragments of lead: and one also comes upon volcanic materials, which lead to the supposition that this mine was subject to the action of fire, and that perhaps it could have been the crater of an ancient volcano."]

10. *Haematites niger cum ochra ferri.* [Black hematite with (weathered) ochre.]

11. *Haematites niger radiatus.*

12. *Galaena plumbi.* This ore was examined a few years ago by the learned Swedish mineralogist Baron Harmelin.

[13. Br 3:208–209 "I stayed in Providence during the following days until the morning of the 18th, when I continued on my way toward Newport. There are, daily, in both Newport and Providence, sloops, or single-masted vessels that come and go between these two cities, and this trip, because of the charm and beauty of Narragansett Bay, is one of the most delightful, accomplished when the wind is favorable within the space of four to six hours. But since the wind was contrary and there was no compelling reason for going by sea, I accepted the gracious offer of Mr. Brown, who insisted upon accompanying me in his carriage as far as Bristol, which is halfway."]

[14. Br 3:210 ". . . to which one passes by a causeway, or palisaded road. . . ."]

[15. Br 3:210 ". . . in Papa-squash, . . ."]

[16. Br 3:210 ". . . which served for our dinner and supper, . . ."]

[17. Br 3:211 ". . . and its expression was utterly repulsive and shapeless, for which it was given the name of toadfish."]

[18. Br 3:211 "Finally, after it had reached a prodigious size, one of the bystanders placed it on a rock, and when he dropped a stone straight down upon it, it burst, making a noise like the explosion of a pistol."]

[19. Br 3:211–13 "Reflecting on the nature of this phenomenon, it occurred to me to examine this fish carefully, and, by means of various experiments, to seek out the reason why it swells in such an extraordinary fashion when it is taken out of the water; but, unfortunately, seeing no more of them, even though we stayed to fish for a long time after dinner, I could only formulate conjectures which, striking me as not completely unlikely, I deem well to add here.

"Most fish, in addition to the faculty of swimming, are provided with a bladder that they can at will fill with air or empty, and which they use to rise to the surface or to plunge into the depths of the water. The toadfish seems to be furnished with the same bladder; however it must be larger in proportion to his size and capable of greater expansion. The sea lobsters and crabs that live in great numbers on the sea bottom are perhaps enemies of these fish, which, being slow swimmers and of an ungainly shape, would perhaps remain prey if they didn't have the escape of being able to rise quickly to the surface of the water by filling the aforesaid bladder with air, whereby by rendering themselves specifically much lighter than water, not only can they rise quickly themselves, but they are even able to drag up their enemy, who by that means is forced to abandon his prey. For that reason they swell when they are thrown upon the ground, believing thereby to rise to a fluid in which they can maneuver and swim. And this is perhaps also the reason why the various species of fish, as soon as they are removed from the water, suck in continuously the outside air."]

20. Guglielmi Rondeletii, *De piscibus,* Lib. 15, Chap. vii, *De orthragorisco, sive Luna pisce.* Lugd. 1554, p. 424.

21. *Systema naturae Linnaei, & Amoenit. academ.,* Vol. I, p. 309, Plate 14, Fig. 3. [*Sphaeroides testudineus* (Linn.)]

[22. Br 3:213 ". . . the day being clear and the sea calm, . . .]

[23. Br 3:213 ". . . where the bay opens to the west to its full extent. The panorama there was delightful. To the north one saw the bay and the village of Bristol and to the northwest that of Providence and the adjacent cultivated slopes; to the west, beautiful Prudence Island, and to the east the island of Rhode Island and the Bay of Mount Hope."]

[24. Br 3:214 ". . . and having fortunately found a sloop near Prudence Island, it was decided that I would continue my journey on it, and that they would return immediately to Papa-squash with the (small) boat."]

[25. Br 3:214 ". . . and having enjoyed for a little while the extremely charming view of the islands and the continent that surrounds Narragansett Bay, we went down to the seashore, where I took leave of my companions, went aboard the sloop, and in less than two hours was in Newport."]

[26. Br 3:215 "Before the Revolution Newport (had) 1200 houses."]

[27. Br 3:217 "The inhabitants are for the most part merchants. . . ."]

[28. Br 3:215 "The ladies are no less attractive than in Providence, and by many they are judged even more beautiful, which the inhabitants attribute to the sea air and to the mist to which this city is very subject, and which, according to them, renders complexions finer and more lively."]

[29. Br 3:216 ". . . I left Newport for Providence on one of the packets that continually go from one to the other of these cities and continued my journey toward Boston, where I arrived the following morning." (Fn.) "From Boston I made another run to Portsmouth in New Hampshire, and from there I returned through Boston to New York. I remained there about a month and then went to Philadelphia, where I spent the winter most pleasurably, both for the less severe climate and the excellent company. When spring came, I went again to New York to seek passage to Europe, and finally, thanks to the Minister for Spain, Mr. Gardoqui, I left on the 16th of May, 1787. . . ."]

30. Br 3:217–18 "The first settlements in the State of Rhode Island had their origin (like those of Massachusetts) in religious disputes and in that spirit of intolerance that then reigned among the fanatic Presbyterians of New England."]

[31. Br 3:217 "The people of Salem had wanted him as minister from the time that he first arrived in America, but the magistrates, who were acquainted with his fanatic spirit of innovation, were opposed to this choice; nor did they fail to remonstrate a second time. But the people gave no heed to their suggestions, and his predecessor Mr. Skelton having died just a little previously, they ordained him minster of the aforementioned church."]

[32. Br 3:218 ". . . not only from the Church of England, but also from the other American Presbyterian churches."]

[33. Br 3:218 ". . . persuaded Mr. (John) Endicott, one of the magistrates and one of the followers of his doctrines, . . ." See Hough, art. cit., p. 60, fn. 10 for more details on this episode.]

[34. Br 3:219 ". . . this trivial cause. . . ."]

[35. Br 3:219 "Banished thus from Massachusetts, he withdrew to the south with his companions to the country then occupied by the Indians and established his residence in a place called Moshawsick, which he named Providence, like other persecuted sectarians considering it a refuge provided him by God."]

[36. See Hough's interesting speculation (art. cit., p. 61, fn. 11) that Castiglioni's information on the baptism of Ezechiell Holyman may have come to him through someone like Jeremy Belknap who had access to transcriptions of John Winthrop's as yet unpublished *Journal of the Settlement of Massachusetts.*]

[37. Br 3:219 ". . . whom he judged to be anti-Christians."]

[38. The exact date of Roger Williams' death is uncertain, but it must have occurred between January 16 and March 15, 1682–83 (*DAB*). The reader is warned for a final time of the factual unreliability of Castiglioni's historical summaries.]

[39. Br 3:221 "Upon his arrival he was, by unanimous agreement, made governor. . . ."]

[40. Br 3:221–22 "The company established by this charter took the name of Governor and Society of the English Colony of Rhode Island and Plantations of Providence in New England, to which were granted the privileges of forming new laws, creating the governor and magistrates, and other concessions so broad that, inasmuch as they conform to the democratic ideas of the new government, they are still in effect after the Revolution." (The state continued to operate under its liberal 1663 Charter of Rhode Island and Providence Plantations until the year 1842.)]

[41.Br 3:225–26 "The soil is fertile and the country is divided into various plantations. The same products are also cultivated here as in Rhode Island, cheeses are made that yield little to the best of England and the European continent, and they are traded with the other American states."]

[42. Br 3:226 "The soil is very fertile, but rocky, and a great deal of effort is required to render it suitable for farming, since the rocks and stones that encumber it have to be removed. With them are made the little walls that surround the fields. This island, too, contains at the present time only a few bearing plantations."]

43. In the *American Museum,* I, p. 305, the population is also counted as 59,670. According to another note, the population was 58,000 in 1775 and 50,000 in 1783 [cf. *American Museum* 3(1788): 453], the drop resulting from the war ([Filippo Mazzei,] *Recherches sur les Etats Unis,* Pt. III, p. 210).

[Br 3:229 "Rhode Islanders are no different in their customs from those of Massachusetts and the other states of New England. In Newport and Providence many are employed in commerce, and in the rest of the state they apply themselves to agriculture, in which they made great progress."]

[44. Br 3:229–32 "Commerce consists mainly of horses, corn, and lumber, which go to the Antilles in exchange for sugar and molasses; and there is also trade in codfish on the Newfoundland Banks, as well as in whale oil, in imitation of the inhabitants of Nantucket. The brother of the aforementioned Mr. Brown was the first in America to begin to manufacture the beautiful spermaceti candles which for their beauty and the light they give are by many preferred to wax. In short, the commerce of Newport was second to that of none of the principal American cities, and there were very many engaged in business; but a new issue of paper money made last year destroyed the hopes of resurgence of this state, which at the present time finds itself in the greatest confusion.

"The State of Rhode Island, being one of the smallest in the United States, could not of course contain people capable of directing political affairs—except for the few inhabitants of Newport and Providence, and these naturally were by preference employed in legislation. The country dwellers, however, enticed by some who sought to sacrifice the good of the state for their particular motives, asked for an issue of paper money. The wiser among the members of the Assembly opposed this proposal ruinous to the state, but the people, believing that they had resisted the introduction of paper money in order to be merchants the year after the new election, chose uncouth and ignorant men as legislators only because they were favorable to this new issue. They began by approving the paper money, which quickly spread about, and its credit unsupported by any stable fund, very soon lost its value. To maintain the credit of this money they passed a law whereby everyone was forced to accept this paper money at the value of current money, and by this most unfair law through which they gave a real value to an imaginary object they increasingly ruined the finances of the state and forced many businessmen of Newport to close their stores and withdraw from commerce. Thus a government directed by ignorant and prejudiced people brought about the ruin of a state, which, although small, would have been able to compete with the others in wealth and trade. . . .

"What has been said regarding the islands of Narragansett Bay will serve to give an idea of the progress of agriculture in this state, so that it would be useless to enumerate again here the products of this state.

"The natural products of Rhode Island, like those of Connecticut, do not differ from the products of Massachusetts and the other New England states. The iron mines found (as I have already said) seven miles from Providence are very rich, and perhaps others still undiscovered exist in the various parts of this state. At a short distance from Providence there is a reddish stone used to make funeral monuments and a kind of white marble not unlike our so-called building marble. Furthermore, I was told that at about 30 miles toward the sea there was recently discovered a quarry of green and yellowish marble which takes a high polish and is very durable, and which perhaps will be some day an item of trade with the neighboring states."]

45. Notes are of two sorts, namely, of the United States in general and of the particular states. The first of these came out by order of Congress in order to meet the expenses of the war, and they held up until, with the waning of public confidence, their value declined to the point of being reduced almost to nothing. The same happened with those of the separate states, which were not backed by the pledging of any fund, so that they served only the private advantage of certain individuals who by that means defrauded their creditors, paying them with bills authorized by the legislature, but which had no trade value. Another evil resulted from the certificates, or notes, issued by the legislative bodies to soldiers and other persons instead of money. The latter had to sell them at a time when they had lost credit. Now businessmen own them and collect interest on them according to face value, so that the state bears the whole burden without having obtained the effect of helping those who had lent service and risked their lives for the

Republic. [Hough, p. 64, fn. 14, documents this sad chapter in Rhode Island economic history.]

46. The unfortunate consequences of a bad administration have been felt even more recently, since Rhode Island was one of the states that refused to ratify the new Constitution.

Chapter XVIII – The United States in General

1. From recent notices that have reached us from that region one learns that finally North Carolina has also ratified the Constitution.

Dates of ratification of the abovementioned Constitution by the other states that have accepted it:

States	*Date of ratification*			*Votes Pro*	*Con*	*Proportion of favorable votes*
Delaware	1787	3	Dec.	Unanimous		. . . .
Pennsylvania		13	Dec.	46	23	More than 5/8
New Jersey		19	Dec.	Unanimous		. . . .
Georgia	1788	2	Jan.	Unanimous		. . . .
Connecticut		9	Jan.	128	40	More than 5/7
Massachusetts		6	Feb.	187	168	More than 1/2
Maryland		28	Apr.	63	12	More than 4/5
South Carolina		23	May	149	73	Almost 2/3
New Hampshire		21	June	57	46	More than 1/2
Virginia		25	June	89	79	More than 1/2
New York		26	July	30	25	. . . . . . 6/11

[The remainder of §1. of this chapter of the *Viaggio nell'America Settentrionale* (pp. 116–51) is a translation of the Constitution.]

2. The Ohio River is navigable for 1174 miles from Fort Pitt to its mouth. The country along this river and between the Alleghany Mountains, Lakes Ontario and Erie, and the Illinois and Mississippi Rivers contains 233,200 square miles, that is, almost the area of England and France. The region situated between the Illinois river and Lakes Huron and Superior, and the Mississippi to the St. Anthony Falls, contains 129,030 square miles, or almost the area of England and Ireland. The region of St. Anthony Falls toward the south from the Lake of the Woods to the headwaters of the Mississippi contains 50,000 square miles, like Holland, Flanders, and Ireland. In fine, the thirteen United States of America contain 207,050 square miles, almost equal to Germany, Flanders, Holland, and Switzerland. *American Museum,* Vol. III, p. 453.
3. [Gian Rinaldo] Carli, *Lettere americane,* Letter I.
4. [Corneille de Pauw,] *Recherches philosophiques sur les Américains.*
5. See Chap. XI, §5, where Kentucky is discussed.
6. *Felis concolor* Lin., and Schreb., *Saügth.* [*Felis concolor couguar* Kerr]
7. *Ursus lotor* Lin. [*Procyon lotor* (Linn.)]
8. *Didelphis marsupialis* Lin. [*Didelphis virginiana* Kerr]
9. *Magnolia glauca* Lin. [*Magnolia virginiana* L.]
10. *Illicium anisatum* Lin. [*Illicium parviflorum* Michx.]
11. *Calycanthus floridus* Lin. [!]
12. *Panax quinquefolium* Lin. [!]

13. Compare, for example, the *Flora japonica* of Thunberg with the *Flora virginica* of Gronovius.
14. Among the oaks, for example, the evergreen oak of Carolina (*Quercus phellos* Lin.) [Castiglioni here surely means *Quercus virginiana* Mill.] might be compared to our holm oak (*Quercus ilex* Lin.), but it is different because the American one has entire, not dentate, leaves and even denser and heavier wood. Thus our common oak differs little from American white oak (*Quercus alba* Lin.), but the latter has great variety in the leaves and acorns and not so hard a wood. See these and similar observations in the respective articles on plants.
15. In Vol. I of *The American Museum* printed in Philadelphia in 1787, p. 305, the inhabitants of the United States are brought up to 3,102,670; but in the same periodical, Vol. III, of the year 1788, p. 453, a more moderate and plausible count is given, namely:

New Hampshire	102,000
Massachusetts	360,000
Rhode Island	58,000
Connecticut	202,000
New York	238,000
New Jersey	138,000
Pennsylvania	360,000
Delaware	37,000
Maryland	170,000
Negroes	80,000
Virginia	252,000
Negroes	280,000
North Carolina	164,000
Negroes	60,000
South Carolina	102,000
Negroes	80,000
Georgia	78,000
Negroes	20,000
Total	2,781,000

of whom 2,261,000 are white, and the other 520,000, negro slaves.
16. The commotions now rife in Europe will serve not a little to increase the population of the United States. The outbreak of disturbances in Geneva has already contributed, and 70 Swiss families have transported themselves here, as can be seen from the following paragraph from a letter written from Philadelphia on July 16, 1788, and reported in *The American Museum,* Vol. IV, p. 101: "Seventy families of Swiss arrived in this port a few days ago in one vessel. They all paid their passages before they sailed, and are clothed and furnished with every comfort and accessary [*sic*] of life. As they come from an industrious, frugal and moral country, enjoying a republican form of government, this colony will be highly acceptable. They intend to settle together, on a body of new lands, about thirty or forty miles from the mouth of the Conegocheague [Conecocheague, Franklin Co., Pa., tributary of Potomac].
17. Vol. I, p. 213, fn.
18. [Guillaume Thomas Francois] Raynal, *Histoire philosophique et politique des etablissements des Européens dans les deux Indes*] Vol. III, Bk. xviii, Chap. 95 (Geneva ed., in 4°), p. 410.

19. This famous man died in Philadelphia on the 17th of April of the current year 1790 at the age of 84 years and 3 months.
20. Nathanael Greene, major general in the United States army, who died from a sunstroke in June 1786.
21. Henry Knox, general in the artillery.
22. Henry [George] Clinton, now governor of the State of New York.
23. Benjamin Lincoln, general in the American army.
24. Richard Montgomery of New York, who was killed in the siege of Quebec.
25. General in the American army.
26. Horatio Gates, major general, who captured General Burgoyne at Saratoga.
27. Samuel Adams, senator in Massachusetts, was one of the keenest defenders of liberty, and John Adams, his cousin, was Minister Plenipotentiary of the United States in Holland and then in England.
28. John Jay, Minister of the United States in Spain, and now Secretary in the Department of Foreign Affairs.
29. John [James] Madison, who was a member of the Virginia Congress and later one of the delegates for the reform of the federal government.
30. Thomas Jefferson, Minister Plenipotentiary of the United States in Paris.
31. R. [Thomas] Paine, author of the treatise entitled *Common Sense,* which contributed much to the Revolution.
32. The sons of the intelligent botanist John Bartram live near Philadelphia and have collections of plants and seeds.
33. Humphry Marshall, a Pennsylvania Quaker, who has written a fine treatise on the trees and shrubs of North America under the title of *Arbustum Americanum.*
34. Manasseh Cutler, Presbyterian minister in Ipswich Hamlet in Massachusetts, who published a description of plants of that region and their uses in Vol. I of the *Proceedings of the American Academy* of Boston.
35. Dr. James Greenway, inhabitant of Virginia, who has made a fine collection of dried plants with descriptions according to the Linnaean system.
36. Certain authors, judging on the basis of decreasing fertility of cleared lands in America, have supposed that in time they would be completely exhausted, so that they could no longer serve for the sustenance of human beings. Such an assertion clearly demonstrates an utter ignorance of agriculture, since it is known that any terrain, although very fertile at first, after a number of years needs rest or the help of fertilizers. This latter method will be introduced into all parts of America with the increase of population, as has already been done near Philadelphia and the most populous cities of the United States. The writers who insisted upon finding all America degenerate were not satisfied with supposing it is so in the human species and in animals, but strove to discredit even the fertility of its lands; and this is what happens to all those who presume to subject nature to the rules of their systems.

[37. Castiglioni's "17th and Last Book" of the ms. *Viaggio* (Br 3:235–87) is a biographical appendix introduced by the following paragraph: "After having spoken of my travels in the thirteen United States of North America, it is appropriate not to relegate to silence those men who, by means of arms or pen, contributed to this fortunate Revolution. To these I shall add those who, although they did not participate in the Revolution, deserve to be distinguished for their extraordinary talents, and, finally, also a few of those who won fame either for their unusual manner of thought or action, or even for their serious crimes and treacheries. In order to avoid confusion, an alphabetical order of family names will be chosen, beginning with statesmen, then going on to military men, and finally those who distinguished themselves in the arts or sciences."

However fresh and interesting Castiglioni's thumbnail biographies of distinguished Americans may have seemed to his contemporaries, most of what he says, when it is not factually deficient, is banal for the modern reader conversant with American history. The passages reproduced below are salvaged as Castiglioni's personal observations or as echoes of contemporary opinions or hearsay.

Statesmen

John Adams: ". . . During a voyage from America to Europe, he scorned working at the pump, to which all the other passengers submitted in order to obviate the imminent danger of sinking, arguing that that was not befitting a person who had public status in Europe. Granted the truth of this fact, if his ambition led him, as is probable, to study and application, the Americans readily forgave him this little defect as recompense for the services he has rendered his country.

"Mr. Adams is 40 to 50 years old, short and corpulent; and his kindly but simple face gives no indication of the range of his knowledge."

Samuel Adams: ". . . Lean, small, a great talker, and crudely dressed, he reveals at first sight both by his words and behavior the turbulent and intolerant character of those individuals who, like death-dealing instruments of war, if they are necessary in disturbed times, should be removed from the sight of men in times of peace."

Benjamin Franklin: ". . . He is about 70 years of age, and his face is even-featured, venerable, and sincere. His manners are simple. He is likable and courteous, but at the same time a skillful and wise statesman. He has a natural son who was governor of New Jersey before the war and is now an officer in the British navy, whose son, also natural, lives with his grandfather and served as secretary for American affairs in Paris. Thus this family was of equal service to the American Republic and the English, and, although arisen from nothing and continued by illegitimate means, held respectable offices in both parties."

John Hancock: "There is perhaps no name more celebrated, and perhaps with less reason, than that of Hancock. He was a moderately wealthy Boston businessman, of a fiery temperament, one of the first to take a firm stand against the English, and one of the three proscribed when proposals of peace were made to the Americans. He was repaid for this proscription with the lofty office of President of Congress, which he held for a number of years in a row. A lover of festivity and amusements, in which he spent the greater part of his fortune, he made himself greatly beloved by the people, who are satisfied with appearances, and although he is of limited talents, he was for many consecutive years elected and confirmed as governor of the State of Massachusetts. . . .

"Mr. Hancock must be 70 years of age, or more. He is most polite with strangers, takes pleasure in holding a respectable office; and he loves show even at the cost of wrecking his own finances. His talents are more those of a courtier than a statesman, and one knows of no great plan that has ever come forth from his mouth or pen."

Patrick Henry: ". . . His knowledge extends not only to politics and government but also to literature and the sciences, the study of which he still pursues in hours free of affairs.

He is a man of about 50 years of age, and his features, fine but not too noble, show the liveliness of his talent."

John Jay: ". . . An old friend of his, who had received his subsistence from him, and who, born of a very poor Virginia family, was accepted in the Spanish army through the intercession of Jay and participated in the sieges of Majorca and Gibraltar as adjutant to the Duke de Crillon, attacked him for selfish reasons, and in a volume of satirical letters printed in America sought to discredit the well-founded reputation of the aforementioned minister. Happy he, if by his writings he succeeded in defending himself against these accusations, and if the elegant style of the accuser was unable to dazzle the eyes of impartial readers!" [For the sordid exchange between Jay and his *bête noire* Lewis Littlepage see Frank Monaghan, *John Jay,* New York & Indianapolis: Bobbs-Merrill, 1935, passim, and *DAB,* s.v. "Lewis Littlepage."]

Thomas Jefferson: ". . . Mr. Jefferson, chosen ambassador of the United States in France to succeed the illustrious Franklin, . . . accepted the charge conferred upon him and went to Paris. (I was myself at that time in Paris, and I had the honor of meeting him in Dr. Franklin's home.)

". . . Mr. Jefferson is a man of about 50 years of age, lean, of a serious and modest appearance. His uncommon talents are not readily visible at a first encounter, but as one talks with him about the various subjects in which he believes himself to be informed, he very quickly gives evident proof of his judgment and application. . . ."

John [Henry] Laurens: ". . . I did not have the fortune of meeting him, but I did have the good luck of meeting his two daughters, who add to a good education the talent of perspicacity and a wide range of knowledge."

John [James] Madison: ". . . He is a man of about 30 years of age, of likable manners and unaffected modesty."

Robert Morris: ". . . Mr. Morris is now the wealthiest merchant in America, but he shares his fortune with friends who are welcomed to his table and into his home without ceremony, but with complete cordiality. He devotes his mornings to business and evenings to joviality and conversation. He has given a good education to his children, two of whom are now traveling in Europe; and he will leave his wealth to whoever is capable of making good use of it. Many persons have not failed to speak badly of him, asserting that he made his fortune by illicit means. Among others, M. Chastellux, ill-informed, fell into this error. It is certain, however, that he is esteemed by all his correspondents as most exact, punctual, and clear in his dealings – qualities forming the active and honest businessman. He has of late gotten much involved in politics, and, being very influential both because of his money and a natural, unstudied, eloquence, he was made head of the Republican party, or of the city inhabitants – a party that exerted a great influence in legislation in the year 1787; and he succeeded in obtaining from the State the legal foundation of the Bank of North America in Philadelphia.

"He is a man of more than 50 years of age, with a rustic and peasant-like face, fond of the table and the bottle, which he gladly shares with his friends."

Gouverneur Morris: ". . . All those who have the good fortune to know him marvel at his talents and can only profit from his conversation and his pleasant company. As courteous and refined as a European, free as an American, he combines the talents of French *bon ton* and republican frankness, and is welcomed with pleasure in Philadelphia society."

Charles Thompson [Thomson]: ". . . I do not know whether he was born in Philadelphia or in some other city of the United States, or perhaps in Europe; nor whether he held public offices before the war. It was natural, however, for his talents to be recognized, since he was made Secretary of Congress from its very beginning. He filled this difficult office, and still fills it, with the universal approval both of his fellow countrymen and foreigners who are capable of a proper appreciation of his talents."

Soldiers

Ethan Allen: ". . . When the war ended, he got it into his head to be an author and wrote a book that was printed in Vermont with the pompous title of *The Oracle of Reason.* In this book, following the ideas of the deists, he presumes to refute the doctrine of Christianity and inveighs strongly against the opinions of the latter, which he dares to call fanatic and ridiculous. In this work he followed, and in many places copied, whole passages from works of this type already published, which he stuck together, along with ideas of his own easily distinguishable for their extravagance and faulty reasoning. I did not have an opportunity to meet this curious fellow, who, living in the southern parts of the state, was not on the route that I took through this region. But from what I heard from those who had known him, he is one of those rustic men endowed with some talent and much presumption, who would be less harmful to humanity if they were more ignorant."

Benedict Arnold: ". . . Some people, and M. de Chastellux among others, maintain that he was instigated to change party by his wife; but beyond the fact that she was demonstrated to be completely innocent by the trials and unaware of what her husband had done, persons worthy of trust assured me that she not only disapproved of what he had plotted but was furthermore almost ashamed of being the wife of a traitor. She is of the Shippen family, one of the most respected in Philadelphia, and being very comely, was much courted in England in spite of the blotch on the honor of her husband."

George Clinton: ". . . Some charge him with being very unsociable, with not spending in vain pomp, with failure to pay court to strangers. But if he occupies the time that he might give to conversation in attending to business, if he gives in charity to the poor the money that he would otherwise throw away in costly dinners and luxury, the nation must venerate this supposed defect as a virtue, and enlightened foreigners will be glad to see him sacrifice his time for the benefit of the state. In fact, the people do render him justice and speak of this man with great esteem. I did not have the fortune to meet him since he flees presentation to strangers, because they would distract him from his methodical manner of living; but persons who know him intimately assure me that he really deserves the praise given him, and that beyond the already mentioned fields of knowledge, he possesses an extensive background in the sciences, which he cultivates in his hours of leisure.

"Governor Clinton is about 50 years of age—or more. Both he and his wife are always simply dressed, and his office inspires in him no haughtiness or sense of superiority."

Horatio Gage [Gates]: ". . . Proud of having acquired for himself an immortal fame by the capture of Burgoyne, he would have been thoroughly happy if the war had ended at that time and he were not compelled to experience the variable turns of fortune on other occasions. But having gone to command in the South, unsuccessful in several encounters, not only was he unable to add other laurels to his brow, he even sullied those he had won in the North, and led many to attribute to a sheer stroke of good luck the deed that perhaps previously was ascribed to his superior talents in military art."

Nathanael Greene: ". . . All in America unanimously give due praise to this general, saying that he alone could have in some part taken the place of the immortal Washington. In fact, as testimony to the fine defense he mounted in the southern states, he was presented by the State of Georgia with a vast estate near Savannah, where he went to live with his family. I went to see him at his new home, and in talking with him I found him very well informed about the history of the wars of Italy and much more so about that of his native country and its political situation. But accustomed to a cold and healthful climate and confident in his sturdy constitution, the following summer, while he was attending to his slaves on his new rice plantations, he suffered a sunstroke, a fatal affliction in that unhealthful climate, soon lost consciousness, and, in only two days, his life. The Georgians, who really esteemed him, paid solemn respect to his remains. His death was mourned by all Americans, who retain a lively memory of one of the greatest and best educated generals of their army."

[John] Paul Jones: ". . . When the war ended, with the money acquired in his various depredations, he went to live in Paris, where he still resides. I had the good luck to meet him in the home of Mr. [Henry] Smeathman, author of a fine memoir on the termites of Africa, the reading of which I attended along with many others.

"Paul Jones is about 40 years of age, short, and has none of the ferocious appearance with which some have painted him in affected portraits. He loves the pleasures of life, and readily finds compensation amid the luxuries of Paris for the harsh labors of his excursions on the sea."

Henry Knox: ". . . Entering the army, he very quickly distinguished himself from the multitude by his range of knowledge and courage. In the course of the war, in which he lost the fingers of his left hand, he commanded the artillery, and was so skillful at directing the artillerymen that by the end of the war the French themselves were amazed at their readiness and activity. His wife always accompanied him in the field and insisted upon sharing the fortunes of war with him. After it was over, it is reported that, upon taking his leave of the other officers, he said laughingly to one of them (who had also been a bookdealer), 'Now we can return home and reopen our shops'—so little influence had the well-deserved distinctions had toward rendering him haughty. He is now Secretary of War, lives in New York with his wife, and those who happen to know him are received in their home with complete cordiality.

"He is a man of about 50 years of age, of fine stature, but corpulent, with pleasant manners and a face more noble than his humble origins."

Charles Lee: "A native of Virginia, he possessed all the qualities opposite to those of Knox. Born of good family, proud of his origin, and full of *amour-propre,* he presumed to dispute with Washington the supreme command of the army. Irreligious and malignant, he dared place in sacrilegious scorn the name of the Savior of the World on one of his trusty dogs. Overbearing with his inferiors, satirical with his equals, he made himself hated by everybody, loved by no one, and feared by a certain few who, by their adulation, courted him and called themselves his friends. When, however, the hoped for command did not materialize and Washington won out over all his plans to deprive him of his charge, he withdrew to Virginia, where, abandoned by his associates, he died in a few months. Those who knew him do not deny his great talent, but this was combined with such bizzarre behavior and such a wicked heart that it might have done great harm to the Republic had the general command of the army fallen into his hands."

Benjamin Lincoln: ". . . From peaceful country life he was called once more to command the troops gathered in the internal regions of Massachusetts by order of the state to repress the incipient rebellion; and, in fact, his prudence in avoiding bloodshed and his firmness when the means of conciliation proved useless succeeded quickly in putting down the rebellion that had broken out and demonstrated that it would have been difficult to choose a better man for this task.

"General Lincoln is already a man of advanced age, but of sturdy physique, simple in his dress, but of a good and cordial character."

John [Richard] Montgomery: ". . . His death was greatly mourned in America, and Congress ordered that a marble funeral monument with an inscription be made for him in France, to be placed at the portal of St. Paul's Church in New York.

"His widow, of the respectable Livingston family, lives in New York, much esteemed both for her own endowments and those of her late husband."

[Israel] Putnam: ". . . After peace was established, he withdrew to live on a property of his near Dover on the Piscataqua River in New Hampshire until he was governor of that state in 1786. Inclined to the profession of arms and an outright fanatic owing to a military fixation, instead of thanking the state for having conferred on him the governor's office, he offered greater thanks for having been elected commander of the militia. (It should be noted that this charge is always connected to that of governor and is not the most important, since there are no troops to command.) Constantly imbued with his martial spirit, he drew up new regulations for the militia, traveled over the state in order to review them, and attended their exercises. However, who would ever have said that these ideas, which distracted the farmers from their work, were to be advantageous to that republic in peacetime? And that precisely a military governor would be necessary in those circumstances? And yet this is exactly the way it turned out, because, after the contagion of the rebellion arisen in Massachusetts spread to adjacent New Hampshire, the dissidents gathered, ran to surround the city hall in the town of Exeter, and might perhaps have done the same damage if the leaders of the rebellion had not been quickly arrested by a military stratagem of the governor. . . .

"In sum, although he is somewhat bizzarre in his military ideas, no one can deny that he has talents sufficient for filling the highest offices of the Republic."

[Joseph] Warren: ". . . For his heroic defense and his honorable death he received from Congress the title of general; and a funeral monument with an inscription was decreed for him."

Castiglioni closes his biographical appendix with briefer mentions of other notable Americans, cast into the following categories:

Philosophers and Mathematicians

David Rittenhouse, Benjamin Rush, Samuel Willard, Samuel Williams, James Bowdoin.

Historians and Writers

Jeremy Belknap, Thomas Paine, Francis Hopkinson.

Natural History

The Bartrams, Humphry Marshall, Manasseh Cutler, James Greenway.

Poetry and Fine Arts

Poetry: John Trumbull, Joel Barlow, David Humphreys.

Painting: John Singleton Copley, Benjamin West.

Luigi Castiglioni's

BOTANICAL OBSERVATIONS

Translated by Antonio Pace

Edited by
JOSEPH & NESTA EWAN

Luigi Castiglioni's Place in North American Botany

LUIGI CASTIGLIONI's plant catalogue appended to his *Viaggio* served as promotion literature. His influence on the progress of North American botany was negligible because of his language, place of publication, and his ultraconservative species concept. Noteworthy, however, are his interest and observations on plant relationships between eastern Asia and eastern North America. Jonas P. Halen had mentioned affinities of the floras in his dissertation *Plantae Camschatcenses* (Upsala, 1750) which had been supervised by Linnaeus. These had been topics of conversation among naturalists he visited in the United States. Castiglioni's observations were also influenced by Kaempfer, whose work he often cites.

The first American notice of the *Viaggio,* calling it a "reputable account," was anonymous, by Caleb Cushing in *North American Review* 13 (1821): 108. Although his travels ranged from the Green Mountains of Vermont to Charleston, South Carolina, François Michaux had preceded him in Vermont, Manasseh Cutler, whom he met in Boston, had ascended Mt. Washington in 1784 and had published on New England plants 5 years before Castiglioni. Virginia and Carolina plants had early entered the literature. Although the southeastern United States were poorly known botanically when Castiglioni toured those states, his conservative opinion on what were new species led him to assign plants he encountered to long-recognized Linnaean species. He expressed the opinion on several occasions that needless multiplication of names already burdened the literature. Those few species in his catalogue which Castiglioni indicated with the capital letter "N," signifying *Nobis* or "my own," he believed to be undescribed. These presumed new species, however, have all been reduced to synonyms by later botanists.

Castiglioni's object in adding the plant catalogue to his travel narrative was to present and evaluate the potentials each plant held for its bark, fiber, juices, fruits, or seeds, should the plant be grown and harvested in his native Italy. Characteristic is his account of White oak, *Quercus alba,* that the wood "hard, compact, and of good quality, is used in framing wooden houses, building ships, and a great many other purposes; and although the ships made of this oak are not as durable as those made with northern European oak, they are nevertheless best among the ships built in the provinces of United States of America."

For ready reference he arranged genera, not by a theoretical classification under either the popular Linnaean or the novel scheme of Jussieu, but by pragmatical alphabetical arrangement, as if the book were to be consulted by the entrepreneur in Milan, alert to the expanding economy of his country. As a good commentator, Castiglioni offers methods of growing, harvesting, or utilizing the plant product, first as reported in the historic writings of Charlevoix, Kalm, John Bartram, or Carver, among others, then supplemented by his own considered observations. Included in these observations were his experiences in his Italian garden, resting surely on his having taken back seeds or plantings in the hope of introducing farm or garden subjects.

We know from his narrative that he made at least two dried plant collections during the course of his travels, but lost each when fording swollen rivers, one in

South Carolina. His surviving herbarium in Milan, however, is of highly satisfactory specimens which he had gathered in a medicinal or "physick" garden in Italy. What, then, was lost would have added importantly to our early field records for the territories he visited. In this Milan herbarium are specimens of *Aristolochia pistolochia, Liriodendron,* and *Gleditsia triacanthos,* American species known in Europe long before Castiglioni visited the United States. There are good specimens of *Acer, Morus,* and *Sambucus,* for example, but none of these is a North American species.

Modern equivalent botanical names, and any notes added by us, are enclosed in square brackets, their *only* use in the observations. The full names of authors and the titles of Castiglioni's citations will be found in Castiglioni's References: e.g., Duham. will be found as Duhamel . . . , Pluk. as Plukenet . . . , etc.

Understandably, Castiglioni had difficulty with synonyms in available literature. Except in a few conspicuous cases we have not attempted to check the accuracy of his citations.

The generic entries have been reproduced precisely as in the *Viaggio* except that we have *italicized* only the primary (numbered) phrase names, special observations, and book and journal titles. The punctuation and abbreviations of the generic entries are as found in the *Viaggio,* except that "β" is given as "b."

Observations on the Most Useful Plants in the United States

ACER

1. *A. RUBRUM foliis quinquelobis, subdentatis, subtus glaucis; pedunculis simplicissimis aggregatis.* Lin.

a. foliis subtrilobis.

Acer Virginianum folio subtus incano, flosculis ex viridi rubentibus. Hermann *Parad. Bativ.* tab. 1. pag. 1. Acer Virginianum folio majore subtus argenteo, supra viridi splendente. Duham. *Arb. & Arbust.* n. 6. Catesby Tom. I. tab. 62. Trew. *Plant.select.* tab. 86.

Scarlet-flowering maple in the United States. [*Acer rubrum* L.]

b. foliis quinquelobis.

Acer glaucum. Marshall *Arbust. Amer.* Acer foliis quinquelobis subdentatis, subtus glaucis, floribus pedunculatis simplicissimis. Trew. *Pl. sel.* tab. 85.

White maple, Silver-leaved maple, Rock maple in the United States. [*Acer saccharinum* L.]

2. *A. SACCHARINUM foliis quinque-partito-palmatis, acuminato-dentatis, subtus pubescentibus.* Lin.

Acer *Duham.* n. 5. Acer foliis acutioribus, utrinque pallide virentibus, & lanatis, angulis lateralibus fere obsoletis.* Gronov. *Fl. Virginica* pag. 161.

Sugar Maple, Sugar tree in the United States. *Erable à sucre* in Canada. [*Acer saccharum* Marsh.]

*The figure of the leaf is correct, but Plukenet's synonym cited there belongs to type b. of the Red Maple Spec. 1.

3. *A. PENSILVANICUM foliis trilobis, acuminatis, serrulatis; floribus racemosis.* Lin.
Acer foliis quinquelobis, inaequaliter serrulatis; florum racemo composito erecto, pedicellis subdivisis. Du Roi, n. 6; Duham., n. 11, tab. 13, fig. 11.

Variat capsulis rufescentibus.

Dwarf mountain maple, Moosewood in the United States. [*Acer pensylvanicum* L.]

4. *A. STRIATUM foliis sub-quinquelobis, duplicato-serratis, acutis; floribus spicatis* N[obis].
Acer striatum Du Roi. Acer cortice striato, foliis basi ellyptica, apice trilobo, racemo pendulo simplici. Lauth, *Diss. de Acere,* n. 10. Acer Canadense. Marshall.

Striped maple, Moosewood, Deerwood in the United States. [*Acer spicatum* L.]

5. *A. NEGUNDO foliis compositis; floribus racemosis.* Lin. Acer foliis compositis, floribus racemosis Gronov. *Virg.* pag. 161. Duham. n. 10, fig. 10.

Ash-leaved maple in the United States. [*Acer negundo* L.]

Red maple (Spec. 1), like our opulus,* varies a great deal in the leaves and blossoms, so that the varieties were multiplied by writers, as many as four being counted by Mr. Lauth in his dissertation on maples.†

These varieties depend mainly upon whether or not the blossoms are provided with imbricated scales,‡ or whether they are masculine or hermaphroditic. But since, after observing European maples, I became convinced that maple blossoms called male ought rather to be called *sterile* blossoms because of an accidental lack of pistil and ovule§ (which occurs perhaps also in other plants of the Linnaean class *Polygamia*), I abandoned these distinctions. Hence the species I observed are reduced to only two, namely, the scarlet-flowered maple (Spec. a) and the so-called White or Rock maple (Spec. b). The first of these grows sometimes to the height of 70 English feet; its leaves are divided sometimes into three, sometimes five lobes, and it has blossoms of a very pretty scarlet color. The second reaches a height of about 50 feet, its leaves are larger, divided into five lobes, green above and silver-colored underneath, and it has blossoms of deep red, followed by the fruit, which fall from the tree in the very early summer. The first likes clayish soil, and the second is very abundant in swamps and flooded areas; but it is also found in stony elevations, whence it got the name of Rock maple. When the leaves begin to dry in the fall, both of them make a beautiful spectacle in the woods from the red color they take on, and in the spring, if one makes a hole in the trunk, a juice comes out from which sugar is derived. This sugar, however, is not as good nor as esteemed as that obtained from the Sugar maple = (Spec. 2). There grows upon these trees a kind of agaric [Polypore], or fungus [*Fomes fomentarium*], which, when dried in the sun, forms excellent tinder that both the Canadians and the Indians use to light their pipes. The wood of the Red maple is used

**Acer campestre* Lin.

†Lauth, *Dissertatio de Acere* (Argentorati, 1781).

‡Imbricated, i.e., overlapping like roof tiles.

§Scopoli, too (*Flora carniolica,* 2nd ed.), found in the *Opulus* (*Acer campestre* Lin.) flowers, now hermaphroditic, now completely or partly male, some of which had a rudimentary ovule.

to make dishes, combs for carding flax, legs for chairs and beds, and other kinds of furniture. This wood is sometimes grained, especially in those protuberances that form on the trunk, of which I was shown one at Cataraqui on Lake Ontario two feet in diameter. The grained wood is called Curled maple, and it is highly prized by inlayers, who use it the same way protuberances of [*A. opalus* Mill.] are used in our country. With the bark both wool and linen can be stained dark blue by boiling in water and adding a portion of copperas [ferrous sulphate]; and with the same bark is made also an ink of good quality.* This tree is very slow in growing and very hard to multiply from seed, but it can be propagated easily by layering and it can be grafted onto our native maple.†

Sugar maple (Spec. 2) grows in elevated locations to the height of 60 to 70 feet by a diameter of 2 or 3 feet, and its leaves are very similar to those of the maple called *platanoides* by Linnaeus. It differs from the Red maple principally in having leaves that are less whitish underneath and blossoms of a grass-green color. From the sap proper‡ of this tree is obtained in North America a reddish sugar not much different from cane sugar, and perhaps heartier and more healthful. To extract the sap incisions are made in the trunk, ordinarily of an oval shape and in such a way that the greater diameter is almost horizontal. At one of its extremities, which must be lower than the other so that the fluid can collect, a knife or a piece of wood is thrust along which it runs, dropping into a receptacle placed below. The cut must penetrate the wood at least to the depth of three inches, since the liquid is obtained from this and not from the bark. The incisions are made in the fall after the trees have dropped their leaves, and they can continue until the middle of May when the blossoms begin to appear, although the cuts do not yield sap until the freezes are over. Mr. Duhamel, speaking on the basis of information obtained by Mr. [? Jean-François] Gaulthier [1708–56], adds that, although it may have frozen over night, the liquid will come out the following day if the warmth of the sun produces a thaw. Hence a cut made on the south side gives more sap, especially if the plant is protected against cold winds and well exposed to the sun. Hence it follows that the most abundant yield is from the middle of March to the middle of May. Cuts located on the lower part of the tree give a larger quantity of sap, and if only one a year is made, the plant does not suffer perceptibly. Old trees yield less sap, but it produces more sugar. It is noteworthy, too, that the liquid always emerges from the upper lip of the cut.

It is drunk just as it comes from the tree, and it is healthful and tasty, especially in the spring, although later, that is, in May, it often has a disagreeable grassy taste that the Canadians call "gout de sève," and it is then said to be as purgative as manna.§ With this liquid is made a sweet and refreshing syrup that is mixed with

[*Kalm was a prime source for Castiglioni. Much of this is taken from *Travels* (London, 1772) 1: 131–32.]

†*Acer pseudoplatanus* Lin.

‡In plants two humors are found: lymph and sap proper. Lymph is clear and tasteless, and sap proper is often colored, tasty, and fragrant. Such are Manna, gums, and resins. See Duhamel, *Physique des arbres,* Tom. I.

§See "Mémoire sur les érables de M. Fougeroux de Bounderoy," in *Mémoires de la Société d'Agriculture de Paris* (1787, Trim. de printemps).

water, but it quickly turns acid and it cannot be kept for long. In fact, this same liquid exposed in a barrel to the heat of the sun changes into a very good vinegar. The yearly sugar harvest in Canada amounts to between 12,000 and 15,000 pounds, and the sugar is made in the following manner. After a sufficient quantity of liquid (for example, 200 pints) has been collected with due precautions, it is poured into vats that are set to boil, the froth being removed periodically. When it begins to thicken, the vats are taken from the flames and set on coals, and the liquid is stirred continuously to keep it from scorching and to hasten the evaporation. When it has reached the consistency of a thick syrup that changes to sugar upon cooling on a spoon, it is poured into molds. These are of earthenware, or of birch or alder bark, and shaped into cones or little boxes. When it is thoroughly cooled, it is taken out of the molds. It has a reddish color and an excellent flavor if it has not been cooked excessively, in which case it takes on the taste of toasted sugar. Some refine it with egg white, and others add 2 or 3 pounds of flour for every 10 of cooked syrup, thus making it lighter in color. For this reason it is preferred by those who do not recognize the adulteration.

In addition to the method indicated above for making sugar from this species of maple, there is another used in America that is somewhat different. I shall include it here, along with other information on how to extract molasses from the same sugar, how to make from it beer, wine, and vinegar, according to the periodical printed in Philadelphia with the title *American Museum* [4 (1788): 349–50, by "Agricola"]. To produce sugar make an incision in many trees simultaneously in the months of February and March and collect the sap that comes out in earthenware or wooden containers. Pour off the liquid and boil in a vat, which must be placed directly over the fire so that the flame does not come at it from the sides. Skim the liquid as it boils, and after it is reduced to a thick syrup let it cool, pour it off again into another container letting it set for two or three days, in which time it will become ready for the process of reduction to granular form. In order to accomplish this, the vat is half-filled with syrup and brought to a boil, putting in it a little piece of butter or fat the size of a nut to keep it from overflowing as it boils. One can easily tell when it has boiled enough to be granulated by cooling a small portion of it. Then the syrup must be put in cloth bags so that the more liquid part can run off, leaving behind the sugar already reduced to a paste. This sugar, refined by the method used for that produced from cane, can become fully as white and tasty.

Molasses can be obtained in three ways: (1) from the thick syrup obtained from the first boiling after it has been poured off and prepared for the second boiling; (2) by dissolving the dry sugar in water; (3) from the last liquid that comes out of the trees (which can never be reduced to granular form), thickened by means of evaporation. In order to make beer, boil a quart of maple molasses in four gallons of water. After the liquid has been brought down to 30° Réaumur, add as much yeast as necessary to make it ferment. One can also put in malt or an appropriate amount of bran. If to this is added a spoonful of spruce pitch, the liquid will become very pleasant and healthful. From it is made a kind of wine by boiling four or five gallons of sap and one of water, increasing the water in proportion to the density of the sap, and adding yeast. After everything has fermented completely, it is placed in a cool spot in a tightly closed container, and, so they say, after it has been kept for two or three years, it becomes an excellent wine in every respect equal to delicate European wines. This wine can be made more fragrant by mixing in small pieces scraped from magnolia root,* or from other aromatic substances. The same sap exposed to the open air and sun will become vinegar in a short time.†

Maple sugar is used for the same purposes as cane sugar; with it are made sweetmeats; it is prescribed for colds and chest afflictions, and in the internal regions of North America it is commonly used with tea. However, since the sugar produced from sap collected in May melts easily on humid days, the Canadians usually make Venus's-hair syrup [oil of capillaire, *Adiantum capillus-veneris* L.] out of it. Both the Canadians and the Indians mix this sugar with grain or corn flour; they put up a supply for long trips, and this mixture, called 'Quitsera' by the Indians, furnishes good nutrition. They also eat the sugar on bread, so that in the spring every family stores away a good harvest of it for their own use. During the war, when it was hard to get cane sugar, maple sugar was used instead. Some farmers harvest a large quantity of it every year, and sometimes a single individual has obtained up to 300 English pounds of sugar from his trees.

The Pennsylvanian maple (Spec. 3), although very common in the northern regions of Massachusetts, is not found at all along the sea coasts south of New Hampshire, although it grows on the mountains of Pennsylvania, whence its name. The Brunswick and Saint George woods are full of them. They occur in two varieties, one with red seeds and the other with white seeds. This shrub forms clumps from 8 to 10 feet high, its leaves divided into three lobes‡ simply dentate.§ The blossoms are small and of a grass-green color, and the seeds are likewise small, often joined together, and hanging in the form of clusters. In Massachusetts it is called Moosewood because moose, and likewise deer, are very fond of its leaves. It is difficult to propagate from seeds, but easy by layering, and although it is very common in America, it is not much known in the gardens of Europe. It is true, however, that it has no practical use, nor any particular beauty of blossom or leaf.

Striped maple (Spec. 4) is no less common than the preceding one in the woods of northern regions, growing, however, to a greater height and having leaves somewhat similar to it, but much larger, more deeply segmented, doubly dentate and sharp at the point, with blossoms and larger seeds not joined together in clumps but each attached separately to a common peduncle.|| Another easier distinction is the bark, striped white and green in young branches and white and dark in adult ones. This streaking,

**Magnolia glauca* Lin.

†*American Museum,* Tom. 4, p. 349.

‡"Lobe" is the term for each segment of a leaf–for example, leaves with three lobes, four lobes, etc.

§"Dentate" is the term for the edges of a leaf whose segments are irregular and obtuse. If they are round, they are called "scalloped" (*crenatum*), if sharp and turned toward the point, *serratum,* i.e., saw-toothed.

||It is not possible to distinguish clearly between the different parts of plants exclusively with words already adopted in the Italian language. It is necessary, therefore, to invent new ones, which I thought best to translate as literally as possible from the Latin terms of Linnaeus. So, for example, I have taken in order to denote the *petiolus,* that is, the stem of leaves, the name "picciuolo," distinguishing it from the stem of flowers and fruit, to which I have given the name "peduncolo," deriving it from *pedunculus,* the name adopted by Linnaeus. And "piedicello" (*pedicellus*) means

which depends upon the splitting of the epidermis, is not constant in all individuals of this species, since sometimes variations may be seen even in shoots that come from the same root. It is also called Moosewood or Deerwood, and it is frequently confused with the preceding, although, as I have already said, it differs from it in many essential respects. The bark from young branches is very resistant, and even when it is removed from the tree in bad season it is always tough, whence the Indians, according to Carver,* make from it cords as strong and durable as those of hemp. Its wood, white in color and tough-grained, is comparable to that of the more used maples, but since it does not grow to a large size, it cannot serve for all purposes. Because its leaves are very large and it ladens itself heavily with seeds, it is necessary to support its branches, which are easily shattered by the wind.

It can be propagated from seeds by placing them in good soil in October and protecting the young plants from the sun. It doesn't sprout so easily when it is sown in the spring since the seeds, by drying out in the winter, lose the capacity to sprout. It can also be propagated by layering and from shoots, and it can be grafted onto the common maple. The graft, however, does not turn out too well, since the subject, a tree with a tall trunk, always swells excessively, and the streaking of the bark is interrupted. For that reason if one wishes to graft he should make the graft as close as possible to the earth in order to conceal its defect, and also so that the striped maple may produce its own roots for nourishing itself. Even before my voyage to America I got from London two specimens of this maple which produced many blossoms for me that same year. The first ones, which came out of the ends of the branches, were all hermaphroditic and perfect. Subsequently, after seed-set was past, there came out below many spikes of blossoms quite like the preceding ones except that they lacked pistils. This fact, which I saw repeated in the years following, seems to confirm my opinion that these latter blossoms are imperfect and that therefore they should be called sterile blossoms, and not, indeed, male, as Linnaeus calls them. [Castiglioni here was confronted with varying floral combinations in *Acer* where bisexual or perfect flowers, and unisexual or imperfect flowers, may be borne on the same or separate individuals (i.e., a monoecious or dioecious condition) or combinations thereof (i.e., a polygamodioecious condition).]

The maple called *Negundo* (Spec. 5) is very easily distinguished from every other of this genus because it has compound leaves† and male blossoms separate from the female on two different trees, whence Mr. Adanson‡ made of it a new genus under the name of *Rulac.* This is the tallest of all the maples, reaching a height of 50 feet in moist and shaded terrains. Its leaves, now by threes, now by fives, resemble those of the ash, and for this reason the Americans gave it the name of Ash-leaved maple.

---

the partial stem of flowers joined in clusters. Many of these names I owe to the precise translation of the *Elementi di Botanica* by the learned Don Casimiro Ortega, chief botanist of His Catholic Majesty, felicitously accomplished by Dr. Gua[l]teri, Royal Professor of Botany in Parma [Giambattista Gualteri (1743–1793)].

*Carver, *Travels.*

†That is, many little leaves joined together on a common petiole, like those, for example, of the rose.

‡*Familles des plantes.*

The male flowers are supported by long peduncles and they have five and more stamens*; and the female ones, almost completely devoid of style, show only two stigmas† located on the ovary. The flowers hang in long clusters, and the latter are followed by winged seeds more curved than those of other maples. The *Negundo* is not found in the northern states, but it is very common in Virginia and even in Pennsylvania. If one makes incisions in this tree in the spring, a sweet and sugary liquid comes out similar to that of Species 2, and, according to what some writers say, the inhabitants of Virginia use it. In fact, Father Charlevoix says in his history of America that sugar is produced from a liquid drawn from the ash, which Mr. Kalm correctly surmises must be the *Negundo.* I myself saw the liquid flowing abundantly from the cut branches of one of these trees, but I didn't understand from the inhabitants that sugar is extracted from it. Because of its beautiful leaves which last very late, it should be propagated in gardens and groves, and since it is quite large and of very good wood, it deserves our attention as a forest tree. It has not been successfully grafted onto other maples, but it can be propagated by layering and from branches that rarely die; and in only three years it rises to a height of six or seven feet. It is not difficult even to reproduce it from seeds, inasmuch as, if one obtains them fresh from America in the fall, and puts them in the ground as soon as they arrive, they sprout very readily, as was my experience in the spring of 1789.

All the maples mentioned here hold up well in our winters in Lombardy; and the Red, the Sugar, and the Negundo, more than the others, should be valuable to us because of the use that can be made of them.

ACORUS

A. CALAMUS Lin.

Acorus verus, sive Calamus aromaticus officinarum. Bauh. *Pinax,* pag. 34.

Sweet flag and Spicewort in the United States. [*Acorus calamus* L.]

Aromatic Calamus is a plant too well known in our spice shops to merit a detailed description, and both in Europe and in America grows in swamps. For that reason I would have refrained from mentioning it if in the United States it were used not only in medicine but in the household. It abounds in the marshes near Ipswich in Massachusetts and flourishes in June, called by the inhabitants there Sweet flag or Spicewort.‡ Its roots, grafted and mixed with water, are given in America to children for stomach and belly pains, and its leaves are woven into chair seats as is done with reeds and straw in our country.

*Italian botanists used to call them "*sommitadi*" and "*stamigne.*" However, I believe more appropriate the term "*stame,*" which is an Italian word and closer to the Latin.

†Stigma: the end of the pistil, which often looks like a wound and is supported by the style.

‡In our country it is commonly called *Erba cannella* [Cinnamon grass] because of the odor of its leaves.

ACTAEA

A. RACEMOSA racemis longissimis; fructibus siccis. Lin. Christophorianae facie herba spicata. Pluken. *Amalth.* tab. 383 fig. 3.

Richweed and Black snakeroot in the United States. [*Actaea racemosa* L.]

This plant is called Richweed and also Black snakeroot, and is a kind of Christophoriana quite common in Virginia and in other parts of North America. It has a very sharp taste and is used particularly for scirrhous tumors. Mr. [Cadwallader] Colden, in his description of the plants of New York, relates that the decoction of this root, taken by mistake instead of that of the *Aralia* called *racemosa* for an attack of listlessness, produced in the patient an acute crisis accompanied by cold sweat, after which he regained his health. That agrees well with what Linnaeus says in his *Materia Medica*—that this herb, like many of the *Umbelliferae,* is suspect and almost poisonous, so that it must be used with the greatest precaution.

ADIANTUM

A. PEDATUM frondibus pedatis; foliolis pinnatis; pinnis antice gibbis, incisis, fructificantibus. Lin.
Adiantum fruticosum Americanum, summis ramulis reflexis, & in orbem expansis. Pluk. *Almag.* tab. 124, fig. 2. Adiantum Americanum Cornuti *Pl. Canad.* pag. 7 tab. 6.

Maidenhair in the United States, *Capillaire* in Canada. [*Adiantum pedatum* L.]

The American Venus'-hair grows in the woods everywhere between Montreal and Cataraqui. The stem rises straight up without any leaves and at the top it divides into many little branches which, bent into a round shape, are furnished with obtuse little leaves notched around the edge. The Indians made much use of its decoction for the cough, and from them the Canadians learned to use it under the same circumstances. In the more internal regions, near the St. Lawrence River, it often replaces tea, and I tried it myself, finding it of a very delicate flavor. Under the French government a large quantity of this Venus'-hair used to be shipped every year to Europe, since it was considered better than ours.

AESCULUS

1. *AE. PAVIA floribus sub-octandris, spicis erectis; capsulis inermibus.* N[obis]. Pavia Duham. *Arb. & Arbust.* pag. 98. Trew *Pl. Selec.* tab. 15.

Deer's-eye, Buckeye, Poison root, and Scarlet-flowering horse-chestnut in the United States. [*Aesculus pavia* L.]

2. *AE. LUTEA floribus octandris, spicis pendulis; capsulis inermibus.* N[obis]* [See Li, 2].

*The Linnaean phrase [*nomen specificum legitimum,* the specific differential character, *Species plantarum,* 344] regarding the Indian chestnut should be changed as follows: *Aesculus (Hippocastanum) floribus heptandris, spicis erectis, capsulis spinosis.*

Hippocastanum lactescens gemmis majoribus; ligno foetido Encyclop. Lausanne Art. Marronier.

New River Horse-chestnut and Yellow-flowered horse-chestnut in the United States. [*A. octandra* Marsh.]

The *Pavia* or Horse-chestnut with red flowers (Spec. 1) grows only to a height of 12 or 15 feet. It leaves resemble those of the Indian chestnut, and the flowers, arranged in spikes, have a very beautiful red color. These are quite different in the form of the petal* from those of the Indian chestnut, and especially because the number of stamens is not constant, there being sometimes seven sometimes eight of them; so that some people have made a separate genus of it. The flower is followed by a smooth dark-colored capsule shaped like a pear and divided internally into four or five little cells containing as many seeds covered with a tough reddish skin resembling chestnuts. The fact is, however, that invariably some of the seeds abort, and generally only one seed turns out perfect. The name Poison-root was given to this shrub because of the notion held in America that its root is poisonous, a notion that I found based on no fact and upheld only by popular hearsay. I have heard, on the other hand, that this root is saponaceous and is used to wash linen, which to me seems all the more likely because, as I observed, when the seeds are left for a long time in water, they make it soft and viscous.† It can be ornamental because of the beauty of its scarlet blossoms, but the wood is of no use. It is capable of being propagated from seeds provided they do not have far to travel, in which case they rarely succeed. Layerings have to be carried out in the spring, and by the following fall they will already have enough roots to be transplanted. It may be grafted onto the Indian chestnut, but subsequently the graft dies or becomes deformed on account of the difference in stature between the two plants. Hence this method should not be used except to obtain seeds, from which may be grown Pavias from the root. Linnaeus, and even Mr. Reichard,‡ place the *Saamóuna* [*arbor*] of Piso [p. 175], as a synonym of *Pavia,* fooled by the fact that both have quinate leaves, while *Saamóuna* is an entirely different tree, namely, *Bombax pentandrum* of Linnaeus himself, called the Silk cotton-tree by the English and Fromager by the French.

The Yellow-flowered Horse-chestnut (Spec. 2), although in many respects similar to the one just described, must be considered as a different species. In fact, it grows to a greater height, has larger seeds quite like those of the Indian chestnut, spikes not upright but pendent, and blossoms almost always provided with eight stamens. For that reason it was called *Aesculus octandra* by Mr. Marshall, a name that I felt obliged to change, because the number of eight stamens is not absolutely certain, and it is also common to *pavia.* This species is found in abundance in the western parts of Georgia near the city of Augusta where *pavia* is not seen, which, on the other hand, is very common in the regions near the sea. Its root is likewise considered poisonous, and it is saponaceous; and both the flowers and the wood have a disgusting,

*"Petal" is the word for the segment of a flower.

†Scopoli, in his *Flora Carniolica,* says that the fruit of the common Indian chestnut shelled and ground serves like soap for washing linen.

‡*Systema Plantarum,* Tom. II, p. 137.

though not very strong, odor. It can be propagated like the *Pavia,* and can be more successfully grafted onto the Indian chestnut, on which it grows very vigorously, being a tree of medium height.

ANCHUSA

A. VIRGINICA floribus sparsis; caule glabro. Lin.
Anchusa minor lutea Virginiana, Pucoon indigenis dicta, qua se pingunt Americani. Plukenet. *Almag.* 30. Lithospermum Virginianum flore luteo duplici ampliori. *Morison Hist.* 3, pag. 447 tab. 28 fig. 4.

The Pucoon of the Indians of Virginia. [*Lithospermum canescens* (Michx.) Lehm.]

The *Anchusa* of Virginia is an herb resembling the *Anchusa officinalis* of Linnaeus, called bugloss in spice shops. Its leaves, unevenly distributed, are oblong, narrow, obtuse at the ends, and hairy. The flowers, which come out of the axils of the leaves, are tubulous and yellow in color. From the root of this herb the Indians extract a red dye which they use to paint their faces and bodies. The *Lithospermum Virginianum* described by Morison* is believed by Gronovius and Reichard† to be a simple variety of this species of *Anchusa,* the double flowers of which Morison speaks depending merely on the greater fertility of the soil in which it grows.

ANDROMEDA

1. *A. ARBOREA racemis secundis, nudis; corollis rotundo-ovatis.* Lin.
Frutex foliis acuminatis, floribus spicatis, uno versu dispositis Catesby *Carol.* tome I tab. 71; Seligmann tome 2, pag. 42.

Sorrel-tree in Virginia; Pepper-bush in Massachusetts. [*Oxydendrum arboreum* (L.) DC.]

2. *A. NITIDA pedunculis aggregatis; foliis alternis, ovatis, integerrimis, sempervirentibus* N[obis].
Andromeda nitida Marshall. Arbust. Amer.

Evergreen shining-leaved andromeda and Caroline red-bud in the United States. [Fetterbush, see Harper, ed. Bartram's *Travels,* 438. *Lyonia lucida* (Lam.) K. Koch].

Obs.: *Affinis Andromedae marianae.*

Andromeda arborea (Spec. 1) is the largest of the species group, although as its name indicates it does not ordinarily exceed 10 or 15 feet in height. It is very abundant in the woods of Massachusetts near Falmouth and Brunswick. At the ends of

*Morison, *Hist. Plant.,* Tome II, p. 447, tab. 28 fig. 4 [Tome III, not II].
†*Systema Plantarum,* Tome I, p. 389.

its branches it produces pretty spikes of tiny pitcher-shaped blossoms like those of the strawberry tree.* The wood is very durable, and in Massachusetts is considered the best to which to attach fishing hooks. Furthermore, the decoction from its leaves is used to reduce the heat of fever.

Andromeda nitida (Spec. 2) is one of the most beautiful shrubs to look upon when it is in bloom. It has leaves that are evergreen, lanceolate,† alternate,‡ and glossy; and the blossoms, which emerge from the lower part of the branches in dense clusters, acquire, when they open, a pretty red color. They also emanate a very pleasant odor and are much frequented by bees, which draw from them honey in abundance.

I might have added many other species of *Andromeda* to these two, like *calyculata, paniculata, racemosa, mariana,* and *plumata* of Marshall, all of which are widespread in the United States, but since they have neither been recognized yet as useful nor as having any particular beauty, I have omitted them—all the more because these plants are very difficult to propagate and almost never come up from seed.

ANNONA

A. TRILOBA foliis lanceolatis; fructibus trifidis. Lin.

Annona fructu lutescente levi scrotum arietis referente. Catesby *Carolin.* tome 2, tab. 85; Trew *Pl. Select.* tab. 5.

Papaw-tree and Custard-apple in the United States. [*Asimina triloba* (L.) Duval]

Of all the species of *Annona,* the papaw is the only one that can do well in our climate, since it is native to Pennsylvania and grows well in France and some parts of England, to which it has been taken. It likes a rich, moist, shady terrain protected from the cold winds, and it can easily be obtained from seed, which generally sprout the second year. Care must be taken to put the plants inside in wintertime the first three years. It is a small tree 12 to 20 feet tall with large oval leaves arranged alternately on the branches which, contrary to the other annonas, do not last through the winter. The flowers are of a dark color and are composed of six petals, three of which look shorter than the others. The fruit are often two, and even three, joined together in the form of a cucumber, so that they resemble the scrotum of a ram. When they ripen they are easily detached from the peduncle. They are soft, of a yellow color, and contain about 12 reddish kernels. The flowers emerge with the leaves in April, and the tree exudes a strong and disgusting smell so perceptible even in the fruit that only Negroes and Indians are willing to eat it. It is said nevertheless that they find the flesh of this fruit healthful and tasty, even though the skin that covers it contains an extremely strong acid.

**Arbutus Unedo* Lin.

†Lanceolate: spear-like, that is, oval with pointed ends.

‡Alternate: that is, arranged alternately on the branches.

APOCYNUM

1. *A CANNABINUM caule erectiusculo herbaceo; foliis oblongis; paniculis terminalibus.* Lin.
Apocynum foliis ovatis acutis, subtus tomentosis. Gronov. Fl. Virg.
Indian hemp in the United States. [*Apocynum cannabinum* L.]

2. *A. ANDROSAEMIFOLIUM caule erectiusculo herbaceo; foliis ovatis utrinque glabris; cymis terminalibus.* Lin.
Apocynum canadense foliis androsaemi majoris. Morison *Hist. Plant.* Tome III, pag. 609 tab. 3 fig. 16.
Dog's bane, Umbrella-weed in the United States. [*A. androsaemifolium* L.]

The *Apocynum* (Spec. 1), called "Indian hemp" in America, was by them much used, who got from it strands for making rope and cloth. The first settlers in New Jersey, also, according to what Kalm states, used to use this species of *Apocynum* for making sacks and nets. It forms a very high shrub with ovate, sharp-pointed leaves woolly underneath, and producing at the ends of the branches flowerlets of an herbaceous color and very long, but slender, siliques. It is found in the United States from Virginia to Canada.

The *Apocynum* with androsaeme leaves (Spec. 2), also called Flycatcher plant, is confused by some not versed in natural history with the *Dionaea muscipula* of Linnaeus merely because of its property of catching flies that land on it, although this takes place in quite a different manner.* The woods near Falmouth are all full of these handsome shrubs, which produce white flowers streaked with red that emit a most pleasing fragrance. Flies and ants, coming to rest on these blossoms to suck out their honey, get their legs so tangled up in certain triangular fissures situated between one [and] another of the stamens that they cannot pull them out. This same property is common also to other plants of this family, as, for example, the *Asclepias Syriaca,* already known in our gardens under the name of "Silk grass."

Both these apocynums are easily propagated from seed, they send out copious shoots from the base; and the second, especially, in fertile and moist soil, will produce a very beautiful effect in gardens.

ARALIA

1. *A. SPINOSA arborescens, caule, foliolisque aculeatis.* Lin. Angelica arborescens spinosa, seu arbor Indica fraxini folio cortice spinoso, Commelin. *Hort. Medic. Amstel.* Tome I, pag. 89 tab. 47. Aralia. Duham. *Arb. & Arbust.*
Shot-bush and Pigeon-weed in Massachusetts and New Hampshire, Greenbriar, Prickly-ash, Tooth-ash-[ache]-tree in Virginia and New York. [*Aralia spinosa* L.]

*See the entry on the *Dionaea.*

2. *A. NUDICAULIS caule sub-nudo; foliis binis ternatis.* Lin. Christophoriana Virginiana, Zarzae radicibus furculosis, and fungosis Pluk. *Almag.* tab. 238, fig. 5.

Sarsaparilla in New Hampshire. [*A. nudicaulis* L.]

3. *A. RACEMOSA caule folioso herbaceo, levi.* Lin.
Panaces carpimon, seu racemosa Canadensis. Corn. *Canad.* pag. 74 tab. 75.

Spikenard in the United States. [*A. racemosa* L.]

Aralia spinosa (Spec. 1) is a small tree 8 to 10 feet in height that grows in America near brooks. Its trunk, as well as the branches, and the petioles of the leaves, are surrounded by various crowns of short thorns. It has compound leaves, likewise thorny, the flowers are gathered in clumps of a greenish and not very pretty white; and the berries, when they are ripe, take on a deep red color. This plant sends out a strong odor and has a stimulating taste, hence its decoction was used among the Indians to treat rheumatic pains and also dropsy.* It sprouts readily from seed in the second year, but the young plants at first will have to be kept in the shade, getting them used to the sun a little at a time. It can also be propagated from the shoots that it puts out abundantly from the base, provided, however, that they have some root.

The *Aralia* (Spec. 2) called sarsaparilla is a small herb quite common in the woods of New Hampshire and Massachusetts. Its root winds around a great deal, and it produces a bare stem, that is, without leaves, which divides into three peduncles supporting as many clusters of flowers. Another stem is subdivided into two or three petiolules with ternate or quinate leaflets, with a similar terminal division. The blossoms are white and small, and the berries are red [no, black]. The name sarsaparilla, belonging really to a species of *Smilax,* was improperly given in the United States to this *Aralia* perhaps because of the similarity of the roots and a like effect in treating illnesses. In fact, the root is covered with a pulpy bark with a balsamic odor and is said to be even more effective than true sarsaparilla. The Indians apply the moistened and softened bark to wounds, and they also extract from it a hearty drink that they use mainly during long trips. It is propagated by seed.

Aralia racemosa (Spec. 3) is a perennial herb whose branches spread horizontally and which produces laterally clusters of berries that ripen in the month of September and which are sweet and wholesome. The root is balsamic and was used by the Indians to cure not too far-advanced ulcers by cooking it and adding water from time to time until it was reduced to a mucilaginous substance that they applied to the affected part. It is said, too, that, if you swallow the juice as you chew it, it is good for kidney pains and stomach disorders. This root is tuberous,† and possesses a milky, pleasant-smelling juice.‡

*Colden, *Plantae Coldeng[h]amiae,* p. 108. [This was published by Linnaeus with whom Colden corresponded, and to whom he sent specimens, many lost to pirates].
†That is, with nodules, like truffles (*Tubera*).
‡See [Linnaeus,] *Amoenit. Acad.* tom. 4. p. 513.

ARECA

A. OLERACEA foliolis integerrimis. Lin.
Palma nobilis, sive regalis Jamaicensis, & Barbadensis, Ray. *Hist.* p. 1361.
Palmetto Royal in the Carolinas, Cabbage-tree in Jamaica, *Palmiste-franc* and *Chou-palmier* in the French Antilles. [*Sabal palmetto* (Walt.) Lodd.]

This palm is not found in the continental United States, but it is very common in the islands near Charleston in South Carolina and in Savannah, Georgia, especially in places flooded by the sea. It grows to a great height, and its leaves, as with the other palms, come directly out of the trunk, are four to five feet long, palmate, and folded like a fan at the tip. The trunk produces a great quantity of blossoms, which are followed by fleshy fruit the size of a cherry with a single seed. Perhaps this handsome palm, which is very useful, could be propagated in warm and maritime regions of Italy. The central shoot formed by the tender curled leaves resembles in its shape and taste the cole called *Cappuccio,** is similarly eaten in various ways, and, when seasoned with vinegar and pepper, has an excellent taste. Hence the name Cabbage-tree and *Chou-palmier* by which the English and the French of the Antilles call it. The trunk of this palm, although spongy and light, lasts better than any other wood in places almost continuously flooded by the sea, and in Charleston it is even preerred for making wharfs along the rivers. Another curious property of these trunks was discovered during the war when the Americans were defending Fort Moultrie on Sullivan Island, whose fortifications were made of palmetto. The cannon balls sank into its soft substance and, instead of wrecking the fortifications, make them more solid by becoming embedded in them.

ARISTOLOCHIA

A. SERPENTARIA foliis cordato-oblongis, planis; caulibus infirmis, flexuosis, teretibus; floribus solitariis. Lin.
Aristolochia Pistolochia, sive Serpentaria virginiana caule nodoso. Pluk. *Almag.* tab. 148. Serpentariae virginianae radix. Officin.

Rattlesnake-root in the United States. [*Aristolochia serpentaria* L.]

Among the plants used for rattlesnake bites this is one of the most valued. It grows in the internal regions of Pennsylvania and Virginia in fertile and shady terrain. It forms a scandent† plant varying greatly in the shape of the leaves, which are now oblong and heart-shaped, now auriculate,‡ now simply oval. The flowers tubulous, irregular, and somewhat contorted, of a dark red color; and the seed pods are quite small. The roots of this *Aristolochia* have an aromatic and stimulating flavor,

**Brassica oleracea*; var. *capitata.* Lin.
†Scandent: which winds about trees like the bean plant.
‡Auriculate: having two leaflets at the base, like those of [Solanum] *Dulcamara* [L.].

and, in addition to the aforementioned quality as a remedy for rattlesnake poison, are said to be useful during acute and intermittent fevers. Almost the same efficaciousness is attributed to those of the Linnaean *Aristolochia arborescens* [L.] (probably the *Aristolochia frutescens* described by Mr. Marshall), which is one of the most beautiful and rarest species of this genus. [Castiglioni was misled by Linnaeus who proposed two names for a single species: *Aristolochia arborescens* L., *Species plantarum,* 960, is documented by the illustration in Plukenet, *Phytographia* "t. 78, f. 1?", a poor illustration of *A. serpentaria.* Linnaeus, 961, for *A. serpentaria* cites *Phytographia* t. 148, f. 5, which is the reprod. of a drawing by John Banister with Banister's descriptive phrase, see Ewan, *Banister,* fig. 17. Marshall's *A. frutescens* is *A. durior* Hill]. We owe this note, as well as those regarding many other medicinal herbs, to the discovery of America, which not only furnished us information about new useful plants but has also made known to us by analogy the properties of our own plants of similar genus. For example, no one would have suspected the common European *Polygala* to be alexipharmic if the effect of the American *Polygala Senega* [see p. 424] had not been known. Who would have believed that the tips of our spruce could yield a kind of beer and our maples sugar, if congeneric American trees had not indicated the possibility? Hence we applaud the opinion of various writers who recommend that efforts be made to obtain from the Indians the knowledge they have of the use of plants, because, although such knowledge has been exaggerated by some who praised it as superior to the European, it merits examination nonetheless; and in the hands of able physicians and naturalists it can furnish in the future, as it has furnished in the past, advantageous discoveries.

ARUM

A. VIRGINICUM acaule, foliis hastato-cordatis, acutis, angulis obtusis. Lin. Arum aquaticum foliis amplis, sagittae cuspidi similibus, pene viridi; radice tuberosa, rapae simili, fervida, & acerrima. Clayt. n. 228. Gronov. *Fl. Virg.* pag. 142.

Tuc-kah-[h]oo, Taw-ho, Taw-hill by the Indians; Wake-robin in the United States. [For early confusion of the term "Tuckahoe" by early writers, see Ewan, *Banister,* 173, 377, and fns. 30, 31 and 33 on 392–93. *Peltandra virginica* (L.) Kunth].

The *Arum* of Virginia, like all the species of this genus, grows in marshy terrains. Its roots are huge, and pigs go after them so eagerly that they often immerse themselves completely in water in order to eat them. The Indians, too, made use of them, preparing them, according to Kalm, in the following manner. They would dig a trench about 10 feet long in which they placed the roots, covering them with a little earth on which they kept a great fire going until they thought them sufficiently cooked. It is said that these roots prepared this way have a taste similar to that of potatoes. It is, as Kalm observes, hard to imagine how men were able to discover that these roots, which are bitter and poisonous when raw, would lose under fire their deadly quality and become good to eat. It is true, however, that similar discoveries were made in other countries, so that the roots of *Calla palustris* are used instead of bread in certain northern regions of Europe, the Indians of South America and the Antilles make manioc from the *Yucca,*[*] the Hottentots eat another kind of *Arum,* and the ancient Egyptians used the cooked roots of the *Colocasia.*

ASCLEPIAS

A. SYRIACA foliis ovalibus, subtus tomentosis; caule simplicissimo; umbellis nutantibus. Lin.

Apocynum majus, Syriacum, rectum. Cornuti. *Canaden.* tab. 90.

Silk-grass, Silk-weed in the United States and Cotonier in Canada. [*Asclepias syriaca* L.]

The species of *Asclepia* native to North America are numerous; but among these the first place for beauty, fragrance of its blossoms, and utility is held by the one termed *syriaca* by Linnaeus because Clusius had called it so in his history of plants. This species, already very common in our gardens, is known there under the name of Silk-grass on account of those fine, bright, white hairs attached to the seeds. Its blossoms form quite a thick globe and have a very pleasant odor. In America it is found along the fences that ring the fields, where it can be seen in bloom at the beginning of July. It also grows in Canada, where the inhabitants call it *Cotonier.* The Canadians, so Kalm says, eat the young shoots in the spring like asparagus without feeling any ill effects, although lactescent plants like this one are usually suspect. He also says that from the blossoms they obtain a kind of dark, but very tasty, sugar, plucking them when they are still covered with dew, squeezing out the juice, and then boiling it. Pillows are stuffed with the fuzz or silk of its fruit, and excellent candle wicks can be made from it that rarely require trimming; and they don't give off a bad odor when they are extinguished. The beauty of this silk has given various people the idea of trying to spin it,† but so far no one has succeeded in weaving it by itself because the hairs are too short and not very tough. On the other hand, the mountaineers of Virginia made cloth from the outer covering of the stalks of this plant. It propagates from shoots from the base, which in good soil sometimes even spread excessively in all directions.

During the first days of August 1785 I collected in America on this Asclepia a white caterpillar with transverse yellow [green], and black stripes. It had two long black horns on the first ring near the head and two others at the tail; and on the sixth of the same month it changed into a green chrysalis spotted with golden dots which I was very sorry to lose after a few days. From the form of the caterpillar and from the bare and gold-marked chrysalis I conjecture that it belongs to a butterfly of the Linnaean order of *Equites.* [*Danaus plexipus* (Danaidae), the Monarch butterfly.]

[*LC here confused *Yucca* for yuca, Manioc, as did many early writers. See Ewan, *Banister,* fn. 33 on p. 393, and 398.]

†Among them the Prince of S. Severo in Naples. See *Voyage en Italie* by M. La Lande.

AZALEA

1. *A. NUDIFLORA foliis ovatis, corollis pilosis; staminibus longissimis.* Lin. Azalea scapo nudo, floribus confertis terminalibus, staminibus declinatis. Trew Pl. selec. tab. 48. Azalea foliis ovatis, corollis pilosis, staminibus longissimis. Kalm, *it.,* pag. 110. Duhamel, *Arb. & Arbust.,* pag. 85, tab. 3.

Honeysuckle in the United States. [*Rhododendron nudiflorum* (L.) Torr.]

2. *A. VISCOSA foliis margine scabris, corollis piloso-glutinosis.* Lin.

Swamp-pink in Massachusetts. [*R. viscosum* (L.) Torr.]

The *Azalea* (Spec. 1) called *nudiflora* because it is laden with blossoms before the leaves are formed is very common in the woods of Georgia, especially between Savannah and Augusta. It grows to a height of from four to five feet and produces at the ends of the branches a great quantity of these blossoms, which have a very good odor. Their color varies a great deal, some being pink, others red and orange, with all the shades in between. In America this shrub is called Honeysuckle, a term in English proper to *Caprifolium,* inasmuch as there is some resemblance between these flowers.

Azalea viscosa (Spec. 2) is distinguished from the first by a kind of gluten all over the plant, and especially the blossoms. Many have confused these two species, perhaps fooled by the synonym of Catesby reported by Linnaeus under *viscosa,* and which belongs to *nudiflora.* But from the following observations it appears to me that the distinction made by Linnaeus ought to be retained, unless it should be found that both come from the same seed, a fact of which I am not aware. The differences are: (1) *nudiflora* has a pistil shorter than the stamens, whereas it is longer than they in *viscosa*; (2) the blossoms of *viscosa* are more slender, white, covered with hairs, and ending in a tiny gland viscous to the touch; (3) the leaves of *viscosa* come out at the same time as the blossoms, they are smaller than on *nudiflora,* and they have petioles just as hairy as the flowers. The *viscosa* seemed to me to be more fragrant and its shrub prettier to look at, so that although its flowers do not have as beautiful a color as the other, it can be very useful as an ornamental in gardens. The two varieties of *viscosa* named by Mr. Marshall, namely, *Azalea viscosa* and the *Azalea viscosa palustris* differ only in the terrain in which they grow.

BARTSIA

B. COCCINEA foliis alternis, linearibus, utrinque bidentatis. Lin.
Bartsia foliis alternis *Amoen. Acad.,* Tom. 1 pag. 160. Pedicularis, sive Cristae Galli affinis Virginiana, Ajugae multifido folio apicibus coccineo, floribus pallidis in spicam congestis. Pluk. *Almag.* 283 tab. 102 fig. 5. [*Castilleja coccinea* (L.) Spreng.]

Only once did I come upon this curious herb, and it was in low and damp places on the road from Boston to Lancaster. It is unusual in that it has blossoms of a greenish color. But those leaflets called *bractaeae* by Linnaeus, which accompany the blossoms on some plants, have a very pretty red at the tips, so that they can easily be taken for the flowers, as happens with [*Salvia*] *horminum.** Mr. Richard says that the fructification of this species of *Bartsia* was not yet well examined, so I compared it with the *Genera Plantarum* of Linnaeus† and found a perfect agreement in every respect, except that the lobes of the calyx are sometimes not emarginated,‡ and the stigma seemed split rather than obtuse. Its leaves are irregularly cut and arranged alternately on the stem. Like them are the bracts which, as I have said, are half green and half red. The small, longish blossoms are whitish with green tips, and the seeds, enclosed in a bivalvular capsule,§ keep themselves covered by the calyx in such a way that one can't tell without breaking it when they are mature. Gronovius describes it in the following terms: *Bartsia flore pallido, [. . .] tenui, membranaceo, in capitulum congesto, perianthio longo viridi, ad finem coccineo, occultato, cui subest folium tripartitum, primo viride, postea ad finem etiam coccineum. [. . .]*

BETULA

[See Li (1957) 207]

1. *B. LENTA foliis cordatis, oblongis, acuminatis, serratis.* Lin.
Betula julifera fructu conoide, viminibus lentis. Gron. *Virg.* pag. 146, Duham. *Arb. & Arbust.* n. 2.

a. rubra

Yellow birch and Red birch in the United States. [*Betula lenta* L. and *B. nigra* L.]

b. papyrifera

White paper-birch in the northern states. [*B. papyrifera* Marsh.]

c. populifolia

Aspen-leaved birch in the northern states. [*B. populifolia* Marsh.]

d. humilis

Dwarf birch in the United States. [*B. pumila* L.]

2. *B. NIGRA foliis rhombeo-ovatis, acuminatis, duplicato serratis.* Lin.
Betula nigra Virginiana. Pluk. *Almag.* p. 67. Betula foliis ovatis, oblongis, acuminatis, serratis. Duham. *Arb. & Arbust.* n. 3.

Black birch, Sweet birch, and Sugar birch in the United States. [*B. nigra* L.]

Betula lenta (Spec. 1), so called by Linnaeus because of the flexibility of its shoots, so closely resembles our European White birch‖ that it may be merely a simple variety of it. Both vary in the color of the bark and in the form of the leaves, so that many kinds are counted that depend perhaps on the quality of the soil and the age of the plant. It is abundant in the northern regions of Massachusetts and is used

**Salvia horminum* Lin.
†*Linnaei Genera Plantarum* ed. J. Reichard.
‡Emarginated: with the outside edge cut in a concave line.
§Bivalvular: twofold.
‖*Betula alba* Lin. [*B. alba* L.]

in many ways, just like the White birch in northern Europe. In cold regions this tree reaches a height of 50 feet and is covered with a white outer layer under which is the bark, which is the most useful part. With it the Indians build their light canoes, whence it was called *Bouleau canot* by the French in Canada. They also make with it baskets, pouches, cups, dishes, buckets, and other utensils that they sometimes decorate with spruce roots,* porcupine quills, and deer hair dyed in various colors. With larger pieces of this bark they also cover their wigwams, or cabins; and the colonists of the more internal regions have imitated these ways, covering their wooden houses with this bark. Variety a called Red and also Yellow on account of the yellowish-red color of the bark, is used in the environs of Cambden near Penobscot Bay for tanning hides. The other variety called *papyrifera* (Var. b) has a more flexible and whiter bark but reaches only a modest height. The third, with poplarlike leaves (Var. c) grows in the states of New Jersey and Pennsylvania and has leaves somewhat more triangular than the others and almost like those of the *Populus tremula.* [The American species is *Populus tremuloides* Michx.] Finally, the last (Var. d), which I found in great abundance in the neighborhood of Montreal in Canada, is not unlike the preceding ones, and especially the second, except that it is smaller.

The Black (Spec. 2) is easily distinguished from all the other birches not only by the shape of the leaves, which are ovate, acuminate, doubly toothed, and by the dark color of the bark, but also by the pleasant odor of both leaves and branches. These qualities caused it to be given various names, namely *Bouleau merisier* by the Canadians because of the resemblance of its leaves to those of the wild cherry,† and Black birch and Sweet birch by the inhabitants of the United States. In the woods of St. George they extract from this plant in the spring a liquid that they prepare like spruce beer and from which can be produced a kind of sugar, so that it was distinguished also by the name of Sugar birch. The bark has a pungent taste resembling somewhat that of the root of the *Polygala senega.*

In addition to these two species one finds in North America *Betula pumila* of Linnaeus, which has obovate‡ leaves fluted at the margins, and the alder,§ distinguishable into three varieties called by Mr. Marshall Betula [-] Alnus, 1. *glauca* [unidentified], 2. *maritima* [*Alnus maritima* (Marsh.) Muhl.], and 3. *rubra* [*Alnus serrulata* (Ait.) Willd., Hazel alder], which I shall only mention since I am not aware that any particular use is made of them in America.

BIGNONIA

1. *B. CATALPA foliis simplicibus cordatis ternis; caule erecto; floribus diandris.* Lin.

Bignonia Urcu foliis, flore sordide albo, intus maculis purpureis, & luteis adsperso,

**Pinus canadensis* Lin. [*Tsuga canadensis* (L.) Carr.]
†*Prunus avium* Lin. *Merisier* of the French.
‡That is, with the narrowest part near the petiole.
§*Betula alnus* Lin. *Onizza* in Lombard.

siliqua longissima, & angustissima. Catesby *Carolin.* Tom. I pag. 49. Seligmann tab. 98.

Catalpa tree in the United States. [*Catalpa bignonioides* Walt.]

2. *B. RADICANS foliis pinnatis, foliolis incisis; caule geniculis radicatis.* Lin. Bignonia Americana fraxini folio, flore amplo phoeniceo. Tournefort pag. 164. Duham. *Arb. & Arbust.* n. 1. [*Campsis radicans* (L.) Seem.]

*b. minor**

Bignonia fraxini foliis, coccineo flore minore. Catesby *Carolin.* Tom. I tab. 65. Duham. *Arb. & Arbust.* n. 2.

Climbing trumpet-flower in the United States. [See Li, 3]

3. *B. SEMPERVIRENS foliis simplicibus lanceolatis; caule volubili.* Lin. Gelsiminum, sive Jasminum luteum odoratum Virginianum, scandens, sempervirens. Catesby *Carolin.* Tom. I tab. 53. Seligmann Tom. 2. tab. 6.

Yellow jasmine in the two Carolinas and in Georgia. [*Gelsemium sempervirens* (L.) Ait.]

Bignonia catalpa (Spec. 1) is a tree known already for many years in the gardens of Europe and lately propagated by me and my brother Count Alfonso in certain woods of the region of Milan, particularly in those recently planted in the sandy terrain of the *brughiera*† of Mozzate, where already for some years more than 2000 of these trees have flourished happily. Linnaeus, in his *Species plantarum,* confused three different plants under the species of *Catalpa* with the synonyms of the authors he cited. In fact *Bignonia longissima* of Mr. Jacquin‡ is a different species from *Catalpa,* and to *longissima* belong also the synonyms of Brown[e]§ and Plumier.|| The *Cambulu* of the Malabar Garden of Van Rheede# must be a tree of a genus completely different from *Bignonia,* since it forms a fleshy fruit with a hard pit. Hence the true Linnaean synonyms of *Catalpa* reduce themselves to those of Miller,** Duhamel,†† and Catesby.‡‡ Likewise the *Kawara-Fisagi* found in Japan by Koempfer§§ is the same as our *Catalpa*; however it differs in possessing leaves hairy on both sides and in its smaller size, so that the Chevalier Lamarck|||| made of it a variety. This is one of the many plants## common to the eastern coasts of North Asia and America and which prove the analogy of those two climates. *Catalpa* is native to the internal regions of the

[*Here and in 21 other instances Castiglioni follows the practice of Linnaeus in his *Species plantarum.* He provides a varietal designation, "b", with or without a name, and like Linnaeus with apparent inconsistencies.]

†This is what in the region of Milan they call the uncultivated places that produce heather (*Erica vulgaris* of Linnaeus, *Bruyère* of the French).

‡*Plant. Amer.* p. 25.

§*Bignonia arborea foliis ovatis verticillato-ternatis, siliqua gracili longissima.* Jamaic., p. 264.

||*Bignonia arbor, folio singulari undulato, siliqua longissima & angustissima.*

#[See Rheede in References.]

***Diction.,* N. 2.

††*Arb. & Arbust.* pag. 104.

‡‡Catesby *Carol,* Tom. I pag. 49 Seligmann Tom. I tab. 98.

§§*Amoenit. exot.* p. 841.

||||*Encyclopédie méthodique: art.* "Bignone."

##See Chap. XVIII §2.

United States, being rarely found in regions near the sea, and not growing spontaneously north of 43° latitude. Nevertheless it withstands great cold, and our plants did not suffer at all from the extremely severe January of 1789. It grows to a height of 40 feet in moist and sandy soil and produces very wide heart-shaped leaves, which are ordinarily arranged in a triangle about the branch. It blooms in the month of June, and its flowers, in great clusters, are white, streaked inside with yellow, and spotted with red.* The siliques [capsules] that follow are round and very long and full of small winged oblong seeds.

A few years ago the *Catalpa* was common in the gardens of Pennsylvania, but quite a few of them were pulled up when the rumor spread that the negro slaves were using them to poison their companions. However, this plant was wrongfully inculpated as poisonous since, although it belongs to a family of suspect plants† and has a heavy and disgusting odor, the decoction of its wood provokes only vomiting without producing any other ill effect. On the other hand in Japan, according to the testimony of Koempfer and Thunberg,‡ the decoction of the siliques is given to asthmatics, and the leaves are used as a cataplasm in nervous afflictions. The beauty of its thick foliage, the width of the leaves, the abundance of the flowers and their pleasing odor (quite different from that of the wood and the leaves), make this tree valuable in gardens. Its soft and easily cut wood render it, in my experience, as suitable for carving as the linden; and, on account of its ready growth, it can easily replace the alder as firewood in thin and sandy terrains, its broad leaves serving better to fertilize the soil. Some authors give instructions on propagating it by layering and from cuttings, but since it is now very easy to get from fresh seeds, this will be the best way of obtaining it in quantity–all the more so because by covering them with a little moderately decent soil they sprout with no difficulty and in two years can be transplanted in the woods.

Bignonia radicans (Spec. 2), called Trumpet flower and Red jasmine, is one of those plants that entwine themselves about trees, forming a tortuous and woody trunk like that of the grapevine. It is equipped with little roots with which it attaches itself to the bark of trees, and likewise to walls. It was therefore introduced into gardens to cover masonry walls, for which purpose it is preferable to the five-leaved ivy, [*Parthenocissus quinquefolia* (L.) Planch.], commonly called Canada vine, since this *Bignonia* produces beautiful green pinnate leaves and copious flowers. The latter come out as clusters in the shape of long orange-red tubes, and in America they are frequented by those tiny little [Humming] birds called *colibrì*, that thrust their beaks into them to suck out the honey. It is found in low damp places of Virginia and the two Carolinas and has been propagated in gardens solely for its beauty, since no economic advantage that I know of has been drawn from it. Its leaves, when chewed, according to Cornuti,§ have a fungus taste.

The evergreen *Bignonia* (Spec. 3), called Yellow jasmine, native to the swamps

*The flowers have for the most part only two perfect stamens, the other two being castrates, i.e., with no anthers.

†This is the natural order of the *Personatae.*

‡*Flora Japonica.*

§Cornuti *Histor. Plantarum Canadensium* p. 102.

of Carolina, is one of the most precocious plants in those regions. Like the preceding one, it winds itself around trees; but it is smaller and more delicate. Its leaves are simple, lanceolate, and evergreen, The blossoms that emerge from their axils are of a very pretty yellow and fragrant, and their tubes are open like bells. Children in America make wreaths with these flowers, with which they decorate the rooms, filling them with a sweet fragrance. But being of a delicate structure, they wilt quickly. The siliques [capsules] are oval, short, and very tiny; and the winged seeds they contain resemble in form those of wild pine. The four stamens are all of the same height, so that in this respect it differs from other plants of the class Didynamia. It is used in gardens in America, but since it is very sensitive to cold, one can't have it in northern regions; and I think that in our climate it couldn't hold up in the open without some protection, and it would be necessary to propagate it in vases in order to bring it inside during the winter.

CALYCANTHUS

C. FLORIDUS petalis interioribus longioribus. Lin.
Beureria petalis coriaceis oblongis, calycis foliolis reflexis. Ehret *Pict.,* tab. 13. Butneria Anemones flore. Duh. *Arb. & Arbust.* Tom. I. Basteria foliis ovatis oppositis, floribus lateralibus, caule fruticoso ramoso. Miller. *Dict., & Icon.* tab. 60. Frutex Corni foliis, floribus instar Anemones stellatae, petalis crassis rigidis, colore sordide rubente, cortice aromatico. Catesby *Car.* Tom. I pag. 46.

Obs.: *Semina non caudata.*

Sweet-scented shrub and Carolina allspice in the United States. [*Calycanthus floridus* L.]

Calycanthus, one of the most charming and highly prized shrubs of the southern United States, grows to a height of 10 or 12 feet, and before the leaves appear is completely covered with dark red flowers that give off a very pleasing fragrance very like that of strawberries, or rather of pineapple, yielding a stronger and more pleasing odor when they are somewhat wilted. They are composed of many petals, of which the internal ones are the longest; and since they resemble a little those of the anemone, Duhamel gave *Calycanthus* the name *Butneria anemones flore.* The seeds, dark, oval, smooth, are enclosed in a pear-shaped chestnut-colored capsule [-like receptacle] formed by the calyx of the flower. The leaves are oval, opposite, and entire, and of a glossy dark green. The wood and the leaves have an aromatic fragrance, and since it is a shrub of beautiful foliage, it is used in South Carolina to form hedges in the little alleys of gardens. *Calycanthus* is found in the two Carolinas, in Georgia and also in the internal regions of Virginia, where I came upon it in the Southwest Mountains, so called, near the Blue Mountains at 37° 50′ latitude. I got several small plants out of the seed I collected in America, which didn't suffer at all from the most severe cold, even though they were only two years old; and they bloomed at the beginning of May in the third year after coming up from seed. Calycanthus, too, is one of those genera common to the United States and Japan, where a species is found little different from this one called *Obai** in that country and *Calycanthus praecox* by Linnaeus. *Calycanthus* was first introduced into Europe by the celebrated Catesby.

CASSINE

C. PERAGUA foliis petiolatis serratis, ellypticis, acutiusculis, ramulis ancipitibus. Lin.

Cassine corymbosa foliis ovato-lanceolatis serratis, floribus corymbosis axillaribus. Miller *Diction. Icon.* tab. 83 fig. 1.

Evergreen cassine, Japan-tea, South Sea tea in the southern states. [*Ilex cassine* L.]

This shrub likes warm climates and grows only in the states of South Carolina and Georgia. It is of modest height, its leaves are thick like those of boxwood, of a beautiful dark green, elliptical in shape; and they are kept even in the winter. The flowers come out early in the spring, and the berries, which are very plentiful and of a red color, ripen only the following spring. This is thought by botanists to be the famous plant whose ground-up leaves are known in Europe under the name of Paraguay plant, or even Jesuit tea; and, in fact, that conjecture seems quite probable, since *Cassine* is very much like the Paraguayan in odor and a similar use is made of it in Carolina. In Paraguay the natives used to take a quantity of these fresh leaves and, immersing them in the river, would drink the water contained in their hands, which, impregnated with the flavor of the leaves, would induce a vomiting healthful in illnesses resulting from indigestion or accumulation of bile. Moreover, the decoction of the leaves served as tea for them; and the Jesuits in the missions over there, and the Spaniards and Portuguese in those regions, especially in Lima, also used it that way. In the provinces of North America *Cassine* was put to the same use during the war but was completely abandoned afterwards when Chinese tea was again introduced. Cassine tea is very diuretic and therefore excellent for stones, nephritic pains, and perhaps also for podagra. The Indians of Florida and the two Carolinas used to make use of the infusion of this plant, which they called *Apalachine*, to inebriate themselves before going into battle. They prepared it by toasting the leaves, steeping them in water, and letting the liquid ferment until it took on a reddish color. This shrub also serves for making hedges and walls of greenery in gardens, because it can be cut with shears like Hornbeam and Boxwood. In Lombardy perhaps it can survive the severity of the winter if one chooses settings that are more protected from cold winds. It is worthwhile to make an effort to propagate it, since it is a shrub from which advantages may be derived for medicine.

CEANOTHUS

C. AMERICANUS foliis trinerviis. Lin.

Evonymous novi belgii, Corni foeminae foliis. Commelin. *Hort. Med.* pag. 167 tab. 167.

*Koempfer. *Amoenit. exot.* p. 878.

American tea, New Jersey tea in the United States. [*Ceanothus americanus* L.]

The American *Ceanothus,* which I frequently saw in bloom in autumn near the St. Lawrence River, is a small shrub four or five feet high with branches covered with ovate three-nerved leaves. The flowers, which come out at the ends of the branches, are very small, white, and of a curious structure; and they are followed by bivalvular capsules containing a single seed in each section and like those of rue in external form. The root, which is thick and red outside, is used in red dyes, and the decoction from it is considered in America an excellent remedy not only for simple gonorrheas, which, according to some, it terminates in a few days without bad consequences, but also for chronic syphilis. The leaves of *Ceanothus,* immersed in a boiling decoction made with the branches and leaves of the same and then left to dry at a moderate temperature, are often used by the people in America instead of tea, which it greatly resembles in taste—especially the kind that is called commercially red or bohea tea. Since, as I have discovered, it survives our coldest winters, this shrub can be cultivated in our country, if one takes care, however, to keep it in vases for the first few years, for the reason that, being small and slow growing, it could be damaged by some accident.

CELASTRUS

C. SCANDENS inermis, caule volubili; foliis serrulatis. Lin.
Evonymoides Canadensis scandens, foliis serratis. Duham. *Arb. & Arbust.*

Bourreau des arbres in Canada; Staff tree in the United States. [*Celastrus scandens* L.]

The climbing *Celastrus* winds itself around trees and goes up to a height of 10 and 15 feet, dangling its long branches from which emerge clusters of greenish flowers. The fruit that follows consists of round three-pointed capsules of a yellow-reddish color which, opening into three valves when they are ripe, show seeds of a lively red. The first time that I observed it was on the mountain of Montreal in the month of September, at which time it was laden with fruit that contrasted very beautifully with the green of the leaves. I have not yet succeeded in obtaining this species of *Celastrus* from seed, but I believe it will not be difficult to make it sprout in quantity if the seed is fresh. It can be useful only as garden decoration to cover bowers or little grottoes; but one must be careful to keep it away from valuable trees, since it entwines itself about them so tightly as to penetrate their bark, for which reason it took the French name of *Bourreau des arbres.* The Virginia *Celastrus* is little different from this species.

CELTIS

C. OCCIDENTALIS foliis oblique ovatis, serratis, acuminatis. Lin.
Celtis fructu obscure-purpurascente Duham. *Arb. & Arbust.*

Nettle-tree in the United States. [*Celtis occidentalis* L.]

This tree is quite common in moist and fertile terrains of North America, where it reaches a great height. This is a species of the plant called *Frigerio** in our country, to which Italian botanists have given the name Lotus, on the supposition that it was the famous African lotus mentioned by Homer, whose fruit was considered so excellent.† The American lotus differs mainly from ours in that it has leaves with a sharper point turned to one side and an uneven base, with fruit of a dirty red color when it is ripe. The bark of the young tree is often smooth and of a dark color, but rough and whitish on old trees. It grows marvelously from seed and I have a number of plants that grow here as in their native country. The flowers come out in mid-April, and they are partly hermaphroditic, partly sterile, since (like those of the maple) they often lack pistils. The sterile flowers (called "male" by Linnaeus) usually have six stamens and six segments in the calyx, although this number is not constant and in rare instances is found also in the hermaphrodites. The latter, however, ordinarily have five stamens and five segments. Among the plants grown from seed I collected in America there are some that during the third year put out very long and flexible shoots that bent down toward the ground under their weight like the branches of the African willow [*Salix babylonica* L.]. The wood of the American lotus can serve for the same purposes as our own. As a matter of fact, it grows more rapidly, loses its leaves much later in the fall, and is quick to put them on in the spring. Its berries have a sweet taste, but somewhat astringent, and according to Mr. Marshall are used in America for acute dysenteries.

CEPHALANTHUS

C. OCCIDENTALIS foliis oppositis, ternisque. Lin.

Globe flowering shrub, Pond dogwood, and Button-bush in Massachusetts; and Buttonwood in New York. [*Cephalanthus occidentalis* L.]

Cephalanthus grows everywhere in low, damp places near brooks and ponds, rising to a height of six to eight feet on a branchy trunk, with opposing, and sometimes ternate ovato-lanceolate leaves. The flowers come out of the ends of the branches and are spherical, white in color, and of a pleasant odor. They are composed of many tiny blossoms provided with a calyx divided into four parts at the tip containing a monopetalous corolla, four stamens, and a pistil. They make a pretty sight and produce little globes formed of conical seed joined at the points in a center like those of the plane tree. In fact the similarity of the fruit led in New York to giving this shrub the name of Buttonwood, by which name the American plane is denoted in

**Micacoulier* of the French. *Celtis australis* of Linnaeus. *Bagolaro* in some places in Lombardy.

†The Englishman Mr. [Thomas] Shaw was the first to discover the true African Lotus of the ancients, which is a species of jujube (*Zyzyphus*) [*Ziziphus*], called *seedra* by the Tunisians. It is abundant in the district of Jereed, which was formerly included in the country of the Lotophagi. See Shaw, *Voyage* (French trans., Bk. iv, p. 123); and Linnaeus Reichard. *Rhamnus Lotus.* [Reichard's ed. of Linnaeus' *Species plantarum* etc., see Castiglioni's References.]

Massachusetts. It grows easily from seed and holds up very well in our climate, where it blossomed in the third year.

CERCIS

C. CANADENSIS foliis cordatis, junioribus pubescentibus N[obis]. [Castiglioni adds to Linnaeus' descriptive phrase.]
Siliquastrum canadense. Tournef. *Inst. B[R.] H.* Duham. *Arb. & Arbust.* N. 3.
Obs. *Folia adulta glabra evadunt.*
Redbud, Judas-tree in the United States. [*Cercis canadensis* L.]

The *Siliquastrum* of North America is very common in the woods, where it reaches a height of more than 15 feet. The small difference that there is between this and the Judas-tree, which is the European Siliquastrum,* consists in that the former has leaves ending in a sharper point and much smaller blossoms. However, it makes up for this lack by the larger quantity of flowers that it produces both from the branches and the trunk, so that in the spring it looks very beautiful and is comparable to peaches in full bloom. The blossoms are of a vivid red color and cover the whole tree before the leaves come out; for this reason they use it in South Carolina to adorn gardens. It can be adopted for the same use in our country, since it sprouts readily from seed—from which I obtained a number of plants.

CHIONANTHUS

C. VIRGINICA pedunculis trifidis, trifloris. Lin.
Amelanchiér Virginiana Lauro-Cerasi folio. Catesby *Carol.* tab. 68.
Snowdrop, Fringe, or Paper-tree in the United States. [*Chionanthus virginica* L.]

Chionanthus is one of the most curious plants of United America for the structure of its white flowers, which have very long and fine corolla segments, on account of which it has gotten the names of Snowdrop, Fringe-tree, and Paper-tree. I saw it in Georgia in April laden with blossoms in uncultivated and sandy areas near Augusta, but in those warm climes it reaches only a modest height and begins to bloom early. On the other hand, in the temperate regions of Virginia and Pennsylvania it forms a handsome shrub of secondary size that rises to a height of 10 to 12 feet, which shows how favorable our climate of Lombardy ought to be for it. However, it is found only in small quantity in states north of New York, and it is completely unknown in the Province of Canada. It usually sprouts from seed the second year, and one will do well to protect it during the first winters. The Indians treat wounds with the crushed bark of *Chionanthus* because it closes them, so they say, almost without suppuration.

**Cercis siliquastrum* Lin. *Gainier* [in] Franc[e].

[Br 3:106]

COLLINSONIA CANADENSIS

Collinsonia, [Linnaeus] *Hort. Cliff.* 14 tab. 5; Colden, *Noveb.* n. 8. Kalm, *Travels,* vol. 1, p. 154; [Linnaeus], *Mat. med.,* p. 40. Collinsonia floribus pallide luteis foliis ovato-oblongis acute serratis, Clayt. no. 894 [in] Gron., *Fl. Virg.* p. 6.

This plant was discovered by Mr. Bartram, who sent it to Europe for the first time. It got the name *Collinsonia* from Mr. Jussieu, who was in London, in memory of Mr. Peter Collinson, a London merchant, member of the Societies of London and Sweden, and a dedicated amateur of natural history. It has a pleasant, but excessively sharp, odor, which produces a headache when one lingers in or simply passes through a wood in which there is a quantity of them in bloom. It grows as a small shrub in rich and good terrain, and, according to Mr. Bartram, Pennsylvania and other provinces in the same climate are the original region of this plant. It is not true, however (as Mr. Kalm asserts) that it was not found by Clayton, proof to the contrary being the citation reported above from the aforementioned author. It was found in Virginia by Clayton [earlier by Banister who called it *Melissa*], in Pennsylvania by Bartram and Kalm, in New York by Colden, and according to Linnaeus, it is also found in Canada. In New York it is called Horse weed because horses eat it in the spring. The odor is compared by Colden with that of *Melissa,* and according to him, the root serves to sooth pains after childbirth. Mr. Bartram recognizes this plant as an excellent remedy for any kind of lumbar pains and good for application to parts affected and become red because of cold. Mr. Kalm reports further that Mr. Conrad Veisser [Johann Conrad Weiser, 1696–1760], finding himself in the company of some Indians in Pennsylvania, one of the latter was bitten by a rattlesnake, and the other companions having boiled *Collinsonia* and given the decoction to the afflicted one, he recovered happily. Kalm, Vol. 1, p. 155.

COREOPSIS

C. VERTICILLATA foliis decomposito-pinnatis linearibus. Lin. Chrysanthemum marianum scabiosae tenuissime divisis foliis, ad intervalla consertis. Pluk. *Mantis.* tab. 344 fig. 2.

[*Coreopsis verticillata* L.]

Coreopsis is a plant with radiate flowers of the class *Syngenesia* of Linnaeus. The leaves of *verticillata* are bipinnate, of slender linear *pinnae.* It produces yellow flowers with a dark disk, the flowers sustained by a short calyx whose external leaflets are shorter than the others. This biennial plant, native of Virginia and Louisiana, is very delicate, and, according to the Chevalier Lamarck,* in Paris, where it grows in the Botanical Garden, it dies easily in the winter. *Coreopsis* would not be worth listing among the economical plants of North America were it not for the use that the Indians made of it, extracting from the yellow leaflets that surround the flower a red dye with which they colored their dress.

CORNUS

C. FLORIDA arborea; involucro maximo, foliolis obcordatis. Lin.
Cornus mas Virginiana flosculis in corymbo digestis, a perianthio tetrapetalo albo radiatim cinctis. Pluk. *Almag.* pag. 120. *Phytog.* tab. 26 fig. 3. Catesby *Carolin.* tab. 27.

Dogwood in the United States. [*Cornus florida* L.]

The Dogwood called *florida* is very common in the United States. In the Carolinas it blooms in March or at the beginning of April, producing tiny little flowers joined together like a little umbrella and surrounded by four broad leaves of a white, sometimes of a rather reddish, color that form the involucre of the flowers. The plant is almost completely covered with them in the blossom season, and in the fall it is laden with little red berries. It grows to the height of an average shrub in temperate regions, but in cold climes it rarely exceeds five or six feet. The bark of this shrub was used advantageously in America for intermittent fevers on account of its styptic and bitter taste. The excrescences and knots on the trunk are very hard, for which reason they have many uses in the crafts; and the young shoots, since they are straight and smooth, are used for making distaffs.

Many other species of Dogwood are common in America, such as the Dogwood with alternate branches,† White dogwood‡ (a species very similar to our Sanguino,§ differing from it only in possessing purplish-white berries), Swamp dogwood|| (perhaps a variety of the White), Silk dogwood,# and, finally, the Canada dogwood** (a small perennial plant very common in the United States). Since all of these species are, to my knowledge, of no particular use, a simple mention of them will suffice.

CORYPHA

C. MINOR frondibus palmatis, flabelliformibus, plicatis, subbifidis; filis interjectis paucis; stipitibus inermibus. Jacq. *Hort.* Tom. 3 pag. 8 tab. 8 Sabal. Adanson. *Familles des plantes,* pag. 495.

**Encyclop. Méthod.* Art., *Coriope,* Bk. ii.
†*Cornus alterna* [not] Lin. [but *C. alterna* Marsh. = *C. alternifolia* L.f.]
‡*Cornus alba* Lin. [*C. stolonifera* Michx.]
§*Cornus sanguinea* Lin. [*C. foemina* Mill.]
||*Cornus candidissima* (Marshall, *Arbust. Amer.*) [*C. racemosa* Lam.]
#Cornus sericea (Lin., *Mant.*). [*C. amomum* L.]
****Cornus canadensis* Lin. [*C. canadensis* L.]

Palmier nain des marais among the French in the Antilles; Palmetto in South Carolina. [*Sabal minor* (Jacq.) Pers.]

Linnaeus did not describe this species of *Corypha* which at first sight resembles very much the dwarf palm of Spain [*Chamaerops humilis*] except that its leaves are larger and have a spineless petiole. However, the fruit-bearing parts examined by M. Jacquin show it to be of the Linnaean genus *Corypha.* Its roots are fibrous, producing palmate leaves folded fanlike and joined together at the base. From among these leaves arises the spadix bearing clusters of whitish flowers, which are succeeded by spherical black berries a little larger than a pea. The dwarf *Corypha* [*Sabal*] is common in the marshes of the Carolina, mainly near Wilmington. The inhabitants call it Palmetto, distinguishing with the name Palmetto royal the Cabbage palm or Areca. [Castiglioni in a ms. draft had called this "Chamerops americana" as a new name. For synonomy of *Sabal* see Sargent, *Silva* (1896) 10:38.]

CUPRESSUS

1. *C. THYOIDES foliis imbricatis, frondibus ancipitibus.* Lin.

Cupressus nana mariana, fructu coeruleo parvo. Pluk. *mant.* p. 61 tab. 345 fig. 1.

White cedar in Massachusetts. [*Chamaecyparis thyoides* (L.) BSP.]

2. *C. DISTICHA foliis disticibis patentibus.* Lin.

Cupressus Virginiana foliis Acaciae deciduis. Com. *Hort. Med.* tom. 1 pag. 113 tab. 59. Duham. *Arb. & Arbust.* Cupressus Americana. Catesby *Carol.* tom. 1 tab. 11.

White cypress [Bald cypress] in the United States. [*Taxodium distichum* (L.) Rich.]

Cupressus thyoides (Spec. 1) grows abundantly in the marshes of New Jersey on the eastern shore of the Delaware River, with the result that those flooded areas have the name of cedar swamps. The name White cedar was given to it because of its resemblance to the Virginia juniper, there called Red cedar.* It sometimes reaches the height of a large tree, although usually it is only of modest stature; and its branches, covered with small narrow and pointed leaves are half way between those of the Juniper and the Thuja. The tiny round fruit are hardly distinguishable from the berries of the junipers, because the scales are somewhat angular. The wood of the Cupressus thyoides is softer than that of the Acacia-leaved cypress (Spec. 2), but durable nevertheless and not subject to termites. For this reason, and also on account of its lightness, it is much used in building to cover roofs, in ship construction, and for fences. It is also easily worked on the lathe, and various small utensils are made of it. This tree does not require much cultivation, it sprouts easily from seed, and since it grows rapidly in somewhat damp terrains, it could be propagated profitably in the uncultivated and flooded valleys of Lombardy.

The Acacia-leaved cypress (Spec. 2) is a very handsome and useful tree of

*On the meaning of the name "cedar" see the entry "*Juniperus.*"

South Carolina and Georgia. The swamps of those regions are full of them, where these trees reach a height of 70 to 80 feet by 3 to 4 feet in diameter, with foliage arranged pyramidally like those of the common cypress. Unlike the other cypresses and almost all the other resinous and coniferous trees, it has the property of losing its leaves in the winter as does the larch. These leaves are rather wide, pinnate, and of a light green color. The cones are almost round and about an English inch in diameter. They are often found joined in clusters and contain hard, angular seeds attached beneath the scales.

It is an unusual fact that this cypress produces near its foot conical protuberances of a substance quite like that of the trunk, from which there issue neither branches nor leaves. M. Fougeroux de Bondaroy speaks about that at length in a memoir of his on cypresses that deserves to be consulted for the interesting information assembled in it.*

In South Carolina it is called White cypress, a term that in the middle states is sometimes given to the *Cupressus thyoides* already described, so that a great deal of confusion results in the popular names. Although it is native to warm climes, it is also hardy in temperate ones, and in France there is along a brook around the hamlet of Monceau, formerly belonging to the celebrated Duhamel, a beautiful avenue of these trees that began to bear cones in 1779.† The wood, though light, holds up better than any other in water, so that out of it are made those small slabs with which roofs of houses are covered in America; also buckets and vases. It is, furthermore, an excellent wood for construction, to which use it is commonly put in Carolina. The resin that oozes from its cones emits a very fragrant odor and leaves on paper a very bright orange-red color that might perhaps be of use for varnishes.

DATURA

D. STRAMONIUM pericarpiis spinosis, erectis, ovatis; foliis ovatis, glabris. Lin. Stramonium, vel datura fructu rotundo spinoso flore albo simplici. Tournef. *Inst. R. H.* Knorr *Deliciae* tab. 13.

Noce metella (Mattioli); *Pomme épineuse* of the French; Thornapple in the United States. [Jamestown or Jimson weed, *Datura stramonium* L.]

Stramonium, a plant native to America, has multiplied so in every part of Europe that it is useless to give any description of it, since it is known even by persons not trained in natural history.

[From Br 2:316] This narcotic plant, whose effects were experienced by those poor ignorant women who were thought to be witches, who, imbued with the idea of conversing with the Devil and transported into believing themselves to be in that condition by an overheated imagination by rubbing their temples with stramonium oil, overcome

Mémoires de la Société d'Agriculture de Paris (1786 Trimestre d'été).

†See [Lamarck], *Encyclop. méthodique,* art. "*Cyprés.*"

by its soporific virtue, would fall immediately into a deep sleep in which, their minds continuing to wander in the preconceived notion, they imagined themselves straddling broom handles and flying off to their conciliabules.

I would have made no mention of this plant were it not for the use made of it by certain Indian nations, mainly the Appomatox, who used to live on the shores of the river of the same name now included in the State of Maryland [Virginia!] When they were about to choose one of their chiefs, they would take a number of youths and shut them up in a place from which they could not escape. Every day they would give them a decoction of *Stramonium,* increasing the dose until they became delirious and then reducing it in order to restore to them little by little the use of their reason. This served as a trial for choosing those who were to fill the highest offices; and one of the young men was always allowed to die in delirium by giving him larger doses. Hence the people would believe that that had come about by divine punishment, since he was not worthy of presiding over the nation. They used to perform this trial on the occasion of celebrating the feast called Husque-hannah. [See Ewan, *Banister,* 395, note 53 on "Huskinaugh"]

DIONAEA

D. MUSCIPULA. Lin.

Dionaea. Ellis. *Act. Upsal.* Tom. I, pag. 98 tab. 8 Lamarck. *Encyc. method.*

Flytrap in the United States. [*Dionaea muscipula* Ellis]

There is perhaps among American plants none that so pleasantly intrigues the curious observer as the *Dionaea,* which grows in the damp fields of certain parts of North Carolina, chiefly near Wilmington [currently only near the South and North Carolina border]. The leaves of this little plant, scattered about close to the ground, are divided into two almost round lobes and provided at their margins with a number of curved bristles, with the upper surface covered with tiny glands and three or four spines, or very short points. These leaves are held up by winged petioles like those of Orange leaves. In the middle arises the stem, which bears five to seven white blossoms of five striped leaflets. From the little glands on the leaves there probably oozes a sweet liquid to suck which flies and other insects alight, and, upon irritating by their movements the sensitive fibers of the leaves, these close and hold them with the marginal bristles until they reopen after the insect has stopped moving and set it free. Such a phenomenon seems to prove that the motion of leaves in many species of plants depends upon irritation rather than upon relaxation of the fibers, as various authors have asserted. The *Dionaea* is for good reason called by Linnaeus a *miraculum naturae,* and on account of this singularity was repeatedly sent to Europe, but very rarely with a happy outcome.

Mr. Ayton [Aiton], director of the Royal Garden of Kew in England, told me that he had seed sent from America every year, since the plants germinated in

England died before they could be brought to maturity. Upon my return from America I shipped several of these little plants, a number of which were meant for Count Florida-Bianca, but because of the violent motion of the boat [!] and because they were too young, having been transported from North Carolina a short time previously, they all died. I sent some absolutely fresh seed from America, and as soon as they arrived they were planted in moss and kept moist, but in spite of everything nothing came up. [See J. Ewan in *Festschrift für Claus Nissen* (Wiesbaden, Guido Pressler, 1973), 173–84, for recent historical account.]

DIOSPYROS

D. VIRGINIANA foliorum paginis concoloribus. Lin.
Guajacana Loto arbori affinis Virginiana, Pishamia dicta, Pluk. *Almag.* pag. 180 tab. 244 fig. 5. Guajacana, sive Pishamin Virginianum. Duh. *Arb., & Arbust.* n. 3.

Persimmon tree in the United States. [*Diospyros virginiana* L.]

The American *Guajacana* is not much different from that of southern Italy* except that in the American plant the leaves are larger, a little more oblique at the base, slightly hairy beneath, the flowers are isolated, and the fruit much larger and juicier. It grows in the swamps and woods of Pennsylvania and Virginia [and Southward] and its fruit begins to look ripe toward the end of September. It is of the shape of a large round plum, of a beautiful yellow color, and held by a very short peduncle to which the calyx is fastened. In the fruit there are hard, closely-packed seeds, and the pulp, which is very juicy, has a sweet, honeyed flavor if thoroughly mature and wilted by frost, although the persimmon rarely loses entirely the bitter unripe-medlarlike taste it leaves on the tongue for a long time when it is still green. In some parts of Virginia this fruit is plucked when ripe, and kneaded with bran, large cakes are made of it that are cooked by holding near the fire until the crust is browned. They are then kept in a dry place until the following spring, at the beginning of which they are reduced to a powder that is soaked in water for two or three days. Then after the mixture has been boiled, the liquid is drained off while still lukewarm and poured into a barrel with the addition of yeast to make it ferment, and in about a week this liquor is good to drink. The inhabitants use it instead of beer. It has a sweet and heady flavor and keeps on improving in quality even after a long time.

The Philosophical Society of Philadelphia proposed in November of 1788 that an experiment be performed on the fruit of the persimmon for the extraction of brandy, and Mr. Isaac Bartram was delegated to run the experiment. [He suggested that the U.S. could become independent of the West Indies for rum.] The method that he proposed according to his experimentations is the following: In proportion to the quantity of fruit prepare barrels open at one end. At the other end make a hole about four inches from the circumference, in which place a spigot in such a way that when the barrels are set upright on two wooden blocks the liquid can be drawn off by means

**Diospyros Lotus* Lin. *Falso loto.* Mattioli.

of the spigot. Inside, over this hole, put little pieces of wood covered with straw two or three inches thick in order to keep the pulp of the fruit from plugging it. The barrels being thus arranged, fill one of them half-full with well-crushed persimmons and add water until the mixture comes to two-thirds the height of the barrel. Then cover the barrel using the removed end as a cover and let stand in this manner for nine days. In this time the pulp or lees will separate out as a result of the fermentation, and then the liquid can be extracted by the spigot at the bottom, letting it drop into a barrel. When this is full, close it carefully with the bung in order to prevent a second fermentation, in which case the liquor would become acid and useless for distillation. Having thus extracted the vinous part from the first barrel, add water to the two-thirds point as before, mixing it well and stirring it well with the lees and shaking it in order to get all the juice out of the fruit. Then fill the second barrel half-full of crushed fruit like the first one and, instead of pure water, add that impregnated with juice from the stirring taken from the first barrel. Then allow it to ferment and proceed as with the first barrel—and so on from the second to the third until all the fruit is used up. Keep the vinous liquid collected in the barrels for a month before distilling it (unless meantime it threatens to become acid), since Mr. Bartram observed that the liquor distilled right after fermentation was not as spiritous as that which had been allowed to rest. A persimmon tree is capable of producing about two bushels of fruit, and from each bushel is drawn about a gallon of brandy.

Among the many plants that the English use in their beautiful dyes, the gum of this tree was also found to be very useful, so that before the war the Society of Arts and Manufacturers of London had proposed a reward of £20 sterling to whoever transported the largest quantity of it to England (not less than 50 pounds) and with the least expense. Moreover, they say that the little cakes made with the pulp of this fruit and dried in the sun are a good remedy for dysenteries, that the decoction of its leaves is astringent, and that its wood has a tough fiber and is good for many uses. The seed of this tree I collected in America grew easily in Lombardy, and the numerous plants that I possess are not only very vigorous but withstood the extremely cold winter of 1788–89 in a new wood where several had been planted. It is easily propagated from seed and can be grafted (as I have proved) onto the European *Guajacana*. It must be noted, however, that the small plants must be transplanted in the spring and never in the fall, since under these circumstances the winter freeze does them great harm. I hope that by planting the seed and cultivating this tree in rich and fertile soil, by espaliering it like the other fruit trees, and perhaps by grafting it repeatedly upon itself, its fruit will abandon its disgusting bitterness and become larger and more tasty. The wood of this tree is fit for many uses, it makes a good fire, and the ashes are rich in alkali. The leaves rot easily, reduce themselves to good fertilizer, and help the grass grow in the fields.

It is probable that the *Diospyros kaki* of Japan described by Koempfer* is a variety of the persimmon. Certainly it is very similar in the leaves, and size, color, and taste of the fruit, although perhaps it differs in having its flowers three by three, so that Mr. Thunberg, one of the most distinguished disciples of the great Linnaeus,

**Amoenitates exoticae,* p. 805.

made a new species of it under the name of *Diospyros kaki,* forming two varieties.* In Japan the fruit of the *kaki,* sprinkled with flour or sugar, can be conserved for a long time like figs, and the same could no doubt be done with that of the persimmon, which ought thus to lose its bitterness. As we have said regarding the maple and the lotus (*Celtis,* Lin.), the Guajacana should be removed from the class of *Polygamia Dioecia* of Linnaeus, and then it would belong to that of the *Octandria,* where the aforementioned Mr. Thunberg put it.

[Br 3:158]

DIRCA PALUSTRIS

Moosewood. It is a small shrub that grows on knolls near ponds and marshes. The English in Albany call it Leatherwood because its bark is tough and pliable like leather, and the French in Canada, *Bois de plomb.* The bark is used by the Indians to make rope, various kinds of baskets, and it is certainly suitable for such uses, because of its remarkable toughness similar to that of Linden bark. The English and the Germans in various parts of America and the French in Canada use it in all those circumstances in which the bark of the linden is employed in Europe. The wood too, is very tough, and I don't know whether the branches can be detached without cutting them with a knife. They are used for rods and stakes. *Dirca* blooms in April. Kalm, Vol. 2, p. 12. [*Dirca palustris* L.]

DRACONTIUM

D. FOETIDUM foliis subrotundis concavis. Lin.
Arum americanum betae folio. Catesby *Carolin.* Tom. II pag. 71 tab. 71.

Skunk- or Polecat-weed in the United States. [*Symplocarpus foetidus* (L.) Nutt.]

Linnaeus changed a number of times the location of this plant in his various editions, placing it now in the genus of *Dracontium,* now in *Pothos,* both of which are in his class *Gynandria.* In fact, the fetid *Dracontium* [*Symplocarpus*], if it agrees with the other dracontiums in having a pistil furnished with a style, and almost round berries wrapped separately in the funguslike pith of the spadix, nevertheless approaches the genus *Pothos* in having only four stamens and a single seed in each berry. It is common in American marshes and damp fields, where in the months of April and May it can be spotted because of its blossoms ranging from red to yellow. This plant emits a disgusting odor not unlike that of the American Skunk, or Polecat,† from

*Thunberg, *Flora Japonica* (Leipzig, 1784) p. 157.
†*Viverra Mephitis* Lin. = [*Mephitis mephitis* (Schreber), and other species.]

which is derived its name of Polecat- or Skunk-weed. The pulverized roots and leaves are said to be excellent for asthma and are administered in doses of 4 or 6 grains for children and up to 20 for adults. This remedy (according to Mr. Cutler, [(1785), 409] was learned from the Indians, who administer it at the end of the paroxysm, repeating the same dose in the morning for several days. They then allow as many days to pass before continuing its use, and so on until recovery. Mr. Colden adds that this *Dracontium* is an excellent antiscorbutic, and that the Indians say that bears, upon coming out of their dens in the spring, motivated by natural instinct, eagerly eat its leaves, for which reason the Swedes in America give it the name *Byorn-Blad* or *Byorn-Retter,* that is, Bear-leaf or Bear-root.

[Br 2:319]

ERYNGIUM

E. FOETIDUM foliis gladiatis serrato-spinosis: floribus multifidis. Linn.

This plant was pointed out to me by Dr. [James] Greenway [1703?–94], a Virginia physician (of whom I shall speak below) as an excellent remedy for rattlesnake bite; and Mr. Clayton, in his *Flora virginica,* after having alluded to the aforementioned quality, adds that in the treatment of fevers it is on a par with *Contrayerva* [*Dorstenia*]: *Ad morsus serpentis caudisoni, et aliorum venenatorum optimum censetur remedium. In febribus idem praestat quod Contrayerva.* Gron. *Fl. virg.* [ed. 2] p. 40[41]. [*Eryngium yuccifolium* Michx.]

FAGUS

1. *F. SYLVATICA foliis ovatis, obsolete serratis. Lin.*

b. atro-punicea.

Fagus sylvatica atro-punicea. Marsh. *Arb. amer.* pag. 46.

American beech tree in the United States. [*Fagus grandifolia* Ehrh.]

2. *F. CASTANEA foliis lanceolatis, acuminato-serratis, subtus nudis.* Lin.

Fagus Castanea dentata. Marsh. *Arb. amer.* pag. 46.

American chestnut tree in the United States. [*Castanea dentata* (Marsh.) Borkh.]

3. *F. PUMILA foliis lanceolato-ovatis, acute serratis, subtus tomentosis; amentis fili-formibus, nodosis.* Lin.

Fagus Castanea pumila. Marsh. *Arb. amer.* p. 47. Castanea pumila virginiana, fructu racemoso parvo, in singulis capsulis echinatis unico. Catesby *Carol.* Tom. I tab. 9.

Chinquepin or Chinkapin in the United States. [*C. pumila* (L.) Mill.]

Similar to our European is the American beech (Spec. 1), which I found only in the northernmost parts of Massachusetts, where it reaches a great height and serves for the same uses as ours. I find, however, that Mr. Marshall describes as belonging to the American beech that variety known in the gardens under the name of Copper-leaved beech, whence I suppose that this beautiful species that I did not observe is perhaps native to the more internal regions of the states of Pennsylvania and New Jersey. This Copper-leaved beech is highly prized for its extraordinary color and is still rare in Europe, where in gardens it is grafted onto the common beech. It could very well be that its color is constant and might be obtained from seed, and therefore might form a new species. [Copper beech (*F. sylvatica* cv. *atropunicea*) originated in several European gardens and comes true from seed to a limited extent. The American beech is not known to produce colored foliage.]

The American Chestnut (Spec. 2) is a mere variety of our chestnut and forms a very handsome tree of 60 and even 80 feet high. The bur is about the same size as ours but contains up to six and seven chestnuts, which are consequently very small. They are eaten boiled and roasted like ours, and even raw, and sometimes in the more internal regions they are roasted like coffee. In any case their taste is inferior to that of European chestnuts. The wood is easy to split lengthwise, but is used a great deal for making fence stakes, since it lasts longer than that of American oaks. The charcoal is employed in forges, and, in short, its wood serves all the purposes that the European Chestnut does.

The dwarf chestnut called Chinkapin (Spec. 3) is a shrub that does not exceed a height of 10 to 12 feet. Its leaves are smaller than those of the common chestnut and somewhat fuzzy underneath. It produces very small burs which for the most part contain only one chestnut scarcely the size of an average grape and with a sharp point. Americans are little concerned about gathering them, so that they serve as fodder for pigs and other animals. Whenever they are put on the table, they are eaten raw, being in fact sweet and very tasty. Catesby says that the Indians stocked them for the winter. Its wood is good only for the fire, but in this respect, it is inferior to the chestnut.

FOTHERGILLA

C. [sic.] gardeni. Linn.

Fothergilla Gardeni. Marshall *Arb. Amer.* pag. 47. [*Fothergilla gardeni* Murr.]

Fothergilla was discovered not many years ago in South Carolina by Dr. [Alexander] Garden and was sent for the first time by Mr. John Bartram to Mr. Peter Collinson in London under the name of *Gardenia.* However, since this designation had already been given by Linnaeus to the lovely Goa jasmine, so called, it was named in honor of the famous English botanist Dr. [John] Fothergill, the memory of its discoverer being preserved in the trivial name *gardeni.* This little shrub, which at first sight resembles the alder, grows in the vicinity of marshes in the Carolinas, rising to a height of barely two or three feet, putting out many shoots from the base, and winding about a great deal with its roots. The leaves are alternate, oval, somewhat dentate at the tips; and the flowers, which come out in spikes from the ends of the branches, lack a corolla and are furnished with 16 to 18 long, very white stamens. Its fruit are quite like those of *Hamamelis,** of only half the size, however, and contain two smooth, hard, oblong seeds of a white color. This shrub can be propagated from seed, and also from roots, and can serve an ornamental purpose, since its blossoms are very pretty and come out early in the spring.

FRANKLINIA
(Tab. XII)

[Castiglioni's plate XII is the first published illustration of *Franklinia.* It precedes Wm. Bartram's drawing in his *Travels* (1791).]

F. ALATAMAHA. Marsh.

Calyx (1) Perianthium monopetalum, 5-partium, persistens, laciniis concavis, subrotundis.
Corolla (2) Petala quinque ob-ovata, magna, basi unita.
Stamina (3) Filamenta numerosa, corollae inserta, & basi coalita in corpus cylindricum. Antherae binae.
Pistillum (4) Germen subrotundum, vix sulcatum. Stylus cylindricus, staminibus longior. Stigma obtusum.
Pericarpium (5) Capsula ovata, quinque-locularis.
Semina (6) Plurima, ovato-compressa.

[*Franklinia alatamaha* Marsh.]

Franklinia is a new acquisition for lovers of natural history, so named in honor of Benjamin Franklin, a handsome shrub discovered by 1760 by John Bartram on the shores of the Alatamaha River in Georgia. Fifteen years later it was taken to Pennsylvania by his son William Bartram, who cultivated it in his garden near Philadelphia and from the seed obtained plants that in the fourth year began to bloom and in the fifth produced mature seed. It grows to a height of about 20 feet, dividing into many branches arranged alternately like the leaves, which are oblong, narrow at the base, and saw-toothed. The flowers come out of the ends of the branches, are composed of five wide white petals adorned in the center by a thick crown of yellow stamens sometimes up to five English inches in diameter when they are fully opened. They have the delightful fragrance of orange blossoms and produce a dry capsule of about the size of a hazelnut that opens into five segments. According to the observations of Mr. Marshall, verified by me, *Franklinia* ought to form a new genus between the *Stewartia* and *Gordonia* in the *Monadelphia polyandria* class of Linnaeus. One can hope with good reason that this shrub can hold up in our Lombardy climate, since it flourishes vigorously in that of Pennsylvania.

*See the entry on *Hamamelis.*

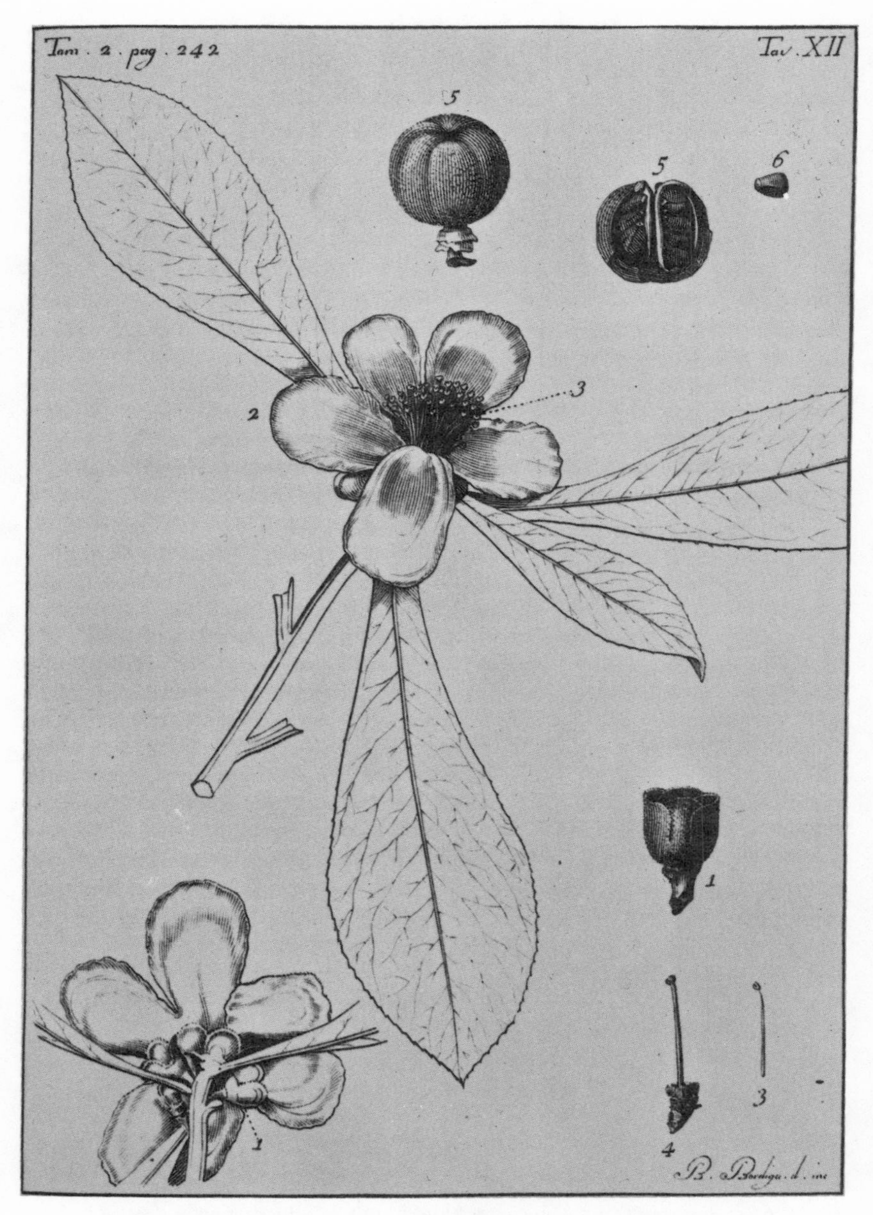

Plate XII. Earliest published illustration of Bartram's Franklinia.

FRAXINUS

[See Li (1957), 3.]

1. *F. AMERICANA foliolis integerrimis, petiolis teretibus.* Lin.
Fraxinus Caroliniensis foliis angustioribus, utrinque acuminatis pendulis. Catesby *Carol.* tom. I tab. 80.

Red ash in the United States. [White ash, *Fraxinus americana* L.]

b. alba

Fraxinus alba. Marsh. *Arb. Amer.* p. 51. Fraxinus acuminata. Lamarck *Encycl. method.* n. 5. Fraxinus ex Nova Anglia pinnis foliorum in mucronem productoribus. Duh. *Arb. & Arbust.* n. 6.

White ash in the United States. [*F. americana* L.]

c. pensylvanica

Fraxinus pensilvanica. Marsh. *Arb. Amer.* pag. 51.

Sharp-keyed ash in the United States. [Red ash, *F. pennsylvanica* Marsh.]

2. *F. NIGRA foliolis dentatis; floribus calyciferis* N[obis].
Fraxinus nigra. Marsh. *Arb. Amer.* p. 51. Fraxinus Caroliniana. Lamarck *Encycl. méthod.* n. 7.

Black ash in the United States. [*F. nigra* Marsh.]

b. juglandifolia

Fraxinus juglandifolia. Lamarck n. 6. Fraxinus Caroliniana latiori fructu. Duh. n. 5.

c. pubescens

Fraxinus pubescens. Lamarck n. 8. Fraxinus Ornus Americana. *Hort. Reg. Paris.*

d. sambucifolia

Fraxinus sambucifolia. Lamarck n. 9.

There are certain genera of plants, as, for example, the ash and willow whose species differ so little from one another and so easily vary in different climes and terrains that it is almost impossible to distinguish true species from simple varieties. The celebrated Linnaeus says, speaking of the willow: *Species hujus generis difficillime extricantur, solum palustre, arenosum, alpestre, calidum mutavit mira metamorphosi species, ut de iisdem haesitarint saepius Botanici.* And the same difficulty is encountered at present with the genus *Fraxinus,* ash, whose American species are made to number as many as five by the most recent botanists, whereas Linnaeus had recognized only one under the name *Fraxinus americana.* It is true, however, that the differences on which these new species were established are not, as Linnaeus says, essential, consisting principally in the greater or lesser width of the leaves and fruit, variations very well known also in other genera of plants, especially the willow, oak, and the American White nut [*Carya*], the last of which would form by itself four or five species if one were to consider these small differences. *Primaria caussa* (so says Linnaeus in his *Critica Botanica*) *cur nomina specifica antecessorum fallacia evaserint, sola in eo consistit, quod partes, & notas naturales, ac certas a ludicris distinguere recusarint. Cum autem assumpserint omnes notas accidentales, & naturales indifferenter, indeque constituerint ob minimam notam novam speciem, orta fuit tanta confusio, tanta nominum barbaries, tanta specierum* *falsarum accumulatio, ut facilius esset stabulum Augiae purgare, quam Botanicen.* Motivated by these reasons, I was led to reduce to only two species the ashes of United America, taking the specific difference from the dentations of the leaflets; hence to *Fraxinus americana* of Linnaeus (which has entire leaves) belongs *Fraxinus alba* of Marshall, called White ash in America, that differs from the Linnaean species only in having wider leaves and growing to a greater height; and to it must be referred also *Fraxinus acuminata* Lamarck, which is the *Fraxinus pennsylvanica* Marshall, different only for its longer and narrower seeds. The second species which, keeping the name of Marshall, I have called *Fraxinus nigra,* has dentate leaves, and from this specific difference it can easily be distinguished, all the more so if constant in all its varieties were what was observed by M. Lamarck in *Fraxinus caroliniana* and *pubescens,* namely, flowers provided with calyx. It would thus form a species between the common ash with bare flowers and [*F.*] *ornus* or Manna ash,* whose flowers have the corolla in addition to the calyx. To this Spec. 2 are referred the ashes *juglandifolia, caroliniana,* and *pubescens* of M. Lamarck, and perhaps also the one called *sambucifolia* of the same author, whose difference consists in having sessile leaves, a difference not very noticeable in the ash, which has leaves provided with extremely short petioles.

The American ash (Spec. 1) grows to a height of 40 and 50 feet by 18 and more inches in diameter. Its wood, especially that of variety (b) called White ash is preferred by carriage makers for making wheels and is used like our own by turners. The inside bark and the seeds are used to promote urination.

The Black ash (Spec. 2) serves the same uses as the first, except that it is smaller. The seeds of the ash, as likewise the leaves and flowers of this and other American plants, are often subject to being transformed into curious and grotesque figures by the numerous tribes of galliferous insects that abound in those interminable woodlands. On 7 December 1786 I was at the home of Mr. Hultgreen,[†] then a minister of the Swedish church in Philadelphia, a person very well informed in natural history, who showed me among the many plants in his *hortus siccus* a branch laden with seeds. These were of lanceolate form quite similar to those of the ash, except that in the midst of these there were others in the shape of balls the size of half a Neapolitan medlar and made of a substance resembling a mass of dried leaves. I remained for a while in doubt as to what tree that branch belonged, but observing it carefully and breaking a few of those balls I discovered very easily that it was the work of certain insects that had destroyed the seed of the ash to make of it a nest for themselves.‡

**Fraxinus ornus* Lin. This should be called rather *F. florifera*; and in fact Scopoli in the *Flora Carniolica* (2nd. ed.) changed the trivial name of *ornus* to *florifera,* while the name *Ornus,* from Micheli, who first illustrated this genus, was given to the *Fraxinus apetala,* to which Scopoli restored it.

[†Rev. Matthias Hultgren, as Wicacoa Mission, Philadelphia, was preparing an account of his residence in North America. It remains a 7-volume unpublished manuscript, vol. 3 on natural history. See E. E. Larson, *Swedish Commentators on America, 1638–1865* (New York, 1963), 69. Amandus Johnson, *Nicholas Collin* (Philadelphia, 1936), 35, says Hultgren sailed from Philadelphia July 2, 1786!]

‡Linnaeus speaks of these monstrosities produced in plants by insects in Vol. III of his *Amoenitates Academicae* in the dissertation entitled *Miracula Insectorum.* I saw another curious example in a *Vaccinium* that I shall speak about in the proper place.

GAULTHERIA

G. PROCUMBENS. Lin.*
Vitis idaea canadensis pyrolae folio. Tournef. *I. R. H.* pag. 608.

Winterberry and Mountain tree in the United States, *Tee-Buske* among the Swedes in New Jersey, and *Pollom* among the Indians in Canada. [*Gaultheria procumbens* L.]

This plant, very common in the woods of Massachusetts and New Hampshire, was so denominated by Mr. Kalm in honor of M. [Jean-François] Gaulthier, a Canadian doctor known for the precise description he gave of the method of making sugar from the maple of those regions. *Gaultheria* is a small shrub about a foot high with ovate evergreen leaves for the most part coming out from the tips of the shoots. The blossoms are white and like those of *Vitis-idaea,* but provided with 10 stamens and a pistil, which are followed by little red berries. The infusion of the leaves is used instead of tea, so that it got the name of Mountain tea from the Swedes. It is also called Winterberry because it keeps its berries during the winter. The Canadian Indians call it *Pollom.*

GLEDITSCHIA [*sic*]

G. TRIACANTHOS caule spinis triplicibus axillaribus. Lin.
Acacia Americana Abruae folio triacanthos. Pluk. *Mantissa,* tab. 352 fig. 1.

Honey locust in the United States. [*Gleditsia triacanthos* L.]

b. aquatica

Gletidsia aquatica. Marsh. p. 54 Gleditsia spinis subsimplicibus, leguminibus monospermis. Gleditsia caroliniensis. Lamarck art. "Fovier."

Water acacia in the United States. [*G. aquatica* Marsh.]

c. inermis

Gleditsia inermis mas, & foemina. Duh. *Arb. & Arbust.* n. 2. [*G. triacanthos* var. *inermis* Willd.]

Gleditsia† is a tree 40 and more feet high. Its foliage is very beautiful and composed of double pinnate leaves of a very deep green. The flowers are not very showy and are of a greenish white. They come out in long spikes in May. Sterile and hermaphroditic ones are found on the same tree and female ones on a different plant. I didn't have the opportunity to observe female plants of Gleditsia, but I noted that on those with hermaphroditic flowers they were less numerous than sterile ones and

*Mr. Reichard, *Syst. Plant.,* Tom. II, p. 297, called this plant *Gualtheria* instead of *Gaultheria* [a misprint].

†It was given this name in honor of the famous German botanist Mr. [Johann Gottlieb] Gleditsch [1714–86].

that the spikes bearing some of the former were shorter and thicker with flowers. I have also called sterile those flowers of *Gleditsia* for the reason already adduced in speaking of the flowers called male by Linnaeus, both of the maples and other plants of the class *Polygamia*. In both the sterile and hermaphroditic ones the stamens are from five to nine, two of which frequently open their anthers before the others; the calyx has three, four, and up to five segments, and the corolla, five petals.*

The variety called *aquatica* (Var. b) discovered by Catesby on Mr. Warring's plantation [Waring in Catesby] near the Ashley River in South Carolina differs mainly in having shorter spines, very often simple ones, that is, without lateral spines principally on the trunk, smaller leaves and oval pods containing a single seed. For this reason M. Lamarck and also Mr. Marshall made of it a different species under the names *Gleditsia aquatica* and *Gleditsia caroliniensis*, since it is found, as I have already said, in the marshlands of Carolina.

The variety called *inermis*, that is, without thorns (Var. c) is noted only by M. Duhamel and described by Linnaeus under the name *Gleditsia inermis*, who added to it the synonyms of Plukenet and Miller, which belong according to the most recent observations, to another completely different species of *Gleditsia* described by M. Lamarck under No. 4 and called by him *Gleditsia javanica*.† The variety called *inermis* is perhaps only due to cultivation and better soil.

I saw *Gleditsia* for the first time on the shores of the little river Aesopus between Albany and New York and then in the town of Rochelle between New York State and Connecticut. The siliques [properly legumes] of this tree are very long, flat, and of a dark brown color, containing a number of ovate, compressed, hard seeds. The internal pulp of the [legume] is green and of a sweet honey-like taste, whence came the name of Honey locust, or Acacia mellifera, for the tree. Some people use these [legumes] in making beer, and in winter they are sometimes given to sheep, which eat them very eagerly. The beauty of this tree and the use that can be made of both its wood and its legumes should induce us to propagate it here where, within my experience, it has survived the hardest winter, even though the tender young plants had been transplanted late in the fall and in a sandy and uncultivated soil. One should see to it, however, that the plants are at least three years old, inasmuch as rabbits gnaw on the tender shoots. It multiplies very readily from seed, and by that means one can have varieties, mainly the one without thorns, which is preferable for many

**Flos sterilis*
Calyx 3–5 fidus.
Corolla 5 petala.
Stam. 5–9.
Flos hermaphroditus
Idem.
Pistillum. Stylus brevis reflexus.
Stigma crassum superius pubescens.
Obs.: *Amentum in culta quandoque monstruosum spina laterali herbacea, flore terminali ex pluribus coalito. Amenta hermaphrodita breviora, confertiora. Calyx & corolla adeo coaliti, ut vix eorum divisio appareat.*

†*Encyclop. méthod.*, art. "Févier."

uses. The long, sharp thorns with which the others are provided render them fit for making unpenetrable hedges, if this tree can withstand frequent pruning which I haven't yet tried. Like [Robinia] *Pseudo-acacia* it can serve as ornament for avenues and gardens, but as with that, care must be taken not to leave just two branches since it is then subject to being split by the wind.

In the seed of *Gleditsia* that I collected in America I found a species of tiny tobacco-colored beetle with black spots that had grown in the seed after boring through the legume. I happened to find the insect in its various metamorphoses (that is, in the state of larva—a little lemon-colored worm, of chrysalis, and of mature insect), to which I intend to give the name of *Chrysomela Gleditsiae,* since I have not found it in the literature.* Probably this creature deposits its eggs on the legume, the worm later penetrating to the seed on which it feeds. In these empty seeds I also found a number of tiny flies half the size of a mosquito of a goldish-green color with white legs near which there were some small greenish worms and some proportionate chrysalides. This I recognized as the *Ichneumon puparum* of Linnaeus,† so called because it lays its eggs in the chrysalides of other insects, especially in that of the butterfly *Antiopa,* for which reason Sig. Scopoli called it *Ichneumon antiopae* in his *Entomologia Carniolica.*

It must be said that this tiny fly enters through the hole already made by the worm of the Chrysomela, in the body of which or in whose chrysalis it lays the eggs from which are born the little worms that feed on the creature killed. The analogy of similar behavior in insects of this kind leaves no room for doubt.

GLYCINE

G. APIOS foliis impari-pinnatis ovato-lanceolatis; foliolis septenis. Lin.
Astragalus perennis, spicatus, Americanus, scandens, radice tuberosa. Morison. *Hist.* 2 pag. 102 tab. 9 fig. 1. Apios Americana. Cornuti *Plantae Canadenses* Cap. 76 pag. 200.

Indian potatoes in the United States. [*Glycine americana* Medic.]

The roots of this leguminous climbing plant that grows abundantly along the St. Lawrence River take the form of knots of varying size joined like a necklace and are eaten by the Indians raw, boiled in water, and roasted as one does potatoes. However, the inhabitants along the St. Lawrence River make no use of them. Not so for

**Chrysomela (Gleditsiae) elytris striatis, nitidis, nigro-variegatis.* N[obis]. *Magnitudo C. 4-punctatae. Antennae thorace longiores, rufae. Caput, & thorax rufi. Thorax punctis, excavatis, pilis flavescentibus rarioribus. Pedes rufi. Larva citrina, capite fusco. Pupa lutea. Variat longitud. 3–4 lin. ped. paris. Cryptocephali genus* Fabric. & Geoff. *Buprestis genus* Scopoli. [Fabricius, *Mantissa,* p. x and no. 31, now *Amblycerus robiniae* (F.) of the family *Bruchidae.* The editors gratefully acknowledge John M. Kingsolver's interest and aid.]

†*Ichneumon Puparum* Lin. [*Systema Naturae,* ed. X (1758) 1: 567.] Obs.: *Larva pallide-viridis. Pupa nigra. Vide* Réaumur, *Histoire des insectes,* Tom. VI tab. 30 fig. 13, 14, 15 Roesel. *Insec.* Tom. II, "Vesp.," tab. 3.

the first European colonists of New Jersey who called this plant *Hopniss* or *Hapniss* with the name given to it by the Indians, from whom they learned to boil the roots which they ate like bread. The blossoms are quite pretty and fragrant, so that it has already been cultivated for many years as an ornamental in European gardens. We denote it by the common name of *Scherzo* or *Riccio di dama.* The Indians more removed from the sea used its legumes as we do peas.*

GORDONIA

G. LASIANTHUS. Lin.

Alcea Floridana quinque capsularis, laurinis foliis laeviter crenatis, seminibus coniferarum instar alatis. Catesby *Carolin.* Tom. I tab. 44 Seligmann Tom. I tab. 88. Gordonia. Ellis *Act. angl.* 1770 [1771]. Hypericum Lasianthus. *Hort. Cliffort.* 380. Gordon. Lamarck *Encyclop. methodiq.*

[*Gordonia lasianthus* L.]

The swamps of Georgia and the Carolinas produce abundantly the *Gordonia,* so called by Mr. Ellis in honor of Mr. [James] Gordon [c. 1708–80], a famous plant dealer in England. This plant grows to a height of 12 to 15 feet, its leaves are lanceolate and saw-toothed, and its blossoms, provided with long peduncles, come out at the ends of the branches from the axils of the leaves. They are white and fragrant and produce ovate capusles, sharp at the point, which divide into five segments and contain winged seeds shaped like those of *Pinus sylvestris.* From a comparison of the generic description given by Linnaeus of *Gordonia* and from the one I gave of *Franklinia,* it is easy to see how much difference there is between the two genera, although some have brought them together into a single one: 1) the calyx of *Gordonia* is formed of five leaves, while in *Franklinia* it consists of a single leaf divided into five parts; 2) the ovary of *Gordonia* is oval, that of *Franklinia* almost round—the style of the former has five angles and ends in five stigmas, and that of the latter is round with a blunt stigma; 3) the fruit of *Gordonia* is pointed, has a calyx that almost half covers it, and the winged seeds are about six in each little locule with the seed toward the base, whereas, *Franklinia* has nearly spherical capsules and its numerous and wingless seeds are set one on top of the other according to the length of the fruit. In addition to these dissimilarities that constitute the essential difference in genus there are many others by which these two plants are easily distinguished, since the flowers of *Gordonia* have a longer peduncle, and are not so large as in *Franklinia,* and the leaves are more dentate and narrower. The capsules of *Gordonia* are covered with silvery hair and are smaller. This plant can be propagated in damp locations if one takes care to protect it from the cold for the first few years; but it is hard to raise from seeds, which don't come up from the ground until the second year. *Gordonia* is a handsome tree of medium height; it begins to bloom in May, and continues all summer.

*Kalm, Vol. I, p. 274.

GUILANDINA

G. DIOICA inermis; foliis bipinnatis, basi apiceque simpliciter pinnatis. Lin. Bonduc canadense non spinosum mas, & foemina. Duhamel *Arb. & Arbust.* Gymnocladus canadensis. Lamarck. *Encyclop. méthodiq.* Art. "Chicot."

Chicot in Canada, Nikar or Coffee-tree in the United States. [*Gymnocladus dioica* (L.) K. Koch]

Guilandina is a very rare tree in North America, found only and seldom in the internal parts of Canada and in the region of Kentucky. It grows to a height of about 30 feet, dividing into many branches covered with an ashy-colored bark and provided with very long bi-pinnate leaves with oval leaflets. The blossoms come out in clusters and are of a whitish color, male and female on different plants. The females produce one cylindrical legume about five inches long, pulpy and divided internally into many transverse little chambers containing very tough ovate seeds. Because of this cylindrical, pulpy, and multilocular fruit, the Chevalier Lamarck thought it necessary to form a new genus different from *Guilandina* under the name of *Gymnocladus*. This name, coming from *gymnos* (nude) and *clados* (branch), is equivalent to the name *Chicot* by which it is distinguished by the French in Canada since, upon losing in winter its long leaves that make up its total foliage, it looks like a lopped tree. The inhabitants of Kentucky roast its seeds and use them to make a kind of bad coffee,

[Br 2:324]. It withstands our Lombard winters and deserves to be propagated, if only for its unusualness. It likes a dry soil.

HALESIA

1. *H. TETRAPTERA foliis lanceolato-ovatis; petiolis glandulosis.* Lin. Frutex Padi foliis serratis; floribus monopetalis albis companiformibus, fructu crasso tetragono. Catesby *Carolin.* Tom. I tab. 64. Seligmann. Tom. II tab. 28. Halesia fructibus membranaceo-quadrangulatis. Ellis *Act. angl.* Tom. 51 tab. 22 fig. A.

Silver-bell tree in the United States. [*Halesia carolina* L.]

2. *H. DIPTERA foliis ovatis, petiolis laevibus.* Lin.
Halesia fructibus alatis. Ellis *Act. angl.* Tom. 51, tab. 22 fig. B. [*H. diptera* Ellis]

Halesia (Spec. 1) is found on the banks of the brooks and rivers along the way that leads from Savannah to Augusta, where I saw it in bloom in the month of April. It is a shrub about 12 feet high and produces very pretty extremely white flowers anging like bells. The capsules are quadrangular, winged, very pointed, and of a yellow-brown color when mature. Their substance is membranaceo-fungous, and they contain a very hard pit.

Species 2 differs from the first in not having the petioles of the leaves provided with glandules; and the leaves are larger and quite smooth underneath. Furthermore, the fruit of this second species has only two wings, although the rudiments of the other two are evident. It seems to me nevertheless that one could make one species out of the two Halesias, since the second is at the very most a simple variety—a fact that could be verified by obtaining many plants from seed. It will serve to ornament copses in springtime.

HAMAMELIS

H. VIRGINICA. Lin.. [*Sic*]
Pistacia Virginiana Coryli foliis. Pluk. *Almag.* pag. 298. Trilopus. Mitchell *gen.* 22. Hamamelis Gron. *Fl. Virg.* Catesby *Carol.* Tom. 3. tab. 2. Duh. *Arb. & Arbust.*

Witch-hazel in the United States. [*Hamamelis virginiana* L.]

Hamamelis puts forth a great number of shoots from the base that divide into many branches furnished with firm oval leaves with fluted margins resembling those of the hazelnut. The flowers, coming directly out of the branches, are of a grassy-yellow color and composed of four linear petals in the midst of which are perceived four tiny stamens and two pistils. The fruit is a kind of a two-horned nut that divides into two little locules, each of which contains a hard, smooth, almost black seed. This singular shrub generally does not bloom in America until its leaves fall in the autumn from the cold and continues until the snow begins to fall. The ovary holds on through the winter, and the fruit matures only in September of the following year; and then, as it begins to bloom once more, the flowers and the mature fruit can be seen on the same branch. For this reason, since it is among the very few plants that bloom in the fall, it will be extremely useful in gardens, although its flower is not very large nor very showy. The Indians considered this shrub one of the most precious items in their medicine. They used to apply to tumors and external inflammations the bark which has a soothing resolvent property, and they made a poultice with the inside bark as a remedy for burning eyes. The aforementioned bark when chewed has at first a bitter and astringent taste, leaving thereafter a pricking sensation on the tongue that lasts for a long time. The properties of this shrub, however, are not sufficiently understood and it may perhaps be, as Mr. Cutler assures us* of great use in medicine. It is easily propagated from seed [LC paraphrases Cutler (1785), 412–13].

HIBISCUS

1. *H. MOSCHEUTOS foliis ovatis, acuminatis serratis; caule simplicissimo; petiolis floriferis.* Lin.
Alcea rosea peregrina, forte rosa moscheutos Plinii. Corn. *Pl. Canad.* pag. 144 tab. 145.

Breast-root in Virginia. [*Hibiscus moscheutos* L.]

**Columbian Magazine,* Tom. I, p. 438.

2. *H. PALUSTRIS caule simplicissimo, foliis ovatis-subtrilobis, subtus tomentosis; floribus axillaribus.* Lin.
Althaea palustris. Bauch. [Bauhin] *Pinax.* pag. 316. Ketmia palustris flore purpureo Tourn. *I. R. H.* p. 100.
[*H. palustris* L.]

3. *H. VIRGINICUS foliis inferioribus cordatis, acuminatis, serratis, superioribus hastatis.* Lin.*
[*Kosteletzkya virginica* (L.) Presl]

Various species of *Hibiscus* are quite well known for the beauty of their broad and vivid blossoms, as, for example, the frutescent *Althaea*† that serves in forming hedges in gardens, *malvaviscus,*‡ *manihot,*§ and the so-called Chinese rose.|| However, among all those that withstand our climate it seems to me that the first place must go to *moscheutos* and *virginic[a],* which every year come up from the base and form a handsome clump.

Hibiscus moscheutos (Spec. 1) is easily distinguished from the other two since it has flowers that come out of petioles of the leaves, which are ovate, acuminate, and saw-toothed. In some parts of Virginia its root is used in the form of an emollient poultice in tumors of the breasts, whence the name of Breast-root.

Hibiscus palustris (Spec. 2) differs little from the first except in that its leaves are a bit woolly underneath and the axillary flowers are not attached to the petioles of the leaves and are provided with longer peduncles.

Finally, *virginic[a]* (Spec. 3) has cordate, acuminate, and dentate lower leaves and hastate# upper ones. The plants obtained from seed I sent from America produced in the second year long flowers attached to the petioles of the leaves and varying from white to flesh-color.

All three of these species are propagated from seed and from roots, and since they come up every year from the base, they are very valuable for the beauty and the abundance of the flowers.

[Br 3:159]

ILEX AQUIFOLIUM
[*Ilex opaca* Ait.]

Holly. It grows in damp places scattered through the forests, and it is one of the less common trees. The Swedes take its leaves, which remain green in the winter,

*It varies in the color of the stems, now white and now reddish; in the flowers, now white, now flesh-colored; and in the divisions of the calyx, that go from 10 to 17.
†*Hibiscus syriacus* Lin.
‡*Hibiscus malvaviscus* Lin.
§*Hibiscus manihot* Lin.
||*Hibiscus rosa-sinensis* Lin.
#In the shape of a three-pointed spear.

and grinding them in a mortar, they boil them with ordinary beer and use them for pleurisies. Kalm. Vol. I, p. 224.

JUGLANS

1. *I. Alba foliolis septenis lanceolatis, serratis, impari sessili.* Lin.

a. ovata

Juglans alba ovata Marshall. Juglans alba fructu ovato compresso cortice squamoso. Gronov. *Virgin.* pag. 150. Duh. n. 11.

Shellbark in the United States; *Chiska-tama* among the Indians. [*Carya ovata* (Mill.) K. Koch. We are indebted to Donald Stone for *Carya* suggestions.]

b. acuminata

Juglans alba acuminata (Marshall). Juglans foliolis lanceolatis glabris, acute serratis, acuminatis, pedunculorum longitudine fere aequalibus. Gronov. pag. 150.

White walnut and Hickory tree in the United States. [*C. glabra* (Mill.) Sweet]

c. odorata

Juglans alba odorata. Marshall. Juglans alba procera fructu minimo, an Juglans alba fructu minori cortice glabro? Clayton *Fl. Virgin.*

Balsam hickory (Marshall). [*C. ovalis* (Wangenh.) Sarg.]

d. minima

Juglans alba minima. Marshall. an Juglans foliolis lanceolatis serratis superioribus majoribus? Gronov. *Fl. Virg.* pag. 150. Nux Juglans Virginiana alba minor, fructu nucis moschatae simili, cortice glabro, summo fastigio veluti in aculeum producto. Pluk. *Almag.* 254 tab. 309 fig. 2.

Pignut hickory in the United States. [*C. cordiformis* (Wangenh.) K. Koch]

e. pacana

Juglans pecan. Marshall, *Pacanier* of the French; Pecan or Illinois hickory in the United States. [*C. illinoensis* (Wagenh.) K. Koch]

2. *I. NIGRA foliolis quindenis lanceolatis serratis, exterioribus minoribus, gemmulis super axillaribus.* Lin.

Nux Juglans Virginiana nigra. Duh. *Arb. & Arbust.* n. 13. Catesby. *Carol.* Tom. I tab. 67.

Black walnut in the United States. [*Juglans nigra* L.]

3. *I. CINEREA oblonga, foliolis cordato-lanceolatis, inferne nervosis, pediculis foliorum pubescentibus.* Lin.

Nux Juglans Virginiana nigra, fructu oblongo prof[u]ndissime insculpto. Duham *Arb. & Arbust.,* n. 14.

Butternut in the United States. [*J. cinerea* L.]

There are very many varieties of *Juglans alba* (Spec. 1), which grows everywhere in Massachusetts and goes under the names of Hickory, White walnut, Shellbark, etc. The variety called *ovata* by Mr. Marshall (Var. a) grows up to 70 and 80 feet high in wet and rich soil, its bark is rough and scaly, and the leaves are for the most part composed of five serrate leaflets with no petiolules. The nuts are almost round, somewhat flat, sharp-pointed, and covered with a coarse husk that divides into four parts, and the shell contains tasty meat segments. The tree is called Shellbark because of its squamous bark.

Variety (b), which Mr. Marshall calls *acuminata,* is not as tall as the preceding, the leaves are composed of five to seven lanceolate leaflets and sharper at the point, and the nuts with the bark are about two inches long and only about one wide. This husk is also divided into four parts and discloses the nuts, which are white and very hard, with four elevated ridges that alternate with the divisions of the husk. These nuts, called Hickory nuts, are very inferior to the preceding, so that some inexperienced people are fooled by them. Variety (c), called *odorata* by Mr. Marshall, forms one of the tallest trees, with flexible and very yielding branches; and its fruit are small, round, with a thin husk and sweet meat segments. There is a variety with wider leaves, and fruit with a coarser husk and quite a small nut. These two varieties are called Common white walnut in New York and Hickory in Pennsylvania. This is the wood most valued for the fireplaces of the gentry and most used by artisans for wagon axles, ax handles, and other farming tools. Variety (d) is a tree 80 and more feet high, called *minima* by Mr. Marshall because it has much narrower and shorter leaves than the others and smaller fruit. These are covered with a thin husk and a very tender shell, and the meat segments are quite large, but of a bitter taste. In the United States it is called Pignut hickory, and its wood is not regarded very highly. Gronovius, speaking of this nut, which he calls Common hickory, says that the aments of the flowers have a rancid odor and that beneath each flower can be seen a bract much longer than the flower itself. Variety (e), finally, called *Pacana* by the Indians, is found only in the internal regions near the Illinois River, and its nuts, stripped of the husks, are oblong, quite smooth, and very much like acorns of the oak, with a tender shell and very tasty meat segments. I haven't seen the plant, although I have had many of its fruits; but I was told that it resembles very closely the preceding variety. It is noteworthy that the White walnut is a sign of rich terrain, as is the pine of a sterile and sandy soil. The White walnut grows readily from seed, but the young plants are very delicate and must be protected carefully during the first few years.

The Black walnut (Spec. 2) grows to a height of 50 to 70 feet and has a grooved bark of a dark color. Its leaves are composed of 15 and more leaflets, the fruit are big and almost round, and the nuts contained within them, grooved and extremely hard. The meat segments are not too large and have an oily and unpleasant taste, so that they would be excellent for producing oil in abundance, if it were not difficult to extract it on account of the hardness and thickness of the shell and of the adhesion of the kernel to it. The wood is used by inlayers and carpenters and takes a nice polish, but its color is too dark, and almost black, so that it is not much esteemed in places where beautiful mahogany wood can be had easily.* With the bark of the Black walnut and the husk of its fruit are dyed wool and dark-colored textiles.

Juglans cinerea (Spec. 3) rises to 40 feet and more and forms a tree rich with

**Swietenia.* Jacquin *Americ.,* & Lin.

beautiful foliage. Its leaves are composed of 11 to 15 leaflets, so that it is easily distinguished from *alba,* which has 5 to 7, as from *nigra,* which has more. The husk of the fruit is hairy, thin, and covered with a viscous substance. The shell is large, oblong, very deeply and irregularly sculpted, and contains indeed soft and sweet meat segments, but very small and rather oily. These trees grow for the most part along the banks of the Connecticut River, near the St. Lawrence River.

The bark of the trunk is of an ashy color and serves, according to Mr. Marshall, as a mild purgative. With the shredded internal bark are woven chairs that last from four to five years, and the husk of the fruit makes a fine dark-colored dye that does not fade easily.

Both *Juglans cinerea* and *nigra* came up for me very nicely from seed, and in spite of the extremely cold winter of last year, 1789, are growing with full vigor.

JUNIPERUS

I. VIRGINIANA foliis ternis basi adnatis; junioribus imbricatis, senioribus patulis. Lin.
Juniperus Virginiana, foliis interioribus juniperinis, superioribus Sabinam, vel Cupressum referentibus. Duh. n. 6. Juniperus Caroliniana. Marshall n. 2.

b. foliis omnibus patentibus
Juniperus Virginiana folio ubique juniperino. Duh. n. 8. Juniperus Virginiana. Marsh. n. 1.

Red cedar, Savin tree in the United States. [*Juniperus virginiana* L.]

The ancients included under the name of Cedar various resinous plants of diverse genus. The Cedar of Lebanon* about which the Holy Scriptures have so much to say is a species of pine, or rather of larch [no: *Cedrus libani*] with evergreen leaves and wood excellent for construction. Heretofore it was found only on Mount Lebanon, whence it was transported to England, the oldest of which, now of an enormous size, can be seen at Chelsea [Physick Garden] near London. The other cedars, distinguished by the Greeks into major and minor, of which there is so much talk in all the ancient authors, belong to the genus of Juniper. In fact Theophrastus says that some also called the Juniper Cedar, and ascribes to them no difference other than that the Cedar has harder and sharper leaves and more fragrant and sweeter fruit.† Pliny mentions three species of cedar, one that he calls "Lycian," which must be the *Juniperus oxycedrus* of Linnaeus; the second called by him "Phoenician," which is the *Juniperus phoenicia* of the same Linnaeus; and a third, that he divides into two species, one fructiferous and the other nonfructiferous, which are the female and the male of the *Juniperus thurifera* of Linnaeus.‡

**Pinus Cedrus.* Lin. [*Cedrus libani* A. Rich.]
†Theophrast., *Hist. Plant. illust. a Stapel & Scaliger,* (Amstelod [Amsterdam], 1644) p. 190.
‡Plin. *Hist. Nat.* Lib. XIII. Cap. v.

N.B. The Lycian juniper of Linnaeus is the same as the Phoenician, and the difference consists in the age or the sex of the plant: *Theophrastus hunc fructicem oxycedrum appellat, & cedrum*

The Red cedar or American juniper (of which I now undertake to speak) has two varieties, one with subulate (or awl-shaped) leaves like the common juniper and the other with subulate leaves near the ground and imbricated ones at the tips of the branches, so that it forms a species between the common juniper and the Phoenician. The little plants I raised from American seed had all subulate leaves and in a plant that I have already had for a number of years and has reached the height of eight feet and more I noted a great variety in the leaves of the various branches. I observed another phenomenon in this plant, which this year has produced berries, although there is no other Red cedar in the garden nor in this neighborhood. That confirms the observation of Mr. Fabricius (cited by Mr. Reichard in the *Systema Plant.*), namely that the Red cedar sometimes produces first only male flowers, and then female, unlike the other junipers that have the male and female on different plants. The bark of the trunk is reddish and divided into thin sheets that wind obliquely around the tree and can easily be detached. The fruit [cone] is smaller than that of the common juniper and of a dark blue color. River banks and other sloping terrains are very favorable to it, but it thrives even in the leanest and most sandy soils and among rocks and crags. It is found in great quantity on the hills near Boston in Massachusetts and reaches there a height of 15 to 20 feet; but it grows spontaneously up to 44° 35′ of northern latitude, because I saw it 18 miles from Fort St. John on the Sorrel River in Canada. Kalm says that the wood of the Red cedar resists rot better than any other, and in fact in various places fences and palisades are made with this wood. Moreover, since it is very light, it furnishes the best material, when the trunks are hollowed out, for making little canoes that turn out to be very good and long-lasting. In New York a number of yachts (small ships that go from New York to Albany on the Hudson River) are built of Red oak* in the lower part always immersed in water and of Red cedar in the upper part exposed to the alternation of wet and dry. In Pennsylvania, where these trees are neither large enough nor common enough to be used for the purposes indicated, they are sawed into slats for covering roofs. The wood is white outside and reddish inside, and it gives off a very pleasant odor; but in time the odor and the color disappear. Near various country homes in Pennsylvania and in New York one can see avenues of Red cedar which, since they are regularly pruned and evergreen, look very nice, especially in winter. They are, however, so slow in growth that Kalm counted 180 rings in a trunk only 13¼ inches in diameter and more than 250 in another only 1½ feet in diameter. At the time of the first settlements it was very abundant near the sea and in the internal regions of Georgia, but the stands of them were destroyed by the ship builders of the Bermuda Islands. It grows easily from seed the second year after planting, as I have found, if one covers it with a little earth and keeps it cool the first year by spreading moss over it. The two-year-old plants, although transplanted in the fall, didn't suffer at all from the coldest winter. It bears cones when it is about 12 years old.

Lyciam: Plinius oxycedrum, & cedrum Lyciam, nam quam alii pro Lycia exhibent meo judicio nihil aliud est, quam novella Juniperi majoris, sive cedri Phoeniciae plantae (Clusius. *Rarior Stirp. Hist.* Edit. 12. Antuerp. 1576. Lib. I Cap. xxviii. pag. 104.

*See entry "*Quercus.*"

KALMIA

1. *K. LATIFOLIA foliis ovatis; corymbis terminalibus.* Lin.
Ledum floribus bullatis confertis in summis caulibus. Trew *Pl. Select.* tab. 38 fig. 1. Chamae daphne foliis tini, floribus bullatis. Catesby *Carol.* Tom. 2 tab. 98.

Laurel in Pennsylvania, Spoon-tree in New Jersey. [*Kalmia latifolia* L.]

2. *K. ANGUSTIFOLIA foliis lanceolatis; corymbis lateralibus.* Lin.
Ledum floribus bullatis fasciculatis ex alis oppositis foliorum. Trew *Pl. Select.* tab. 38 fig. 2. Chamae daphne sempervirens foliis oblongis angustis, foliorum fasciculis oppositis. Catesby Tom. 3 tab. 17 fig. 1.

Sheep poison, Ivy, Dwarf laurel, Lambkill, in the United States. [*K. angustifolia* L.]

The name Laurel, by which Spec. 1 is called in Pennsylvania and New York, is common in United America to all those trees and shrubs which, furnished with wide and tough leaves, keep them in the winter. The two kalmias, myricas, magnolias, and rhododendrons enjoy this name in confusion, for which reason it is impossible to distinguish the plants by the vernacular names, so that botanical nomenclature based on correct principles appears increasingly necessary. *Kalmia latifolia* (Spec. 1) is a shrub of modest height, with shiny ovate leaves and numerous beautiful blossoms of a pale red color that come out in corymbs or clumps from the tips of the branches. It grows luxuriantly in uncultivated terrains and on hillsides but is not found north of 42° latitude. It begins to bloom in May, and at that time its beauty surpasses that of almost all the trees known to us. The Swedes of New Jersey call this shrub Spoon-tree, from the use that the Indians made of it in olden times. The wood is extremely hard and serves for pulley axles and weavers' shuttles, and inlayers and carpenters use it, preferring, however, its roots, since their wood is yellow. Its leaves are poisonous to sheep, cows, and horses; but on the other hand they serve as food for goats, and deer, especially in the winter when the ground is all covered with snow. Mr. Kalm (the first to discover this genus of plant, for which reason Linnaeus gave it the name of *Kalmia*)[*] adds that the leaves of this shrub explode in the fire like those of the laurel, so that if a fire breaks out in a woods, it dies out as soon as it reached the kalmias; and that only their leaves remained intact in 1750, while those of all the [other] trees of Pennsylvania were destroyed by insects.

K. angustifolia (Spec. 2) is very common along the public roads in Massachusetts and is laden with very pretty flowers in the month of June. Its leaves are light green, lanceolate, whole at the margins; and the flowers, which come out in little clumps about the stalk, have a washed-out fleshy color and are, like those of Species 1, cup-shaped. In the various regions of the United States it has the several names of Dwarf laurel, Sheep poison, and Lambkill since for these animals it has the same toxic quality as the first. The best remedy, if it can be given in time, is oil or fat, making them

[*Both *Kalmia latifolia* and *K. angustifolia* were discovered by Banister who sent drawings and specimens to Bobart at Oxford about 1689. Linnaeus based the names in part on Plukenet, *Phytographia* t. 161 f. 3, and f. 4: "D. Banister." See Ewan, *Banister,* p. 182.]

swallow it in quantity, whereby in a short time they recover. This poison is thought to consist in a bitter and corrosive quality, since, according to Mr. Kalm, obvious signs of corrosion have been observed in the intestines of sheep that have died because of it. This shrub, too, is worth propagating in our gardens on account of its beauty; but both this one and the preceding are hard to grow from seed. For this reason we shall have to try to get some young plants from England, where it exists in some gardens.

LAURUS

1. *L. BORBONIA foliis lanceolatis perennantibus; calycibus fructus baccatis.* Lin. Laurus caroliniensis, foliis acuminatis, baccis caeruleis, pedicellis longis rubris insidentibus. Catesby *Carolin.* Tom. I tab. 63.

Bay-tree, and Red-Bay in the Carolinas. [*Persea borbonia* (L.) Spreng.]

2. *L. AESTIVALIS foliis venosis, oblongis, acuminatis, annuis; ramis supra axillaribus.* Lin.

Sweet-Bay-tree in the Carolinas. [*Litsea aestivalis* (L.) Fern.]

3. *L. INDICA foliis lanceolatis perennantibus venosis, planis; ramulis tuberculatis cicatricibus, floribus racemosis.* Lin.

Spicewood in the United States. [*Laurus indica* represents *Persea indica* (L.) Spreng., an endemic of Canary Islands. It is misapplied here to *Lindera melissaefolium* (Walt.) Blume, or, more likely to *Persea palustris* (Raf.) Sarg.]

4. *L. BENZOIN foliis enerviis ovatis, utrinque acutis, integris, annuis.* Lin. Arbor virginiana Pishaminis folio baccata, Benzoinum redolens Pluk. *Alm.* tab. 139 fig. 3, 4.

Benjamin-tree, Wild allspice, and Wild pimento in the United States. [*Lindera benzoin* (L.) Blume]

5. *L. SASSAFRAS foliis integris, trilobisque.* Lin.
Cornus mas odorata, folio trifido, margine plano, Sassafras dicta. Pluk. *Alm.* tab. 222 fig. 6. Catesby *Carol.* Tom. I tab. 55.

Sassafras-tree in the United States. [*Sassafras albidum* (Nutt.) Nees]

Laurus borbonia (Spec. 1) was first called *Borbonia* by Father Charles Plumier, who made of it a new genus, giving it this name in memory of Gaston of Bourbon, son of King Henry IV of France and uncle of Louis XIV, a great lover and promoter of botany. Linnaeus found this plant to be a species of the laurel, so that he kept for it the specific name of *borbonia.** This laurel grows in the moist terrains of the Carolinas and Georgia, particularly near the seashores. Its leaves are evergreen, acuminate, and longer than those of our common laurel, producing in April sterile flowers arranged in spikes, and hermaphroditic ones supported by long peduncles. Its blue

*In order to preserve the memory of a Prince to whom this science owes so much, Linnaeus then gave the name *Borbonia* to a new genus of plants.

berries have a red-colored peduncle and calyx. It does not generally grow very high, but its wood, of a pretty red color, is very hard and therefore much sought after by burners and carpenters for making game tables, chairs, and other items of furniture that take a high polish; and it has the advantage over mahogany, which it resembles in color, of being lighter and easier to work. From this wood is derived a good black dye. Hence for these advantages it ought to be propagated in Lombardy, if our climate turns out to be not too harsh for this plant. It is also called Red bay on account of the color of its wood.

The laurel called *aestivalis* (Spec. 2) because it loses its leaves very early in the fall is a tree of modest size that grows in low and flooded areas of South Carolina and Virginia. Its leaves are oblong, acuminate, and its yellow-colored sessile flowers are umbelliferous, with an involucre of four leaflets like those of the cornel. It is called Sweet bay tree in Carolina because of the fragrance of its leaves. It is as delicate as Species 1.

Laurus indica (Spec. 3) is found in the East Indies, Japan,* and in the United States. It is of a most fragrant odor, much like our own, except that its leaves are less undulate and larger, the young branches are scabrous, and the flowers are alternate and arranged in clusters. The berries are a reddish black color and round, not indeed as round as in our laurel.

In America it is called Spicewood, and *Laurier royal,* and also *Laurier cannellier des sauvages,* by the French. [Philip] Miller tried hard to render this last species fit to withstand the winters of England but with little success, even though he raised many plants from seed, giving thereafter an exact description of their culture in his dictionary. I fear, therefore, that it will be very difficult to grow in the open in our country, except perhaps where olives hold up. The same applies to the two species mentioned above.

Laurus benzoin (Spec. 4) was so denominated by Linnaeus, since he supposed that from this tree was drawn benzoin, a resin known since ancient times in apothecaries' shops; but this resin is due to a tree still unknown.† *Laurus benzoin* is a shrub 10 to 15 feet high; it likes moist terrains, and is quite common in Pennsylvania and in the southern states. Its trunk divides into many small branches and produces thick shoots from the foot, by which it can easily be propagated. Its leaves are oval and entire, they fall in the autumn, and upon being rubbed they have the odor of benzoin, which misled the botanists. The blossoms come out before the leaves; they are tiny, of a greenish yellow, and are sessile in the axils of the leaves themselves. They have a corolla sometimes of six, sometimes of seven petals, and produce red berries that turn black as they ripen. Both the wood as well as the leaves, blossoms, and fruit have the same aromatic odor, for which reason it was introduced into many European gardens. In some parts of North America the oil extracted from its berries is used for colic pains with great relief, according to Gronovius. It holds up very well in

*In Japan it is called *Tamu-no-ki* (see Koempfer, *Amoenitat. exotica,* Fasc. V. p. 906; Thunberg, *Flora Japonica,* p. 173).

†It was later believed that benzoin came from a species of *Croton* that Linnaeus called *Benzoe*[*] and which M. Jacquin recognized as a species of *Terminalia*; but this, too, is not the benzoin tree. The only information we have about it is taken from Valentino's *India litterata,* where he describes it on p. 487. [*"Benzoe," balsam is *Styrax benzoin* Dryander, described in 1787.]

the open in Lombardy and produces a quantity of flowers early in the spring; but up to now all of them have fallen without bearing any fruit, whether because the season is still too cold when it blooms in our climate, or (which is more probable) because it was planted in dry soil in the gardens.

Laurus sassafras (Spec. 5) is the one that yields the true sassafras known for the medical use made of it in America and Europe. I found it very abundant in the woods near Boston in Massachusetts, but it becomes rarer as one goes northward, and I didn't find any of it beyond 44° latitude. It not only becomes rarer as one moves toward the north, but smaller, and from the 15 to 30 feet it reaches in the middle states, it hardly gets up to 6 or 8 in the northern regions. It produces, like almost all the other laurels, copious shoots from the base, but since it does not have enough roots, it is difficult to propagate in this manner. Therefore a better way is by seeds, although it is difficult to gather them because various kinds of birds are very greedy of them. It likes a light, dry soil mixed with much sand and little clay. Its leaves are sometimes divided into three parts, sometimes entire, for which reason Linnaeus made them a variety, relying on the assertion of Plukenet, who calls it *Cornus mas, sive Sassafras Laurinis foliis indivisis.* But inasmuch as this variety is not constant in the same individual, I thought it best to leave it out. The wood and the leaves give off a very pleasant fragrance, so that some people believe it is excellent for keeping moths and other insects away from beds and wardrobes. The bark of the tree is very aromatic and is substituted for drugs by the inhabitants; and with the dried blossoms they make a very tasty and healthful tea. The wood is of no use in the crafts, and it is not even good for burning; but it is excellent in medicine for its sudoriferous, corroborative, and purgative virtues, for which purpose it is used mainly for intestinal obstructions, scurvy, and venereal disease. A quantity of it is shipped every year to England, although the slender price of 11 English shillings for every 100 London pounds render rather paltry the profit from these shipments, since finding and collecting it in the woods is quite expensive. We have not yet acclimated this tree in Lombardy, but it will certainly withstand our winters since it is found further north in America than the other laurels—even more so than *Laurus benzoin,* which, as I have said, flourishes very well in our climate.

LIQUIDAMBAR

1. *L. STYRACIFLUA foliis palmato-angulatis, lobis indivisis, acutis.* Lin. Liquidambar arbor, sive styraciflua aeris folio. Pluk. *Almag.* 224 tab. 4. Catesby *Carol.* Tom. 2 tab. 65.

Sweet gum-tree, White gum-tree, Gum wood in the United States; *Byl-steel* of the Dutch in New York; *Ocosolt* of the Indians of Louisiana. [*Liquidambar styraciflua* L.]

2. *L. PEREGRINUM foliis oblongis, alternatim sinuatis.* Lin. Myrthi Barbanticae affinis americana, foliis asplenii modo divisis. Pluk. *Almag.* tab. 100 fig. 6, 7. Liquidambar foliis oblongis alternatim sinuatis. Duham. n. 2.

Sweet-fern in the United States. [*Comptonia peregrina* (L.) Coult.]

Liquidambar styraciflua (Spec. 1) is a tree that sometimes reaches a height of up to 40 feet. Its leaves are divided into five or seven lobes and very similar to those of our native maple; they have a dark green color and become red in the fall. The blossoms come out early in the spring, followed by globular fruit scattered with many sharp points that are the ends of the cells [locules], each of which contains one or two small, oblong black seeds mixed with a large quantity of yellowish triangular-shaped bodies. The leaves of this tree give off a very pleasing fragrance, and its wood, not very hard and of very fine texture, can be easily carved, but is subject to twisting and checking. It gives a pleasant fragrance to clothes and linens, for which reason it is said that missionaries used it in their censers. From this tree there oozes, both naturally and by means of incisions, a resin of pleasant odor, bitter taste, aromatic, and gray-colored known in apothecaries' shops as *Storacis liquidi resina.** The Indians of North America use it for fevers and apply it to wounds, which they thereby heal in a short time. Its properties consist in being balsamic and warming, and it is said to be an excellent external remedy for scabies, which it cures by drying up the pustules. In Louisiana, where it is called *Ocosolt,* tiny pieces of the bark are mixed in when the resin is drawn from the tree, since that way the perfumes turn out to be more lasting and more pleasing. The so-called oil of liquidambar is obtained from the more liquid part that flows out of the resin by itself as soon as it is extracted and is considered to be more active.† The plants of the northern states of United America yield a very small quantity of it, but on the other hand it is very abundant in the southern regions, where the trees exposed to the sun are all covered with it in the summer. In fact, it appears that this plant likes a rather warm climate since, according to my observations, it is not found growing spontaneously north of 41° latitude. Nevertheless the young plants born from seed I brought from America withstood the cold winter of the year 1789 in the open.

Liquidambar peregrinum (Spec. 2) differs greatly from the preceding one in size and shape, so that if it were not for the flowers and fruit, one would think it of a completely different genus. It forms a small shrub two or three feet high, and its leaves are oblong with a sinuous margin, so that at first sight it could be taken for a species of fern, especially an *Asplenium,* whence it was called *aspleniifolia* by many botanists. The male flowers are gathered in an ament at the ends of the branches and the female flowers are all together in a globe, each covered with a bell-shaped calyx and equipped with two styles. Since these female flowers are hidden among the leaves, they are hard to distinguish; and great care is necessary in collecting the seeds, all the more so since they come easily out of their locules and fall as soon as they are mature. Mr. Marshall says that a decoction of its leaves is used to stop diarrheas, which is confirmed by Mr. Colden,‡ who reports being told that the Indians chewed the root in order to recover from fluxions of blood. It is very common along

*The dry resin of storax, called *Storacis calamitae resina* in the apothecaries' shops, is drawn from a completely different tree—the *Styrax officinalis* of Linnaeus.

†Monardez, *Simplicium medicamentorum historia a Carolo Clusio illustrata* (Antuerpiae, 1579) p. 12.

‡Colden, *Plantae Noveboracenses.*

hedges and in the woods of Massachusetts. These two Liquidambars ought to be propagated in our country, especially the first, not so much for their beauty and fragrance as for the use that can be made of them in medicine.

LIRIODENDRON

L. TULIPIFERA foliis lobatis. Lin.

Arbor Tulipifera virginiana tripartito Aceris folio, media lacinia veluti abscissa. Pluk. *Almag.* tab. 68 fig. 3, tab. 117 fig. 15, and tab. 248 fig. 7. Catesby *Carol.* Tom. I tab. 48. Liriodendron foliis angulatis truncatis. Trew. *Pl. Selec.* tab. 10.

Tulip-tree, Poplar tree, Whitewood, Canoe-wood in the United States. [*Liriodendron tulipifera* L.]

Among the exotic trees known up to now that can be multiplied in our climate first place is due the Tulip-tree, which combines with the singular beauty of its foliage and rate of growth the advantage of becoming a very tall tree whose wood is excellent for many uses. It is found in the United States from the Georgia border up to New York. But I have never found it north of this latter region, although various authors say that it grows natively in Massachusetts. Nevertheless it withstands the coldest climates, because I saw a plant in the garden of the French consul in Boston that produced flowers and fruit in abundance; and it is known that there are in England and France very old trees that flourish vigorously. There are some in our country also, the oldest of which is the one belonging to the Galleari brothers in Treviglio, which has bloomed and produced mature seeds for many years. The Tulip-tree is a tree 70 to 80 feet high with large leaves divided into three lobes that appear cut at the end of the middle lobe. The flowers are pale green lightly tinted with yellowish-red and have the shape of tulips, so that the tree got the name of Tulip-tree. They are composed of a calyx of three concave leaflets and from six to nine petals with many stamens and pistils. The fruit is conical and formed of seeds attached to the little central column. These seeds contain one or two tiny triangular nutlets and end in a long membrane like those of the ash. Mr. Marshall distinguishes two varieties,* one with white wood and the other with yellow, adding that the wood of the former is more tender and splits easily, so that it is used only for game tables, bowls, and other furniture, while the white wood, being heavier and tougher, is used for construction. In view of the immense size of this tree, canoes are made of it in America of one piece by hollowing out the trunks; it was therefore called Canoe-wood. Americans mix the bark of the roots with absinthe in vermouth wine in order to give it an aromatic taste and odor. In fact, not only the roots but the whole tree have such an aromatic fragrance that the native Indians valued it very highly and used it a great deal in

*Linnaeus, basing himself on Plukenet [in turn on drawing of Banister who had sent seeds to Bishop Compton about 1689] also makes two varieties of it, but since more angular leaves with the ends more or less curved are found on the same plant, I do not believe that any weight ought to be given these accidental and small differences.

their medicines. The boiled roots yield a decoction that has sometimes proved helpful in intermittent fevers as well as for rheumatism and podagra. This tree is worthy of all our attention for propagation in Lombardy, both for its medicinal and economic uses and as an ornamental, because its foliage is wide-spreading when there are no other trees near by and for that reason is excellent for avenues. The seed I sent from America sprouted readily after being allowed to soak for about eight days in water, in which they left a yellow tincture. However, the young seedlings must be protected from the strong heat of the sun, and brought inside during the winter for the first two years. It is hard to reproduce from layers, and the trees that come from them do not grow to be as beautiful as those from seed. It likes a light, deep, and somewhat humid soil, but dies quickly in hard and clayey terrains that retain too much moisture.

LONICERA

1. *L. SEMPERVIRENS verticillis aphyllis, terminalibus; foliis summis connato-perfoliatis.* Lin.
Periclymenum perfoliatum virginianum sempervirens, & florens. Rivin. *monopet.* tab. 123 fig. 1; Knorr. *Delic.* G. 3. Lonicera sempervirens. Lamarck *Encycl. méthod.* n. 3.

a. Virginiana
Lonicera virginiana. Marsh. *Arbust. Amer.*

b. caroliniana
Lonicera caroliniana. Marsh. *Arbust. Amer.*
Scarlet honeysuckle in the United States. [*Lonicera sempervirens* L.]

2. *L. PARVIFLORA foliis summis connato-perfoliatis, glaucis; verticillis subaphyllis, staminum filamentis barbatis.* Lamarck.
Lonicera canadensis. Bartram, *Catal.* Marsh. *Arbust. Amer.* n. 4.
Dwarf cherry-honeysuckle in the United States. [*L. canadensis* Marsh.]

3. *L. DIERVILLA racemis terminalibus; foliis serratis.* Lin.
Diervilla Acadiensis fruticosa, flore luteo. Duh. *Arb. & Arbust.*
Yellow-flowering diervilla in the United States. [*Diervilla lonicera* Mill.]

4. *L. SYMPHORICARPOS capitulis lateralibus pedunculatis; foliis petiolatis.* Lin.
Symphoricarpos foliis alatis. Dillen. *Elth.* tab. 278 Duh. *Arb. & Arbust.*
Indian currants and St. Peter's-wort in the United States. [*Symphoricarpos orbiculatus* Marsh.]

Lonicera sempervirens (Spec. 1) with scarlet blossoms is among the most beautiful of this genus. It becomes laden in May with copious red flowers which easily distinguish it from the other species because the edge of the tubes is divided almost regularly, with the result that M. Duhamel did not want to add it to the genus of the

Lonicerae but gave it instead the name of Periclymenum. [Duhamel wanted to retain the name; Banister had used it on a drawing sent to Bishop Compton in 1689, see Ewan, *Banister*, 226, f. 51]. It grows in swampy places, climbing up around plants. It is therefore good for covering walls as well as for ornamenting gardens with its charming flowers that continue all summer long. It is easily propagated from suckers and withstands the winters of Lombardy. There are two varieties of it, one of which, namely, *virginiana* (Var. a), sometimes loses its leaves in the fall, while the other, that is, *caroliniana*, which keeps itself evergreen (Var. b), has smaller blossoms and leaves.

Canadian honeysuckle (Spec. 2) forms a bush adorned with little pale-yellow flowers somewhat red at the base. These flowers come out very early in the spring and have barbed stamens.

Diervilla (Spec. 3) is a shrub two to three feet high whose roots wind about and produce numerous quadrangular shoots furnished with delicately dentate leaves, acuminate, and somewhat hairy at the margin. The yellowish blossoms arranged in clusters come out of the tips of the branches, sometimes from the axils of the leaves, and produce oblong fruit. It blooms at the end of May, and since its flowers are quite showy, it can be propagated to that end in our gardens. This shrub is native to the province of Nova Scotia but is found also in the United States in elevated places, on mountains; and it was one of the many plants that had some fame, though not a lasting one, as a remedy for syphilis.

Lonicera symphoricarpus (Spec. 4), so denominated by Dillenius because its berries are joined together in clumps, is a shrub of very low height that spreads out very wide with its branches and by pruning could easily be reduced to the figure of a round bush as is done with boxwood. It has tiny flowers, but because of the quantity of its reddish berries, it can be introduced as an ornamental into gardens and autumnal thickets. Its branches, and more so the roots, have an astringent quality and are used in intermittent fevers by the Americans, who call it St. Peter's-wort. It is also called Indian currants, perhaps because the latter used to eat the berries. Both *Symphoricarpos* and *Diervilla* are easily propagated; and they are hardy in our climate.

MAGNOLIA

1. *M. GRANDIFLORA foliis lanceolatis perennantibus.* Lin.
Magnolia altissima flore ingenti candido. Catesby *Carolin.* Tom. 2 tab. 61 Duham. *Arb. & Arbust.* n. 1. Magnolia maximo flore, foliis subtus ferrugineis. Trew *Pl. Selec.* tab. 32.

Evergreen tulip-tree, Laurel-tree in the United States. [*Magnolia grandiflora* L.]

2. *M. GLAUCA foliis ovato-oblongis, subtus glaucis.* Lin.
Magnolia laurifolio subtus albicante. Catesby Tom. I, tab. 39. Trew Pl. *Selec.* tab. 9. Duham. n. 9.

Swamp laurel in the United States. [*M. virginiana* L.]

3. *M. ACUMINATA foliis ovato-oblongis acuminatis.* Lin.
Magnolia flore albo, folio majore acuminato, haud albicante. Catesby Tom. 3 tab. 15.
Mountain magnolia and Cucumber tree in the United States. [*M. acuminata* L.]

4. *M. TRIPETALA foliis lanceolatis, petalis exterioribus dependentibus.* Lin.
Magnolia amplissimo flore albo, fructu coccineo. Catesby Tom. 2, tab. 80.
Umbrella tree in the United States. [*M. tripetala* L.]

Magnolia grandiflora (Spec. 1) is doubtless the most beautiful tree of North America, particularly at blossoming time. It grows in the moist and marshy terrains of South Carolina and Georgia, reaching a height of 80 and more feet by a diameter of 2 or 3; and I saw immense ones between Savannah and Yamacraw [Indian reservation up river from, but now within, Savannah; to Vivian Rogers our thanks]. Its leaves are like those of the Cherry laurel,* but much larger and tougher, of a brilliant green above and often tinted with a reddish-brown color underneath. It begins to bloom in May and its huge blossoms (up to 11 inches in diameter) are composed of 8, 10, and 12 petals of a beautiful white color and of pleasing odor, followed by fruit formed by many capsules [carpels] joined in a cone which upon opening let the seeds come out hanging from a white thread. This handsome species of Magnolia is found natively only in the warmer regions of the United States, but under cultivation is hardy even out in the open in Pennsylvania, in France, and in England, where, however, it reaches only a modest height. The oldest of these trees of which I find mention in the literature is the one indicated by M. Poederlè,† existing in the village of La Maillardiére one league from Nantes on the way to La Rochelle. In 1769 (when it was seen by the author) its trunk was more than 3 Parisian feet in circumference and its lowest limbs were about 10 Parisian feet above the roots. It began to bloom at the beginning of the summer, continuing until September; but few of its fruit would reach maturity. According to the information that he obtained in the town, it must have been planted toward 1732. It is hardy through our Lombard winters if one uses a little precaution during the first years. I have a plant which, although young, withstood, with a single layer of straw, the severe cold of January 1789. In addition to its beauty this tree is valuable for the usefulness of its wood which, being white, soft, and pliable, is employed for various purposes. The seeds are extremely bitter, but are remarkable in that the parrots of Louisiana are very fond of them, as Duhamel says, and eat them without suffering any harm, although the other bitter [magnolia] seeds are poisonous to birds. These seeds contain an oil that quickly becomes rancid, and then the seed loses its vegetative power, so that it is very difficult to obtain plants from seed. Therefore a way of propagating it by layering has been introduced in England whereby plants are easily obtained, but they are neither as beautiful nor as vigorous as those from seed. Ordinary garden soil can serve for this tree provided it is not too heavy nor too light. They will have to be watered often but not excessively, however, since the roots rot easily. During the first years the young plants must be shielded from frost and protected against the first cold weather because the buds of this tree are still tender in the fall.

**Prunus lauro-cerasus* Lin.
†*Manuel de l'arboriste, & du forestier belgique* (Bruxelles, 1772) p. 211.

The *glauca* (Spec. 2), the smallest among the magnolias, is very common in the marshy areas of New Jersey, where it is called Swamp laurel. It grows at most to a height of 15 or 20 feet, its bark is smooth and whitish, the leaves are oval, oblong, and entire, of a pretty green color above and bluish or whitish underneath. The blossoms are much smaller than in the other species, as is also the fruit. It blooms very early in the spring and gives off a most pleasing fragrance, so that it is used both in America and in England as an ornamental for gardens and country houses. Since it is native to a more northern province and easily withstands the cold, it ought to be propagated in Lombardy. It is multiplied from seeds more easily than the others, but they must be shipped in sand and sown in a bed of warm manure as soon as they arrive in order to facilitate germination. Although it grows in marshes in its own region, it acquires greater toughness and beauty when it is planted in dry soil. In warmer climates it often keeps its leaves all winter long, but they fall in temperate climates. Its wood is spongy and of no use in the arts, but the seed and bark of the tree have sometimes been used with happy results in rheumatism cases.* There is a variety of the shrub with a double flower in the beautiful collection of Messrs. [James] Gordon and [Thomas] Dermer, celebrated plant and seed dealers in London.

The *Magnolia* called *acuminata* (Spec. 3) is native to Pennsylvania and Maryland, where it grows to a height of 30 or 40 feet in hilly and elevated places, for which reason it got the name of Mountain magnolia. Its trunk divides into many limbs provided with very large leaves; and the blossoms are also large and of a bluish-white color.

[Br 3:108] The fruit is oblong and of the shape of watermelon. This is the one least known in Europe, but in my opinion it would be one of the most fit for survival in Lombardy, since it is native to a region similar in climate. Its wood is orange colored and of a tough texture, but it rots easily upon being exposed to moisture.

Umbrella magnolia (Spec. 4), finally, is found in the swamplands of Georgia, the Carolinas, and also Pennsylvania. Its height is 10 to 20 feet, and at the tip of the young branches, which have the unusual feature of being more slender toward the base, it produces white flowers as large as those of *grandiflora* with petals in part upright and in part upside down. Its leaves are extremely long and, coming out in a ring at the ends of the branches, they represent a kind of umbrella. The trunk is covered with a smooth dark bark, and both it and the blossoms give off a most pleasing fragrance. This species is as delicate as the first, so that the same precautions will have to be exercised to propagate and protect it from freezing during the first few years.

All four of these magnolias deserve our greatest attention in propagating them in our country since there are no trees hardy in our climate that combine so much beauty of foliage with blossoms of so much fragrance and charm.

*Marshall, *Arbust. Amer.*

MESPILUS

[*sensu* Li (1957), 3–4]

1. *M. OXYACANTHA foliis obtusis, subtrifidis, serratis.* N[obis].
Crataegus Oxyacantha. Lin. Reichard. Tom. 2 pag. 494. [*Crataegus oxyacantha* L.]

b. americana.

Mespilus apii-folia. Marsh. *Arbust. Amer.* n. 7.

Parsley-leaved mespilus in the United States. [*Crataegus marshallii* Egglest.]

2. *M. AZAROLUS foliis obtusis, subtrifidis, subdentatis* N[obis].

b. americana

Mespilus Azarolus major. Marsh. *Arbust. Amer.* n. 4.

Great hawthorn in the United States. [*Crataegus azarolus* L.]

c. minor

Mespilus Azarolus minor. Marsh. *Arbust. Amer.* n. 5.

Smaller hawthorn in the United States.

d. aurea

Mespilus Oxyacantha aurea. Marsh. *Arbust. Amer.* n. 6. Mespilus Caroliniana, folio vulgari similis, major, fructu luteo. Trew. *Plant. Select.* tab. 17.

Yellow-berried hawthorn in the United States. [*Crataegus uniflora* Muenchh.]

3. *M. COCCINEA foliis cordatis, repando-angulatis, serratis, glabris.* N[obis].
Crataegus coccinea. Lin. Reichard, Tom. 2 pag. 492. Mespilus Duh. *Arb. & Arbust.* n. 12. Crataegus. Miller. *Dict.* n. 5.

Hawthorn in the United States. [*Crataegus pedicellata* Sarg. and *C. intricata* Lange]

b. viridis

Crataegus viridis. Lin. Reich. Tom. 2 pag. 493. Mespilus coccinea inermis. Marsh. *Arbust. Amer.* n. 1. Var. 1.

Whitethorn in the United States. [*Crataegus viridis* L.]

4. *M. TOMENTOSA foliis cuneiformi-ovatis, serratis, sub-angulatis, subtus villosis; ramis spinosis.* N[obis].
Mespilus cuneiformis. Marsh. *Arbust. Amer.* n. 3. Crataegus tomentosa. Lin. Reichard. Tom. 2 pag. 493. [*Crataegus crus-galli* L.]

b. lutea

Crataegus tomentosa. Miller. *Dict.* n. 10.

Gooseberry-leaved hawthorn in England. [*Crataegus calpodendron* (Ehr.) Medic.]

5. *M. AMELANCHIER foliis ovalibus, serratis, subtus hirsutis.* Lin.

b. nivea

Mespilus nivea. Marsh. *Arbust. Amer.* n. 8. Crataegus racemosa. Lamarck *Encyclop. method.*

Wild service in the United States. [*Amelanchier arborea* (Michx.) Fern.]

c. prunifolia

Mespilus prunifolia. Marsh. *Arbust. Amer.* n. 9. Crataegus arbutifolia. Lamarck *Encyclop. method.*

Plum-leaved medlar in the United States. [*Aronia prunifolia* (Marsh.) Rehd.]

d. canadensis

Mespilus canadensis. Lin., & Marsh. *Arbust. Amer.* n. 10. Crataegus spicata. Lamarck *Encyc. method.*

Dwarf medlar in the United States.* [*Amelanchier canadensis* (L.) Medic.]

6. *M. CRUS GALLI foliis lanceolato-ovatis, serratis, glabris; ramis spinosis* N[obis].

Crataegus Crus galli. Lin. Reich. Tom. 2 pag. 493, an Crataegus Crus galli. Miller. *Dict.* n. 6?

Cockspur hawthorn in the United States. [*Crataegus crus-galli* L.]

b. lucida

Crataegus lucida. Miller *Dict.* n. 7. Mespilus Duh. *Arb., & Arbust.* n. 16. [*C. crus-galli* L.]

7. *M. ARBUTIFOLIA foliis lanceolatis, crenatis, subtus tomentosis.* Lin.

Mespilus arbutifolia. Miller *Dict.* Crataegus pyrifolia Lamarck *Encyc. method.*

b. virginiana

Crataegus virginiana. Miller *Dict.* n. 4. Crataegus Duh. *Arb. & Arbust.* n. 6. [*Amelanchier canadensis* (L.) Medic.]

The many varieties produced in this kind of plant by terrain, climate, cultivation, and perhaps by the mixture of fertilizing dusts [Castiglioni uses an older term here instead of his usual *polline.*] of the blossoms have brought the species of medlars and azaroles so close to one another that is almost impossible to tell them apart. Linnaeus himself was embarrassed in making the distinction between these two genera, perceiving no other difference except in the number of styles and seeds—a difference which, however, is not constant, these styles and seeds varying from one up to five even in the same individuals. This I ascertained in the Canadian medlars, and in the English Whitethorn, which, just as in Germany, has almost always a single style, whence M. Jacquin made of it a new species under the name *Crataegus monogyna.* For this reason I thought it well to combine these two genera after the example of the celebrated Scopoli† and Mr. Marshall—all the more so because the only difficulty one

*The species *Oxyacantha, Azarolus,* and *Amelanchier* are European and are found in America only in their varieties indicated here by [Roman] letters.

†This most diligent botanist, in the second edition of his *Flora Carniolica* (Vindobonae [published by] Krauss, 1772), combined in the class *Icosandria* the orders of *tri-tetra* and *pentagynia* into one that he calls *di-pentagynia,* in which lies the *Mespilus,* of which he says: *Numerus foeminarum in hoc genere lubrica nota est. Mespilus Chamaemespilus Linnaeo pentagynus, mihi cum Hallero, & Jacquinio digynus. Crataegus Oxyacantha Linnaeo digynus, mihi monogynus. In Mespilo Cotoneastro Linnaei styli 3–5. In Aucuparia 3–4. Ergo Mespili characterem naturalem constituent; Calycini dentes, & petala quinque: Stamina quadruplo plura: Styli tot quot locula: Bacca infera umbilicata, calyce, filamentis, & stylis persistentibus terminata.* Therefore he combines with the medlar not only the thorns but also the Rowan tree.

might raise to this fusion, namely, the multiplicity of the species, vanishes if they are properly separated from their numerous varieties. The inconstant shape of the leaves, the thorns and pubescence now present, now lacking, the blossoms now axillary, now terminal, the fruit varying from dark red to yellowish, confuse these plants so much that often one does not know in the literature to which species to refer the specimen under examination, nor how the descriptions, often discordant and incomplete, can be combined. I made an attempt, with no little labor, to clarify this confusion, separating the most distinctive ones and combining those that appeared to me to have great analogy with one another. Nevertheless I don't believe I have determined sufficiently the true species of American medlars—a task that cannot be carried to completion without a multiplicity of observations and experiments, all the more so because among them there must be in my opinion many hybrid species, namely, born from the germ [ovum] of one species fertilized by the pollen from another. Whoever undertakes this task must be on his guard against the passion, now common among botanists, to create new species, since in variant plants specific characteristics must be examined with the greatest attention in order not to fall again into the confusion from which the systematists, above all the immortal Linnaeus, have freed botany.

American hawthorn (Spec. 1, Var. b) is a small shrub that rises barely to five or six feet and is provided with short thorns. The leaves and the fruit are smaller than in the European. This is described only by Mr. Marshall, who makes of it a species under the name of *Mespilus apiifolia.*

The American azerole (Spec. 2, Var. b, c, d) is distinguished by Mr. Marshall into major and minor. The major (Var. b) grows to a height of 12 to 15 feet, has very long thorns, large and heavily veined leaves, and big fruit of a deep red color. The minor (Var. c) is smaller than the preceding in all its parts. To this same species, it seems to me, should be referred *Mespilus oxyacantha aurea* of Mr. Marshall, which differs from the other varieties mainly in having fruit of a yellow color (Var. d), so that I see no difference between this one and the one described and depicted by Mr. Trew in his *Plantae Selectae,* Tab. 17.

The Red thorn (Spec. 3) is found in many regions of North America, grows to a height of 10 to 12 feet, and is armed with long, strong, curved thorns, for which reason it got called Cockspur, a name common also to Spec. 4. The flowers are white, and the fruit is very large and of a pretty red color when it is ripe. If in North America, as wood becomes scarce with the passage of the years, the custom of surrounding fields with wooden fences should have to be abandoned, enclosing them instead with living hedges in the European style, the Red thorn could serve very well for that purpose, even though it has the defect of losing its leaves early in the fall. There is a variety of this species (Var. b) without thorns that Linnaeus called *Crataegus viridis.*

Mespilus tomentosa (Spec. 4) does not differ much from Species 3 aside from having leaves that are less angular and somewhat fuzzy underneath. This species, which grows to a height of 20 and more feet, Mr. Marshall describes under the name of *Mespilus cuneiformis* on account of the shape of its leaves, although this characterization also fits the preceding species. The blossoms of *Mespilus tomentosa* come out of the ends of the branches, and the fruit is red and of medium size. *Crataegus tomentosa* of Miller (Var. b) with greenish-yellow fruit must belong to this species.

Amelanchier (Spec. 5), a common shrub in southern France, is not found in

America, but the varieties noted below native to the United States, distinguished by other authors into as many species, must be referred to this species. *Mespilus nivea* of Mr. Marshall (Var. b), called Wild service in the United States, is a shrub 15 to 20 feet tall, covered with a smooth, whitish, spotted bark. The leaves are oval-oblong, hairy upon coming out of the buds and later smooth and of a pretty green as they mature, the flowers very white and abundant, the fruit large. It ripens in June and has a pleasant taste, so that the shrub ought to be introduced into our gardens for this reason as well as for its beauty. Variety (c), called *prunifolia* by Mr. Marshall, grows in damp places, is smaller than Variety (b), has more subtle dentations in the leaves, and the fuzz remains on them longer. This must be *Crataegus arbutifolia* of M. Lamarck, which, according to him, has white blossoms fuzzy in the center around the styles, maroon anthers, a greenish-colored calyx and pedicels without fuzz, and dark red–almost black–fruit. This Variety (c) blooms toward the end of May, its leaves become red in autumn. A hedge of it is in France in the garden of the Marquis de Poncharost.* Finally, the third variety (Var. d) is the one called *Mespilus canadensis* by Linnaeus and Mr. Marshall and *Crataegus spicata* by M. Lamarck. This is even smaller than the preceding ones and very similar to Variety (c), except that its fruit is of a vivid red color.

Cockspur (Spec. 6) grows to a height of 15 to 20 feet, spreads its branches almost horizontally, and has oval-oblong, but not hairy, leaves of dark green. The blossoms come out later than in the other species, and the fruit, of average size, has a reddish color. Like Species three, this one is furnished with long curved thorns, so that it got to be called likewise Cockspur and is just as good for hedges. There is a species of this (Var. b) that was called *Crataegus lucida* by Miller–*Mespilus virginiana spinis longioribus rectis, foliis quodammodo auriculatis* of Duhamel, No. 16–which differs by its smoother and glossier leaves.

The Arbutus-leaved medlar (Spec. 7) is easily distinguished from the other species because it has leaves that are not saw-toothed but fluted at the edges and fuzzy and whitish underneath. This is called *Crataegus pyrifolia* by M. Lamarck and *Mespilus arbutifolia* by Miller. Miller's *Crataegus virginiana,* which is *Crataegus,* No. 6, of Duhamel, also belongs to this species, under which I have placed it.

All these medlars and thorns are worth being propagated in our country to adorn hedges and copses with the beauty of their blossoms in the spring and of their fruit in the fall. They are easily obtained from seed that sprouts in the second year; and they can be grafted onto our native Whitethorn and Pear–the latter graft improving the fruit.

MITCHELLA

M. REPENS. Lin.

Cham[a]edaphne. Mitchell *gen.* 27. Lonicera foliis subovatis, germine bifloro, corollis interne hirsutis, stylo bifido. Gron *Fl. Virg.* pag. 22. Syringa baccifera myrthi subro-

*Lamarck, art. "Alisier."

tundis foliis, floribus albis gemellis. Pluk. *Amalth.* tab. 444 fig. 2. Catesby *Carolin.* Tom. I tab. 20.

Partridge-berry in Massachusetts. [*Mitchella repens* L.]

The singularity of this tiny shrub consists in its having blossoms paired two by two with the calyx and a common pericarp that changes into a single red-colored berry in which are enclosed two seeds. The flowers are white, funnel-shaped, and similar at first sight to the jasmines; but they become black as soon as they fade. It winds along over the ground and its shoots have glossy, evergreen, nearly round leaves. Given its tiny size, it will be suitable for cultivation in vases or in small garden-plots, where it will look pretty in all seasons. In Massachusetts it is called Partridge-berry.

MORUS

M. RUBRA foliis cordatis subtus villosis, amentis cylindricis. Lin.
Morus foliis subtus tomentosis, amentis longis dioicis. Gronov. *virgin.* 146. Morus virginiensis arbor Loti arboris instar ramosa, foliis amplissimis. Pluk. *almag.* 253 tab. 246 fig. 4. [*Morus rubra* L.]

The Red or American mulberry usually grows on river banks, reaching a height of 20 to 30 feet. Its leaves are ordinarily without marginal teeth and heart-shaped, but sometimes they come out palmate as in the other mulberries, so that the nature of the shape of the leaves is very uncertain and cannot serve to determine clearly the species in this genus. These leaves are of a texture halfway between those of the Black and the Paper mulberry.* In the month of April, on the banks of the Savannah River in Georgia, I saw its blossoms come out in great abundance in the form of aments as long as those of the birch. They were all male on some trees and on others mixed male and female on separate branches. The fruit is very large, resembling that of the Black mulberry of Spain, of a deep crimson color, and very sweet to the taste. Very durable fences are made with its wood, and the inside bark was formerly worked by the Indians of Georgia and the Carolinas, who used to make of it a kind of cloth that was imitated by the first colonists. Silkworms eat its leaves, but they don't like them as well as those of our mulberry, and the silk turns out to be coarser. That is why when it was decided to cultivate silk in Georgia, White mulberries were brought over from Europe.

MYRICA

M. CERIFERA foliis lanceolatis subserratis, caule arborescente. Lin.

a. arborescens

Myrtus Brabanticae similis caroliniensis baccifera, fructu racemoso sessili monopyreno.

Morus papyrifera Lin. [*Broussonetia papyrifera* (L.) Vent.]

Plukenet. tab. 48 fig. 9. Catesby *Carol.* Tom. I tab. 69. Gale. Duh. *Arb. & Arbust.* n. 2. Myrica cerifera. Marshall *Arbust. Amer.*

Candle-berry myrtle in the United States. [Wax myrtle, *M. cerifera* L.]

b. frutescens

Myrtus Brabanticae similis caroliniensis humilior foliis latioribus, & magis serratis Catesby Tom. I tab. 13. Gale. Duh. *Arb., & Arbust.* n. 3. Myrica cerifera humilis. Marshall *Arbust. Amer.* Myrica caroliniensis. Miller. *Dict.*

Bayberry in the United States. [*M. pensylvanica* Loisel.]

I found Variety (a) of the Wax tree for the first time on the banks of the Neuse River 10 miles from New Bern in North Carolina. There it grows to a height of 10 feet and more. Its leaves are lanceolate, just barely dentate, and of a pale green color. Its male blossoms have from four to six stamens,* and the female blossoms, that are on a different tree, produce tiny red berries covered with a white-colored friable substance. This first variety likes warmer climates and is not found north of the Carolinas. Variety (b), on the other hand, is a small shrub three to four feet high common even in all the northernmost of the United States, where I found it up as far as 43° 50′ latitude in the neighborhood of Falmouth in Eastern Massachusetts. The male flowers I examined in Dorchester near Boston, where they were in bloom toward the end of May, had almost all of them from six to seven stamens. It differs from Variety (a) in that it is much smaller, with larger, often dentate, leaves of a darker green color. Both of them produce a sort of wax excellent for making candles obtained by boiling the berries until a thick substance comes to the surface that is skimmed off the vat. This substance, upon being exposed again to the fire, melts and clears itself of dregs, and then acquires a certain transparency and a dark green color. By itself, or mixed with tallow, candles are made from it that are much better than those of pure tallow. They don't buckle during the summer in warm climates, nor do they melt so easily; and they leave a pleasant odor when they are extinguished. If they were mixed with beeswax, they would turn out to be more solid and smoother and would have a prettier color. Bayberry wax is sold for a little more than a shilling a pound in Pennsylvania, and at almost the same price in Massachusetts where it is used by the inhabitants and is not at all an item of trade. Mr. Kalm assures us that the Indians used bayberry roots to soothe toothaches and that in Pennsylvania a soap was made with the wax that was excellent for shaving and fragrant. Since it is difficult to propagate *Myrica* from seed, which rarely sprouts, it will be necessary to send to England for young plants and use the layering method.

NYSSA

1. *N. AQUATICA foliis ovato-lanceolatis, subdentatis, pedunculis unifloris.* N[obis].

Arbor in aqua nascens foliis latis acuminatis, & dentatis, fructu elaeagni majore. Catesby Tom. I tab. 60. Nyssa pedunculis unifloris Gronov. *Virgin.*

*Linnaeus puts it in the class *Dioecia,* in the order of the *Tetrandria,* that is, having only four stamens.

Water tupelo, Blackberry-bearing gum in the United States. *Olivier* among the French in Mississippi. [*Nyssa aquatica* L.]

2. *N. SYLVATICA foliis lanceolatis integerrimis, pedunculis multifloris, floribus dioicis.* N[obis].
Nyssa sylvatica. Marshall *Arbust. Amer.* Nyssa foliis integerrimis. Nyssa pedunculis multifloris. Gronov. *Fl. Virg.* Arbor in aqua nascens, foliis latis acuminatis, & non dentatis, fructu Eleagni minore. Catesby, Tom. I tab. 1.

Obs.: *Arbor dioica.*

Tupelo tree, Sour gum in the United States. [*N. sylvatica* Marsh.]

3. N. OGECHE foliis oblongis, pedunculis multifloris, floribus dioicis. N[obis].
Nyssa Ogeche. Bartram *Catal.*

Obs.: *Arbor dioica.*

Lime tree in the southern states. [*N. ogeche* Bartr.]

Nyssa aquatica (Spec. 1) is a very tall Carolina tree that rises to a height of 80 feet and more. Its leaves are rather large, oval, generally entire, but sometimes furnished with a few teeth at the margin, and covered underneath with a whitish fuzz. The petioles of the leaves are quite long and the fruit is of the size and shape of small olives. The French who live on the banks of the Mississippi, where these trees grow in great abundance in the swamps and in the river itself where the water is not very deep, have for that reason given it the name Olive, and its fruit are kept by them like olives. The wood is white and soft when freshly cut, but light and of good texture when dry, so that it is used for making buckets and bowls. Its roots are very soft and are used like cork to stop bottles.

Nyssa sylvatica of Mr. Marshall (Spec. 2) is not mentioned by Linnaeus, who thought it to be the hermaphrodite of Species 1; and it was distinguished by Catesby and Gronovius. It differs from *aquatica* mainly in having narrower leaves, never dentate, and of a glossy green above, as well as in having blossoms not isolated but in clusters of 6 to as many as 10 on the same peduncle. Moreover, instead of having some individuals male and others hermaphroditic, plants of this species are either with male flowers or female flowers, so that it belongs supposedly to the class *Dioecia* of Linnaeus. This tree is less tall than the preceding, not exceeding 30 or 40 feet by 2 feet in diameter, and is found in elevated places in the states of Pennsylvania, Virginia, Maryland, and the Carolinas. The fruit, with which it becomes laden in the fall, is smaller than in Species 1, of a dark crimson, almost black, color. They have a subacid and somewhat bitter taste, but various animals feed on it nevertheless, among which muskrats, bears, and opossums. The fibers of its wood are tough and curled so that it is hard to split; for that reason it is used for making wagon-wheel hubs and other tools.

Nyssa ogeche (Spec. 3), so named by Mr. [William] Bartram because he found it near the Ogeechee River in Georgia, is described for us by Mr. Marshall as having oblong leaves of a glossy green above and somewhat hairy underneath, with blossoms gathered in clusters like Species 2. Its fruit is almost oval, of the size of a plum, and very tastily tart. I have not examined or seen this last species; it could even be a simple variety of the preceding one.

Nyssas are propagated from seeds, which must be sown [here] as soon as they arrive. They sprout the second year. To help along their emergence they must be put in vases with plenty of watering and, during the first few years, protection against too much heat from the sun in the summer and freezing in the winter. Although they all like humid soils, *sylvatica* holds up better than the others in dry places and ought also to be more hardy and adapted to our climate since it is native to less warm regions.

ORONTIUM

O. AQUATICUM Lin.

Orontium. Lin. *Amoen. Acad.* Tom. 3 p. 17 tab. 1 fig. 3. Gronov. *Fl. Virg.* pag. 53. Arum aquaticum minus, sive Arisarum fluitans pene nudo virginianum. Catesby *Carol.* Tom. I tab. 82.

Taw-kee, Taw-kin, Tak-win among the Indians of New Jersey. [*Orontium aquaticum* L.]

The root of this kind of *Arum* is large and is found in marshes and on river banks. The leaves, which come out of the root, are 8 to 10 inches wide, are attached to extremely long petioles and covered with a very fine fuzz. The shaft or peduncle that supports the flowers is as long as the leaves, of a pale color scattered with dark dots. At the tip there is a sort of cylindrical clump formed by the female flowers and above this the spike of male flowers as in the plants of this family. Pigs, deer, and cows eat its leaves greedily in the spring, and the Indians collect the seeds which, boiled repeatedly in water, they eat like peas.

[Br. 3:160] When the Swedes gave the Indians milk or butter, they would boil or fry the seeds.

Some of them also made bread of it, and the first colonists of New Jersey maintained that of all the vegetables eaten by the Indians this seemed to them the tastiest food. This plant should be introduced into the marshes of Europe.

PANAX

P. QUINQUEFOLIUM foliis ternis quinatis. Lin.

Aureliana canadensis. Catesby Tom. 3 tab. 16. Araliastrum foliis ternis quinque-partitis, Ginseng, sive Ninzin officinarum. Trew. *Pl. Select.* tab. 6 fig. 1.

Ginseng in the United States, *Garent oguen* among the Indians. [*Panax quinquefolius* L.]

Ginseng grows everywhere in humid and uncultivated places of North America and produces a stem divided into three branches, each of which is furnished with five ovate and dentate leaves. In the midst of the three branches there rises a peduncle supporting an umbrella of white flowers, now male, now hermaphroditic, which are followed by red heart-shaped and umbilicate berries containing two seeds. The root is rather long, fusiform, dark outside and white inside, with a strong and aromatic flavor. This root, so much used in China, found in the deserts of Chinese Tartary, was discovered in Canada by certain French botanists and then by the English in their colonies, whence it began to be transported to Europe and from there to China. Following the example of the English, the inhabitants of the United States, after winning their independence and having opened a new commerce with China, shipped a large quantity from a boat that sailed from New York; but perhaps because of insufficient care in collecting and drying the roots this ginseng was not too highly valued by the Chinese, who offered a rather low price for it. Ginseng blooms in the months of May and June and its berries ripen toward the end of August; but it is difficult to collect the seeds since not all the plants produce them and the berries drop as soon as they are mature. When that happens and the leaves begin to wilt, it is time for the harvest, whereas by delaying the leaves disappear and one cannot know where the roots are. After being harvested, they are exposed to the air to dry (for which two or more months are required according to the dryness or raininess of the season) and turned over once or twice a day to keep them from softening or rotting. The [anon.] author in *American Museum,** speaking of the way to harvest Ginseng, recommends that the roots not be washed because they lose thereby a good deal of their efficacy, as may be perceived from the water, which remains impregnated with their flavor. He also suggests that they be dried in the shade, spread out on boards in a ventilated place, carefully shaking off the dirt when it is thoroughly dry. The Chinese and the Tartars use a different method in harvesting these roots and which in part contradicts the statement of the aforementioned author. The Chinese collect the roots when the plants are not in bloom and wash them lightly, taking care not to break the skin. Then they take a pan in which they bring water to a boil and they put in the roots, leaving them there for three or four minutes in such a manner that the skin does not crack nor suffer in anyway, and the inside of a root, upon being cut, has the color of straw. They dry and clean them with a cloth and set up the pan again over a low flame, spreading the roots about in it to dry them a little at a time and turning them over frequently until they acquire a certain elasticity, but without becoming too dry. Then, arranging them in parallel lines, they wrap them in a wet cloth, which they tie up tightly with a cord. After two days, during which these rolls are kept near the fire, they are untied, and the roll is made up again, placing the roots that were in the middle at the circumference in order to make them dry slowly and evenly until they are all so dry that they ring like pieces of wood when they are thrown upon a table. The heaviest ones and those that have a straw or light brown color are the most highly valued. To preserve them they take a chest lined with a thin sheet of lead and put it in another larger one, filling the space between the two chests with pulverized quicklime to keep insects from getting through;

*Vol. 2, p. 576.

and everything is carefully closed up. The method used by the Tartars is much simpler. At harvest time the roots are buried as they are found for 10 or 15 consecutive days. Then they are washed carefully and cleansed of dirt with a brush. Afterwards they are immersed for a moment in the almost boiling decoction of a sort of yellow millet that tints them somewhat with its own color. They also dry them in the sun, but, then although the roots keep their virtue, they do not maintain the color to which the Chinese give great importance. When the roots are thoroughly dry, they must be stored in a dry place to keep them from being spoiled by moisture. The Asiatics regard Ginseng as a panacea or universal remedy, and the Chinese in particular consider it as the most potent means of recovering health. This root used to be sold at three pounds of silver per pound by weight–by which is meant, of course, that of the best quality and best preserved. M. Lamarck says* that in the translation Dr. Wandermont made of a Chinese book wonderful virtues are attributed to it, for example, in dysenteries, stomach disorders, paralyses, convulsions, weakness, and internal [*rientrato?*] smallpox. He adds also that it stimulates perspiration, increases natural warmth, and so strengthens even the dying that it gives them time to take other remedies for recovering their health. These exaggerated virtues of Ginseng root render it so valuable in the eyes of the Chinese that, according to what Father Jartoux [†] relates, in 1709 the Emperor of China employed 10,000 Tartars to harvest it. In America this remedy is used for asthma and weaknesses of the stomach; and in Canada, where it grows near the St. Lawrence River, they make with the leaves a kind of aromatic and rather bitter soup that is nauseous to many people. It is to be noted that in well-cultivated regions Ginseng has almost disappeared, so that the harvesting of it has become expensive in America, too. For this reason it would be very useful to raise it there, all the more so because it does not require much labor. It grows from seed, but rarely sprouts before the third year; and the root is not usable until after the plant has borne seeds.

[Br 2:321] *PERSICARIA URENS* [*Polygonum hydropiper* L.] rather *Polygonum urens*, has a very strong taste, and kills all the fish if it is put in the water in large quantity and left there for some time. [For another contemporary reference to such fish-kills, see Edward C. Carter, ed., *The Virginia Journals of Benjamin Henry Latrobe* (New Haven, Conn., Yale Univ. Press, 1977) 2: 272]

PINUS

1. *P. STROBUS foliis quinis, margine scabris; cortice levi.* Lin.
Pinus canadensis quinque folia, floribus albis, conis oblongis pendulis, squamis abieti

**Encyclop. Méth.* art. "Ginseng."
[†Petrus Jartoux, 1668–1720, first described and illustrated Ginseng according to E. Bretschneider, *History of European Botanical Discoveries in China* (London, 1898) 1: 20.]

fere similibus. Duh. *Arb., & Arbust.* Pinus americana ex uno folliculo setis, longis, tenuibus, triquetris, ad unum angulum per totam longitudinem minutissimis, crenis asperatis. Tschudi *Arb. resineux* conif. n. 5

White pine in the United States; Weymouth pine in England; *Pin du Lord Weymouth* in France. [*Pinus strobus* L.]

2. *P. TAEDA foliis trinis.* Lin.

Pinus foliis longioribus tenuioribus ternis, conis maximis laxis. Poederle pag. 238.

Black pine, Frankincense pine in the United States. [*P. taeda* L.]

b. echinata

Pinus elatior conis agminatim nascentibus, foliis longissimis ternis ex eadem theca. Gronov. *Virgin.* pag. 152. Pinus virginiana praelongis foliis tenuioribus, cono echinato gracili. Pluk. *Almag.* 297. Miller *Dict.* n. 12. *Arb. & Arbust.* n. 15. Tschudi n. 16. Poederle. *Arboris. Belg.* Suppl. pag. 237.

Bastard pine in the United States. [*P. echinata* Mill.]

c. rigida

Pinus rigida Marsh. *Arb. Amer.* Pinus foliis ternis, conis longioribus, squamis rigidioribus. Miller. *Dict.* n. 10.

Common black pine and Pitch pine in Massachusetts. [*P. rigida* Mill.]

d. palustris

Pinus palustris. Marsh. *Arbust. Amer.* Pinus foliis ternis longissimis. Miller. *Dict.* n. 14. Pinus americana palustris patula, longissimis, & viridibus setis. Tschudi, n. 19. Pinus americana palustris trifolia foliis longissimis. Duham. *Arb. & Arbust.* n. 18.

Marsh pine in the United States. [*P. palustris* Mill.]

3. *P. SYLVESTRIS foliis geminis, primordialibus solitariis, glabris.* Lin.

b. norvegica [Nobis]

Pinus canadensis bifolia conis mediis ovatis. Duham. *Arb. & Arbust.* n. 8.

Norway pine in Massachusetts. [*P. resinosa* Ait.]

c. Novo-caesariensis [Nobis]

Pinus Virginiana. Marsh. *Arbust. Amer.* Pinus virginiana binis brevioribus, & crassioribus setis, minori cono, singulis squamarum capitibus aculeo donatis. Pluk. *Almag.* Pinus virginiana foliis geminis brevioribus, conis parvis, squamis acutis. Miller *Dict.* n. 9.

Jersey pine in the United States. [*P. virginiana* Mill.]

d. flava [Nobis]

Pinus foliis longissimis ex una theca binis. Gronov. *Virgin.* Colden. *Noveborac.* 231.

Yellow pine in New York and Maryland. [*P. echinata* Mill.]

4. *P. BALSAMEA foliis solitariis, duplici serie pectinatis, subemarginatis, strobilis oblongis.* N[obis].

Pinus foliis solitariis, subemarginatis, subtus linea duplici punctata. Lin. & Gronov. *Fl. Virg.* Miller. *Dict.* n. 3. Abies taxifolio odore balsami Gileadensis. Duh. *Arb. & Arbust.* n. 3. Tschudi n. 3.

Balm of Gilead, Fir tree in the United States. [*Abies balsamea* (L.) Mill.]

5. *P. AMERICANA foliis solitariis pectinatis, sub-emarginatis, ramis juniori-bus hirsutis, strobilis subrotundis.* N[obis].
Pinus Abies Americana. Marsh *Arbust. Amer.* Abies Americana foliis subemarginatis bifariam dispositis, strobilis subrotundis. Miller, *Dict.* Abies minor pectinatis foliis virginiana, conis parvis subrotundis. Pluk. & Duh. *Arb. & Arbust.* n. 6. Tschudi n. 6.
Hemlock pine, Hemlock fir in the United States. [*Tsuga canadensis* (L.) Carr.]

6. *P. CANADENSIS foliis solitariis linearibus, obtusiusculis. submembranaceis.* Lin.

a. alba
Abies piceae foliis brevioribus, conis parvis biuncialibus laxis. Duhamel n. 8.* Abies Tschudi n. 8.
White spruce and New Foundland spruce-fir in the United States, *Epinette blanche* among the French Canadians. [*Picea glauca* (Moench.) Voss]

b. nigra
Abies piceae foliis brevibus, conis minimis. Duh., n. 7.† Abies Tschudi, n. 7.
Black spruce and Red spruce in the United States; *Epinette noire* among the French Canadians. [*Picea mariana* (Mill.) BSP]

7. P. LARIX foliis fasciculatis obtusis. Lin.

b. rubra.
Pinus Larix rubra. Marsh. *Arbust. Amer.*
Red larch tree in the United States.

c. nigra.
Pinus Larix nigra. Marsh. *Arb. Amer.*
Black larch tree in the United States.

d. alba.
Pinus Larix alba. Marsh. *Arb. Amer.*
White larch tree in the United States. [all are Tamarack, *Larix laricina* (Du Roi) K. Koch]

The pine, fir, and larch were combined by Linnaeus in the genus of the first because of their similar fructification, on which are based the distinctive characteristics of the genera. Nevertheless certain authors have insisted upon retaining the old division, among whom Duhamel, who, although recognizing the analogy in fructification, decided to make the distinctions in order not to overburden the genus of the pines with too large a number of species. This happens, however, only because simple varieties are confused with species, inasmuch as, by separating the former, the latter are reduced all told to the bare number of 13 counting pines, larches, and firs.‡ The variations produced in pines by terrain and climate were noted in Sweden by that diligent observer of nature, Linnaeus, in his handsome dissertation entitled *"Arboretum svecicum"* (*Amoenit. Acad.*, Vol. 5, p. 183) where he says: *Pinus sylvestris habitat per*

*This is the Canadian *Epinette blanche* that Duhamel attributes to his species No. 7.
†This is the *épinette noire.*
‡See remarks at the entry "Mespilus."

totam Sveciam, excepta Scania campestri, a qua usque ad Alpes Lapponicas adscendit. In angustiis longum, integerrimumque truncum, in apricis ramosissima, in rupestribus vero, & cespitosis pigmaea, ac incompta evadit arbor; e nella nota: Hinc opinionem vulgi ortam esse existimo, nempe quod plures species Pini apud nos crescerent. The most constant characteristic for distinguishing the species is offered by the leaves, which grow either singly, namely, one by one, or by twos, threes, or more joined together. There are nevertheless some exceptions even in this feature, since there is *Pinus sylvestris* that sometimes has two instead of three leaves, so that perhaps the varieties of the American *Pinus sylvestris* (Spec. 3) and those of the *Pinus taeda* (Spec. 2) might form a single species, which ought to be verified by abundant sowing.

White pine (Spec. 1) is easily distinguished by its smooth and whitish bark, by its leaves that come out by fives from a single sheath, and by the shape of its cones —long, pendent, and composed of soft and flexible scales like those of the fir. It grows luxuriantly in various parts of Massachusetts and the United States, reaching a height of 70 feet and more in northern regions and growing less vigorously in warmer climates. It was called Weymouth pine because Lord Weymouth was the first to have it brought from America and to begin to cultivate it. Thereafter it was extensively propagated in England, where, in the reign of Queen Anne a law was passed to preserve these trees and to encourage plantations of them in America, since it has been recognized as one of the best woods for the use of the navy. The wood is white, of a hardness halfway between the larch and spruce,* light and tough, and therefore excellent for ship masts, for building wooden houses, and for floors and for wainscoting in homes of brick. This useful wood not only serves the needs of the country but constitutes, moreover, an important article of trade in the northern states, whence, after being sawed up into boards, it is shipped every year to the southern states and the Antilles. White pine grows readily, likes good solid soil, and more than any other species of pine deserves being propagated by us for forming avenues and for the usefulness of its wood. It is also found on the mountains of the province of Fakonia in Japan, as Mr. Thunberg notes in his *Flora Japonica.*

Black pine (Spec. 2), called *taeda* by Linnaeus on account of the quantity of pitch that it produces, is subject to many varieties. In the swamps of temperate climates it grows to a great height and produces long leaves, and large, long, and spiny cones. It abounds in resin, and its wood is sawed into boards for use in construction. Because of the smell of its resin and on account of the site where it grows, it is called Frankincense pine and Virginia swamp pine. On the other hand, the swamps of the warm climate of South Carolina render the Black pine (Var. d) of moderate height, and its leaves are then very long, the cones are quite large and long, but not spiny, and the wood is no good for construction. In rocky and mountainous places of Massachusetts it is a middling-sized tree with black bark, short cones, oblong, spiny, obtuse scales. It gives off a very pleasant fragrance, but its wood is not used (Var. c), whereas in the vast sandy plains of North Carolina it reaches a height of 60 to 70 feet (Var. b), producing the very long leaves that vary from two to three[; and] long, slender, and very spiny cones; and the wood is of good quality. Many other less notable differ-

**Pinus picea* Lin. [*Picea glauca* (Moench.) Voss].

ences are found in these trees, which practically form a series amid the varieties mentioned above. In general, Black pine is the best for producing resin and pitch, especially its two varieties *rigida* and *echinata.** All these varieties could be propagated in our country in barren places and marshes where other plants do not grow well.

Species 3, which is our European *Pinus sylvestris,* presents three distinct species in America also. The first (Var. b), called Norway pine in the United States, grows in Eastern Massachusetts, where it rises to an extraordinary height; it is chosen even over White pine for shipbuilding, and especially for masts. These huge pines are rare in regions near the sea and are found inland at some distance from river banks, for the most part not far from Penobscot, where these enormous trees were reserved for the use of the Royal Navy. The other two varieties are the one called New Jersey pine (Var. c) and the Yellow pine of Maryland (Var. d). New Jersey pine is very similar to our common pine except that sometimes it produces three leaves from the same sheath and the scales of the cones end in short, curved spines. A great deal of pitch is obtained from this tree, but since it is small and the wood is subject to borers, it is used only for firewood. Maryland Yellow pine, very abundant in the woods near Annapolis, is likewise of moderate size with a crooked and irregular trunk. Its leaves are very long and have the peculiar property of giving off an oily and rather unpleasant smell. It is good only for yielding pitch, which is neither abundant nor of good quality. It is called Yellow pine from the yellowish-green color of its leaves. I don't recommend the cultivation of the American varieties of *Pinus sylvestris* where the European ones are abundant, nor can either the height or size of Variety (b) induce us to propagate it in our country, since we know that cold climates are best for these trees, and the same species that forms in our country a tall but not lofty tree becomes immense in the forests of Russia and Sweden. However, the comparison of the American varieties with the European, and of all these with the varieties of Black pine, will serve, if for nothing else, to establish surer limits (if indeed they exist) between these two species, since there is great analogy among them, varying as they do from two to three leaves of greater or lesser length, and with cones, spiny or unarmed, and of diverse shape and size.

[Br 3:161–62] There is something else worth noting about these trees that was noticed by myself and others. In the great heat of summer, cows put themselves in the shade of these trees in preference to the oaks, White and Black nut trees [*Carya* spp.], planes, etc., whose foliage is much denser and thicker, and if there is only one pine in a wood, as many cows lie about it as can be covered by its shade. Some people are therefore inclined to suppose that the resinous exhalations are beneficial to cattle and that for this reason they prefer it to other trees.

Pinus balsamea (Spec. 4) does not differ much from our fir† since, like it, it has pectinate, flat, and emarginated leaves, and might perhaps be considered a sim-

*On the manner of extracting these products see Chap. X.

†*Pinus abies.* It should be noted that in all the editions of Linnaeus that I examined the *trivial*

ple variety of the European one, there being no difference other than wider, more obtuse, and thicker leaves and a stronger odor. This tree is common in the woods of Massachusetts, near Montreal in Canada, and in other places in the United States, where it is called Balm of Gilead [as in Michaux. *Silva*] and Silver fir. It puts out a great number of branches, and its rather large cones open on the tree itself and drop in the autumn as do those on our fir. The surface of the trunk, or rather the bark that lies beneath the epidermis, is covered with tiny vesicles formed by a swelling of the cellular tissue near the vessels that carry the sap proper, which vesicles are full of a clear and very fragrant turpentine used for wounds and which, from the resemblance of the odor to the Balm of Gilead, caused the same name to be given to this tree; what is more, in England the turpentine from *Pinus balsamea* is sold under the name of Balm of Gilead and is very highly prized. This fir forms a very handsome tree when it is young, but in the gardens of England, where it was transplanted, it quickly deteriorated and is now little esteemed for that reason. I believe, however, that by propagating it in cool, hilly places and even in our woods, or perhaps drawing off by incision the turnpentine that becomes too abundant in fertile soils, it could thrive as well here as in America.

The fir called Hemlock (Spec. 5) is very common in the woods of Massachusetts and reaches there a great height. Its leaves are of a dark green, and the tiny cones are about the size of a hazelnut and almost round. The Hemlock was confused with the preceding (Spec. 4) by Linnaeus, and by others it was mistaken for *Pinus canadensis* (Spec. 6), which is a kind of Spruce; but it is different from these as can be seen from a comparison of specific characteristics. The Indians derive from the turpentine of this tree a red color that they use to tint things they make of wood, with the bark they make seats and other furniture, and they use it to cover their wigwams, or cabins. After their example the inhabitants of the woods of St. George in Eastern Massachusetts cover their wooden houses with it, and they also use it for dressing hides. The wood is not much esteemed because it is full of checks and therefore of little use. It is hard to guess why the colonists gave this tree the name Hemlock, a name proper to the *Cicuta,* to which the fir described here bears no similarity. Hence one may suppose that they named it so ascribing to it the same pernicious qualities as that plant. We must try to propagate in our country this very handsome tree, which reaches a height of 40 to 50 feet in the northern regions of the United States.

Spruce (Spec. 6) is a type of *Pezzo** differing little from our native one. Two main varieties of it are known in America—one called White (Var. a) and the other

---

names of the fir (*Abete*) and spruce (*Pezzo*) were wrong, the former being called *Pinus picea* and the latter *Pinus abies,* whereas the synonyms say the opposite. The fir, then, which is the *Sapin* of the French and the *Abies* of the ancients, is the one that has leaves arranged comblike, flat, obtuse, and slightly incised at the tip, and upturned cones. The spruce, which is the *Pesse* or *Sapin de Norvège* of the French and the *Picea* of the ancient Italians, has leaves surrounding the branch in an irregular manner, almost round, slender, and sharp at the tip, and pendent cones. The first is called *Abiezzo* by the Lombards, the second, *Pescia.*

*In spite of the fact that our *Pescia* is called *Picea* in the *Vocabolario della Crusca,* I have preferred the name *Pezzo,* adopted by Mattioli, the Sienese botanist.

called Black (Var. b). The major difference between these two varieties consists in that the first has longer leaves, greenish white [staminate cones] and cones, and the second has shorter, thicker leaves of a darker green and flowers [pistillate cones] and seeds of a reddish or black color. In the northernmost regions of the United States, and in Canada and Nova Scotia, they sometimes grow to a great height in moist and light soil, so that its wood can even serve as masts for small ships. The greatest advantage derived from this tree, however, is spruce beer, which is almost the only beverage in Canada, Nova Scotia, and Massachusetts. The inhabitants of the woods of this latter region fill a vat with the tender shoot-tips of spruce and then pour in water that they boil until a very heavy decoction results, to which they add a large quantity of liquid residues of sugar called molasses, from which ensues a reddish colored beer with a medicinal taste. Others, however, especially in Canada, mix the molasses with the essence or distilled spirits from Variety (b), called Spruce (the best for this purpose) and then obtain a limpid, effervescent beer of a nice yellowish color with a much more pleasant taste. This is the spruce beer in use at the tables of the gentry in Montreal and Quebec and which is also sent to Europe, principally England, where it is consumed in large quantities. The immortal Captain James Cook in his trips around the world found Spruce growing luxuriantly on the coasts of New Zealand[*] and its marvelous efficacy in curing the most inveterate sea scurvy was realized at that time, so that he recommended the essence of Spruce as one of the best remedies to take along on long voyages. This beer was also made recently in England with the branches of Spruces that had been propagated there in gardens, and M. Broussonet presented some at the Royal Society of Agriculture of Paris.† The aforementioned M. Broussonet gives a recipe used in America for making beer that conforms with the method that I saw employed. Take, he says, a 50-pint vat, fill it with Spruce branches, and after drawing off the decoction with the water, add 4 pints of molasses until the molasses is well dissolved. Pour everything into an 80-pint barrel, mixing in the essence of Spruce and making the mixture ferment with beer yeast. The European Spruce was also tried out and a good beer was obtained from it, which might have been expected because of the great analogy and similarity of Spruce and *Pezzo,* so great that at first sight they are not easily distinguishable. This most healthful drink ought to be known also in Mediterranean regions, especially in territories where the inhabitants are subject to putrid diseases and epidemics. The Indians weave baskets with Spruce roots and use them like cord for sewing the pieces of birch bark with which they cover the frames of their canoes.

The American larch (Spec. 7) is distinguished into three varieties by the color of the fruit, namely, Red (Var. b), Black (Var. c), and White (Var. d). I found it only in the northern parts of Eastern Massachusetts, where it is by some called improperly Juniper. It is no different from our Larch except that it is smaller and has tiny cones

[*Cook did not say that he found Spruce in New Zealand. On 1 April 1773, on his second voyage he directed that a beer be made of the condensed juice of a tree resembling Black spruce, *Dacrydium cupressinum* Soland. mixed with *Leptospermum scoparium* Forst., see J. C. Beaglehole, *Jour. Capt. James Cook* (Cambridge Univ. Press, 1961) Vol. 2: 114 and fn. 1.]

†*Mémoires d'Agriculture de la Société R[oyal] de Paris* (1786, Trim. de printemps) p. 15.

with smooth, round scales. As far as I know no great use is made of this tree because it does not attain a respectable size.

Although the pines [conifers] can be counted among the sturdiest of trees, flourishing in the most barren terrains and in the coldest regions, they are nevertheless among the most delicate in the first years of their early growth. Perhaps for this reason nature provided them with most abundant seeds, very few of which can succeed in overcoming the difficulties of growing. The young plants suffer from the sun and the rain, drying out in light and arid soils and rotting in clayey ones. Baron Tschudi,* who applied himself particularly to the cultivation of resinous-coniferous trees, gives the method of carrying out these seedings that I shall report here briefly. It consists in preparing little wooden boxes with holes in the bottom and not more than eight Parisian inches high, with an inside lower layer of pottery fragments and another of good fallowed soil coarsely mixed with sifted construction dirt. On this one sows the [conifer] seeds barely covering the smallest ones with good light earth and a little thicker layer the species that have larger seeds. Expose the boxes to the east so as to protect them from the sun and rain, and as soon as the pines sprout, when summer nights are clear, let them enjoy the dew, and water them, sprinkling them with a broom most sparingly and only whenever you see that the soil moved with the finger is dry below. In autumn you must remove carefully the mossy crust on the surface, scattering on it a little dry dirt, and put the boxes on stones in a place protected from the north wind by some wall or hedge, exposing them gradually to the sun. If the cold is severe, cover them around, and even lightly on top, with dry straw. In the spring of the third year plant them in a greenhouse with the ball of earth about the roots, and there, too, take care to water them little and to keep straw or moss around the foot of each one in order to protect them against drying out without giving them too much moisture. After four or five years they can be planted in their places with the ball of earth around the roots. The American species of pine that in my opinion are most worthy of being propagated in our country are *strobus, balsamea, americana,* and *canadensis,* since they all have some particular use. In fact, I am waiting for some of the plants that I own to reach a suitable size for transportation to the heath of Mozzate,† where a total of about 2000 Pines, Firs, Spruces, and Larches that I transferred there from our Alps have been growing luxuriantly for a number of years. The analogy between the American and European species gives me almost certain expectation of good success.

PLATANUS

P. OCCIDENTALIS foliis lobatis. Lin.
Platanus occidentalis. Catesby. Tom. I tab. 56. Platanus occidentalis, sive virginiensis. Duh. *Arb. & Arbust.* n. 3.

**Traité des arbres résineux-conifères* de M. le baron de Tschudi (Metz. 1768).
†See the entry on *Bignonia catalpa.*

Plane tree, Buttonwood, Water beech, in the United States, *Water bak* or *Was-bok* among the Swedes of New Jersey. [Sycamore, *Platanus occidentalis* L.]

Platanus occidentalis is very common in the neighborhood of Boston and many of them can be seen near public streets, as likewise in low places and near the banks of rivers and brooks. The bark of the tree is whitish and comes loose in wide patches in the fall and winter, a new one forming underneath that grows and spreads during the following spring. The leaves are very large, very much like those of the grape, and less deeply cut than those of the oriental Plane of the ancients [*Ficus sycomorus* L., a fig]. It blossoms in the month of June and then produces spherical fruit about one inch in diameter hanging in a long peduncle and composed of numerous slender seeds joined together at the base, whence it got the name of Buttonwood. This fruit remains on the tree until the following spring, and in April it drops the seeds, which are transported a great distance by the wind. With the bark of the Plane tree the Indians made buckets, and bowls for gathering blueberries; and the Americans saw up the trunks into boards for various uses. This tree is planted in gardens and near homes so that one may enjoy the advantage of a thick shade in the summer; and it is excellent in forming avenues, since the branches span a wide circle. I didn't find the Plane tree in Massachusetts except in the parts south of the city of Portsmouth. It grows from seed in the second year provided it is put in vases, kept well watered, and the seeds are spread over the dirt, covering them with moss. To separate easily the seed of the Plane tree from the fuzz that envelops it, rub it with the hand on a somewhat shaggy cloth, since the fuzz attaches itself to the cloth and the seed can be collected nice and clean, which is very convenient for planting it. As soon as they begin to grow, the plants must be protected from the sun, and in three years, if they are in good soil, they reach a height of more than three cubits, as I myself found out. It is easily layered by burying its branches and holds up excellently in our climate, as was the case with my young Plane trees that have withstood the most severe winters.

PODOPHYLLUM

P. PELTATUM foliis peltatis, lobatis. Lin.

Podophyllum. Trew. *Pl. select.* tab. 29. Anapodophyllon Canadense Morini. Catesby. Tom. I tab. 24.

May apple in the United States. [*Podophyllum peltatum* L.]

This plant has large round leaves divided into many lobes that come directly out of the root, rising to a height of about a foot and a half. The blossoms are composed of many white petals, and the spherical ovary is surrounded by many yellow-colored stamens. Its fruit is of the size of a small apple and contains many seeds. The Virginians and other inhabitants of North America eat it since it has a sweet and tasty flavor, and call it May apple because it ripens during this month. The root, according to Catesby, is a strong emetic, and for that reason it is called Ipecacuanha in Carolina where it is used instead of the real Ipecacuanha [*Cephaelis ipecacuanha* Rich.]. It grows in the more fertile soils near hedges and roads and is easily propagated from roots, which reproduce the leaves and fruit annually. Linnaeus lists another species under the name of *Podophyllum diphyllum* [*Jeffersonia diphylla* (L.) Pers., Twin-leaf] discovered in Virginia by Mr. Collinson, but since I have not seen it, and since it was not clearly defined by Linnaeus himself, who raises the question whether it might not be a species of *Sanguinaria,* I shall make no further mention of it.

POLYGALA

P. SENEGA floribus imberbibus, spicatis; caule erecto herbaceo, simplicissimo, foliis lato-lanceolatis. Lin.
Radix Senega. Lin. *Amoenitat. Acad.* Tom. 2 pag. 139 tab. 2.

Rattlesnake root in the United States; *Senega, Seneka,* and *Sennegar* among the Indians. [*Polygala senega* L.]

Senega is very similar to Persicaria* and has a perennial, fibrous, woody, flexible root furnished at the top with many protuberances out of which come the stalks. These are simple stalks with alternate, lanceolate leaves terminating in a spike of small papilionaceous white blossoms that are followed by tiny little capsules containing for the most part two black seeds with a white lateral appendage. This is a plant famous for its efficacy, and the origin of its fame is as follows. The Indians of North America used a root they called *Senega* or *Sennagar* to treat the bite of the rattlesnake, and they used to sell it reduced to a powder to the Europeans who settled there, wanting never to let them know what the plant was that produced this root. For many years efforts were made in vain to discover it and the roots of various plants were tried out, but they were all useless, or at least inferior to the Senega of the Indians. Finally in the year 1736 Dr. [John] Tennent [c. 1700–c. 1760], a Scottish physician [b. in England], succeeded in discovering from information obtained from the Indians in Pennsylvania that the Senega root belonged to the *Polygala caule simplici erecto, foliis ovato-lanceolatis alternis, integerrimis, racemo terminali erecto* described by Gronovius in his *Flora virginica* on p. 80. Beyond the alexipharmic property already mentioned, Dr. Tennent found in this root a particular effectiveness in cases of pleurisy, for which he received a reward of 75 Pennsylvania pounds sterling† from the magistrate of Philadelphia. The same Dr. Tennent, according to what he says, used it with happy results‡ for hydropsy, asthma, podagra, colds, and a kind of consumption endemic in Virginia. It is nevertheless likely that the virtues of Senega have been exaggerated just the way all new remedies are hawked at first as sure and almost universal. It would not be even just or reasonable, however, to deny to Senega an unusual effect inasmuch as, though the applications tried in Italy with these roots have not been very successful, their small, or complete lack of, efficacy must rightfully be attributed to their excessive drying out or age. In fact, since the virtue of this root consists principally in an acrid acid

***Polygonum persicaria* Lin.
†See Lin., "Diss. de Senega," *Amoenit. Acad.* [2: 139, t. 2.].
‡*Essays on the Pleurisy* (Philadelphia, 1786) in 8°.

so strong that it causes vomiting in the person who takes a tincture of it, it is natural for it almost entirely to dissipate in time (as happens with many other plants)–which must have occurred in the roots tried out in Italy, since they produced in the patients none of the symptoms mentioned by Dr. Tennent. Therefore propagating and testing this plant in our country will not be in vain if the freshly prepared roots can have the same power that was found in them in America and confirmed in cases of pleurisy and poisonous snake bites by a great number of experiments and by the commendation of the magistrate of Philadelphia, so that Linnaeus was prompted by all these authentications to say that Senega ought to be kept in drug shops as one of the most necessary remedies in the same way that one finds there opium, mercury, and quinine.

Although Senega is the most effective herb against snake bite, many others in America are considered valid for the same purpose. I shall give here a catalogue of them with their Linnaean names and the local ones, since most of them do not deserve a separate article.

1. *Aristolochia serpentaria* Lin.*
Rattlesnake root in America. [*Aristolochia serpentaria* L.]

2. *Praenanthes alba.* Lin.
Doctor Witt's snakeroot in America. [*Prenanthes alba* L.]

3. *Veratrum luteum.* Lin.
Unicorn's horn, Rattlesnake root in America. [*Chamaelirium luteum* (L.) Gray]

4. *Osmunda virginica.* Lin.
Fern rattlesnake root in America. [*Botrychium virginianum* L.]

5. *Cunila mariana.* Lin.
Dittany in America. This is also a febrifuge. [*Cunila origanoides* (L.) Britt.]

6. *Sanicula marylandica.* Lin.
Black snakeroot in New York. [*Sanicula marilandica* L.]

7. *Uvularia perfoliata.* Lin.
Its root is used ground and squeezed in water in New York State and serves in poultices to bring abscesses to a head. [*Uvularia perfoliata* L.]

8. *Aletris farinosa.* Lin.
Star grass, Star root in Virginia. It is also a febrifuge and something of a laxative. [*Aletris farinosa* L.]

9. *Eryngium foetidum.* Lin.*
Rattle-snake master in the United States. [*Eryngium yuccifolium* Michx.]

*See the entry on it above.
†The information about plants from no. 9 on inclusive was given to me by Dr. [James] Greenway [1703?–1794] a Virginia physician and botanist who lived in Dinwiddie County three miles from Petersburgh. There he assembled a very handsome collection of dried plants, and he is very well informed in botany.

[Br 2:319] This plant was pointed out to me by Dr. Greenway, a Virginia physician (of whom I shall speak below) as an excellent remedy for rattlesnake bite; and Mr. Clayton, in his *Flora virginica,* after having alluded to the aforementioned quality, adds that in the treatment of fevers it is on a par with *Contrayerva* [*Dorstenia*]: Ad morsus serpentis caudisoni, et aliorum venenatorum optimum censetur remedium. In febribus idem praestat quod Contrayerva. Gron. *Fl. virg.* p. 40[–41].

---

10. *Gnaphalium plantaginifolium.* Lin.

Rattle-snake plantain in the United States. [*Goodyera* spp.
Castiglioni here was confused by the specific epithet. Robert Brown's name for the several species of orchids known as Rattlesnake plantain appeared in Aiton, *Hortus Kewensis* in 1813.]

[Br 2:320] This very common plant, according to Carver, [*Travels,* (London, 1778), 320] used by the Indians against rattlesnake bite, was discovered to be one of the best remedies against the poison of the Negroes.* One of them, having been condemned to death in South Carolina, promised to reveal this secret if he were absolved of punishment. When this was granted him, he showed various people this plant, that was recognized as Rattlesnake plantain. [not *Gnaphalium plantaginifolium* but *Goodyera* spp.]

---

11. *Serratula spicata.* Lin.

Throatwort in the United States. [*Liatris spicata* (L.) Willd.]

It is told that an Indian suffered a rattlesnake bite and recovered very quickly after taking two spoonfuls of this decoction. It is also used for sore throats and in the form of poultices and gargles.

12. *Collinsonia canadensis.* Lin.

Horseweed in the United States. [or Horsebalm, *Collinsonia canadensis* L.]

13. Helianthus (Spec. nova). [*Hypericum,* an early Virginia generic name].

St. Andrew's cross in Virginia. ["St. Andrew's cross" is applied, not to a Sunflower, but to *Ascyrum hypericoides* L.]

This plant was discovered by Dr. Greenway and tried out by him on a woman who had lost consciousness because of a rattlesnake bite. Using solely a decoction of it, he brought her back to health in a few days. This species [not of *Girasole,* a sunflower] is also used a great deal for fevers.

*The Negroes have various poisons of which they make an abominable use, often destroying one another, and sometimes avenging themselves for the cruel treatment of their masters. These poisons, which act little by little upon the internal organs, produce a kind of degeneration that ends with death.

POPULUS

1. *P. NIGRA foliis deltoidibus, acuminatis.* Lin.

b. virginiana

Populus virginiana foliis cordatis, obsolete crenatis, utrinque glabris. *Mém. d'agricul. Trim. de Printemps. 1786.*

Black poplar in the United States. [*Populus deltoides* Marsh.]

2. *P. CANADENSIS foliis oblongis, obtuse-dentatis, subtus albicantibus.* Populus foliis oblongis, obtuse-dentatis, subtus albicantibus. *Mém. d'Agricult. 1786,* an Populus deltoides Marsh. *Arbust. Amer.* n. 1.

Cotton tree in the United States and *Peuplier liard du Canada* of the French. [*P. deltoides* Marsh.]

3. *P. BALSAMIFERA foliis ovatis, serratis, subtus albidis; stipulis resinosis.* Lin. Populus foliis ovatis, acutis, serratis. Gmelin. *Fl. Sibir.* Tom. I pag. 152 tab. 33. Populus nigra folio maximo, gemmis balsamum odoratissimum fundentibus. Catesby *Carolin.* Tom. I tab. 34.

Tacamahaca, Balsam tree, and also Balm of Gilead in the United States. [*P. balsamifera* L.]

4. *P. HETEROPHYLLA foliis cordatis, junioribus villosis.* Lin. Populus magna virginiana, foliis amplissimis, ramis nervosis quasi quadrangulis Duh. *Arb. & Arbust.* n. 9.

Virginian poplar tree in the United States, *Peuplier de Caroline* of the French. [*P. heterophylla* L.]

The genus of the poplars is also one of those whose species are hard to distinguish from varieties and therefore have been multiplied and confused. Thus the Virginia Black poplar (Spec. 1, Var. b) seems to me a variety of the European Black poplar, even though M. Fougeroux de Bondaroy in the *Mémoires de la Société d'Agriculture* printed in Paris makes a new species of it. This tree grows to a height of 70 to 80 feet forming a round top, its leaves are supported by long petioles often tinted with red, and they are almost heart-shaped, fluted at the margin, and smooth on both sides. The resemblance of its leaves to the *heterophylla* of Linnaeus (Spec. 4) leads me to suppose that the poplar in question might be the same one that M. Poederlè* describes under the name of *Peuplier du Canada.* Perhaps this poplar ought to be considered a variety of Spec. 4 since it has heart-shaped and not deltoid leaves and excrescences that form quadrate young branches. But since these differences are often found also in Spec. 1 and its wood is most usable, which is not the case with Spec. 4, I thought it best to put it with the common Black poplar until a more diligent examination brings out some constant difference. The wood of this variety of Black poplar is excellent, easily worked, and is said to be better than that of other poplars, so that it has been much propagated in various parts of France.

Canadian poplar (Spec. 2), which Mr. Marshall called *Populus deltoides,* dif-

**Manuel de l'arboriste belgique,* p. 288.

fers mainly from *Populus balsamifera* in that it has a smooth and lighter colored bark, smaller buttons, leaves narrower and sharper at the point. It reaches a great height and its flowers form seeds provided with a very white and very abundant hair more so than in the other poplars, from which it got in Carolina the name of Cotton tree. The wood is white, tough, elastic, and used a great deal in construction; and whenever the tree is very large, the Indians of Louisiana make one-piece canoes of it. It is called *Peuplier liard* in Canada, where it survives the most severe cold; and it must be cultivated in a moist and not too sunny terrain.

Populus balsamifera (Spec. 3), called Tacamahaca, is a tree of average height very common on the shores of the Connecticut and Charleston Rivers in New Hampshire, where a number of them can be seen planted along the roads. Its trunk is light brown, the ovate and saw-toothed leaves are dark green above but paler and somewhat whitish underneath. Out of its buds comes a resin more fragrant and balsamic than that of the Black poplar, and this is extracted by the Indians by slitting the trees during the winter. They used it for the treatment of various illnesses, but at the present time, to my knowledge, the inhabitants make no use of it. The celebrated botanist Johann Georg Gmelin [1709–55] found this poplar in Siberia and notes on the authority of [Georg Wilhelm] Steller [1709–46] that the Russians of Irkutsk steeped the buds in grain spirits, from which by distillation they drew a pleasant liquor excellent for the *disuria* produced by the Celtic disease.

Populus heterophylla (Spec. 4) is a rather large tree whose young branches have longitudinal excrescences [lenticels] that form from four to five elevated ridges. Its leaves are very large, very tough, fluted at the margin, heart-shaped, of a light green color, and somewhat hairy underneath when they first come out. These leaves vary in form, wherefore Linnaeus gave it the name of *heterophylla.* The poplar under consideration is very common in the botanical gardens of Europe, where it is valued for its broad leaves which are kept until later in the autumn than those of our poplars. It is, however, more subject to boring by the larva of the moth called *Vinula* by Linnaeus, which comes about perhaps because of the greater porousness of its wood, which is no good at all.

All these poplars can be propagated from branches and layerings like the common Black poplar, and like it, they all like moist and light soil.

PRINOS

1. *P. VERTICILLATUS foliis longitudinaliter serratis.* Lin.
Aquifolium foliis deciduis. Duh. *Arb. & Arbust.* Tom. 1 pag. 62. Prinos Gronov. *virgin.* pag. 54.

Winterberry in the United States. [*Ilex verticillata* (L.) A. Gray]

2. *P. GLABER foliis apice serratis.* Lin.
Cassine foliis lanceolatis, alternis, sempervirentibus; floribus axillaribus. Miller *Diction.* tab. 83 fig. 2.

Colberry in southern United States. (Gallberry, Inkberry, *Ilex glabra* (L.) A. Gray]

Prinos verticillatus (Spec. 1) is very common in the swamps of Virginia and other parts of the United States, where it reaches a height of 8 to 10 feet, dividing into many branches toward the top. Its leaves are lanceolate, pointed, saw-toothed, and alternate. The blossoms come out of the axils of the leaves in grassy-green and white clusters, and they are followed by nearly round berries of a red color when they are ripe which crown the branchlets—for which reason it got named *verticillatus* by Linnaeus. It is called Winterberry in America because its fruit remains on the plant through that season, and therefore it is worth propagating in our gardens. In America a poultice for bringing buboes to a head is made with the inner bark of this shrub. Between this and the Carolina holly* there is so little difference that Duhamel described this *Prinos* among the hollies under the name of *Aquifolium foliis deciduis.*

Prinos glaber (Spec. 2) differs from *verticillatus* in having saw-toothed leaves toward the tip.† It is even smaller, its leaves are larger, glossy, of a dark green color, and they stay on in the winter. The flowers are attached to short peduncles, and the berries are black in color. I found it common in the marshy places of the two Carolinas, whose inhabitants boil these berries in water and obtain a dye which, mixed with copperas, serves to blacken stockings and the fabrics they make. That black, however, is neither pretty nor lasting and easily takes on a reddish color. It can be propagated like the preceding plant as a garden ornamental, both of them susceptible to propagation by means of the seeds, which, if they are not put in the ground as soon as they are picked, will sprout only the second year. They like a moist, shaded, and light terrain. Linnaeus cites as a synonym of *Prinos glaber* the *Cassine vera floridanorum arbuscula baccifera &c.* of Catesby, *Carolin.,* 2 p. 57, which was referred by Duhamel to his *Aquifolium caroliniense, foliis dentatis, baccis rubris*—the *Ilex cassine* of Linnaeus.

PRUNUS

1. *P. DOMESTICA pedunculis subsolitariis; foliis lanceolato-ovatis convolutis, ramis muticis.* Lin.

b. americana

Prunus americana. Marshall. *Arbust. Amer.*

Sweet plum tree in the United States. [*Prunus americana* Marsh.]

2. *P. VIRGINIANA floribus racemosis, foliis deciduis, basi antice glandulosis.* Lin. Cerasus latiore folio, fructu racemoso purpureo majore. Catesby *Carolin.* Tom. 2 tab. 94. Cerasus sylvestris, fructu nigricante, in racemis longis pendulis phytolacaceae instar congestis. Duhamel *Arb., & Arbust.* Prunus cerasus virginiana. Marsh. *Arbust. Amer.*

**Ilex cassine.* Lin.

†According to the observations of Mr. Boettger, *Prinos glaber* belongs to the genus *Ilex* of Linnaeus. See Reichard, *Systema Plantarum Linnei: Addenda,* Vol. IV, p. 65.

Wild cherry, Black cherry in the United States. [*P. serotina* Ehrh.]

3. *P. CANADENSIS floribus racemosis; foliis eglandulosis, lato lanceolatis, rugosis, utrinque pubescentibus.* Lin.
Cerasus racemosa, foliis amygdalinis americana. Pluk. *Almag.* tab. 158 fig. 4. Prunus cerasus canadensis. Marsh. *Arbust. Amer.*

Choke cherry in America. [*P. virginiana* L.]

4. *P. PUMILA floribus subumbellatis, foliis angusto-lanceolatis* Lin.
Cerasus canadensis pumila oblongo angustoque folio, fructu parvo. Duham. *Arb., & Arbust.* n. 17. An prunus declinata. Marsh. *Arbust. Amer.*

Dwarf plum in the United States, *Ragouminer, Nega,* and *Minel* in Canada. [*P. pumila* L.]

5. *P. LUSITANICA floribus racemosis; foliis sempervirentibus eglandulosis.* Lin.

b. serratifolia

Prunus Laurocerasus serratifolia. Marsh. *Arbust. Amer.* Laurocerasus americana amygdali odore. Duham. *Arb., & Arbust.* n. 5.

Wild orange in Carolina. [*P. caroliniana* (Mill.) Ait.]

I found in the month of September near Montreal in Canada a kind of wild plum whose fruit, large, somewhat oval, and of a yellowish-red color, was just then ripe and being taken to the city to be sold. Its rather acidulous flavor is not very tasty and therefore it is rarely eaten at good tables; but it is preserved with sugar in various ways. There are many varieties of the plum, called *Prunus domestica* by Linnaeus, that grow natively in North America. Mr. Marshall enumerates four, namely, the *Prunus americana,* with large red or yellow fruit; *angustifolia,* or Chickasaw plum, with thin-skinned red or yellow fruit; "Mississippi," with very large red and rather sour fruit; and the *maritima,* the fruit of which is small and round.

The American Wild cherry (Spec. 2), called also Black cherry, grows to a height of 40 feet and more on a trunk about a foot and a half in diameter. Its leaves are oblong-ovate, saw-toothed, acuminate, and provided at the base with glandules [extrafloral nectaries]. The blossoms come out in long, slender clusters, are white, and followed by tiny fruit of a scarlet color when ripe, with a bitter and disgusting taste. This tree has a very handsome appearance and would deserve to be propagated in Europe not only because of its beauty, especially when it is in bloom, but also because of its usefulness, since its wood is smooth, firm, and of a pretty red approaching that of mahogany, so that carpenters and inlayers use it for the most magnificent furniture. The fruit, though bitter, is greedily eaten by birds; and it is put in brandy made from wine or sugar in order to give it a pleasing taste. The infusion of the bark of this tree is used by the Massachusetts farmers as a purgative, and it is said to be very effective for jaundice.

Canada Dwarf cherry (Spec. 3) rises barely to six or eight feet and divides into many shoots furnished with wide, lanceolate, rather hairy leaves without glandules at the base. Its flowers are likewise in clusters, and the fruit, red as in Species 2, is not so bitter, but, on the other hand, it is so sour as to scrape the palate and throat.

The Canada Dwarf plum (Spec. 4) forms a tiny shrub hardly a foot and a half high. It winds around in the soil with its root, and its long, reddish shoots have narrow, lanceolate leaves somewhat whitish underneath. The flowers are almost umbrellalike and the fruit tiny, of a very deep red color, and very sour.

Species 3 and 4 can serve only as ornamentals for thickets, and Spec. 4, in view of its smallness, can be put in garden plots.

The Carolina *laurocerasus* (Spec. 5), finally, is a shrub of average height with lanceolate, narrow, saw-toothed leaves of a pretty glossy green that are kept in the winter like those of the common *laurocerasus.** The blossoms come out in March in very dense white clusters, and the fruit is small and black when it is ripe. I saw one in bloom in Mr. Watson's garden near Charleston in South Carolina that looked as pretty as can be because of the contrast between its white clusters with the deep, glossy green of the leaves. The name of Wild orange with which it is distinguished by the Carolinians is all the more improper because true wild oranges[†] grow in the same region. Mr. Marshall makes a new species of it under the name of *Prunus serratifolia,* but from its resemblance to the Portuguese *laurocerasus* I decided to admit it as a variety of the *Prunus lusitanica* of Linnaeus. If this can be propagated in our country (as has occurred with the common *laurocerasus* that came originally from Trebizond [Turkey]), it will have to be placed in a sunny spot protected from the winter cold and brought inside during the winter for the first few years.

PTELEA

P. TRIFOLIA foliis ternatis. Lin.

Frutex virginianus trifolius ulmi samaris. Pluk. *Almag.* pag. 159. Dillen. *Elth.* 147 tab. 122 fig. 148. Catesby Tom. II tab. 83. Ptelea Duham. *Arb., & Arbust.*

[Wafer ash, *Ptelea trifoliata* L.]

Ptelea grows 10 to 12 feet high, its trunk dividing into numerous branches covered with a smooth, gray-colored bark. The leaves come three by three, eliptical, tapering at the ends, dark green above and lighter underneath. The flowers are grassy white and come out in a kind of umbrella with four or five petals and four or five stamens, a short style, and the pistil flattened laterally. This grows subsequently in a round membrane with a swollen center where the seed is contained, which fruit therefore resembles a great deal that of the elm. According to Linnaeus there is a five-leaved variety, but this I have never seen. The seeds of *Ptelea* are sometimes triangular, that is, they have three membranaceous wings. Mr. Reichard notes that in *Atti della Societá Economica di Lautern* there is an observation that *Ptelea* has male plants separate from the female [due to abortion of stamens]; however, I found all my plants to produce perfect flowers. *Ptelea* was discovered in Virginia by John Banister, who sent seeds

**Prunus laurocerasus* Lin. Called *Lauro imperiale* in Lombardy.

[†"True wild oranges originated from Spanish introduction of the bitter-sweet orange, *Citrus aurantium* L., widely disseminated by the Indians, or persisting and spreading from André Michaux's garden near Charleston, S.C.]

to England; but nearly all the plants grown from them died during a cold winter, so that later, in 1724, Catesby sent some more, which introduction propagated this shrub in England. The leaves when rubbed have a disgusting odor, but the blossoms, on the other hand, have a charming fragrance and make a pretty sight because of the quantity of them. For this reason, and also because of the unusualness of the seeds and the beautiful green of the leaves, it deserves a place in copses. In Canada its leaves are considered vulnerary, and taken like tea they are said to be vermifugal. It is easily propagated from seed, and in our country it does very well outside.

PYRUS

P. CORONARIA foliis serrato-angulatis, umbellis pedunculatis. Lin.
Malus sylvestris floribus odoratis. Gronov. *virgin.* 55. Duham. *Arb. & Arbust.* n. 4.

Crabapple in Virginia. [*Pyrus coronaria* L.]

This apple grows to a height of 12 to 15 feet in the woods of Virginia, the two Carolinas, and Georgia. In April it is laden with numerous large, pink blossoms of a very pleasant odor, which are followed by tiny apples of a very sour and disgusting taste. This fruit is collected and preserved candied with sugar; and sometimes from it is distilled a kind of spirit called crabapple brandy. This is one of the North American shrubs that ought to be propagated as a garden ornamental, since it will unquestionably withstand our climate.

QUERCUS

1. *Q. PHELLOS foliis lanceolatis, integerrimis, glabris.* Lin.
Quercus, sive Ilex marylandica folio longo angusto salicis. Catesby Tom. I tab. 16; Seligmann Tom. I tab. 32. Quercus virginiana salicis folio longiore, fructu minimo. Pluk. *Amalth.* & Duham. n. 19. Quercus Phellos longifolia. Lamarck *Encyclop. method.* Art. Chêne. Quercus Phellos. Miller. *Diction.* n. 13. Quercus Phellos angustifolia. Marsh *Arbust. Amer.*

Willow oak, Water live oak in the Carolinas. [*Quercus phellos* L.]

b. latifolia

Quercus humilis salicis folio breviore. Catesby Tom. I tab. 22. Seligmann Tom. I tab. 44. Quercus Phellos latifolia. Marsh. *Arb. Amer.* Quercus Phellos brevifolia. Lamarck.

Broad leaved willow oak in the Carolinas. [*Q. laevis* Walt.]

c. sempervirens

Quercus foliis oblongis non sinuatis. Catesby Tom. I tab. 17. Seligmann Tom. I tab. 34. Quercus virginiana. Miller *Diction.* n. 17. Quercus Phellos sempervirens. Marshall *Arbust. Amer.* Quercus Phellos *Arbust. Amer.* Quercus Phellos obtusifolia. Lamarck.

True Live Oak, Evergreen willow oak in the Carolinas. [*Q. virginiana* Mill.]

2. *Q. PRINUS foliis obovatis, utrinque acuminatis, sinuato-serratis, denticulis rotundatis uniformibus.* Lin.
Quercus Castaneae foliis procera arbor virginiana. Catesby Tom. I tab. 18. Seligmann Tom. I tab. 36. Duham. *Arb. & Arbust.* n. 18.

Chestnut oak in the United States, *Mangu-me-nauck* of the Indians. [*Q. prinus* L.]

b. platanoides

Quercus foliis cuneiformi-ovatis superne latioribus, serraturis angulosis sub-inequalibus, inferna superficie albida. Lamarck.

[*Q. bicolor* Willd. *teste* Li.]

c. humilis

Quercus humilis virginiensis Castaneae folio. Pluk. & Duham. n. 20. Quercus Prinus humilis. Marshall.

Dwarf chestnut oak, Chinquapin oak in the United States. [*Quercus prinoides* Willd.]

3. *Q. NIGRA foliis cuneiformibus obsolete trilobis.* Lin.
Quercus, forte marylandica, folio trifido ad Sassafras accedente, Catesby Tom. I tab. 19. Seligmann Tom. I tab. 38. Quercus nigra integrifolia. Marshall n. 7. Quercus nigra latifolia. Lamarck.

Black oak in the United States. [*Q. marilandica* L.]

b. aquatica

Quercus folio non serrato in summitate quasi triangulo. Catesby Tom. I tab. 20. Seligmann. Tom. I tab. 40. Quercus nigra trifida. Marshall n. 6.

Water oak, Maryland Black oak in the United States. [*Q. nigra* L.]

4. *Q. PUMILA foliis obtuse sinuatis, setaceo-mucronatis, sub-quinquelobis, subtus albicantibus.* N[obis]. Tab. XIII.
Quercus pumila bipedalis foliis oblongis sinuatis, subtus tomentosis. Gronov. *virgin.* pag. 150. Quercus pumila. Banister, an Quercus rubra nana? Marshall. [Castiglioni found the reference to *Quercus pumila* Banister in Gronovius, although it was published first in Ray *Historia* (1688) 2: 1927. The name preceded Marshall's by three-quarters of a century.]

Shrub oak in the United States. [*Q. ilicifolia* Wangen.]

5. *Q. RUBRA foliis obtuse sinuatis setaceo-mucronatis, utrinque viridibus.* N[obis].
Quercus Aesculi divisura, foliis amplioribus aculeatis. Catesby Tom. I tab. 23. Seligmann Tom. I tab. 46. Quercus rubra. Miller *Dict.* n. 11. Quercus rubra maxima. Marshall *Arb. Amer.* n. 9. Quercus rubra maxima. Marshall *Arb. Amer.* n. 9. Quercus rubra latifolia. Lamarck.

Red oak, Grey oak, Pennsylvania black oak in the United States. [*Q. rubra* L.]

b. hispanica

Quercus rubra, seu hispanica hic dicta, foliis amplis, varie, profundeque incisis. Clayton *Fl. Virgin.* n. 785. Quercus Aesculi divisura foliis amplioribus aculeatis. Pluk.

Plate XIII. Scrub oak, the "Quercus pumila" of Banister (*Quercus ilicifolia* Wang.).

Phytograph. tab. 54 fig. 4.* Quercus rubra ramosissima. Marshall n. 10. Quercus rubra dissecta Lamarck. Var. b.

Lowland Spanish oak in the United States. [*Q. palustris* Muenchh.]

c. subserrata

Quercus virginiana rubris venis muricata. Pluk. *Phytograph.* tab. 54 fig. 5. Duhamel n. 17. Quercus Caroliniensis virentibus venis muricata. Catesby Tom. I tab. 21 fig. dextra. Seligmann Tom. I tab. 42 fig. dextra. Quercus rubra montana. Marshall *Arb. Amer.* n. 11. Quercus rubra subserrata. Lamarck. Var. c.

Upland Spanish oak, Scarlet oak in the United States. [*Q. coccinea* Muenchh.]

6. *Q. ALBA foliis oblique pinnatifidis, sinubus, angulisque obtusis.* Lin. Quercus alba virginiana. Catesby Tom. I tab. 21 fig. sinistra. Seligmann Tom. I tab. 42 fig. sinistra. Quercus alba Banisteri. Duh. *Arb., & Arbust.* n. 16. Quercus alba major. Marshall n. 1. Quercus alba minor. Idem. n. 2.

White oak in the United States. [*Q. alba* L.]

b. palustris

Quercus alba palustris. Marshall n. 3.

Swamp white oak in the United States. [*Q. bicolor* Willd.]

The Willow-leaved oak (Spec. 1) is distinguished mainly in three notable varieties. The first of these is *phellos* of Linnaeus, properly called, which grows to a great height in moist places. Its leaves, entire, smooth, narrow, and very long, have short petioles, and its acorns are quite small. In the more southern regions, when the winter is not too severe, it keeps its leaves, but its wood is soft and coarse-grained, so that it is not of much use. The second variety (Var. b) differs little from the preceding one except that it has wider and shorter leaves. It is found in lean and dry soils, and its acorns are also very small. The third (Var. c) grows in the two Carolinas and in Georgia and reaches a height of 40 feet and more, especially near the sea. Its leaves are oblong, entire, blunt at the tips, dark green, and they are kept during the winter. This plant is the best of the North American oaks and, furthermore, one of the most valued woods in those regions. It is a very tall tree, leafy, of very handsome appearance, so it would be excellent for making avenues in barren and sandy terrains where other trees might have difficulty adapting. Its wood is so compact and heavy that it does not float on water, and being tough and durable, it is considered the most suitable for the framework, or skeleton, of ships. It could be therefore, a profitable item of trade for those regions if transportation to Europe were less difficult, or rather less dangerous, since large beams and trunks of this extremely heavy wood, rolling from one side to the other of the ship in stormy weather, can knock apart the sides to the point of putting it in danger of sinking—which has happened more than once. What is more, some people have told me that there is not one example of a ship laden with this lumber arriving undamaged in Europe. The Indians (as Catesby says) stored up the acorns from this oak, which are quite sweet, and used them to thicken the soup that they made with deer meat, and eating them in other ways. He says, too, that they

*The same phrase name was used by Catesby for Species 5; but Plukenet's illustration belongs to this variety of the same Species 5.

extracted from them a tasty and healthful oil almost like that obtained from sweet almonds. Such a useful tree, and one that is content with barren soil, ought to be transported to Italy, especially to those regions where flourish the Cork* and the Holm-oak,† which it closely resembles.

The Chestnut-leaved oak (Spec. 2) is a tree 40 feet and more high with a whitish, furrowed bark easily detachable from the trunk, obovate‡ leaves pointed on both sides and fluted at the margin, huge acorns with very wide, but short, cups. It likes good, moist, and light soil; but it is not so common in the woods, and I found some only in Massachusetts on the way from Boston to Lancaster. Its leaves resemble so much those of the Chestnut that one tree can be taken for the other, if attention is not paid to the flowers and the fruit. Its wood, though not of fine and beautiful grain, is very useful for making fence posts and for still other purposes; and it supplies excellent firewood. In addition, pigs are very fond of its large acorns. Variety (b) is the one described by M. Lamarck under the name of *Quercus prinus platanoides* and differs from its species because it has shorter leaves, wider at the tip, somewhat whitish underneath, with deeper, blunter, and less regular indentations. He calls it *platanoides* because the bark comes off like that of the Plane tree, a property, however, common to the preceding one. Finally, the third variety (c), called Chinquapin oak§ in America, is a small shrub a few feet high. Its leaves are dentate and somewhat sinuate, and the acorns much smaller than in the varieties already described.

Black oak (Spec. 3) is distinguished from the others in that it has leaves nearly always divided into only three lobes toward the tip, a feature that serves to separate it from the Red oak (Spec. 5) and White oak (Spec. 6), which have leaves divided into many lobes. The term Black is given in America to two different oaks—the Red oak|| being called common Black oak in Pennsylvania, while in Maryland this name is given to the true Black oak of Linnaeus, which is the present one. Of this latter there are in America two varieties: one has large, almost sessile leaves ending in three to five obtuse lobes at the tip and producing acorns of average size; the other (Var. b), called *aquatica* because it grows in flooded areas of Maryland, is a tree of greater size than the preceding, with narrower, oblong leaves divided into three lobes at the tip, and with tiny acorns so bitter that not even pigs will eat them. The wood of both these varieties of Black oak isn't good for much and is used in America only as firewood. Both grow very luxuriantly in thin, sandy, and flooded terrains, especially along the road that goes from Annapolis to Alexandria. They are a sure sign of barren subsoil, just as, on the contrary, woods of White walnut, White pine, and Red maple are proof of the fertility of the terrain.

The Dwarf oak (Spec. 4, tab. XIII) was described by Gronovius under the

**Quercus suber.* Lin.
†*Quercus ilex.* Lin.
‡*Ob-ovatum, idest obverse-ovatum.* Lin. *Philos. Botan.* That is, egg-shaped, but with the narrower part attached to the petiole.
§Chinquapin is the name of the American Dwarf chestnut (see the entry *Fagus* above).
||See Species 5.

name *Quercus pumila*; but it was omitted by Linnaeus, and is probably the one that Mr. Marshall names *Quercus rubra nana.* It seems to me, however, that this is a true species different from the Red, although at first sight it does resemble it a great deal, since the same never exceeds 8 or 10 feet in height and has a tortuous and uneven trunk. Its leaves, regularly (Fig. I) divided into five lobes and ending in threads at the tips, are dark green above and woolly and white underneath. It produces tiny, rather short, acorns (Fig. 3) almost two-thirds covered by the cup, which is also very small and globe-shaped. I was unable to investigate whether in America any use is made of this shrub abundant in the woods of Massachusetts, so that it should not be propagated in our country except in ornamental thickets for its unusualness.

The Red oak (Spec. 5) varies greatly in the shape of its leaves and in the size of the acorns, plants varying widely from one another often being obtained from the seed of a single tree, as Miller also notes in his *Dictionary.* Three main varieties of it are distinguished in America, one of which rises to a height of more than 70 feet, with large, bluntly sinuous leaves with sharply pointed lobes ending in a bristle produced by the prolongation of the veins of the leaf. The acorns are large and the cup short and thick. The other variety (Var. b), found in marshy places near streams, is a tree not as tall as the preceding, with smooth gray-colored bark, narrower leaves deeply sinuate almost to the central rib, with a longer stem, and very small acorns. This variety is called Spanish oak in America. Then the third variety (Var. c), called Upland Spanish oak, grows in thin and elevated terrains to a height of more than 50 feet, with a rough and whitish bark. Its leaves are less deeply sinuate than in Variety (b), of a paler color, and almost regular in the lobing, so that they look somewhat like those of the Chestnut-leaved oak, except that they terminate in threads like the other Red oaks. This name was given to them because they have reddish veins in the wood and because the leaves become more or less deep red colored before they fall in the autumn. The wood of these oaks, although of inferior quality, is used nevertheless for roof shingles and fence posts, as well as for construction and ship building. The bark, used in tanning hides, is preferred to the other oaks for this purpose; and, what is more, a few years ago in England a way was discovered of staining fabrics in various colors with them. It is to be noted that the wood of the Spanish oak is the worst of all, since it is very susceptible to borers.

White oak (Spec. 6) is the one that more than any other resembles our *Rovere* [*Q. petraea* L. ex Liebl.]. It reaches a height of 60 to 70 feet by 3 to 5 in diameter and is covered with a scaly white bark. Its leaves are narrow at the base, deeply and obliquely sinuate, of a light green color underneath, and borne on very short petioles. The acorns, of smallish size, have a very small cup. Its wood is hard, compact, and of good quality, and is used in framing wooden houses, building ships, and a great many other purposes; and although the ships made of this oak are not as durable as those made with the northern European oak, they are nevertheless the best among the ships built in the United States. Sometimes specimens are found with quite sweet acorns, and then they are much sought after by pigs, who prefer them to all the others except those produced by the Willow-leaved oak, of which I have already spoken. Furthermore, in the marshes there grows a variety (Var. b) with wider, less sinuate, leaves, with bigger round acorns, held two by two by a long, stout peduncle, and with an ashy bark. This variety, called there Swamp white oak, although it grows to a considerable height, has such porous wood that it cannot serve for the construction either of buildings or ships.

All the American oaks (except perhaps the Willow-leaved) will survive the winters of Lombardy since a number of them already flourish both in England and in France, and they could easily be propagated from freshly gathered seed; but since it is shipped from America wrapped in paper it dries out and therefore rarely arrives in condition to sprout. One would do well to obtain a few young plants from England. I tried to send acorns from America, freshly plucked and wrapped in moist moss, but since care was not taken to keep the moss moist during the voyage, the embryos dried out, and out of several hundred only a few sprouted.

RHUS

1. R. *GLABRUM foliis pinnatis, serratis, lanceolatis, utrinque nudis.* Lin.
Rhus virginicum panicula sparsa, ramis patulis glabris. Dill. *Elth.* tab. 243. Catesby *Carolin.* Tom. 3 tab. 4. Rhus angustifolium n. 4. Rhus canadense folio longiori, utrinque glabro n. 3 Duhamel *Arb., & Arbust.* Rhus glabrum caroliniense. Marshall *Arb. Amer.* n. 2. Var. I.

Sumach in the United States, and *Vinaigrier* in Canada. [*Rhus glabra* L.]

2. *R. TYPHINUM foliis pinnatis, argute serratis, lanceolatis, subtus tomentosis.* Lin.
Rhus virginianum. Dillen. *Elth.* tab. 253. Duhamel n. 2. Rhus Typhinum. Miller n. 2. Marshall n. 3.

Stag's horn sumach in the United States. [*R. typhina* L.]

3. *R. COPALLINUM foliis pinnatis, integerrimis, petiolo membranaceo articulato.* Lin.
Rhus obsoniorum similis americana, gummi candidum fundens non serrata, foliorum rachi medio alata. Pluk. *Almag.* tab. 55 [56!] fig. I.

Lentiscus-leaved sumach in the United States. [*R. copallina* L.]

4. *R. VERNIX foliis pinnatis, integerrimis, annuis, opacis, petiolo integro, aequali.* Lin. (Tab. XIV).
Toxicodendron carolinianum foliis pinnatis, floribus minimis herbaceis. Duhamel n. 3. Toxicodendron pinnatifolium. Miller *Dict.* n. 4. Rhus Toxicodendron Vernix. Marshall n. 1.

Varnish-tree, Poison ash in the United States. [*R. vernix* L.]

5. *R. TOXICODENDRON foliis ternatis; foliolis petiolatis, angulatis, pubescentibus, caule radicante.* Lin.
Toxicodendron triphyllum, folio sinuato pubescente. Duhamel n. 2. Hedera trifolia

Plate XIV. Poison Swamp Sumac (*Rhus vernix* L.).

canadensis. Cornuti *Canadens.* 96 tab. 97. Barrelier *Icon* 228. Rhus Toxicodendron. Marshall *Arb. Amer.*

Poison oak in the United States. [*R. toxicodendron* L.]

Spec. 6. Lin. [follows:]

6. *R. RADICANS foliis ternatis, foliolis petiolatis, ovatis, nudis, integerrimis; caule radicante.* Lin.

Toxicodendron triphyllum glabrum. Duhamel n. 1. Rhus Toxicodendron radicans. Marshall n. 3.

Poison vine in the United States. [*R. radicans* L.]

There are plant genera that seem to be particular to a given region, a large number of species being found there. For example the Proteaceae, the geraniums, and mesembryantheums are very numerous in Africa, *Cereus,* and *Passiflora* in South America, the vacciniums, medlars [*Crataegus spp.*], and sumacs in North America. The latter, which are abundant in the United States, vary greatly according to terrains, hence the species are excessively multiplied in the literature.

Rhus glabrum (Spec. 1), there called Sumac, is one of the common plants in North America, where it is found in great abundance in uncultivated places and near roads. It rises to a height of 15 feet and more, with a branching irregular trunk and pinnate leaves glossy above and whitish underneath that become red in autumn. Among the flowers, some are without stamens and gathered in panicles of a greenish color. However, these panicles vary from green to scarlet, so that Mr. Marshall made two species of them. The seeds are of a pretty red color and covered with a soft, acid substance that children suck without suffering any harm, and which, on the contrary, is said to be good for sore throats. On account of this acidity it is called *Vinaigrier* in Canada. The Indians used this fruit instead of smoking tobacco, and that custom was imitated not only by the Americans, but latterly also by the English, who have sought it extensively in America. It is said to be better than tobacco itself, and that those who are used to smoking this sumac find the best tobacco disgusting. The fruit is prepared for this use by gathering it in the month of November, exposing it to the air spread out on a cloth, and then drying it in an oven after bread has been baked. Upon being taken from the oven, it is spread again on the cloth and left there for 24 hours, after which it is fit for use. From the boiled seed is obtained an extremely black dye; and some people use it for dressing hides. The wood, when it is several years old, is streaked with yellow and greenish lines, and would be excellent for veneering furniture if it were of a closer texture. This wood, boiled with iron ocher, gives silk a more lasting brown color than that obtained from India wood or *Campuccio,* or even from the oak gall, since it is not subject to being changed by acids. Not only is it very easy to propagate, according to my experience, but even though the soil may be barren and sandy, in a short time it covers it with the quantity of shoots that it puts out from the base. It is therefore most useful in holding back earth that is too loose on the slopes of sandy hills.

The Hairy sumac (Spec. 2) is easily distinguished from the preceding because its young branches are all covered with short thick hair like velvet. It grows 10 or 12 feet high on a very branching and rather irregular trunk, and the blossoms are followed by a large number of red and very hairy seeds. It is common in Pennsylvania, Virginia, and other parts of the United States and is no less valuable than the preceding for the beauty and unusualness of its panicles and its leaves, which turn red in the fall. The acid fruit of this sumac (according to [Valmont de] Bomare) are steeped in cold water and given in successive doses for various kinds of hemorrhages, and its leaves, ground up and applied, prevent old whitlows from becoming gangrenous. I have already raised this shrub for a long time, which multiples without any attention, putting out a great number of shoots in any kind of terrain. It is therefore better than Species 1 for bracing banks and holding back soil, so that the celebrated Count Buffon recommends it highly for this purpose. He also says that he made good use of it to shade young plants in freshly seeded woods. Mr. Wewelinchoven* found that this sumac is better than willow for preventing the erosion of river banks.

The sumac called Copal (Spec. 3) grows in Pennsylvania in light, stony soils up to a height of 10 feet, dividing into many flexible branches. The shape of its leaves, which have an oval membrane in place of the common petiole [rachis], easily distinguishes it from the other American sumacs. The flowers, which come out in panicles from the axils of the leaves, are larger than in the other species, white with yellow stamens, and become clusters of reddish seeds scattered with gray, varying in the greater or lesser intensity of color. Various people, the illustrious Linnaeus among others, believed that true gum copal was obtained from this shrub, but afterwards this product was attributed to the [legume] *Hymenaea courbaril* Lin., which subsequently was also recognized as not being the tree of gum copal,† or at least not the only plant that yields it. M. Geoffroi, speaking of this gum in his *Materia medica,* says that it is produced by eight different Mexican plants described by Hernandez,‡ among which the one that yields the best gum is the *Copalli-quajutl,* which has leaves like the oak and which has not hitherto been examined by other botanists nor described in any system. Hence although it is certain that the *Copalli-quaiutl* of Hernandez is not the sumac we are talking about, it is however not unlikely that it, too, produces a kind of copal, since this sumac (like the other two species, 1 and 2) yields with incisions a viscous gum that should be investigated. [For note on use for tooth pain, and by early Virginians as vinegar, see Ewan, *Banister,* 241–42.] The Copal sumac grows readily from seed and flourishes vigorously in our climate, producing many flowers in the second year after seeding.

The Varnish sumac (Spec. 4) reaches a height of 12 or 14 feet, is provided with many branches, and its leaves (Table XIV, Fig. 1) are composed of 7 to 9 glossy, oval leaflets, pointed at the tip, and frequently not exactly opposite. The flowers come out of the axils of the leaves in tiny, sparse, grass-green panicles. These are described by Linnaeus and by other authors as male and female on different trees; however, the plants I grew from seeds I collected in America produced perfect or hermaphro-

*Poederlè *Manuel de l'arboriste belgique.* art. "Sumac." p. 366.
†Aublet, *Plantes de la Guiane Françoise,* Vol. I, p. 178, art. "Hymenaea."
‡*Hist. plant. Mexic.* [see P.C. Standley, *Contrib. US Natl. Herb.* 23 (1923): 551.]

ditic flowers, although, to tell the truth, the pistils on them were very small, and, what is more, with barely visible stigmas.* Perhaps the sterility of many plants that had a defective pistil gave rise to the uncertainty on the part of the authors. This sumac is also one of those plants equally common to North America and Japan, in which kingdom is extracted that beautiful and to this day unique varnish called *laque* and *vieux laque* by the French which the Japanese use to cover their wooden objects. That most diligent observer Koempfer, in his rare work *Amoenitates exoticae,*† describes this tree under the name of Sitz, or Sitz-dsiu, commonly called *Urus* and *Urus-no-ki,* and gives the following information about the uses they make of it there:

> Its leaves, which have a wild taste and produce a perceptible warmth on the tongue when chewed, stain paper a ferruginous color. The flowers give off a very pleasant orange odor, and the seeds are the size of a lentil, covered with a tenuous and glossy membrane of a whitish color. When the bark is split with a knife, a milky juice mixed with a transparent fluid‡ spurts out from different vessels, turning black upon contact with the air. The branches, the leaves, and the peduncles of the flowers yield, upon being broken, the same fluid, which produces warmth to the tongue without bitterness and without any particular taste. This can be said in spite of the fact that this tree exhales a vapor so strong that it produces excoriations on the skin of children that come near it—which also happens to others after they have touched the wood. In order to collect the *Urusi,* or the varnish, little incisions are made into the three-year-old shoots from which the liquid drips, new gashes continuing to be made until they are completely dry. Then they are cut, and from the root rise new shoots that yield a new harvest after three years. It is grown in abundance in the provinces of Xicoco and Figo, where it is propagated with cut stalks, which put out roots when they are planted in the ground and produce varnish after the three-year period. That harvested in the area of the city of Jassino is considered the best in the country—in fact, in the world. Japanese varnish, which is the most valuable, is so scarce that it would not suffice for the work done there if the wood were not covered first with a layer of more ordinary varnish called *nam-rack,* brought there from the Kingdom of Siam. This latter is obtained in the province of Corsama and the Kingdom of Cambodia from the tree called there *tonj-rack,* that is, the Rack tree, whose fruit, which is the *Anacardium* of the drug shops, is called *luck-rack,* and the varnish, *nam-rack.* This is drawn from the trunk by inserting a little tube into the incision, from which the liquid issues in great abundance.§ The native varnish

*See Tab. XIV, Fig. 1, a branch; Fig. 2, the blossom; Fig. 3, the calyx, Fig. 4, the five stamens attached to the corolla, Fig. 5, a stamen magnified; Fig. 7, the berries; Fig. 8, the seed.

†Koempfer, *Amoen. Exot.* (Lemgov) p. 791, Tab. 792.

‡That is, its own juice and sap.

§The *Anacardium* of the drug shops mentioned here by Koempfer was thought to be the fruit of *Avicennia tomentosa* of Linnaeus. However, M. Lamarck (*Encyclop méthod.,* art. "Badamier"), supported by the description given by Rumphius in the well-known *Herbar. Amboinense* of the *Caju-Sanga,* Vol. II, p. 259, Tab. 86, which he calls Varnish tree, judges it to be a species of *Terminalia,* to which he gives the name of *Terminalia vernix.* One must not, as M. Lamarck has done, confuse this tree with our varnish sumac, inasmuch as Koempfer himself speaks of both of them—that is, of the sumac that produces the Japanese varnish and of the *Anacardium* that produces the inferior varnish called "of Siam" and "of Cambodia," as we have seen above.

> (that is, that of our sumac, continues Koempfer) has hardly any need of preparation, and in Japan all they do is to pass it through paper, folded over but as thin as a cobweb and manufactured for this purpose, in order to purge it of its heterogeneous and coarser parts, twisting and squeezing it carefully. Once it has been refined, it is mixed with a small quantity of toj oil, extracted from the seeds of the tree called *Kiri.** Then the varnish, stored in wooden vases, is transported to the various parts of Japan without danger of its spirit's evaporating except from the surface, which quickly becomes covered with a black skin. It is sold not only this way, but also colored with native Chinese cinnabar and red earth, and even tinted with ink. Both these varnishes, the Japanese as well as that of Siam, give off a poisonous vapor that makes the lips swell and the head ache, so that those who work with it are in the habit of covering their mouths and noses with a cloth.

The ease with which the sumacs are propagated would be enough to assure us, beyond the evidence of Koempfer, that we can have very quickly and without any great effort large numbers of this useful plant. The poisonous qualities of contact and exhalation seem to be exaggerated, at least in part, since many persons, among whom I myself, handle it without suffering any harm. Moreover, even if the varnish produced the adverse effects indicated by Koempfer, it would not be hard to protect oneself against them, as is done with mercury vapors, much more active and pernicious. As for the toj oil extracted from the Kiri tree, or from the aforementioned *Bignonia tomentosa,* one might make up for it with other oils, even mixing up different kinds. In any case a plant that yields such a precious product deserves to be tested in our country. [For use as dye see Ewan, *Banister,* 202.]

[*R.*] *toxicodendron* (Spec. 5) grows barely three or four feet high, and its leaves, which come out three by three, are sometimes entire, sometimes sinuate, and a little woolly underneath. It produces small flowers of a grassy color, and its berries are gray, resembling those of the varnish sumac. There is much talk in the literature about the poisonous quality of this plant, to which was given for that reason the name of *toxicodendron.* In the *Philosophical Transactions* there is a letter of Mr. Moore[†] to Dr. [William] Sherard in which it is related that some people became unconscious after burning some of this wood in a room, so that, if a neighbor had not happened to open the door and given them help, they probably would have died. The exhalations alone of the plant are said to cause headaches in some persons, and touching it reportedly causes peeling of the skin and also swelling and burning of the eyes, although others handle it without feeling any ill effects—which can come about on account of the greater or lesser density of the pores of the skin, as well as for differences in the condition of the plant and the season. When the branches are cut, a milky fluid comes out that quickly turns black upon exposure to the air. It grows everywhere in the United States, and also in Canada, where it is distinguished by the name of *Herbe à la puce*—a name too favorable, according to Duhamel, for a plant of such per-

*This is the *Bignonia tomentosa* of Thunberg, *Flor. Japonic.* [*Paulownia tomentosa* (Thunb.) Steud.]
[†Thomas Moore, "pilgrim botanist" was sent to New England to collect for a group of British botanists including Paul Dudley and William Sherard. He was a disappointment to them. The letter dealt actually with *Rhus vernix,* though both are poisonous.]

nicious quality. Some people cultivate it in their gardens solely as a curiosity, since it has neither a pretty flower nor a remarkable appearance; and, unfortunately, like other noisome plants, it multiplies with extreme ease.

Rhus radicans (Spec. 6) is similar to *toxicodendron,* the principal difference between them consisting in the little roots that it puts out from the branches with which it attaches itself to plants, and in the smooth leaves without fuzz. Duhamel speaks of it as No. 1,* but then mistakenly attributes to No. 2 (*Rhus toxicodendron.* Lin.) the property of propagating itself by radicant shoots, which is proper only to the present one. It, too, grows in the United States and in Canada, and is no less poisonous than the other. It is told that in a German city it happened some years ago that everyone in a certain family suffered from headaches and peeling skin without knowing why until it was discovered that it came about because they used to spend time in the garden under a little green arbor covered with this sumac planted there in place of the Canada vine [*Parthenocissus quinquefolia* (L.) Planch., Virginia Creeper). Perhaps this confusion arose from the similarity of the names by which they were distinguished by certain authors [Cornut for one], who called the Canada vine *Hedera quinquefolia canadensis* and the radicant sumac *Hedera trifolia canadensis*—in addition to the fact that at first sight they are not very different from each other. Recently the French physician M. du Fresnoy discovered that the infusion of its leaves or the distilled juice of the same were a specific remedy for the most inveterate cases of ringworm and for paralysis of the lower regions. However, we shall have to wait for these facts to be confirmed, since we have already seen poisons introduced a number of times as excellent remedies to discover later the falseness of the virtues for which they had been extoled.

ROBINIA

1. R. *PSEUDACACIA racemis pedicellis unifloris; foliis impari-pinnatis, stipulis spinosis.* Lin.
Pseudacacia vulgaris. Duhamel.
Locust tree in the United States. [*Robinia pseudoacacia* L.]

2. R. *HISPIDA racemis axillaribus; foliis impari-pinnatis, caule inermi hispido.* Lin.
Pseudacacia hispida floribus roseis. Catesby *Carol.* 3 p. 20 tab. 20. Robinia rosea. Marshall *Arbust. Amer.*
[*R. hispida* L.]

Robinia pseudacacia (Spec. 1) is common in North America from the southern states up to 44° latitude, and, although it does not grow spontaneously in more northern regions, it is easily propagated there and withstands the coldest winters. This is a tree from 40 to 50 feet tall, big in proportion, with very long branches and pinnate leaves, and oval leaflets of a pretty green with two hard and extremely sharp thorns

*Art. "*Toxicodendron.*"

at the base of the petioles of the leaves. Its white leguminous blossoms come out in clusters, and these are followed by short, flat legumes containing a bare two or three dark and very tough seeds. The wood of *pseudacacia,* although rather soft when green, becomes hard upon drying, and is used for shipbuilding, fences, carriage axles, and for very many other purposes, so that it may be numbered among the most useful North American trees. It is also an excellent firewood; and it is said that its shade not only does not hinder, but even encourages the growth of grass. Therefore, in the United States it is planted to this end in dry and sandy places. With its blossoms, which give off a very pleasant fragrance, they make a very tasty syrup; and both for these and for its beautiful leaves it was introduced as an ornamental tree along many avenues and in many gardens. It has been propagated for this purpose in Europe, also, where in some places it has multiplied to the point good use can be made of its wood; and in Germany it was proposed to cut its leaves with certain shears attached to a pole as feed for cattle, which are very fond of it. However, oxen eat its leaves attached to the twigs, unconcerned about the thorns, as I myself have found out; and therefore it can be useful when there is a shortage of fodder. To so many good qualities must be counterpoised the fact that it has weak limbs, so that they are easily broken by the wind, and that in Massachusetts it is subject to a kind of worm that bores into the wood and kills it. This worm is an inch long, of a white color, and with a dark head, belonging to some coleopterous insect of the genus *Scarabaeus.* They say that this insect was formerly unknown in Massachusetts and that it was introduced there from Virginia. But what is certain is that almost all the Pseudacacias of Massachusetts die from this affliction, and that the remedies tried up to now to destroy the worms were equally harmful to the insect and the plant. The only way to get rid of it would be to study the history of this beetle in order to recognize it in the flying insect stage, in which case it would be easy to catch it and destroy it, as has been successfully done in our country with the grapevine beetle during these last few years.* M. Saint-Jean de Crèvecoeur, in his memoir on the cultivation and use of *pseudacacia,*† did not speak of this disease, perhaps because he was too inclined to magnify the advantages of this tree with a description elegant rather than exact, following in that respect the poetic style adopted in his well known book entitled *Le Cultivateur américain.* It can be propagated with the greatest ease from the numerous shoots that come out of the roots, but not so easily from seed. It grows very rapidly, mainly in sandy, light terrains, even though they may be thin and dry; and it can also be cut like a hedge to protect fields. About 500 of these plants flourish successfully in the sandy terrain of the moor of Mozzate, and many of them produce flowers and mature seeds. Of all the trees that develop quickly it has the most solid and best wood. In the catalog of plants introduced or to be introduced into France placed at the end of the fine memoir by M. Thouin on the cultivation of exotic trees,‡ there is talk of a thornless *pseudacacia* as a variety of the present one. However, I do not know where there is a single specimen. The attempt should be made to propagate this vari-

*See the *Atti della Società Patriotica* (Milano) Vol. II, p. 56.
†*Mémoires de la Société d'Agriculture de Paris* (1786 Trimestre d'hyver).
‡*Mémoires de la Société d'Agriculture de Paris* (1786 Trimestre d'hyver).

ety, which would be much more useful than the thorny one, since it could be made into a harvestable rootstock in sandy places and the leaves could easily be gathered as food for cattle, which would be a tremendous contribution.

Robinia hispida (Spec. 2), called *Robinia rosea* by other authors, is a tree of average size with the trunk and branches covered with rough reddish hairs. Its leaves are pinnate, with leaflets wider than those of Species 1, and of a faded yellowish color. From early spring until autumn it continues to produce beautiful leguminous flesh-colored blossoms larger and more abundant than those of *pseudacacia,* but almost odorless. Although they have quite well formed stamens and pistils, nevertheless they very rarely produce any legume—which is true not only in the gardens of Europe but also in its native country. It is native to South Carolina, where it grows in rich and marshy terrains. It can be grafted onto Species 1, but the graft must be made as far down as possible, inasmuch as it will produce its own roots from the point of the graft. It is much more delicate than *pseudacacia* and often suffers from severe winters, even plants already adult and vigorous dying. Its branches are very fragile, and it can serve only for adorning gardens and copses, for which use, however, it can be put ahead of all the shrubs.

RUBUS

1. *R. ODORATUS foliis simplicibus, palmatis; caule inermi multifolio, multifloro.* Lin.
Rubus odoratus. Cornut, *Canaden.* tab. 150. Duham. n. 14.
Superb raspberry in the United States. [*Rubus odoratus* L.]

2. *R. OCCIDENTALIS foliis ternis, subtus tomentosis; caule aculeato, petiolis teretibus.* Lin.
Rubus idaeus, fructu nigro, virginianus. Banister. Duhamel n. 12. Dillen. *Eltham.* tab. 287. [A specimen from Banister is in the Morisonian Herb., Oxford. A plant, probably from Banister seed, grew in James Sherard's garden, "Eltham."]
American Raspberry and Blackberry in the United States. [*R. occidentalis* L.]

3. *R. HISPIDUS foliis ternatis nudis, caulibus, petiolisque hispidissimis, strigis rigidulis.* Lin.
Rubus hispidus. Miller *Dict.* n. 7.
Dewberry bush in the United States. [*R. hispidus* L., a collective species]

*Rubus odoratus** (Spec. 1) is very common near new plantings and on the slopes of hills in Massachusetts, where I found it in bloom in the month of July. It is a shrub four or five feet high, thornless, with very large palmate leaves and big blossoms of a vivid red color. Its fruit is almost always imperfect and hardly any of the granules ripen, so that, mixed as they are with dried stamens, they cannot be eaten. This shrub has glutinous leaves, and especially so the petioles, that leave a smell of roses on the

*By some it is called *Framboisier odorant.*

fingers. For this reason, and because of the beauty of the leaves and flowers that it continues to produce for a long time, it was propagated in European gardens. Like our *Lampone* [*R. idaeus* L.] it is easily multiplied from roots.

Rubus occidentalis (Spec. 2) is a small shrub seven to eight feet high whose stalks often bend back toward the ground putting out new roots. The blossoms come three by three, whitish, and a little hairy underneath; and the blossoms, which are white, produce small deep red, almost black, fruit. Both this fruit, like that of *Rubus fruticosus,** commonly called Blackberry in America, are taken to genteel tables; and by squeezing out the juice a kind of wine is made in Pennsylvania called Blackberry wine. This liquor, which is very tasty, is obtained by mixing this juice with an equal quantity of fresh and pure water and adding to it three pounds of sugar for every gallon by English measure, then letting it sit until it is fit to drink.

Finally, *Rubus hispidus* (Spec. 3), called Dewberry bush because it resembles the small European bramble,† is a shrub that winds about a great deal with its branches. It has leaves like those of the common briar, except that they are smaller, as are also the blossoms and the fruit. It is called *hispidus* because it is covered with stiff hairs.

RUMEX

R. BRITTANICA floribus hermaphroditis; valvulis integerrimis omnibus graniferis; foliis lanceolatis; vaginis obsoletis. Lin. [*Rumex orbiculatus* Gray, or *R. verticillatus* L.]

Perhaps this herb is no different from the *Rumex verticillatus* of the said Linnaeus, nor perhaps also from the *Rumex sanguineus* common in Europe in our country. There are two distinct kinds in America, one with a root black outside, and the other yellow with an orange or saffron color inside. It grows in marshy places, with large, lanceolate, sharp-pointed leaves and ribs tinted with red. It is an excellent remedy for curing ulcers of the mouth by rinses with a decoction of the roots, according to the experience of Mr. Colden. This was one of the greatest secrets of the New York Indians which they did not want under any condition to reveal to the Europeans and which was discovered accidentally.‡ The virtue of this plant is similar to that of the *Herba brittanica* of the drug shops, which is *Rumex aquaticus* of Linnaeus.

SAGITTARIA

1. *S. SAGITTIFOLIA foliis sagittatis acutis.* Lin.

Sagitta major. Scopoli *Fl. Carniol.* [*Sagittaria latifolia* Willd., or *S. cuneata* Sheld.]

This, too, is a marsh plant used by the Indians, who used to eat its roots. These

*Rubus fruticosus. Lin. The common bramble. *Rovedo* in Lombardy.

†*Rubus caesius.* Lin.

‡Colden, *Acta Svaecica* (1743, 1744).

are oblong and big, and they prepared them by boiling them or roasting them under ashes. . . .

[Br 3:162–63] Nils Gustafson, a man about 90 years of age, told me that he often ate them when he was a boy, and that at that time he liked them very much. He said, moreover, that the Indian women used to travel all the way to the islands (I don't know whether these islands, mentioned by Kalm, are possibly Long Island and Staten Island) in order to dig the roots out of the ground and take them home. I myself got some of these roots, which I had roasted, and which in my opinion were very palatable although rather dry, their flavor resembling that of potatoes.

The Swedes, says Kalm [Vol. I, p. 386], made use of it in those days; and Kalm himself went so far as to taste them and found them to be of good flavor, resembling potatoes. Pigs eat them greedily and cattle are very fond of the leaves. The American *Sagittaria* is a simple variety of the European, there being no difference other than that the American has bigger roots.

SALIX

S. BABYLONICA foliis serratis glabris, lineari-lanceolatis, ramis pendulis. Lin. Salix orientalis flagellis deorsum pulchre pendentibus. Tourn. *Cor.* 41. Duhamel n. 20.

Weeping willow in the United States. [*Salix babylonica* L.]

This tree, which formerly was thought to grow only in the Orient, was also found on the banks of the Ohio in North America. [It was grown in Hampton Court gardens in 1692, but its date of introduction into North America is evidently unrecorded. It was probably introduced into the Ohio Valley by French settlers.] Because of the beauty of its long drooping branches, it is used as an ornamental in gardens,* where it is known under the name of Weeping willow and African willow. But in America a greater worth has recently been discovered in it, consisting in the virtue of curing intermittent fevers. Mr. Hutchins,[†] a United States geographer, transmitted himself the information to me that the bark of this willow was most useful to him in arresting the fever by which his traveling companions in the environs of the Ohio were afflicted. They were given the decoction of this bark, which in a few days produced a salutary effect, and this experiment was repeated with a happy outcome in Philadelphia, also. It is true that the common willow [forerunner of aspirin], and, in fact, al-

*This willow would be very useful if its long shoots were not fragile. Presumably boiling might make them more flexible.

[†Thomas Hutchins (1730–1789) military engineer served as officer of Pennsylvania colonial troops in "Western country" 1757–59; member of American Philosophical Society 1772–. In 1781 Congress appointed him "geographer to the United States."]

most all bitter plants, are useful for fevers, but their action is much much less potent and lasting than that of quinine, so that after the discovery of this remarkable medicine almost all the other known febrifuges were abandoned. The same, however, should not happen to the Babylonian willow, if we are to believe the experiments made in America, since its potency was found there to be almost equal to that of quinine.

SANGUINARIA

S. CANADENSIS. Lin.
Chelidonium majus canadense acaulon. Cornut. *Canad.* 211. Ranunculus virginiensis albus. Raj. *Supplem.* 314.

Redroot and bloodroot in the United States, *Turmerick* and *Pucoon* among the Indians. [*Sanguinaria canadensis* L.]

The root of *Sanguinaria* is long and thick, and from it come the blossoms, which are provided with a single digitate leaf that envelops the stem. The blossom consists of a calyx with two leaves [sepals] and eight petals, many stamens, and a short pistil. The latter produces an ovate silique [capsule] containing many tiny seeds. This plant is used by the Indians, who extract from it a deep yellow color that they employ to paint their bodies. They call it *Turmerick* and *Pucoon,* and the Americans call it Bloodroot and Redroot because externally it is deep red, although inside it has an orange-yellow color. It grows in damp places and is said to be useful for jaundice. (Kalm, Vol. I, p. 712].

SARRACENIA

1. *S. PURPUREA foliis gibbis.* Lin.
Sarracena foliis brevioribus, latioribus. Catesby *Carolin.* 2 pag. 70 tab. 70.

[Pitcher plant, *S. purpurea* L.]

2. *S. FLAVA foliis strictis.* Lin.
Sarracena foliis longioribus, & angustioribus. Catesby *Carolin.* 2 pag. 69 tab. 69.

Trumpet flower, Sidesaddle flower in the Carolinas. [*S. flava* L.]

Sarracenia purpurea (Spec. 1) grows in swampy places and in the midst of stagnant water, where I saw it for the first time in bloom on my trip from Boston to Lancaster. The flower is red, of the shape of a large buttercup, and supported by a long stem. The stamens are very numerous, and the pistil, whose stigma broadens out in the shape of an umbrella, covers all the stamens. This extraordinary pistil seems granted to it by nature in order that fertilization not be prevented by the surrounding water, inasmuch as it is often buried under water. The leaves are no less unusual than the blossom and come out of the roots in groups of four or six around the stem. They have the form of a swollen tube whose mouth is covered with a kind of tongue or valve that closes it. These leaves, filling themselves with water, serve perhaps to store the moisture necessary in case water is lacking, and for this reason I believe that

Sarracenia could be grown even in dry places, if one takes care to fill the bases of its leaves with water. [Philip Miller and his contemporaries were still unaware of insectivory. LC did not understand requisite soil conditions.]

The yellow *Sarracenia* (Spec. 2) grows in the swamps of South Carolina. In early April it produces yellow flowers, not as large as those of *purpurea.* Its leaves are very long, tube-shaped, more slender and less tumid than in the other species, but likewise covered with a tongue or valve at the end. These plants almost never come up from seed, and Miller suggests that in order to obtain them the roots be taken up together with the soil and brought to Europe after being put in terra-cotta tubes, care being taken to sprinkle them frequently. Once they have arrived, plant them in vases with light, friable soil mixed with wood fragments and moss, placing these vases in larger vases likewise filled with water. By this method he says that he obtained some plants that blossomed in England. He adds that, whether they do come up from seed, many years pass before they produce flowers, since this is a very slow-growing plant. For this reason he recommends that roots that have already bloomed be gotten from America.

SMILAX

1. *S. SARSAPARILLA caule aculeato, angulato; foliis inermibus, ovatis, retuso-mucronatis, trinerviis.* Lin.
Smilax viticulis asperis virginiana, folio hederaceo laevi Zarza nobilissima. Pluk *almag.* tab. 111. fig. 2 Duhamel. n. 3.

Sarsaparilla in the United States. [*Smilax walteri* Pursh]

2. *S. LAURIFOLIA caule aculeato, tereti; foliis inermibus, ovato-lanceolatis, trinerviis.* Lin.
Smilax laevis laurifolio, baccis nigris. Catesby *Carol.* Tom. I tab. 15. Seligmann tab. 30. China altera aculeata foliis oblongis cuspidatis. Plumier *Plant. American.* tab. 85.

[*S. laurifolia* L.]

3. *S. TAMNOIDES caule aculeato, tereti; foliis inermibus, cordatis, oblongis, septemnerviis.* Lin.
Smilax Bryoniae nigrae foliis, caule spinoso, baccis nigris. Catesby Tom. I tab. 52. Seligmann Tom. 2 tab. 4

China root in the United States. [*S. bona-nox* L.]

4. *S. PSEUDO-CHINA caule inermi, tereti; foliis inermibus, caulinis cordatis, rameis ovato-oblongis, quinquenerviis.* Lin.
Smilax aspera nodosa, radice rubra majore. Plumier *Plant. American.* tab. 82.

Bastard China in the United States. [*Smilax tamnifolia* Michx.]

Smilax is a very abundant one in North America, and the various botanical authors count up to 10 species more or less different in the shape of the leaves and color of the fruit, and with or without thorns. Nevertheless, I shall speak of only four species that in some respect deserve our attention, the others not being known as fit for any use.

The first, the well-known Sarsparilla (Spec. 1), grows in Virginia and the southern parts of the United States forming an angular and thorny stalk with ovate, pointed leaves with only three nerves. The flowers hang from long peduncles, and the berries are tiny and red. Its cylindrical, slender, and yellowish root is divided into various knobs and runs along horizontally near the surface of the ground. Everyone knows about the great use made in both America and Europe of the decoction of this root for syphilis and other diseases as a diuretic and purgative. It should be noted that that of the warmer climates is more potent, so that the Sarsparilla from Peru and Mexico is preferred to that from the United States.

The Laurel-leaved *Smilax* (Spec. 2) also has a thorny, but not angular, stalk, and its leaves are ovate-lanceolate with three nerves. The flowers stand up supported by short peduncles, and the mature berries have a black color. This plant grows in damp places to a height of more than 16 feet, winding itself about trees like the other smilaxes, and with its large leaves, heavier than in the other species, it forms an impenetrable barrier to the rays of the sun and to the force of the wind, so that (according to Catesby) the places where it abounds serve as shelter for cattle both in the summer and in the winter. There is a kind of blue magpie* that is very fond of the berries.

Smilax tamnoides (Spec. 3) has a round, thorny stalk, thornless, heart-shaped, oblong leaves with seven nerves, and produces black berries, but hanging from very long peduncles. It grows 20 feet high, climbing up trees, and has tuberous roots divided into many knobs. Immediately upon being taken from the soil they are soft and full of juice, but upon drying in the air they become as hard as wood. In South Carolina this plant is called Sweet China-root, although it is different from the true Sweet China,† a plant native to Persia, China, and Japan. The Carolinians eat the tender shoots of *Smilax tamnoides* like asparagus and with the roots make a drink to which they attribute many of the qualities proper to Sweet China.‡

The false Sweet China (Spec. 4) has a very thick, round, thornless stalk, with cordate leaves on the trunk and ovato-oblong leaves on the branches, and black berries attached to very long peduncles. The root is a winding one, thick, knotty, and of a red color. Many people in the United States use it instead of Sweet China, whose medicinal virtues it is also said to possess.

All the smilaxes are easily propagated from seed, and more easily from layers, but they must be kept in good, well exposed soil.

[Br 2:322]

SOPHORA TINCTORIA L.

Wild Indigo. Enticed by the resemblance of this plant to true indigo, certain individuals tried to obtain the same color, but the experiments performed up to now have not

**Corvus cristatus.* Lin. [Blue jay. *Cyanocitta cristata* (Linn.)]
†*Smilax China.* Lin.
‡See Catesby, Vol. I, p. 52.

been successful and the juice obtained from it has not been found to be of any use in dyeing. The same is confirmed by Clayton in his *Flora virginica* [ed. 2, 64] where he says: *Tentarunt ex hac planta smegma Indigo dictum conficere, verum successus minime respondeat.*

[False indigo, *Baptisia tinctoria* (L.) R. Br.]

SPIRAEA

1. *S. TOMENTOSA foliis lanceolatis, inaequaliter serratis, subtus tomentosis; floribus duplicato-racemosis.* Lin.
Spiraea americana floribus coccineis. Duh. n. 2. Spiraea pentacarpos integris serratis foliis parvis, subtus incanis virginiana. Duhamel. n. 6. Ulmaria pentacarpos integris serratis foliis parvis, subtus incanis virginiana. Pluk. *Almag.* pag. 393 tab. 321 fig. 5. [*Spiraea tomentosa* L.]

b. alba.
Spiraea tomentosa alba. Marshall.

Indian pipeshank in the United States. [*S. tomentosa* forma *albiflora* Macbr.]

2. *S. HYPERICIFOLIA foliis ob-ovatis integerrimis, umbellis sessilibus.* Lin.
Spiraea hypericifolio non crenato. Duhamel n. 3. Pruno sylvestri affinis canadensis Pluk. *Alm.* 408 tab. 218 fig. 5.

[*Spiraea hypericifolia* L., introduced]

3. *S. OPULIFOLIA foliis lobatis, serratis, corymbis terminalibus.* Lin.
Spiraea opuli-folio. Duhamel n. 5. Evonymus virginiana Ribesii folio, capulis eleganter bullatis. Commel. *hort.* 1 pag. 169 tab. 87.

Ninebark in the United States. [*Physocarpus opulifolius* (L.) Maxim.]

4. *S. TRIFOLIATA foliis ternatis, serratis, subaequalibus, floribus subpaniculatis.* Lin.
Filipendula foliis ternatis. Gron. *Virg.* pag. 77.

Indian physic in the United States. [*Gillenia trifoliata* (L.) Moench]

Woolly spiraea (Spec. 1), so called because its leaves are covered underneath with a white fuzz, is very common in the vicinity of Portsmouth, the capital of New Hampshire (where I found it in bloom) and also in other parts of the United States. It grows to a height of four or five feet, with a reddish trunk covered with a light fuzz. The leaves are lanceolate, saw-toothed, of a pretty green above, and veined and white underneath. The tiny flowers come out of the ends of the branches in long, rich, red-colored spikes. Mr. Marshall has a variety under the name of *Spiraea tomentosa alba* differing from the preceding in that it has leaves of a more delicate texture, somewhat woolly on both sides, and with white-colored flowers. This variety is called Indian pipeshank in America because they put its pithy stalks to that use. I think that a kind of Spiraea with a white blossom somewhat like *Spiraea salicifolia* of Linnaeus that I found in abundance in New Hampshire might be the variety mentioned by Mr. Marshall, although the fuzz he described is hardly visible in the dried plants in my herbarium. The *Spiraea callosa* of Mr. Thunberg,* called *Niko, Simo-stuke,* and *Simo-tski* in Japan, according to a comparison of the description with the plants I observed, seems to me to be a variety of *tomentosa,* too.

The Hypericum-leaved *Spiraea* (Spec. 2) is a shrub five to six feet tall with a dark brown bark. The leaves are entire, oblong, smooth, and opposite, and the yellow-colored blossoms form little umbrellas attached to the stalk. It has been known for a long time in European gardens, especially in England, under the name of *Hypericum frutex* and is much sought after for the beauty of its blossoms.

The *Spiraea* called *opulifolia* (Spec. 3) because of the resemblance of its leaves to *opulus*† (commonly called also Water elder and Snowflake) grows to a height of five or six feet. The leaves are three-lobed, somewhat fluted at the margin, and saw-toothed; and the blossoms come out of the end of the branches in the form of white corymbs with some pale red dots. The bark of its trunks is dark and scaly, and since it separates into various thin sheets, it was called Ninebark by the Americans.

Finally, *Spiraea trifoliata* (Spec. 4) differs from these mentioned above in that each year it renews its stalks from the root like *filipendula* and has leaves three by three. Its blossoms have very large white petals speckled with red and a quantity of stamens barely as long as the tube of the flower. It is called Indian physic, and its root, which is bitter and nauseous, has the property of purging and of exciting vomiting like ipecac—requiring, however, a much larger dose. As an emetic it is given in 40-grain doses.

All the spiraeas can serve as garden ornamentals because of the attractiveness of their blossoms, which last a long time; and they can be propagated from seed, but much more easily by dividing the roots.

STAPHYLEA

S. TRIFOLIA foliis ternatis. Lin.
Staphylodendron virginianum trifoliatum. Duhamel n. 2.

Bladdernut in the United States. [*Staphylea trifolia* L.]

I found this shrub, which grows to a height of 8 to 10 feet, for the first time in the woods situated between lakes George and Champlain almost at the northern end of the State of New York. It differs from the European *Staphylea*‡ in the ternate leaves and fruit vesicle, which is smaller and contains much smaller, glossier, and harder seeds. Its clusters of white blossoms and the curious shape of its fruit make it worthy of being placed in ornamental copses.

**Flora Japonica,* p. 209 [*S. japonica* L. f.]
†*Viburnum opulus.* Lin.
‡*Staphylea pinnata.* Lin.

STEWARTIA

S. MALACODENDRON. Lin.

Stewartia. Catesby *Carolin.* 3 tab. 13. Duhamel. *Arb.* 2 pag. 284. Malacodendron. Mitchell *gen.* 16.

[*Stewartia malacodendron* L.]

Stewartia, as we saw at the entries on *Franklinia* and *Gordonia,* has a great affinity with those two genera of plants—they, too, peculiar to North America. From a comparison of the generic Linnaean characteristics one can easily perceive the differences between *Stewartia* and *Gordonia*—consisting in the fact that *Stewartia* has a calyx with only one sepal, almost round pendent anthers, a hairy bud, a style of the length of the stamens, and fruit with five lobes and five valves, each containing a single ovate and compressed seed.*

Stewartia differs further from *Franklinia* in that it has unmatched and almost round anthers, a style of the same length as the stamens, and a stigma divided into five rows; and also fruit which, although almost round, dry, and divisible into five parts, contains only one seed in each valve.† This shrub grows natively in Virginia and in a few places in Pennsylvania, reaching a height of 10 or 12 feet. Its leaves are oval, pointed, dentate, and a little hairy underneath. The large whitish flowers with five petals resemble those of *Malvaviscus* and possess the peculiarity of having one petal spotted with yellow. This shrub looks pretty when it is covered with blossoms, which happens in May . It likes a fertile and moist soil and withstands very well the winters of England and France when it is adult. It is difficult to obtain from seed, which rarely develops, and the young plants die quickly when moisture is lacking or the sun is too strong.

THUYA

T. OCCIDENTALIS strobilis laevibus; squamis obtusis. Lin.

Thuya Theophrasti. C. Bauhin. *Pin.* Duhamel n. 1.

White cedar in the United States. [*Thuya occidentalis* L.]

Thuya grows in North America only north of 42° latitude, since it likes cold climates, where it reaches a height of 30 to 40 feet in rather moist places and especially along river banks. The thickness of the trunk is not always proportionate to the height, and frequently one sees extremely tall trees that are only eight or ten inches in diameter. The leaves are very small, imbricate, and the little branches seem compressed, presenting an almost flat surface on both sides. The flowers [male cones] are tiny, in fact hardly visible, and the strobiles, or [female] cones are small, oblong, and composed of smooth scales blunt at the ends. Under each scale is a tiny oblong, winged seed. The main, and almost sole difference, between the oriental *Thuya* and the one

*See the entry "*Gordonia.*"

†See the entry on the *Franklinia.*

we are talking about consists in that the former has strobiles with uncinate scales and big ovate seeds without a membrane. The oriental *Thuya* is known in our gardens under the name of Chinese *Thuya,* since it is native to those regions, although the western one is also found in Chinese Tartary, as M. Gmelin attests in the first volume of his *Flora Sibirica.* * In fact, the latter was believed by many authors to be the *Thuya* or *Thya* described by Theophrastus, which they would not have supposed if this species were not also found in the ancient Continent. By what right Caius Bauhinus[†] and others subsequently gave the ancient Greek name of *Thuya* to this tree it is difficult to judge, since the tree indicated by that name by Theophrastus appears to be a species of cypress or juniper.‡ The first plants of the occidental *Thuya* to be seen in Europe came from Canada at the time of Francis I, King of France, and were cultivated in the royal garden of Fontainebleau, where the celebrated Clusius§ saw them and transported a few plants into Flanders. This wood is used in Canada to make palisades for forts, fences for gardens, and floors for rooms. The Indians make of it frames for their canoes which they cover with birch bark, since the wood of *Thuya* is flexible and very light; and for this reason they make with the branches brooms that they go and sell in the cities. *Thuya* is not lacking in medicinal qualities and is used for cases of rheumatism by boiling its fresh leaves with lard and applying them to the affected part; and also for tertiary fevers and coughs by drinking the decoction of the leaves. In short it is sudorific and aperient and approaches *Sabina* [*Juniperus*] in its qualities. Thuya is an evergreen and therefore produces a fine effect in copses in wintertime and in gardens. It also yields a kind of transparent, but very soft, resin and until now useless. It multiplies easily from seed and also from layerings. But it must be situated in moist, or at least cool, places, inasmuch as in dry and exposed terrains it does survive, but in the summer loses many of its leaves and the foliage is left thin.

TILIA

T. AMERICANA floribus nectario instructis. Lin.
Tilia foliis majoribus mucronatis. Gronov. *virgin.* 58. Duhamel n. 5.

b. caroliniana
Tilia caroliniana. Marshall.

Black lime-tree, and Linden tree in the United States. [*T. caroliniana* Mill.]

The American Linden grows to a considerable height, spreading about many branches exactly like the European one. Its bark is dark brown, the wide leaves heart-shaped, sharp-pointed with saw-toothed border, green or dark above and lighter underneath, where they are somewhat hairy. The flowers, which have a long bract or particular leaf attached to a common peduncle as in the European Linden, have

**Fl. Sibirica,* Vol. I, p. 182 [1747].
†See the entry "*Juniperus.*"
[‡Caspar Bauhin, *Pinax* (Basil. 1671), 487.]
§Charles (Carolus) de L'Ecluse [or l'Escluse!]

in addition a nectary* at the base of the petals. The fruit is a round capsule containing a single seed. There is a variety of this tree that differs in its whitish bark, oblique cordate leaves, and smaller flowers, to which belongs the so-called Basswood, White-wood, and *Sugumuck* (a tree found in the woods of eastern Massachusetts), since it resembles completely the Linden in its trunk and leaves. The wood of the *Sugumuck* is white, soft, and very light. With the inner bark of its branches the Penobscot Indians make cord, and from it they derive a sewing thread. As for the American Linden properly speaking, however, its wood is used for various purposes, and the infusion of its blossoms has been employed advantageously for epilepsy because they have the quality of being cephalic like those of the European Linden.

TILLANDSIA

T. USNEOIDES filiformis, ramosa, intorta, scabra. Lin.
Cuscuta ramis arborum innascens caroliniana, filamentis lanugine tectis. Pluk. *Almag.* 126 tab. 26 fig. 4. Caragate musciforme n. 10. Lamar[c]k *Encyclop. méthodiq.*

Moss in the southern states. [Spanish moss, *Tillandsia usneoides* L.]

This plant, previously described under the name of *Renealmia* by Gronovius and under that of *Cuscuta* by Plukenet is parasitic, growing in humid and swampy regions of the Carolinas on the branches of very old trees, from which it hangs in long strings with thin, fleshy, and ash-colored leaves. It has all the appearance of a tree moss and is so called for that reason in those regions. Although it looks arid and dry, it is nevertheless juicy and green inside, so that it is collected in the winter as fodder for cattle, especially in the vicinity of the Tar River between Halifax and Tarborough in North Carolina. [This epiphyte—not parasite—was reported as used for winter feed for cattle before 1692 by Banister although he had not seen the plant.] It is noteworthy that, although *Tillandsia* is very abundant on oaks and other trees that lose their leaves in the winter, it is never seen growing on resinous plants, a property common to other parasitic plants.

VACCINIUM

[A particularly complicated, hybridizing genus.
Castiglioni had especial difficulty with synonyms.]

1. *V. CORYMBOSUM floribus corymbosis, ovatis, foliis oblongis acuminatis, integerrimis.* Lin.
Vaccinium corymbosum. Marshall.
Obs. *Frutex humanae altitudinis.* [*Vaccinium corymbosum* L.]

*This is what Linnaeus called in flowers everything that cannot be said to be either a calyx, a corolla, a stamen, or a pistil.

b. myrsinites

Vaccinium myrsinites. Lamarck. *Encyclop. meth.* art. Airelle n. 6. [*V. myrsinites* Lam., a distinctly southern species]

Obs. *Frutex sesquipedalis.*

Blueberry in Massachusetts. [V. corymbosum L.]

2. *V. LAEVIGATUM floribus corymbosis, bracteatis, corymbis alternis; foliis lanceolato-oblongis, acuminatis, subserratis, utrinque glabris.* N[obis]

Obs. *Frutex orgyalis. Differt a V. corymboso.*Lin. *foliis subtus magis venosis, utrinque glabris; a V. ligustrino.*Lin. *floribus corymbosis bracteatis, foliis amplioribus magis venosis.*

High blueberry in Massachusetts. [*V. corymbosum* perhaps var. *glabrum* Gray]

3. V. LIGUSTRINUM *racemis nudis, caule fruticoso, foliis crenulatis, oblongis.* Lin.

Vaccinium ligustrinum. Marshall. [*Lyonia ligustrina* (L.) DC.] Vaccinium pensylvanicum. *Horti Reg. Paris.* Lamarck *Encyclop. method.* art. Airelle n. 7.

Obs. *Frutex bipedalis.*

Whortleberry, Blueberry in Massachusetts. [perhaps *V. angustifolium* Ait., or var.]

4. *V. FRONDOSUM racemis filiformibus foliosis, foliolis oblongis, integerrimis.* Lin.

Vaccinium frondosum. Marshall. Vaccinium foliis ovatis integris deciduis, racemis foliosis. Gronov. *virgin.*

Common whortleberry in Massachusetts, Indian gooseberry in Pennsylvania. [perhaps *V. stamineum* L.; or unripe *Gaylussacia*]

5. *V. OXYCOCCUS foliis integerrimis revolutis, ovatis, caulibus repentibus.* Lin.

b. hispidulum. [*V. macrocarpon* Ait.]

An. Vaccinium hispidulum? Lin. [no]. Vaccinium Oxycoccus. Var. b. Lamarck *Encyclop. method.* Vitis idaea palustris virginiana, fructu majore. Raj. 685. Vitis idaea palustris americana. Plukentius *Almag.* 382 tab. 320 fig. 6.

Obs. *Structura Oxycocci europaei, sed majora omnia. Squamae caulinae, setaceae, imbricatae.*

Cranberry in Massachusetts, Mossberry in the United States, *Atoca* and *Atopa* among the Canadian Indians. [*V. oxycoccus* L.]

The species of *Vaccinium* known in North America under the names of Whortleberry, Blueberry, and Cranberry are very numerous. They are very common there, covering like the European heather uncultivated areas. However, I intend to speak here of only five species, as those that are most worthy of our attention.

Vaccinium corymbosum (Spec. 1) develops into a shrub six to eight feet tall and grows in damp and marshy places. Its leaves are entire, oval-oblong, and somewhat hairy underneath. The fruit, or berries, are black when ripe and of a somewhat tart, but very pleasant, flavor. A variety of this (Var. b), which grows in elevated terrains, produces fruit of a black color tending toward blue called Blueberry in America and much used at tables in Massachusetts along with other fruit. Puddings are even made of it by mixing it with corn flour and a sufficient quantity of molasses.

Vaccinium laevigatum (Spec. 2) was not described by any author as far as I know. It is a shrub of the height of *corymbosum,* from which it differs in that it has leaves smooth on both sides, narrower, and more veined underneath. The fruit of this species is larger than that in the preceding and is used the same way. This one is called the High blueberry in order to distinguish it from *myrsinites.*

Vaccinium ligustrinum (Spec. 3), so named on account of the similarity of its leaves to those of *ligustrum,* grows to a height of barely two feet, has narrow, smooth leaves glossy on both sides; and its fruit, of a dark black color, are smaller than those of *myrsinites.* It is very abundant in uncultivated areas of Eastern Massachusetts and is used at table like the preceding, except that its fruit ripens about two weeks later. In America it is called Black whortleberry.

Vaccinium frondosum (Spec. 4) is also very common in Massachusetts, where it grows to a height of three or four feet on a branchy and often gnarled trunk. The leaves are entire, oblong, and quite small; and the blossoms, which come out underneath the leaves, are tiny, oval, and red-colored before they open. It produces red-colored oval berries, soft and juicy, but bad tasting. On the 14th of June, 1785, as I was coming from Chelsea, a place not far from Boston, I saw among some bushes of this *Vaccinium* some blossoms much larger than usual formed of a fleshy substance and provided with calyx, corolla, stamens, and pistil in the most complete perfection. These were produced by the sting of certain insects which, by drawing an excessive quantity of nutritive juice, had caused this montrosity, preserving remarkably the symmetry and proportion of the parts. This insect must be of the genus of those that produce oak galls.

The American *Vaccinium oxycoccus* (Spec. 5, Var. b) grows abundantly in the midst of the moss in swamps and produces oval, oblong, glossy leaves that remain green even in winter. The fruit is large, round, of a red color and tart flavor. It differs from the European *oxycoccus* in that it has branches covered with bristly imbricate scales and is much larger in all its parts. Linnaeus made of it a new species under the name of *Vaccinium hispidulum*; but M. Lamarck put it with *oxycoccus,* which I, too, thought it proper to do, since there is no difference other than in the scales of the branches. The fruit of this *Vaccinium* keeps for a long time, and, prepared with lots of sugar, is eaten daily with roast duck, pork, and other meats. Jams are also made of it that are shipped to Europe and much used during sea voyages. It is called Cranberry in America and *Atoca* or *Atopa* by the Indians in Canada.

Vacciniums are not easy to propagate from seed, and, like the heathers, are hard to keep and multiply in gardens.

VERATRUM

V. LUTEUM racemo simplicissimo, foliis sessilibus. Lin. Reseda foliis lanceolatis, caule simplicissimo. Gron. *Virg.* pag. 158.

[*Chamaelirium luteum* (L.) Gray]

This species of White hellebore has a bulbous root and wide, lanceolate, smooth, tough, nerved radical leaves. The stalk, that comes up in the midst of the leaves, is

also provided with some narrow, lanceolate leaflets without petiole, and smaller and not curved, as are those that come out of the root. At the end of the stalk it produces the tiny yellowish flowers that are followed by oblong, straight, compact capsules containing many oblong, compressed, blunt seeds provided with a membrane.

[Br 3:164–66] This is very common in low and marshy places in North America. In New Jersey the Swedes call it Dack, Dockor, or Dockretter, that is Childroot, because children make toys with its leaves and stem; and the American colonists call it [illeg.] and Hellebore. This plant is poisonous, and cattle never touch it except occasionally at the beginning of spring when pastures are still bare, so that cows, attracted by the large leaves, which are very early, taste them almost in spite of themselves. If they do, this food is very often fatal to them, and geese and sheep die after eating them. The root, which is thick and tuberous, and contorted causes vomiting when it is chewed. Dogs upon eating it, quickly become sick, but recover by vomiting if done at once, otherwise they die. If the aforementioned root is thrown away raw, there is no animal willing to taste it; but, on the other hand, if it has been boiled first, its sweet flavor draws animals to taste it. However, in spite of the harm that derives from its poisonous quality, this plant is used to preserve the kernels of corn from the voracity of birds. If corn seed is sown the day after a night-long steeping in a cooled decoction of this root and *maize thieves,*[*] crows, or other birds eat it, they become delirious and fall to the ground, which so frightens their companions that they no longer dare return to feed in the same field.† It is necessary, however, to be careful that ducks or other fowl do not taste it accidentally, since otherwise they would become ill, or die, if they eat it in quantity. Some people, after boiling the root, wash parts affected by scurvy, which is said to cause pain and an abundant discharge of urine, but then cures the sick person. This decoction is also employed in America to rid children of those most disgusting insects [lice] by dipping combs in it before using them. This was also one of the many plants that acquired some notoriety as a remedy for rattlesnake bite.‡

ULMUS

U. AMERICANA foliis aequaliter serratis, basi inaequalibus. Lin.
Ulmus fructus membranaceo, foliis simplissime serratis Gron. *Virg.*
[*Ulmus americana* L.]

The American elm is a slow-growing tree that rises to a height of 30 to 40 feet on a trunk of proportionate size. It differs from the European elm only in having simply saw-toothed leaves, and not doubly like ours; and smaller seeds. It is remark-

[*Maize thieves or Maize birds were blackbirds, esp. Redwings.]
†Kalm [Travels], vol. I, p. 382 [in Forster ed. (1772) 1: 370–72.]
‡See item *Polygala senega.*

able for the beauty of its branches, which are numerous, very wide-spreading and pendent almost like those of the African willow [*Salix babylonica* L.], so that it would be preferable to the European for making avenues and other ornamental plantings. In Lancaster, Massachusetts, I saw some of immense size in an avenue next to the house of Mr. Willard, and there are many others near farmhouses. Its wood is not inferior to that of our native elm, and therefore the attempt should be made to cultivate it, since it can easily be obtained from seed, and also by grafting onto the European elm.

XANTHORHIZA

X. SIMPLICISSIMA. Marshall.

Calyx nullus.

Corolla pentapetala; petalis lanceolatis acutis.

Stamina. Nectaria quinque, filiformia, Antherae subrotundae.

Pistillum. Germina 7–11, ovato-compressa, basi unita. Styli totidem, subulati, apice reflexi. Stygmata acuta, simplicia.

Pericarpium. Capsulae 7–11, ovato-compressae, uniloculares, bivalves, apice dehiscentes. Semen unicum, ovale, sub compressum.

> Obs. *Numerus petalorum, & staminum variat a 5 ad 6. Classis Pentandria polygynia prope Myosurum. Ordo naturalis multissiliquarum Aquilegiam inter, & Aconitum juxta fragmenta methodi naturalis Linnaei.*

[*Xanthorhiza simplicissima* Marsh.]

Xanthorhiza is a shrub of South Carolina, its roots are slender, cylindrical, winding, and of a very vivid yellow color. The slender stalks rise to a height of about two feet, for the most part without branches and are covered with a light brown bark. Its leaves have four lateral lobes and one at the tip which are deeply cut at the margin and bound together by means of long petioles, so that at first sight they look like pinnate leaves. The blossoms come out of the ends of the branches the preceding year in panicles or compound racemes, with partial pedicles generally provided with three flowers. The flowers are small and of a maroon color, and they produce little heads of compressed capsules, each of which contains a single seed. This shrub, discovered a short time ago, was named in some plant catalogues in honor of M. Marbois, formerly French consul in the United States, but Mr. Marshall, who first described it systematically, decided to keep the name *Xanthorhiza* by which he had first called it. The generic natural description I gave at the beginning of this entry is taken from what Mr. Marshall says about it in his *Arbustum Americanum,* since I did not have an opportunity to examine this new plant in America. He adds that the three flowers that generally are found on each pedicel are not all fructiferous, but that usually one of the lateral ones aborts, from which he infers that perhaps some of these flowers may be of different sex and therefore sterile. Mr. Marshall thinks that a yellow color useful for dyeing can be extracted from the roots and stalks of this plant—which seems quite likely given their vivid color.

YUCCA

1. *Y. ALOIFOLIA foliis crenulatis strictis.* Lin.
Aloe Yuccae foliis caulescens. Pluk. *Almag.* 19. tab. 256. fig. 4.
Palmetto royal[*] in South Carolina. [*Yucca aliofolia* L.]

2. Y. FILAMENTOSA foliis serrato-filiferis. Lin.
[*Y. filamentosa* L.]

Yucca aloifolia (Spec. 1) grows in South Carolina in places near the sea and hedges are made around gardens with it, especially in the vicinity of Charleston. Its blossoms, resembling a pyramid of pendent white tulips, make a nice decoration, and it was propagated in our country for that purpose. It survives easily in vases, which, however, must be taken in during the winter.

Yucca filamentosa (Spec. 2) is very much like *Yucca gloriosa* of Linnaeus, except that it is smaller and has narrower leaves. The peculiarity that distinguishes it consists in the detachment of very white slender filaments from the leaves that twist and form a strange ornament on the leaf itself. At the present time it is still rare in our gardens, where it can easily survive in the open, as I have discovered with some young plants raised from seed. It is native to Virginia and North Carolina, and I saw it in many places on river banks, especially between Halifax and Wilmington.

ZANT[H]OXYLUM

Z. CLAVA HERCULIS foliis pinnatis Lin.
Zant[h]oxylum Lentisci longioribus foliis, Evonymi fructu capsulari. Catesby *Carolin,* I tab. 26. Seligmann I tab. 52.
[*Zanthoxylum clava-herculis* L.]

b. americanum.
Fagara Fraxini folio. Duham. *Arb., & Arbust.* pag. 229 tab. 97. Xant[h]oxylum fraxinifolio. Marshall.

Toothache tree in the United States. [*Zanthoxylum americanum* Mill.]

Zanthoxylum is a shrub 10 to 12 feet tall all covered with a reddish bark and armed at each knot with two short, strong thorns. Its leaves are composed of 9 to 11 ovato-oblong, opposite and almost sessile leaflets with a few thorns underneath. The flowers are sometimes male and sometimes female on different individuals, and the latter produce oval capsules containing a single round, smooth seed. Variety (b) differs from the species in that it has lanceolate, saw-toothed leaflets provided with longer petioles. The leaves have a pleasant orange fragrance when they are rubbed, and the bark and capsules, of a strong and warming flavor, are used in America to soothe

[*Castiglioni here merely reflects Linnaeus' confusion of *Yucca* and *Sabal.* See Edmund and Dorothy Smith Berkeley, *Dr. Alexander Garden of Charles Town* (Chapel Hill, Univ. North Carolina Press, 1969), 109–111.]

toothache, so that it got the name of Toothache tree. Tincture of *Zanthoxylum* is also recommended for rheumatic pains, and the seeds ooze a very abundant oil which perhaps might be good for something. It grows easily from seed; and since it withstands even our coldest winters, it can easily be propagated in gardens.

ZIZANIA

Z. AQUATICA panicula effusa. Lin.

Arundo alta gracilis, foliis e viridi caeruleis, locustis minoribus. Sloane *Jamaic. Hist.* tom. I pag. 110 tab. 67. [Sloane's illustration is of *Arundo donax* L.!]

Wild oats in the United States and Folle avoine in Canada. [*Zizania aquatica* L.]

I saw this species of *Zizania* rising from the water in great abundance for the first time at the beginning of September, 1785, in the St. Lawrence River at the village called Vaudreuil. It rose two or three feet above the surface of the river and was provided male flowers. The grains, however, milky and immature, were oblong like those of oats, but arranged at the sides of a simple narrow spike. This grain is extremely abundant in the more internal parts of North America and very useful to the Indians, who harvest it in the following manner. Toward the time that the grains, losing their milky fluid, begin to approach maturity, they go out among the *Zizania* plants with their canoes and binding several of them together with bark cords beneath the spikes, leave them that way for two or three weeks. At the end of September they return, and each family, distinguishing the bundles that belong to them from the manner in which they are tied, collects the seeds. This is done by bringing the edge of the canoe up to the clump and making the grains fall inside from the spikes by striking them with a piece of wood. After collecting the grain in this fashion, they smoke it, shell it, and keep it until the new harvest in bags made of deer or young buffalo hides. In addition to the usefulness that derives from this grass for the nutriment of human beings, a large number of birds of various kinds find in it their food, and become very fat and tasty on it. Mr. Carver, to whom we owe this information, thinks that this grass, which he calls Wild rice, is found only in the more internal parts of North America – which is contradicted by various worthy botanists, Mr. Kalm among others, who found it at Fort Frédéric[*] and at Prairie[†]; and Mr. Clayton, who came upon it in Virginia. It is true, however, that in this latter region it never grows very tall and the inhabitants make no use of it.

[*At the south end of Lake Champlain.]
[†Prairie de Magdalene, five miles above Montreal, on St. Lawrence River.]

References

Castiglioni's References

"Agricola." "Advantages of the Culture of the Sugar Maple-Tree." *American Museum* 4 (1788): 349–50.

Anon. "On the culture of Ginseng." *American Museum* 2 (1787): 576–77.

Adanson, Michel. *Familles des plantes.* 2 vols. Paris, 1763–(1764).
Facsimile edition with introduction by Frans A. Stafleu. Lehre: J. Cramer, 1966.

Amoenitates Academicae. See Linnaeus, who is by convention credited with authorship of student dissertations prepared under his supervision.

[Castiglioni cites no author]. *Atti della Società Economica di Lautern* (quoted in Reichard).

[Castiglioni cites no author]. *Atti della Società Patriotica di Milano* 2 (ca. 1785): 56.

Aublet, Fusée. *Histoire des plantes de la Guiane Françoise.* 4 vols. Paris, 1775.

Banister, John. Castiglioni reported that on his "departure from England to America" Joseph Banks gave him a "printed copy" in English of Banister's "collection" which Bishop Compton had sent to John Ray (letter James Greenway to Benjamin Smith Barton, January 31, 1793, at American Philosophical Society). These records had been published in Ray, *Historia plantarum* 2: 19[26]–1928, Banister's catalogue of 1679–1680. His later records were scattered through Vol. 3 (1704). Banister's drawings were published in Leonard Plukenet's *Almagestum, Mantissa,* and *Amaltheum,* collected in his *Phytographia.* Linnaeus cited many Virginia records from Ray, from Plukenet, and from Robert Morison, *Plantarum historiae universalis Oxoniensis* 3 (1699).

Barrelier, Jacques. *Plantae per Galliam Hispanium et Italiam observatae,* edited by A. de Jussieu. Paris, 1714. Cited as Barrelier, *Icon.*

Bartram, Isaac. "A Memoir on the Distillation of Persimmons." *American Philosophical Society Trans.* 1 (1771): 231–34.

[Bartram, John Jr.] "Catalogue of American Trees, Shrubs, and Herbaceous Plants . . ." Philadelphia, 1783, a broadside. Reprinted in *An Account of the Bartram Garden.* Philadelphia: Newman F. McGirr, 1929.

Bartram, William. *Travels through North & South Carolina, Georgia, East and West Florida.* Philadelphia, 1791. Naturalist's edition, edited with commentary and annotated index by Francis Harper. New Haven: Yale University Press, 1958. Castiglioni may have seen Bartram's *Travels* in manuscript.

Bauhin, Caspar. *Pinax.* Basel, 1671.

Boettger, Christoph Henrich (Böttger). *Verzeichness . . . Baume und Stauden, welche in den angelegten englishchen Parks und Garten. . . .* Cassel, 1777.

Bomare. *See* Valmont de Bomare

Bossu, Jean Bernard. *Nouveaux Voyages aux Indes Occidentales.* Paris, 1768. Translated by Johann R. Forster. 2 vols. London, 1771.

Browne, Patrick. *Civil and Natural History of Jamaica.* London, 1756.

Broussenet, Pierre Marie Auguste. [on spruce beer]. *Mémoires d'Agriculture de la Société Royal de Paris.* 1780. Trimestre de printemps.

Buffon, George Louis le Clerc. Probably "Mémoire sur la conservation et le rétablissement des forêts," *Mém. de l'Acad. Sci. Paris* (1739): 140–56; or "Mémoire sur la culture des forêts," *ibid.* (1742): 233–46.

Carver, Jonathan. *Travels through the Interior Parts of North America.* London, 1778. Many other editions.

Catesby, Mark. *The Natural History of Carolina, Florida and the Bahama Islands* 2 vols. London, 1771. Partial reprint with intro. by George Frick, and natural history notes by Joseph Ewan. Savannah, Ga.: Beehive Press, 1974.

Charlevoix, Pierre-François Xavier de. *Histoire et Description générale de la Nouvelle France, avec le journal historique d'un voyage . . . l'Amérique Septentrionale* 3 vols. Paris, 1744.

Clayton, John. *See* Gronovius. Clayton's specimens and catalogue were sent to Gronovius who published Clayton's descriptive phrase-names usually as synonyms. See Edmund and Dorothy Smith Berkeley, *John Clayton, Pioneer of American Botany.* Chapel Hill: University of North Carolina Press, 1963.

Clusius (L'Escluse), Carolus. *Rariorum aliquot stirpium per Hispanias observatarum historia.* Antwerp, 1576.

Clusius, Carolus. *Rariorum plantarum historia.* Antwerp, 1601.

Colden, Cadwallader. "Plantae Coldenghamiae in provincia Noveboracensi Americes sponte crescentes," *Acta Societatis regiae scientiarum Upsalensis* 4 (1743): 81–136; 5 (1744–50): 47–82.

———. "*Acta Svaecica*" (1743–44). Did Castiglioni here abbreviate the preceding title?

Commelin, Jan. *Horti medici Amstelodamensis rariorum plantarum descripti et icones.* 2 vols. Amsterdam, 1697–1701.

Cornut, Jacob. *Canadensium plantarum . . . historia . . .* Paris, 1635. Reprinted with intro. by Jerry Stannard. New York, Johnson Reprint Co., 1966.

Crèvecoeur, Michel Guillaume Jean de. "De Robinia Pseudacacia," *Mémoires de la Soc. d'Agriculture de Paris.* 1786 Trimestre d'hyver.

Crèvecoeur, St. John de. *Le Cultivateur américain.* Paris, 1784. This was a translation of Hector J. St. John, pseud. for M. G. Jean de Crévecoeur, *Letters from an American Farmer describing certain provincial Situations, Manners and Customs, not generally known . . .* London, 1782: Philadelphia 1793.

Cutler, Manasseh. "An account of some of the vegetable productions, naturally growing in this part of America (New England), botanically arranged," *Mem. American Acad.* 1 (1785): 396–493. The same article appeared also in *Columbian Magazine* 1 (1787): 431–.

Dillen, Johann Jakob (Dillenius). *Hortus Elthamensis.* 2 vols. London, 1732. James Sherard's garden at Eltham specialized in exotic plants, many American.

Duhamel du Monceau, Henri Louis. *Traité des arbres et arbustes qui se cultivent en France en pleine terre.* 2 vols. Paris, 1755. Reprinted 1785.

———. *Physique des arbres, où il est traité de l'anatomie des plantes et de l'économie végétale.* Paris, 1758. Vol. 1.

DuRoi, Johann Philippe. *Dieharbkesche wilde Baumzucht . . .* 2 vols. Braunschweig, 1771–72.

Ehret, Georg Dionysius. *Plantae et papilliones rariores depictae et aeri incisae.* London, 1748–59. A folio of 65 paintings.

Ellis, John. "Dionaea muscipula descripta," *Nova Acta Societ. Upsalensis* 1 (1770): 98–101, t. 8. This appears also in Ellis' *Directions for bringing over seeds and plants . . . to which is added the figure and botanical description of Dionaea muscipula.* London, 1770.

———. "A copy of a letter from John Ellis . . . to Dr. Linnaeus . . . a new genus to which Mr. Ellis gives the name Gordonia." *Philos. Trans. Royal Soc. London* 60 (1771): 518–23. LC cites the article from *Act. angl.: Acta philosophica Societas Regiae in Anglia, anno 1665 . . . 1681.* Amsterdam.

Encyclopedia Lausanne.

Fabricius, Johan Christian. *Mantissa insectorum sistens eorum species nuper detectus . . .* 2 vols. (Copenhagen, 1787).

Fougeroux de Bondaroy, Auguste Denis. "Sur le Thuja de Théophraste," *Jour. de Physique* 18 (1781): 354–56.

Fougeroux de Bondaroy, Auguste Denis. [On *Cupressus* and advantages of culture]. *Mémoires de la Soc. Agric. Paris.* 1786, Trimestre d'été: 59–88. [on *Populus*] *ibid.,* 1786, Trim. de printemps. "Memoire sur les érables de M. Fougeroux de Bondaroy," *ibid.,* 1787 Trim. de printemps.

Garden, Alexander. See Edmund and Dorothy Smith Berkeley. *Dr. Alexander Garden of Charles Town.* Chapel Hill: University of North Carolina Press, 1969.

Geoffroy (Geoffroi), Claude Joseph. *Tractatus de materia medica sive medicamentarum simplicium historia, duritute, delecti et usu* 3 vols. Paris, 1741.

Gmelin, Johann Georg. *Flora sibirica.* 4 vols. St. Petersburg, 1747–69.

Gronovius, Johan Frederick. *Flora virginica.* ed. 2. Leiden, 1762. Ed. 1, not used by Castiglioni was published in two parts (1739, 1743). Facsimile editions, Arnold Arboretum, 1946.

Gualtari, Giovanni Battista. *Elementi di botanica.* See Ortega.

Hermann, Paul, *Paradisus batavus.* Leiden, 1705.

Hernandez, Francisco. *Rerum medicarum Novae Hispaniae thesaurus.* Rome, 1649, or 1651. Annotated ed. of the botanical part, *Historia de las plantas de Nueva España* by Isaac Ochoterena. 3 vols. Mexico City, Institutuo de Biologia, 1942–46, reproduces the original illustrations.

Hutchins, Thomas. *Topographical description of Virginia, Pennsylvania, Maryland, and North Carolina.* London, 1778.

Jacquin, Nicolaus Joseph von. *Enumeratio plantarum, quas in insulis Caribaeis vicinaque Americes Continente detexit novas* . . . Leiden, 1760. Castiglioni cites as *Plant Amer.*

Jacquin, Nicolaus Joseph von. *Hortus botanicus Vindobonensis seu plantarum rariorum* . . . 3 vols. Vienna, 1770–76.

Jartoux, Pierre. "Lettre . . . touchant la plante de Ginseng." in Jean Frédéric Bernard, ed., *Recueil de Voyages au Nord continent divers mémoires très utiles au commerce* . . . 6 vols. Amsterdam, 1715. Vol. 4: 83–96, 2 folding plates. At least 2 later editions. Or:

Jartoux Pierre. "The description of a Tartarian plant, called Ginseng; with an account of its virtues . . . Taken from the tenth volume of letters of the missionary Jesuits, printed at Paris in 8°, 1713," *Philos. Trans. Royal Soc. London* 28 (1714): 237–47.

Kaempfer, Engelbert. *Amoenitates exoticae.* Fasiculo V. Lemgo, 1712.

Kalm, Pehr. *En resa till Norra America* . . . 3 vols. Stockholm, 1753–61. Castiglioni probably used translated *Travels* by Johan Reinhold Forster. 2 vols. London, 1772. Edited by Adolph B. Benson with new material from Kalm's diary notes 2 vols. New York: Wilson-Erickson, 1937.

______. *Itinera priscorum scandianorum in America* . . . (Abo, 1757). (Dissertation, Abo, Georg A. Westman respondent). Translation by Esther Larson in "Selections of the work of Pehr Kalm" in American Philosophical Society Library, Philadelphia.

Knorr, Georg Wolffgang. *Deliceae naturae selectae* . . . *beschreiben von Philipp Müller.* Nuremberg, 1766. 38 col. plates; Pt. 2 (1767). 53 plates.

Koempfer. *See* Kaempfer.

Lamarck, Jean Baptiste Pierre-Antoine de Monet de. *Encyclopedia méthodique Botanique.* 3 vols. and suppls. Paris, 1783–89.

Lalande, de M. *Voyage en Italie.* ed. 3, 7 vols. Genève, 1790.

Lauth, Thomas. *Dissertatio de Acere.* Strassbourg, 1781. 40 p.

Linnaeus (Carl von Linné). *Critica botanica, in qua nomina plantarum generica specifica, et variantia, examini subjiciuntur.* Leiden, 1737.

______. *Hortus Cliffortianus* . . . Amsterdam, 1737.

______. *Materia medica. Liber I. de plantis.* Amsterdam and Stockholm, 1749. Ed. 4, Leipzig and Erlangen, 1782.

______. *Species plantarum* . . . Stockholm, 1753. Facsimile edition with Introduction and Notes by W.T. Stearn. (London, 1957–59). J.J. Reichard published the 4th ed. as *Systema plantarum.* Frankfurt a. M., 1779–80, in 4 parts. This also contained later editions of *Systema vegetabilium* (1774) *Mantissa* (1767–71) and *Genera Plantarum* (1764).

______. *Philosophia botanica in qua explicantur fundamenta botanica* . . . (Stockholm and Amsterdam, 1751. Facs. reprint. Lehre, 1966.

______. *Amoenitates academicae* . . . 7 vols. Stockholm, 1787–90. Dissertations prepared under Linnaeus' direction.

Marshall, Humphry. *Arbustrum Americanum: the American Grove, or, an alphabetical catalogue of forest trees and shrubs* . . . Philadelphia, 1785. Facsimile with French edition (1788), introduction by Joseph Ewan. New York: Hafner, 1967.

Mattioli, Pier' Andrea (Matthiolus). Castiglioni does not indicate which of the works, published 1563–1611, he consulted.

Miller, Philip. *Figures of the most beautiful usefull and uncommon plants described in the Gardeners Dictionary* . . . 2 vols. London, 1760. folio, 300 colored plates.

Miller, Philip. *Gardeners' Dictionary.* ed. 8. London, 1768. First edition to incorporate Linnaean binomials. The edition used by Castiglioni.

Mitchell, John. "Dissertatio brevis de principiis botanicorum et zoologorum . . . plantarum quaedam genera recens condita," *Acta Acad. Nat. Cur. Ephemerides* 8 (1748): 187–224. See Edmund and Dorothy Smith Berkeley, *Dr. John Mitchell, the Man who made the Map of North America.* Chapel Hill: University of North Carolina Press, 1974. The *Acta* title is given there in one of its variants as *Acta Physico-Medica Academicae Caesare [Leopoldense] Ephemerides.*

Monardes, Nicolas. *De simplicibus medicamentis ex occidentali India delatis.* Translated and abridged by Charles l'Escluse (Clusius). Antwerp, 1574. See Francisco Guerra, *Nicolas Bautista Monardes, Su vida y su obra.* Mexico, D.F., Compania Fundidora de Fierro y Acero de Monterey, S.A., 1961.

Morison, Robert. *Plantarum historiae universalis Oxoniensis.* Oxford, Vol. 2, 1680, Vol. 3, 1699. Vol. 3 completed after Morison's death by Jacob Bobart, the younger, contained Banister's records from Virginia.

Moore (More). *See* Sherard.

Ortega, Casimiro Gomez de, and Antonio Palau y Verdera. *Elementi di botanica* (Madrid, 1785), transl. by Giambattista Gualteri. Parma, 1788.

Piso, Guillaume. *De Indiae utriusque et naturali et medica* . . . Amsterdam, 1658.

Plinius Secundus, Cajus (Pliny). *Naturalis historiae libri 37.* Venice, 1469, the principal edition.

Plukenet, Leonard. *Opera omnia botanica phytographia.* London, 1691–1705. These are assembled plates from *Almagestum botanicum* 1696; *Almagesti botanici mantissa,* 1700; and *Amaltheum botanicum,* 1705. The *Phytographia* was reprinted in 1720.

Plumier, Carolus. *Plantarum americanarum fasciculi 10* . . . ed. J. Burmannus. Amsterdam, 1755–60.

Poederlè, Eugene Joseph. *Manuel de l'arboriste et du forestier belgique.* Brussels, 1772.

Raj. *See* Ray.

Ray, John. *Historia plantarum* . . . 3 vols. London, 1686–1704. Vol. 2, 1688, contains Banister's "1680" Catalogus. Vol. 3 [Suppl.) contains many later Banister records.

Réaumur, René Antoine Ferchault de. *Mémoires pour servir à l'histoire des insectes.* 6 vols. Paris, 1734–1742.

Reichard, Johann Jakob. *Systema plantarum* . . . 4 pars. Frankfurt, 1779–80. This was a new edition of Linnaeus' works including *Systema vegetabilium, Species plantarum, Mantissa,* and *Genera plantarum.*

Rheede tot Draakenstein, Hendrik Adrian van. *Hortus indicus malabaricus* 12 vols. Amsterdam, 1678–1703.

Rivinius (Bachmann, Augustus Quirinus). *Ordo plantarum, quae sunt flore irregulari monopetalo.* Leipzig, 1690.

Roessel (Rösel) von Rosenhaf, August Johann. *De naturlyke histoire der insecten* 4 vols. Harlem en Amsterdam, 1761. Colored plates.

Rumphius, Georg Everhard. *Herbarium amboinense, plurimus complectens arbores, frutices, herbas, plantas terrestres et aquaticus* . . . edited by Jo. Burmannus. Amsterdam, 1750. *Auctuarium,* (1755).

Scopoli, Giovanni Antonio. *Flora Carniolica* 2 vols. Vienna, 1760. edition 2 (1772).

Scopoli, Giovanni Antonio. *Entomologica Carniolica exhibens insecta* . . . (Vienna, 1763).

Seligmann, Johannes Michael. *See* Trew, C.J.

Shaw, Thomas. *Travels or Observations relating to several parts of Barbary and the Levant.* Oxford, 1738. Castiglioni used French edition, *Voyages de Monsr. Shaw, M.D.* La Haye, 1743.

Sherard, William. "A farther account [of that of Paul Dudley which precedes] of the Poyson Wood Tree of New England," *Philos. Trans. Royal Soc. London* 31 (1720–21): 147–48.

Sloane, Hans. *A Voyage to the Islands Madera, Barbados, Nieves, S. Christopher and Jamaica, with the natural history* . . . 2 vols. London, 1707–25.

Tennent, John. *Essay on Pleurisy.* Williamsburg: Wm. Parks, 1736. Reprinted New York: James Parker, 1742.

Theophrastus Eresios. *De historia plantarum libri X. graece et latine* . . . *commentariis* . . . *a Stapel; accesseriunt Jul. Caes. Scaligeri* . . . Amsterdam, 1644.

Thouin, Andrea. "Liste d'arbres étrangers acclimatés en France." *Mém. de la Soc. Royal d'Agricult. de Paris* 1786, Trimestre d'hyver, 60–95.

Thunberg, Carl Peter. *Flora Japonica* . . . Leipzig. 1784.

Tournefort, Joseph Pitton. *Institutiones rei herbariae.* 3 vols. Paris, 1700. Ed. 3 with an appendix by Jussieu 3 vols., Paris, 1719.

Tournefort, Joseph Pitton. *Corollarium institutionem rei herbariae.* Paris, 1703.

Trew, Christoph Jakob. *Plantae selectae* . . . 10 parts. Augsburg, 1750–73. With drawings by Ehret. Castiglioni also used Johannes Michael Seligmann, *Hortus nitidissimus* . . . *quas* . . . *collegit* . . . *C. J. Trew.* Nuremberg, 1767.

Tschudi (Tschudy), Jean Baptiste Louis Théodore, Baron de. *Traité des arbres résineux conifères; extrait et traduit de l'anglais de Philipp Miller.* Metz, 1768.

Valentini, Michael Bernhard. *Historia simplicium reformata* . . . *a J. C. Becker. Latio restituta* . . . *accedit India laterata* . . . *Latinatate donata* . . . (Francofurti ad Moenum, 1732).

Valmont de Bomare, Jacques Christophe. *Dictionaire raisonné universel d'histoire naturelle* . . . 6 vols. Paris, 1775, or ed. 3, 9 vols. Lyon, 1776.

Wandermont. Not located.

[Wangenheim, Friedrich Adam Julius von. *Beschreibung einiger Nordamerikanischer Holz-und Buscharten mit Anwendung auf deutsche Forsten.* Göttingen, 1781. Cited by Dr. Li for *Quercas ilicifolia.]*

Editors' References

Britton, Nathaniel Lord, and Addison Brown. *An Illustrated Flora of the Northern United States, Canada, and the British Possessions.* 3 vols. New York: Charles Scribner's Sons, 1896–98.

Desmond, Ray. *Dictionary of British and Irish Botanists.* London: Taylor and Francis, 1977.

Dictionary of American Biography, ed. by Allen Johnson. New York: Scribner's, 1946–.

Dictionary of National Biography, ed. by Leslie Stephen and Sidney Lee. vols. Oxford: At the University Press, 1921–.

Dryander, Jonas. *Catalogus Bibliothecae Historico-Naturalis Josephi Banks.* 5 vols. London, 1796–1800.

Ewan, Joseph and Nesta. *John Banister and his Natural History of Virginia 1678–1682.* Urbana: University of Illinois Press, 1970.

Fernald, Merritt Lyndon. *Gray's Manual of Botany, Eighth (Centennial) Edition* . . . New York: American Book Co., 1950.

Gleason, Henry A. *The New Britton and Brown Illustrated Flora.* . . . 3 vols. New York: Hafner, 1963.

Hitchcock, Albert S. *Manual of the Grasses of the United States.* Ed. 2, revised by Agnes Chase. Washington, D.C.: USGPO, 1951.

Li, Hui-Lin. "Castiglioni's Plant Names," *Jour. Washington Academy of Sciences* 47 (1957): 1–5.

Linnean Society. *Catalogue of Printed Books and Pamphlets.* London, 1925.

Little, Elbert L., Jr. *Check List of Native and Naturalized Trees of the United States (including Alaska).* Agriculture Handbook no. 41. Washington, D.C.: USGPO, 1953.

Meisel, Max. *A Bibliography of American Natural History, The Pioneer Century, 1769–1865.* 3 vols. New York: Premier, 1924–29.

Royal Geographical Society. *Catalogue of the Library,* compiled by Hugh R. Mill. London, 1895.

Sargent, Charles Sprague. *The Silva of North America.* . . . 14 vols. Boston: Houghton, Mifflin, 1892–1902.

Small, John Kunkel. *Manual of the Southeastern Flora.* New York: Publ. by the Author, 1933.

Stafleu, Frans A. *Taxonomic Literature.* . . . Utrecht: International Bureau for Plant Taxonomy and Literature, 1967.

Stafleu, Frans A., and Richard S. Cowan. *Taxonomic Literature.* . . . ed. 2. Vol. I: A–G. Utrecht: Bohn, Scheltema & Holkema, 1976. Vol. II: H–Le (1979).

Index

Abenaki, 40
Abercorn, Ga., 126, 129
"Acacia mellifera" (*Gleditsia*), 92, 386
Academy of Sciences, Boston, 21
Acadia (Nova Scotia), 15
Acer, 346–51
Achiugan, 76
Acorus, 351
Actaea, 213, 352
Adams, John, xxxii, 21, 267, 335
Adams, Samuel, xxxii, 21, 267, 335
Adanson, Michel, 350
Adiantum, 352
Aesculua, 352–53
Agaric, 83, 346
Agamenticus Mts. (Mass.), 44
Agkistrodon, 287
Agricultural Society of Philadelphia, 228
Aiton, William, xix, 375
Alabama River, 131
Albany, N.Y., 87, 88–89, 90, 91, 217
Albemarle, George Duke of, 154
Alder, 58
Aletris, 425
Alexander (son of Massasoit), 14
Alexander, Colonel ______, 318 n. 74
Alexandria, Va., 112, 193, 196
Allen, Ethan, 67, 70, 71, 280, 337
Allen's Ordinary, 117
Allenstown, N.H., 56
Alligator, 119, 125–26
Alligator Creek, 119
Alston, Francis, 121
Alston, William, 121
Altamaha River, 131
Amadas, Captain Philip, 176
Amat di San Filippo, P., xxvii
American Academy of Arts and Sciences, 21
American Philosophical Society, 225, 228
American Revolution, peace treaty, 47
American tea, 368
Amherst, N.H., 57
Amoretti, Carlo, xxi, xxii
Amoskeag Falls, N.H., 57
Amsterdam, Holland, 98
Anabaptists, 14, 18
Ananas, 163
Anchusa, 354
Andreani, Count Paolo, xvii
Andromeda, 118, 129, 354
Anguis, 117
Annapolis, Md., 112, 208, 209
Anne, Queen of England, 19, 87
Antlion, 188
Apalachicola River, 131
Apocynum, 356
Apples, 18, 108, 194, 232–33, 237
Appomatox River, 115
Aquia, Va., 114
Aralia, 356
Arasapha, Fort, 99

Arduino, Giovanni, xxi
Argall, Sir Samuel, 98, 192
Argenteau, Count Florimund Merci d', xvii
Aristolochia, 358, 425
Arnold, Benedict, 258, 337
Arum, 359
Asclepias, 360
Ash, 383–384
Ash, American, insects on, 384
Ashepoo River, 122
Ashley, Lord Anthony, 154
Ashley River, 122, 157
Asimina, 355
Atoca, 457
Atopa, 457
Attleboro, Mass., 255
Augusta, Ga., 129–30, 141, 144, 147
Azalea, 122, 129, 361
Azarole, 406, 408

Baccalare, 8, 19
Bagaduce River (Me.), 34
Bagaduce, Me., 34, 41, 48
Bailly, Jean Sylvain de, xvii, xviii
Bald cypress, 373
Balm of Gilead (fir), 416, 419–20
Balm of Gilead (poplar), 427–28
Balsam, 427–28
Baltimore, Cecil Lord Calvert, 207, 208, 223
Baltimore, Md., 111, 189, 206, 208, 209, 210, 213
Banister, John, 116, 359, 371, 396 fn., 403, 431, 456
Banister, John, Colonel (grandson of John), 116
Banks, Sir Joseph, xv, xvii, xix, xxi, xxv, 188
Baptisia, 451–452
[Barbé-] Marbois, François de, 460
Barbel, 69, 76
Barclay, Mr. ______, 319
Barley, 171, 182
Barlow, Captain Arthur, 176
Barlow, Joel, 267, 339
Barrington, Mass., 257
Bartram, Isaac, 376
Bartram, John, 129, 267, 371, 380, 381
[Bartram, John] (not Collinson), 424
Bartram, William, 267, 381, 412
Bass, 70, 76
Basswood, 456
Bastard china, 450–51
Batavia, S.C., 122
Bath, Me., 31, 42
Bay, 118
Bayard, Nicholas, 283
Bayberry, 411
Bay-tree, 397
Beacon Hill, 16
Bear, 69, 210; skin, 209–10
Bear-leaf, 379
Bear-Root, 379
Beauharnais, Eugène de, xxxiii
Beaver, 82, 176, 210; skins, 141
Beccaria, Giambatista, xxiv, xxv
Beccaria, Marquis Cesare, xxv, xxviii, xxxi, 314
Bechlen Bertholf, Baron de, 74
Beech, 58, 379–380
Beer, spruce, 19, 33; making of, 29
Beetle, 56, 127, 247
Beetle infestation, on *Robinia,* 445
Belknap, Jeremy, xv, 267, 278, 279
Benjamin-tree, 397, 398
Bennington, Vt., 63
Benzoin, 213
Berkeley, Va., 190
Berkley, Lord John, 99, 154, 241
Bethabara, N.C., 175
Bethania, N.C., 175
Bethlehem, Pa., 174, 213–217, 230
Betula, 362–63
Beverages, 19
Beverly, Mass., 26
Bicrofft, (Dr.) ______, 128
Biddeford, Me., 29
Bignonia sempervirens (Gelsemium), 122, 364
Birch, 31–32, 33, 35, 37, 40, 58, 75, 362–363
Birch beer, 33
Blackberry, 446–47
Blackberry-bearing gum, 412
Blackbird, 28, 205
Black lime-tree, 455

Black River, 121
Black snakeroot, 352, 425
Black walnut, 392–93
Bladdernut, 453
Blanchard, François, xix
Blandford, Va., 115
Blome, Richard, 153
Bloodroot, 449
Blueberry, 32, 457, 458
Bluebird, 28, 217
Boccage, ______ du, xvii
Bois de plomb, 378
Bolton, Mass., 24
Bolton's Ferry, S.C., 121
Bomare, Valmont de, 441
Bondaroy, Auguste-Denis Fougereaux de, xvii
Boonesborough, Ky., 199
Bosomworth, Thomas, 141
Boston, Mass., 5, 10, 13, 14, 16–25, 33, 43, 52, 96, 121, 187, 255, 256, 259
Boswell, ______, 128
Botrychium, 425
Bouleau canot, 363
Bouleau merisier, 363
Boundary House, S.C., 152, 173
Bourbon laurel, 118, 397
Bourreau des arbres, 368
Bowdoin, James, 339
Bowman, Mr. ______, 290
Braddock, General Edward, 113
Bradford, William, xxviii, xxxi; letter, 313–314
Brambilla di Civesio, Count Cesare, xxix
Breast-root, 390
Brewer, Captain James, 36
Briar, 58, 213
Briar Creek, 130
Brignoli, Professor ______, xxvi
Broad River, 150
Broadbay River (Me.), 31
Bristol, Pa., 229
Bristol, R.I., 257
Brook, Lord ______, 251
Broussonet, Pierre Marie Auguste, xvii
Brown, ______, 268, 331
Brown, John, 256, 257, 258
Brunswick, Me., 31, 42
Buckeye, 352, 353
Buckwheat, 214, 233, 246, 249, 317 n. 65
Buffon, Count Georges Louis Leclerc de, xvii, 91, 264, 441
Bull, William, 140
Bundling, 253–54
Bunker Hill, Mass., 22
Burgoyne, General John, 70, 71, 87, 88
Butterflies, 25, 130, 173, 217
Butternut, 58, 250, 392, 393
Button-bush, 369
Buttonwood, 369, 423
Byl steel, 399
Byorn-Blad, 379

Cabbage, 233
Cabbage-tree, 358
Cabot, Sebastian, 97
Caecilia, 117
Calvert, Cecil, 207, 308
Calvert, Charles, 207, 208, 308
Calvert, Leonard, 207, 308
Calvi, Felice, xxvii
Calvin, John, 13
Calycanthus, 148, 185, 266, 366
Cambridge, Mass., 22–23, 60, 251
Camden, Me., 32–33, 41
Campbell, Lieutenant Colonel Archibald, 126
Campsis, 364
Canadian ivy, 213
Candle-berry, 411
Candles, spermaceti, 256, 262, 331 n. 44
Canè, Nicola, xxviii
Canoes, 37–39, 69, 75
Canoe-wood, 401
Canonicus, 260
Cantù, Cesare, xxvii
Capawach, 15, 44
Cape Ann, 9–10
Cape Cod, 10, 13, 15
Cape Fear River, 119
Cape Hatteras, 176
Cape Henlopen, Del., 211
Cape May, N.J., 243
Capillaire, 349, 352
Carabus calidus, 56
Carcajou, 82

Cardinals, 119
Carey, ______, 81
Caribou (reindeer), 82
Carli, Count Gian Rinaldo, xxxii, 265
Carolina allspice, 366
Carolina Red-bud, 354
Carp, 81
Carpenter, Samuel, 211
Carr, Sir Robert, 99
Carteret, John, 99, 241
Carteret, Philip, 241
Carteret, Sir George, 99, 154, 157, 241
Carver, John, 14
Carver, Jonathan, xxxi, 350, 426, 462
Carya, 392, 393
Caryophyllum root, 243
Casati, Giovanni, xvii
Casco Bay (Mass.), 30
Cassine, 367
Cassini, Jacques Dominique de, xvii
Castanea, 379–80
Castiglioni, Alessandro, xxvii
Castiglioni, Beatrice, xxvii
Castiglioni, Count Alfonso, xii, xiii, xiv, xv, xviii, xx, xxiv, xxvi, 364
Castiglioni, Count Carlo Ottavio, xxiv, xxvii
Castiglioni, Marietta, xii
Castiglioni, Sig. Don Ottavio, xii
Castilleja, 361
Castleton, Vt., 65, 248
Catalpa, 92, 363, 364, 365
Cataraqui, 48, 74, 77–80, 347
Catawba River, 151, 173
Catesby, Mark, 32, 175, 361, 364, 367, 380, 386, 412, 423, 432, 435
Catfish, 76
Catholicism, sentiment against, 60–61
Catta ant lion, 188
Cattle, 194, 200, 231, 233, 235, 445
Cavendish, Vt., 64
Ceanothus, 76, 367–68
Celastrus, 368
Celtis, 369
Cephalanthus, 213, 369
Cercis, 370
Chamaecyparis, 87, 373
Chamaelirium, 425, 458
Chambly (Fort), 72
Champlain, Lake, 47
Charles I, King of England, 14, 59, 98–99, 207, 249
Charles II, King of England, 88, 99, 154, 160, 241, 251, 260
Charles River (Mass.), 22–23
Charleston, Md., 206
Charleston, S.C., 119, 121, 128, 129, 132, 134, 148, 158, 160–162, 163, 164, 165, 177, 182
Charlestown, Mass., 14, 21–22, 26, 30, 63
Charlestown, N.H., 58, 64
Charlevoix, 351
Charlotte River, 120
Charlotte, N.C., 173
Charlottesville, Va., 183, 185, 186
Chastellux, Marquis François Jean de, xxxi, 216, 267
Cheese, 261, 330 n. 41
Cherries, 18, 194, 200, 430
Chester (Fort), 240
Chestertown, Md., 209
Chestnut, 379–380
Chickasaw plum, 430
Chickens, 194
Chicot, 388
Childroot, 459
China root, 450, 451
Chinkapin, 380
Chinquepin, 380
Chionanthus, 148, 370
Chiska-tama, 392
Chokecherry, 430
Chou-palmier, 358
Christian Spring, Pa., 215
Christina, Del., 211, 212, 240
Chrysomela Gleditsiae, 188, 386, 387
Chub, 76
Cider, 19, 235, 256
Clams, 89, 100
Clarendon, Edward, Count of, 154
Clarendon, Vt., 64
Clark, Thomas D., xxix
Clarke (John?, Dr.), 27
Clayton, John, 371, 379, 452, 462
Climbing trumpet-flower, 364
Clinton, George, 97, 267, 337
Clinton, Sir Henry, 162
Clover, 197, 200

Cobb's Ordinary, 117
Cobham, ______, 36
Cocheco River (N.H.), 55–56
Cockspur, 407, 409
Codfish, 8, 19, 26, 30, 51, 262; preparation, 31
Codington, William, 260
Coffee, 326 n.49
Coffee-tree, 388
Cohoes Falls, N.Y., 88
Coins, 309–310
Colberry, 429
Colchester, Va., 113
Colden, Cadwallader, 63, 352, 357 n., 371, 400, 447
Coles, Colonel Isaac, 183
Coles, Colonel John, 183, 184
Coligny, Gaspard II de, 154
Colleton, Sir John, 154
Collinson, Peter, 371, 380, 424, 426
Collinsonia, 371
Colonists, lives of, in woods, 32–33
Compton, Bishop Henry, 403
Comptonia, 400
Concord, N.H., 56–57, 66
Condorcet, Marquis Marie Jean Antoine Nichola de Caritat, xvii
Congregationalists, 18
Conifers, 422
Connecticut River, 52, 58, 60, 63
Contoocook, N.H., 58
Cook, Captain James, 8, 421 n.
Cook's Inn, 147
Cooper, Lord Ashley, 157
Cooper River, 157
Coosawhatchie River, 122
Copal, 441
Copley, John Singleton, 268, 339
Coreopsis, 371
Cormorant, 120
Corn, 25, 26, 33, *passim* 129–262; preparation, 230, 318 n.68
Corniani, G. B., xxvii
Cornus, 372
Cornwallis, General Charles, 162, 180
Cortland Manor, 107
Côteau St. François, 75
Cotonier, 360
Cotton, 171, 181, 215
Cotton, Rev. ______, 325
Cotton tree, 427
Cougar, 82, 265
Court de Gébelin, Antoine, 248, 324
Crabapple, 432
Craddock, Matthew, 14
Cranberry, 457, 458
Crataegus, 406, 409
Craven, Lord William, 154
Crèvecoeur, Saint-Jean de, 445
Cricket, 31
Croton sebiferum, 163
Crown Point (Fort), 47, 69, 70–71, 72, 85
Cucumber tree, 404
Cunila, 425
Curculio, 182
Currencies, 309
Cusani, Francesco C., xxx
Custard-apple, 355
Cutler, Manasseh, xv, xvi, xxii, xxiii, xxiv, 26, 267, 278, 379, 390

Dack, 459
Damariscotta, Me., 31
Dan River, 183
Danaus plexipus, 360
Dartmouth, N.H., 60
Datura, 374
Davenport, John, 251
Deal, England, 5, 11
Dedham, Mass., 255
Deer, 82, 100, 149, 210; skins, 48, 141, 215
Deerfield, N.H., 56
Deer's-eye, 352
Deerwood, 346, 350
Delaware, Lord Thomas West, 192
Dermer, Thomas, 405
Dermestes, 305 n.58
De Segnier, ______, xvii
Detroit (Fort), 48
Dewberry, 446, 447
DeWitt, Simon, 313
Dexter, Aaron, xv
Diderot, Denis, xvii
Diervilla, 402
Dighton, Mass., 23

Dionaea, 375
Dioscorea sativa, 163
Diospyros, 376
Dirca, 378
Dittany, 425
Dockor, 459
Dockretter, 459
Dog's bane, 356
Dogwood, 148, 243
Dorchester, Mass., 14, 23–24, 251
Dover, N.H., 55–56, 59
Dover Castle (England), 5
Drake, Commander Francis, 176, 177
Drayton, John, 122
Dryander, Jonas, xxi
Dublin, N.H., 57
Ducks, 194
Duhamel, du Monceau, Henri, 347, 404, 443, 444
Dumfries, Va., 114
Dung beetle, 127
Dunkers, 230
Durham, Conn., 249
Dyes: *Acer rubrum* 347; *Diospyros* 377; *Juglans cinerea* 394; *Juglans nigra* 393; *Persea borbonia* 398; *Rhus glabra* 440; *Xanthorhiza* 460

Eagle, 81, 122–23
East River, 93
Easton, Pa., 217
Eaton, Theophilus, 251
Ebenezer, Ga., 129
Ebenezer Creek, 129
Edenton, N.C., 117, 179
Edisto River, 122
Edward (Fort), 87
Edward, Count of Clarendon, 154
Eggleston, W. W., xxviii
Elizabeth I, Queen of England, 97, 176
Elizabeth Island, 44
Elizabeth Point, N.J., 239
Elizabeth Town, N.J., 239, 241
Elk, 82; skin, 40
Ellis, John, 388
Elm, 16, 459
Endicott, John, 330
Enniscorthy, 184, 185
Enoree River, 150
Ephrata, Pa., 230
Epinette blanche, 417
Epinette noire, 417
Epping, N.H., 56
Erie, Lake, 47
Eryngium, 379, 425
Estaing, Count Jean Baptiste Charles Henri Hector d', 126
Euhawes, S.C., 122
Euler, Leonhard, 267
Evergreen tulip-tree, 403
Exeter, N.H., 56, 61–62
Exports, 268

Fabricius, Johan Christian, 25, 56
Fagopyrum, 214
Fagus, 379–80
Fair Haven, Vt., 67
Fairfield, Conn., 242
Fallep Islands, 76
Falmouth, Me., 29, 42, 47
Falmouth, Va., 114
False indigo, 451–452
False sweet China, 451
Faxon, C. E., xxviii, xxx
Fayetteville, N.C., 119, 179
Fenwick, George, 251
Ferdinand, Archduke of Austria, xxv
Fern rattlesnake root, 425
Ferrario, Giulio, xxiii
Fetterbush, 354
Fevers, 243–44, 320–21, n. 21–27
Fir, 30, 35, 416, 419–430
Fireflies, 42
Firmian, Count Karl Joseph von, xii
Fish, as food, 179, 210
Fishdam Ford, S.C., 150
Fishing Creek, 150
Fishing eagle, 122–123
Fishkill, N.Y., 92
Fish poison, 415
Five Mile Point, Vt., 70
Flax, 182, 214, 249, 261, 37, n. 65
Flemish Cape, 5
Flint, 203

Flycatcher plant, 356
Flytrap (*Dionaea*), 119, 375
Foglia, Father ______, xiv
Foile avoine, 462
Fomes fomentarium, 346
Fossils, 115, 201, 265
Fothergill, John, 380
Fothergilla, 380
Foulke, Dr. ______, 246
Fox, 82
Francis, Mr., 328
Frankincense (pine), 416, 418
Franklin, Benjamin, xv, xvii, xviii, xxiv, xxv, xxvi, xxxii, xxxiii, 21, 186, 228–29, 266, 267, 323, 335
Franklinia, 381, 388, 454, Pl. XII, 382
Fraser, General Simon, 88
Fraxinus, 383–384
Frederica, Ga., 141
Frederick (Fort), 71
Fredericksburg, Va., 114
Fredericktown, Md., 205, 206, 208
Freeman, James, 18
French, Moses, 62
Fresnoy, André I. G. du, 444
Friday's Ferry, S.C., 150
Fringe-tree, 370
Frisi, Paolo, xvi, xvii, xviii, xxv
Frogs, 86
Frontenac (Fort), 77
Fungus, 346

Gallberry, 429
Gallop, Canada, 77, 81
Ganaraski, Canada, 79
Gannet, 9
Garden, Alexander, 380
Garoqui, Mr., 329
Gates, General Horatio, 70, 88, 267, 337
Gaulteri, Giambattista, 349–50
Gaultheria, 385
Gaulthier, [? Jean-Francois], 347, 385
Gay Head, Mass., 53
Gelsemium, 364
Geoffroi, Etienne François, 441
George I, King of England, 248
George II, King of England, 140
George, Duke of Albemarle, 154
George, Fort (Me.), 34
George, Fort (N.Y.), 87
George River (Me.), 42
George's Pond, Me., 31
Georgetown, S.C., 121, 166
Germantown, Pa., 213
Geum, 243
Gillenia, 452, 453
Gillon, Commodore Alexander, 122
Ginn, Captain (James?), 35
Ginseng, 81, 90, 108, 266, 413–415
Gleditsia, 385
Globe flowering shrub, 369
Gloucester, Va., 180
Glycine americana, 387
Gnats, 36, 72
Gold Coast, 48
Golphintown, Ga., 145
Goodyera, 426
Gooseberry, 70
Goose Brook (N.H.), 58
Gordon, James, 388, 405
Gordonia, 387–388, 454
Gorg Harbor, N.Y., 71
Gorges, Fernandino, 277
Gout de sève, 347
Grackle, purple, 308 n. 2
Grain, *passim*; trade, 108; grinding, 209, 212, 215
Grapes, 143, 149, 166, 185
Grasshoppers, 31
Grassi, Father Giovanni, xxii
Graves, The, 10
Gravesend, England, 140
Green, Dr. ______, 66
Greenage, 128
Greenbriar, 356
Greene, General Nathanael, xxxii, 126, 148, 175, 258, 267, 337
Greenland, 216
Greenland, N.H., 28, 56
Green Mountains (Vt.), 64
Greenway, James, 116, 267, 379, 426
Gregory, ______, xxxi, 32, 41
Greville, Sir Richard, 177
Gronovius, Johann F., 354, 364, 398, 412
Ground nut, 172
Guilford, N.C., 175

Gustafson, Nils, 448
Gustavus Adolphus, King of Sweden, 98
Gymnocladus, 388

Habersham, John, 128
Hager, John, 214
Haidt, John Valentine, 312
Halesia, 129, 148, 389
Half Moon, N.Y., 88
Halifax, Canada, 34
Halifax, N.C., 117, 179, 181
Hamamelis, 390
Hampton, Mass., 28
Hancock, John, xxxii, 21, 335
Harpers Ferry, Va., 190
Harriot, Colonel ______, 290
Harrods, Ky., 199
Hartford, Conn., 249, 250, 251
Hartford, Md., 206
Hartsfield, Pa., 225
Harvard College, 21, 23, 60, 238, 248
Hawkins, Commander Sir John, 176
Hawthorn, 406–407
Hayward, ______, 122
Head-of-Elk, Md., 206
Heart, Captain John, 202
Heart, Captain Jonathan, 202
Helsingburg (Fort), 240
Hemlock, 30, 31, 32, 33, 36, 37, 58, 417, 420
Hemp, 182, 187, 189, 205, 249, 256, 261, 317 n. 65
Henderson, Richard, 199, 306
Hendless Creek, 148
Henlopen (Cape), 240
Henrietta Maria, Queen of England, 207
Henry IV, King of France, 207
Henry VII, King of England, 97
Henry, Patrick, 335
Hernandez, Francisco, 441
Heron, 122
Hibiscus, 171–72, 390–391
Hickory, 392, 393
Hicks Ford, Va., 116
Hill, Samuel, 250
Hillsboro, N.C., 179
Hoarkill (Fort), 211, 240
Hogohechie River, 131
Holly, 391
Holyman, Ezechiell, 259
Honey locust, 385
Honeysuckle, 148, 361, 402
Hooker, Thomas, 251, 325
Hopkins, Edward, 251
Hopkinson, Francis, 267, 339
Hormelin, Baron d', 328
Horsebalm, 426
Horse-chestnut, 352–353
Horse Neck, Conn., 247
Horses, 108, 194, 231, 233, 235, 262
Horseweed, 426
Horshoe Crab, 22
Hough, Samuel J., xxviii, xxxvi
House of Hope (Fort), 98
Howe, General Robert, 126
Hudson, N.Y., 90, 91
Hudson, Henry, 98
Hudson River, 87, 93, 102
Hultgreen, Matthias, 384
Hummingbirds, 18, 273, 365
Humphreys, Lieutenant Colonel, David, 268, 339
Huron, Lake, 47
Huss, John, 174
Hutchins, Thomas, 321, 448
Hutchinson Island, Ga., 126
Hypericum, 426

Icebergs, 6–7, 8
Ichneumon, 387
Ilex, 367, 391, 428–429
Imports, 326 n. 49; 327 n. 4
Independence (Fort), 92
Indian chief, visit to, 37
Indian clothing, 43
Indian crab, 22
Indian currents, 402
Indian foods, 43, 100
Indian gooseberry, 457
Indian hemp, 356
Indian pepper, 172
Indian physic, 452, 453
Indian pipeshank, 452–53
Indian potatoes, 387

Indian use: Acer saccharum 349, Adiantum 352; Aralia 357; Aristolochia 359; Betula 363; *Cassine* (*Ilex*) 367; *Castanea* 380; *Chionanthus* 370; *Collinsonia* 371; *Datura* 375; *Diervilla* 403; *Dirca* 378; *Gaultheria* 385; *Gillenia* 453; *Glycine* 387; *Goodyera* 426; *Hamamelis* 390; *Kalmia* 396; *Liatris* 426; *Liquidambar* 400; *Liriodendron* 401; *Lithospermum* 354; *Myrica* 411; *Orontium* 413; *Peltandra* 359; *Polygala* 424; *Populus* 428; *Quercus* 435; *Rhus* 440; *Rumex* 447; *Sanguinaria* 449; *Sagittaria* 447; *Symplocarpus* 379; Tacamahaca 428; *Thuja* 455; *Tilia* 456; *Tsuga* 420; *Veratrum* 459; *Zizania* 462
Indians, 43, 100, 131–41, 151, 153, 191, 200, 219, 232, 248, 259, 260, 266
Indigo, 170–71, *passim* 118–82
Inkberry, 429
Ipswich, Mass., 26–27
Iron, 210, 256–57, 331 n.44
Iron, smelting, 42
Irondequac, 79
Isle aux Noix, 71
Ivy, 396

James I, King of England, 13, 97, 98, 191
James II, King of England, 157
James River, 115
Jamestown, R.I., 261
Jamestown, Va., 191
Jamestown weed, 374
Japan-tea, 118, 367
Jartoux, Father, 415
Jay, John, 97, 267
Jefferson, Thomas, xxxii, 185–86, 191, 196, 228, 265, 267, 336
Jeffersonia, 424
Jesuits, 73
Jesuit's tea, 118
Jews, 95
Jimson weed, 374
John's Ordinary, Va., 184
Johnson, Canada, 76
Johnson (Fort), 162
Johnson, Robert, 140, 167
Johnson, Sir John, 76
Johnson, Sir William, 101
Jones, John Paul, 338
Joppa, Md., 206
Judas-tree, 122, 370
Juglans, 392, 393
Juniper, 394, 395

Kaempfer ("Koempfer"), Engelbert, 364, 442, 443
Kageneck, Count de, 74
Kalm, Peter, 90, 96, 101, 205, 214, 319, 320, 321, 322, 351, 356, 359, 360, 371, 395, 397, 411, 448, 462
Kalmia, 92, 206, 396
Keene, N.H., 58
Kennebec River (Me.), 31, 42, 44
Kennebunk, Me., 42
Kensington, Pa., 225
Kenty, Canada, 78, 80
Keowee, S.C., 148, 152
Keowee River, 152
Kichlein's Inn, Pa., 214
Kinderhook, N.Y., 90
Kingston, Va., 116
Kittery, Me., 29
Knox, General Henry, xxxii, 21, 267, 338
Kosteletskya, 391

Lacerta plica, 123
Lachine, Canada, 74, 81
La Coruña, Spain, 259
Lafayette (Fort), 92
Lafayette, Marquis Marie Joseph Paul Yves Roche Gilbert du Motier de, 209
La Galette (Fort), 47, 48, 77
Lake of the Blessed Sacrament, 86
Lake Champlain, 65, 67, 69, 85, 86
Lake George, 70, 85–87
Lake Kasumpy, 60
Lake St. François, 75, 81
Lake of Two Mountains, 75
Lake of the Woods, 47
Lake Winnepesaukee (N.H.), 60
Lamarck, Jean Baptiste, 372

Lamberth's Inn, 130
Lambkill, 396
La Motte Island, 71, 85
Lampropeltis triangulum, 278
Lancaster, Mass., 24–25
Lancaster, Pa., 230
Land's End, England, 5
Lane, Ralph, 177
Laprairie, Canada, 73, 81
Larch, 417, 421
La Rochefoucauld-Liancourt, Duke François Alexandre Frédéric de, xvii
Larus, 6
Laurel (*Kalmia*), 396
Laurel-tree, 403, 404
Laurens, John Henry, 336
Laurier cannellier des sauvages, 398
Laurier royal, 398
Laurocerasus, 122, 431
Lead, 257
Lead mine, 249
Leatherwood, 378
Lee (Fort), 92
Lee, ______, 34
Lee, Charles, 338
Les Trois Rivières, 71
Lever, Sir Ashton, xix
Lewis, Colonel Nicholas, 185
Lexington, Mass., 22
Li, Hui-Lin, xxviii
Liatris, 426
Lime tree, 412
Lincoln, General Benjamin, xxxii, 47, 126, 267, 338
Linden, 16, 455
Lindera, 397, 398
Linen, Spinning and weaving, 215; washing, 353
Linnaeus, Carolus, xiii, xv, xix, 22, 66, 74, 122, 123, 130, 163, 171, 173, 188, 214, 217, 233, 244, 250
Linseed, 108, 215
Liquidambar, 399, 400
Liriodendron, 401
Lispinard, Leonard, 283
Lithospermum, 354
Litsea, 397, 398
Little, Daniel, 35–36, 378
Little, (David?), 42
Littlefield, Colonel (Noel Moulton?), 29
Littlepage, Lewis, 336
Live-oak, 432, 435
Livingston Manor, 91, 92, 107
Lizard, 123
Locke, John, 155, 156, 157, 164
Lockwood's Folly, 120
Locust tree, 87, 444–446
Lomellini, Marquis Agostino, xvii
London, England, 5
Londonderry, S.C., 158
Londonio, Carlo Giuseppe, xxii
London's Ferry, 88
Long Island, N.Y., 90
Long Saut, Canada, 76
Longueuil, Canada, 81
Lonicera, 402
Ludlow, Roger, 251
Lumber, 30, 108, 127, 141, 165, 179, 256, 262
Luther, Martin, 216
Lynn, Mass., 26
Lynn River (Mass.), 26
Lynx, 82, 210
Lyonia, 354

MacAllaster, Captain ______, 119, 120
Macdoval (MacDowell?), ______, 189, 303
Mackerel, 19
MacLean, Lieutenant ______, 79
Madambeatic, Lake (Me.), 32
Madison, James, 196, 267, 336
Magnolia, 118, 121, 266, 403–405
Magnolia root, in maple wine, 349
Mahattan, 93ff
Maidenhair, 352
Maize thieves, 205
Major-bag-wa-duce (Me.), 34
Malaria, 243, 244, 321 n. 21–27
Mammoth, 201
Manchester, Vt., 63
Mangu-me-nauk, 433
Manini, Lorenzo, xxxii
Manzoni, Alessandro, xxx
Maple sugar, 347–349
Maples, 30, 32, 35, 58, 346–351
Marble, 331 n. 44

Marblehead, Mass., 10
Marbois, François de [Barbé-], 460
Maria Theresa (Empress), xii, xvi, xxiv, xxvi
Marl, 256
Marlboro, (N.H.), 58
Marlborough Grove, Ga., 126
Marraro, Howard R., xxviii
Marriage customs, 33, 35
Marshall, Humphry, 267, 355, 359, 361, 369, 381, 393, 394, 400, 412, 452, 460
Marten, 82
Martha's Vineyard, 44, 52
Martyn, Thomas, xix
Masko-nan-gi, 81
Mason, John, 59, 277
Massachusetts Bay, 10
Massachusetts Company, 14
Massasoit, 14–15
Maurepas, Frédéric, 71
May apple, 423
Mayflies ("Ephemera"), 72
Meat, salted, 182
Mecklenburg, S.C., 158
Medford, Mass., 26
Medici, Cosimo de', xxv
Meherrin River, 116
Meisel, M., xviii
Melia azedarach, 163
Melons, 171
Merrimack River, 28, 44, 56–58, 60
Mesmer, Friedrich, xvii, xviii
Mespilus, parsley leaved, 406
Metacomet, 14–15
Mica, 310
Middleton, Arthur, 122, 291
Middleton, Henry, 121, 122, 290
Middletown, Conn., 249
Miller, Charles R. D., xxviii
Miller, Philip, 398, 450
Miller's Town, Va., 189
Mineral water, 230, 243
Mink, 82
Minuit, Peter, 310
Missionaries, 35
Mississippi River, 47, 131–32
Mitchella, 409
Mitterpaker, Ludwig, xxi, xxii
Mobile River, 131
Mockingbirds, 187
Molasses, 326 n. 49; 327 n. 4
Molasses (from maple sugar), 348
Monadnock Mountains (N.H.), 57, 58, 59
Monarch butterfly, 360
Monoculi, 22, 96
Montgomery, General Richard, 97, 267, 338
Monticello, 185
Montmorency (Canada), 88
Montreal, Canada, 72, 73, 74, 79, 82
Moore, Thomas, 443
Moose, 82
Moosewood (*Acer*), 346, 349, 350
Moosewood (*Dirca*), 378
Moravians, 174, 175, 213–217
Morison, Robert, 354
Morris, Robert, xxxii, 336
Morrison, A. J., xxviii
Morus, 410
Mosquitoes, 33, 36, 72, 320 n. 12
Mossberry, 457
Moth, 188, 217
Moultrie (Fort), 162
Moultrie, William, xxxi, 132
Mount Petersboro (N.H.), 57
Mount Pleasant, Md., 112
Mount Pleasant, S.C., 122–23
Mount Vernon, Va., 112–13
Mountain tree, 385
Muddy River (Mass.), 23
Mulberry, 123, 129, 143, 185, 410
Musa paradisiaca, 163
Muskrats, 76, 100, 210
Mussi, Giuseppe, 213
Mustela, 82
Myrica, 410–411

Nantucket, 15, 44, 52, 53
Napoleon I, xxiv, xxvi
Narraganset, 14
Nassau (Fort), 98
Natali, Giulio, xxviii
Natchez (Mississippi Territory), 131
Natick, Mass., 43
Nazareth, Pa., 174, 214, 215
Negroes, 20, 31, 97, 127, 166

Negundo, 346, 350
Nettle-tree, 368–369
Neuchâtel, Switzerland, 123
Neuse River, 118
New Amsterdam, N.Y., 98
Newark, N.J., 239
New Bern, N.C., 118, 178, 179, 180
New Bordeaux, S.C., 149
New Brunswick, N.J., 239
Newburyport, Mass., 27, 52
New Casco, Me., 30
New Castle, Del., 211, 212, 218, 219
Newcastle, Me., 31
Newfoundland, 5–7, 8
New Gothenburg, Del., 240
New Haven, Conn., 247, 248, 249, 251
New Holland, 98
New Jersey tea, 368
New Meadow River (Me.), 31
New Plymouth, Mass., 13–15
Newport, R.I., 255, 256, 257, 258, 260, 261, 262
Newport, Captain Christopher, 191
Newton, Va., 189
New York, N.Y., 91, 93–97, 111, 213, 226, 239, 241, 246, 247, 259
Niagara (Fort), 48, 74, 79, 88
Nichols, Gov. ______, 93
Nicholson (Fort), 87
Nikar, 388
Ninebark, 452, 453
Ninety-six, S.C., 148–49
Ninety-Six Creek, 148
Noddles Island, Mass., 22
Norfolk, Va., 196
North Yarmouth, Me., 30, 42
Norwalk, Conn., 247
Nottingham, N.H., 56
Nottoway River, 116
Nova Scotia, 34
Nyssa, 411–413

Oak: 25, 32, 432–38; Black, 112, 148, 433, 436; Chestnut, 25, 433, 436; Dwarf, 25, 433, 436; Live, 127, 144, 432; Red, 25, 433, 437; Scrub or Shrub, 25, 433, 436, Pl. XIII, 437; White, 25, 203, 215, 435; Willow-leaved, 118, 120, 123, 432, 435
Oats, 74, 148, 171, 182, 209, 233
Occoquan River, 113–14
Ochre, 257
Ocosolt, 399–400
Ogeechee River, 128, 131
Oglethorpe, General James, 126, 129–30, 140–41, 174
Oil of *Capillaire*, 349
Okra, 171–72
Old Nation's Ford, 151
Old York, Me., 29, 42
Oldham, John, 250
Olives, 143, 166
Olivier, 412
Onions, 249
Onisci, 5
Ontario, Lake, 47–48, 77
Opheodrys vernalis, 278
Opossum, 244–246, 265, 321–322, n. 28, 29
Orange, Prince of, 99
Orangeburg, S.C., 149
Oranges, 163
Orchards, 261
Orontium, 413
Osborne, Va., 115
Osley, ______, 215
Osprey, 122–23, 291 n. 86
Oswegatchie River, 77
Oswego (Fort), 48, 89, 90
Otter, 82, 210
Owen, Griffith, 211
Oxford University, 116
Oxydendrum, 354
Oyster shells, 112, 123, 203
Oysters, 101–102

Paine, Robert Treat, 267
Paine, Thomas, 267
Paintonborough, Va., 183
Palm, dwarf, 120, 122
Palmetto, 128, 373
Palmetto Royal, 358, 461
Palmier nain des marais, 373

Pamlico, 176
Panax, 413–415
Papaw-tree, 355
Papegoya, Johan, 240
Paper-tree, 370
Paraguay grass, 122
Paraguay tea, 118
Partridge-berry, 409, 410
Passenger pigeon, 32
Passy, 228
Pattens, Colonel ______, 150–51
Patterson, ______, 184, 301
Patuxent River, 112
Paulus Hook, N.J., 111, 239
Pauw, Corneille de, 265
Pavia, 353
Pavón, J., xxi
Pawtuckaway Mts. (N.H.), 56, 60
Peach bark, 243
Peach brandy, 197
Peach orchards, 237
Peaches, 25, 114, 115, 182, 266
Peale, Charles Willson, 209
Pecan, 392
Pecanier, 392
Pee Dee River, 121
Peekskill, N.Y., 92
Pekan, 82
Peltandra, 359
Pemaquid River (Me.), 31
Pemberton, Phineas, 211
Pembroke, N.H., 56
Pendleton, Edmund, 145
Penn, John (brother of William), 313
Penn, John (son of William), 131
Penn, William, 100, 208, 211, 218, 219, 223, 225, 226, 241
Pennacoock, N.H., 56
Penobscot Bay (Me.), 32, 41
Penobscot Island, 37
Penobscot Mountains, 32
Penobscot River (Me.), 34–35, 41, 44
Penobscot Village, Me., 28, 37, 41, 52
Pepper-bush, 354
Perch, 69, 76
Persea, 397
Persimmon, 114, 115, 376–377
Persimmon beer, 115
Petersburg, Va., 115, 116, 182, 193
Peuplier, 427
Phalaena, 217
Philadelphia, Pa., 96, 183, 189, 194, 200, 206, 212, 213, 223–226, 244, 246, 259, 263, 268
Philipsborough, N.Y., 92
Philipse Manor, 107
Phryganea, 188
Physocarpus, 452–53
Phytolacca, 213
Picea, 417, 420
Pierce's Inn, Ga., 129
Pigeon, 32
Pigeon-weed, 356
Pigs (swine), 117, 181, 194
Pike, 69, 81
Pine: 30, 35, 58; Black, 111, 144, 181, 243; White, 5, 16; ships; masts, 30; 415–416, 417–419
Pines as shade for cattle, 419
Pinus, 415–416, 417–419
Piscataqua River (N.H.), 28, 44, 55–56, 59–60
Pitch, 117, 118, 119, 141, 165, 179, 182; method, 181
Pitcher plant, 449
Pitt (Fort), 218
Pitt, William, 93, 162
Pittsburgh, Pa., 200
Plane trees, 16, 256, 422–423
Plant collection, 85, 152
Platanus, 422–423
Plover, 115
Plowden, Sir Edmund, 98
Plums, 194, 266, 429, 430
Plymouth, England, 13
Plymouth, Mass., 259
Plymouth Company, 97–98
Pocahontas, 191–192
Pocahontas, Va., 115
Pocataligo River, 122
Podophyllum, 423–424
Poederlè, Joseph C. G., 404
Pointe aux Barrils, 81
Pointe au Baudet, Canada, 75
Pointe Claire, 74
Pointe de l'Isle, 74
Pointe du Lac, 75
Pointe Maligne, 76

Poison ash, 438
Poison ivy, 213
Poison oak, 440, 443
Poison root, 352, 353
Poison swamp sumac, 439
Poison vine, 440, 446
Poisonous plant (kalmia), 396
Polecats, 100
Polecat-weed, 378
Politics, Massachusetts, 45–46
Pollom, 385
Polygala, 66, 424
Polygonum, 415
Polypore, 346
Polyxena, 25
Pomme epineuse, 374
Pond dogwood, 369
Ponpon River, 122
Poplars, 58, 88, 427–428
Populus, 427–428
Porcupine quills, 40
Pork, 29, 210
Portsmouth, N.H., 24–25, 28–29, 42, 52, 55, 59, 60, 61, 121
Postell, ______, 129
Potatoes, 233
Potentilla, 243
Potomac River, 112–14
Poughkeepsie, N.Y., 91
Powhatan, 115, 191
Prenanthes, 425
Presbyterians, 13–15, 18, 50, 252–53
Presumpscot River, 30
Prickly-ash, 356
Pride of China, 163
Priestley, Joseph, xix, 18
Prince George (Fort), 148
Princeton, N.J., 238, 239
Princeton College, 238
Printz, Johan Björnsson, 240
Pritzel, George A., xxvii
Protesilaus, 130
Providence, R.I., 255, 256, 257, 258, 262
Prunus, 429–31
Pseudoacacia, 200
Ptelea, 431
Puccoon, 354
Pudsey, England, 216
Pullen Point, Mass., 10
Pumpkins, 171
Purry, Jean Pierre, 123, 158
Purysburg, S.C., 123, 125, 158
Pusey, Caleb, 211
Putnam, Israel, 267, 339
Pynchon, William, 251
Pyrus, 432

Quakers, 226–228
Quebec, Canada, 68, 73, 74, 82
Quercus, 432–38. *See* Oaks
Quinine, 243
Quitsera, 349

Raccoon, 238–39, 265
(Rail) Soree, 115
Raleigh, Walter (Sir), 97, 154, 176, 177, 191
Ramsey, Nathaniel, 267
Randolph's Bridge, 122
Rapide Plat, Canada, 76, 81
Raspberry, 58, 446, 447
Rattlesnake, 65–66, 85
Rattlesnake master, 425
Rattlesnake plantain, 426
Rattlesnake remedies, 425–426
Rattlesnake-root, 358, 424
Rawdon-Hastings, Lord Francis, 148
Ray, John, 116
Raynal, Guillaume Thomas François, 267, 268
Reading, Pa., 230
Red bay, 118, 397
Red cedar, 26, 88, 118, 176–77, 243, 394, 395
Red china, 243
Red jasmine, 18, 365
Red thorn, 408
Redbud, 370
Redroot, 449
Rehoboth, Mass., 255, 257
Reichard, 431
Resin, 117, 118, 119, 141, 165, 179, 182; method, 181
Rheede, Hendrik A. D. van, 364

Rhineback, N.Y., 91
Rhode Island University, 255
Rhododendron, 361
Rhus, 438–44
Rice, 117–80
Richelieu River, 71
Richmond, Va., 115, 183, 193
Richweed, 352
Rio May, 154
Rising, Johan, 99, 240
Rittenhouse, David, 267
Roach, 188
Roanoke River, 117
Robert Brothers, xvii
Robertson, William, 265
Robin, 217
Robinia, 87, 444–446
Rock crystal, 88
Rockfish, 70
Rocky River, 173
Roland, ______, 28, 41
Rolfe, John, 192
Roman, Jean-Joseph-Thérèse (Abbé), xvii
Rondelet, Guillaume, 5, 258
Roxbury, Mass., 23, 251, 255
Rubus, 446–47
Rudbeckia, 76
Ruiz Lopéz, H., xxi
Rulac, 350
Rum, 33
Rum-soconga Island (Me.), 36–37
Rumex, 447
Rush, Benjamin, xxiv, xxvi, 230–35, 267
Rush River, 149
Russel, Thomas, 21
Russell, Thomas, 21
Rutland, Vt., 63, 65
Rye, 25, 33, 182, 209, 214, 233, 317 n. 65, 319 n. 75
Ryebread, 29

Sabal minor, 120, 373
Sabal palmetto, 358
Sabin, Joseph, xxviii
Saccardo, P. A., xxvii
Sacchi, Father, xiii
Saco, Mass., 29
Sagadahoc, 15, 28, 31, 44
Sage's Ordinary, 118
Sagittaria, 447
Sago, 128
St. Andrew's cross, 426
St. Augustine, Fla., 128, 163
St. Croix River, 44, 47
St. George (Fort), Me., 42
St. George woods (Me.), 31, 41
St. Johns, Canada, 47, 70–72, 81–82
St. Lawrence River, 47, 77
St. Léger, Baron Barry de, 74
St. Mary's River, 131
St. Peter's wort, 402
St. Regis, N.Y., 76
Salem, Mass., 25–26, 52, 259
Salem, N.C., 174, 175, 180
Salisbury, Mass., 28
Salisbury, N.C., 174, 179
Salix, 448–449
Salmon, 19, 35
Salt, 210
Saluda River, 148–49
Sampit River, 121
Sand flies, 128
Sandstone, 213
Sandy Creek, S.C., 150
Sandy Hill, S.C., 122
Sandy Hook, N.J., 243
Sanguinaria, 449
Sanicula, 425
Santee River, 121, 158
Saratoga, N.Y., 70, 87, 88, 102
Sargent, Charles Sprague, xxviii
Sarracenia, 449
Sarsaparilla, 357, 450–451
Sassafras, 31, 87, 176, 213, 397, 399
Satilla River, 131
Savane, Canada, 72–73
Savannah, Ga., 126, 127, 128, 129, 144
Savannah River, 125
Savin, 394
Sawmill, 31, 56
Say, Lord ______, 251
Sayle, Captain William, 156, 157
Scarboro, Me., 29
Schenectady, N.Y., 90
Schiavo, Giovanni, xxviii
Schreber, Johann Christian Daniel, 91

Scopoli, Giovanni, xv, xvi, xxix, 387
Sea dogs, 7
Sea flea, 5
Sea lion, 41
Seals, 7
Seguin Island, 9
Senega, 424, 425
Service, Wild, 406, 408–409
Shagpoke, 214
Shakers, 14, 50
Shaw, Thomas, 369
Sheep, 194, 261, 396
Sheepscot River (Me.), 31
Shellbark, 19, 392
Sherard, William, 443
Shingles, 119
Ship-beams, 435
Shippen, Edward, 211, 219
Shot-bush, 356
Shrewsbury, Vt., 64
Sidesaddle flower, 449
Sierra Leone, 48
Siliquastrum, 370
Silk, 129
Silkgrass, 42, 356, 360
Silk Hope, 128
Silk-weed, 360
Silverbell, 389
Simkins, Arthur, 148
Siskin, 28
Skelton, Mr., 330
Skins, dressing of, 215
Skunk, 91
Skunk-weed, 378
Slate, use, 16
Smallpox, 147
Smilax, 118, 450–451
Smith, Captain John, 191, 192
Snakeroot (Doctor Witt's), 425
Snakes, 56–57, 65–66, 85, 123, 184, 185; Glass, 116; Green, 56; Milk, 56; moccasin, 116; Striped, 78
Snowdrop, 370
Snowflake, 453
Society of the Adventurers of London, 97
Sophora, 451
Soree, 115
Sorel River, 71, 85, 100
Sorghum, 249, 319 n. 78
Sorrel-tree, 354
Sour gum, 412
South Amboy, N.J., 239
South Hampton, N.H., 59
South Kingston, R.I., 260
South Sea tea, 367
Southampton Courthouse, Va., 116
Southwark, Pa., 225
Spar, 88
Sparrow, North American, 28
Spelts, 233
Spermaceti, 262; candles, 256
Spicewood, 397, 398
Spicewort, 351
Spikenard, 357
Spinus, 28
Spiraea, 452–453
Spokohummah, 132–134
Spoontree, 396
Springfield, Mass., 251
Springs, 190
Spruce, 33, 58, 417, 420
Spruce beer, 19, 33; making of, 29
Spruce pitch, 348
Spruce roots, use, 37, 75
Squanto, 14
Squirrel, Flying, 27; Gray, 26–27; Striped (Chipmunk), 27
Staff tree, 368
Stalactytes, 187
Stanton River, 183
Staphylea, 453
Star grass, 425
Star root, 425
Staunton, Va., 187
Stevens (Fort), 58
Stevens, Phineas, 278
Stewart, ______, 268, 300
Stewartia, 454
Stiles, Ezra, 248, 323
Stillwater, N.Y., 87, 88, 102
Stokes, Jonathan, xv, xvi, xix, xxv
Stone, Samuel, 251
Stono River, 122, 159
Story, Thomas, 211
Stow, Mass., 24–25
Stower's Town, Va., 189
Stratford, Conn., 247
Stratham, N.H., 56

Striped squirrel, 27
Stroudwater, Me., 29
Stroudwater River, 30
Stuart, John, 9
Stumpel, ______, 158
Sturgeon, 35
Stuyvesant, Peter, 99, 240
Sudbury, Mass., 24, 255
Sugar, 326 n.49
Sugar maple, 32, 200, 347–349
Sugar tree, 347–349
Sugumuck, 456
Sullivan, General John, 62
Sumac(h), 213, 438–444
Sunflower, 76
Superior, Lake, 47
Surinam, 99
Svenssöner, 223
Swammerdam, Jan, 96
Swamp laurel, 403
Swamp-pink 361
Swamp sumac, 438–39
Swan, Major ______, 24
Sweet bay, 122, 397, 398
Sweetbay-tree, 397, 398
Sweet-fern, 30, 400
Sweet flag, 351
Sweet gum, 92, 399
Sweet potatoes, 117, 128, 129, 143, 171
Sweet-scented shrub, 366
Swen, sons of, 223
Swine, 181
Sycamore, 423
Symplocarpus, 378

Tacamahaca, 58, 427, 428
Tak-win, 411
Talc, 57, 92, 202, 213
Tallow tree, 163
Tar River, 117
Tarboro, N.C., 117, 181
Tarrytown, N.Y., 92
Taunton River, 23
Taw-kee, Tawkin, 411
Taxodium, 373, 374
Taylor, ______, 268
Temple, N.H., 57
Teniers, David, 89
Tennent, Gilbert, 316
Tennent, John, 424, 425
Theophrastus, 455
Thomason, Charles, 336
Thomaston, Me., 42
Thompson, Captain ______, 201, 306, 307
Thomson, Charles, xxxii
Thornapple, 374
Thouin, André, 445
Throatwort, 426
Thuja, 35, 36, 37, 87, 454
Thunberg, Carl, 453
Ticks, 149
Ticonderoga (Fort), 47, 70–71, 85
Ticozzi, S., xxvii
Tilghman, Colonel Tench, 209
Tilia, 455
Tillandsia, 456
Tinctimingo, 133, 134, 292
Tinder, 346
Toadfish, 257–258
Tobacco, 52–55, 114–209 *passim*; cultivation, 196–197, 305
Tocqueville, Alexis Charles Henri Maurice Clérel de, xxxiv
Toddy, 19
Tomaselli, R., xxix
Tomato, 172
Tomochichi, 126–127, 140
Toothache-tree, 356, 461, 462
Tournefort, Joseph Pitton de, xiii
Trade, barrels, 250; beef, 250; codfish, 20, 30; corn, 254; flour, 317 n. 65; grain, 108; horses, 250, 254; lumber, 108, 250; onions, 250, 254; salt pork, 250; wheat, 108, 254
Travel, on Sunday, 27–28
Treat, ______, 35–37, 41
Trent River, 118
Trenton, N.C., 118, 237
Trinity Fort (Del.), 240
Trumbull, John, 267, 268, 339
Trumpet flower, 365, 449
Tryon, William, 178, 247
Tuckerman, Henry T., xxviii
Tukasse-king, Ga., 129
Tulip tree, 92, 112; bark, 243, 401

Tully-finny River, 122
Tupelo, 412
Turkey, 150
Turkey buzzard, 118; vulture, 118
Turner, Robert, 224, 225
Turnips, 233
Turtle, 100
Tyger River, 150

Ulmus, 459
Umbrella magnolia, 405
Umbrella tree, 404
Umbrella-weed, 356
Unicorn's horn, 425
Unitarians, 18
Universalists, 61
Upper Coos, 60
Usnea, 287 n. 32
Usselinx, Willem, 240
Uvularia, 425

Vaccinium, 32, 456–58
Vacovia, N.C., 175
Vane, Sir Henry, 260
Van Rensselaer family, 90
Van Rensselaer Manor, 107
Varnish sumac, 441–43
Varnish tree, 438, 441
Vaudreuil, Canada, 74
Vaughan, Benjamin, 230
Vaughan, John, xxi, xxv, 92
Vaughan, General ______, 92
Veiser, Johann Conrad, 371
Venus'-hair, 349, 352
Veratrum, 458
Vereen's Inn, N.C., 120
Vernon, ______, 14
Verplanck, N.Y., 92
Verri, Alessandro, xii, xiii, xiv
Verri, Pietro, xii, xiii, xiv, xvi, xxv, xxx, xxxiii
Verri, Teresa, xii
Vestri, ______, xvii
Vinaigrier, 438, 440
Vinegar, 348–49
Vinula, 428
Virginian poplar, 427
Vison, 82
Vries, David Pietersz de, 240
Vultures, 118

Waccamaw River, 121
Wafer ash, 431
Wagtail (Bluebird), 28, 217
Wake-robin, 359
Waldoboro, Me., 31
Walker, Captain Robert, 116
Wall, Major ______, 116
Walmesley, Charles, xix
Walnut: Black, 92, 200, 213; White, 213
Walpole, Mass., 255
Walpole, N.H., 58
Wampum, 39, 43, 89
Wandermont, Dr., 415
Waring, Mr. (Warring), 385
Warren, Dr. Joseph, 22, 339
Warren, Me., 31
Warwick, Earl of, 260
Washington College, 209
Washington, Colonel William, 122
Washington (Fort), 92
Washington, George, xxxii, 23, 48, 112–13, 196, 209, 258, 263, 267, 268
Washington, Major ______, 128
Wassaqusset, 14
Water acacia, 385
Water beech, 423
Water elder, 453
Watertown, Mass., 24, 251
Wax myrtle, 411
Wax tree, 118
Weasel, 82
Weathersdon March, Va., 189
Weeping Willow, 448–49
Wells, Me., 29, 52
Wero-anco, 207
Wessagusset, Mass., 14
West, Benjamin, 268, 339
West Indies, 20
Weston, Mass., 24
Wethersfield, Conn., 64, 249
Wethersfield, Vt., 64

Wewelinckoven, Mr., 441
Weymouth, Mass., 14
Weymouth pine, 416
Whale, 9–10
Whale oil, 20, 52, 256, 262
Wheat, 108, 214, 233, 254, 317 n. 65. *See also* Grain
Wheelwright, John, 58–59, 278
Whipple, William, 278
White, Captain John, 177
White cedar, 16, 87, 373, 454
White cypress, 373
Whitefield, 214
Whitefield, George, 214, 316
White gum-tree, 399
White hellebore, 458
White Hills (N.H.), 56, 59
White Mts., 44
White nut, 383
White walnut, 392
Whitewood, 401, 456
Whortleberry, 457–58
Wild allspice, 397, 398
Wildcat, 210
Wild indigo, 451
Wild oats, 462
Wild orange, 430, 431
Wild pimento, 397, 398
Wild rice, 74, 116, 462
Willard (Samuel ?), 24–25, 267, 339, 460
William (Fort), 11
Williams (Jonathan ?), 267
Williams, Roger, 255, 259–60
Williamsburg, S.C., 158
Willow oak, 432, 435
Willow, weeping, 243
Wilmington, Del., 211, 212
Wilmington, N.C., 119–20, 179–80
Wilton, N.H., 57
Wincasett, Me., 31
Winchester, Va., 189, 205
Windmill Point (N.Y.), 81
Windsor, Conn., 251
Windsor, Vt., 63
Wine, 235
Wine from Maple sugar, 348
Wingina, 176–77
Winterberry, 385, 428
Winyah Bay, 121
Witch-hazel, 390
Withering, William, xix
Wokoken Island, 176
Wolverine, 82
Woodbridge, N.J., 239
Woodpeckers, 175; Red-headed, 175, 213
Woolwich, Me., 31
Worcester, Mass., 255

Yale College, 238, 248, 249; museum collection, 248, 323 n. 6
Yale, Elihu, 248
Yamacraw, Ga., 127–28, 140
Yaocomico, Md., 207
Yeardley, Sir George, 192
Yellow jasmine, 122, 364, 365
York, Pa., 230
York, Duke of, 88, 99, 157, 211, 241
Yorktown, Va., 180
Yucca, 122, 461

Zanthoxylum, 461
Zizania, 74, 116, 462
Zizendorf, Count Nikolaus Ludwig, 174, 215

LUIGI CASTIGLIONI'S *VIAGGIO*

was composed in ten-point Compugraphic Plantin and leaded two points,
with display type in Plantin and Goudy Oldstyle,
by Metricomp;
printed by sheet-fed offset on 60-pound acid-free Warren Oldstyle,
Smythe-sewn and bound over 88-point binder's boards in Joanna Arrestox B,
by Maple-Vail Book Manufacturing Group, Inc.;
and published by

SYRACUSE UNIVERSITY PRESS
SYRACUSE, NEW YORK 13210